Archaeologies of Vision

Archaeologies of Vision

Foucault and Nietzsche on Seeing and Saying

GARY SHAPIRO

The University of Chicago Press

Chicago & London

Gary Shapiro is professor of philosophy and Tucker-Boatwright Professor in the Humanities at the University of Richmond. He is the author of three previous books, including *Alcyone: Nietzsche on Gifts, Noise, and Women* and *Earthwards: Robert Smithson and Art after Babel*.

The University of Chicago Press, Chicago 60637
The University of Chicago Press, Ltd., London
© 2003 by Gary Shapiro
All rights reserved. Published 2003
Printed in the United States of America
12 11 10 09 08 07 06 05 04 03   5 4 3 2 1

ISBN (cloth): 0-226-75046-9
ISBN (paper): 0-226-75047-7

Library of Congress Cataloging-in-Publication Data

Shapiro, Gary, 1941–
    Archaeologies of vision : Foucault and Nietzsche on seeing and saying / Gary Shapiro.
        p.   cm.
    Includes bibliographical references and index.
    ISBN 0-226-75046-9 (alk. paper) — ISBN 0-226-75047-7 (pbk. : alk. paper)
    1. Foucault, Michel.   2. Nietzsche, Friedrich Wilhelm, 1844–1900.
3. Vision.   I. Title.
B2430.F724 S53   2003
121'.35—dc21

                                                                            2002014836

In memory of Irving H. Shapiro and Leo Shapiro

Contents

eleven

twelve

Illustrations

Preface

For years I have been teaching and thinking about philosophy in the post-Kantian, post-Hegelian tradition (what we Anglophones call "continental philosophy" in our insular way). This eventually led to two books on Nietzsche (*Nietzschean Narratives*, 1989, and *Alcyone: Nietzsche on Gifts, Noise, and Women*, 1991), which were attempts to come to terms with such themes as narrativity, the metaphilosophical poetics or tropology of philosophical discourse, the possibility of the gift, the structure of parasitism, and the question of voice as inflected by sexual difference. Like many writers of the last hundred years, I have been haunted sometimes by one of Nietzsche's last letters, where he declares to his first serious commentator, Georg Brandes: "Once you discovered me, it was no great feat to find me: the difficulty now is to lose me" (January 4, 1889). My book of 1995, *Earthwards: Robert Smithson and Art after Babel*, might appear to be such an attempt to lose Nietzsche, since it focuses on a recent artist in the light of a series of issues that are often labeled *postmodern* (a term that I contest in the first chapter of that book, countering it with the deliberately ugly *postperiodization*). But this was at best a partial escape, since the engagements there with Heidegger, Lyotard, and Derrida were hardly independent of their own discoveries of Nietzsche and their attempts to lose him. As I saw it, one of the exemplary themes for Smithson, and one that has been increasingly internalized by the practice of art and its critics (not only because of him, of course), was the questioning of the implicit grand narrative of the history of art, whether in the Hegelian form so powerful in the formation of the discipline of art history, or in influential neo-Kantian approaches like Clement Greenberg's.

Archaeologies of Vision aims at restating the question of what constitutes the history of art in the language of Nietzsche, Foucault, and some of their intermediaries such as Bataille, Klossowski, and Deleuze; but in restating that question, it discovers others, having to do with the possibility of a conception of visual regimes that includes the history of art within it as a variation, in a way analogous to Smithson's provocative proposal that art's history be seen as an episode within geological history and the cosmic tendency toward the increase of entropy. The present book also begins to ask the question of how philosophy's alleged ocularcentrism is addressed, criticized, and transformed in two thinkers who warn us against the panoptical gaze (Foucault) or who incite us to emulate the hundred-eyed Argus (Nietzsche). If vision has been the traditional escape from embodiment, as a "theoretical" sense, it is perhaps worth noting, as these thinkers do, that *theoria* itself has to do with embodied looking and so returns us to what we have sought to evade. Perhaps the greatest limitation of *Archaeologies* is that it takes most of its material and examples from the world of the museum and the gallery that arose with the era of aesthetics in the eighteenth century and is now undergoing a metamorphosis parallel to that of its disciplinary sister. I am conscious of the need to develop further the exploration of what Deleuze might call the diagrams of art and the aesthetic in a broader compass than that envisioned by Kantian and Hegelian philosophy and the "other space" of the museum. That thinking would take up some of Smithson's questions and return to the thoughtful engagement with those encompassing works variously understood in terms of categories such as landscape design and architecture, gardens, parks, and environmental art, which were thought of as exemplary in the same eighteenth century that invented aesthetics; and it would call for an interrogation of how, from the early nineteenth century, aesthetics managed to exclude such powerful works from its purview. But these are projects for other occasions.

As the foregoing genealogy suggests, this book has been growing slowly for some time. Some of the first stimuli came from David Michael Levin, who invited me to write an essay on Nietzsche for his collection *Modernity and the Hegemony of Vision* (1993) and Mark Rollins, who asked me to write one on Arthur Danto for *Danto and His Critics* (1993), in which I contrasted Danto's and Foucault's theorizing about Andy Warhol. I have found Arthur Danto's work to be a continuous challenge, and I am grateful to him for this and much else, despite our disagreements about the *Brillo Boxes*. John Sallis requested an essay for *Research in Phenomenology* (1995), which was the first version of my ocular reading of *The Birth of Tragedy;* in 1999 I had the occasion to sharpen some of my thoughts in the form of a commentary on his book *Shades—Of Painting at the Limit* at a meeting of the Society for Phenomenology and Existential Philosophy. I'm indebted to John Sallis for the example of his own work on the artistic imagination, as well as the opportunities afforded by these occasions. Another talk was presented at the gracious invitation of Paul von Tongeren at a productive seminar on "Nietzsche's Use of Language" at Nijmegen in 2000. Versions of various preliminary sections of the book have been delivered as papers at the American Society for Aesthetics, the World Congress of Philosophy (1998), and two anniversary meetings of the North American Nietzsche Society (1994 and 2000); I am grateful to Richard Schacht, a boundless source of energy in Nietzsche studies, for the invitations to the last-mentioned events. Alan Schrift's insightful scholarship, both published and in conversation, has been an important stimulus in recent years; when he invited me to publish an essay for his collection *Why Nietzsche Still?* it was a welcome opportunity to think further about painting, dreams, and phantasms in Nietzsche and Foucault.

I was enabled to complete this book with the support of a fellowship from the Dedalus Foundation in 2000 and a year's residency at the Clark Art Institute in 2000–2001. Under the inspired directorship of Michael Ann Holly, the Clark proved to be an ideal place to live and work. Its stupendous library of art history offered a number of unexpected discoveries as I explored some of the rhizomatic network in which Nietzsche's and Foucault's discussions of painting and the visual were embedded. Discussions with colleagues from art history and the museum world, and in two joint workshops with the Getty Institute, were exceptional opportunities to share in a discourse that I would otherwise be reading about only retrospectively and externally. My thanks to Michael Ann Holly; to Darby English, who offered tireless and thoughtful assistance of many sorts; and to all of the staff and fellows at the Clark. Jenny King was an intelligent and industrious research assistant. Mark Cheetham gave the manuscript a sensitive and helpful reading, as did one anonymous reader for the University of Chicago Press. In a lecture at Williams College in April 2001, I discussed some of the materials in the introduction, including the contrast of the Taliban and the Teletubbies, a juxtaposition that subsequent events have cast in another light. The University of Richmond helped to support my year at the Clark with a research grant, and it is a pleasure to acknowledge that help and the former Dean of Arts and Sciences, David

Leary, who helped to arrange it. I am grateful to the Faculty Research Committee at Richmond for a grant that allowed me to visit the Dresden Gallery and for other support over the years. Jim Hall, Chair of the Philosophy Department at Richmond, helped in arranging research time, and Stella Jones provided highly skilled assistance. A number of students at Richmond, especially those in courses on philosophy and the visual arts, responded in ways that helped me to shape the project. In the fall of 2001, as a fellow at the Rockefeller Foundation's Villa Serbelloni, in Bellagio, Italy, I devoted some of my time at that scholars' paradise to final revisions of the manuscript. Many thanks to Gianna Celli and to Richard and Jing Lyman for presiding graciously at Bellagio and to the other fellows for companionship and questions about that puzzling word *ekphrasis.*

I am grateful to Bettina Bergo, an accomplished translator of the most difficult French texts, for improving the translation of passages from Foucault's essay on Paul Rebeyrolle, prodding me to get on with the project in a timely fashion, and setting an example of philosophical dedication.

Susan Bielstein at the University of Chicago Press has been a great source of encouragement and support. She has been a friend of the project and a perceptive critic since our original discussion of my plans at a meeting of the College Art Association. All writers should be so fortunate as to have such an editor. Anthony Burton at Chicago has been reliable, ingenious, and resourceful on matters ranging from the book's format to obtaining permission to reproduce images. Lois Crum provided helpful and perspicacious copyediting.

A number of friends and colleagues have offered or been cajoled into lending an ear, giving encouragement and support, or providing references and critical responses to earlier versions of my thoughts on Nietzsche, Foucault, and the visual. I am happy to acknowledge them while absolving them from any responsibility for the final product: in addition to those mentioned above, they include Babette Babich, Tom Bonfiglio, Matthias Bruhn, Judith Butler, David Carrier, John Carvalho, Marco CasaNova, Ed Casey, Daniel Conway, Martin Donougho, Richard Eldridge, Jean-Pierre Faye, Thomas Flynn, Barbara Freeman, Jeremy Gilbert-Rolfe, Hester IJsseling, Michael Kelly, Gina Kovarsky, David Krell, Richard Kuhns, Len Lawler, Michael Leja, Ladelle McWhorter, Rachel Nussbaum, David Owen, Jana Sawicki, Gerd Schank, Holger Schmidt, Alan Schrift, Herman Siemens, Hugh Silverman, Lorenzo Simpson, Mark Taylor, Mariet Westermann, Cynthia Willett, and David Wood.

Earlier versions of some of the sections of this book have appeared as articles or book chapters in the following places: "Art and Its Doubles: Danto, Foucault, and Their Simulacra," in *Danto and His Critics,* ed. Mark Rollins (Oxford: Blackwell, 1993); "In the Shadows of Philosophy: Nietzsche and the Question of Vision," in *Modernity and the Hegemony of Vision,* ed. David Michael Levin (Berkeley: University of California Press, 1993); "*Übersehen:* Nietzsche and Tragic Vision," in *Research in Phenomenology* (1995); "Pipe Dreams: Simulacrum and Eternal Recurrence in Foucault's Ekphrasis of Magritte," *Word and Image* (January–March 1997); " 'This is not a Christ': Nietzsche, Foucault, and the Archaeology of Vision," in *Why Nietzsche Still?* ed. Alan Schrift (Berkeley: University of California Press, 2000); "Nietzsche's Story of the Eye: Hyphenating the *Augen-Blick,*" *Journal of Nietzsche Studies* (fall 2001); "Shades and Shining: Thoughts on John Sallis's *Shades—Of Painting at the Limit,*" *Continental Philosophy Review* (March 2002).

In quoting from Nietzsche, Foucault, and some other writers, I have drawn freely on a number of published translations, and I have occasionally modified them. In a few cases that seemed worth noting, I have commented on some of these modifications in the text or the notes.

References and Abbreviations

Friedrich Nietzsche

References to Nietzsche's writings are given in the following form, when a work exists in English translation: (*GM* II.13; *KSA* 5.317). The first reference is to the numbered parts and sections of Nietzsche's texts; the second is to the volume and page number of the *Kritische Studienausgabe*. Occasional further references of the form 4[194] are to the numbering of notebooks and entries that are given in *KSA*. I have used a number of English translations, sometimes with my own modifications. When there is no English translation, the reference is simply to the *Kritische Studien ausgabe*.

A	*The Antichrist(ian).*
AD	*On the Advantage and Disadvantage of History for Life.*
BGE	*Beyond Good and Evil.*
BT	*The Birth of Tragedy.*
CW	*The Case of Wagner.*
D	*Daybreak.*
EH	*Ecce Homo.*
GM	*On the Genealogy of Morality.*
GS	*The Gay Science.*
HAH	*Human, All Too Human.*
	HAH, AOM Human, All Too Human, Assorted Opinions and Maxims.
	HAH, WS Human, All Too Human, The Wanderer and His Shadow.
NCW	*Nietzsche contra Wagner.*

"MW"	"On Music and Words," trans. Walter Kaufmann. In Carl Dahlhaus, *Between Romanticism and Modernism: Four Studies in the Music of the Later Nineteenth Century*, 106–19. Berkeley: University of California Press, 1980.
SE	*Schopenhauer as Educator.*
T	*Twilight of the Idols.*
W	*Richard Wagner in Bayreuth.*
WP	*The Will to Power.*
Z	*Thus Spoke Zarathustra.*
B	Friedrich Nietzsche, *Sämtliche Briefe, Kritische Studienausgabe.* 7 vols. Ed. Giorgio Colli and Mazzino Montinari. Berlin: de Gruyter, 1986.
KGW	Friedrich Nietzsche, *Kritische Gesamtausgabe: Werke.* Ed. Giorgio Colli and Mazzino Montinari. Berlin: de Gruyter, 1967–.
KSA	Friedrich Nietzsche, *SämtlicheWerke, Kritische Studienausgabe.* 15 vols. Ed. Giorgio Colli and Mazzino Montinari. Berlin: de Gruyter, 1980.

Michel Foucault

References of the form *DE* 2.296 are to volume and page number of Michel Foucault, *Dits et écrits*, 4 vols., ed. Daniel Defert and François Ewald (Paris: Gallimard, 1994).

Other references to Foucault's writings are to page numbers of the following works and editions in French and English; where possible I have provided references to both the English and French editions, in that order.

AK	*The Archaeology of Knowledge and the Discourse on Language.* Trans. A. M. Sheridan-Smith. New York: Harper and Row, 1976.
AS	*L'archéologie du savoir.* Paris: Gallimard, 1969.
BC	*The Birth of the Clinic: An Archaeology of Medical Perception.* Trans. A. M. Sheridan-Smith. New York: Random House, 1975.
CP	*Ceci n'est pas une pipe.* Paris: Fata Morgana, 1973.
DP	*Discipline and Punish.* Trans. Alan Sheridan. New York: Vintage Books, 1979.
DX	*Dream, Imagination, and Existence.* Trans. Forrest Williams and Jacob Needleman. *Review of Existential Psychology and Psychiatry* 19 (1984–85): 1.
F	*The Essential Works of Foucault.* 3 vols. Trans. Robert Hurley and others. Ed. Paul Rabinow. New York: New Press, 1997–2000.

GF   Gilles Deleuze and Michel Foucault. *Gérard Fromanger: Photogenic Painting.* London: Black Dog Publishing, 1999. A bilingual edition. Foucault's essay is translated by Dafydd Roberts.

HF   *Histoire de la folie à l'âge classique.* Paris: Gallimard, 1999.

LCMP   *Language, Counter-Memory, Practice: Selected Essays and Interviews by Michel Foucault.* Trans. Donald F. Bouchard and Sherry Simon. Ithaca, NY: Cornell University Press, 1977.

MC   *Madness and Civilization.* Trans. Richard Howard. New York: Random House, 1967.

Mch   *Les Mots et les choses: Une archéologie des sciences humaines.* Paris: Gallimard, 1966.

NC   *Naissance de la clinique.* Paris: Presses Universitaires de France, 1983.

OT   *The Order of Things: An Archaeology of the Human Sciences.* New York: Random House, 1973.

PK   *Power/Knowledge.* Ed. Colin Gordon. New York: Pantheon, 1980.

"PP"   "Photogenic Painting." In *Gérard Fromanger,* ed. Adrian Rifkin. London: Black Dog Publishing, 1999.

SP   *Surveiller et punir.* Paris: Gallimard, 1975.

"TE"   "Thought and Emotion." In *Duane Michals: Photographie de 1958 à 1982, by Duane Michals.* Paris: Mois de la photo, 1982. Available in French in *DE* 4.243–250.

TNP   *This Is Not a Pipe.* Trans. James Harkness. Berkeley: University of California Press, 1983.

MPA   *The Merleau-Ponty Aesthetics Reader.* Ed. Galen Johnson. Evanston, IL: Northwestern University Press, 1993.

Our eye sees falsely, it abbreviates and compounds: is that a reason to abandon vision and to say it is good for nothing?
—Nietzsche[1]

It becomes necessary to level the artistic structure [*kunstvolle Gebäude*] of the *Apollonian culture,* as it were, stone by stone, till we catch sight of [*erblicken*] the foundations on which it rests.
—Nietzsche[2]

I have the impression that there are two great families of founders. There are the builders who place the first stone, and there are the diggers and excavators. Perhaps in our uncertain space, we are closer to those who excavate: to Nietzsche (instead of Husserl), to Klee (instead of Picasso).
—Foucault[3]

Painting has at least this in common with discourse: when it transmits a force that creates history, it is political.
—Foucault[4]

Introduction

The Abyss of Vision

1 Iconoclasm and Indoctrination: The Taliban and the Teletubbies

Is there evidence of something new in the economy of the senses, in the distribution of thinking and seeing, something that would justify talk of a "visual" or "pictorial turn" in culture and so in the studies that attempt to make sense of it?[5] The term *evidence* itself of course refers us back to the *video*, the "I see"; the Anglo-American legal tradition is one in which visual evidence, supplied by an eyewitness, takes a certain precedence over other forms of supporting argument and information. The evidence should be before our eyes. Such evidence would seem to arise from rather different sources, ranging from the most mundane to the rather theoretical (as in *theoria*, originally an eye-witnessing). First there is the increasing deployment of visualization at every level in the daily life of our mediatized world. By *visualization* I intend to suggest the proliferation of techniques of picturing, showing, reproducing, and displaying the actual, the artificial, and the fantastic. Traditional literacy, based on printed texts, is being displaced or demoted by a culture of the screen, which may be cinematic, video, or computer-based. Newspaper editorials express dismay at the increased use of films in university classes ostensibly devoted to literature and at the rise of media studies, often focused on popular figures, such as courses on Madonna and Princess Diana. Precocious children, who once learned to read before their peers, now find themselves at the computer screen, manipulating an array of images sometimes accompanied by text; stories that were once children's classics, first read aloud and then accessible through the young reader's own efforts, are now encountered originally through video versions, which the younger generation may very well assume to be the definitive ones, bearing the same relation to the text as a contemporary film does to its "novelization." This is indeed, and increasingly, a society of the spectacle, a spectacle that infiltrates and insinuates itself at the most unconscious levels of habit and practice and which is at work in what Plato called *paideia* (the education of youth).

I want to consider two rather extreme attitudes toward the image, which might be taken to stand for a spectrum of contemporary ways of responding to and shaping the world of the eye. There seems to be no escaping the politics of vision. Questions of the censorship or control of images in film, TV, and the Internet are everywhere. As I write, in March 2001, there are reports of a major iconoclastic movement in Afghanistan. The Taliban movement, which has developed out of a lengthy and complex conflict in that country, has destroyed a set of remarkable ancient Buddhist statues; almost all commentators greet the news with righteous indignation.[6] The Taliban claims that after completing the operation, it will also subject the country's museums to an iconological cleansing, eliminating all "idols." The endangered objects are defended sometimes as works of art, sometimes as elements of a cultural or religious heritage. A set of questions could be raised about the issue of whether these are indeed works of art or objects of aesthetic experience—categories introduced in the West only since the eighteenth century. These would be deeply Foucauldian questions, and I trust that the following text will show the value of Foucault's thought for considering such issues. This is, of course, hardly the first instance of massive and official iconoclasm. It is only recently, though, that the images of this process, or at least of the works being annihilated—as in the destruction of Stalinist monuments in the former Soviet Union—have become instantly visible around the world. Except perhaps in Afghanistan, where the Taliban also prohibits television. One characteristic of what I will call a visual regime lies in what it allows to be seen, by whom, and under what circumstances. But it is also a question of a more general structuring of the visible: not just display or prohibition, but what goes without saying, not what is seen but the arrangement that renders certain ways of seeing obvious while it excludes others. We become aware of the violent practices of the Taliban on television, in print, and on the Internet, where images of the statues appear in their former condition, prior to the attacks. It is not difficult to feel outrage about the reduction of these magnificent works to rubble and to feel superior to those who are carrying out the process of annihilation. It is equally easy to forget that western Europe has seen its own share of iconoclasm and that attempts to defend the Buddhas on the grounds that they are works of art relies on a concept of art that was invented only in the eighteenth century; that concept was devised around the time when the museum became a significant cultural institution, which was seen as the natural site for visually interesting objects that had previously been thought of under a host of different categories. The thinkers who developed the foundations of art history, like G. W. F. Hegel, saw the museum as the obvious venue for art; those who were the witting or unwitting heirs of this movement, like Nietzsche, absorbed the culture of the museum and its commitment to preservation. It was left for later thinkers, like André Malraux and Foucault, to begin to theorize that institution and to understand the ways in which its practices of framing, display, inclusion, and exclusion contributed both to our implicit conception of what art is and to the making of art itself. But this is to run ahead of the story. Let us recall that before the era of art and the rise of the museum, the questions associated with iconoclasm were much more pressing. In a recent work of great erudition and philosophical insight, *Likeness and Presence: A History of the Image before the Age of Art,* the art historian Hans Belting reminds us that there is an "age of art," with its own temporal and geographical limits.[7] Before that time, the predecessor of what we call art was the religious image; there was no "art history" but rather a lively theological debate about the powers of images. For images were thought of, in the Orthodox and Byzantine tradition, as being endowed with the power of the divine beings and saints that they were thought to embody. These images were icons, not representations. The iconoclastic conflict that emerged with the Protestant Reformation was anticipated by earlier disputes in which images were denounced and sometimes attacked on the grounds that an illusory power had been claimed for them and that respect for the image was inconsistent with genuine piety. The reformers could draw on the prohibition of idols—a difficult and elastic concept—in the Hebrew Bible, a strictly monotheistic source whose use by the reformers is closely related to the Taliban's reference to the Qur'an to justify their own iconoclasm.[8] If we can begin to understand how iconoclasm could seem like a live cultural option rather than an immediate sign of wild fanaticism, we are on our way to thinking in terms of what, adapting a notion of Foucault's, I will call an archaeology of the visual. That is, we will realize that such terms as *image* and *art* mark distinctive eras with their own sets of expectations and practices regarding what we see and how it is displayed and valued. If the practices of the Taliban are holdovers from before the age of art, how are we to describe our own institutions and attitudes, which, in a time of almost limitless reproduction and the mixing of previously disparate high and low forms, can be thought of as a society of the spectacle or the simulacrum, in any case a time after the age of art?[9] While I address these questions only somewhat indirectly here, by exploring Foucault's response to artists like René Magritte and Andy Warhol, I also explore the project of a visual archaeology implicit in his work; that project ought to be able to help us think about the contemporary scene.

That contemporary scene is omnipresent, at least in the media of the West, and it is one in which we are fervently acculturating the youngest generation. Consider for a moment the spectacle of one- to two-year-old infants, still on the verge of the linguistic but being acculturated and given their earliest lessons in the symbolic by watching the Teletubbies. We might take this to be the pacific and gentle antithesis of iconoclastic violence; but while this may be true of the content of their video pastoral, there is something disturbing in the program's insidious project of insinuating the normality of the contemporary cult of the image. The Teletubbies are terminally cute, infantile figures, toddling about in a world of pleasant green fields and in a fully automated and mediatized house designed for their amusement. Like their implied audience, they are just on the verge of speech, communicating in an all-too-charming lisp. The children who watch them learn a first lesson simply by being glued to the television screen, which presents itself as a source of information and instruction. They begin to absorb some of their basic verbal oppositions (near-far, big-little, high-low) by associating these with the hallucinatory simulacra on the screen. In 1982, a time that can seem like ancient history if we consider how few people had their own computer screens then, David Cronenberg made his prescient film *Videodrome* in which we witnessed the grotesque implosion of the real in a world where humans were transformed into video cyborgs, sprouting televisual screens in their abdomens. Now the Teletubbies all happily possess their own screens in their tummies, and the narrative, such as it is, can dissolve from a scene in which all of the gang is gathered around, into the world that opens up through one of their internal videos. If there is a mirror stage, it may be subject to a cultural transformation in which the entry of the *in-fans* into language will now coincide with her seeing herself as not only open to the reflection of the unified image, but also as a site in which that image (or its image) becomes the locus of screens within screens. Each infant can think of herself as a *mise-en-abîme*. Nietzsche's Zarathustra, at one of the most critical hinges in his grappling with the thought of eternal recurrence, announces that "vision itself is seeing abysses." He says this in "On the Vision and the Riddle," where he is attempting to come to terms with the riddle of vision and the recurrence of the *Augenblick*, or the twinkling of the eye (see sec. 36, chap. 5, below). This is said as a challenge to that small band of courageous searchers and researchers who would follow Zarathustra in his most dangerous quest. Could it be that we are now effortlessly educating our young to see the abyss of vision in preparation for a world of videos within videos? A later Cronenberg film, *Existenz*, portrays a world of virtual reality games where the symbiosis of the human and the image-machine has reached a higher level than in *Videodrome*. Might we expect a sanitized version of this as part of the basic education of the children of those children who are now crossing the threshold of the imaginary and the symbolic by means of the Teletubbies? In Homer's *Iliad* there is a spectacular imaginative construction: Hephaestus forges a magnificent shield for the hero Achilles, a shield that shows moving images of all aspects of life—war and peace. For the ancients this impossible screen was possible only in imagination, and even then it was something that could have been created only by a god at the request of a goddess for her son. Now every two-year-old who watches the Teletubbies can look forward to the possibility of becoming a cyborg with a built-in screen much more versatile than that of Achilles. A program like *The Teletubbies* seems peaceful and wholesome compared to most of the fare on television, including even the cartoons, some of them violent, intended for slightly older children. The use of these images and this new culture of the image appears to be as distant as possible from the iconoclasm of the Taliban. Yet the habits of seeing and the technologically driven shifts in thought and practice represented by such programs (along with their spin-offs in toys and on the Internet) are likely to have consequences much more far-reaching than the destruction of Buddhist images.

How should we begin to think about the different visual regimes, old and new, that hold sway in such varied cultures? Might philosophy have something to say about such things? According to one fairly widespread view, we need to be on our guard against an overvaluation of the visual. It is said that ocularcentrism is an implicit, unthought undercurrent of the Western tradition, or at least of modernity, and that a truly critical philosophy would contribute to exposing its pitfalls and its insidious hegemony. It will become clear that I, following Nietzsche and Foucault, among others, have some serious reservations about this position; at the most basic level, these reservations have to do with what seems to be a failure to distinguish among different modalities and conceptions of vision, among different visual practices and visual regimes. In a time that takes the thought of difference so seriously, there is an anomaly in thinking of vision as always the same, always identical, and so opposing it to other forms of perception and sensibility, which, it is claimed, offer more finely nuanced, more engaged, more historically sensitive ways of engaging with things. But let me briefly rehearse some of the main lines of the philosophical critique of vision in the last century.

We have now become suspicious of the way in which this traditional hegemony of vision established itself so firmly in the West.[10] Vision, as Heidegger saw it, was complicit with the metaphysics of presence. Plato called vision "the noblest of the senses," and the *eidos,* or idea, is in the first instance a visible shape. Even if the truth is ultimately beyond the visible, the best analogies that we can devise for talking about it come from the realm of images and shapes that we see: the cave, the sun, the line. Plato's *Lehre von der Wahrheit,* then, was a doctrine about what could become present, wholly and fully there, and could hardly be divorced from that sense which, unlike touch, taste, smell, or even hearing, seemed to deliver up the object all at once. The light metaphysics of the medievals passes into the natural light to which Descartes appealed and into the *Wesenschau* of Husserlian phenomenology. There is perhaps a trace of this tradition even in Wittgenstein's injunction "don't think but look." The critique of this tendency to assume a vision that makes everything present assumes a variety of forms. Heidegger's response was to replace Cartesian vision with *Umsicht,* a knowing one's way around that was largely implicit and that did not objectify beings in the mode of *Vorhandenheit.* Consistently with this, Heidegger much later insisted that what emerges into the light, what shines forth in the phenomenon, could do so only on the ground of a more fundamental clearing, a *Lichtung* that is a light-ening rather than a light.[11] Similar criticisms of ocularcentrism are to be found in the deeper strands of the pragmatic tradition, in John Dewey, George Herbert Mead, and more recently in Richard Rorty's attempt to dismantle the image of the mirror of nature.[12] From the perspective of psychoanalysis, Freud suggested that the priority of vi-sion was a relatively late development in humans, one that had to do with the assumption of an erect posture that led to the abjection of smell and touch.[13] On this basis, some have argued that the advantage gained in the instrumental manipulation of the environment is at least matched by the alienation from our own bodies and their immediate circumstances attendant upon illusions of distance and objectivity. Er-win Straus gave some phenomenological content to such suggestions by showing the interdependence between the human posture and our form of the visual.[14] Luce Irigaray's trenchant critique of the masculine imaginary proceeds by her holding up a curved mirror, a speculum, to the fantasy of the all-seeing gaze; one might say that she undermines the fantasy of the phantasm itself. For this idea of a vision that seems to behold everything at once, a seeing that seems to take no risks, to be free of embodiment, and to pretend to a neutral position free of all desire—this vision has surely never existed and seems best explicable as a hypertrophy of a traditional masculine fantasy of distance, secu-rity, and self-possession. How appropriate that when the limits of this fantasy have been recognized in the main line of the tradition, such vision has been reserved for a paternalistic God rather than being the possession of men, although it was still thought to be a faculty that we could exercise insofar as we were made in God's image, which might just mean that we were created in the image of his imaging powers. "Now we see through a glass darkly, but then we shall see face to face." Even if human vision is deficient with respect to a higher standard, it is to be measured against that standard; it is telling that it is the *vision* of God to which mystics, theologians, and philosophers aspire, not to the touch or smell of God. Nietzsche attends to just such figures of vision in his dense and celebrated one-page history of philosophy, "How the True World Finally Became a Fable" (sec. 77).

All of this indicates that questions of aesthetics cannot be divorced from what has been thought of as first philosophy. Surely conceptions of *aisthesis* help to constitute our ideas of knowledge, thought, and reality. To imagine that they do not is to let them determine the most fundamental conceptual assumptions and operations while surren-dering the possibility of critical vigilance. Accordingly, if there is a shift in the economy of sensibility, a revaluation of the visual, or a change in how we conceive it, it is likely to have far-reaching consequences. Has there been such a shift? In his encyclopedic work *Downcast Eyes: The Denigration of Vision in Twentieth-Century French Thought*, Martin Jay argues that the tendency of this century, especially among the French, has been to depose vision from its former supremacy. Emblematic of this movement, for Jay, is Foucault's criticism of the medical gaze and of surveillance practices and devices such as Bentham's Panopticon. On this reading, the "empire of the gaze" is in the process of being overturned, then, in the spirit of Heidegger, the pragmatists, and Irigaray, as just sketched.

I want to suggest that we need to move beyond an overly schematic contrast between a malevolent ocularcentrism and a beneficent nonocular orientation. Even if we want to question the implicit and explicit claims made for vision by such thinkers as Plato, Descartes, and Husserl, even if we want to show that similar attitudes underlie dangerous orientations to the environment and to the "other"—for example, those of a different ethnicity, gender, or culture—we should proceed with some caution in identifying these with vision tout court. Consider Jay's argument that Foucault is an antivisual thinker. The claim is that, for Foucault, the Panopticon is the emblem not only of the carceral society, but also of the malignity of vision. Foucault discusses Jeremy Bentham's Panopticon in *Discipline and Punish*, where he takes it as an emblem of carceral society (secs. 62–64). The Panopticon is a device for total surveillance of the occupants of a disciplinary institution. Originally projected as a design for prisons, it is also applicable to schools, hospitals, factories, asylums, and any other sites where a high premium is attached to having an orderly population subject to constant inspection. Jeremy Bentham, the philosophical architect of the Panopticon, claimed that the great advantage of "this simple idea in architecture" was its efficiency not simply in providing a means of surveillance of the institution's inmates, but also in encouraging them to become their own guards, to practice a constant self-surveillance. The "simple idea" is to have a central structure around which cells are arranged in circular fashion, so that an observer in that center can see what is occurring in any single cell at any time. If the inspectors are hidden from the inmates (a maneuver to which Bentham devotes some ingenious attention), the latter must assume that they are constantly observed. Given the efficacy of rewards hoped for and punishments feared, the inmates will tend to become their own guards, anticipating a general surveillance. They become subject to a generalized ocular regime, an architectural realization of the archaic motif of the "evil eye" (sec. 34). This evil eye would be complicit with such suspect notions as the idea of a pure, neutral vision, with the impossible divorce between theoretical subject and an objective world to be manipulated, and with the male gaze as the reduction of the feminine to salacious spectacle. Jay believes that Foucault identifies this apparatus with vision as such and that his attitude is typical of other French philosophers and theorists who have analogous criticisms of vision: "Among French intellectuals in the 1960s and 1970s, it was Michel Foucault who most explicitly interrogated the gaze of surveillance. . . . he provided a panoply of arguments against the hegemony of the eye which augmented and extended those already encountered in this narrative and others still to come. With [this] work, the ocularcentrism of those who praised 'the nobility of sight' was not so much rejected as reversed in value. Vision was still the privileged sense, but what that privilege produced in the modern world was damned as almost entirely pernicious."[15] It is certainly clear that Foucault sees Panoptical and carceral society as "almost entirely pernicious." However, even within the modern world, vision has other modes, some of which constitute forms of resistance to panopticism. Foucault designates a number of artists of the last two centuries as providing various alternatives to surveillance and visual homogenization: these include Manet, Kandinsky, Klee, Magritte, Warhol, Michals, and Fromanger. So it is not a question of denigrating vision; it is rather a question of being alert to the different visual practices, often quite conflicting, that operate in the same cultural space and sorting out their specific structures and effects. Foucault has no arguments against vision in general. He is an archaeologist of the visual who is alert to the differential character of various visual regimes and to the disparate and possibly conflicting visual practices of a single era. But it is thought-provoking that Jay and other critics see Foucault and other recent French thinkers—Derrida, Lacan, and others—as antivisual thinkers in a time that increasingly is thought of as highly visual. Jay's argument has been influential; a recent book on photography by Celia Lury, *Prosthetic Culture: Photography, Memory, and Identity*, which, while finding Foucault valuable as a theorist of power and history, repeats, citing Jay, that Foucault was unalterably critical of the visual mode.[16] In contrast, Gilles Deleuze, perhaps the most insightful commentator on Foucault, says that his friend's thought must be understood as having substituted a binary of visibility and discursivity for the nineteenth century's transcendental aesthetic of space and time (sec. 41). On this reading, Foucault would analyze practices, formations of power/knowledge, indeed all human activities, as having always a double aspect. Neither the visible nor the articulable (in contrast to a Kantian transcendental aesthetic) would be an eternal given; each mode would be susceptible of a historical, or speaking more precisely for Foucault, an archaeological analysis, that would disclose its specific character in varying contexts. Vision would not be generally suspect or denigrated; rather, every situation would be open to visual analysis.

Later I will explore Foucault's conception of visibility in greater depth, mainly by means of attending to a number of his encounters with painting, architecture, and visual imagery. For now, I want to raise two sorts of questions about Jay's thesis, in order ultimately to explore the question of whether there is a "visual turn" in recent Continental philosophy that responds to and can perhaps help to clarify the increasing and changing role of spectacle and image in daily life. One question has to do with times and periodization; is the criticism or denigration of vision a relatively recent affair, one that reaches its height in the twentieth century? Second, with regard to some of the thinkers identified by Jay and others, do they indeed turn *away* from the visual, or should they be described, perhaps, as giving a *new turn* to the relation between thinking and seeing? To the first question, then. Here we can observe a certain ambivalence in the role accorded to the visual in what we might all too simply take to be a uniform tradition. Despite Plato's appeal to analogies of the sun, the cave, and the line, he is quite clear that the intellectual apprehension of the most fundamental things is not accomplished by the bodily sense of vision; vision is "noblest" because it bears the same relation to the other senses, which are inextricably tied to desire and fail to give us the whole whose presence we seek, that *nous/dianoia* does to all the senses, including vision. Similarly, it is clear that Descartes's natural light and Husserl's *Wesenschau* are meant as metaphors. That the metaphors are taken from the visual realm is significant, but again, these are metaphors; if pressed, their authors would no doubt distinguish rational or phenomenological intuition from everyday vision. When we turn to the philosophy of art and aesthetics, it becomes even clearer that there is no valorization of the visual as such that would then provide the ground for a later devaluation of sight. Consider Lessing's *Laocoön,* an attempt to delineate the "boundaries of painting and poetry." Lessing was troubled by what he saw as the tendency to confuse the plastic arts and poetry (the word *literature* had hardly been coined). Specifically, he was disturbed by the notion that painting might tell a story and that poetry might offer us descriptions of visual objects (including works of art). He argued that the two types of art are to be strictly distinguished in terms of their media: painting can show bodies that exist simultaneously in space, while poetry can tell of actions that unfold in time. It is therefore a serious mistake when the poet offers, say, lengthy descriptions of flowers, or the painter undertakes to do more than depict the single most pregnant and meaningful moment of the subject he has chosen. The sculpted Laocoön, unlike his literary twin, fails to cry out (Lessing erroneously supposed) not because the expression of pain is inconsistent with the nobility of the classical soul, but because to show him at just that moment would be to allow an ugliness contrary to the principles of art. Similarly, Lessing has an answer to those who would point to the long descriptive passages in Homer, than whom there could be no more canonical poet; in almost every case, especially in regard to the famous account of the shield of Achilles, the critic points out that these descriptions are really integrated into the narrative. We hear about Achilles' uncanny shield because we see it being made by Hephaestus; it is part of the story, and indeed to describe the shield is to describe the stories enacted on it. (One might imagine that such a shield, acting as a screen for moving images, would be an object of great fascination, bewitching those enemies who stood in the hero's path. Perhaps we might trace the fantasies of abdominal television in *Videodrome* and the Teletubbies back to this source in the ancestor of all our art.) The main tendency of Lessing's argument is to suggest that the verbal has a far greater range than the visual, and in this respect his work exhibits a typical commitment of aesthetics.[17] In *The Truth in Painting,* Derrida points out that this commitment is underlined in the thought of Hegel and Heidegger.[18] Hegel's system of the arts unfolds as a movement from the most material to the most spiritual, from architecture to poetry; while painting is the first of the romantic arts, because it can be seen as sheer expanse and does not participate in the dynamics of gravity in the way that architecture and sculpture do, it is still inferior in imaginative power to music and especially poetry, which dispense with any tangible surface. Heidegger, despite his attempt to formulate an alternative to Hegel's teleology and idealism, still takes poetry to be the most significant of the arts, the one that is the key to all the others. Even Merleau-Ponty, who appears to argue for an irreducible art of the visual in texts like "Cézanne's Doubt" and "Eye and Mind," seems to adhere to the traditional priority of the linguistic in his essay "Indirect Language and the Voices of Silence" (secs. 46–48). So the subordination of the visual (and in some respects its denigration, to use Jay's term) seems to be well established in the economy of aesthetic theory.

Now I want to raise a second question, having to do with whether recent European thought embodies a turn away from the visual and whether it practices a variety of linguistic reductionism. We have heard this charge repeatedly, a charge frequently buttressed by the citation of Derrida's "there is nothing outside the text" outside of its own context and with little attempt to distinguish the positions of different thinkers. We might be struck, however, by the sheer amount of attention that has been devoted to painting and the other arts of the visual by, for example, Foucault, Derrida, Lyotard, and Kristeva, all of whom devote books or major essays to painting. Foucault's *Les mots et les choses* opens with a celebrated discussion of Velazquez's *Las Meninas*, perhaps the only book of philosophy to begin with such an *ekphrasis*. Derrida offers a criticism of the parallel attempts at linguistic appropriation of a painting in his essay "Restitutions." His position constitutes a case for taking the visual more seriously as evidence, noting, for example, that what a celebrated art historian and a major philosopher identify as a pair of shoes looks more like an odd couple of two left shoes. Lyotard argues for the ineluctability of the dimension of sheer presence in the series of dialogues that constitute his book *Que peindre?* and Kristeva, in essays like "Motherhood according to Giovanni Bellini," suggests the ways in which painting functions at the level of the semiotic, on the verge of the symbolic or linguistic.[19]

3 Foucault as Illustrator: The Case of Frans Hals

If there has been something like a visual turn in the humanities or human sciences, it has not yet had much of an effect on the way that philosophical texts are read; more specifically, it does not seem to have altered, as it might, our approach to the history of philosophy. Such an alteration could involve reading the philosophers in the context of the visual culture of their time, critically examining their work as it touches on (or avoids) significant visual material, or even (as in the case of Bentham) as it involves the design of visual works. This is a kind of study that has scarcely been undertaken, although there exist a few indications of how it might proceed; these include, for example, studies of Plato and the art and geometry of his time, Deleuze's examination of Leibniz and the baroque, and surveys of Hegel's actual acquaintance with the museum culture of his time.[20] A large part of this book is devoted to examining Nietzsche and Foucault in the context of what they looked at and how they translated that looking into words. I attempt to read these thinkers diagonally, as Deleuze would say, attending to the visual materials that they discuss, whether glancingly or in greater depth, to their accounts of visuality, and to their deployment of visual figures in their own work or to their analysis of it in the work of others. It is, of course, Nietzsche and Foucault who have contributed as much as any other thinkers to make this kind of reading possible. In organizing this book, I have found it useful to employ a good many cross-references to numbered sections; neither thinker set out to write a treatise on the visual, so it is up to me (and to you, reader) to find our way in and out of the labyrinth. The labyrinth is of course a favored figure for both writers, and there may be some delicious irony in our undertaking a dark and subterranean itinerary for the sake of illuminations about vision.[21]

Such reading yields unexpected results. Let me illustrate by recording a surprising discovery that occurred in the course of writing this book. In a fit of perverse erudition, I was hunting out the second French edition of *The History of Madness* because it contains a short essay, "Madness, the Absence of Work," that appears only there. What I also found, unique to that edition of 1972, is a frontispiece black and white reproduction of one of the great works of Frans Hals, *The Regentesses of the Old Men's House*, painted around 1664 (fig. 1).[22] Nowhere in the book does Foucault comment on the painting, but he does discuss it elsewhere. And nowhere, so far as I can tell, has anyone taken public notice of this appearance of the picture. In an interview, from the time of the second edition, Foucault calls it "one of the most overwhelming [*bouleversement*] pictures ever painted in the West" and refers to a few "beautiful pages" on it by Paul Claudel, a very Catholic writer, whom one might be surprised to find him citing with such respect (*DE* 2.296). Interesting questions are raised then about philosophers and their books; if we think about writing and publishing as material practices, as activities that are carried out by means of pen and paper, printing, computer, or Internet, then we should attend more to what actually appears in philosophical texts. In addition to the specific language (Greek, English, and so on) in which a text appears, there is also its visual arrangement and presentation. This can involve such elements as illustrations, diagrams, and the author's marginal comments or summaries. The first century or two of printing fostered a variety of formats, which gradually yielded to the more homogeneous style that has been expected more recently. For example, the original edition of Hobbes's *Leviathan* has a magnificent title-page illustration depicting a crowned man of absolutely gigantic size, made up of myriad smaller men. It is a graphic picture of the Hobbesian commonwealth, in which individuals agree to surrender their power to a unitary sovereign. Here the sovereign carries out his activities by his incorporation of the many, potentially individual, political wills in a single one. The illustration could be misleading since Hobbes did not hold that sovereignty must always reside in a single human person, although he tended to favor

monarchical government. It also reveals assumptions that are for the most part implicit in the words of the text, for example, the fact that sovereign and citizens are all male. That Hobbes was a Calvinist, and in agreement with the iconoclastic tendencies of Calvinism, makes this use of an allegorical picture, with its debt to Renaissance emblem books, all the more striking. Foucault, too, added visual materials to some of his books; there are many more illustrations for *Discipline and Punish* than appear in the English edition. When his essay on Flaubert's *Temptation of Saint Anthony* appeared in French (the original publication was in German), it was accompanied by thirteen illustrations of "oriental" religions and heresies, keyed to Flaubert's text (the essay itself leans heavily on Flaubert's testimony that he was inspired by a painting of the *Temptation*; see sec. 45).

The Hals painting belongs to the rich and significant genre of the group portrait that flourished in the Dutch Republic. It was made possible by the rise of the bourgeoisie, independence from the former colonial power of Spain, and a set of public and private institutions that allowed a greater proportion of the population to engage in civic activities than could do so under the absolute monarchies. In contrast, it was at almost this same time, 1656, that the court painter Velazquez finished *Las Meninas* as part of his assignment to portray the royal family. A few years after publishing *The History of Madness*, Foucault wrote *The Order of Things*, with its analysis of *Las Meninas*. It was a few years more before the second edition of *The History of Madness* was issued with the portrait of the regentesses. Why did Foucault include this painting by Hals? Many art historians regard this picture and its companion piece, one of the (male) regents of the old men's home, to be the artist's finest works. They now hang together in the former almshouse, which has become the Frans Hals Museum. Hals painted the pair, on commission, when he was a destitute man in his eighties. Although the legend that he himself had become a resident of the paupers' home is no longer believed, it does seem clear that the several applications he made for small monetary subsidies and fuel to maintain a meager standard of living were addressed either to these same trustees or to their colleagues in Haarlem.[23] In *The History of Madness*, Foucault analyzes institutions like hospitals, madhouses, and workhouses that sprang up so quickly in Europe in the seventeenth century. These were places for those who did not work, and the process of confinement was linked to the expulsion of beggars from the cities

Figure 1. Frans Hals, *The Regentesses of the Old Men's Almshouse*, ca. 1664. Frans Hals Museum, Haarlem. Foto Marburg/Art Resource, NY

and to a rigorous ethic of labor as articulated by Calvin and others. Madness, once seen in terms of its relation to the transcendent and to the power of imagination, was now affiliated with the failure to work, and so the failure to work came to be seen as not far from madness. (What then is art, we ask parenthetically, which at this time was becoming more questionable as a form of work?) The institutions develop their own, internal judicial structures, enjoying considerable autonomy in relation to the state. Foucault at his most acute sees madness as a social and historical phenomenon, one that arises correlatively with the institutions of confinement. These official portraits, hung in the almshouse, offer a frightening and devastating glimpse into this world. Or so critics began to say sometime in the late nineteenth century, after a period in which the paintings received almost no written commentary. The paintings came to be seen as the revenge of the poor painter on his subjects, subjects whom he knew in their capacity of doling out a minimal sustenance to him in his old age. The fourth man from the left in the *Regents* painting was said to be drunk, for his face is flushed, his eyes are unfocused, and his hat is worn at a rakish angle. The *Regentesses* fared even worse in the eyes of commentators. With the possible exception of the standing figure at the right, they were thought to exhibit a frightening coldness. One critic, writing in 1902, says: "These five old ladies, so grimly respectable, so austerely benevolent, so reproachfully prim and well-kept, must have been no small terror to their defaulting sisters who appeared before them—as probably Mrs. Hals had done—on a charge of poverty."[24]

In 1963 two Dutch scholars, a psychologist and an art historian, published an essay titled "The Malignity of Hals's Governors" in which they sought to question such judgments of the painting. They argued that the sitters would never have accepted a painting showing them in a strongly unfavorable light; that the "drunken" man was probably the victim of a facial paralysis or deformity, and that wearing one's hat at an extreme angle was a fashion of the times; and that the conventions of Dutch portraiture were such that a fairly strict and realistic representation of subjects was expected, even if it meant showing people with unattractive features.[25] Appealing to authorities in both art history and psychology, they argued that physiognomy is no sign of character. After the publication of this article, there have been very few defenses of the earlier view of the painting, a view that seems essential to Foucault's use of the portrait; he would scarcely assign the position that he did to a work that he thought of simply as a factual transcription of the appearance of five women who shared a certain responsibility.

One loud dissent on the painting has been sounded by John Berger, in his BBC series and later book, *Ways of Seeing*. Berger discusses what he calls the "mystification" of the painting by an art historian he describes as a typical academic. As Berger's footnote tells us, the scholar is Seymour Slive, and we learn from Slive's work that he supports his view of the painting by referring to the two Dutch writers, who marshaled a number of positivistic arguments to deny the malignity of the figures in the two paintings.[26] Berger quotes from Slive's description of the paintings to demonstrate the way in which the critic appeals to presumably universal aesthetic standards to discuss the success of the works; on his reading the paintings are great because of their qualities of formal composition and their insight into the (apparently timeless) "human condition."[27] This is a mystification, Berger says, because it obscures the specific relations of power and wealth that form the content and the context of the painting; and when Slive says that Hals's figures "almost seduce us into believing that we know the personality traits and even the habits of the men and women portrayed," Berger thinks that he is denying the power of these paintings to transmit living human expression. But what is painting, at least painting in the grand style, if it cannot convey a meaningful expression? This is a question that Nietzsche, a keen student of the exchange of glances and the reading of faces, would also want to pose (secs. 33–34).

Foucault refers us to Claudel's judgment of the painting of the regentesses, which describes the work as introducing us to a zone between life and death, more terrifying than hell because of its uncertainty. These are the judges, reminding us of those who will preside over our eternal fate. Claudel writes:

> All the accounts are settled; there is no more money on the table; there is only this book definitely closed whose flat surface shines like bones and whose edges are of burning, fiery red. The first of the regentesses, the one at the corner of the table who had at first appeared to us as the most reassuring, tells us with that indirect look and that open hand that interprets the other which is closed: *It is finished! And that is that! And as for the other four ghouls . . .* but let us first dispose of the one who is bringing the president a card probably bearing our name. We are dealing with a sort of feminine tribunal whose collarettes and cuffs, that isolate and severely outline their masks and hands, accentuate their judiciary character. They have opened session not before a crucifix but before a picture representing the shadowy banks of the river of death. If we succeed

in detaching our attention from that skeleton claw that she spreads out flat on her knee, the hard eyes, the compressed lips, the book on which she leans demonstrate sufficiently that we cannot count on this lady. And as for the president, in the center with her gloves and that fan she holds affectedly, that deceitful face puckered up into a beak by a frightful smile, indicates that here we have to do with something more pitiless than justice, and that is annihilation.[28]

Claudel continues, speaking of "this phosphorescent emanation, the vampire *aura*, that floats from these four figures as from a dead body." We can put a more historical spin on this otherworldly description if we note that one-third of the population of Haarlem had just died of the plague and that there were great pressures on the institutions for poor relief.

Foucault begins the book to which he added this picture with a commentary on Bosch, Breughel, and other fifteenth-century painters of madness and ends it with some remarks on Goya and Van Gogh. He claims that in recent times, madness and literature have been in communication, as in Rimbaud, Kafka, Artaud, and Beckett; but in the fifteenth century, painting was more attuned to the dreams and nightmares of madness. This painting of the regentesses shows that those whose job it is to oversee deviance, to control idleness and madness, cannot help but appear mad themselves. Since madness is constructed in a series of practices and institutions, it involves the supervisors as well as the supervised. In the essay "Madness, the Absence of Work," which he adds along with the Hals painting, Foucault asks what we will *look like* to a future—a possible future of new pharmacological and social techniques—that does not understand the importance that the nineteenth and twentieth centuries attached to madness. So the second edition of *The History of Madness* is, as it were, flanked by a pair of bookends: at one end, the ghoulish regentesses passing judgment on their charges, at the other an essay that asks how we shall look to another age. The regentesses might be thought of as casting an evil eye on the inmates, and there is something mad both in the fear of the evil eye and in those to whom it is attributed. Here we need to make a distinction: Foucault is frequently concerned with visual works or architectural structures, like the Hals painting or the Panopticon, that represent or embody a malevolent gaze; but this is not to say either that he thinks that the entire visual world is oriented in this way or that he judges the entire spectrum of visibility to be under the sway of an evil eye.

Foucault constantly placed his own work under the sign of Nietzsche's thought. The Nietzschean inspiration of Foucault's genealogy is evident and is given a very explicit statement in the essay "Nietzsche, Genealogy, History." I will be suggesting that Foucault's attention to the visual also bears a Nietzschean stamp, and this may not be so obvious. It may seem implausible to think of Nietzsche, whose eye troubles are famous, as having something important to say about the visual world. Foucault seldom speaks of Nietzsche explicitly when he is concerned with visual themes. However, Georges Bataille, one of Nietzsche's self-appointed heirs who is also one of Foucault's great predecessors, can begin to help us establish a point of contact. In his novel *The Story of the Eye*, eyes are glorified and humiliated, tortured and sexualized; the eye becomes a general figure of excess, and eggs, testicles, and much else (in accordance with a traditional symbolism) become virtual eyes, seeing everything, guaranteeing that everything is on display (for a consideration of Foucault's response to Bataille's eye, see sec. 42). These eyes are ophthalmic eyes as well as visual ones; that is, they are eyes of flesh and mucus, eyes that not only weep but are in principle, like no other eye among the animals, always open to the possibility of weeping. In a later preface to this story, Bataille writes of *W.C.*, a book he claims to have written and burned the year before publishing the version we have now. He says: "A drawing for *W.C.* showed an eye: the scaffold's eye. Solitary, solar, bristling with lashes, it gazed from the lunette of a guillotine. The drawing was named *The Eternal Return*, and its horrible machine was the crossbeam, gymnastic gallows, portico. Coming from the horizon, the road to eternity passed through it. A parodistic verse, heard in a sketch at the *Concert Mayol,* supplied the caption: 'God, how the corpse's blood is sad in the depth of sound.'"[29] It is not clear how much resonance Bataille expected this drawing to have with the scene at the doorway in the chapter of *Thus Spoke Zarathustra* entitled "On the Vision and the Riddle." In both cases it seems that something about eternal return is being illustrated by a scene in which there is an archlike structure through which a road runs, and the road is a pathway of eternity. There are differences: Bataille's road runs *through* the guillotine, while two ways *abut* or confront one another at Zarathustra's *Thorweg.* One might also notice that in each case there is a scene that has or contains an inscription. Bataille's putting the eye squarely in the midst of the scene of eternal recurrence reveals a powerful reading of Nietzsche, who would provoke some of his other excursions into a writing and thinking of excess. Bataille's scene is perhaps the devilish inversion of Nietzsche's; for Bataille, the eye of God, mysteriously singular and detached, presides over an eternal scene of execution, while the transformative doorway of the *Augenblick* is transformed into the eternal instrument of punishment and its reminder of guilt. In *Thus Spoke Zarathustra*, Nietzsche sets a highly visual scene at a gateway, one that is inscribed *Augenblick;* this word is best translated as "twinkling of the eye" to preserve its visual connotation, one obscured in ordinary German usage but heightened by the poetic and rhetorical context of *Zarathustra* (see sec. 33). I will also be suggesting that we can read *Zarathustra* as the story of the eyes, although one with a rather different focus than Bataille's.

With this hint, we can proceed to see how it is that Nietzsche might be taken seriously as a theorist of vision. Like other philosophers, thinkers, and writers, Nietzsche constantly speaks of knowing, believing, realizing, and other cognitive activities in terms of a language or rhetoric of vision. The habit is so deeply rooted that we seldom notice it in ourselves or others; we fail to see what we are doing, even when it is right before our eyes. If it does come to our attention, in our own language or in that of others, we may think, rightly, that the practice derives from and is symptomatic of some long-standing and largely unconscious assumptions about the hegemony of vision. Such assumptions have also come in for critique and interrogation by a number of philosophers, especially in the last century, and we will shortly consider some of these critiques. Nietzsche's very shorthand and proleptic anticipation of such critiques is expressed in the question quoted at the beginning of this chapter: "Our eye sees falsely, it abbreviates and compounds: is that a reason to abandon vision and to say it is good for nothing?" Whatever the limits of vision, the point is not to abandon it but to employ it with a sense of those limits; the task may be to rethink the nature of vision and visibility. In a question that we will come back to, Nietzsche has Zarathustra ask, "Is not seeing itself—seeing abysses?" (Z III.2; KSA 4.199). Let me suggest, briefly and schematically, that this rhetorical question is meant to suggest the following points about vision, either as one of our so-called five senses or as a symbol of what it is to sense, know, and understand: (1) vision is never totalizing and absolutely comprehensive; (2) there is no absolute foundation or ground to the abyss *(Abgrund)* which is vision; (3) seeing is never simple; it entails the risk of looking into and sometimes teetering on the edge of an abyss; this can induce vertigo; (4) vision is through and through perspectival; there is no intrinsically privileged place from which to see things; and (5) every act of vision is framed in a larger context of which we may or may not become aware; in other words, the abyss is not just an intensive one, within some specific scene, but also extensive, characterizing the series of frames within which that vision is set. Nietzsche, I suggest, sets himself the task of rethinking vision along these lines. In the chapters that follow, I explore this rethinking especially in two books—*The Birth of Tragedy*, which is concerned both with the nature of Apollonian visionary art and with the perspectival architectonics of the theater, and *Thus Spoke Zarathustra*, which is permeated by an optical discourse, ranging from the initial invocation of the sun as a great, quiet eye to the visual scenario in which Zarathustra attempts to convey the significance of the eternal return of the *Augenblick*, or twinkling of the eye. But in addition to these canonical sources, I explore other discussions of and references to visual art and the visual world that appear throughout Nietzsche's writings, including his notebooks and his letters.

For now I propose to approach this project of rethinking vision by looking at some remarks scattered in a number of Nietzsche's texts. I will juxtapose these with some of the criticisms, implicit and explicit, of the alleged ocularcentrism of philosophy as voiced by thinkers such as Martin Heidegger and Luce Irigaray. A few striking formulations are found in the books sometimes described as Nietzsche's "enlightenment" writings, or works of his "middle period"—specifically *Human, All Too Human* and *Daybreak*. If there is a thematics of vision and visual culture here, it may be analogous to the one sustained by the movement of thought known as the Enlightenment. This is not to say that Nietzsche adopts the metaphysics or aesthetics of presence that characterizes the classical Enlightenment. Indeed, the perspectivism that is explicitly formulated in some of these writings is to be contrasted with the way in which the Enlightenment tends to equate seeing and knowing. In the preface that he added to *Human, All Too Human* in 1886 (eight years after its initial publication), Nietzsche declares himself to be a philosopher of suspicion, describing that suspicion in highly visual terms. He looks more closely where others are naive, and he stays with the surface more rigorously than do those thinkers who posit a reality behind the appearances:

> In fact I do not believe that anyone has looked into the world with
> an equally profound degree of suspicion . . . and anyone who could
> divine something of the consequences that lie in that profound suspi-
> ciousness, something of the fears and frosts of the isolation to which
> that unconditional *disparity of view* [*Verschiedenheit des Blicks*] con-
> demns him who is infected with it, will also understand. . . . What I

again and again needed most for my cure and self-restoration, however, was the belief that I was not thus isolated, not alone in *seeing* as I did—an enchanted surmising of relatedness in eye and desires, a blindness in concert with another without suspicion or question-marks, a pleasure in foregrounds, surfaces, things close and closest, in everything possessing color, skin, and apparitionality [*Scheinbarkeit*]. (*HAH*, pref., 1; *KSA* 2.13–14)

The poles of Nietzsche's "method," then, are a deeply suspicious look and an intense desire that others share his point of view: on the one hand an "evil eye" *(böse Blick)* for that which is questionable, on the other a willingness to suffer illusion for the sake of a common perspective. As should become clear, Nietzsche does not claim that this common perspective is somehow dictated by the materials of vision.

Nothing is more of a commonplace in speaking of Nietzsche than to point out that he is not a systematic thinker and to observe that he is capable of writing apparently contradictory statements on what appears to be the same topic. In *Twilight of the Idols*, he declares that "the will to a system is a lack of integrity" (*T*, "Maxims," 26; *KSA* 6.63). Yet even if Nietzsche rejects system (and the sense of this term would need to be articulated), there now appear to be much greater continuities and firmer structures in his thought and writing than was generally apparent before Heidegger's and Deleuze's studies (to take only two notable examples of works that have contributed to transforming our picture of his work). In the case of everything connected with vision, we will be challenged by the tension between what might provisionally be called systematic and unsystematic tendencies in Nietzsche's thought. He never explicitly provides an extended account of vision, visual art, or visual culture, in the way that he does of tragedy, morality, or philosophy. Yet his writing is suffused with a visual language, which is often developed with great elaboration, and there are many sections of his work, such as those we will consider in *The Birth of Tragedy*, that carry out an analysis of the visual with some rigor.

If *Human, All Too Human* does indeed belong to Nietzsche's "enlightenment" or "positivistic" phase, then it is here, if anywhere, that we might expect to find him adopting some version of the hegemony of vision, where vision is understood in terms of the metaphysics of presence, as a modality of sense that allows for a detached and objective observation of a whole or a totality spread out before us. Yet even in this "enlightened" text, he establishes an important critical distance from such a position. And this is so even despite certain appearances to the contrary. Early in the book, for example, Nietzsche gives an account of the "logic of the dream." This proves to be a rather constant theme in his writings; he already relied on an analysis of the dream in his first book, *The Birth of Tragedy*, treating it above all as a visual phenomenon; here Nietzsche adopts the rhetoric of nineteenth-century psychology and optics. He suggests that when we are asleep (or even when we close our eyes while awake), "the brain produces a host of light-impressions and colors, probably as a kind of afterplay and echo of those effects of light which crowd in upon it during the day." Since we cannot tolerate a mere chaos of impressions, we are unconsciously compelled to organize these random data into "definite figures, shapes, landscapes, moving groups. What is actually occurring is again a kind of inferring of the cause from the effect; the mind asks where these light-impressions and colors come from and supposes these shapes and figures as their causes: it regards them as occasioning these lights and colors because, by day and with eyes open, it is accustomed to finding that every color, every light impression does in fact have a cause that occasions it. . . . as with a conjuror, a confusion of judgment can here arise" (*HAH* 13; *KSA* 2.34). Characteristically, Nietzsche adds that this process of confused inference is all too easy for us and that we live about half our lives still in this condition of interpreting as in fantasy and dream. He would seem to be adopting a Cartesian, Humean, or Russellian account of vision, according to which what we see is a construct, more or less justified, that arises from a series of discrete visual impressions. Ambiguity, confusion, or uncertainty is to be ascribed not to the data but to our own processes of construction and inference.

However, just a few aphorisms later, Nietzsche discusses "Appearance and Thing Itself," in a way that modifies the apparent reductionism of "Logic of the Dream." There he compares philosophers to spectators standing before a painting and attempting to interpret it correctly. They disagree as to whether this painting is an informative indication of the thing in itself (roughly analogous to Locke's view) or whether the connection is completely indeterminate (somewhat like Schopenhauer's position). But both are said to be making the same mistake: "Both parties, however, overlook the possibility that this painting—which we call human life and experience—has gradually *become*, is indeed still fully in course of *becoming*, and should thus not be regarded as a fixed object on the basis of which a conclusion as to the nature of its originator (the sufficient reason) may either be drawn or pronounced undrawable" (*HAH* 16; *KSA* 2.36). If the painting has acquired color over many years, Nietzsche adds, we may forget that "we have been the colorists." So the suggestion here is that vision itself is in flux, that the very idea of there being constant elementary data that serve as the foundation of the forms or gestalts that we see is an illusion. There never was such a firm bedrock of visual impressions that would have served as the basis of inferences, whether conscious or unconscious, everyday or philosophical. Consequently, the thing in itself "is worthy of Homeric laughter." Visual interpretation and imagination, Nietzsche might say in more recent jargon, goes all the way down.

The title of a late Nietzsche text, *Twilight of the Idols*, evokes a time of day that involves subtle shadings and chiaroscuro; it is the *Zwielicht* or *Dämmerung* that might provide an alternative to the all-too-bright and illusory light of the Enlightenment. Nietzsche is concerned with such effects, which would be the optical analog of his notion of sounding out idols with a tuning fork (the "hammer" of the book's subtitle, "How One Philosophizes with a Hammer"). However, it may be difficult at first to see whether he holds a consistent view or whether there is some principle that would make his apparent shift of positions comprehensible. Here, in a chapter called "What the Germans Lack," Nietzsche argues that they require an education in seeing: "One has to learn to *see*, one has to learn to *think*, one has to learn to *speak* and *write:* the end in all three is a noble culture.—Learning to *see*— habituating the eye to repose, to patience, to letting things come to it; learning to defer judgment, to investigate and comprehend the individual case in all its aspects. . . . the essence of it is precisely *not* to 'will,' the ability to defer decision" (*T*, "What the Germans Lack," 6; *KSA* 6.108–9). Here it is not immediately clear to what extent *seeing* functions as a name for a general dimension of all education and culture and to what extent it is modeled on the specific experience of ocular vision. It may be useful to know, however, that drawing had a rather strong position in the Swiss educational system with which Nietzsche became familiar in Basel. As a recent historian of the period observes:

> Drawing was not an idle supplement to education in the Basel of Burckhardt's day. Doubtless because of its importance to technicians and designers in the ribbon industry, it was one of the subjects regularly taught in the city-state's public schools after the educational reforms of 1817. . . . in the popular educational ideas and projects of Johann Heinrich Pestalozzi . . . drawing appears not as a luxury or an optional extra, not as an accomplishment of people of a certain social class, not even as a valuable practical skill, but as a critical part of the education of the child, promoting careful observation and a healthy relation between the subject and the object world.[30]

As this same study goes on to note, the critical term used by Pestalozzi that also turns up in Goethe and Burckhardt to designate the virtue promoted by drawing is *Anschauung;* this is usually translated as "intuition," but we may need to attend to its specifically visual meaning (as in the first sentence of *The Birth of Tragedy*). We might say that we shall have to *see*, in the sense of reading and thinking with care and not leaping to premature judgments. The need for such a philological approach (philology is defined as "slow reading" in the preface to *Daybreak*) could also be signaled by an encounter with what Nietzsche says just a little later in *Twilight*, where he condemns observation for its own sake and couches the entire aphorism in the language of painting, vision, and the eye, suggesting that an overly interested observation will produce a "false optics" and a "squint":

> To experience from a *desire* to experience—that's no good. In experiencing one *must* not look back towards oneself, or every glance becomes an "evil eye" [*jeder Blick wird da zum "bösen Blick"*]. A born psychologist instinctively guards against seeing for the sake of seeing; the same applies to the born painter. He never works "from nature"—he leaves it to his instinct, his *camera obscura*, to sift and strain "nature," the "case," the "experience." . . . What will be the result if one does otherwise? Carries on colportage psychology in, for example, the manner of Parisian *romanciers* great and small? . . . just see what finally emerges—a pile of daubs [*Klecksen*], a mosaic at best, in any event something put together, restless, flashy. . . . Seeing *what is*—that pertains to a different species of spirit, the *anti-artistic*, the prosaic. One has to know *who* one is. (*T*, "Skirmishes," 7; *KSA* 6.115–16)

(Later, in the context of reading *Thus Spoke Zarathustra*, we will encounter again the notion of the resentful and destructive "evil eye" that appears here and which is to be contrasted with Zarathustra's "radiant eye.")

An attempt could be made to harmonize these two statements by pointing out that in the first case Nietzsche is discussing the minimal conditions of culture, not its highest attainments; in the second he is expressly prescribing for the psychologist, who must not remain at the level of naive observation. We might also say that in the first aphorism he addresses the deficiency of the Germans, while in the second he speaks of what the French (or their psychologists) possess in excess. Such a reading would tend to reduce the specifically visual connotations of Nietzsche's language to a customary and general way of speaking about observation and knowledge. Now while Nietzsche can hardly avoid the strong relation between seeing and knowing that is embedded in Western languages and their philosophies, there are other elements at work here. In the first aphorism, Nietzsche focuses on the importance of learning to see *before* one does anything else, and he emphasizes the powerful self-restraint that is necessary in order to resist the temptation to yield to the first stimulus that comes along. In the second, he compares the psychologist to a painter, that is, to one who is actively involved in shaping objects for vision. The painter and his kin are explorers and researchers in the realm of the visual, Nietzsche assumes, and so they must create, shape, and constrain their material. The visionary (or Apollonian) artist is not merely receptive; such a painter may put out of play Dionysian exuberance, intoxication, and multiplicity, but this artist *invents* and does not merely observe. In the passage above, Nietzsche speaks of the painter's use of "his instinct, his *camera obscura*, to sift and strain" his materials. He employs the notion of the camera obscura as a figure to denote the fact that the painter must choose what to represent and how to represent it. Yet the camera obscura was an actual optical instrument used frequently by the old masters, used indeed to frame and delimit their subjects; through a pinhole in a dark chamber, light projected an inverted image of the subject, which could be traced, and altered, by the artist. Whether or not the painter employs such an external device to give order to the picture, the point is that the procedure is never a sheer, unmediated beholding. In this sense, drawing can and does function as an instrument for the painter, an instrument that gives an initial, selective shape to the subject and allows for further development and variation.

5 Realism: Reading from Left to Right

Nietzsche's claim can be illustrated most readily by looking at the work of artists who are regarded as great realists, masters at depicting precisely what is in front of them. A painter whose work might seem to fit this description is Hans Holbein. Nietzsche would have encountered his painting of two Englishmen, *Thomas Godsalve and his Son John*, at the Dresden Gallery (fig. 2); Holbein was a native of Basel, and many of his pictures are there, where Nietzsche would also have seen them (he may also have been aware of Burckhardt's interest in Holbein, which was sufficiently developed that he had a connoisseur's opinions about which of the paintings attributed to him were genuine). This double portrait appears to be a masterpiece of realism. Julia Kristeva

Figure 2. Hans Holbein, *Portrait of Thomas Godsalve and His Son John*, 1528. Gemäldegalerie Alte Meister, Staatliche Kunstsammlungen, Dresden. Foto Marburg/Art Resource, New York

has argued that Holbein's realism, as exemplified in his *Christ Dead in the Grave,* has a strongly depressive dimension, portraying things in the starkest of terms.[31] Death is not present only through such devices as the famous anamorphic skull of *The Ambassadors*, but in the very facticity of the painter's manner. Indeed it is, insofar as there is a painstaking and successful attempt to capture the textures and tones of cloth, fur, skin, metal, and paper. The setting is rather spare, and this allows the painter to develop a number of specific objects and themes. We notice the resemblance of the sitters, something of which we would be aware even without the title's telling us that they are father and son. The clothing is somewhat restrained in comparison with other portraits of the time (we could compare it, for example, with that in the Dresden portrait *Charles de Solier* or the famous painting *The Ambassadors* in London). Thomas's sober black coat nevertheless has a fur lining, as does his cape; John's sleeve displays the fur of his own coat. The writing instruments, including the inkwell and its attachment (perhaps a blotter or seal attached by a red cord), occupy the narrow section of a writing table, the surface closest to the viewer. In the early sixteenth century, such portraits functioned as official or legal depictions of their subjects. Holbein tends to emphasize or exaggerate this dimension of the genre by attaching a date to the painting in the upper left corner. Yet this addendum to the image breaks the realistic frame; the paper with the Latin inscription of the date 1528 seems pasted on the surface of the canvas itself, rather than attached (or inscribed, as it might have been) on the wall behind the sitters. But now that we notice this text, we can hardly avoid thinking about the one that Thomas is composing, and it is perhaps by understanding the role of writing in this painting that we come to see what Holbein has accomplished with his (figurative) camera obscura. The older man has paused for a moment in writing; so far he has penned his name and age in Latin: Thomas Godsalve of Norwich, forty-seven years of age.

We know, as Nietzsche probably would not, that Thomas was a notary and a moderately successful landowner; he was intensely ambitious for his son and managed to have him appointed to governmental positions, culminating in his becoming a knight and comptroller of the Mint under Edward VI. Even without being aware of these things, the philosopher would notice the prominence of the written word in this picture. Writing is the only action that is being (or has been) performed here; the diagonal line suggested by Thomas's pen, passing through the V formed by their two shoulders and through John's prominent nose, links the text of the sitter with that of the painter. That which is within the frame of the picture points to something, the date seemingly pasted onto the canvas with an irregular piece of paper, which makes us aware of the framing conventions themselves. Writing, perhaps especially in paintings of this genre at this time, is a mark of finitude and mortality.[32] There was a concern that having oneself represented in a painting might be an act of vanity, so there is a tendency to make each portrait into a memento mori. By fixing the date of the picture and the age of the sitter, the painter reminds us that this is a portrait valid only for a time; the sitter will age and die, like the painter and like the rest of us. Nothing more can be claimed than to have depicted Thomas and his son as they were in Thomas's forty-seventh year. Might writing play some other roles in this double portrait? John is clutching a folded piece of paper, something that may bear an inscription; perhaps it is his father's letter to Thomas Cromwell, petitioning him in the most diplomatic terms to find a place for his son; it would be John's ticket to higher things. In the minimal space of this painting, writing and its implements are the only foci other than the sitters; there is none of the glorious apparatus that graces the world of *The Ambassadors,* nor are there the rich, patterned background, the ornate clothing, and the dagger that can be seen in the Dresden portrait *Charles de Solier.* Luther had already been preaching of the absolute superiority of the word to the image, and we might find something of the Protestant spirit here. Perhaps the most obvious, global feature of this picture is the arrangement of the two sitters. Rather than facing straight ahead, as in so many double portraits (of royal or distinguished couples or, again, of *The Ambassadors*), these two men both face to the right. Thomas, pausing in his composition, looks straight ahead and a bit upward; John, in his junior position (he is also bareheaded) tilts his head downward and is in a position to read his father's writing. The embroidery on his collar echoes some of the loops and curlicues of the notary's Latin, as if he were himself a text produced by the man with the pen. Several observers have remarked on the unusual double pose of two rightward looks. So far as I know, none has suggested that this may have something to do with our Western practice of reading script from left to right, a practice that we also seem to transfer to the reading of pictures. This implicit convention would have us attend first to John and then to his father; we see that the father is writing and the son is reading. In left-to-right reading of paintings, it is typical (but not inevitable) that while the eye is led into the picture by something on the left, it is something on the right that is of greater importance. Here it is Thomas the writer and his text, a text whose instrument, the pen, completes a zigzag movement by referring us back to the mark of the painter: not a signature in a narrow sense, but the pasted date that makes it impossible to ignore the fact of this image's fabrication. Everything about the painting is structured by the left-to-right pattern, a pattern imposed by the painter through his camera obscura, which manages to produce a meaningful construction from the sparsest materials. This is perhaps an instance of the lesson that Nietzsche alludes to in the aphorism *What one should learn from artists* (*GS* 299):

> How can we make things beautiful, attractive, and desirable for us when they are not? And I rather think that in themselves they never are. Here we could learn something . . . from artists who are really continually trying to bring off such inventions and feats. Mov-

ing away from things until there is a good deal that one no longer sees and there is much that our eye has to add if we are still to see them at all; or seeing things around a corner and as cut out and framed; or to place them so that they partially conceal each other and grant us only glimpses of perspectives; or looking at them through tinted glass or in the light of the sunset; or giving them a surface and skin that is not fully transparent—all this we should learn from artists while being wiser than they are in other matters.

Artists are good at producing framing and perspectives. As Nietzsche's late preface to *The Birth of Tragedy* has it, they help us to see science (or attempts at realism) in the optics of art; but we should go further and see art in the optics of life, that is, we should use it to make the things of our lives, indeed those very lives themselves, "beautiful, attractive, and desirable."

⬛ Hidden Images: Before the Age of Art

One way to learn from the artists that Nietzsche cites as exemplars is to see them as working with media, styles, and genres that (like the sixteenth-century portrait) have a specific historical situation. In *Twilight of the Idols,* he charges philosophers with a failure of historical sense that leads them to produce conceptual mummifications of whatever they theorize (*T*, "Reason," 1; *KSA* 6.74). Surely this would apply to what is said and thought about vision, which has traditionally been taken to be a pure and unchanging mode of perceiving its objects. One example: in *The Birth of Tragedy*, Nietzsche offers what is, in effect, an archaeology of the Greek theatrical experience, explaining the way in which it sets up the possibility for a distinctive form of spectatorship that has fallen into oblivion (secs. 25–29). There are other texts where he articulates a conception of visual culture as something with a history, attempting to free the practices of seeing and of making things to be seen from philosophy's Egypticizing tendencies. Nietzsche's fullest sketch of an archaeology of vision occurs in a long aphorism in *Human, All Too Human* (*HAH, AOM*, 222; *KSA* 5.474–76). Entitled *The simple comes neither first nor last in time*, it begins by considering the history of "religious conceptions," and it does so by interrogating the presuppositions of a gradualist and evolutionary account of the development of religious images or representations of the divine. It is tempting to believe, Nietzsche suggests, that there has been a "gradual evolution of *representations of gods* [*Götterdarstellung*] from clumsy stones and blocks of wood up to complete humanization." Such an evolutionary narrative might be called Hegelian; in any case it brings to mind a host of ways of thinking about the development of culture that were rife in the nineteenth century. They tend to reduce the historical dimension by seeing growth as a teleological process in which the goal is already immanent in a process from the beginning. The result is a narrative that depicts human beings as moving by a series of intelligible steps from a position in which they confront the religious as something mysteriously other and transcendent to one in which they acknowledge their own nature in the highest reality, finally representing it to themselves in the beautiful images of the Greek gods as we know them from fifth-century Athens.

This story, according to which we have come to understand ourselves ever more completely and in which the dimension of sheer otherness is overcome, would suggest that vision and the production of images are destined to approach and capture reality, to make it all present with no unrepresentable residue. This would be to subordinate the visual to the metaphysics of presence. It is to suppose that the deepest intention of visual images has always been to make everything present. This was of course a familiar narrative in nineteenth-century histories of painting and the visual arts; inspired by Italian Renaissance painting and its tradition, critics and historians found it easy to see the history of art as a series of progressive conquests of the world of appearances. The pattern is clearly established in Vasari's *Lives of the Painters,* in which the line from Giotto to Michelangelo is represented as a successive string of discoveries of the visual world with respect to perspective, color, modeling, and texture.

Contained in this narrative is a certain imperial, hegemonic conception of the visual that takes painting to be a kind of science, a paradigm of human knowledge, which must have as its goal to lay everything before us, to open it to our inspection. It is the "empire of the gaze" (as Martin Jay calls it), in which the monocular, absolute perspective of Alberti and his disciples joins hands with Cartesian method and optics. Merleau-Ponty analyzes this reductive approach to vision in "Eye and Mind," demonstrating that Descartes provides "the breviary of a thought that wants no longer to abide in the visible and so decides to construct the visible according to a certain model-in-thought."[33]

In Descartes's optics and in his remarks on painting, we find an account of vision as a deciphering of signs in which visual clues allow us to reconstruct the genuine, geometric order of the world; color, depth, the intermingling of objects, and above all the complicity of the viewer in the scene beheld are excluded from this attempt to construe vision on the model of line drawings, diagrams, and engravings. By the nineteenth century, philosophical modernity had made common cause with an evolutionary history of religion and symbols, so that the movement that Vasari saw as originating with Giotto could now be read back into the earliest forms of the production of images and deployed to explain the history of religion.

It is in this context that we should understand Nietzsche's intervention and interrogation of what might be called the aesthetics of presence and its history of images. The context of his discussion of the history of visual images, then, is the typical belief of the nineteenth century that everything has become visible, that the development of visual representation and its culture have been a steady progress toward the light. In the section from *Human, All Too Human*, Nietzsche describes the early images of the gods not in terms of an aesthetics of presence but as exemplifying a play of the present and the absent, the clear and the obscure, the manifest and the hidden; and he insists that this has nothing to do with an incapacity of the artists or the confusions of an incipient process of image-making that is just finding itself. He tells a story of interruptions and cross-pollination in which the poets, themselves creators of images, provoke changes in the visual imagination:

> [S]o long as the divinity was introduced into trees, pieces of wood, stones, animals, and felt to reside there, one shrank from a humanization of their form [*Gestalt*] as from an act of godlessness. It required the poets, existing outside the the religious cult and the spell of religious *awe*, to accustom the inner phantasy [*innere Phantasie*] of men to acceding to such a thing; overweighed again by more pious moods and moments, however, this liberating influence of the poets again withdrew and the sacred remained, as before, in the realm of the monstrous, uncanny, and quite specifically non-human. (*HAH, AOM,* 222; *KSA* 2.475)[34]

Here Nietzsche gives an account of the "uncanny [*unheimlich*]" status of the cult object. It was not understood to be either a representation or a thing of beauty. It was not yet conceived as a work of art. Indeed, if we are to be precise, the modern conception of fine art as embracing (at least) architecture, sculpture, painting, music, and poetry was probably formulated no earlier than the eighteenth century, as Paul Kristeller reminds us.[35] The cult object might be a natural thing set aside by the priest and provided with a simple framework. The poets come from outside the confines of the cult; as Nietzsche emphasizes in his earliest writings (sec. 14), they are themselves makers of images. They work on men's *innere Phantasie;* and I suggest that we respect the connection between *Phantasie* and the Greek *phantasm,* which has the sense of a visual manifestation (see chaps. 3 and 11). The poets, in Nietzsche's narrative, provoke images or phantasms of the gods in the mind's eye of the community. We can mark Nietzsche's departure from Lessing's division of arts of space and arts of time by noting that he takes it to be a matter of course that the poet can produce the possibility of a change in visual culture. Human beings are tempted to see more of the divinities. But a reaction sets in, probably because of the priestly fear of profaning the mysteries. Now, however, there is a continuing tension between the dimensions of concealment and manifestation. The cult object exists in a strange space between presence and absence. We know something of such a situation through the fairly well documented history of the sacred image in Christianity. In *Likeness and Presence,* Hans Belting has described how holy images were thought of in terms of their actual power as forms through which the divine became present; the images were conceived not primarily as the productions of painters, but as the emanations of God and the saints.[36] They did not exist in order to be seen and contemplated but might be brought out occasionally with great ceremony, for example, once a year on a saint's feast day. There were a series of iconoclastic controversies in which the adversaries of images argued that their powers were overrated. The Reformation was, on the whole, an iconoclastic movement, and the Counter Reformation made a generally unsuccessful attempt to restore the "uncanny" and "mysterious" power of the image. We can make some sense of Nietzsche's attempt to reconstruct the structures of visual presence and absence by keeping this history in mind. Indeed, we might also ask whether Belting's alternative to a more continuous, evolutionary art history is possible only because of an intellectual climate that owes much to critiques by Nietzsche and others of such forms of thinking. Belting takes note of the obstacles faced by such archaeological thinking in describing his own program of unearthing the age of the image:

> It is difficult to evaluate the significance of the image in European culture. If we remain within the millennium with which this book is concerned [approximately 400–1400 C.E.], we are everywhere obstructed by written texts, for Christianity is a religion of the word. If we step outside this millennium into the modern period, we find art in our way, a new function that fundamentally transformed the old image. We are so deeply influenced by the "era of art" that we

find it hard to imagine the "era of images." Art history therefore simply declared everything to be art in order to bring everything within its domain, thereby effacing the very difference that might have thrown light on our subject.[37]

Belting's statement of the dilemma is intriguing. He suggests no easy way out. In effect, he proceeds by working with both texts and visual artifacts (to introduce a term that might include both the image and art as he uses those concepts). The question of how it is possible to escape the blinkers of the era of art is not directly addressed. André Malraux argued in *The Voices of Silence* that techniques of reproduction and the institution of the museum have empowered art to devour the remains of previous epochs in which the objects of the museum were once significant loci of religious or political power.[38] Philosophically, our history has been structured by aesthetics, which has tended to accept "the modern system of the arts," to read it back into earliest history, and then to attempt to establish its conceptual foundations by appealing to universal human faculties, in the style of Kant, or to show that it is the meaning of history itself, in the style of Hegel. Later we will find Foucault implicitly criticizing Merleau-Ponty for being caught within the modernist regime of art, and we will see that Merleau-Ponty's arguments against Malraux are modernist responses to the latter's protoarchaeology (secs. 46–48). Might it be that Foucault speaks with some justice when he maintains that it is only possible to delimit the distinctive structural features of an era or epoch when it has passed away? If Hegel made a superficially similar remark in his *Philosophy of Right*, maintaining that philosophy paints its gray in gray only in the evening when the owl of Minerva takes flight, he does not seem to have envisaged the radical division of eras of art, its predecessors, and its successors that Nietzsche and Foucault discern.

Nietzsche continues by describing a conflict between the "inward and the outward eye"; and if we take the inner eye to be the imagination (as Nietzsche's translators sometimes do), we should realize that the imagination is a faculty of images *(Bilder)*. There is a struggle between rival forms or cultures of *Phantasie:*

> But even much of that which phantasy dares to construct for itself would, translated into outward, bodily representation, nonetheless produce a painful effect; the inward eye [*innere Auge*] is very much bolder and less bashful than the outward (which is why it is difficult, and in part impossible, to convert epic material into dramatic). Religious phantasy for a long time *refuses* absolutely to believe in

the identity of the god and an image [*Bild*]; the image is supposed
to be the visible evidence that the *numen* of the divinity is, in some
mysterious, not fully comprehensible way, active in this place and
bound to it. (*HAH, AOM,* 222; *KSA* 2.475)

Religious fantasy, on this account, resists the innovations of the poets.
The play of conflicting forces can be best described genealogically,
rather than as a continuous development or the unfolding of a meaning
that was there in germ from the beginning. As Nietzsche says in a
lapidary (and deceptively parenthetical) formulation in *On the Genealogy of Morals,* "only that which has no history can be defined" (*GM*
II.13; *KSA* 5.317). This applies to the world of images and visual culture
as much as to practices such as punishment. That the Greeks finally
come to accept and venerate the sculpture that Winckelmann and others
taught the moderns to see as the expression of "noble simplicity and
quiet grandeur [*edle Einfalt und stille Grösse*]" must be seen as one
result of a tangled history, rather than as the expression of the integral
spirit of a people. If Lessing began the work of contextualizing Greek
beauty in terms of the specific media of the different arts, Nietzsche
continues that work (and differs from Lessing) by understanding it as
a fragile product of a complex *agon.* Nietzsche now gives his account
of the "oldest," or most archaic, modality of divine images, one that
conveys the sense of the labyrinthine character of the image together
with its frames:

> The oldest image of the god [*Götterbild*] is supposed to *harbor and
> at the same time conceal the god*—to intimate his presence but not
> expose it to view. No Greek ever truly *beheld* his Apollo as a
> wooden obelisk, his Eros as a lump of stone; they were symbols
> whose purpose was precisely to excite fear *of* beholding him. The
> same applies to those wooden idols furnished with paltry carvings of
> individual limbs, sometimes an excess of them; such as a Spartan
> Apollo with four arms and four ears. In the incompleteness, allusive-
> ness or overladenness of these figures there lies a dreadful holiness
> which is supposed to *fend off* any association of them with anything
> human. It is not at an embryonic stage of art at which such things
> are fashioned: as though in the ages when such figures were revered
> men were *incapable* of speaking more clearly, representing more ac-
> curately. What was the case, rather, was that one thing was specifi-
> cally avoided: direct statement. As the cella contains the holy of ho-
> lies, the actual *numen* of the divinity, and conceals it in mysterious
> semi-darkness, *but does not wholly conceal it;* as the peripteral tem-

ple in turn contains the cella and as though with a canopy and veil shelters it from prying eyes, *but does not wholly shelter it:* so the image is the divinity and at the same time the divinity's place of concealment. (*HAH, AOM,* 222; *KSA* 2.476)

Nietzsche goes on to give an account of how "plastic art in the grand style [*die grosse Plastik*]" emerged only after the Greeks had become accustomed to viewing statues of the victors in the Olympic games, statues that were set up outside the temples. Now that divine and human images stand close to one another, "the eye and the soul of the pious frequenter of the temple" become habituated to their proximity, and so allow the possibility of blending reverence for man with reverence for god. This was not an inevitable historical progression but the consequence of a concatenation of events and circumstances that might very well have been otherwise. Like the genesis of tragedy, it requires a genealogical analysis.

7 Nietzsche and Heidegger on Visual History

In Nietzsche's phenomenological description of these early images, he emphasizes what we might call their flickering quality. That quality is suggested and its possibilities elaborated at many levels in Nietzsche's writing, for example in his use of the titles *Daybreak (Morgenröte)* and *Twilight of the Idols (Götzendämmerung)*, which gesture at the importance of those times in which light is uncertain, outlines waver, objects are in shadow, and the full presence sought by philosophers since Plato is not to be found. What eventually emerges into light and clarity does so on the basis of a background of concealment. Here Nietzsche is very close to Heidegger's understanding of truth as concealing *and* revealing. Heidegger thinks of truth or *aletheia* as unconcealment, choosing to see *a-letheia* as a privative concept; what is negated is concealment or oblivion. What becomes manifest, on this account, is what is wrested away from the tendency toward concealment, originally named as *Lethe,* or the river of forgetfulness. Nietzsche says that "the image is the divinity and at the same time the divinity's place of concealment," sounding like Heidegger when the latter speaks of the uncanny play of presence and absence that is the context of all presencing or manifestation. Nietzsche is explaining, through this reconstruction of the archaic history of the image, or, better, its archaeology, why an aesthetics of presence is untenable, for reasons analogous to those which, for Heidegger, make a metaphysics of presence impossible. I take it that this point is being emphasized and reiterated in a number of ways: through key words such as *Daybreak* and *Twilight*, suggesting that since outlines waver, objects are in shadow, so the full presence sought by philosophers since Plato is not to be found; through the teaching of perspectivism, first developed in a visual context; through the Wanderer's and Zarathustra's dialogues with a personified "shadow"; and through the special role of the *Augenblick*, the momentary glance of the eye, which contrasts with the all-too-imaginary totalizing gaze.

Heidegger wants to enclose Nietzsche within his own history of philosophy, whose principle is the metaphysics of presence. On that analysis, Nietzsche would simply be reversing or inverting Platonism; if Plato took the essential reality that can become present to be the *eidos* (originally a visible outline or shape), Nietzsche's reversal would consist in claiming that the eminently present is the world of the senses, which Plato disdained. But here, and in an analysis of the visual dynamics of the Greek temple, Nietzsche finds a tension of visual presence and absence in the Hellenic world that parallels what Heidegger discovers in archaic *aletheia*. We might recall Heidegger's reading of the myth of the cave in the *Republic;* there he attempts to exhibit the strategies by which Plato insinuates the hegemony of the sense of vision. By articulating this set of moves, he wants to suggest how some of the alternatives neglected or excluded by Plato might be developed. In "Plato's Doctrine of Truth," Heidegger systematically emphasizes and discloses the visual import of terms such as *eidos* and *theōria*, which help to constitute the metaphysics of presence. For Heidegger, the scene of instruction that centers around the cave story is the point at which philosophy committed itself to an ocular metaphysics of presence, casting into oblivion or outer darkness the more originary sense of *aletheia* with its own dimension of oblivion.

Heidegger's reading of the history of metaphysics as a visual obsession both parallels and differs from Nietzsche's, so it is worth considering his reading of this crucial moment in its founding. He begins his rethinking of Plato's image of the sun and its heritage by telling us what Plato did *not* do:

> In the "allegory of the cave" the force of the clarification does not spring from the image of being enclosed in a subterranean vault and imprisoned in this enclosing; it does not even spring from the aspect of the openness outside the cave. The image-making interpretative force of the "allegory" is gathered together for Plato rather in the role of the fire, the firelight and the shadows, the brightness of the

day, the sunlight and the sun. Everything depends upon the shining of the phenomenal and the possibility of its visibleness. To be sure, unhiddenness is named in its various stages, but one can only consider it in the way it makes the phenomenal accessible in its outward appearance *(eidos)* and the way it makes this self-showing [*Sichzeigende*] *(idea)* visible.[39]

The nerve of Heidegger's story of philosophy, the plot of his metanarrative, consists in claiming that we have never ceased to be in thrall to the Platonic principle that "everything depends on the *orthotes*, the correctness of the glance."[40] The culmination of this story, for Heidegger, lies in Nietzsche's declaration that truth is the kind of error that is necessary for life: "Nietzsche's concept of truth is an example of the last reflection of the extreme consequence of the changing of truth from the unhiddenness of beings to the correctness of the glance [*Blick*]. The change itself takes place in the definition of the Being of beings (i.e., according to the Greeks, the presence of what is present) as *idea*."[41] If life is seen from the perspective or optics of art, and that means in terms of the perspectiv*ism* that characterizes art, then it seems that Heidegger has taken a rather large step in identifying the kind of error that is necessary for life with the "correct glance," presumably a glance that allows no flickering, no alternatives, and no play of presence and absence. He has overlooked what Nietzsche has to say about the glance itself.[42] I propose to open an inquiry into the glance, the gaze, and other modes of vision by exploring Nietzsche's continuing fascination with a painter of perspective and depth, Claude Lorrain.

one

Between Sun and Cyclops: Nietzsche at the Dresden Gallery

8 Eye Trouble

> My eyes get worse every day, and, unless someone comes along and helps me, I shall probably be blind by the year's end. So I shall decide not to read and write at all—but one cannot stick it out when one is completely alone.
>
> Nietzsche[1]

To his mother, to his friends and colleagues, Nietzsche writes repeatedly of his failing eyes and his fear of blindness. Two months before the letter to his mother, he said to his old friend Franz Overbeck that "matters concerning the eyes are increasingly doubtful. Schiessen's remedies have not helped. Since last summer there has been a change that I do not understand. Spots, veiling, also a flood of tears" (B 7.33; Schiessen was one of his several ophthalmologists). Nietzsche had too many reasons, among them human, all-too-human, reasons, for associating his own destiny with that of his vision—one might say, with vision itself. His struggle to see, in the literal and more than the literal sense of the word, was a constant of his career. There is something poignant in Nietzsche's discussion, in *Schopenhauer as Educator*, of some of the typical weaknesses of the modern scholar, for he construes the scholar as a nearsighted fellow; his own optical deficiency becomes a metaphor for a general circumscription of intellectual vision. The scholar, he says, has a

> sharpsightedness for things close up, combined with great myopia
> for distant things and for what is universal. His field of vision is usu-
> ally very small and he has to hold his eyes close to the object. If the
> man of learning wants to go from one point he has just subjected to
> scrutiny to another, he has to move his whole seeing-apparatus to
> this new point. He dissects a picture into little patches, like one who
> employs opera-glasses to view the stage and then has a sight now of
> a head, now of a piece of clothing, but never of anything whole. He
> never gets to see these patches joined together, his perception of
> how they are connected is only the result of an inference, and thus
> he has no very strong impression of anything universal. . . . he
> would be tempted to assert that an oil-painting is a disorderly heap
> of blots. (*SE* 6; *KSA* 1.395–96)

Perhaps Nietzsche could be on his guard against scholarly myopia because he knew the disease of the eyes of which it is an extended version; his own effort was to see more and to escape the parochial limitations of a single perspective.

If we follow Martin Heidegger's reading of Nietzsche as the culmination of Western thought's pursuit of presence, we could read this struggle for vision as a symptom of philosophy's impossible desire. Heidegger suggests that the history of this tradition should be read as the tragic unfolding of a hubris that enters the stage with Plato's story of the cave and the sun. If Nietzsche's work constitutes the last act of this tragedy, then these laments for his failing eyes would support an analogy with the fate of Oedipus. Both would have staked everything on their ability to subdue the world by means of their gaze, and both would have eventually submitted to a blindness that signified the limits of their vast aims. In this book I am investigating what Nietzsche thought and said about vision, the activity of seeing with our eyes and also with our whole being, for he understands vision not as the activity of a disembodied eye (or "I") but as the project of a human who is situated in a place, a time, a culture, and a body that is imbricated in all of these contexts.

In his last year Nietzsche complains of his failing vision and expresses the fear that his remaining time for reading and writing will be severely limited by his problems with his eyes. Apologizing for a delay in responding to his friend Carl Fuchs, he scribbles this on a postcard in August 1888, less than five months before his breakdown:

> Esteemed friend, it is scarcely describable how little time I have, above all with my *eyes* to thank you for your rich letters. It is almost the high tide of all sorts of necessities with me that absorb my little bit of the faculty of vision all too completely. Happily, you are not acquainted with this physiological misfortune. I need number 3 glasses for reading and writing—if my three ophthalmologists had been right, I would have been blind for years. In fact, each day I have only a *very small* number of hours for reading and writing; and if the weather is dark, no time at all. To deal with this in the economy of a great work demanding a learned culture is a problem. (*B* 8.394)

Precisely during this time, Nietzsche became increasingly concerned with one painter, Claude Lorrain. He had no access to Claude's pictures at this time, and we do not know how much he would have been able to make of them if he had encountered them in a gallery. So we seem to be dealing with memories of vision, of phantasms that haunted Nietzsche at a time when he was planning the philosophical architectonics of what he projected as his major work, *The Transvaluation of Values*. It might seem to be an odd choice. Lorrain is a painter of peaceful ideal landscapes, idyllic visions of a perfected version of the Roman Campagna, a painter who turned out such works in a methodical, businesslike way in response to a constant demand from wealthy aristocrats and clerics (including a pope). Such paintings might not seem to be those which would first come to mind to the thinker of the will to power. And we might also wonder whether Nietzsche, especially with his poor eyes, could have much to tell us about the visual world and how we see it. Or could it be that being always on the verge of losing his vision gave this thinker a capacity for seeing this power in all its splendor and fragility?

9 Glances of the Golden Age

Why Claude Lorrain? The answers begin to appear in Nietzsche's writings, notes, and letters. For Nietzsche Claude is the painter of tranquility, of scenes that give the sense of peace and assurance, of what he was to call the halcyon, reintroducing that word into the German language.[2] As his eye troubles increase and the vision of his youth becomes a memory, one way to designate such beauties is to invoke the name of Claude. A perfect landscape, a perfect day, become for Nietzsche a Claude Lorrain. In *Ecce Homo* he rejoices in the atmosphere of Turin, his *"proven* place," declaring: "Never have I experienced such an autumn, nor considered anything of the sort possible on earth—a Claude Lorrain projected into the infinite, every day of the same indomitable perfection" (*EH*, "Books," "*Twilight*," 3; *KSA* 6.356). What was Nietzsche remembering? He would have seen two Claudes in Dresden, at the celebrated gallery of old master paintings; Dresden was not far from Leipzig, where he was a student for two years and where he saw Wagner's operas. The Dresden Gallery possesses two Claudes that were also exhibited in Nietzsche's time, a *Landscape with Acis and Galatea* (fig. 3) and a *Landscape with the Flight into Egypt*. The first of these is the more dramatic and has attracted the most comment. At first glance, it portrays a seductive utopia, a rugged coastline, a smoking volcano in the distance, a rising or setting sun—there are uncertainties about some of Claude's suns—that radiates a golden glow over everything and speckles the sea with brilliant highlights. In the foreground are an amorous couple, protected only in minimal fashion by a rudimentary canopy. Architecture has not yet made a serious incursion into this world of idealized simplicity. Perhaps the strongest impression, as with so many of Claude's paintings, is of vast distance and peace, a horizon "projected into the infinite," in which the sun is not so much an object as the site or condition of what Nietzsche's Zarathustra was later to call an "abyss of light" (Z III.4; *KSA* 4.207). Claude is justly renowned for his creation of spaces that seem to recede into the infinite and for capturing the magical shimmering of sunlight on the sea; both are striking aspects of this painting. We can imagine Nietzsche, perhaps at twenty, the student of classical languages, being entranced by this idealized representation of archaic Greece, with its indication of a mythical world, a golden age. Philology, he was beginning to feel, had a tendency to turn everything into the materials of *Wissenschaft*, fodder for dry treatises from which one could never sense the life of the ancient world. Here was a painting that spoke of that lost time. The painting had similar effects on others. Dostoyevsky was one of those passionate visitors to the Dresden Gallery, and he has left an account of how the painting might impress one sensitive visitor. In the course of his anguished confession in *The Possessed*, Stavrogin recalls Claude's picture as representing the golden age:

I had a dream which was totally surprising to me because I had never dreamed anything like it before. . . . In the Dresden Gallery there is a painting by Claude Lorrain, called in the catalogue *Acis and Galatea* if I am not mistaken, but which I always called *The Golden Age*, I don't know why. I had seen it before and just three days earlier I saw it again in passing. As a matter of fact, I went to the gallery simply in order to look at it and it was perhaps for that reason alone that I stopped at Dresden. It was this picture that appeared to me in a dream, yet not as a picture but as though it were an actual scene.

. . . As in the picture, I saw a corner of the Greek archipelago the way it was some three thousand years ago: caressing azure waves, rocks and islands, a shore in blossom, afar a magic panorama, a beckoning sunset—words fail one. European mankind remembers this place as its cradle, . . . here was mankind's earliest paradise, gods descended from heaven and united with mortals, here occurred the first scenes of mythology. Here lived beautiful men and women! They rose, they went to sleep, happy and innocent; the groves rang with their merry songs, the great overflow of unspent energies poured itself into love and simple-hearted joys. . . . The sun poured its rays upon these isles and the sea, rejoicing in its fair children. Oh, marvelous dream, lofty illusion![3]

As Stavrogin's last words and his fearsome life suggest, the beauty of the scene cannot be the final truth about human possibilities. Life in "civilized" Europe, which provides the setting for such Dostoyevskyan themes as spite, envy, murder, prostitution, gambling, and the sexual abuse of children is no longer "happy and innocent." It is significant that the painting comes back to Stavrogin as a memory, a dream, a vision; not directly present, it is recalled or impresses itself involuntarily on the mind through a dream. So the memory of Claude comes to Nietzsche in Turin. And the painting itself is a recollection, a reconstruction of a lost dream, here humankind's dream of a golden age. But we do not need to go outside the painting to see that such a dream is shadowed by malign and destructive forces. Above the lovers, up in the rocks to our right is the Cyclops Polyphemus, playing a flute or pipes and minding his herd. Polyphemus is the same monocular giant who was later blinded by Odysseus; Homer emphasizes the Cyclops's brutishness by showing his insensitivity to language, whose multiple meanings are wielded so adroitly by Odysseus, leaving the wounded giant crying that "nobody" has injured him. The story in Ovid (and in earlier sources, going back to Theocritus) is that Polyphemus became

Figure 3. Claude Lorrain, *Landscape with Acis and Galatea*, 1657. Gemäldegalerie Alte Meister, Staatliche Kunstsammlungen, Dresden. Foto Marburg/Art Resource, New York

jealous of Acis and slew him in order to capture his lover.[4] Neither Dostoyevsky nor Nietzsche alludes to this sinister side that sometimes darkens a Claude painting, but we can imagine that Nietzsche, who certainly knew his Ovid and the pastoral tradition, found the narrative dimension of the picture significant. Even the natural setting suggests a certain foreboding in the darker clouds that are gathering in the right-hand section of the sky. Might he have been struck by the fact that it is a Cyclops who casts a single envious or evil eye upon the lovers? In *The Birth of Tragedy*, Socrates' role in the destruction of Greek tragedy is described as an effect of his "one great Cyclops eye," which was unable to tolerate the multiplicity of perspectives and abyssal depths opened up by tragedy (see chap. 4 below, esp. secs. 27–29). At the point depicted in the painting, time seems tranquilly suspended. It is not clear whether Polyphemus has seen the lovers yet; in any case he has not instigated his attack. Most of Ovid's telling of the story consists in Galatea's relation of the Cyclops's song, in which he woos her and threatens her lover. Since the text describes him as singing this song to the accompaniment of his pipes, this could be the moment depicted here (however, Galatea's narration also describes the lovers as taking refuge in a cave at this point). The sun, invoked by Zarathustra as a great radiant and generous eye, is bathing the scene, probably in its early morning light. Perhaps the sun and the eye of Polyphemus can be thought of as two polar extremes of optical possibility. Polyphemus sets the stage for this interpretation, for in Ovid's version of his song to Galatea, he apologizes in this way for his unusual countenance: "True, I have but one eye in the middle of my forehead, but it is as big as a good-sized shield. And what of that? Doesn't the great sun see every-thing here on earth from his heavens? And the sun has but one eye."[5] While the Cyclops proposes an identity between his eye and the sun, we might find his vision to be already deformed by his failure to ap-preciate a plurality of perspectives. He is, in a sense, already blind, a point emphasized in Galatea's narration when she says that Poly-phemus had already disregarded a prophetic warning that Odysseus would blind him one day. We might notice that these two eyes present a deep contrast as well as similarities. Each is single, and each avoids the complexity of human vision, which is suited to depths and perspec-tives. The sun is beyond the human, because it makes vision possible; the other, Cyclops's one eye, embodies that degraded extreme at which sight recoils in envious hatred and contempt for what would otherwise be an object of admiration. This would be the contrast between the evil eye of folklore and its radiant other (the opposition plays a major role in *Zarathustra* and is especially worth noting in the different ways of *seeing* eternal recurrence—I use the term both literally and metaphorically). Each of these optical stances can be construed as a form of the gaze, a vision that totally encompasses its object. Nietzsche is a proponent of perspectivism, of the position that there is no uniquely privileged gaze. He becomes a critic of the philosophical tradition, insofar as the latter assumes that such a gaze is possible or even necessary. While the tendency within the main lines of that tradition has been to take the language of vision deployed by such thinkers as Plato, Descartes, and Hegel in a figurative sense, so that it becomes simply another way of talking about knowledge and understanding, we must pause, in reading Nietzsche; for he, insisting that knowledge and understanding are fully embodied activities, cannot allow himself such a reduction of the senses to the pure intellect. And his own reading of his predecessors, as in a famous section of *Twilight of the Idols*, called "How the True World Finally Became a Fable," will suggest that each of the major stages of metaphysics can be understood as an optical regime, in which, for example, Plato poses as the sun, Christianity trades on the contrast between seeing now through a glass darkly and then face to face, and Kant claims to perceive the traces of the sun's truth through northern fog and mist.

The date given for the Claude painting is 1657. The painter and his work are contemporary with Descartes; the philosopher, who died in 1650, had as his project the legitimating of a singular point of view, the construction of a universal method of vision, one parallel to his system of coordinate geometry with its unique point of origin. Claude was a master of the system of perspective that entered European painting in the quattrocento and whose spirit contributes to the Cartesian worldview, indeed to the construction of the very idea of a worldview; as Heidegger argues, the conception of a *Weltbild*, a total picture of the world, becomes possible only in this era.[6] The structure of such a picture is apparent in Claude's work in the framing devices he typically employs: clumps of trees or rocks at the sides of the painting, which provide something like a stage set or coulisse to center and highlight the recession of the landscape into the distance; scholars have suggested that, along with other painters of his time, he derived these motifs from the conventions of the ancient and contemporary versions of the Roman stage.[7] Claude was an innovator in several ways in producing a pictorialized conception of nature. He was among the first, along with Salvator Rosa, to paint pictures in which the narrative content, as divulged possibly by the title, seems to play a rather minor role in relation to the natural scene—or what we *take* to be the natural scene. For Claude clearly follows a series of conventions, developing a certain perspective, in both the technical and the more figurative senses of that term. By providing the viewer of the painting with an elevated point of view, he produces the impression that the world is spread out before the spectator and implicitly confirms that spectator in a position of detachment, one appropriate for a city dweller fantasizing about nature. Claude, as in this painting, typically placed the vanishing point on a horizon about two-fifths of the way up from the bottom of the picture and employed a complex system of triangulated perspective that intensifies the sense of vast recession in the landscape for which his works are noted.[8] In comparison with landscapes as they appear in paintings of the two centuries before him, Claude articulates a space in which the horizon is not reached by a gradual series of stages, but in which there are relatively abrupt and dramatic variations from foreground to middle distance to the far distance. A recent and compelling study of the history of landscape architecture plausibly argues that Claude's painting (along with the work of a few others, such as Rosa) plays an enormous role in the very formation of our concept of the natural, as expressed first in the picturesque eighteenth-century English landscape garden, in the great American parks of the nineteenth and twentieth centuries, and in the barrage of photographs, postcards, and other images that instruct us as to what we are to look for in "nature."[9]

When Michel Foucault attempts to give us an insight into the "classical" or Cartesian age at the beginning of *The Order of Things*, he does so not by a direct analysis of Descartes, but through the exploration of another contemporary painting, *Las Meninas*, that also deploys (and perhaps deforms) the system of Renaissance perspective. His aim is to show what is missing from Descartes's universe by demonstrating the exclusions when even a masterly painter of the era attempts to inventory all the varied forms of representation: the possibility of representation itself still cannot be accounted for (see chaps. 7 and 8). If Nietzsche were to ask what sort of account the Claude painting gives of vision itself, the inventory would be rather different. No one is looking at us, the spectators; we can maintain the illusion that we are gazing through a window into a vanished or imaginary world. The lovers are absorbed in each other, the Cyclops still occupied with his own affairs. The source of light is portrayed boldly; Claude dares to show the sun itself, although his sun is typically rising or setting, as here. The "great noon" of which Nietzsche speaks in Zarathustra is perhaps not to be captured on canvas. It may be that the sun cannot be depicted directly; the painter needs to approach it slyly, as Socrates suggests men might be led out of a cave step by step in order to approximate to such a vision of what would otherwise be too dazzling for them. As a synoptic survey of visual modalities, much is ignored or excluded. Yet between the sun and the Cyclops, the painting embodies two forms of the gaze, the radiant and beneficent power of the sun and the reductive, evil eye that seeks only its own narrow advantage.

Claude's paintings were a reminder for Nietzsche that vision could be ultimately beneficent, even if it also harbored possibilities of degeneration. There is an elegiac tone in his references to Claude, references that intriguingly become more frequent in the last year or so of his life, as he laments his own decayed vision; we latecomers, knowing of his impending collapse, are tempted to read these passages as rather desperate bids for a peace and stability that was slipping away all too quickly. At least five times, in letters to friends and colleagues during the last year of his life as a writer, Nietzsche invokes Claude, speaking of him more frequently than of any other painter during this time. Claude sometimes designates a musical work or passage of the highest "classical" sort. In *Nietzsche contra Wagner*, Nietzsche cites his own discussion, some ten years earlier, in which he argued that music was typically the late and unexpected fruit of a great culture.

> Of all the arts that grow up on a particular cultural soil under particular social and political conditions, music makes its appearance *last*, in the autumn and deliquescence of the culture to which it belongs: at a time when the first signs and harbingers of a new spring are as a rule already perceptible; sometimes, indeed, music resounds into a new and astonished world like the language of an age that has vanished and arrives too late. . . . It was only Mozart who gave forth the age of Louis the Fourteenth and the art of Racine and Claude Lorraine in *ringing* gold. . . . So that a friend of delicate metaphors might say that all truly beautiful music is swan-song.—Music is thus *not* a universal language for all ages, as has so often been claimed for it, but accords precisely with a measure of time, warmth and sensibility that a quite distinct individual culture, limited as to area and duration, bears within it as a universal law. (*HAH, AOM,* 171; *KSA* 2.450)[10]

Notice here, by the way, that Nietzsche employs a certain framework for understanding the history of art; while allowing what we might see as a very generalized form of the Hegelian idea that there is some general correspondence between art and its age, he is suspicious of making this connection too close, suggesting that the different arts might express the age at quite different times, sometimes even after the era has passed. He has already sketched what Foucault would call an archaeo-logical model for understanding the history of Greek art in *The Birth of Tragedy*, in which he used the image of excavating the distinct cul-tural layers of a site. Nietzsche's colleague, Jakob Burckhardt, had al-ready developed his own critique of the Hegelian tendencies of the nascent discipline of the history of art, and it is a theme that we will find Foucault developing much more explicitly. Even Nietzsche's ap-parent concession to Hegelianism, the reference to "a measure of time, warmth and sensibility" that a culture "bears within it as a universal law," is qualified by the limitation with respect to "area and duration"; and to speak of such cultural productions as exhibiting a certain law is to use a language closer to that of twentieth-century structuralism than to Hegelian talk of the expression of spirit. Here Nietzsche makes use of this sense of distance or gap between a culture and its art to suggest that in the visual realm, Claude is specially suited to mark such synco-pations of culture and taste. We have already seen that Claude's paint-ings were generally understood to be suffused with an elegiac at-mosphere. Here Nietzsche seems to invoke that atmosphere doubly, suggesting both the relation of "late" music to an earlier culture and, so far as Claude is emblematic of that culture, implying that the golden high point of that time was already infused with a certain sense of mourning and distance. The example becomes more poignant when we think of his failing eyesight. It is music, whose nuances Nietzsche can still perceive, that is called upon to recapitulate an experience of vision that has become increasingly difficult. Might Nietzsche's impaired and failing eyesight have led him to identify in some way with the Cyclops, who lacks the stereoscopic vision that we take as normative? Might the giant's fated blindness be a warning to him, given his own degenerating vision? It is interesting that the Cyclops, a figure for crude, brutal, and uncivilized desire in Homer, becomes more appealing in later versions. Theocritus, in *Idyll 11*, makes Polyphemus into a lovelorn singer, a tradition that Ovid expands and elaborates by having Galatea recite his song to Scylla. I confess my own sympathy with the Cyclops's predica-ment. My two eyes, with drastically different capacities, have never focused together, and so I seem to lack the normal sense of depth (and, a fortiori, of the abyss). An ophthalmologist tells me that in infancy (in the state prior to speech) I must have made a series of unconscious adjustments that protected me from falling into the schizoid optical catastrophe of attempting to combine two radically different simultane-ous images; I must have devised some technique of switching back and forth from one eye to the other that gave me some approximation or equivalent of depth perception.

Could it be that vision always carries along with it its own defect, a tendency to ruin and dissolution? Might it share in the infirmities, and therefore in certain unexpected possibilities, that Nietzsche and much of the philosophy of the twentieth century find in the experience or assertion of self-knowledge and self-identity? Is the "I see," the *video*, infected with difficulties analogous to those of the *cogito*, the "I think"? To summarize one of these philosophical developments rather starkly, Martin Heidegger claims that the truth of the "I think" is "I will die" (taking "truth" here in the Hegelian sense of the ultimate, destined, but initially unsuspected outcome of a process). For each of us to come to terms with the existence that is asserted implicitly or explicitly by the "I," even taking the "I think" in that implicit Kantian sense in which it is simply that which *can* accompany all my perceptions, is to know our own finitude. Jacques Derrida offers a demonstration of a similar point by considering the "I" as a linguistic performance. All language, he argues, must make sense in the absence of its object, of what it purports to be about. "It rained on Friday" will necessarily be intelligible even when the rain has stopped and also the next day and the next week, and whether it actually rained on Friday or not. This will be true not only of statements about the weather and the stock market but also of utterances or inscriptions that involve a reference to the speaker or the author, the "I" of the "I am." As Derrida puts it in *Voice and Phenomenon:*

> When I say *I*, even in solitary discourse, can I give my statement meaning without implying there, as always, the possible absence of the object of the discourse—in this case myself? When I tell myself "I am," this expression, like any other according to Husserl, has the status of discourse only if it is intelligible in the absence of its object, in the absence of intuitive presence—here, in the absence of myself. Moreover, it is in this way that the *ergo sum* is introduced into the philosophical tradition and that a discourse about the transcendental ego is possible.[11]

This is, of course, the germ of Derrida's claim about the relation between writing and speech. There is a classical argument, put forward by Socrates in Plato's *Phaedrus*, for example, that writing suffers from the deficiency of having to make sense in the absence of its author, and its meaning is therefore rendered intrinsically indeterminate. Derrida accepts the account to the extent that it points to the disconnection between meaning and the living presence of the "father" of the words (Socrates' expression), but he finds the structure to be characteristic of all discourse, including its spoken or virtually spoken forms (as when we "think," or speak silently to ourselves). These conditions do render all discourse somewhat indeterminate, but not utterly so, making it both possible and necessary for any utterance to be clarified, amplified, contextualized, or qualified by further significant behavior. Anything I write must make sense even if I am dead, and the practice of the signature, where I claim something as my own (for example in a legal context, signing a check or a last will and testament), in fact rests on the supposition that my thoughts and intentions, realized verbally, will be able to survive me.

If the truth of the *cogito* is "I will die" or "I am dying," could the truth of the *video*, "I see," be that I will cease to see? Certainly human vision is an ephemeral and variable matter. While the elegiac dimensions of a Claude painting may put us in mind of vanished beauties, such as the perfect (but possibly imaginary) sunsets of our youth or the perfections (certainly imaginary) of the golden age that is the youth of humanity, the banal sights of everyday life are also fleeting and the power of sight itself not something on whose stability we can count. I may blink, fall asleep, or discover that tears are welling up in my eyes; the scene itself may change, as sunset gives way to darkness. These considerations, of course, form classical objections (as in Plato) to basing our knowledge and our actions on the changing world of the senses.[12] Yet if a thinker—Nietzsche, for one—is suspicious about the availability of some other world, then he or she may find it necessary to understand vision in all of its fragility, a project that may even gain an added impetus if one's own vision is subject to defects that are not universally human. I suggest that for Nietzsche the truth of the "I see" is what he calls the *Augenblick*, the moment of vision, the twinkling or glance of the eye. Later I will devote more attention to this term, which plays a major role in *Zarathustra* and, specifically, in the idea of eternal recurrence; it is the *Augenblick* that is said to recur eternally (chap. 5). For now, I want to emphasize two things: (1) in Nietzsche's writing, the term *Augenblick* often has a specifically visual sense or dimension, and this is rather important in what he took to be his most important book, *Thus Spoke Zarathustra;* and (2) part of the sense of the term, as Nietzsche uses it, is to suggest the fragility of vision, the fact of passage and change, a fact that has roots both in the contingency of the viewer and in that of the objects of sight.

This contingency is one of which Nietzsche is acutely aware. In *Ecce Homo* he claims that he is an expert in illness and convalescence, in decadence and its opposite. If we were to challenge his qualifications to speak of the visual realm, we would, in all consistency, have to challenge almost everything that he has to say about illness and health—which would amount to disqualifying most of his thought. His argument on the contrary is that an understanding of the possibilities and limits of a power can be heightened by the experience and awareness of its limits. So while the aphorism from *Daybreak* that follows, *In prison*, can be read as a confession of his own condition, the passages from the later *Ecce Homo* suggest a power of analysis that can be enabled by that condition:

> My eyes, however strong or weak they may be, can see only a certain distance, and it is within the space encompassed by this distance that I live and move, the line of this horizon constitutes my immediate fate, in great things and small, from which I cannot escape. . . . Now it is by these horizons, within which each of us encloses his senses as if behind prison walls, that we *measure* the world, we say that this is near and that far, this is big and that small, this is hard and that soft: this measuring we call sensation—and it is all of it an error! (*D* 117; *KSA* 3.110)

> This dual descent, as it were, both from the highest and the lowest rung on the ladder of life, at the same time a *decadent* and a *beginning*—this, if anything, explains that neutrality, that freedom from all partiality in relation to the total problem of life, that perhaps distinguishes me.
>
> My eye trouble, too, though at times dangerously close to blindness, is only a consequence and not a cause: with every increase in vitality my ability to see has also increased again.
>
> Looking from the perspective of the sick toward *healthier* concepts and values and, conversely, looking again from the fullness and self-assurance of a *rich* life down into the secret work of the instinct of decadence—in this I have had the longest training, my truest experience; if in anything, I became master in *this*. Now I know how, have the know-how, to *reverse perspectives*; the first reason why a "revaluation of values" is perhaps possible for me alone. (*EH*, "Wise," 1; *KSA* 6.264–66)

It is the self-medicated patient who knows something about the limitation of his eyesight and his perspectives who can say something about their significance.[13] Nietzsche knew that his visual perspective was deficient, but he claims that such knowledge is more productive than the complacent confidence in what is taken to be normal, where the normal in fact constitutes the bars of a prison. Later Foucault will explore the attempt to deploy a general regime of carceral vision.

On November 13, 1888, two months before his collapse, Nietzsche writes to his friend and former colleague the Basel church historian Franz Overbeck, reporting on his extraordinary happiness in Turin and perhaps, like any traveler, remarking on the weather. Yet weather tends to become an index of the state of the soul: "Perhaps you are already into winter: we are almost there—the neighboring mountains are already covered by a light wig of snow. I hope that the winter will correspond to the fall: here at least that was a true wonder of beauty and the fullness of light [*Lichtfülle*]—a perpetual Claude Lorrain [*in Permanenz*]. I have relearned the whole concept of 'beautiful weather,' and shudder to think of my stupid dependence on Nizza" (B 8.468). Yet Nietzsche knows, as we all know, that there can be no eternal Claude Lorrain. Here the memory of the paintings—there seem to have been no actual Claudes to see in Turin—becomes a kind of defense against "time and its 'it was.'" But Zarathustra knew that such beautiful views, such glances and twinklings of the eye, were necessarily fleeting. In a chapter that is initially puzzling, "The Tomb Song," we at first find it difficult to see just whose passing is being lamented, who is buried on the isle of the dead. A careful reading suggests that it is certain visions: "O you visions and apparitions [*Gesichte und Erscheinungen*] of my youth! O all you glances [*Blicke der Liebe*] of love, you divine moments of vision [*Augenblicke*]! How quickly you died. Today I recall you like dead friends" (Z 110; *KSA* 4.142). What might seem to be the simplest of facts, of phenomenological basics, the passage of time, becomes for Nietzsche (as for Augustine and Hegel), the subject of philosophical wonder but also of mourning. Those past and passing moments are to be understood as a "perpetual perishing" (in John Locke's words). Recognition of the inevitability of transience takes the form of understanding that transience in terms of the human experience of loss; and while we take such losses seriously in the case of death, Locke's figure of speech suggests that perishing is universal. In "The Tomb Song," Nietzsche describes his dead friends as visions, glances, and twinklings of the eye. He curses his enemies, those unnamed forces responsible for perpetual perishing, because "you have cut short my eternal bliss, as a tone that breaks off in a cold night. Scarcely as the gleam of divine eyes it came to me—passing swiftly as the twinkling of an eye [*Kaum als Aufblinken göttlicher Augen kam es mir nur,— als Augenblick*]" (Z II.11; *KSA* 4.143). Lost visions, divine memories, may be recalled by paintings such as Claude's, or in even more secondary fashion, by the memory of those paintings; but paintings and memories, however glorious, will be imbued with a sense of loss.

11 "Claude Lorraine-like Raptures and Tears"

Thus Spoke Zarathustra will attempt to come to terms with the sorrows, regrets, and thirst for revenge stirred up by "time and its 'it was'" by insinuating the uncanny and disorienting thought of eternal recurrence, a thought worked out, in part, in the visual terms of a scenario entitled "On the Vision and the Riddle." I am suggesting that we can begin to see why this elaboration of the thought takes the form it does by looking at the role Claude plays in Nietzsche's spectrum of meanings. Claude's painting becomes a figure of beauty, the beauty that we would madly wish to transform into a permanent possession; when we see that this is impossible, we can do nothing but lament its ephemeral quality. So in St. Moritz, Nietzsche writes to himself in 1879: "The day before yesterday, toward evening, I was completely submerged in Claude Lorraine-like raptures and continuously broke into heavy tears. That I am still able to experience this! I had not known that the earth could display this, and I had thought that the good painters had invented it. The heroic-idyllic is now my soul's discovery: and now the whole bucolic of the ancients is unveiled and accessible to me— until now I understood nothing of this" (*KSA* 8.610).[14]

Let us recall for a moment that Claude's painting has a fairly definite place within the European tradition of pastoral and utopia. He is generally recognized as being one of the foremost painters of ideal landscapes, indeed as probably the most important artist of the genre. Having been born in Lorraine (as Claude Gelée), he settled in Rome while still in his twenties and quickly became well known for his landscapes, which derive in part from the Italian land and sea. His paintings were soon in great demand, and he seems to have led an orderly life, producing them with businesslike regularity. The market was so strong that imitations appeared while he was still young, and so he maintained a book of drawings in order to authenticate his works. The initial appeal of Claude's work to wealthy urban patrons, including prominent clerics, is in keeping with the times. The seventeenth century, most of which Claude spanned with his life, was a time of rapid social change and upheaval. It is the period that Foucault was to mark by such events as the confinement of the mad and the rise of Cartesian systems of ordering the world; it was also the time when "witches" were persecuted, a symptom of a general uncertainty about the relation between the new ways and the old. In this environment the notion of utopia, whether expressed in words or images, came to have a strong attraction for those who were confronting the problematic transition to a society marked by capitalism, Galilean science, the rise of the nation state, and the accompanying transformations of Christianity. The utopia, or "nowhere," that became a standard point of reference in the culture of this time was a place where, variously, reason ruled (as in Sir Thomas More and Francis Bacon) or natural human innocence flourished in a primeval setting that was relatively untouched by the degenerate practices of civilization.[15] Claude's paintings offered dreamlike visions and virtual wish fulfillments to those seeking some assurance of the possibility of a better, more tranquil world, a place where desire was not in conflict with culture, where there was as yet no conflict between nature and culture. Claude achieves this effect in part by minimizing the role of human beings in his landscapes. They are usually present, but in rather reduced size, and even when their iconographical significance touches on critical themes of religion and myth, this can easily be overshadowed by the landscape. The other painting by Claude in the Dresden Gallery, the *Landscape with the Flight into Egypt*, for example, was for many years thought to be just one more pastoral landscape, as its subject went unrecognized. Nietzsche's notebook entry above is not completely explicit with respect to the question of whether he gave any special attention to the narrative dimension of Claude's work, its role as history painting. When he uses the term "heroic-idyllic," he could be thinking of the fact that many of Claude's works, as well as those of other painters of "ideal landscapes," are based on classical and biblical texts, presenting moments from stories in which characters of some magnitude act in challenging circumstances. The painters of the time tended to accept some version of Aristotle's notion of mimesis, in which it is heroic figures who reveal themselves in action. As we shall see in the next chapter, Lessing's *Laocoön* is a reaction against what he saw as the tendency to make paintings overly literary; but he did allow for the depiction of a favored moment, which would crystallize the essential dimensions of a more extended action in a single scene. Many since Claude's time have tended to see in those land- and seascapes wondrous and dreamy manifestations of what Nietzsche was to call "the transfigured world of the eye" (a philosopheme that plays a role in the studies of the poetic image that culminate in *The Birth of Tragedy*; see chaps. 2 and 3).

Claude's critics, such as Sir Joshua Reynolds, sometimes suggestedthat he "had shown more discretion, if he had never meddled with [mythological] subjects."[16] Yet human beings do make appearances in

Claude, who drew on the Bible, Ovid, Virgil, and other canonical sources to legitimate and title his paintings; in this, of course, he was following the practice of his day. A social and cultural inventory of *Acis and Galatea* would indeed confirm Dostoyevsky's reading of the painting in terms of the golden age. There is no evidence of agriculture, political organization, or metallurgy (although ships do appear in the distance); the lovers are protected by the most elementary of shelters, one that bears a certain resemblance to the vulva and so can be seen as a natural haven. In general, Claude's pictures show no signs of anything like a tragic social conflict; the rather obscure presence of Polyphemus in the Dresden painting is not the sign of a problematic relation among human beings, but of a threat posed by the relatively incalculable forces of nature, like the smoldering volcano in the background.

Nietzsche says that he came to an understanding of the ancient idyllic and bucolic modes through "Claude Lorraine-like raptures," experiences that showed him that the beauties of the great landscape painters were not simply idealized constructions but also objects of possible experience. This puts him in the odd company of those eighteenth-century enthusiasts of the picturesque who traversed the English countryside with their "Claude glasses," devices with tinted lenses that were intended to bring out the painterly possibilities in the landscape. Nietzsche is also taking a position rather distant from his own contemporary John Ruskin, who ridiculed the eclectic quality of Claude's pictures, which he said involved the conglomeration of unrelated figures, themes, architecture, and natural settings.[17] Nietzsche would, of course, have already been familiar with the literary tradition of idyll and bucolic as represented by writers like Theocritus and Virgil. Some of the poems in *The Gay Science* (the title alludes to *la gaya scienza*, the Provençal term for poetry) are playful and satiric send-ups of this genre and are adapted from the earlier "Idylls from Messina" (a reference to the Sicilian origin of the Theocritean idyll). But the "raptures" here were neither those of literature nor of painting, but of landscape, although we must take into account the fact that Nietzsche was able to "see" the landscape through the eyes of Claude or the words of Virgil. When we read Nietzsche's words about his discovery of the "heroic-idyllic," written in 1879, we should also think of *Thus Spoke Zarathustra*, composed just a few years later, which might be thought of as dramatizing a heroic action in an idyllic setting.

We should not ignore the fact that Claude's work has a significant literary history of which Nietzsche was certainly aware. In Goethe's *Conversations with Eckermann*, which Nietzsche calls "the best German book that there is," these remarks are recorded; they are typical of Claude's reception in the nineteenth century. "'Here, you see, for once a complete man,' said Goethe, 'who thought and felt beautifully, and in whose mind lay a world such as you will not easily find out of doors. The pictures have the highest truth, but no trace of actuality. Claude Lorraine knew the real world by heart, down to the minutest details, and used it only as a means to express the world of his beautiful soul. That is the true ideality which can so use real means that the truth evolved produces an illusion of actuality.'"[18]

Nietzsche's understanding of Claude was also mediated by Jakob Burckhardt. Burckhardt had concluded his *Cicerone*, the guide to Italian art that Nietzsche read, used, annotated, and recommended to friends, with a stirring passage on Claude; Claude is seen, along with Poussin, as the culmination of modern painting, specifically in the genre of landscape. The passage is worth quoting at some length both for its interest for Nietzsche and as an example of how Claude was seen in the nineteenth century:

> His landscapes are less powerfully constructed than those of [Poussin] but there is an inexpressible magic in them. As a finely attuned soul, Claude perceives the same voice [*Stimme*] in nature which is mostly destined to console human beings and he repeats her words. Whoever immerses himself in his works—indeed their equally beautiful completion makes this into a task to be thankful for—will find no further words necessary. . . . Whoever meets these two masters [Claude and Poussin] again outside of Italy will find them awakening a homesickness perhaps much more strongly than the most brilliant modern landscapes—a homesickness that only slumbers for a while, but never dies, after seeing unforgettable Rome. The writer of these pages has had the experience. He wishes that those who read him, will agree and take this companion with them over the Alps, will have the same quiet happiness of soul that he enjoyed in Rome; this memory comes back to him even from the weak reproductions that are overpowered by those great masterpieces.[19]

Here Claude's elegiac qualities become a means of taking an elegiac leave of all the art of Italy.

The notebook entry concerning "Claude Lorraine-like raptures" is probably the basis of the aphorism in *The Wanderer and His Shadow* where Nietzsche speaks of "Poussin and his pupil" (no doubt Claude). It bears the elegiac title *"Et in Arcadia ego,"* echoing that of two of Poussin's most renowned works, the later of which poignantly juxtaposes pastoral beauty with intimations of mortality (the phrase was also the epigraph for Goethe's *Italian Journey*).[20] Rather than commenting directly on either of the paintings, Nietzsche begins by describing a scene he saw in the mountains, presumably in Switzerland. The vivid account emphasizes framing mountains, craggy rocks, a lake, varied flowers and grasses, and a pastoral scene with cattle and picturesque youthful herders. He then tells us how the scene led to his spontaneous production of what the ancients called a phantasm:

> The beauty of the whole scene induced in me a sense of awe and of adoration of the moment of its revelation; involuntarily, as if nothing were more natural, I inserted into this pure, clear world of light (in which there was nothing of desire or expectation, no looking before and behind) Hellenic heroes; my feeling must have been like that of Poussin and his pupil: at one and the same time heroic and idyllic.—And that is how individual men have actually *lived,* that is how they have enduringly *felt* they existed in the world and the world existed in them; and among them was one of the greatest of men, the inventor of an heroic-idyllic way of philosophizing, Epicurus. (*HAH, WS,* 295; *KSA* 2.686–87)

Here the speaker is receptive in taking in the beautiful scene; but he is also productive in peopling it with heroic figures. So he becomes a virtual painter himself and comes to understand Poussin, Claude, Epicurus (and perhaps Goethe) as kindred spirits. A vision, a twinkling of the eye, is sufficient to trigger an awareness of how the world can be transfigured. Here that transfiguration is identified with a way of thinking, one that Nietzsche could practice himself. What he learns from his own powers of invention in populating the scene is something about the painters' power of invention and, by analogy, something about that of Epicurus, who *invented* a way of thinking. Thought is creative, like painting; it is not simply the passive recording or classification of information. Even if thought has a receptive moment, devoid of "desire or expectation," like the Kantian experience of beauty, it realizes itself as thought only through spontaneous construction. So, in just a few years, Nietzsche will be practicing a creative thinking by means of the visual figure of the *Augenblick*.

12 Nietzsche and the Time of the Museum

In ways that Nietzsche himself helped to clarify, we all inherit a complex of cultural perspectives, habits, and attitudes of acting, perceiving, and interpreting. He was not alone in taking the context of the museum for granted as the setting for painting; along with many others, he might be thought of as a prisoner of the museum as well as its beneficiary. The Dresden Gallery had an enormous impact on several generations of European and especially German thinkers about the arts, including Winckelmann, the Schlegels, Hegel, Schopenhauer, and Dostoyevsky; their texts on the gallery form the background for later visitors, including Nietzsche. Yet we have no direct and specific records of what he thought about the works in the Dresden Gallery, other than his important meditation on the *Sistine Madonna* (sec. 21), although in addition to Claude Lorrain he does discuss or mention Raphael, Albrecht Dürer, Hans Holbein, Peter Paul Rubens, and Anthony van Dyck in ways that allow us to construe his responses to their work.

For educated Germans and other Europeans, Dresden was a city of both sights and sounds, the arts corresponding to what philosophy has traditionally regarded as the two theoretical senses. Wagner's *Musikdrama* aspired to be a *Gesamtkunstwerk*, embracing the visual forms of dance, costume, and scenography. So while we might think of Nietzsche as being attracted to Dresden mainly by its musical offerings, the city contained much more. When the Schulpforta student, then seventeen years old, hears that his sister Elisabeth is paying an extended visit to the city, he writes to say that she must visit the Dresden Gallery at least once or twice a week and write each time about at least two or three paintings (*B* 1.203). We do not know whether Elisabeth followed her brother's directions, but we do know that young Fritz's recommendations were consistent with the attitude taken toward this collection by figures such as Hegel, Schopenhauer, and Dostoyevsky.

We now tend to take the museum for granted as the obvious place where works of art are displayed and the place to encounter and learn about the visual; it was not always so. Sometime around the end of the eighteenth century, and with accelerating force in the next two hundred years, the museum became the canonical context for viewing and understanding works of visual art. Royal and aristocratic collections of paintings and other artworks were typically part of larger assemblages of precious, rare, or strange objects, including armor, jewels, and exotic artifacts brought back from Asia, Africa, and the Americas. The collection of old master paintings in the Dresden Gallery grew from the holdings of Augustus I, elector of Saxony, whose *Kunstkammer* (hall of art) was set up in the palace at Dresden in 1560.[21]

By 1855, when Gottfried Semper's new gallery was complete, the pictures were presented in a space that displayed them rather lavishly. Photographs of the gallery from 1900 and earlier show heavy curtains, plush benches, and paintings with large gilt frames. As a twentieth-century director of the Gallery observes, Semper's design "reverts to the romantic idea of the 'holy of holies.' "[22] Within the collection, the holiest of these holies was undoubtedly Raphael's *Sistine Madonna*, and it was framed accordingly, being set aside in a room that bore some resemblance to a chapel. If an art pilgrimage was to be undertaken to Dresden, this was then, as now, the center and masterpiece of the collection.

In retrospect, the installation of Raphael's *Sistine Madonna* in the Dresden Gallery in 1754 was a major turning point in the aesthetic culture of Germany, one that contributed directly and indirectly to the development of aesthetic theory from Winckelmann to Nietzsche. The painting's entrance into the collection was a challenge to an iconoclastic strain in German Protestant culture that had persisted since the Reformation, when extremists smashed holy images to demonstrate their impotence. (Calvin's Geneva marked the moment of its true foundation from the day in 1535 when sacred images were destroyed and broken.)[23] In *Likeness and Presence,* Hans Belting tells what we might call a Foucauldian story about a succession of visual regimes. Rather than supposing that there is a single continuous subject, art, which has been developing, evolving, or unfolding along lines that are somehow intrinsic to itself (let us call that a Hegelian account for now), he asks us to recall that until the Reformation Christian images were regarded not so much as works of art to be appreciated aesthetically, but as icons that expressed the real presence and power of the divine. There were a series of iconoclastic controversies, but the notion was not in play that a painting might be best encountered as an object to be seen simply in terms of its beautiful forms or as a vivid picture of what it represented. It was with the growing criticism of the veneration and alleged power of images around 1500 that a new way of construing visual artifacts emerged. Luther was very clear in insisting that God communicated through the word, not by means of visual images; he responded to the destruction of images by arguing that the best antidote to an undue valorization of the image was to preach the word, explaining that images were at best reminders and illustrations of religious truths.[24] Yet as the *Sistine Madonna*'s fame grew, aided by publicists like Winckelmann, it became the focus of a controversy that continues the earlier disputes over images in a changed form. Some critics raised the specter of the iconophilic tradition, suggesting that even (or especially) in the frame of the art gallery, it served as a temptation to the cult of images, a cult that the Counter Reformation had vigorously attempted to revive. Friedrich Schlegel wrote with some irony that hostile observers were saying that the work encouraged its admirers (or idolaters) to convert to Catholicism; shortly afterward he himself converted. The main effect of the painting's special place in the Dresden Gallery and of its apotheosis by a number of the early German romantics seems to have been this: it was now acceptable to celebrate visual likenesses of the divine and to bask in beautiful images, where the image was no longer understood as a real presence but as a specifically human artifact designed for aesthetic ends. In *Human, All Too Human,* Nietzsche was to write a somewhat ironic coda to a long tradition of panegyrics of this painting (sec. 21).

It was this gallery, then, a temple of art and not of religion, that was one of Nietzsche's crucial introductions to the visual culture of his day.[25] What is it to see art within the perspective of the museum, to enjoy and study it not as a religious or political sign or gesture, but as a purely artistic or aesthetic phenomenon, whatever that may be? How is the museum enabled by an aesthetic theory like that of Kant's, which Schopenhauer somewhat mistakenly took himself to be extending, a theory that segregates works of art from theoretical and practical life? How might it be inspired or legitimated by the Hegelian philosophy of art, which sees the historical succession of works and styles as a progressive effort of self-understanding by the human spirit? What happens when art becomes a subject for knowledge and aesthetic appreciation, when a medieval devotional image or sculpture is removed from its religious context and placed among a variety of productions from many different times and cultures? When, as Hegel says, we reach the modern era and "the knee does not bend" at such sights, then something has been lost and we tend to agree that "art on its highest side is a thing of the past." Michel Foucault gave some thought to the institutions of the museum, the library, and the archive; he began to develop an account of how these shaped both the production and reception of pictures, books, and other cultural artifacts. In his sketch of a number of distinct visual regimes (like Belting's discussion of the ages of images and of art), Foucault raises the question of how these ways of seeing involve specific formations of power and knowledge, including forms of resistance to hegemonic institutions and practices; Warhol's images, he suggests, can be read not simply as endorsements of American popular icons and commodities, but also as ways of eviscerating them of their standard meanings (see secs. 45 and 74–77).

13 A Tour of the Dresden Gallery

We might see some tension between two strands in Nietzsche's imagined response to *Acis and Galatea.* There is the romantic, almost kitschy indulgence in fantasies of the ideal landscape, fantasies that could have great appeal in the rather cramped and conservative culture of Biedermeier Germany. Yet there is also a focus on "the transfigured world of the eye," the shining and luminosity that come to be identified with Apollo in *The Birth of Tragedy*. There Nietzsche turns much more explicitly to the example of a painting, in the form of Raphael's *Transfiguration*, in order to explain Apollonian art. Another painting in the Dresden Gallery, by Claude's Dutch contemporary Vermeer, has a strong Apollonian dimension. Consider *Girl Reading a Letter at an Open Window*, a painting in which light has an extraordinary force, so that what is displayed is display itself (fig. 4). It is as if the yellow or ochre drapery on the right is struck by the light and recoils at the point of contact. As Edward Snow has noted, it seems that the light has forced the window open, thrust the red curtain back, produced a shadow to claim the girl, and concentrated itself in the glow that it lends to the wall.[26] The curtains add a dramatic touch and may recall the story of Zeuxis and Parrhasius.[27] As is usual with Vermeer, the light that enters through the window is a pure shining, unencumbered by any landscape or view. There is a similar effect, as Foucault notes, in Velazquez's *Las Meninas* (*OT* 6; *MCh* 22).[28] The fruit at the bottom of the picture tumbles out of its bowl, suggesting an abundant giving, like that of the light. There are so many fabrics here—the two curtains, the very rich oriental rug, the girl's dress—whose twists and turns allow them to assume and exhibit the most differentiated shadows and structures. It is as if they are all stand-ins or substitutes for the canvas, and we could be reminded that what has caught and transformed light in these manifold ways is nothing but a simple piece of cloth. It is an emblem of *Verklärung* or transfiguration. The spectral image of the girl reflected in the window is a shining of the shining, an image trapped in the crossbars of the windowpane. Traditionally, at least following Alberti in the fifteenth century, painting is thought of as a window that we look through at some scene; but in this picture we see nothing through a window while the draperies and the horizontal rod underline the artifice of the scene; what we see of the window is the pane crisscrossed by its internal framing mechanism; it contains a ghostly image of the girl. Evanescence has been captured in a translucent net. Here windows—or paintings—are not clear, unmediated avenues to some external scene or presence but places in which reflections, visions, and shades are generated. The ontology of the window is put into question by the flickering quasi-presence. Framing is emphasized repeatedly by the window glass and the curtains. The same light that casts a shadow behind the window generates this ephemeral image, a shade of oneself

Figure 4. Johannes Vermeer, *Girl Reading a Letter at an Open Window*, ca. 1659. Gemäldegalerie Alte Meister, Staatliche Kunstsammlungen, Dresden. Alinari/Art Resource, New York

as it might be grasped in a vision or a dream, perhaps an alternative self with another fate. Perhaps it is the invisible girl made visible, the one who is reading and responding to the letter. We might imagine that this is a more somber girl, one who reads the letter as announcing the end of something; the upper part of the letter very noticeably catches the light. Did Nietzsche notice something about the power of light in this painting? Unlike Claude's light, the radiance in this painting is indirect; the sun itself is not depicted.

Nietzsche's tours of the Dresden Gallery would have given him the opportunity to reflect on a spectrum of ways in which vision is thematized, explored, or put into question by painting. Like any museumgoer, he would have found himself drawn to a nude, to Giorgione's *Sleeping Venus;* since her eyes are closed, the viewer can gaze at her without being disturbed, as one might be by realizing that the subject, as we call her, of the painting can look back (in this voyeuristic scenario, it is "one" who looks, not "we"). Everything about this picture conspires to make the woman available; the gently rolling landscape echoes her curves, and so the whole world of the painting acquires an erotic glow (one might say that Claude achieves something of this effect without prominent nudes). Yet eventually one realizes that one is looking, and one begins to reflect on the intensity and interest of this look. Nietzsche might have thought, not necessarily for the first time, that Kant's definition of the aesthetic as being devoid of interest was best seen as a hieroglyphic of Kant's soul, not the report of someone who has seen the desirable body of this painting, a body that invites us by inviting the gaze. Eventually he was to come across that sentence of Stendhal, "[B]eauty is the promise of happiness," which he was to deploy against Kant and Schopenhauer (*GM* III.6; *KSA* 5.346–49). Schopenhauer had preceded Nietzsche in Dresden and had littered his main work with memories of what he had seen there, illustrations of his idealism of the will. Art, he taught, had the magical property of allowing us entry into a world of pure contemplation. He had lingered over the Giorgione, and paintings like it, and had gone back to his scholarly retreat to write: "No object transports us so rapidly into purely aesthetic contemplation as the most beautiful human countenance and form, at the sight of which we are instantly seized by an inexpressible satisfaction and lifted above ourselves and all that torments us." Why is this, Schopenhauer asks. It is, first, because art in general allows us to contemplate the will in nature. We begin to do this simply by observing the play of gravity and mass in architecture. Yet it is the human form that of all *visible* things (Schopenhauer uses such terms for what others might call the empirical or phenomenal) is most expressive of the will. And it is the form of the will that we ourselves are. The claim about bodily beauty is not simply that art encourages a kind of detachment, so that *even* in the case of beholding a desirable body we find ourselves bracketing our erotic desires; it is rather that this form of art, the depiction of human beauty, is the *most* likely to send us into a contemplative state.[29] Surely this claim becomes more difficult to sustain when the nude returns our gaze. Look at Venus as she sleeps. Reclining, unclothed, slumbering, she has no defenses against the viewer. There is more to her situation: as so frequently, a figure on the left of the painting is in a somewhat weaker position than one placed to the right. Perhaps this has something to do with the general Western practice of reading from left to right; frequently our attention is attracted initially by a figure on the left of the painting who leads us to one on the right in a more decisive or commanding attitude or posture. This is the case in another Dresden painting that takes up the themes of vision, desire, and self-knowledge, Poussin's *Narcissus*. Poussin deploys a pastoral setting to demonstrate the folly of falling in love with one's own image. The nymphs on the left are simply spectators, and the arm of the nymph facing us points directly to Narcissus, who is seen in the act of gazing at himself. He holds out his hand to his own reflection, failing to understand who he is and at whom he is looking. Might the painting be an allegory of the impossibility of truly coinciding with oneself, an illustration of the fatality that attaches to such a quest? In the background Echo is turning to stone, a metamorphosis provoked by Narcissus's failure to respond to her beauty. Just behind Narcissus is a dog, attentively standing guard, although his eyes are focused upward, showing us that he does not understand where the real action of the picture is.

In Dresden there are a number of portraits of individuals or small groups in which the subjects look out at us. One of these, by Hans Holbein, shows the artist's characteristic sense of the uncompromising thereness, or *haecceitas*, of the visual world. A distinguished man gazes at us resolutely, with a sense of confident power that is also touched by an awareness of the need to maintain one's guard. We know that this is Charles de Solier, Sieur de Morette, soldier, diplomat, and French ambassador to England, where Holbein painted him in 1535 when he was fifty-five years old. Holbein's de Solier is richly dressed and has all the accoutrements of office and success. Standing foursquare against an elegant hanging, his body, with its broad shoulders and massive arms, forms an impregnable rectangle or living shield. There is no effort here to hide the slight asymmetry of the face; while de Solier looks at us in a disarmingly direct way, his face not turned in the slightest from the picture plane, this absolute frontality allows us to see the minor irregularities of eyes, nose, and beard, a theme dramatized in the difference between the two hands, one bare and one gloved, which hold his dagger, the emblem of his power. This gaze asks us to acknowledge the new realism of Holbein, which takes an unflinching look at its people and asks us to do the same. That realism reaches a kind of peak in his completely unsentimental painting of *The Dead Christ* in Basel, a work that Nietzsche would have seen and perhaps recalled when he was imagining his madman obsessed with the death of God. The famous anamorphosis of the skull in the London *Ambassadors* also insists on the relation between death and realism. In 1799 Caroline Schlegel wrote that if any portrait was destined for eternity, it was this one.[30] Nietzsche acknowledges Holbein's realism in a notebook entry that speaks of "women who resemble those of Holbein not merely externally and perhaps have nothing essentially different in their heads and hearts" (*KSA* 8.398).

Who sees and who fails to see? The Dresden Gallery has an early El Greco, *Christ Healing the Blind Man*, which was painted during the artist's Venetian apprenticeship. The theme suggests that vision is inherently defeasible, that it can come as a gift, that it is not to be taken for granted. Christ's eyes are directed at the blind man, and another bystander stares into the latter's face at close range. There is an intense exchange of looks by a group of men, perhaps the disciples, who are amazed by the miracle. In the foreground a small dog is drawn in a very different direction, sniffing some bags (of food?) and again, as in Poussin's painting of *Narcissus*, marking the difference between human and merely animal vision.

At the Gallery one sees without being seen, or at least that is the enabling fiction of the institution. But sometimes the possibility of being a voyeur is itself made into an explicit theme. If we had not thought of this as we contemplated (or desired) Giorgione's nude, we would encounter it in a curious painting by Franciabigio, *David's Letter to Uriah*. We are struck at first by something like a split-screen effect, with two distinct scenes and two different groups of spectators, as we eventually come to see. On the left is a women's bath with a number of nude figures, on the right a complex group of men on the steps of a classical building. The wall of the women's bath has been cut away to allow us to look in, and especially because we realize that those on the right have no inkling of this scene, we find ourselves in the position of the voyeur, seeing what is closed off and prohibited. The painting depicts two distinct events in the story of David and Bathsheba. Reading from left to right, we come to understand that David spied upon Bathsheba in the first scene; the internal framing of the bath episode makes us complicit in his voyeurism. By the time of the second scene, David has consummated his desire and is in the process of giving Uriah an assignment that he expects will send him to his death. Is this also analogous to what we do to hide the consequences of our guilty visual knowledge? This all-too-busy painting, with its complex group of figures, would seem to ask this question, in part by providing a number of spectators—or voyeurs—on the balconies of the two main buildings. And again the innocence of animal vision is highlighted in the foreground, where a soldier leans on his horse and they seem to gaze into each other's eyes. In *Zarathustra* Nietzsche was to ask what price we pay for vision, comparing the evil eye with its radiant other.

It may seem a bit forced to approach Nietzsche by means of Claude, a painter whom he seems to mention rather casually. And one might wonder whether Claude is simply too Apollonian to serve as an emblematic artist for the disciple of Dionysus. Yet the references in the late letters associate these landscapes with some of Nietzsche's most significant experiences, for example, with the explosion of writing of his last months, in other words with what was most important to him. In December 1888 he writes to Emily Fynn from Turin, praising the city and remarking on the wonderful letters he is receiving from correspondents such as Strindberg and a Russian princess. As he often does, Nietzsche introduces Claude's name by means of the always available topos of the weather: "I think that you are having the same sublime weather that we have been having since September? It seems to me that I live in a continuous Claude Lorrain in colors. Also I have in my whole life altogether never *created* so much as here in the last twenty days—who knows! Great things of the first rank. . . . And without a shadow of weariness, rather in the midst of complete cheerfulness and *good food*" (B 8.506–7). Again, Claude comes to be associated with a great sense of well-being, a feeling of being nourished in multiple ways by one's surroundings, and with the joy of effortless writing. This was the time during which he completed *Twilight of the Idols, Ecce Homo, The Case of Wagner,* and *The Antichrist(ian),* the last of which was projected first as the initial book and then apparently as the whole of *The Transvaluation of Values.* During an earlier stay in Rome, between the composition of *Zarathustra II* and *Zarathustra III,* Nietzsche writes to Overbeck that he has found very little to sustain and interest him in the metropolis, except that "[a]n ancient head of Epicurus and one of Brutus gave me something to think about, and equally three landscapes by Claude Lorrain" (B 6.379).[31] Nietzsche had earlier associated Claude and Epicurus (along with Poussin) with the invention of a heroic-idyllic way of philosophizing. The head or bust of Epicurus that Nietzsche saw is no doubt the one in the Capitoline Museum. Recent research discloses that such busts of philosophers were employed for inspirational and didactic purposes in the recruitment and pedagogical practices of the philosophical schools.[32] Whether Nietzsche had an intimation of this or not, he seems to have taken the head as a provocation to an inventive thought. Claude, too, gave Nietzsche much to think about, certainly the possibility of a glorious experience of the eyes and of at least a temporary sense of harmonious peace with the natural world. Was it also something having to do with the question of what vision is and what art can do to illuminate that vision? These are concerns that run throughout several strands of Nietzsche's thought: his sensitivity to some paintings as offering shining visions and means of interpreting them; his exploration of the theatrical frame of vision, and its implications for framing beyond the theater; and his interrogation of the depth of vision itself, the phenomenology of the life of the gaze, the glance, the evil and the radiant eye that is a constant theme of *Thus Spoke Zarathustra.*

two

Nietzsche's *Laocoön:* Crossings
of Painting and Poetry

14 Aesthetics: Nietzsche contra Lessing

The project of reconstructing aesthetics appears very early in
Nietzsche's work. Writing to Erwin Rohde in October 1869,
Nietzsche tells his friend that he looks forward to seeing him
because

> a great abundance of aesthetic problems and answers has
> been brewing in me during the last year, and the space of
> a letter is too narrow to explain it properly to you. I use
> the opportunity of *public* lectures to work out small parts
> of the system, as I did in my inaugural lecture ["Homer
> and Classical Philology"]. Naturally, Wagner is useful to
> me, in the highest sense, as a prime example of what aes-
> thetics until now has been unable to grasp. Above all it's
> necessary to surpass Lessing's *Laokoon* in a powerful way:
> something that one should scarcely say without inner an-
> guish and shame. (*B* 3.63)

We know of, course, that this aesthetic effervescence will lead in the first instance to *The Birth of Tragedy* and to the unpublished writings that surround it. But in this brief statement of Nietzsche's battle plans, why should Lessing's *Laocoön* occupy the position of that which must be overcome? Lessing is mentioned only briefly in the final version of the *Birth*, and with no explicit reference to his aesthetics; there is no engagement there with the examples or canonical works that Lessing describes in order to articulate his distinctions between poetry and painting, that is, the Laocoön statue itself or the specific passages in Homer that Lessing discusses. I suggest that Nietzsche is thinking of Lessing's attempt to delimit the boundaries of painting and poetry, of the visual and verbal arts. But let us think for a moment not of the *Laocoön* but of Lessing's general approach to tragedy and drama, which he took to be modeled on Aristotle's and yet adapted to the needs of a contemporary theater of *Burgers*. So Lessing plays a role like that which Nietzsche attributes to Euripides, whom he describes as having brought the spectator onto the stage, meaning (at least) that his figures are more like the ordinary citizens in the audience than the heroes of Aeschylus and Sophocles. For Lessing the dramatic critic and theorist, the drama is a story unfolding in time; the roles of spectacle and music are peripheral, and the chorus gets scant attention. The only significant unity, he argued against the French, is that of action, so that the plot, as in Aristotle, is the soul of tragedy. To speak in Aristotelian terms, Nietzsche gives music and spectacle a status at least equal to that of plot; but he also shows that the art can be conceived in terms of powers other than imitation. But the relative demotion of plot and imitation and the elevation of music do not entail the degradation or elimination of images. In this vein, Nietzsche's deepest difference with a thinker like Lessing will be with respect to the original division of experience and its categorization into such binaries as those which are developed more explicitly in the *Laocoön* than in his writings on drama. Ultimately Nietzsche will be rethinking Lessing's insistence on a firm distinction between arts of space and arts of time, between painting and poetry. And, like Wagner, he will be challenging Lessing's protomodernist program that prohibits the mixing of the arts.

Yet initially there is the appearance of a rough parallelism in the dualities that structure these two great works of German aesthetics, the *Laocoön* and *The Birth of Tragedy*, representing two variations of the forms taken by the tyranny of Greece over Germany. Lessing's distinction between painting, as the representation of bodies in space, and poetry, as the expression of thought and emotion in language, seems to bear some resemblance to the contrast between the Apollonian art-force of beautiful appearance and the Dionysian one that is musical. It might even be suggested that Nietzsche is reworking Lessing's contrast between arts of space and arts of time, with music replacing literature as the preeminent temporal art (so far, Nietzsche would be following Schopenhauer's contrast between representation and will, which leads to the special position accorded to music in the latter's theory of art). Let us recall some of the major moves, explicit and implicit, of Lessing's aesthetics, in order to see why and how Nietzsche thinks that he must subvert it, despite these superficial parallels. (I use the word *aesthetics* here in what I take to be a fruitfully wide or ambiguous sense, a sense to be justified in what follows, as pertaining both to the theory of art and to *aisthesis*, understood as the use of the senses and, more generally, of the nature of sensibility, as in Kant's transcendental aesthetic. Nietzsche uses the word this way when he opens the *Birth* by saying, "We will have gained much for the science of aesthetics . . .") What is at stake here is both Nietzsche's conception of art and his attempt, stretching throughout all of his texts, to develop a distinctive conception of sensibility, including visual sensibility. Part of Nietzsche's project of overturning Platonism, as Eric Blondel and others have suggested, lies in articulating another way of ranking and distinguishing the senses, one that moves away from the ocularcentric model that has, as many now say, reigned over Western thought at least since Plato baptized sight as "the noblest of the senses."[1] Yet I want to claim that Nietzsche's rethinking of the senses does not entail so much a demotion of vision as a rethinking of the visual. We will see that he understands tragedy as a highly visual art, a perspective that does indeed place him in opposition to Lessing, not to mention Aristotle and much of the critical tradition (chap. 4).

15 Modernism and Its Discontents: Nietzsche after Greenberg

Lessing and Nietzsche might seem to be allies of a sort in their opposition to a certain conception of the Greeks. Lessing criticizes Winckelmann for attributing (what he sees as) the sculpted Laocoön's failure to cry out when he and his sons are being crushed and strangled by monstrous snakes to the "*edle Einfalt und stille Grösse*" (noble simplicity and quiet grandeur) of the Greeks. But Lessing knows that as *literary* figures Greek heroes cry out, groan, and lament, and even the gods can be wounded and emit a scream; it's all in Homer. And a play like Sophocles' *Philoctetes* is largely given over to the cries of a man suffering from a poisoned wound that constantly renews itself. It is precisely these features of epic and tragedy that Socrates censures in the *Republic* when he proscribes the representation of heroes crying in distress or pain and the mimesis of women who "are ill, or in labor, or in love."[2] Lessing's argument is that Winckelmann must have confused the characteristics of visual art with the character of the Greeks as a people. Laocoön restrains his cries because the sculptor follows the laws of beauty, which will not tolerate the ugliness of a mouth distended by a great expression of pain, fear, or anxiety. In Lessing's terms Edvard Munch's *Cry* would not be a successful work of fine art. Most of the text of the *Laocoön* is devoted to working out and exemplifying the principles that hold for the different arts of painting and poetry. Painting presents objects seen simultaneously in space by means of line and color; poetry uses the successive property of time in order to narrate action and express feeling.[3] It is all much too neat, and recently readers have paid a good bit of attention to the subtitle of the book, "An Essay on the Boundaries [*Grenzen*—which the English translators take as "limits"] of Painting and Poetry," because it indicates that what appears as a metaphysics of genre, deducing the qualities of each art from the definition of its medium, masks a politics of genre, really a police action of criticism, designed to keep each art (but especially painting) in its place. That Lessing is continually rediscovered by those who want to enforce the rules of genre is not surprising; Irving Babbitt's *New Laokoon* (so important for T. S. Eliot) was followed by Clement Greenberg's "Towards a Newer Laocoon" and by Michael Fried's classic and enigmatic essay of 1967 "Art and Objecthood," which attempts once more to enforce a certain purity of visual art, protecting it against a deviation into theater.[4] Greenberg appeals to Lessing as one of the primary theorists of the modern; also invoking Kant, he argues that each distinctive art, inquiry, or practice must be understood in terms of its own specific limits and presuppositions. On this basis, he sketches a history of modern painting in terms of its acceptance and deployment of the flatness of the canvas, opposing this to the supposed earlier attempt to make the boundaries of the painting function as a virtual window frame that reveals some slice of the world.[5]

And now in opposition to Lessing and to such theories of genre, Nietzsche invites us to hear the stirrings of Wagner's orchestra; and we are also asked to behold all the other elements, including spectacle, that constitute the *Gesamtkunstwerk*, as well as the complex *griechische Musikdrama* as understood by Wagner's erstwhile philosophical publicist. Does not the very first paragraph of the main text of *The Birth of Tragedy* begin by declaring the necessity of a certain transgression or crossing of boundaries, an intercourse between two art-forces that would otherwise be distinct? "We shall have gained much for the science of aesthetics, once we perceive not merely by logical inference, but with the immediate certainty of intuitive vision [*unmittelbaren Sicherheit der Anschauung*], that the continuous development of art is bound up with the *Apollonian* and *Dionysian* duality—just as procreation depends on the duality of the sexes, involving perpetual strife with only periodically intervening reconciliations." To the extent that the Apollonian and the Dionysian parallel painting and poetry for Lessing, they are not to be kept apart but become most fruitful in their antagonism and occasional union. If Lessing is a modernist, then Nietzsche could be styling himself and Wagner as postmoderns, were the term available to him. In this postmodern perspective, a theory of genre and medium would be replaced by an agonistics that would attempt to chart the ways in which various art impulses, forms, and styles vie with one another, creating new configurations as they alternately subsume or break free from each other. Yet as Nietzsche tried out various ways of sorting out the abundance of aesthetic thoughts that occupied him in the years 1869–72, he sometimes sounds like a modernist; the agonistic perspective is suggested or implicit at various points, but the formulation of the opening sentence of the *Birth* requires Nietzsche to work through a series of other possible ways of construing the interrelation of the arts.

While the contrast of Apollo and Dionysus does not appear fully explicit until the essay "The Dionysian Worldview" in the summer of 1870, some of the lectures and writings of the preceding months already display Nietzsche's uneasiness with categories like Lessing's, although the latter's name does not appear in this context. In "Das griechische Musikdrama," a lecture of January 1870, Nietzsche describes the Greek actors, audience, and poet as athletes of the pentathlon, simultaneously practicing several arts that we moderns unfortunately take to be distinct. He condemns as an unfortunate modern habit the expectation that we cannot respond to art as whole human beings but only as eyes or ears (*KSA* 1.518). There is already the germ of the thought that Nietzsche will develop later when he argues that a theory of art requires that we see the creation and response to art as the work of fully embodied human beings. Borrowing the term *Musikdrama* that Wagner used to distinguish his work from the traditional European opera, Nietzsche attempts to show how distant his nineteenth-century audience is from the work of the Greeks; if they want to comprehend Aeschylus, they must have a sympathetic experience of Wagner.[6] The notion of the *Gesamtkunstwerk*, whether Greek or contemporary, clearly involves a transgression of the boundaries that Lessing and modernism thought to draw between painting and poetry (or other forms of art). The visual, insofar as it is part of such art, is not static and is not necessarily to be divorced from language and narrative. Similarly, drama does not simply tell a story unfolding in time but presents a series of tableaus that have a sculptural dimension. In this spirit Nietzsche had already written in fall 1869, around the time of his letter to Rohde announcing the necessity of a break with Lessing, that "we are unfortunately in the habit of enjoying the arts in isolation: madness of the picture gallery and the concert hall. The *absolute arts* are an unhappy modern trick [*Unart*]" (*KSA* 7.22).

16 Images, Words, and Music

The Apollonian-Dionysian distinction is incommensurable with Lessing's attempt to ascertain the boundaries between painting and poetry because poetry, on Nietzsche's account, is not necessarily under the dominion of either god. In "The Dionysian Worldview," he describes epic poetry as Apollonian, because the epic poet, like the sculptor, works with "the transfigured [*verklärte*] world of the eye." "Beholding, the beautiful, shining [*Das Schauen, das Schöne, der Schein*] circumscribes the realm of Apollonian art: it is the transfigured world of the eye, that is artistically created in the dream behind closed eyelids. The *epic* attempts to place us in this dream-state: we should see nothing with our eyes open and turn to the inner images [*Bildern*] to whose production the rhapsode seeks to tempt us with ideas" (*KSA* 1.563). In *The Birth of Tragedy*, Nietzsche will be examining Raphael's *Transfiguration* as an exemplary model of this "transfigured world of the eye." Homer makes "the form or the group or the image appear clearly to us" and so shares his "dreamlike condition" with his listeners (*KSA* 1.563). Lessing argues that Homer never offers images for their own sake; on this account, Homeric description is always subordinate to action. Rather than to attempt to picture Helen's features for us, Homer is wisely content, Lessing points out, to show the Trojan elders responding to her beauty and agreeing that she is worth the war. What appears as a counterexample to Lessing's principle, the lengthy ekphrasis of Achilles' shield, is shown to exemplify the point; for the shield is described only within the context of its creation, and the priority of action to static image is carried so far that Homer speaks of figures on the shield as in motion. If we try to picture the shield, we could think of it on the model of the moving images of film or video (not that Lessing had such analogies available to him). Nietzsche consistently describes Homer as a poet of images, and he does not attempt, like Lessing, to show that these are always in the service of action. Homer presents us with a legendary difficulty in assessing the relation between words and images; according to tradition he was blind, and yet he was a master of making things come vividly before the eyes of his listener or reader; the first, enormously influential model of poetic ekphrasis, the description of the shield of Achilles in the *Iliad*, was supposed to have been written by a blind man (and so it is doubly uncanny, the description of an impossible visual work by a man who could not see). Nietzsche sidesteps the issue of Homer's blindness by agreeing, in the wake of the Homeric question that gave a powerful impetus to German philology in the century before him, that "Homer" was not an individual but an aesthetic creation that fit the need of his audience for a single source of their national poems. Nietzsche the philologist knows that, in Derrida's words, we are always dealing with "more than one language"; and Foucault is indebted to him, in part, for the critical question "what is an author?" Young Professor Nietzsche, lecturing on "Homer and Classical Philology" at Basel in 1869, characterizes "Homer" (or at least the *Iliad*) as a collection of images: "The *Iliad* is no garland, but an assemblage of flowers. There are the greatest possible number of images [*Bilder*] stuck into a space, but the collector was unconcerned with whether the grouping of the collected images was always pleasing and rhythmic. He knew, to be sure, that the whole came to nobody's attention, but only the single detail" (*KGW* II.1.264). Nietzsche goes on to say explicitly that the plot or structure *(Plan)* of the poem is a later addition, one even subsequent to Homer's fame, and that the quest for the "original structure" of the poem is a search for a will of the wisp.[7] While this critical judgment does not speak directly to Lessing's contrast of images deployed for their own sake with images in the service of action, it does suggest a deeper affinity between the exemplary poet and the plastic artist than Lessing would acknowledge. Nietzsche's account of the lyric, on the other hand, sees it as tending toward the musical, and so having an affinity with the Dionysian. Given the traditional tripartite division of poetry into epic, lyric, and dramatic genres, this leaves the possibility that drama will be the site for the combination or confrontation of the two gods of the arts. When Nietzsche declared in his later preface to the *Birth* in 1886 that the work was too Hegelian, he may have been thinking of these sorts of conceptual moves.[8] Young Nietzsche quotes with approval from A. W. Ambros's history of music, which describes the Greek stage as being like a bas-relief, comparing it to the scenes on the pediment of the Parthenon (*KSA* 1.527–28). He concludes the lecture "The Dionysian Worldview" by saying that "what we hope for from the future was already once reality—in a past that is over two thousand years old" (*KSA* 1.532). He might have agreed in part with Michael Fried, who, under the inspiration of Clement Greenberg, argued that the minimalist art of the 1960s that violated the limits of its genre ceased to be sculpture but collapsed into theater. Nietzsche of course challenges his audience to open themselves to the experience of such multidimensional theater.

One of Nietzsche's many studies for the *Birth* is traditionally known by the title "On Music and Words," although it might also be called "On Music and Images."[9] The polemical point of this draft is to demonstrate that music cannot be used to illustrate poetry; more generally, Nietzsche is attempting to establish that while music can generate a world of images, such images by themselves cannot generate music. In this text Nietzsche uses a number of terms to designate images, such as *Bild* and *Vision*, all of which have a distinctly visual meaning. Although he had declared himself a critic of Lessing, the shape of the argument in this study seems surprisingly similar to that of *Laocoön*'s contrast between painting and poetry. While Lessing had argued for the limited character of painting or the visual arts when compared with the infinite expressive possibilities of poetry, "On Music and Words" could be read as developing a different binary opposition, opposing music to *both* poetry and painting. It is perhaps the most iconophobic of Nietzsche's early writings.[10] The notion that Dionysian music can generate Apollonian images will be central to *The Birth of Tragedy*, but there is an emphasis here on the impotence of the image, a need to deny its power, that is reminiscent of the passion involved in Lessing's parallel comparison of painting and poetry. What is crucial to the world of images is that it be self-contained; for once its borders have been opened to other spheres of experience, it can no longer maintain its power of illusion:

> How could the Apollonian world of the eye, wholly absorbed in visual contemplation, be able to generate a tone which after all symbolizes a sphere that is excluded and overcome by the Apollonian abandonment to shining [*Schein*]? The joy in shining [*die Lust am Scheine*] cannot generate out of itself the joy in non-shining. The delight of seeing [*die Wonne des Schauens*] is a delight only because nothing reminds us of a sphere in which individuation is broken and annulled. (*KSA* 7.363; "MW" 110; I have, somewhat unconventionally, translated *Schein* as "shining" for reasons that will be explained later [secs. 19, 20])

Although there is a voluptuous pleasure involved in submitting to the world of images, it is a fragile one. Merleau-Ponty will speak of "the madness of vision," suggesting that it can constitute a kind of monomania, excluding all the other senses.[11]

17 The Silence of Saint Cecilia

In order to demonstrate the relations between the world of images and that of music, Nietzsche produces his first description or ekphrasis of a painting by Raphael, *The Ecstasy of Saint Cecilia* (fig. 5); eventually he will describe two others, joining the ranks of the many German writers who contributed to the artist's apotheosis in the nineteenth century. If the ancient world of Greece and Rome was the first focus of his valorization of an artistic culture, the Italian renaissance was not far behind.[12] And if some other more distant societies, including Islamic Spain and India, were later to play the role of more affirmative cultures, there is no reason to think that Nietzsche was ever acquainted with or thought seriously about the visual aspects of these traditions. In the painting Saint Cecilia, patron saint of music, has abandoned her instruments because her attention has been completely captured by a choir of angels. Surrounded by a number of saints, she directs her gaze heavenward to the celestial music. Her organetto is falling from her hands, and other instruments lie broken at her feet.[13] Schopenhauer cites the painting at a crucial point in *The World as Will and Representation*, where it marks the transition from the aesthetic to the religious realm. After a lengthy and passionate account of the way in which the arts, ranging from architecture to music, can lead to an escape from the tyranny of the will into a contemplation of ideas or of the will itself, Schopenhauer now points to the limits of art. The artist or the art-lover stops at this point, delighting in the episodic release from desire yielded by aesthetic experience; it is only a partial relief because "it does not deliver him from life for ever, but only for a few moments. For him it is not the way out of life, but only an occasional consolation in it, until his power, enhanced by this contemplation, finally becomes tired of the spectacle, and seizes the serious side of things. The *Saint Cecilia* of Raphael can be regarded as a symbol of this transition."[14] And indeed Cecilia is abandoning her instruments for the sake of the higher harmonies that she hears from above. On Schopenhauer's reading these finer sounds must be understood as transcending the musical world altogether and indicating, instead, that which can be neither pictured

in images nor expressed by voice or instrument, the holy or religious life that involves a total sacrifice of the will. Schopenhauer does not explicitly comment on the play of the visual and the musical that is the reason for Nietzsche's invocation of the painting, although the latter's description is shot through with his conceptual apparatus, as well as suggesting, in context, a difference with his predecessor on some important points. For example, Schopenhauer speaks of "the will's passage into visibility" and of "degrees of visibility," and he contrasts the world of representation, or *Vorstellung*, with that of the will itself, whose only copy is found in music.[15] But while Schopenhauer sees the painting as occupying a transitional place where art passes over into religion, or super-art, Nietzsche understands it as marking the boundary between an art of images and an art of musical tones; this suggests that here too, even before *The Birth of Tragedy*, Nietzsche is skeptical about the possibility of the realm of total surrender of the will that Schopenhauer saw in religion:

> Populate the air with the *Phantasie* of a Raphael and contemplate, as he did, how St. Cecilia is listening, enraptured, to the harmonies of angelic choirs; no sound issues from this world, though it seems to be lost in music. But if we imagined that this harmony did actually acquire sound by virtue of a miracle, whither would St. Cecilia, Paul, and Magdalene, and even the singing angels, have suddenly disappeared from us? We would immediately cease to be Raphael, and even as the instruments of the world lie broken on the ground in this painting, our painter-vision [*Malervision*], conquered by a higher one, would pale and vanish like shadows. (*KSA* 7.363; "MW" 109–10)

Music can generate images; images cannot generate music. (Hegel said something similar in ranking music as a more subjective or spiritual art than painting and sketching the form of a transition from painting to music.) Our experience of seeing *Saint Cecilia* is both actually and virtually silent. We have no sense of the music that she played before dropping her instruments; any attempt to imagine the song of the angels above will come to nothing. We come to understand, as in another notable ekphrasis, Keats's "Ode on a Grecian Urn," that while heard melodies are sweet, unheard ones are always sweeter (sweeter even than those heard with the mind's ear). Jakob Burckhardt had com-

Figure 5. Raphael, *The Ecstasy of Saint Cecilia*, 1514. Pinacoteca Nazionale, Bologna. Alinari/Art Resource, New York

mented on the way in which Raphael had deftly represented the triumph of one kind of music over another in a necessarily silent medium: "all are listening to the choir of angels only indicated in the air above. Raphael gave song to this wonderfully improvised upper group, whose victory over instruments is here substituted for the conquest, impossible to represent, of heavenly tones over the earthly, with a symbolism worthy of all admiration."[16] Burckhardt was an enthusiastic reader of Schopenhauer and was Nietzsche's richest personal contact with the visual arts, at least during the latter's Basel period; his account of *Saint Cecilia* seems to focus more on Schopenhauer's contrast between earthly art and unearthly religion than on Nietzsche's opposition between plastic and musical arts. While Lessing demarcated boundaries between painting and poetry, Nietzsche chooses another image to evoke the relationship between music and the arts of the image: "While it is certain that a bridge leads from the mysterious castle of the musician into the free country of images—and the lyric poet walks across it— it is impossible to proceed in the opposite direction, although there are said to be some people who have the delusion that they have done this" (*KSA* 7.362; "MW" 109). In place of Lessing's boundaries (which, he acknowledged, could endure some very moderate incursions, if strictly limited to the frontiers), Nietzsche sees the basic division of the arts as a one-way street open only to the musician.

And Nietzsche reads this in a painting, one that he would have seen in a copy by Denys Calvaert in the Dresden Gallery. As will be evident when we explore his other encounters with Raphael, he understands this painter as one who both goes to the limits of his art and articulates and thematizes those very limits. In this sense, there would be a modernist dimension in Raphael, following Greenberg's account of modernism, and Nietzsche would be a modernist critic of painting. It is in this vein that Foucault will speak of Manet. Yet Nietzsche would not be a modernist critic *überhaupt*, for music is expressly not subject to the strictures that *Saint Cecilia* is said to demonstrate for the pictorial art.

If music can generate images, however, that does not mean that there is always a happy relationship between a musical work and the text or action (in the case of the opera) that might accompany it. Nietzsche considers the case of song: "the song [*Lied*] is just a symbol and related to the music like the Egyptian hieroglyph of courage to a courageous soldier. Confronted with the supreme revelations of music, we even feel, willy-nilly, the *crudeness* of all imagery [*Bildlichkeit*] and of every emotion that might be adduced by way of an analogy. Thus, for example, Beethoven's last quartets put to shame all of visuality [*Anschaulichkeit*] and the whole realm of empirical reality" (*KSA* 7.366; "MW" 112). Note that Nietzsche's text permits little doubt that he is emphasizing the visually suggestive *Schau* of *Anschaulichkeit*; and this renders plausible a similar reading of related words such as *Anschauung*, which appears in the first sentence of *The Birth of Tragedy*. The point is even applied to the last movement of Beethoven's *Ninth Symphony* and its use of Schiller's poem "An die Freude." Nietzsche claims that we are uninterested in the sense of the words and of any images they might provoke, "because, rendered wholly impotent [*depotenziert*] through music for image and word [*Bild und Wort*], *we simply do not hear anything of Schiller's poem*" (*KSA* 7.366; "MW" 113). While he says that some people have argued that Beethoven's work marks a breakthrough allowing music an entrance into the "conscious mind's" image and concept *(Bild und Begriff)*, Nietzsche understands Beethoven as having marked the nature of the relationship by the words that introduce the song of the choir, "Ach Freunde, nicht diese Töne . . . ," by which he means to justify not the language, words, and images of Schiller's poem but the choral song itself; what Beethoven needed at this point was not the specific sense of a particular poem but the "more pleasing" joyful sound of the human voice.

There would then be a deep analogy between the self-imposed and self-referentially marked limits imposed by both Raphael and Beethoven in Nietzsche's examples. Each would be gesturing at the apparent possibility of his art breaking through into another dimension, while carefully guarding it from doing so. While the *Saint Cecilia* would be demonstrating the impossibility of images moving into the territory of the musical, the *Ninth* would be exhibiting the inadequacy of any specific words or images to its own music. At this point in his argument, Nietzsche might appear closest in his method to Lessing and his modernist heirs, in celebrating two supreme works of art that make a theme of their own limits. For the pair of the *Laocoön* group and Homer, Nietzsche would substitute *Saint Cecilia* and Beethoven's *Ninth;* and he would replace the opposition of painting and poetry with that of the Apollonian (including painting and most poetry) and Dionysian music. Yet this appearance is deceptive, since Nietzsche sees the relation between music and images as a one-way bridge or street; the claim is not that Beethoven's music exemplifies the total irrelevance of the image to music but that the specific and supreme work that he analyzes is not to be understood in terms of the meaning of its accompanying words or the images to which they give rise.

By the time of *The Birth of Tragedy,* the figure of the unidirectional bridge from "the mysterious castle of music" to "the free land of images" has been dropped for another way of portraying the relationship of the Apollonian and the Dionysian. If Nietzsche never gives up his view that the musical can generate images, but that the converse is not the case, the insistence on the impotence of the image is no longer quite so explicit. If we think of Nietzsche as wrestling with the heritage of Lessing's aesthetics, we can consider the train of writings culminating in the *Birth* as a series of attempts to describe the limits, boundaries, or forms of relationship among distinct forms of art. In this sense, no matter how sharply Nietzsche differs with Lessing on such issues as whether poetry is or can be an art of images, he still accepts the necessity of distinguishing among the different arts and specifying their relations, and he borrows from Lessing the conception that there are fundamentally two forms of art, one of which is preeminently imagistic; so here we might see Nietzsche as adopting a Schopenhauerian revision of Lessing, according to which the most significant contrast is to be drawn not between painting and poetry, but between music and all the other arts.

It seems that the birth of *The Birth of Tragedy* is to be dated from Nietzsche's having focused on the very figure of sexual relations and birth as a way of understanding the affiliations and ruptures of two very different forms of art. What is distinctive about the *Birth,* in relation to his earlier studies, is that Nietzsche has not only transformed the *terms* of Lessing's binary aesthetics but that, after provisionally trying out one version of the sort of exclusionary principle involved in the former's idea of *Grenzen,* he has now also advanced a new conception (or figure) for understanding the *relations* between those terms. The thoughts about aesthetics that were bubbling and brewing in Nietzsche's thought, at least since 1869, come forth at the New Year of 1872 with the declaration "that the continuous development of art is bound up with the *Apollonian* and *Dionysian* duality just as procreation depends on the duality of the sexes, involving perpetual strife with only periodically intervening reconciliations." The pregnancy of his thoughts leads to the thought of pregnancy.

While Nietzsche compares the relation of the Apollonian and the Dionysian to the attraction and conflict of men and women, Lessing employs sexual examples and metaphors to a quite different end, in order to insist on the boundaries appropriate to the arts. *Laocoön* is permeated by iconophobia, a fear of the power of the visual image. In contrasting the "wise Greeks," who kept images under control by civil law, with the moderns, who tend to allow the image a freer play, Lessing occasionally sides with the "pious iconoclasts," who had a certain holy fear of the image. For the ancients, he claims, beautiful men and beautiful statues helped to create one another, while "with us the highly susceptible imagination of mothers seems to express itself only in producing monsters."[17] This leads Lessing to recall that the mothers of many of the great men of antiquity dreamed, while pregnant, of having sexual relations with serpents; this was the result, he claims, of their seeing images of gods accompanied by these symbols of their divinity. It is this seductive power of the image that needs to be kept in check. Thinking of passages like these, W. J. T. Mitchell observes that Lessing produces a gendered account of the arts, leading to this opposition: "Paintings, like women, are ideally silent, beautiful creatures designed for the gratification of the eye, in contrast to the sublime eloquence proper to the manly art of poetry. Paintings are confined to the narrow sphere of external display of their bodies and of the space which they ornament, while poems are free to range over an infinite realm of potential action and expression, the domain of time, discourse, and history."[18]

The vision of snakes, whether in the representation of Laocoön and his sons caught in their coils, in perverse dreams, in the image of the Medusa's head, or in Orestes' confrontation with the furies, is almost always an index of the terrors that can come through sight (keep in mind that Nietzsche calls the idea of eternal recurrence, a recurrence of the *Augenblick*, the moment of vision, or twinkling of the eye, a "Medusa's head"; see sec. 38). Glancing ahead to the narratives of *Thus Spoke Zarathustra* that adumbrate the idea of eternal recurrence of the *Augenblick*, we find Nietzsche, too, deploying serpentine imagery. The second part of "On the Vision and the Riddle" relates the continuation of a vision in which a shepherd lies choked by the head of a serpent, that image which arises so frequently whenever it is a question of establishing or testing the limits of the visual. As disgusting as the dreams of serpentine copulation, and perhaps with an analogous sexual meaning, this image literalizes the Medusa's head of the thought of recurrence. While Nietzsche's story of the shepherd is indeed a verbal and not a visual text, it is highly charged with visual appeal (or repulsion). Although it might survive Lessing's strictures, insofar as it narrates incidents that involve ugliness rather than simply describing the ugly in itself, the passage does not deal with the visual in a merely accidental fashion but thematizes it in a complex way (sec. 37). The account of the shepherd is a very different form of combat with the snake than Laocoön's heroic resistance (in either the sculptural or the literary versions that Lessing cites), and it challenges the exclusions demanded by "the laws of beauty." Nietzsche's aesthetics, since it is directed against the policing of the senses and the genres that Lessing's work exemplifies, involves a defense of vision and visual art, both as taken by themselves and as intertwined with other senses and arts. Derrida suggests that traditional aesthetics, from Plato to Hegel and Heidegger, gives a special priority to the arts of language, and Lessing's attempt to fix the boundaries of the arts certainly places him squarely in that tradition; yet insofar as Nietzsche takes poetry to be an art of images and contrasts both poetry and painting with music, he would be challenging and deforming this tradition (like Schopenhauer, whom he follows here in some respects). This was the lesson he learned from Wagner and that he retained until the end, despite his about-face with regard to almost everything else concerning the maestro's work and persona.

It is not just a rhetorical flourish that Nietzsche employs when he says in that first sentence of *The Birth of Tragedy* that we must see what he is leading us to "with the immediate certainty of intuitive vision [*Anschauung*]." Not only the prose of *The Birth of Tragedy*, but also the story that it tells of the birth of tragedy, is in large part a story of becoming visible, of the arrangement and projection of visual images, whether actual, virtual, or hallucinatory. Later, in his 1886 preface to his first book, Nietzsche was to call it "image-mad and image confused [*bilderwüthig und bilderwirrig*]" (*BT*, pref., 3; *KSA* 1.14). These images are perhaps literary in the first instance; but Nietzsche was also concerned with specifically visual pictures, and his drafts show that he was thinking of even more paintings and drawings than he explicitly mentions.[19] The *Birth* is about the genesis of a certain kind of vision and of the framework or setup whose structure makes that vision possible. At crucial points in developing his articulation of the Dionysian or of the tragic, Nietzsche gives the reader specific directions to use the visual imagination. This is remarkable because the contrast of the Dionysian with the Apollonian might lead us to think of the former as a nonimagistic force, affiliated with the nonimagistic art of music. But in giving us instructions on how we ought to realize or comprehend the Dionysian, Nietzsche moves not from the visible to the musical, but the other way around: "Under the charm of the Dionysian not only is the union between man and man reaffirmed, but nature, which has become alienated, hostile, or subjugated, celebrates once more her reconciliation with her lost son, man. Freely, earth proffers her gifts, and peacefully the beasts of prey of the rocks and deserts approach. The chariot of

Dionysus is covered with flowers and garlands; panthers and tigers walk under its yoke. Transform Beethoven's 'Hymn to Joy' into a painting; let your imagination [*Einbildungskraft*] conceive the multitudes bowing to the dust, awestruck—then you will approach the Dionysian" (*KSA* 1.29; *BT* 37). "Transform Beethoven's 'Hymn to Joy' into a painting": this is the kind of transformation that Nietzsche allows in "On Music and Words." Yet to say that we will "approach" the Dionysian in this way seems rather odd in the light of Nietzsche's earlier strictures on moving from the world of images to that of music. What was once a one-way street seems to have become a circular path, in which music can provoke images that in turn lead to an understanding of music. How strange it seems, in the light of what he wrote just a year or so earlier, to hear that we will approach the Dionysian by constructing such a history painting. In *The Birth of Tragedy*, the agonistic interplay of image and music has become supple enough to accommodate and encourage such translations. We are left wondering what sort of picture this might be; what visual memories from his visits to the Dresden Gallery or from Burckhardt's prints and engravings might be at work here? In the Dresden Gallery there is a painting, *The Drunken Silenus*, by Van Dyck, but Silenus is accompanied by just a few figures helping him stumble away from the scene of his dissipation. Later Nietzsche will declare that Rubens and Van Dyck are for him the greatest of all painters (*B* 5.236), and he will compare Delacroix to Wagner (*EH*, "Clever," 5; *KSA* 6.289), so we might imagine the painting along some such lines, perhaps a huge Rubens bacchanalia or a Delacroix with many writhing bodies in the style of his *Death of Sardanapalus*. In his preface of 1886, Nietzsche called his book "image-mad and image-confused." Let us not dismiss Nietzsche's visualizations too quickly on the basis of that later reservation. Is there not an implicit principle here that nothing is grasped in its full import until it has generated the vision appropriate to it?

three

"This Is Not a Christ": Art in
The Birth of Tragedy

19 Transfiguring the *Transfiguration*

When he invites us to imagine Beethoven's "Ode to Joy" as
a painting or a sculpture, Nietzsche is performing a kind of
inverted ekphrasis, one that should be carefully compared with
his reading of Raphael's *Transfiguration* in the *Birth* (fig. 6).
In this genre of ancient rhetoric, a visual work of art becomes
the subject of a discourse, serving to generate a speech or a
text that clarifies the original and sometimes vies with it, suggesting that the rhetorician can provide a verbal equivalent of
the work of the artist. It is symptomatic of this condition that
the first canonical and exemplary ekphrasis in the Western
tradition is a description of an imaginary work of art written
by a blind man—Homer's lines on the shield of Achilles,
which perform the amazing feat of animating and putting
movement into what would ordinarily be a static, engraved
piece of metal. There is something uncanny in the fact that
writers on ekphrasis return continually to this doubly impossible example. In Rome Pliny the Elder had no compunctions

about describing lost works of art (in his *Natural History*), and even in the seventeenth century, Franciscus Junius was producing elaborate descriptions of ancient paintings that we would have to call exercises in the painterly imaginary. Ekphrasis often dwells on that which is not strictly visible in the painting or sculpture, taking the seen as a sign of unseen meanings.[1]

Nietzsche gives two extended accounts of individual paintings (the other is of another Raphael painting, the *Sistine Madonna*), so they will receive some detailed attention here. Before rereading this text, we should recall that the *Transfiguration* occupies a special place in Raphael's work and in the veneration of Raphael practiced by figures like Vasari, Goethe, and Jakob Burckhardt; Vasari, for example, called Raphael a "mortal god."[2] It was Raphael's last painting, and a dispute continues concerning how close it was to completion at the time of his death and what the role of his studio was in painting and completing it. Vasari tells us that it was displayed with Raphael's body in the painter's studio; in this account it is the painting that lives:

> Having made his confession and repented, Raphael ended his life on Good Friday, the same day he was born. He was thirty-seven when he died; and we can be sure that just as he embellished the world with his talent so his soul now adorns heaven itself. As he lay dead in the hall where he had been working they placed at his head the picture of the *Transfiguration* which he had done for Cardinal de' Medici; and the sight of this living work of art along with his dead body made the hearts of everyone who saw it burst with sorrow. In memory of Raphael, the cardinal later placed this picture on the high altar of San Pietro in Montorio, where because of the nobility of everything Raphael ever did it was afterwards held in great reverence.[3]

Burckhardt finds Raphael to be the zenith of Renaissance art and offers a reasoned defense of this judgment in his *Cicerone*, a guide to art in Italy. It is a guide that Nietzsche follows in a number of respects, one that he frequently recommended to friends and acquaintances. For Nietzsche, Raphael is always an exemplary painter, generally *the* exemplary painter, a valuation that he shares with Burckhardt. According to the historian, the great art of the Renaissance does not emerge as

Figure 6. Raphael, *Transfiguration*, 1520. Vatican Gallery, Vatican State (Rome). Alinari/Art Resource, New York

the result of any external influence, such as the imitation of classical models. At the end of the fifteenth century, art

> rose to the highest stage to which it was allowed to attain. Out of the midst of the study of life and character, which was the task of this century, complete beauty raised itself up newborn. . . . Then and there it springs forth, unexpectedly, like a flash of lightning, not as the mere fruit of a determined effort, but as a gift of heaven. The time had come. . . . There is indeed only a brief time for the full bloom. We may say that the short lifetime of Raphael (1483–1520) witnessed the rise of all that was most perfect, and that immediately after him, even with the greatest who outlived him, the decline began.[4]

Even Leonardo and Michelangelo show signs of this decline. Leonardo tends toward the fanciful, as in the introduction of dreamy landscapes (for example, in the *Mona Lisa*), while Michelangelo (as in the *Last Judgment*) indulges in the symbolic. According to Burckhardt, Michelangelo's restless need to create new forms sets the stage for the excesses of Mannerism. Raphael stands alone as having avoided these failings. He uses allegory but refuses to allow it to intrude on his works. In light of the controversy over the *Transfiguration*, which is the culminating point of Burckhardt's discussion of Raphael, who is in turn the highest flowering of Renaissance painting, it is noteworthy that he insists on unity as one of the painter's distinctive achievements: "In Raphael the detail strikes so powerfully that one thinks it the essential part; yet the charm of the whole is infinitely the most distinctive point."[5] Burckhardt was able to reserve a unique position for Raphael by following a different method in his art-historical writings than he did in his other works. He first separated the two enterprises. Hayden White suggests some of the motives behind Burckhardt's method: "Art objects were self-referential, and although the quality, mood, style, of an age might be reflected in them, in order to enjoy them one did not have to consider the problem of the artifact's relation to the milieux in which it arose. In fact, Burckhardt's decision to exclude a consideration of the visual arts from his *Civilization of the Renaissance in Italy* may well have been a product of his desire to discourage the notion that high art was dependent in any significant way on the external circumstances in which it was produced."[6] Having established a historical method that treats the artwork as a relatively independent form of expression, Burckhardt proceeds to identify one artist, Raphael, who was supreme in achieving such independence for his works. Throughout the *Cicerone*, which is divided into sections dealing with architecture, sculpture, and painting, he adheres to a three-stage conception of the history of art, in which classical and early Christian beginnings are followed by the achievements of the High Renaissance, giving way in turn to the slow decline of the baroque; this historical pattern is grafted onto a ranking of the arts adopted from Schopenhauer, in which architecture, sculpture, and painting exhibit progressively more spiritual forms and content.[7] If Raphael's *Transfiguration* marks one of the high points of his career, that means that in this narrative it also marks one of the high points of all visual art; in producing this narrative, Burckhardt can be seen as rewriting Vasari with Schopenhauer's conceptual grid.

In his *Untimely Meditation* on *The Advantage and Disadvantage of History for Life*, Nietzsche thinks critically about the Hegelian philosophy of history, and implicitly about the Hegelian aesthetics, by means of the case of Raphael. Raphael's sudden death at the age of thirty-seven has always (like Mozart's death and perhaps that of Keats) seemed to be one of the great tragedies of art. History seems unfair; there appears to be an obvious gap between what is and what ought to be. Yet a Hegelian will play upon the question, which might occur to anyone, whether some of these artists might indeed have achieved all that it was given to them to accomplish. Hegel asked similar questions about the great men of history, like Alexander, Caesar, and Napoleon, and argued that it was fitting that such world-historical figures died or disappeared shortly after their major actions. More generally, Hegel and some of his followers attempted to show that in the last analysis the history of the world was identical with the judgment to be passed upon the world. At the end of history, we will comprehend the achieved identity of what is and what ought to be. In his essay on history, Nietzsche apologizes for repeating once more the "obsolete and old-fashioned" objection that history says only "it was," while morality says "you ought not to have done something." But this means that

> history amounts to a compendium of factual immorality. How far astray he would go who regarded history as being at the same time the judge of this factual immorality! Morality is offended, for example, by the fact that a Raphael had to die at thirty-six: such a being ought not to die. If, in the face of this, you wanted to come to the aid of history as apologists of the factual, you would say: he had expressed everything that was in him, had he lived longer he would have produced only a repetition of the beauty he had created already, and so forth. (*AD* 8; *KSA* 1.310)[8]

To make such arguments, Nietzsche says, is to take on the role of devil's advocate, to worship the idol of the factual. And it is to argue from ignorance, "for it is only because you do not know what such a *natura naturans* as Raphael is that you are incensed to know that it once was but will never be again." The point is not merely that the devil's advocate (or Hegel) is too shortsighted to understand what Raphael might have done but that none of us could have anticipated what his later work would be like. The painter is the example here because he died so young (in the course of the discussion, Nietzsche argues against the facile use of another form of the Hegelian argument, which describes certain figures—possibly Goethe—as outliving themselves). Yet the fact that Raphael is Nietzsche's example of a *natura naturans*, that is, of a creative force from whom we must learn, says something about the seriousness with which he proposes to understand the paintings of the master. Three of his pictures (including the *Sistine Madonna* and the *Saint Cecilia*) are subjects of rather detailed discussion, an attention Nietzsche gives to no other painter. More specifically, it tells us that Nietzsche sees Raphael's work as highly instructive. Here Nietzsche (somewhat naively, some might say) adopts a traditional conception of genius. But that use of the concept might be reformulated by saying that he takes Raphael's work to be exemplary: we should not only assume the possibility that it will modify our concepts; we should give it every opportunity to do so.

For Nietzsche Raphael is indeed an exemplary painter, and the pictures that he discusses, especially the *Transfiguration*, are exemplary paintings. Consider this distinction between an example and an exemplar. An *example* of a concept or theory is something that is supposed to illustrate the concept or theory. If we eventually decide that it is a poor example, we simply discard it and employ another. But something is an *exemplar* if we are committed to seeing it as in some important sense constitutive of what it exemplifies; if we were to change our mind about the meaning of what we had taken to be an exemplar, we would be changing our minds about the domain that it was supposed to characterize. If we significantly revise our conception of *Oedipus the King*, we will revise our conception of Greek tragedy. Similarly, Raphael's *Transfiguration* seems to play the role of an exemplary painting. For Burckhardt it is one of the supreme works of the artist, who is himself exemplary of the Renaissance, and Burckhardt, a determined critic of Hegelianism, sees great art as essentially timeless.[9] If we were to see this painting in a significantly different way, it would change our idea of what painting is. As we will see, Nietzsche changed his view of this painting and of Raphael over the course of the next sixteen years, but it is only in the *Birth* that he is explicit about how his understanding of this work helps to establish a concept of pictorial art.

The special status of Raphael is overdetermined for Nietzsche. Schopenhauer had concluded *The World as Will and Representation* by urging us to turn our attention away from our desperate, ravenous will to live, "to turn our glance from our own needy and perplexed nature to those who have overcome the world." And here, on the last page of his major work, he summons up an image of those who have indeed overcome: "Then, instead of the restless pressure and effort; instead of the constant transition from desire to apprehension and from joy to sorrow; instead of the never-satisfied and never-dying hope that constitutes the life-dream of the man who wills, we see that peace that is higher than all reason, that ocean-like calmness of the spirit, that deep tranquility, that unshakeable confidence and serenity, whose mere reflection in the countenance, as depicted by Raphael and Coreggio, is a complete and certain gospel. Only knowledge remains; the will has vanished."[10] If Nietzsche begins his first book with an ekphrasis of a Raphael painting in order to establish a non-Christian way of reading it, then he is setting out his own philosophy by an alternative understanding of an image.

While Raphael's paintings were taken as exemplary by all or almost all of the thinkers, especially Germans, with whom Nietzsche was constructing a dialogue, the question of how to interpret his last, most problematic picture was a subject of lively discussion. If Raphael is a *natura naturans*—"one of the great naive ones" Nietzsche calls him in the *Birth*—then what appear to some as the painting's flaws ought to be reexamined to see whether they can be reinterpreted in terms of a strong new reading of the work. Critics have long been divided on the question of whether the picture constitutes a unified work. It is usually seen as conjoining two distinct scenes, based on two Gospel texts that narrate different episodes (Matt. 17; Mark 9:20–27).[11] At the bottom, a boy with a wild-eyed expression flings up his arm and is the focus of a confused and agitated group of disciples, family, and onlookers; he is the possessed subject of the story. The biblical text tells us that Jesus rebuked the disciples for failing to heal the boy because of their unbelief. In the upper half of the painting, Jesus floats above the mountain, attended by Moses and Elijah. Matthew says that he "was transfigured before them: and his face did shine as the sun, and his raiment was white as the light." The spectacle has witnesses; Peter, James, and John accompany Jesus to the mountain and see not only the transfiguration but also a "bright cloud," from which a voice issues declaring, "This is my beloved Son, in whom I am well pleased; hear ye him." The painting involves several levels of spectatorship: while the disciples above appear awestruck and shield their eyes from the dazzling light, most of the crowd below clearly have their gazes fixed on the demoniac boy or on one of the fervently gesticulating figures in their midst. On the left are two witnesses who have been variously identified, most likely as patron saints of the church for which the painting was commissioned.[12] Only we see the entire tableau.

Some critics have argued that Raphael does not succeed in unifying the two somewhat disparate segments of the painting, but many have claimed that the artist has daringly created a higher unity by combining them. From the latter perspective, the work marks a new departure in Raphael's art that leads away from classicism to a style that can allow ruptures and discontinuities. It would be the opening of the door that led to Mannerism. Nietzsche would certainly have read Goethe's *Italian Journey;* recounting his visit to Rome along with a group, he writes of the painting: "[T]he quieter members of the group were annoyed to hear the old criticism that it has a double action. . . . it is odd that anyone should ever have found fault with the grand unity of this conception. . . . How, then, are those upper and lower parts to be separated? The two are one: below, the suffering part, in need of help; above, the effective, helpful part, both of them linked together. To express the sense of this in another way: can the connection between the conceptual and the real be severed?"[13] Goethe's remark about the conceptual and the real can be read as anticipating Nietzsche's contrast of the Apollonian and the Dionysian, which he finds represented in the painting. Yet his account of the unity of the picture will be rather more complex. Ultimately the tension between the upper and lower scenes is kept from blatant contradiction or from falling apart into two separate episodes by the Apollonian principle of individuation. The painting teeters on the edge of falling into a split-screen effect, saved by Apollo, the master of images.

It was a major task of German aesthetics and art theory to explain in general how art brought together opposites into a higher unity; and since Raphael was generally thought to be a perfect artist or genius, the *Transfiguration* posed a special problem for an aesthetics that wanted to make contact with the canon. Hegel's account in his *Aesthetics* relies on his speculative understanding of Christianity to generate a reading of the deeper unity of the work:

> [I]t is a familiar and often repeated reproach against Raphael's *Trans-figuration* that it falls apart into two actions entirely devoid of any connection with one another, and in fact this is true if the picture is

considered *externally:* above on the hill we see the transfiguration, below is the scene with the child possessed of an unclean spirit. But if we look at the *spirit* of the composition, a supreme connection is not to be missed. For, on the one hand, Christ's visible transfiguration is precisely his actual elevation above earth, and his departure from the disciples, and this must be made visible too as a separation and a departure; on the other hand, the sublimity of Christ is here especially transfigured in an actual simple case, namely in the fact that the disciples could not heal the child without the help of the Lord. Thus here the double action is motivated throughout and the connection is displayed within and without in the fact that one disciple expressly points to Christ who has departed from them, and thereby he hints at the true destiny of the Son of God to be at the same time on earth, so that the saying will be true: Where two or three are gathered in my name, there am I in the midst of them.[14]

The image is saved by the action of the Hegelian philosophy; on the verge of splitting apart, the picture is shown to have a higher unity, just as Christ through his movement of departure and return rescues a world whose passions and confusions tend to disrupt and shatter all unities. What Christ does on the theological level Hegel repeats, saving the image from fragmentation and misunderstanding (one might also say that as a philosopher of religion he rescues Christianity from itself, insofar as it threatens to collapse into nothing but an episodic narrative). All of this of course depends on an iconological reading of the painting that makes sense of it in terms of the Christian story. Nietzsche's approach to the picture will be quite different, since he will apparently ignore almost all that we know, or think that we know, about what these scenes represent. Perhaps if art needs to be saved from anything, it is from a dialectical system that makes the validity of the image contingent upon a cosmic story about salvation. I want to suggest that there is a certain cunning in Nietzsche's failing to name the incidents and events here by referring to the biblical texts or even to the barest outlines of the Christian story, a cunning designed to highlight the image as such. Foucault does something similar, but he provides a more explicit account of his procedure, when he asks us to look at first at Velazquez's *Las Meninas* without attempting to name the figures that people the scene or to construct a narrative about them that goes beyond what we see on the canvas (sec. 52).

The painting continues to generate ingenious attempts to preserve its unity; these all testify to the enormous strength of the principle laid down by Plato and Aristotle that a true work of art must be a unity, preferably an organic unity such that disturbing any part necessarily alters the whole. So even when forced to the extreme of admitting that a painting like the *Transfiguration* fails to meet the standard, the principle is saved by attributing its discrepancies or gaps to its being left unfinished and completed by other hands, a favored strategy in the case of Raphael's last painting (Nietzsche later comes close to this position; sec. 22).[15] Raphael remains a supreme genius who created only masterpieces at the height of his career, and any incoherence is explained by attribution to external circumstances. Another strategy of a quite different sort arises from widening the iconographical and iconological context to include social, historical, scientific, or even medical references and associations that were not known or thought relevant earlier. While the painting has traditionally been seen as depicting the boy during an epileptic fit or an episode of demonic possession, a recent reading by a physician suggests that we see him in the immediate aftermath of the fit; so Raphael has connected the two scenes by having Jesus, the miraculous healer, float above the work he has just done. While this interpretation would cast the painting in a more unified light, it does not seem to have been suspected by Nietzsche (or any other critic of the painting) until quite recently.[16]

Nietzsche introduces his ekphrasis in section 4 of the *Birth*, where he is describing the Apollonian form of art:

> In a symbolic painting, Raphael, himself one of these immortal "naive ones," has represented this disempowerment of shining to the level of appearance [*Depotenziren des Scheins zum Schein*], the primitive process of the naive artist and of Apollonian culture. In his *Transfiguration*, the lower half of the picture, with the possessed boy, the despairing bearers, the bewildered, terrified disciples, shows us the reflection [*Wiederspiegelung*] of suffering, primal and eternal, the sole ground of the world: the "shining" here is the reflection [*der "Schein" ist hier Wiederschein*] of eternal contradiction, the father of things. From this shining arises, like ambrosial vapor [*Duft*], a new visionary world, invisible to those wrapped in the first shining—a radiant floating [*Schweben*] in purest bliss, a serene contemplation beaming from wide-open eyes. Here we have presented in the highest artistic symbolism, that Apollonian world of beauty and its substratum, the terrible world of Silenus; and intuitively we comprehend their necessary interdependence. Apollo, however, again appears to us as the *principium individuationis*, in which alone is consummated the perpetually attained goal of the primal unity, its redemption through shining. With his sublime gestures, he shows

us how necessary is the entire world of suffering, that by means of it an individual may be impelled to realize the redeeming vision, and then, sunk in contemplation of it, sit quietly tossing in his bark, amid the waves. (*BT* 4; *KSA* 1.39–40)

When he wrote this passage, Nietzsche could have seen this painting only in reproductions or copies, for he had not yet visited Rome; but he would have seen (at least) Raphael's *Sistine Madonna* and the copy of *Saint Cecilia* that are in Dresden. However, he was familiar with Burckhardt's paean to Raphael and to the *Transfiguration* in particular; for both are to be found in the *Cicerone*. Young Professor Nietzsche would have heard his admired senior colleague expounding such views in lectures and conversations.[17] If he knew the work only vicariously and without seeing its actual color and size, he was certainly no further from it than he was from the performance and spectacle of fifth-century Greek tragedy, which he was struggling to understand. The experience of tragedy, he argues, has been distorted by over two thousand years of rationalism and requires an archaeological reconstruction. By means of one absent work of art, he is seeking to imagine the experience of an even more distant one.

What is striking in Nietzsche's ekphrasis is the repeated stress on *Schein*, which I have translated as "shining." Most English translations, for example Walter Kaufmann's, use the term "appearance" or "semblance" here, and sometimes gratuitously enlarge the phrase to "mere appearance." The phrase *Schein als Schein*, which appears occasionally, might possibly be translated in this way. But Nietzsche's emphasis is not so much epistemological as ontological; Apollo is the shining or brilliant god, the one who manifests himself through light. Something appears, but it is not primarily an appearance *of* something; and if its status as *Schein als Schein* is sometimes emphasized, it is not to suggest its cognitive deficiency but the brilliant way in which it offers itself. This shining is akin to that of the phantasm, whose nature is simply to shine or appear, without representing anything.[18] Heidegger picks up a line from Mörike, "selig scheint es in ihm selbst," to suggest something similar.[19] The shining, in both cases, is understood as neither active nor passive, but in the middle voice. The vision is not named as caused by some other agent nor as an effect produced in an observer. Appearing is *phainesthai*, the middle-voice form (it appears in and through itself) that Heidegger says we must think if we are to understand the phenomenon and phenomenology. "*[P]hainomenon* means what shows itself, the self-showing, the manifest. *Phainesthai* itself is a 'middle voice' construction of *phaino*, to bring into daylight, to place in brightness. . . . Thus the meaning of the expression 'phenomenon' is *established as that which shows itself in itself,* what is manifest."[20] It shines forth in itself, by itself, through itself; in this sense it is not a "mere appearance" that must be referred to the cause that it may accurately or inaccurately represent. Nietzsche, the classicist, is already thinking in these terms, as he describes the phenomenon as a theophany.

Nietzsche transfigures the *Transfiguration* by identifying the floating figure as Apollo. In this respect he effectively concurs with Schopenhauer, who allowed that history painting, when it deals with scenes from the Old or New Testaments, runs the risk of restricting the painter "to a field chosen arbitrarily, and not for artistic but for other purposes." However, he asserted that paintings that employed the history or mythology of Judaism and Christianity could transcend these limits, if they used them in order to reveal the ethical spirit of Christianity, and he expressly mentions Raphael and the early Correggio as artists who do this.[21] Surely one reason Nietzsche so admires this painting is that its hovering central figure lends itself to being seen as not merely a luminous apparition but as the principle of apparition itself. In this respect, the painting would indeed display an Idea in Schopenhauer's sense. As the latter describes it, "the Idea is not really *this spatial form which floats before us,* but its expression, its pure significance, its innermost being, disclosing itself and appealing to me" (my emphasis).[22]

What makes Nietzsche's identification particularly shocking is that this scene of transfiguration is, from a theological perspective, not just any depiction of Christ but a depiction of the very moment in which his divinity, concealed until then, becomes openly manifest. Raphael is showing Christ as both son of God and miraculous healer. Nietzsche may not have known that this painting was one of a pair commissioned by Cardinal Giulio de' Medici, the other being Sebastiano del Piombo's *Raising of Lazarus,* also showing Jesus as miracle worker. We can imagine Nietzsche seeing the competition between Sebastiano and Raphael in terms of the agonistic spirit that he so often celebrates among artists; but any mention of this is strangely lacking in the discussion of this great "naive" artist. (As the protégé of Michelangelo, Sebastiano was in competition with Raphael, but since the picture of Lazarus was completed first, Raphael had the opportunity to respond to it and go a step further in his own work.)[23] Moreover, to name the figure as Christ would be to become involved in metaphysical and theological questions of how the radiant appearance is caused by, grounded in, or expressive of some deeper principle.[24] Raphael had made a design for the work in which God the father did appear in the upper level of the painting and Jesus was shown as transfigured, but without a scene involving the possessed boy. In this respect the artist had already begun the work of expelling the transcendent that Nietzsche observes in the painting.[25]

Hegel attempted to make an entire logic and an aesthetics out of the Christian notion of the incarnation; he would never have thought of Jesus as a phantasm, except as a remote possibility within the realm of a very late, playful, and ironic art that had become free, after having reached the highest pinnacle of expression, to turn back and dismantle its own principles in a display of virtuosity. Hegel's theory of painting requires a sharp distinction between classical and romantic art, where the former is understood in terms of the relatively remote perfection of the Greek gods, and the latter involves the full incarnation of the divine within the most concrete forms of human experience; so Christ's crucifixion, even in its grotesque expressions, is among the most profound subjects of painting on this view. To the extent that Nietzsche was aware of the contrast between Hegelian and Schopenhauerian aesthetics here, his reading of Raphael marks a clear choice between them. In the first section of *The Birth of Tragedy*, Nietzsche invoked Apollo as the god who shines forth; from the Apollonian perspective, the everyday world is contrasted not with a transcendent world that does not appear (as in the dualistic religions of Judaism and Christianity) but with a world of dreams and visions that appear more intensely and vividly than our mundane surroundings:

> This joyous necessity of the dream experience has been embodied by the Greeks in their Apollo. Apollo, the god of all plastic energies, is at the same time the soothsaying god. He, who (as the etymology of the name suggests) is the "shining one" [*Scheinende*], the deity of light, is also ruler over the beautiful illusion of the inner world of *Phantasie*. The higher truth, the perfection of these states in contrast to the incompletely intelligible everyday world, this deep consciousness of nature, healing and helping in sleep and dreams, is at the same time the symbolical analogue of the soothsaying faculty and of the arts generally, which make life possible and worth living. (*BT* 1; *KSA* 1.27)

That Apollo is invoked here as healer and helper as well as the shining one helps to explain Nietzsche's reading of the *Transfiguration:* the floating, radiant figure (shining forth in and from himself) is the one who offers the healing and redemption demanded by the suffering crowd around the possessed boy. Indeed, viewing Apollo as a healing god could strengthen a reading of Raphael's painting that takes it to depict the moment just after the boy has been delivered from his affliction. The physician-critic Gordon Bendersky offers an analogous interpretation, seeing the transfigured Christ as a medical healer; he suggests that this involves a play on names and words that constitutes a variation on Raphael's own name, whose Hebrew meaning is "God heals," as well as on that of Giulio de' Medici.[26] Raphael would then, on a Nietzschean reading, be proclaiming himself a devotee of Apollo. Even sixteen years later, Nietzsche would say something along these lines of the artist: "[A] Christian who is at the same time an artist does not exist. . . . Let no one be childish and cite Raphael as an objection, or some homeopathic Christian of the nineteenth century: Raphael said Yes, Raphael did Yes, consequently Raphael was not a Christian" (*T*, "Skirmishes," 9; *KSA* 6.117; cf. *WP* 845). Nietzsche, like some other philosophers, occasionally compares himself with a painter and sometimes aspires to an affirmation that he identifies with Raphael: "I want to proceed as Raphael did and never paint another picture of torture [*Marterbild*]" (*GS* 313; *KSA* 3.548). What might this mean, since Raphael's last picture seems to contain an image of suffering and agony and since Nietzsche will go on to depict images of torture in both external and internal theaters of cruelty in *Toward a Genealogy of Morality?* Presumably it is a vow not to portray suffering for the sake of suggesting (as does Schopenhauer) that it is the last word about life.

Already in the first section of the *Birth*, with the appearance of the therapeutic Apollo, Nietzsche is opening up some distance between himself and Schopenhauer, whose idiom he continues to speak. The god, with his arts of healing and his beautiful manifestations, can "make life possible and worth living"; the point of art is not to allow us to contemplate and so escape from the will but to provide an impetus for a fuller and richer existence. Just as Nietzsche's visionary Apollo eludes Schopenhauer's pessimism, so the vocabulary of Indian thought, also adapted from Schopenhauer, is deployed for ends contrary to the context from which it is borrowed. If Schopenhauer and the Indians speak of our being immersed in the realm of *maya,* or illusion, Nietzsche will point out the constructive and healing dimension of this illusion or shining. And while Nietzsche may have found some common cause with Indian thinkers in their principle that dreams are truer than waking reality, he does not accompany them in their next step, in which they assert that dreamless sleep is even more profound than the oneiric state. It is only "in an eccentric sense" that Nietzsche says we might agree with Schopenhauer "when he says of the man wrapped in the veil of maya" that he holds on to the principle of individuation like a sailor in a storm-tossed sea trusting completely in his frail bark (*BT* 1; *KSA* 28).[27] It is an eccentric sense because Schopenhauer sees the principle and the shining phenomena it engenders as desperate defenses against the chaos of the raging seas, to be followed ideally by a contemplative objectification of the will; Nietzsche accepts the contrast between individuation and chaos, but he affirms that these images and visions can make human life a plausible project.

20 Floating and Shining

The two levels of the *Transfiguration* make it eminently suitable to demonstrate the way in which Apollonian art has the capacity to represent, include, and transcend the Dionysian. Of course it represents the Dionysian only by giving it Apollonian form; in a stricter sense, it could be said that the Dionysian cannot be represented, but only embodied or performed. As Burckhardt and other critics observe, Raphael has been audacious in juxtaposing the two distinct scenes from the Gospels, which are not clearly set in the same physical place in the biblical text. Burckhardt sounds shocked by Raphael's daring in constructing a "monstrous" *(ungeheuer)* tableau: "Here, by a dramatic contrast, which one may call monstrous, the supernatural is far more forcibly put before us than by all the glories and visions of other painters. Two entirely different scenes are combined in the picture—a piece of audacity not to be recommended to everyone."[28] Burckhardt is especially impressed with the way in which Raphael handles the floating figure; he argues that this Christ is the first successful floating form in Italian art and that "the form and expression of Christ reveal one of the great secrets of art, which sometimes elude the endeavors of centuries."[29] The secret has to do with the representation of a floating and radiant being, and here Nietzsche seems to be in agreement with Burckhardt if he is not indeed following him. The imagination of the reader of the biblical text will be provoked by the description that "his face did shine as the sun, and his raiment was white as the light" (Matt. 17:2); this requires a presentation of Jesus that, according to Burckhardt, "presupposes a brilliant self-contained illumination of the form, and therefore the absence *(Aufhebung)* of all shadow, as well as of all modelling."[30] But this is impossible, for it would defeat the principles of painting, at least of the style that Raphael is practicing; it would take us into the world of overwhelming illumination evoked in Dante's *Paradiso*, which must remain on a literary level (it is understandable that the *Inferno* lends itself, however imperfectly, to pictorial representation). A trace of that dazzling experience is evident in the self-protective gestures of the three disciples who shield their eyes, while the two witnesses on our left, who observe the scene from a more removed standpoint, perhaps embody an aspect of our own position as spectators (although unlike us, they do not see the entire scene, which includes the possessed boy and the crowd below).

According to Burckhardt the pictorial solution to this demand to depict the impossible was for Raphael to substitute a floating Christ for the nonmodeled and nonshadowed figure suggested by the text. We must be able to see something extraordinary while recognizing, through the figures of the blinded disciples, that something beyond the limits of vision has manifested itself. Raphael's triumph in depicting floating is evident in the folds of Christ's drapery, buoyed up and billowing in the air. If this painting works at the limit between pure luminosity and the illumination that plays between light and shade, the *Saint Cecilia* was also a painting at the limit, in that case the limit or boundary between the visible and the musical, the latter being a form of the invisible. In the *Transfiguration* there is a tangle of the verbal and the visual modes, one that Lessing might have wanted to disarticulate. The biblical text requires a series of transformations or transfigurations in order to be translated into the form of a painting. Not only is the narrative condensed into simultaneous presentation of two separate episodes, but a radiance that could not be captured in painting is provided with an affective equivalent and a reminder (through the disciples who are blinded by the dazzling light or who dare not look) that a translation has been attempted. Lessing might point out that this is roughly parallel to Laocoön's being able to cry out in Virgil but not in sculptural form; the story has been adapted to the limits of the medium. Lessing might have difficulties with the conjunction of the two scenes because they are narratively sequential and distinct, although he might be open to the suggestion that they really form one scene after all. Yet this is not an end of the exchange of words and images, for Burckhardt, Nietzsche, and the historians of art produce their own verbal versions of the visual artifact, translating it into new and unanticipated contexts.

Burckhardt and Nietzsche seem to agree that, within the conventions of his art, Raphael comes as close as possible to producing a figure that exemplifies *Schein als Schein*. About one hundred years later, apparently inspired by Nietzsche's thought of recurrence (and perhaps even by this ekphrasis in the *Birth*), Michel Foucault will see the floating pipe in one of Magritte's "This Is Not a Pipe" series as playing a role that closely parallels the floating Christ. Like Lucretius, whom Nietzsche invokes on the first page of the *Birth* to testify to the ancients' understanding of dreams, he will speak of hovering simulacra and phantasms. But recall that for Nietzsche this floating figure is not Christ. The levitating apparition is named as Apollo, the radiant and shining god, the god of appearances and visual manifestations. Nietzsche would then be transfiguring the *Transfiguration*. With Magritte in mind, we could think of the painting as effectively being retitled *This Is Not a Christ*. This suggests that there may be a surrealist dimension in Raphael (or at least in Nietzsche's reading) and that Magritte may not be wholly unconcerned with religious themes. When we look more closely at Foucault's analysis of images, it will be worth considering the parallel between the role of the dream in his thought and Nietzsche's: for Foucault's first book begins with an account of dreaming, employed to found a theory of art that attempts to deduce its basic forms from the fundamental phenomenological structures of the dream (sec. 43).

The evisceration of a Christian divinity implicit in Nietzsche's account reflects a movement that others have found within Renaissance art. As Hans Belting demonstrates in *Likeness and Presence: A History of the Image before Art*, the Byzantine icon was not thought of as merely the representation or likeness of the saint but as the saint's very manifestation.[31] Typically, icons were not generally displayed but kept under wraps and taken out only on special occasions, such as the feast day of the saint. As Italian art moved away from Byzantine thought and practice, so this story goes, it came to construct the image as a likeness, not a reality; it would be one step more to arrive at a point where, in the terms of German aesthetics as adapted by Nietzsche, it was able to acknowledge and even to celebrate *Schein als Schein* (Belting identifies the *Sistine Madonna* as one of the primary loci of this transformation).

I said earlier that Nietzsche regards the *Transfiguration* as a supreme exemplar of Apollonian art. This is true, but it overlooks the specific context within which he makes this claim. In section 4 of the *Birth*, Nietzsche is still examining the relation between Apollonian art and the dream, developing the contrast between the two great natural art impulses of dream and intoxication, presided over respectively by Apollo and Dionysus. Specifically, he is attempting to show how the "naive" artist can be understood by deploying such concepts and distinctions. In the course of the discussion, he implies not only that such an artist is inspired by dreams and dreamlike states but also that we require such art in order to show us what dreams are. Art is not merely a form or consequence of the dream but also the first way that we have of gaining access to it. Or as Freud said, just a generation later, the poets and artists showed the way long before his own work of *Traum-deutung*.[32]

Nietzsche does not speak of the naive artist in any pejorative sense; indeed, his writings are full of praise for Raphael, who is frequently cited as a supreme artistic genius (although some of Nietzsche's later notes, as we shall see, take a more critical turn). In the German aesthetic tradition whose language Nietzsche speaks here, the "naive" artist is to be understood in terms of Schiller's distinction between the naive and the sentimental.[33] Schiller's most minimal formulation is that the naive poet is nature, while the sentimental poet seeks nature. The naive artist is there in the material, in the work itself; we might say that such artists are self-effacing, except that since they have never been the themes of their own work, there is no call for effacement. The sentimental artist is concerned with his or her own feelings and responses; they become a constituent of the work that cannot be ignored. In considering the naive artist, Nietzsche generalizes considerably on Schiller's formulation; he wants to understand the artist who is enthralled by the content and structure of the dream while apparently indifferent to his own role within it.

The dreamer whom Nietzsche imagines is so immersed in his vision that "in the midst of the illusion of the dream world and without disturbing it, he calls out to himself: 'It is a dream, I will dream on'" (*BT* 4; *KSA* 1.38). Today this might be called an instance of lucid dreaming, in which the subject chooses to prolong, explore, and even take an active role within the dream. Nietzsche, however, emphasizes the element of submission or acceptance in the dreamer's attitude. And he suggests that we can interpret such phenomena by following "the dream-reading Apollo," who is also the god of radiance and painting. As Nietzsche's ekphrasis of Raphael suggests, Apollo is not only the god who inspires such visions but also one of their prime subjects. Reflecting on the dream, in a philosophical voice that harks back to Schopenhauer, while also informed by Schiller's celebration of *Schein*, Nietzsche offers the formulation that "the truly existing primal unity, eternally suffering and contradictory, also needs the rapturous vision, the pleasurable illusion, for its continuous redemption." Empirical and phenomenal reality are simply appearance or illusion in this perspective; but then the dream is "a shining of shining, hence a still higher appeasement of the primordial desire for shining" (*BT* 4; *KSA* 1.39).

It is at this point in his argument that Nietzsche invokes Raphael and the *Transfiguration* in order to explain how the artist and the painting display "the disempowering of shining to the level of pure shining." Without such display would we be able to comprehend the dream process or the activity of the Apollonian artist? On Nietzsche's reading, what Raphael depicts is the process of naive art itself; it is still naive insofar as it is not sentimental, not concerned with the persona and feelings of Raphael himself, but it is naïveté raised to a higher level, insofar as it reveals the very structure of naïveté.

The *Transfiguration* remains a problematic image. There are some figures in the painting that do not seem to fit into the biblical narratives and are overlooked by Burckhardt, Nietzsche, and most recent critics. In the foreground of the lower scene, a rather majestic woman is kneeling and pointing to the boy; but her head is turned away from him while she gazes steadily and perhaps sternly at the disciples. A few observers have suggested that her very classical pose is reminiscent of figures of Sibyls, so she might be understood as making a prophetic or revelatory statement. Her *contraposto* posture necessarily involves movement, but she appears more stable and calm than do the rest of the frenzied crowd in the lower half of the painting. In contrast, the other figures, almost all male, display their agitation in their excited gestures. The Sibyl-like woman figures prominently in a theological reading of the *Transfiguration,* according to which it reflects an atmosphere of apocalyptic expectation that was influential in ecclesiastical circles around this time. Inspired in part by writings falsely attributed to Joachim of Fiore, who had perhaps introduced the first of many philosophies of history based on a pattern of three ages (Father, Son, and Holy Spirit), this movement took the biblical scene of transfiguration as having a symbolic significance for the coming transformation of the world. Both Raphael's *Transfiguration* and a painting of this title by his rival, Sebastiano del Piombo, were eventually displayed in the church of San Pietro in Montorio.[34] Whatever the specific iconographical context may be, the female figure suggests an assurance and a knowledge somewhat inconsistent with Nietzsche's characterization of the lower half of the picture (Rudolf Preimesberger identifies the woman as Mary Magdalene, whose presence here would recall the fact that she will be the first to see the risen Christ).[35]

There is another puzzling feature nearby on the canvas. Just above and to the right of the Sibylline woman's head, we can make out just the head of a man who is shrouded in darkness; he is scarcely visible in the deep shadow of the mountain, which is the setting for the transfiguration itself. Like the woman in the foreground, he seems much less agitated than those who are concerned with the possessed boy. Unlike all of the others in the lower half of the painting, his attention is directed neither at the boy nor at anyone in the crowd of distraught and passionate people around him. While the other figures are all intensely engaged with one another, this one is strangely isolated. Alone among all the characters in this work, he could be looking out at us, the spectators. His expression, so far as we can make it out, is one that suggests a sadness and resignation at the suffering of the world that is being played out before him. Quite detached from all the action, his role, like that of the painter, is to acknowledge what is seen here where anguished humanity enacts its drama. As the darkest figure in the painting, he is at the opposite pole from the illuminated Christ, and like him, his gaze is not attached to any of the other actors in the scene. The contrast might remind us of one in Claude's *Acis and Galatea* between the radiant sun and the vengeful Cyclops. The dark man is perhaps Christ's shadow; the pairing of the two would create a structure that summarized and paralleled the opposition of the upper and lower scenes of the painting. The figure of the shadow will be personified later in *The Wanderer and His Shadow* and in *Zarathustra;* this strange man of the shades could be the visual analog of those characters. While Nietzsche might not have seen this tenebrous figure in whatever reproduction was accessible to him, his presence is consistent with the philosopher's understanding of the painting.

If we take a quick philosophical inventory of the *Transfiguration*, as read by Nietzsche, it is certainly a very rich work. It is self-referential, since not only does it shine, manifest, and display itself, but this action of shining is signified in the figure of Christ—or Apollo—who embodies this shining. In this pure shining, he is a floating phantasm, or as a painted figure of artifice, he is, by Pierre Klossowski's definition, a simulacrum (secs. 68–70). The *Transfiguration* also involves a series of variations on the theme of seeing and not seeing, embodied in the many different looks and exchanges of looks by the characters. Nietzsche takes note of this dimension of the painting only as he describes its two levels and scenes, because his focus is on the shining manifestation of "Apollo." When he comes to discuss the revered *Sistine Madonna*, he offers an explicit analysis of the different ways in which the painting can be read, suggesting that it is doubly or multiply coded for rather different groups of viewers.

21 Double-Coding the *Sistine Madonna*

What we saw as internal to the *Transfiguration* now becomes a dimension of the *Sistine Madonna*'s relation to its viewers (fig. 7). In an aphorism entitled *Honorable painting* [*Ehrliches Malerthum*], Nietzsche describes Raphael as having achieved a canny way of satisfying

Figure 7. Raphael, *Sistine Madonna*, 1512–13. Gemäldegalerie Alte Meister, Staatliche Kunstsammlungen, Dresden. Alinari/Art Resource, New York

the demands of his patrons while preserving his own integrity. The ironic suggestion is that honesty is preserved by duplicity. The painter, we are told, "did not compromise by so much as an inch with the pretentious, ecstatic piety of many of his patrons; he preserved his honesty even in that exceptional picture, originally intended for a processional banner." The double coding works through the duality of perspectives offered to the viewer by means of the two figures at the Madonna's sides:

> He wanted for once to paint a vision [Vision]; but it was to be such a one as noble young men without "faith" too might and would have, the vision of a future wife, of a clever, noble-souled, silent and very beautiful woman bearing her first-born in her arms. Let the old, who are accustomed to prayer and worship, here revere something suprahuman [Übermenschliches], like the venerable graybeard to the left of the picture; we younger men, so Raphael seems to cry to us, shall go along with the lovely girl on the right, who with her challenging and in no way devout look [Blicke] says to the viewer of the picture: "This mother and her child—a pleasant, inviting sight [Anblick], isn't it?" This face and this look reflects the joy in the face of the viewers; the artist who invented it all in this way has the enjoyment of his own joy and adds to it the joy of the recipients of his art. (HAH, WS, 73; KSA 2.585–86)

The conventional religious viewer sees the figures on the sides of the painting as Pope Sixtus and Saint Barbara; the healthy young man sees a graybeard and an attractive young woman. So the look of the "lovely girl" is virtually our look, and we can imagine the artist smiling at the way in which he has managed to share his appreciation of the beautiful young woman with her child with us (us healthy young men!), while providing a pious image for the old and the reverent. There is an abyssal effect here, leading to the realization that a complex relationship both links and contrasts a number of ways of seeing: our own take on the painting, that of another class of viewers, that of the figures within the painting, and that of the artist. It is effects like these that the Nietzschean art critic Michel Foucault will articulate in his reading of Velazquez's Las Meninas. And Nietzsche, in The Birth of Tragedy, has already suggested a way of understanding the position of the theatrical spectator in terms of a multiple vision (secs. 27, 28). Honest painting involves not only avoiding allegiance to values or ideals that one rejects; it also requires an honest sensitivity to the fact that vision is always multiple, that there is no single or absolute perspective. If the Italian painters of the Renaissance introduce a system of absolute spatial perspective, involving a single vanishing point, the wisest or most honest among them will realize that this technique ought not to be used in such a way as to preclude other forms of pluralizing our perspectives.

Or so we see the painting under Nietzsche's guidance. But not every viewer will share his response to the figure of Saint Barbara, "the lovely girl on the right." Assuming that we can hold in suspense our knowledge of the religious identity of these personages, still Barbara's look seems modest rather than "challenging." With her demurely downcast eyes and her folded hands, she appears more devout than Nietzsche allows. So she appeared to Louise, in August Schlegel's dialogue on painting: "The young saint, who folds her hands on her chest so tenderly and gracefully, turns her face away from the Madonna, looking over her shoulder and lowering her eyes. She is too timid to look around, too meek and more concerned with herself. . . . The young woman flees into her inwardness and prays for the salvation of her own soul. She has a very lovely little head, made just right to express pious wishes and loving devotion."[36] Or might Nietzsche be seeing this apparent modesty as the appropriate way in which a well-brought-up young woman would present the charms of another? She would be acknowledging before the young man that she has something to be reticent about. Then Barbara's expression would not be awe before the queen of heaven but the rather coy look of a go-between. Other aspects of the picture that might contribute to a religious reading are never mentioned in this ekphrasis. Mary, Sixtus, and Barbara are all standing or walking on clouds in an unusual heavenly space, which is further defined and complicated by the drawn curtains and the emblematic architectural fragment that reminds the viewer of Barbara's connection with a city. While these may all intensify the visionary aspect of this *Vision*, they present some obstacles for those who would ignore the theological dimension of the painting. And what are we to make of the angelic faces that are just visible in the background of the picture? Surely these are not images of all the children that the young male viewer, whom Nietzsche imagines, desires from his future wife. Nietzsche is not denying that the painting has a religious theme, simply insisting that it can be read in a number of ways, at least one of which ignores and subverts the devotional character of the picture. He was not alone in seeing the Virgin as a somewhat earthly young woman. Goethe and Heinse think of her as an attractive young mother, while Herder, who wrote a poem about the painting, saw her as an idealized country girl *(Landmädchen).* Winckelmann compared Mary to an ancient goddess, emphasizing her embodiment of an idealized human love. Ludwig Feuerbach, consistent with his reinterpretation of religion as a practice of this world, characterized Raphael's Madonna as having "a sort of human cheerfulness, a round beauty, an almost Junonian health." As Wolfgang von Löhneysen comments with regard to Nietzsche's account of the painting, he "was not as untimely as he believed himself to be."[37] So even if we have some lingering doubts about the account of Barbara, Nietzsche was in good company in the way that he saw the central figure.

Nietzsche finds a similar double coding in the face of the infant Jesus:

> Raphael, the honest painter who had no wish to paint a state of soul in which he did not believe, has outwitted his *believing* viewers in a very cunning fashion; he has painted that natural phenomenon which is not all that rare an occurrence, the eyes of a man in the head of a child, and in this instance the eyes of a valiant man ready to assist in some emergency or difficulty. To these eyes there belongs a beard; that it is missing, and that two different ages of life speak out of one face, is the pleasing paradox which the faithful have interpreted in the sense of their belief in miracles: which the artist was entitled to anticipate from their art of interpretation and imposition of what they wish to see.

Honesty again manifests itself in duplicity, that is, in fashioning an image that can be read in several ways. Although a number of those who had commented on the painting anticipated Nietzsche's sense of the Madonna's earthly attractions and the complex look in the child's face, none seems to have explicitly developed the conception of a painting that was designed to allow and encourage at least two distinct ways of viewing and interpreting.[38]

Nietzsche had earlier dismissed those who wanted to see something *Übermenschliches* in this painting. Did he know that one of the other characters in August Schlegel's dialogue had detected just this quality in the complex face of the child, suggesting that more is at stake than the play between infant and grown man? "The eyes seem to be two immovable stars; they are deeply set, and the forehead is full of reflection. And yet one cannot say that this boy is already a man. It is not an overripeness, but *Übermenschlichkeit*. For so far as the divine can reveal itself in childish guise, it has happened here and I cannot think of the man who corresponds to this child."[39] Zarathustra gives a series of speeches in which he teaches of the *Übermensch*; the first, "Of the Three Metamorphoses," outlines a progressive set of transformations from the camel to the lion to the child. Does that passage offer an echo of the child in whom some saw this quality?

Noticeably absent from Nietzsche's account of the *Sistine Madonna* is any mention of the two putti resting on their elbows on the thin ledge at the bottom of the scene. These little angels with their pensive charm have acquired an independent life in the world of images, being reproduced on calendars, greeting cards, and advertisements. They add to the painting another variation of the gaze, one that Schopenhauer felt called to comment on. A frequent visitor to the Dresden Gallery while he was writing *The World as Will and Representation*, Schopenhauer was struck by the look with which Raphael had endowed his angels and explained it in terms of his notion that the prepubescent child, not yet under the sway of sexual desire, is naturally much more open to learning and to disinterested looking than the adult: "The innocent and clear glance of children, at which we revive ourselves, and which sometimes in particular cases reaches the sublime, contemplative expression with which Raphael has adorned his cherubs, is to be explained from what we have said. Accordingly, mental powers develop much earlier than the needs they are designed to serve, and here, as everywhere, nature proceeds very appropriately."[40] Later, in *Parerga and Paralipomena*, Schopenhauer would name these cherubs more specifically: "[A]s children we behave far more like purely knowing than willing beings. Hence the serious contemplative look [*der ernste schauende Blick*] of many children, which Raphael has used so happily for his angels, especially for those of the *Sistine Madonna*."[41]

In not mentioning the two putti, Nietzsche also overlooks the ledge on which they are leaning, and so he omits any consideration of the internal framing devices of the painting, including the curtain that hangs from a narrow rod. Yet it is precisely this framework that helps to create the sense that we are beholding a vision or apparition, rather than a scene in heaven. On Nietzsche's double reading, the painting presents a vision of the ideal wife for young men and a religious vision for the pious. This conception of a double-coded picture echoes and transforms the debate that raged at the time of the romantics as to how the *Sistine Madonna* could be an exemplary work of art if it were originally painted for a church. Belting suggests that Raphael has managed to frame a vision in such a way that painting as an art displaces painting as a technique in the service of the cult of the image. The curtain, on this interpretation, is what might be expected to alternately conceal and reveal a cult image. Alternatively, a curtain that has been drawn back could be seen as opening onto a further space, allowing us to see through a window or similar aperture. However, if the curtain reminded contemporary viewers, who were familiar with such conventions, of the way in which an image might be displayed, what they saw in the picture would have defeated the expectations connected with the cult. What appears is neither a sacred image nor a window onto a realistic scene. Instead, the Madonna stands on a cloudbank, one that dissolves into hazy angelic faces. The impression is of a "celestial vision," and "[t]he work appeals to the inner vision, rather than creating the window illusion that has to be taken at face value. . . . The curtain is drawn aside from an image that is in reality the *idea* of an image, and thus it partakes of a different order of reality. The visible work is a symbol of an ideal beauty. . . . The work loses its aura as an 'original' in the religious sense—an image exercising power over believers by its actual presence. Instead, it becomes an 'original' in the artistic sense, in that it authentically reflects the artist's idea."[42] Nietzsche might have employed his own archaeology of the *Bild* (sec. 6) to explain this play between image and art; his sensitivity to the double coding of the picture could be understood as his way of recognizing not merely that the painting is the occasion for a conflict of interests in religion and secular beauty but that the opposition between these two is being acted out here. On this reading, the *Sistine Madonna* becomes one of the crucial hinges between what Belting calls the era of the image and the era of art. Art would not be emancipating itself from religion, as the conventional story (told by Hegel, Burckhardt, and others) has it, but establishing itself as the successor to the image. The temptation to tell a continuous story of the development or history of art is provoked in part by the fact that both images and art occur in the same site or with the same objects (in the church, involving sacred figures); but they are better thought of on the archaeological analogy of two distinct cultures that have occupied the same geographical territory. The later one is built over the ruins of the earlier. As Nietzsche says in another context, although with a telling reference to the visual, "if a temple is to be built, a temple must be destroyed."

22 The Death of (Metaphysical) Art

Raphael remains an exemplary painter for Nietzsche after the *Birth*, but the painter no longer occupies quite the position to which the romantics, Hegel, Schopenhauer, and Burckhardt elevated him.[43] The Christian theme that was willfully ignored in the *Birth* returns to haunt him. As in his interpretation of the *Sistine Madonna*, Nietzsche becomes suspicious of the way in which Raphael and other artists can be used to promote religious moods and sentiments in a seemingly secularized context. Schopenhauer made such gestures, ending the final book of *The World as Will and Representation* when he said of those who have overcome the world that they experience "that peace that is higher than all reason, that ocean-like calmness of the spirit, that deep tranquility, that unshakeable confidence and serenity, whose mere reflection in the countenance, as depicted by Raphael and Correggio, is a complete and certain gospel. Only knowledge remains; the will has vanished."[44] Within the world of the romantics, there was a Raphael cult. Friedrich Schlegel worshiped in Dresden at the altar of the *Sistine Madonna*, and it is responses like his that Nietzsche was no doubt taking into account when he attempted to show that Raphael's honest painting could produce a complex work allowing both religious and secular readings. Schlegel's religion of art contributed to his conversion to Catholicism, and if Nietzsche could be critical of Protestantism for its iconoclasm, he could also point out the insidious way in which art could prepare the way for religion without making explicit claims that might trigger critical hesitations. The religion of art thus becomes a target of analysis: "[W]hen a philosophy demonstrates to us the justification of metaphysical hopes and the profound peace of soul to be attained through them, and speaks for example of 'the whole sure evangel in the glance of Raphael's Madonna,' we go out to meet such assertions and expositions with particular warmth of feeling; the philosopher here has an easier task of demonstration, for he here encounters a heart eager to take what he has to offer" (*HAH* I.131; *KSA* 2.124). Nietzsche's quotation is close to, but not identical with, Schopenhauer's words and captures the spirit of much of the nineteenth century's enthusiasm for Raphael. In this aphorism, *Religious after-pains*, he proceeds to declare that "scientific philosophy" must be wary of following such "presentiments" that seem to be suggested by morality and art, and so of uncritically adopting an organon at the local gallery.

Just as Nietzsche later attained a critical distance from Wagner, so he came to see that Raphael's *Transfiguration* was not the timeless emblem of Apollonian art that it seemed to be in *The Birth of Tragedy*. One sign of this appears in *Human, All Too Human*, where he reluctantly criticizes the introduction of *"The Beyond in Art"*:

> It is not without profound sorrow that one admits to oneself that in their highest flights the artists of all ages have raised to heavenly *transfiguration* [emphasis added] precisely those conceptions which we now recognize as false. . . . if the rainbow colors at the extreme limits of human knowledge and supposition grow pale, that species

of art can never flourish again which, like the *Divina Commedia*, the pictures of Raphael, the frescoes of Michelangelo, the Gothic cathedrals, presupposes not only a cosmic but also a metaphysical significance in the objects of art. A moving tale will one day be told how there once existed such an art, such an artist's faith. (*HAH* I.220; *KSA* 2.180)

In the *Birth*, and in the other discussions of Raphael, it seemed as if the artist could be excused for employing Christian iconography and the paintings could be read as if something quite different was depicted. Jesus could appear as Apollo, Saint Cecilia could mark the gap between visual images and music, and the Madonna could be taken to be simply an attractive, nubile young woman. The "moving tale" that Nietzsche thinks will "one day be told" has already been told by Hegel, who observed that art no longer evoked the devotion it had in earlier days. When the knee no longer bends before the image of the Virgin, then art becomes a matter of education, culture, and science.[45] Several questions arise here. Has Nietzsche abandoned the apparently nonmetaphysical reading that he was able to give of works like the *Transfiguration*? Or is he perhaps recognizing that his own earlier interpretation was itself a metaphysical one? Even if Raphael's paintings can be read in several ways, Nietzsche's point may simply be that such works would never have been created unless the artists (or their patrons or audience) were imbued with faith in the beyond. Whether other artists, working with new themes, can approach those "highest flights" of the past would remain an open question; but he seems to suggest that there can be no truly great art without a metaphysical base. Yet perhaps art can transfigure without attempting "heavenly transfiguration." In *The Transfiguration of the Commonplace*, Arthur Danto, who acknowledges an affinity with Hegel's story of the completion of art, has suggested that even works of Pop Art like Andy Warhol's *Brillo Boxes* can transform the most ordinary and banal of subjects or content by raising them not to the status of heaven, but to that of art itself (see sec. 74). To use Hegel's expression, the question Nietzsche leaves us with here is whether art "on its highest side" is definitely a thing of the past.

Another aphorism, this one from *Daybreak*, marks a similar archaeological reservation and explicitly suggests the possibility of a new form of transfiguration. "*Transfiguration*.—Those that suffer helplessly, those that dream confusedly, those that are entranced by things supernatural—these are the three divisions into which Raphael divided mankind. This is no longer how we see the world—and Raphael too would no longer be able to see it as he did; he would behold a whole new transfiguration" (D 8; KSA 3.21). Less than ten years earlier, Nietzsche had taken the division of the painting into two great parts (not three) as its way of exemplifying the way in which art can display a metaphysical truth. Now he sees art as tied much more closely to time and history. This would exclude on principle telling the kind of story that Burckhardt does, in which certain artists and their works attain a supreme value independent of their time and place (it would exclude the theoretical assumptions that allowed Burckhardt to construct such different kinds of narrative in the *Cicerone* and in *The Civilization of the Renaissance in Italy*). Surely Nietzsche is thinking back to his own use of the painting less than ten years earlier. And he now has a different evaluation of the work, which he sees (as contemporary art historians tend to do) not as a supremely accomplished masterpiece, but as a somewhat transitional one, arising from Raphael's attempt to teach himself a new style. Nietzsche seems to acknowledge that in the *Birth* he assumed, along with Vasari, Burckhardt, and so many others, that the Greeks and the Renaissance offered two forms of timeless perfection in the plastic arts. Now such views would seem to fall under the same critique that Nietzsche administered to the entire philosophical tribe when he said that their family failing was the lack of a historical sense (*HAH* 2; *KSA* 2.24). In *Daybreak* he implicitly qualifies his view of the painter as one of those "great naïve ones." He disagrees with Michelangelo, who described himself as "nature" or talent as opposed to the other artist's "study" or learning. Nietzsche responds:

> [F]or what is talent [*Begabung*] but a name for an *older* piece of learning, experience, practice, appropriation, incorporation, whether at the stage of our fathers or an even earlier stage! . . . Raphael, like Goethe, was without pride or envy, and that is why both were great *learners* and not merely exploiters of those veins of ore washed clean from the siftings of the history of their forefathers. Raphael vanishes as a learner in the midst of appropriating that which his great competitor designated as *his* "nature": he took away a piece of it every day, this noblest of thieves; but before he had taken over the whole of Michelangelo into himself, he died—and his last series of works is, as the *beginning* of a new plan of study, less perfect and absolutely good precisely because the great learner was interrupted in his hardest curriculum [*Pensum*] and took away with him the justificatory ultimate goal towards which he looked. (D 540; *KSA* 3.308–9)[46]

The *Transfiguration*, of course, is the most celebrated of Raphael's last series of paintings. So Nietzsche is taking his distance from Burckhardt and from a number of the painter's admirers in suggesting that there is something indeterminate about the style of this work and those others at the end of the painter's life. Yet he also differs with the critics who find it verging on incoherence insofar as he places it within a narrative about Raphael's development. Perhaps the most significant suggestion in this aphorism, entitled simply *Learning*, is that there are no absolute beginnings in art. Every artist inherits forms, conventions, and styles; the best artists are those who continue to learn and to teach themselves. They work, no doubt largely unconsciously, to become who they are. Yet even if Nietzsche now gives a greater weight to the dimension of becoming in the work of Raphael and other recognized masters, he is not a Hegelian; that is, he does not claim that there is a single continuous process of artistic development in which there is "a justificatory ultimate goal," above and beyond the goals that individual painters may set for themselves.[47]

The very title of *Daybreak (Die Morgenröte)* suggests that new forms of vision, new ways of seeing are at hand. Nietzsche's epigraph for the book from the Rig-Veda reinforces this thought: "There are so many dawns that have not yet glowed." If the book is mainly concerned with the "prejudices of morality" (the subtitle), its aphorism on the *Transfiguration* is also concerned with how the moral and postmoral epochs show themselves, with the sort of figuration they employ. Even Raphael, Nietzsche says, would "behold a whole new transfiguration." The suggestion is that there are a series of transformations in the way we see things, both in moral terms and in the more literal sense of vision. If ever since the *Birth*, Nietzsche has been using changes in visual culture to render plausible the idea that our fundamental moral concepts might alter or be transformed into extramoral concepts, he is now less inclined than before to exempt any mode of vision from the archaeological perspective, including that of the divine Raphael. In a jotting from the summer of 1884, there is a harsher observation about the artist: "Christianity has it on its conscience that it has *corrupted* many well-developed [*volle*] men, for example Pascal and earlier Meister Eckhart. It finally corrupts even the concept of the artist: it has spread a timid hypocrisy over Raphael, in the end even his transfigured [*verklärter*] Christ is a fluttering, fanatic little monk [*schwärmerisches Mönchlein*] that he does not dare to show naked. Goethe's got it right there" (*KSA* 11. 151; 26[3]). Burckhardt's magnificent floating has been reduced to a fluttering. If Nietzsche once realized that Raphael's *Transfiguration* could no longer be seen as a timeless exemplar of the Apollonian redemption of appearance, he now finds it gushing rather than glorious. On one interpretation, the *Transfiguration* reflects an apocalyptic current of thought, owing much to Joachimist prophecies, that was strong in some monastic circles around the time of its production; in that case the suggestion that this figure of Christ is a foolish enthusiast could be a prescient observation.[48] It seems that Nietzsche not only acknowledges the indelibly Christian character of this painting, which he had once described as the manifestation of Apollo, but is also finding it impossible to imagine himself, even in the most hypothetical way, as its appreciative spectator; the suspension of disbelief is no longer an option. It turns out that the idea of transfiguring this transfiguration was a fantasy that could not be sustained. What was necessary, Nietzsche eventually saw, was a frontal attack on Christianity rather than an attempt to undermine it aesthetically.[49]

Nevertheless, Nietzsche's debate with himself over Raphael continues. He changes his mind fairly frequently about Raphael's relation to sensuality and sometimes seems to be arguing with himself on the question of his ability to embody and to portray a robustly sexual human being. As for the artist's vitality itself, he takes the painter, as so frequently, to exemplify the energetics of all art: "Artists, if they are any good, are strongly put together (even bodily), excessive, powerful animals, sensual; without a certain overheating of the sexual system no Raphael can be conceived" (*KSA* 13.295).[50] About a year earlier he had suggested in a note that Raphael (perhaps because of his intense sexuality?) had been able to create a very appealing form of the young woman (*Jungfrau*, or virgin, which might also designate Mary, as in the *Sistine Madonna*): "Raphael discovered the classical type of the *Jungfrau* through the completion of the vulgar type—through the absolute opposition to beauty as da Vinci sought it in the *exquisite* instances of the type and the *rarity* of expression. A sort of completely human cheerfulness, a rounded beauty, an almost Junonian health. She will always be popular" (*KSA* 13.122). And yet he responds just a few months later, apparently haunted by these images of female beauty, with a scathing critique of Raphael's paintings, saying that they frame these images of women in a way that conflicts with their character:

> The *physiological falsity* in Raphael's pictures.
>
> A woman with normal secretions has no need for salvation. That all these natures who have turned out well and advantageously should concern themselves eternally with this anemic saint of Nazareth runs contrary to natural history. He belongs to a different species:

such as Dostoyevsky is acquainted with—sensitive, corrupted, and distorted abortions with idiocy and fanaticism [*Schwärmerei*], with *love* . . . (*KSA* 13.267)

The discourses that attempted to make sense of art in terms of radiant shining and the dream, or by means of a perspectivism that allowed for multiple ways of taking the same work, have been replaced, or at least overshadowed, by what begins to sound at best like an anticipation of Freudian aesthetics and at worst like a form of physiological reductionism. Yet in all of this internal controversy, Raphael remains the type of the strong artist, and his women remain supremely desirable. But his Christ, who could once be double-coded as Apollo, has become a weak, fluttering, sickly little fanatic. Falling in line with the judgments of the early romantics and Burckhardt, this artist served as the model of his youth, even if Nietzsche had given a rather different account of Raphael's greatness, constructing ingenious rereadings of the *Transfiguration*, the *Sistine Madonna*, and *Saint Cecilia*. In the same period of about a year in which this new judgment of the once exemplary painter crystallizes, we find him recalling Claude Lorrain in language that suggests no hesitation or reservation about the beauty of his paintings or the insights that they offer into nature.

23 The Knight, Death, and the Devil

One other picture is summoned up in *The Birth of Tragedy*, and like the *Transfiguration*, it is one to whose creator Nietzsche later returned. Indeed, it is the single visual work with which Nietzsche has been most closely identified, in large part because it is the one that just after the First World War was thought by Ernst Bertram and Thomas Mann to sum up what the philosopher could teach about the fate of Germany. Albrecht Dürer's *Knight, Death, and the Devil* (fig. 8) offers a significant contrast to Raphael's painting; the placement of the two at the beginning and end of the *Birth* constitutes a diptych in which a German print and an Italian painting face off against one another. Later Nietzsche will denounce Germany and Christianity for their reaction against the Renaissance. And while he does not suggest this here, he could have contrasted Dürer's Christian knight from the age and country of Luther with the magical "Apollo" of Raphael. While the *Transfiguration* suggests redemption through a wonderfully radiant shining, the presentation of *Schein als Schein*, Nietzsche invokes the Dürer print in order to intensify the sense of resolute determination in the

Figure 8. Albrecht Dürer, *Knight, Death, and the Devil*, 1513. Engraving. Städelesches Kunstinstitut, Franfurt am Main, Germany. Foto Marburg/Art Resource, New York

absence of all hope. After analyzing the unusual, almost miraculous rise of tragic culture, and its death at the hands of Socrates and Euripides, Nietzsche jumps ahead to the Germany of his day, which he finds mired in banality. The general theme of section 20 of the *Birth* is the failure of contemporary Germany to learn from the Greeks. Nietzsche expresses his admiration for "the noblest intellectual efforts of Goethe, Schiller, and Winckelmann" but laments that since their time the project of coming to terms with the Greeks "has grown incomprehensibly feebler and feebler." The list of German intellectual and cultural heroes is worth pausing over: Winckelmann was seen as having opened up the way to the visual world of the Greeks, and Goethe was regarded as having taken up his heritage in emphasizing the importance of plastic form, as in his *Italian Journey*. "The cultural power of our higher educational institutions has perhaps never been lower or feebler than at present," Nietzsche observes. The journalist triumphs over the professor, and the latter, in self-defense, adopts the manner of the former. Professors of classics are traitors to the Greek spirit who become correctors of old texts, microscopic philological historians of language, or appropriators of the ancients from an unquestioned horizon of satisfaction in the present (it is not difficult to see why classicists either attacked or ignored *The Birth of Tragedy*). "We can understand why so feeble a culture hates true art," and so it is not surprising that even "heroes like Goethe and Schiller could not succeed in breaking open the enchanted gate which leads into the Hellenic magic mountain." What is at stake is the flatness and banality of a culture that Nietzsche also attempted to lay bare in his lectures "On the Future of our Educational Institutions" and that he would dissect in his "untimely" essay *David Strauss, the Confessor and Writer*. Are there any prospects for a renewal by way of a fresh infusion of the Greek spirit? Nietzsche refuses to abandon hope: "Let no one seek to diminish our belief in the impending rebirth of Hellenic antiquity, for this alone allows us to hope for a renewal and purification of the German spirit through the fire-magic of music." This is clearly an allusion to the "magic fire music" in act 3 of Wagner's *Die Walküre*. Wagner was invoked as the tutelary spirit of the *Birth* in Nietzsche's preface; consulted along the way for his judgments on music; appealed to implicitly, if not by name, in the attempt to make sense of the Greeks through the example of his *Musik-drama;* and in the section before this one, he appeared as the living successor of Bach and Beethoven in the creation of a Dionysian German musical culture that offered an opposition to Socratic culture, experienced by the latter as "terrifying and inexplicable . . . overpowering and hostile" (*BT* 19; *KSA* 1.127). Much of Nietzsche's analysis of the Greek theater and his attempt to articulate a parallel between it and Wagner depends on the visual dimension of the *Gesamtkunstwerk* (see chap. 4). Now Nietzsche summons up an episode and an image from Wagner as he is on the verge of proposing a visual symbol for the situation of the devout follower of Goethe, Schiller, and Winckelmann in the Germany of the 1870s; this symbol will function in contrast to Raphael's glorious return to the Greek world of the dream. The "magic fire music" of *Die Walküre*, a burst of sonic intensity with a corresponding visual spectacle, allows him to hope; but without this we are in the situation of Dürer's knight:

> In vain we look for a single vigorously developed root, for a spot of fertile and healthy soil: everywhere there is dust and sand; everything has become rigid and languishes. One who is disconsolate and lonely could not choose a better symbol than the knight with death and the devil, as Dürer has drawn him for us, the armored knight with the iron, hard look, who knows how to pursue his terrible path, undeterred by his gruesome companions, and yet without hope, alone with horse and dog. Our Schopenhauer was such a Dürer knight; he lacked all hope, but he desired truth. He has no peers. (*BT* 20; *KSA* 1.130–31)[51]

It is important to find a "symbol" of Germany's cultural situation, and in choosing Dürer's famous picture, Nietzsche offers a specific reading of the image and one that is not as uncontroversial as its brevity might suggest. Here he marks both his indebtedness to Schopenhauer and his distance from him. Schopenhauer is the Dürer knight; in his world art and religion offer avenues for suspending, quieting, or eliminating the irrational will and so freeing us, in some degree, from our suffering. Schopenhauer creates a stark image of the world, a black and white image, we might say, like Dürer's. Schopenhauer's articulate and influential pessimism offers no prospect of cultural renewal but at best a heroic resignation to the pain of the world. We can admire his intrepid resolution, Nietzsche says, but we want something more, and we see its possibility, as in Wagner's music, which represents a transformation (perhaps a transfiguration) of Schopenhauer. This transfiguration would lead to a new picture: "[H]ow suddenly the wilderness of our tired culture, which we have just painted [*geschildert*] in such gloomy colors can be transformed, when it is touched by Dionysiac magic! . . . Our eyes gaze in confusion after what has disappeared, for what they see is something that has emerged from a pit into golden light, so full and green, so luxuriantly alive, so immeasurable and filled with longing." From black and white to color; from Dürer's print to Greek polychrome or Italian hues. As an initiate of Dionysus, Nietzsche calls upon us, his "friends," to "put on the wreaths of ivy, put the thyrsus into your hands, and do not be surprised when tigers and panthers lie down, fawning, at your feet" (BT 20; KSA 1.132).

Nietzsche was grateful when he received a (genuine) copy of the engraving from a patrician admirer in 1875.[52] To Malwida von Meysenburg he confides that although he rarely takes pleasure in pictures, this one "stands near to me, I scarcely know why"; and he confirms that it was his discussion of the image in the Birth that led to the gift (B 5.36). Later Nietzsche passed the engraving on as a wedding gift to his sister Elizabeth and Bernhard Förster to be taken along into the wilderness of Paraguay (B 7.46–47). He had also given a print of Dürer's Melancholia to Cosima Wagner in 1870, indicating his interest in a group of three engravings usually thought to form a series organized around the four humors (these include the St. Jerome in His Study and one putative lost picture). Knight, Death, and the Devil is indeed a powerful image. Death and the Devil are truly gruesome and monstrous figures. The Devil combines the features of a number of beasts, real and imaginary, in his hairy face, projecting snout, horns, and tail; with his pickax he stands ready to spear any unwary soul. Death confronts the knight mockingly with an hourglass; time is always running out. And in death we will lose our faces, as Death has lost lips and nose. Snakes are intertwined in his crown and around his neck. The landscape is forbidding, full of jagged rocks and twisted dead or thinning trees. Compositionally the picture balances the strong vertical line of the erect knight and the horizontal of his horse with the marked diagonals of his lance and sword, which themselves echo the lines of the landscape. Dürer's characteristic signature appears on a tablet with the date, 1513, leaning against a stump on which there is a skull. This dated work reminds us of both our mortality and the artist's. Ironically, Nietzsche may have exaggerated the pessimistic content of Dürer's picture. Certainly the knight has an "iron, hard look [Blick]" and walks a "terrible path." But are death and the Devil his "companions," and is he "without hope"? The figures of Death and the Devil are certainly gruesome, yet Erwin Panofsky argues that they should be seen not as actual threats to the knight, but as "spooks and phantoms," which he recognizes as such.[53] Indeed, the knight rides resolutely ahead, looking a bit to his left and ignoring the leering, crowned apparition of Death on his right. He has seen through these traps and lures, as Saint Anthony sees through the temptations that he is presented with in other representations of the period. The knight, on this reading, embodies the virtuous Christian soldier as he was described in Erasmus's *Enchiridion*, whose title invokes a stoic heritage. And hope is present in the picture, if distant, in the form of the turreted castle on a mountain far in the distance; it is the "fortress of virtue," as Panofsky sees it, following Erasmus. The road will be steep and difficult but not impossible. If death and the Devil are seen as "spooks and phantoms" (or "phantasms"— Erasmus had spoken of "*terricula et phantasmata*"), then the picture becomes a more complex allegory of vision. We may be tormented by specters, it would suggest, but we can become aware of their spectrality. This would again contribute to a chiasmic relation with Raphael's *Transfiguration*; while the latter celebrates the visionary, this picture introduces it as a dangerous hallucinatory distraction. We might think of Luther's own highly visual experience with the Devil, while sitting on the privy. And Kierkegaard, in *The Concept of Anxiety*, argues in good Protestant fashion that the Devil is much more threatening as a sudden visual apparition than as a speaking being. If he speaks, then we can respond to him and he can be confounded by our words, and those of Scripture. If he simply and suddenly appears, he has a much more radical power to interrupt, tempt, or threaten us.[54] Yet in the face of such a vision, we can become valiant knights, who refuse to be distracted from our mission. Might one read Schopenhauer as also seeing through the snares of the world, realizing that death is a deliverance and that the threats and temptations of the Devil (the hopes and fears that constantly torment the will) are nothing but "spooks and phantoms"? Dürer's engraving thus becomes another document of what Belting calls the "crisis of the image": visions are *only* visions, and the life of the good Christian is subordinate to the word, as Luther argues. Yet a question might be raised: does not Panofsky's reading of the picture, drawing heavily on literary sources (Erasmus's *Enchiridion* and the correspondence of Erasmus and Dürer), already assume such a dominance of the word? In *The Birth of Tragedy*, Nietzsche is contesting the traditional primacy of the bare text, at least in the case of Greek tragedy. His argument is that if we reduce the dramas to the text, following the direction initiated by Socrates and codified in Aristotle's *Poetics*, then the place of the chorus and indeed everything that Aristotle characterized as music and spectacle becomes unintelligible. Could the point not be made with reference to works of visual art? Indeed, Burckhardt offers a gentler version of this perspective in warning against the danger of seeing the plastic arts too exclusively through the lens of iconographical and literary knowledge.[55] Yet Panofsky's reading has the merit of focusing attention on the rider's resolute stare. We might notice that the complex of rider, horse, and dog stands out against the immediate background; the diagonal lines of the knight's weapons are reinforced by the middle ground of the landscape, and his vertical posture is in tune with the castle in the upper distance. Death and the Devil may indeed be "spooks and phantasms" within the world of this very architectonic picture.

24 Nietzsche and the Little Black Dress: All the Costumes of History

If Schopenhauer could sally forth in the armor of a knight, it does not follow that this is a style that Nietzsche will adopt or encourage others to wear. In *Human, All Too Human,* he expresses doubts about the possibility of dressing oneself today in Dürer's clothing, just as he doubts the possibility of a higher, metaphysical art. The passage is interesting because its ostensible subject is fashion, the way in which contemporary European men and women present themselves by means of their clothing; it deals with the images that we create for ourselves every day. It offers a hint of an aesthetics of the quotidian, one that might help us to clarify the relations of high and low culture. In this section, *Fashion and modernity* (*Mode und modern, HAH, WS,* 215; *KSA* 2.647–50), Nietzsche suggests that national costumes are still found "wherever communications are poor, the landscape is meager, and the priesthood is powerful." Where these are in decline, fashion reigns, and so it is to be understood in its association with European virtues, although it may be their shadow-side, since the meaning of fashion is simply to exhibit one's belonging to a respectable social stratum. Fashionable male dress suggests a certain uniformity, an effort at diminishing vanity, and a discreet abstention from appearing overly individual or as a member of a certain class, ethnicity, or nation. European women, on the other hand, want through their dress to be recognized as members of a superior class. Yet as women become more inward, they can be expected to follow the male pattern. Nietzsche, the fashion prophet, foresees the spread of the little black dress. Given these aspirations, it is not at all unreasonable for the work of fashion to be concentrated in a single city, Paris. This is simply part of the division of labor, one in which our potentially most personal images are mass produced for us by a small circle of designers. Germans might feel uncomfortable with this, but what are they to do?

If, out of hatred for this claim by a French city, a German elects to dress differently, as Albrecht Dürer dressed, for example, let him consider that the costume he is wearing, though Germans formerly wore it, they invented it just as little as they invented the fashions of Paris—there has *never* been a costume which denoted a German as a German; he should also consider what he *looks* like in this costume and whether the really modern mind, with all the lines and folds the nineteenth century has inscribed in it, might not take exception to someone's wearing clothes like Dürer's. (*HAH, WS,* 215; *KSA* 2.650)

It was, of course, the question of German culture that had led to Nietzsche's admiration for Schopenhauer's following the heroic example of Dürer's knight, that is, wearing his clothing or armor.[56] Now he seems to be distancing himself even further from Schopenhauer's costume than he had before. As with Nietzsche's changing response to Raphael, the question of what it means to assume the habit of Dürer and his knight is an indication of some shift in his positions being worked out once more in terms of a significant image. The *Birth* was published in 1872, Nietzsche received his print in 1875, and the note on fashion was published in 1880; by the time of *Thus Spoke Zarathustra,* Nietzsche will criticize historicist culture as providing a grab bag of costumes and disguises that mask the fact that contemporary humans have no authentic selves (Z II.14; *KSA* 4.153–55). And in *Beyond Good and Evil,* he will suggest that the costume shop of history can be turned to advantage by donning its contents in the spirit of "a carnival in the grand style" (*BGE* 223; *KSA* 5.157). Now Nietzsche had the visual model of a Venice far past its prime but marketing its own past, to serve as the alternative to a European dress code and image industry that was becoming all too homogenized. Perhaps the paintings of Europe, the works of Raphael and others that Nietzsche refers to, have become images to be "tried on, put on, taken off, packed away, and above all *studied.*" If we cannot wear the costume of Dürer, for example, in all seriousness, we can still don it temporarily, perhaps through the agency of institutions like the museum and disciplines like the history of art.

The tendency of Nietzsche's later reflections on what he once took to be exemplary images and works of art is to demote them to the status of examples. The modern European can wear a simple and severe outfit or can indulge in the appearances of "all the names of history" (as Nietzsche declared in his last letter to Burckhardt, that supreme historian of images, that he was "all the names of history"). Yet the move toward a radically historical or archaeological conception of the image was already there in *The Birth of Tragedy*, not with regard to works of art like Raphael's and Dürer's but in the analysis of tragedy itself. Louis Marin suggests that the *Transfiguration* is the visible form of the tragic myth; but we should remember that tragedy itself is a visual medium on Nietzsche's analysis. And so we can still inquire, as he does in his first book, how it comes to shine or show itself.

four

Übersehen: Architecture and Excess
in the Theater of Dionysus

Oh these Greeks! We sigh; they upset all our aesthetics
Nietzsche, *BT* 7; *KSA* 1.54

25 Optical Illusions

Toward the end of *The Birth of Tragedy,* Nietzsche sketches
the possibility of a rebirth of tragedy and tragic culture. It is
Wagner, of course, that Nietzsche seems to have in mind most
specifically. His seductive language reaches a kind of cre-
scendo; all along he has been inviting the reader to share his
sense of what ancient tragedy was, and now, jumping over two
thousand years to the present, he evokes the Wagnerian world.
The constant implication is that one's tastes and sensitivities
are crucial in determining whether one is hopelessly caught
in the anemic Alexandrian world of modernity (sometimes
here called "the culture of the opera," later to be known as nihilism) or is a candidate for redemption through art. At a certain point, Nietzsche begins to speak of (and, in a sense, *to*) a

"friend" who is genuinely attuned to music and musical drama (these "friends"—actual, hoped for, unknown, sometimes identified with future readers—who people Nietzsche's books are crucial for the reader's seduction).[1] What is extraordinary is that while the reception and criticism of this book has been so overshadowed by the ideas of the Dionysian and the musical, here, in one of his most intimate appeals to his reader, Nietzsche attempts to delineate the nature of the musical drama that is being reborn, by an appeal to what and how such a friend will *see*. This friend will acknowledge that in "the effect of a true musical tragedy, purely and simply, as he knows it from experience," it will be

> as if his visual faculty [*Sehkraft*] were no longer merely a surface faculty but capable of penetrating into the interior, and as if he now saw before him, with the aid of music, the waves of the will, the conflict of motives, and the swelling flood of the passions, sensuously visible [*sinnlich sichtbar*], as it were, like a multitude of vividly moving lines and figures; and he felt he could dip into the most delicate secrets of unconscious emotions. While he thus becomes conscious of the highest exaltation of his instincts for visibility and transfiguration [*Sichtbarkeit und Verklärung*], he nevertheless feels just as definitely that this long series of Apollonian artistic effects still does *not* generate that blessed continuance in will-less contemplation which the plastic and the epic poet, that is to say the strictly Apollonian artists evoke in him with their artistic productions: to wit, the justification of the world of the *individuatio* attained by this contemplation—which is the climax and essence of Apollonian art.

So these visible forms (or virtually visible, if we attend to Nietzsche's "as if" and "as it were") do not reinforce the sense of individuation that the author believes he has already established as the goal of Apollonian art. Yet this passage does indicate that music, while not a strictly Apollonian art, like painting and epic poetry, shares this characteristic with the Apollonian: it evokes "sensuously visible" images, although now highly mobile ones. Music's capacity to generate images has already been asserted in "On Music and Words." And as transfiguration is the meaning of the strictly Apollonian arts, so it is here in the musical theater. The friend "beholds the transfigured [*verklärte*] world of the stage and nevertheless denies it. He sees the tragic hero before him in epic clearness and beauty, and nevertheless rejoices in his annihilation. . . . He sees more extensively and profoundly than ever, and yet wishes he were blind" (*BT* 22; *KSA* 1.140–41).

The world of the Wagnerian stage is transfigured. Now that the

Transfiguration of Raphael has shown us something about the structure of artistic vision, transfiguration itself becomes a figure for intense visual experience in Nietzsche's account of tragedy. We can transpose Nietzsche's account of the levels of vision involved in beholding this painting to the situation of the Wagnerian audience. Then the characters on the stage would be like the figures in the painting, transfigured by appearing in a new and remarkable light. And just as those in the lower level of the painting do not see the spectacle over their heads and the disciples shield their eyes, so some spectators fail to see what is going on and others wish themselves blind. How strange that a complex intertwining of sight and blindness would in some way be the key to understanding the new Wagnerian music! But Nietzsche has already prepared the ground for this move in his analysis of the Greek theater and of tragedy. There is no theater without vision; as we are often reminded, our words *theory* and *theater* derive from the Greek *theoria* that signifies the act of beholding or witnessing.[2] Behind the strange complicity of vision and blindness that Nietzsche expects his friend to experience in the musical drama of his day, there is the similar structure that he articulates in the Greek theater. Oedipus and Teiresias are not only figures of the stage but also figures for what it is to see the visions of tragedy. Homer, too, was blind, according to a significant legend; yet Nietzsche describes him as the most visual of Greek poets.

The dream, and dreamlike visions, are luminously clear, on Nietzsche's account, yet there is something illusory about them. One of the aims of *The Birth of Tragedy* will be to provide a key to the interpretation of such dreams and visions by situating them in their contexts. Let us assume for now that these brilliant visionary experiences are exceptional in relation to our general optical experience, in which the dominant theme is the duality of concealing and revealing, light and shadow, dawn and dusk. When clarity emerges, it always does so out of a context of darkness. This is the analysis that Nietzsche gives of the appearance of the tragic hero in the *Birth*, whose apparently clear outlines he ascribes to something like an optical illusion. We should not take the language of optics to be a mere metaphor, for Nietzsche is emphasizing that the appearance of the tragic figures on stage is very much a visual phenomenon. His account of the hero's appearance is an explanation of the latter's transfiguration by an analogy with an optical illusion:

> suppose we disregard the character of the hero as it comes to the
> surface, visibly—after all, it is in the last analysis nothing but a
> bright image [*Lichtbild*] projected on a dark wall, which means ap-

pearance [*Erscheinung*] through and through; suppose we penetrate into the myth that projects itself in these brilliant reflections [*hellen Spiegelungen*]: then we suddenly experience a phenomenon that is just the opposite of a familiar optical phenomenon. When after a forceful attempt to gaze on the sun we turn away blinded, we see dark-colored spots before our eyes, as a cure, as it were. Conversely, the bright image projections [*Lichtbilderscheinungen*] of the Sophoclean hero—in short, the Apollonian aspect of the mask—are necessary effects of a glance into the inside and terrors of nature; as it were luminous spots to cure eyes damaged by gruesome night. (*BT* 9; *KSA* 1.65)

So clarity is a kind of illusion; a beautiful illusion, but illusion nonetheless. We naturally recoil from a look into the abyss, and yet Zarathustra will challenge his listeners, "[I]s not all seeing—seeing abysses?" The abyss is dark, empty, and endless; like the extreme of light, it requires a counterbalance, one supplied by an architecture of the theater, as the antidote to light will be produced by a natural reflex of the eye. Vision is a dangerous, risky business; Nietzsche will also suggest that his "most abysmal thought," the eternal recurrence, is a Medusa's head (sec. 38). The terrors of "gruesome night" call out for some medicine for the eyes. In the theater, the site of beholding, it is possible to construct a kind of machine for seeing, one that, like a camera obscura, uses the extremes of light and dark to produce a model form of vision that will both lead us into the depths and provide a shining escape from the nausea and vertigo that they provoke. Now I will develop an analysis of Nietzsche's understanding of the theater as an optical device, in a sense that ranges from the extended or metaphorical sense of vision to the actual arrangements for viewing the chorus and the actors. This is what Foucault and Lyotard would designate by such terms as *dispositif* or diagram.

26 Aesthetics of Presence

In his account of the dream and the visionary experience, Nietzsche provides an analysis of a conception of vision that can be construed as a form of the aesthetics of presence. Following Heidegger and Derrida, we have come to see the persuasive power of a history of Western philosophy that emplots it as the persistent attempt to valorize the absolutely present, whether in the form of the Platonic ideas, the Cartesian *cogito*, or the Hegelian absolute spirit. If we call this tendency the metaphysics of presence, we will see that it is accompanied by a corresponding aesthetics, one that takes clarity and the radiant image to be central to aesthetic experience; such would seem to be the nerve of Plato's admiration for classical and Egyptian style, Aristotle's identification of the plot as the soul of tragedy, Kant's conception of beauty in which design plays a paradigmatic role, and Hegel's definition of the beautiful as the "sensuous shining" of the Idea. Nietzsche's Apollonian art can be seen as a distillation of this tradition, with the very significant proviso that it exists only in and through its antagonism with another artistic impulse, the Dionysian, which opens onto the complex, the abyss, and the depths of gruesome night. In his later writings, Heidegger develops a bipolar account of truth, according to which whatever is seen and understood is what emerges or is wrested from an abyssal context or background; *aletheia* (or truth) is what arises out of *Lethe*, originally the river of oblivion. Similarly, whatever comes into the light requires a *Lichtung*, a clearing or lightening that provides a space for it. Nietzsche will eventually call himself the first tragic philosopher, and we can make sense of this self-description by taking it as a generalization of the bivalence (and ambivalence) of the insight that he has about tragic vision.

What, then, is tragic vision in Nietzsche's radical theory and revisioning of tragedy? In the "Attempt at a Self-Criticism" that he added to *The Birth of Tragedy* in 1886, Nietzsche says that his book was "image-mad and image-confused [*bilderwuthig und bilderwirrig*]" (*BT*, "Attempt," 3; *KSA* 1.14). No doubt he is referring to the images of his own rhapsodic prose in 1872, a voice that "should have *sung* and not spoken!" (*BT*, *P*, 3; *KSA* 1.15), and it is a judgment with which Nietzsche's readers have tended to concur. But in addition to bursting with these poetic images, the book thematizes and interrogates the notion of the image itself, in the sense of that which appears, and appears quite specifically to sight, beginning with the very first sentence, in which the fluctuating relations of the Apollonian and Dionysian forces are compared to the eternal war of the sexes. Throughout the book Nietzsche insists that we *see* what he is proposing or revealing to us, and this insistence is already marked in the same opening sentence, which says that we will have made an advance in aesthetics "once we perceive not merely by logical inference, but with the immediate certainty of vision [*Anschauung*]" the roles of the two great artistic drives (*BT* 1; *KSA* 1.25). If the translation of *Anschauung* as vision, rather than, say, intuition, seems tendentious, it appears less so when we recognize the pervasive visual language as well as the visual thematics of the *Birth*, dimensions that have been somewhat overshadowed by the book's obvious celebration of the musical. And if we are tempted to dismiss such language and concerns as merely "metaphorical" (as if we knew what that status was), and as standing in at least a potential conflict with the apparent melocentrism of this work (thus confirming its status as "image-mad and image-confused"), we should recall that in the *Birth* Nietzsche says that "for a genuine poet, metaphor is not a rhetorical figure but a vicarious image [*stellvertretendes Bild*] that he actually beholds in place of a concept" (*BT* 8; *KSA* 1.60). In the framing essay of 1886, Nietzsche still emphasizes the visual dimension of his analysis of tragedy in this summary of its "artist's metaphysics": "The world—at every moment [*Augenblick*] the *attained* salvation of God, as the eternally changing, eternally new vision [*Vision*] of the most deeply afflicted, discordant, and contradictory being who can find salvation only in *shining* [*Schein*]" (*BT* "Attempt" 5; *KSA* 1.17).

Even if Nietzsche now looks at his youthful book with "a much older, a hundred times more demanding, but by no means colder eye" it still has the significance of placing things in the proper perspective, or nested set of perspectives, namely *"to look at science with the optics of the artist, but at art with that of life"* (*BT* "Attempt" 2; *KSA* 1.14). The terms in which the older Nietzsche formulates the import of his first book call for some comment. *Schein*, as explained earlier, should be read as "shining," not as the more neutral epistemic "appearance" (sec. 19). The *Augenblick*, the moment of vision or twinkling of the eye, does not play a large role in the 1872 version of the *Birth*, but it does become significant in most of the crucial texts concerning eternal recurrence; and as the highly visual concern with the *Augenblick* in *Zarathustra*'s chapter "On the Vision and the Riddle" indicates, the sense of a look, the phenomenological sense of the experience of a blink or twinkling of the eye, ought to be heard in this term. *Vision*, although orthographically equivalent to the English word, has the specific sense of that which is visionary, of seeing something beyond the mundane. *The Birth of Tragedy*, as Nietzsche's later account confirms, is indeed a visionary text.

Both the texture of Nietzsche's prose and the narrative it relates of the birth of tragedy are concerned with becoming visible, with the arrangement and projection of visual images, whether actual, virtual, or hallucinatory. If, as Giorgio Colli suggests in the afterword to his edition, the *Birth* can be read as a kind of written equivalent of a Greek mystery ritual, we should remember that often the crucial or culminating stage of those rituals was the display of some scene or object charged with meaning (*KSA* 1.902–3). Nietzsche's story is precisely one of a birth, a passage from the hidden to the manifest of something that suddenly becomes visible (and noisy). It tells of how the cult and rituals of Dionysus, penetrated and impregnated by Apollo, give birth to a set of images, visions, and appearances. This story is also an archaeological inquiry; it is an attempt to unearth the specific practices that make possible what was seen in the Greek theater. And it is an architectural mapping of the relations of space and power, one that articulates a fundamental way of building and structuring a matrix for vision.

Although the Dionysian is said to be a nonimagistic force, affiliated with the nonimagistic art of music, Nietzsche asks us specifically to visualize this power. Just a few lines after one of these instructions to transform music into painting, an injunction to translate Beethoven's *Ninth Symphony* into a painting, the Apollonian art of sculpture appears (Apollo is called the *Bildnergott* at one point) in order to help us appreciate the meaning of the Dionysian mysteries.[3] The Dionysian man, Nietzsche says, "is no longer an artist, he has become a work of art: in these paroxysms of intoxication the artistic power of all nature reveals itself to the highest gratification of the primordial unity. The noblest clay, the most costly marble, man, is here kneaded and cut, and to the sound of the chisel-strokes of the Dionysian world-artist rings out the cry of the Eleusinian mysteries: 'Do you prostrate yourselves, millions? Do you sense your maker, world?'" (*BT* 1; *KSA* 1.30). Here the musical, aural world of Dionysus is something of a secondary accompaniment to the activity of the sculptor. Man is reshaped and reconfigured in a material and visible form while the sculptor's radio plays Beethoven's *Ninth*.

In urging us to imagine a painting or a sculpture, Nietzsche performs a kind of inverted ekphrasis. It is curious that Nietzsche, the classicist, never refers explicitly to this genre, although some of his most important passages, such as the appropriately named chapter "Of the Vision [*Gesicht*] and the Riddle," from *Zarathustra*, could be understood as ekphrases of imaginary scenes. As the paradigmatic instance of literary ekphrasis, Homer's description of the shield of Achilles, makes clear, the object of description need not be an actual work; indeed, given Homer's legendary blindness, it is remarkable that the touchstone for all future ekphrases would be one of an imaginary work of art by a man who could not see. Nietzsche does not speak of Homer's blindness, and one can imagine that it might be difficult for him to reconcile it with his status in the *Birth* as the supreme Apollonian poet. "How is it," he asks, "that Homer's descriptions are so much more vivid [*anschaulicher*] than those of any other poet? Because he visualizes [*anschaut*] so much more vividly" (*BT* 8; *KSA* 1.60). But perhaps he glancingly alludes to the legend when, after remarking on "the incredibly precise and unerring plastic power of their [i.e., the Greeks'] eyes, together with their vivid, frank delight in colors," he concludes that "we can hardly refrain from assuming even for their dreams (to the shame of all those born later) a certain logic of line and contour, colors and groups, a certain pictorial sequence reminding us of their finest bas-reliefs whose perfection would certainly justify us, if a comparison were possible, in designating the dreaming Greeks as Homers and Homer as a dreaming Greek" (*BT* 2; *KSA* 1.31). The implicit thought may be that, especially among the Greeks, even the blind have visions, an idea that is to be distinguished from the looser and more common notion that they may, like Teiresias or the old Oedipus, have powers of knowledge and prophecy denied to those with sight. More significantly, Nietzsche describes Greek dreams in sculptural and architectural terms. We are tempted to think of the dream as much too fleeting and ambiguous to be grasped by these categories, but Nietzsche's use of them here underscores his conception of the dream as Apollonian, the product of the sculptor god. If there is an architecture of dreams, a context that allows the emergence of "a certain logic of line and contour," then we might also suspect that an architectural setting will be essential to making sense of tragedy, in which dreamlike visions are so important.

Let us look once more at the structure that Nietzsche finds within Raphael's *Transfiguration*, which turns out to be an analog of that of tragedy, with the emphasis on how each one issues in certain visions, illusions, or images. The painting is a vision; in principle we might analyze the structure that allows that vision to appear to us and by virtue of which we receive it, just as Nietzsche will analyze the underlying setup of Greek tragedy (the festival, the space of the theater, the orchestra, the scene, the mask). To follow out that path would be to articulate the space in which the painting is found (church or museum), how the work is framed and presented within that space (labeling, lighting, arrangement in rooms and on the wall), and the expectations aroused in the spectators when they enter into the viewing space. As Nietzsche reads it, the *Transfiguration* is a *mise-en-abîme* of appearance and of painting, foreshadowing both Zarathustra's announcement that "all vision is seeing abysses" (in "On the Vision and the Riddle") and the ways in which Foucault, with Velazquez's *Las Meninas* or Magritte's *This Is Not a Pipe*, or Derrida (in at least one of his voices), with van Gogh's *Old Shoes*, attempts to read certain paintings as emblems of painting itself.

In the crucial eighth section of the *Birth,* Nietzsche addresses Schlegel's conception of the chorus as the "ideal spectator [*Zuschauer*]" of the tragedy. This is a view that Nietzsche can endorse, but only if it is taken to mean that the chorus is "the only *beholder* [*Schauer*], the beholder of the visionary world of the scene [*Scene*]" (*BT* 8; *KSA* 1.59). Here we need to be aware that the *skene* is the small stage on which the actors appear, and it is on the *skene* that Nietzsche locates the Apollonian vision of separate characters that constitutes a "visionary world." In the dense analysis of the structure or setup of the tragic theater that follows, there is a rigorous explication of what is comprehended in such beholding or seeing; it involves not only the question of who sees but also the place of seeing and the content of what is seen. One standard reading of the *Birth* sees Nietzsche as reversing the order of importance of the "parts" of tragedy that Aristotle delineated, specifically as displacing what the *Poetics* called the "soul" of tragedy, the plot *(mythos),* and substituting music or melody *(melos)* for it. In a thoughtful essay on the *Poetics,* for example, P. Christopher Smith writes: "Nietzsche alone, in his brazen radicality, succeeds in taking down the visual and intellectualist surface of Greek tragedy and in exposing for us the acoustical foundations beneath it, and this two millennia after Plato's very nearly successful efforts to obliterate these acoustical foundations once and for all and, with them tragedy as such."[4] This view is in need of some qualification. For Nietzsche it is not a question of acoustics versus optics (or of finding a "foundation" for tragedy), but rather it is a matter of asking just how we are to understand the optical. Smith's contrast of the two modes seems to presuppose that we know quite well what the visual dimension is, while I take Nietzsche to be rethinking accepted notions of the visual. If Nietzsche does indeed revalue the position of music in tragedy, he also puts a new construction on the visual aspect of what happens in the theater, what Aristotle called the spectacle *(opsis),* which he held, along with music, to be one of the two least essential elements of tragedy; in the winter of 1869–70, Nietzsche notes: "*Contra Aristotle,* who reckons *opsis* [appearance or spectacle] and *melos* [song or music] only among the *hedysmata* [sweetenings or sensuous attractions] of tragedy: and already completely legitimizes the drama that is [merely] read" (*KSA* 7.78).[5] The reversal is quite explicit, and Nietzsche not only denies the centrality of plot but further claims that the conception, reigning from Aristotle through Lessing and Hegel, that tragedy is mainly concerned with action *(Handlung)* is fatally flawed. As he says in his lecture "Das griechische Musikdrama," given in the period of the gestation of the *Birth*, all modern drama, in its emphasis on plot and intrigue, derives not from ancient tragedy but from the Greek new comedy:

> Compared with that, ancient tragedy was poor in action and tension [*Handlung und Spannung*]; it can even be said that in its early stages of development, there was no aim at acting [*Handeln*], at *drama*, but rather at suffering [*Leiden*], or *pathos*. . . . in Greek drama the accent rests on suffering, not on acting. . . . We have no criterion by which to estimate the judgment of the Attic public on a poetic work, because we do not know, or do so only in the slightest way, how suffering, or generally the life of feeling in its outbreaks, was brought to effective expression. (*KSA* 1.527–28)[6]

The *Handlung*, on Nietzsche's reading, is that which gives rise to visions. The two artistic divinities, Apollo and Dionysus, preside over the two types of art, the visual and the musical, that Aristotle (and most of the tradition following in his wake) relegated to accessory positions in relation to the favored art of poetry. From this perspective the traditional contrast between Plato and Aristotle is enormously exaggerated. If Plato's claim was that the staging of tragedy is a very dangerous thing, Aristotle's achievement was to develop a hermeneutics of tragedy such that the danger could be avoided by reading tragedy so that performance, in both its optical and its acoustical dimensions, was at bottom irrelevant. If we go to tragedy with this Aristotelian framework in mind, the danger of staging will have been eliminated. Aristotle rehabilitates tragedy, then, not by arguing for the acceptability of what Plato condemned, but by changing the subject. The first full title of Nietzsche's book, *The Birth of Tragedy out of the Spirit of Music*, emphasizes only *melos* and not *opsis*. The "Self-Criticism" makes it fairly clear that one motive for revising the title to *The Birth of Tragedy, or Hellenism and Pessimism* was Nietzsche's radical change of heart and tune with regard to Wagner. But an effect of the change is to downplay the earlier stress on music, which will now allow the reader to focus on the "artist's metaphysics," in which the world appears "as the eternally changing, eternally new vision of the most deeply afflicted, discordant, and contradictory being who can find salvation only in *Schein*" (*BT* "Attempt" 5; *KSA* 1.17).

Suffering, rather than acting, has to be seen as the condition of the spectators and of the chorus; and it is this suffering, in its musical and choreographic expression, that manifests itself in visions. But to explain the apparatus or structure that enables this requires the complex analysis that Nietzsche offers in section 8 of *The Birth of Tragedy*; it is a part of the text that is not so rhapsodic as much of the rest but which is perhaps the most definitive statement in Nietzsche's book about the actual genesis of tragedy. In fact we should speak here of structure rather than genesis; for if the discussion indeed presupposes everything that has been said about the Apollonian and Dionysian artistic impulses, it proceeds now not by way of narrative, but by offering an account of the synchronic relations of audience, chorus, actors, within a space divided into *theatron* (the space for the spectators), *orchestra* (the circle within which the chorus sings and dances), and *skene* (the rather small and narrow space from which the individual actors emerge and within whose precincts they remain).[7] As Nietzsche says in *Twilight of the Idols*, architecture is itself neither Apollonian nor Dionysian, and so this is also the case of the architecture of the Greek theater (using the latter word now in the broad, contemporary sense, which would include all of the parts just mentioned).[8] On one hand, as a formative or plastic art, it lies within Apollo's realm; on the other, Nietzsche remarks at one point that the bowl-like shape of the theater could be reminiscent of the valleys in which Dionysus manifested himself to his followers (*BT* 8; *KSA* 1.60). But neither of these possible identifications, nor the fact that the tragic theater was indeed the theater of Dionysus, nor the common Athenian saying that "tragedy has nothing to do with Dionysus" ought to be regarded as definitive. What *happens* in the theater is strongly Dionysian, but the structure of the theater, including its architecture and the expectations and identifications linking (and dividing) audience, chorus, and actors is a matrix in which Apollo and Dionysus are allowed to play out their complex and fragile mutual epiphanies. To understand the Greek theater is to see it as one possibility within a spectrum of architectural possibilities.

The chorus itself in "its primitive form" (but Nietzsche implies that this identification continues through the classical development of tragedy) is said to be the self-reflection or self-mirroring *(Selbstspiegelung)* of Dionysian man. If this is simply a metaphor—or perhaps an image—to suggest that the audience, insofar as it is Dionysian, can identify with the chorus, the account of the visual aspect of tragedy and its architectural context that immediately follows surely has to do with that which is seen; and even if these visions appear mainly to the mind's eye, it is as visions that they appear:

> This phenomenon [of *Selbstspiegelung*] is best made clear by imagining an actor who, being truly talented, sees the role he is supposed

to play quite palpably before his eyes. The satyr chorus is, first of all, a vision [*Vision*] of the Dionysian mass, just as the world of the stage, in turn, is a vision of this satyr chorus: the force of this vision is strong enough to make the eye insensitive and blind to the impression of "reality," to the men of culture who occupy the rows of seats all around. The form of the Greek theater recalls a lonely valley in the mountains: the architecture of the scene [*Scene*] appears like a luminous cloud formation that the Bacchants swarming over the mountains behold from a height—like the splendid frame [*Umrahmung*] in which the image of Dionysus is revealed to them. (*BT* 8; *KSA* 1.60)

Visions in the theater have a frame, but so do phantasms experienced by Bacchants in the mountains. What Nietzsche implies here is that all visions are framed in some way and that those who want to understand them must articulate the structure of the frame rather than simply focus on what might appear to be the immediate content of the vision—whether it is dream, artfully generated theatrical vision, or hallucination. We should realize that when Nietzsche speaks of aesthetics at the beginning of the *Birth*, the term refers to *aisthesis* as well as to works of art; he is interested in the Apollonian and Dionysian ways of manifestation or appearing. To put a somewhat Kantian construction on it, he is proposing something like a "transcendental aesthetic," in which the two divinities preside over specific realms of experience whose differences and intersections may be analyzed in order to articulate the possibility of the forms of art. The architectural frame, neither Apollonian nor Dionysian, is the field in which tragedy allows these forces to play themselves out. Here Nietzsche explains several levels of framing. The entire theater is set off from the rest of the world, like a "lonely valley in the mountains"; the valley or the theater is the world for now, so that everything beyond its periphery recedes into forgetfulness. This architecture is commanding, as each spectator's eyes are made blind with respect to the other men of the city who surround him; not seeing others like himself, overlooking them, he also forgets himself. Architecture can be a way of virtually reconstituting the sense of self. Yet the appeal to a natural setting here is curious. We know of the Bacchants "swarming over the mountains" from Euripides' *Bacchae;* Nietzsche has implicitly appealed to our knowledge of a *theatrical* event in order to provide a *natural* analog of theatrical experience. Within the limits of the theater, the spectators' attention is further framed by their focus on the vision of the satyr chorus and the *skene* or stage. The architecture of the *skene* appears as a "luminous cloud formation" because the stage seems to rise up mysteriously out of the *orchestra*, which is the place of the chorus. The Bacchants would behold a luminous cloud formation down in the valley as a "splendid frame" for the revelation of Dionysus. So the theater becomes a complex optical device for presenting such Apollonian visions of the Dionysian. The frame within a frame within a frame (the *skene* surrounded by the *orchestra* surrounded by the *theatron*, or rows of seats) exhibits a spectacular economy of means in order to produce the tragic spectacle. In response to Aristotle, Nietzsche would be suggesting not merely that he dismissed the spectacle much too easily but that he never understood what it was.

Later in section 8, Nietzsche again speaks of the frame, when he narrates the development from the pretragic Dionysian chorus to "drama" (the latter word is typically in quotation marks in the text to mark Nietzsche's reservations regarding construing tragedy as action rather than passion or suffering). While Dionysus was not at first present to the chorus, but merely imagined, "Later the attempt was made to show the god as real and to represent the visionary figure [*Visionsgestalt*] together with its transfiguring frame [*verklärenden Umrahmung*] as something visible for every eye—and thus 'drama' in the narrower sense began" (*BT* 8; *KSA* 1.63). If tragedy is the epiphany of the god, following Nietzsche's analogy between the theater and the valley in which Dionysus appears to his disciples, then the god does not appear except by means of a "transfiguring frame." Apollo (or Christ) also required a transfiguring frame of a different sort in Raphael's painting. That figure becomes a focus of visionary experience by appearing above a mountain, being surrounded by awed viewers, and appearing in contrast to the confused scene below. Making allowances for the different media of painting and architecture, the *Transfiguration* appears to operate through principles of framing very close to those of the theater. Tragedy is transfiguration in more than a metaphorical sense; it involves a vision in which startling and luminous figures manifest themselves in a setting that invites their presence. The verb *umrahmen*, which generates the noun *Umrahmung* (frame) may mean either to frame or to reframe. If Nietzsche writes of a transfiguring framing or reframing, he emphasizes the variability of the frame, a variability that he applies in a wider sense to the entire argument of the *Birth*, when he says in 1886 that it dared for the first time "*to look at science with the optics of the artist, but at art with that of life.*" In the passage quoted above from section 8, not only the vision but also the frame become visible; this is the architectural sense of "frame" that Nietzsche employed earlier in saying that "the form of the Greek theater recalls a lonely valley in the mountains." There the comparison is between "the architecture of the scene" and Dionysus appearing in a cloud formation as the Bacchants look down from a height. Recall that the *skene* is elevated somewhat over the circular orchestra, while the spectators look down on both from the semicircular *theatron*. So the spectators can both look down at the scene, the tragic vision, from their place in the *theatron*, identifying with Bacchants on a mountainside, and at the same time, insofar as they identify with the theatrical chorus, they can be virtually looking up, from *orchestra* to *skene*. The framing can be thought of as a reframing, since every frame within or outside another frame is the reframing of what we would see without it. In tragedy the frame is transfiguring; setting off the actors in their costumes and masks from the surrounding space, it makes "the eye insensitive and blind to the impression of 'reality.' " Blindness again is the condition of tragic vision. Of course, more than architecture is involved here; the frame in the more comprehensive sense includes the festival of Dionysus at which the tragedy is performed and the marking off of a space separate from the mundane that is implicit in attending the theater.

28 The Theatrical *Dispositif*

It will not be easy to find philosophical resources to clarify Nietzsche's conception of framing and reframing. Lessing, whose aesthetics Nietzsche set out to revise, has an idea of the theater that seems tied to the proscenium stage and so lacks the possibility of explaining the more complex framing effect of Greek architecture. In the *Critique of Judgment,* which Nietzsche studied in the years before writing *The Birth of Tragedy,* Kant mentions the frame only to minimize its importance, apparently as an afterthought. The frame, which includes architectural structures, is just one form of the more general category of *parerga,* or ornament: "Even what we call *ornaments* [*parerga*], i.e. what does not belong to the whole presentation of the object as an intrinsic constituent, but [is] only an extrinsic addition, does indeed increase our taste's liking, and yet it does so only by its form, as in the case of picture frames, or drapery on statues, or colonnades around magnificent buildings."[9] Kant does recognize that the frame may have a formal significance, and so he distinguishes it from mere "finery" such as a gold frame attached to a picture simply to draw our attention to it. Yet he seems oblivious of the way in which a frame may function as part of a framing, a process in which it would be more than an "extrinsic addition" to the work. That he mentions colonnades as examples of such *parerga* suggests something problematic in his conception of architecture, despite the fundamental role played by his notion of a philosophical architectonic and the way in which he has absorbed the Cartesian conception of philosophy as a kind of absolute building.[10] Jacques Derrida has raised the question of the frame in Kant (and so in the vast amount of aesthetic theory deriving from him) by inquiring about how this marginalization works.[11] Determined to clear a space for beauty, Kant wants to exclude all that is extraneous but that might be confused with it. Yet, isn't the frame necessary simply to identify what is intrinsic about a work? And if so, does it not also become an intrinsic aspect? By what criteria, then, do we identify the intrinsic and the extrinsic? Part of the problem seems to be that Kant wants to speak of the frame as a static element that can be added to or subtracted from the work; but framing, in Nietzsche's sense, is an activity, a function, a dimension of the work. For characters to appear as figures of the tragedy, some setting or frame is required; if this is not the specific architecture of the Greek theater, then it must be some other set of conditions, an alternative *dispositif* by which the world of the theater establishes some boundaries between itself and the rest of the world (even if permeable in some ways). Nietzsche goes a long way in the direction of acknowledging and analyzing the function of the frame; it is no longer unthought but is thematized.

Nietzsche does not introduce the terms *perspective* and *perspectivism* in the first edition of *The Birth of Tragedy*; however, the preface of 1886 does contain the well-known formulation that is usually translated in terms of "perspective," although the word Nietzsche uses is "optics" *(Optik)*. If the dominant thought there is that one perspective may contain and transform another, we might understand the articulation of the double-viewing position of the audience—actually from the *theatron* and virtually from the *orchestra*—as involving a somewhat different form of perspectivism: the realization that one could simultaneously or almost simultaneously entertain different views of the same scene, identifying with distinct spectatorial positions. It is more than a distinction of physical locations or focus, although it does involve that; think of the effect, for example, of seeing now with the right and now with the left eye (especially if they have somewhat different optical strengths and weaknesses) or of shifting attention so as to behold things in sharp or in soft focus. Here the audience is said to be now "seeing as" the citizens in their seats in the *theatron* and now as the chorus in the *orchestra*. The difference in location marks two different roles: on the one hand, the Athenian head of household, participant in the assembly and war; on the other, the reveling, dancing, celebrating follower of Dionysus. This doubling of vision is made possible by the transfiguring frame.

In thinking of the framing effect of tragedy and the work of the poet, we must understand the audience or spectators as also being constituted by the frame. What is transfigured is the viewing subject, the *Zuschauer*, as well as the visions presented. This is precisely how Greeks (or Greeks of the tragic age) become what they are; and when tragedy declines, they become something different, because the tragic frame is replaced by a series of others: the Euripidean dichotomy of reason and emotion, Socratic inquiry, Platonic dialogue, New Comedy, or the new sacrificial drama of Christianity. These setups or frames (and their more recent successors, the modern theater and opera) can be understood in terms of their contrasts with the tragic structure that is sketched in *On the Genealogy of Morality*. Jean-François Lyotard, in pages that reveal his own debt to Nietzsche, writes of the *dispositif* that simultaneously establishes space, subject, and objects of attention: "[I]n the set-up [*dispositif*] of the *politeia*, you have first of all the enclosure of a space. . . . the city closes itself off as though into a circle. . . . in the middle there is an empty space . . . 'de-reality.' . . . movement to the inside will be filtered exactly as spectators are filtered at the entry to a play. They will be filtered according to a certain number of codes, the set of which defines what is known as citizenship."[12]

Lyotard is writing about the *dispositif* of painting, and he illustrates it by these analogies drawn from the theater and politics. Nietzsche writes of the frame of theater and compares it to the work of the painter and to the way in which a certain community (of Dionysian man) is constituted. First there is the question of what a character is. For the poet, "[a] character is not something he has composed out of particular traits, picked up here and there, but an obtrusively alive person [*Person*] before his very eyes, distinguished from the otherwise identical vision of a painter only by the fact that it continually goes on living and acting" (*BT* 8; *KSA* 1.60). The person may be obtrusively alive, but a *Person* may also be a persona, a mask. "The Dionysian excitement is capable of communicating this artistic gift to a multitude, so they can see themselves surrounded by such a host of spirits while knowing themselves to be essentially one with them. This process of the tragic chorus is the *dramatic* proto-phenomenon: to see oneself transformed before one's own eyes and to begin to act as if one had actually entered into another body, another character" (*BT* 8; *KSA* 1.61).[13]

Transformation through vision, through having visions, is one of the chief concerns of the *Birth*. Another of Nietzsche's observations suggests that the frame renders possible a distinctive and transformative mode of vision: "A public of spectators as we know it was unknown to the Greeks: in their theaters the elevated, terraced structure of concentric arcs of the spectators' space [*Zuschauerraumes*] made it possible for everybody to actually *see beyond* [*übersehen*] the whole world of culture around him and to imagine, in absorbed contemplation, that he himself was a chorist" (*BT* 8; *KSA* 1.59). *Übersehen* is a complex verb; it can mean to overlook, either in the sense of scanning and surveying or in that of neglecting, failing to see, and forgetting. Given Nietzsche's penchant for emphasizing the active and transformative sense given by *über-* in words like *überwinden* and *Übermensch*, his *übersehen* may actually combine both of these meanings. We might also translate this term as "super-vision," if we could concentrate on the sense of an extra or excessive seeing rather than on the more usual sense of surveillance or superintendence; the position of the Athenian audience is not that of the supervisors in the Panopticon (although Foucault's analysis of the panoptical diagram owes much to Nietzsche; see secs. 60, 63). The spectators, in their specially arranged and framed space, look beyond the ordinary world of their culture to imagine themselves one with the chorus, whose spectacle they see, and to see the visions that the chorus sees as if they were their own (the spectators'). This would not be a mere neglect or failure to see the surroundings (their neighbors or whatever of the city might be visible from their seats); it would rather be akin to the "active forgetfulness" that Nietzsche celebrates in *On the Genealogy of Morals* (*GM* I.10; *KSA* 5.271). Seeing beyond may entail not only having a vision but also being able to behold a vision within a vision. At the close of section 8, Nietzsche takes the vision of Euripides' Admetus within the play *Alcestis* to be parallel to the vision that appears to the spectator in the tragic theater. He sees a veiled figure before him; filled with foreboding, he begins to anticipate something uncanny. And the figure is revealed to be Alcestis, brought back from the dead. This, Nietzsche says, is analogous to the spectator's seeing Dionysus appear on the stage after having already identified with his sufferings: "[T]he world of the day becomes veiled, and a new world, clearer, more understandable, more moving than the everyday world and yet more shadowy, presents itself to our eyes in continual rebirths" (*BT* 8; *KSA* 1.64). The framing of tragedy enables a seeing beyond; the birth of tragedy is the condition of a continual rebirth of the visionary.

Such is the fruit of the tragic architecture of the Greeks. One way in which Nietzsche differs from other philosophers who have invoked architectural terms and concepts is in his rejection of foundationalism. Descartes claimed that true philosophical building could not begin without a thorough clearing of the ground and the construction of absolutely firm foundations. When Nietzsche speaks in architectural language, he envisions the building process as much more fluid and flexible. In the essay "On Truth and Lie in an Extra-Moral Sense," composed just after *The Birth of Tragedy*, Nietzsche questions the Cartesian protocols. After describing the way in which humans attempt to stabilize the flux of perceptions by means of concepts and schemata, he describes them as builders: "As a genius of construction, the human raises himself far above the bee in the following way: whereas the bee builds with wax that he gathers from nature, the human builds with the far more delicate conceptual material which he first has to manufacture from himself."[14] Yet this construction has no firm foundation; every human architecture (whether in stone or in ideas) builds on the shifting sands of perception, custom, climate, and culture. If the Greeks achieved something unusual in their theatrical architecture, they did so, like all builders, in contingent and hazardous circumstances. And if Nietzsche sometimes becomes enthusiastic about vast, monumental architecture that seems to build for an eternity, part of his admiration lies in his realization that none of these structures are necessary; none will last forever, none are ordained by the nature of things.

Given Nietzsche's use of Euripides at this critical point in the argument of the *Birth*, and his reliance on the *Bacchae* for his portrayal of Dionysus, in which that play is seen as a retraction of the main thrust of Euripides' work, it might be surprising that the playwright is identified with the death of tragedy. Without reiterating here everything that Nietzsche says about the fatal collusion of Euripides and Socrates in that death or assassination, recall Nietzsche's fundamental criticism of Euripides: he "brought the *spectator* onto the stage" (*BT* 11; *KSA* 1.76). Clearly, part of what Nietzsche has in mind here is that Euripides' characters are no longer the noble tragic figures of Aeschylus and Sophocles but are more like the ordinary Athenian. Yet just because of that fact, because the spectator sees someone more like his everyday self on the stage, he will not go through the complex process of identifying with the chorus and then vicariously sharing its visions. The theatrical setup, the framing, has been disrupted or deconstructed. Euripides has reframed the theater. The delicate fabric of vision has been torn apart; because the distance between spectator and character has disappeared, the audience has lost the play of multiple perspectives that tragedy briefly made possible.

Just a few paragraphs later, however, we learn that Nietzsche's first formulation of Euripides' assassination of tragedy was only provisional. Now it is said that he never respected the spectator in general, but only two, himself and Socrates. What happens when Socrates looks at tragedy? "Let us now imagine the one great Cyclops eye of Socrates fixed on tragedy, an eye in which the fair frenzy of artistic enthusiasm has never glowed. To this eye was denied the pleasure of gazing into the Dionysian abysses" (BT 14; KSA 1.92). The Cyclops eye of Socrates is not capable of the complex vision required by the tragic frame, a vision that involves *übersehen* and that identifies with the chorus so as to behold their visions through them. Just as he cannot gaze into the abyss, so he cannot dwell with the shining figures that are projected out of that abyss. He is blind to everything but the tragic plot, which he finds confused. But the apparent confusion is an error of optics or perspective: he fails to see that the plot is only one thread in a complex fabric, and he looks so intensely that he overlooks the frame and the architecture within which the plot functions. In this way Socrates also fails to see the luminous manifestations of the characters and their retreat into shadow for what they are when seen within the frame. He is neither fully sighted nor blind but monocular, a victim of his own tunnel vision. Socrates' maxims—that virtue is knowledge, that no one does wrong knowingly, that the virtuous man is the happy man—all of these establish the frame of a new setup, which could be called the theater of dialectic and virtue. This is precisely what Socrates plays out in his own life, turning himself into a theatrical figure in the Athenian *agora;* he constitutes a "new Socratic-optimistic stage world" (BT 14; KSA 1.95). Socrates' own theater was in place well before Aristophanes recognized it in The Clouds. The trial and death are only the final, most memorable act of the drama: "[T]he image of the *dying Socrates,* as the human being whom knowledge and reason have liberated from the fear of death, is the emblematic shield [*Wappenschild*] that, above the entry gate of science, reminds us all of its mission" (BT 15; KSA 1.99). Like other dramaturgs, Socrates needs to leave behind an image; if the shield of Achilles was the intense, visual condensation of the epic world, the Socratic *Wappenschild* is a vivid series of images, "the last days of Socrates," as painted by Plato (Or by Jacques-Louis David. More specifically, in a discarded draft for the *Birth*, Nietzsche compared the image of the dying Socrates to Saint John in Bernardo Luini's fresco in Lugano; KSA 14.52).[15]

Nietzsche's image of the "one great Cyclops eye of Socrates" also suggests how he might respond to recent critiques of vision by some feminist critics. Luce Irigaray, to take one prominent thinker, has sought to show that the main tradition of Western philosophy is dominated by a masculine imaginary, much of which centers on a certain visual imagination. Certainly Jacques Lacan's account of the mirror stage seems to be an appropriate target of such an analysis. Seeing himself in the mirror, and recognizing himself as the one mirrored, the infant comes to view himself as an integral and autonomous being; now he has a counterweight to the chaotic, multidirectional, and disruptive impulses, needs, and experiences that would otherwise work to fragment his sense of himself (I follow Lacan here in using masculine pronouns in order to suggest the plausibility of Irigaray's critique). On the stage of the mirror, the infant spectator sees only himself and rejoices only in himself. Irigaray suggests that Lacan's scenario is symptomatic of a fascination with the visual that has dominated Western thought at least since Plato. Vision, on her analysis, has this attraction because it lends itself to the fantasy that the viewer is independent of the object, that the eye (serving as the model for the mind's eye) is detached from what is seen in a way that the organs and experience of smell, touch, and taste can never be. Plato's praise of vision as "the noblest of the senses" appears in this context as the expression of a desire to construct the knower as hovering freely over and above the scene surveyed. In this respect Irigaray offers a powerful reading of the figures of the cave and the sun in the *Republic;* Plato's story, on this account, is aimed at suppressing the residues of dependence on the body (specifically, the maternal body) in order to constitute the soul as a pure knower. Irigaray evokes the desire underlying Platonic myth and argument:

> *Only the divine vision is without liabilities,* encompassing the All, with no trace of opaqueness left. Light that nothing resists, going through *any paraphragm,* reaching everywhere, without deviation of any sort. Ever identical to itself in its rectitude. Not allowing itself to be bent by any mirror since it knows itself throughout time (as) the one who has the most power of all. Gazing upon itself (as) that which in reality is brightest. Good, alien to all shadow, outshining the sun itself: its clearsightedness will never be dazzled by any stars, for it overflows that orbit, encircling the All which turns around in the space of its field.[16]

Even Nietzsche, who said that his goal was to overturn or reverse Platonism, is described as being under the sway of similar fantasies. In

Irigaray's lyrical love letter to Nietzsche, one that at times expresses that knowing anger and rage reserved for lovers, she (or her persona) suggests that he too is still a victim of the masculine imaginary, and in its specifically visual form. If the sea is the counterpart to the empire of the air, which is the place of Zarathustra's (and Nietzsche's) phantasmatic transcendence, it is a place of depths and multiplicity that will always foil the simplistic gaze: "The sea shines with a myriad eyes. And none is given any privilege. Even here and now she undoes all perspective. Countless and shifting and merging her depths. And her allure is an icy shroud for the point of view."[17] Allusively, Irigaray seems to suggest that even Nietzsche's perspectivism is not subtle enough to do justice to the complexity of the sea (or feminine) which is both radiant and of impenetrable depths.

However, Nietzsche's perspectivism does constitute a serious challenge to the Socratic, Cyclopean vision. Suspicious of the monocular, disembodied simplifications of the philosophical tradition, he insists on the (at least) double point of view of the tragic spectator, and he offers a way of understanding vision that departs from the Platonic tradition. The earlier Athenian audience, Nietzsche claims, does *not* see itself on the stage; that was the innovation of Euripides, which Socrates turned into an interpretation of the Delphic "know thyself." What was deficient about that project was its narrow conception of what the self might be, as well as its assumption that it would yield itself up to an internal vision as it seemed to do on the Euripidean stage. In Nietzsche's account the spectators see as if they were in two distinct positions; they get outside of themselves (they are ecstatic) because of their multiple perspective. This may be the first statement of Nietzsche's perspectivism; if so, it is permeated with the visual dimension of that notion, even more explicitly than are the later forms of that idea. This constitutes a revisioning of vision, suggesting that it is not sight itself that is necessarily complicit with the masculine imaginary as described by Irigaray. We might even find Nietzsche in a certain agreement with Irigaray, for the figure of the Cyclops seems to intimate something of the phallus in its most unreflective mode. The Cyclopes of the *Odyssey* live solitary, brutish lives, and what vision they have is at the mercy of circumstances, or more specifically, dependent upon the action of the wily Odysseus, the man of many turns *(polytropos)*, who is adept with the multiple meanings of the symbolic. There would be a delicious irony in Nietzsche's identifying Socrates, the paradigmatic hero of reflection and self-knowledge, with the blind and blinded Cyclops, who seems to embody the crudest form of desire. What is at stake, I am hoping to insinuate, is not the question of contrasting a deluded, self-important vision with the other allegedly more sensitive and nuanced senses, but the possibility that there are other ways of experiencing and theorizing the visual than are found in philosophy's mirror stage or Cyclopean perspective.

30 Postclassical Framing

According to Nietzsche's narrative, once Socratic and Alexandrian culture is constituted, it produces its own artistic and theatrical forms. The paradigm of these is "*the culture of the opera*," which could give its name to the entire era (*BT* 19; *KSA* 1.120). While Nietzsche takes the defining characteristic of opera, that is, of its frame or setup, to be the fact that speech dominates its music, a key symptom of the degeneracy of the operatic genre is its inability to generate visions; this deficiency leads it to substitute laboriously manufactured images in their place. (In reading these analyses, we need to keep in mind the German sense of *Vision*, as opposed to *Bild*; the former always suggests something visionary, something beyond the everyday power of sight.) On the one hand, "[b]ecause [the creator of the opera] is unable to behold a vision, he forces the machinist and the decorative artist into his service" (*BT* 19; *KSA* 1.123). On the other hand, in "a true musical tragedy" (like Wagner's), things become "sensuously visible, as it were, like a multitude of vividly moving lines and figures" (*BT* 22; *KSA* 1.140). Tragic culture, Nietzsche has already proclaimed, depends not only upon a rebirth of music *simpliciter*, but on a music that accepts its destiny of producing visions and images. "Music at its highest stage must seek to attain also to its highest objectification in images [*Verbildlichung*]" (*BT* 16; *KSA* 1.108).

While one line of thought in *The Birth of Tragedy* would draw a sharp distinction between the Apollonian and the Dionysian and would appeal to the authority of Schopenhauer to establish the absolute independence of music from the visual and phenomenal world, another tendency (also sometimes appealing to Schopenhauer) insists on the complicity of music and image, as here. Part of the complexity of Nietzsche's argument, which is essential for understanding his conception of the frame of tragedy, as well as its alternatives and successors (Euripides, Socrates, the opera), has to do with the separability of two elements or dimensions of the Apollonian. Apollo is said at various times to be the god of images and visions and also of the *principium individuationis*. But in the actual "strife" and "reconciliation" of Apollo and Dionysus that is tragedy (to recall again the book's first line), images and visions function precisely in order to contest any presumed autonomy and independence of the individual: "In several successive discharges [*Entladungen*] the primal ground of tragedy radiates this vision of the drama which is by all means a dream apparition [*Traumerscheinung*] and to that extent epic in nature, but on the other hand, being the objectification of a Dionysian state, it represents not Apollonian redemption through mere appearance but, on the contrary, the shattering of the individual and his fusion with primal being" (*BT* 8; *KSA* 1.62).

Perhaps the most general contrast between tragedy and the other forms of theater or framings has to do with the status of the individual. The question to which tragedy is the answer goes something like this: how can images and visions be deployed, apparently contrary to their original tendency, in order to subvert the status of individuality? If we were to look for a theatrical analysis of the opposition between Dionysus and the Crucified that Nietzsche poses so frequently, it might hinge on the way in which Christ retains his individuality, an individuality reinforced by his solitary presence on the cross and his resurrection. It is a process that Nietzsche explores again in *On the Genealogy of Morals*, where he contrasts the cultural ethos of the ancient theater with the civilized man who turns his aggression against himself. All antiquity was oriented to the spectator of an "essentially public, visible world which cannot imagine happiness apart from spectacles and festivals." But in civilization man turns against himself; for the external festival, he substitutes an internal theater of cruelty or a "torture chamber," one in which self-laceration reaches such heights that "divine spectators were needed to do justice to the spectacle" (*GM* II.7; *KSA* 5.305). The philosophical versions of this internal theater range from Stoic imperatives to examine our conduct and emotions to Augustine's explicit repudiation of pagan theater in favor of the internal theater of reflection, repentance, and confession to the "metaphor" of the mind as a dark chamber or camera obscura in empiricist philosophy, where each of us examines the contents of what passes before us on our own stage. As Schopenhauer formulates it, things are no more outside us than objects in the theater are outside the theater.[18] The process of theatrical subjectification began with Euripides and continues in what Nietzsche, after the enthusiasm for Wagner had died, called "theatrocracy," a condition in which theater is elevated over the other arts and in which theater panders to the lowest common denominator of the audience; here theater becomes a "revolt of the masses."[19]

About a year after publishing *The Birth of Tragedy*, Nietzsche wrote a brief account of his search for an "honest [*ehrlich*]" position in relation to ancient tragedy (*KSA* 7.565–69). The untitled text coincides with the time of the controversy between Wilamowitz and Rohde; the former had attacked the *Birth* in a pamphlet called *Zukunftsphilologie* (parodying Wagner's *Zukunftsmusik*), and Nietzsche's friend had replied, accusing Wilamowitz of philological indiscretions of his own, in an essay entitled *Afterphilologie*, which might be translated as *Assbackwards philology*. Nietzsche was also concerned that his teacher and sponsor, Ritschl, found the *Birth* too undisciplined, and his essay reads as if it were directed to a skeptical but not entirely unsympathetic reader like Ritschl. He says that the difficulty of establishing such a position is enormous and must contend with the "monstrous defect" that we do not see the tragedies as performed but must reconstruct them from texts. The danger is that the enthusiastic reader will project contemporary concerns or personal fantasies onto these texts. In this situation perhaps the best that can be done is to admit our hermeneutic distance from the Greeks and acknowledge our need of some mediating voice. Nietzsche provides an intriguing set of alternative perspectives that can be employed in this way. Most contemporary scholars use Goethe as a guide to the Greeks, he says, while others seek the aid of Raphael. Certainly Winckelmann and the line of German criticism that he helped to inspire could be seen as approaching the Greeks through a conception of Raphael's classicism, while those who followed Goethe emphasized the naturalness of the Greeks and celebrated their freedom from Christian guilt. But Nietzsche's own path was to understand ancient tragedy through his experience of Wagner's operas, and he specifically cites a summer 1872 performance of *Tristan*. He was immediately struck by the vast difference between modern theater (with actors in Shakespearean or Schillerian roles) and Wagner, with respect to their sculptural presentation ("nach der *plastischen* Seite der Darstellung"). In other words, what Nietzsche observed in Wagner had to do with what he *saw* on the Wagnerian stage, the gestures, movements, and postures of the performers, which he describes in this way: "Quite independently of the talent of the actors, an involuntary effort was noticeable to preserve a *quiet grandeur* even in the most passionate moments: in essence one saw noble, soberly moved, for the most part almost motionless sculptural groups. It occurred to me that modern restlessness had surrendered to the sculptural impulse [*Plastik*]." Nietzsche suggests that Wagnerian music has the effect of slowing down gestures and movement, while the traditional opera, with its stretches of recitative, speeds them up. The *"quiet grandeur"* to which he refers alludes to Winckelmann's notion of the Greeks as a people of "noble simplicity and quiet grandeur [*edle Einfalt und stille Grösse*]." While the Wagnerian experience leads him to hope for a great future for "our sculptural pursuits," the opera now appears useless for this and is in fact complicit with the degeneration of modern culture: "On the other hand, the opera was completely unsuited to foster a purification of the sculptural sense: for its singers were instruments with clothing, its movements fundamentally indifferent and therefore determined by convention. Or rather, one could say that the moderns, seduced by their favorite art of opera, have accustomed themselves to conventional expression in dress, gesture, and so on: that the [royal] courts are imitations of the world of the opera and that gradually the entire civilized world has become the pale imitation of an earlier courtly culture" (*KSA* 7.567). Aeschylean drama must have made an impression similar to that of the Wagnerian, Nietzsche continues. The movements of the actors were slow and dignified and emphasized their distance from the spectators. He even infers that Aeschylus's sculptural scenes must have been the preliminary stage of the work of Phidias, "because the plastic arts always follow after a beautiful reality with slow steps" (*KSA* 7.568). The argument, then, is that fifth-century tragedy is the origin of sculpture like that of the Parthenon, just as the opera is to blame for the ignoble gestures and attire of the modern world. However implausible these explanations may appear, they show that Nietzsche attributes an enormous importance and influence to what is seen on the stage, whether of tragedy or daily life. Closer to Plato than he might comfortably acknowledge, he insists on the formative significance of the visual scenes produced by the arts. He first formulated some ideas along these lines several years earlier, while reading Gottfried Semper, an architect and aesthetic theorist associated with Wagner. In 1869 Nietzsche celebrates Aeschylus as a fashion designer: "Aeschylus discovered the elegance and dignity of the toga, in which the priests and the torchbearers followed him. Previously the Greeks had dressed barbarously and were not acquainted with the freely falling garment" (*KSA* 7.15).

In *Richard Wagner in Bayreuth*, Nietzsche continues to emphasize the plastic dimension of Wagnerian art. Wagner will renew not only music, in the narrower sense, but also the visual culture of modernity. Music and the realm of the visual are two aspects or manifestations of a single thing, like Schopenhauer's will and representation: "The relationship between music and life is not only that of one kind of language to another kind of language, it is also the relationship between the perfect world of sound and the totality of the world of sight. Regarded as a phenomenon for the eyes, however, and compared with the phenomena of life of earlier times, the existence of modern man exhibits an unspeakable poverty and exhaustion, despite the unspeakable gaudiness which can give pleasure only to the most superficial glance" (*RW* 5; *KSA* 1.456). Wagner is said to have discovered that the soul of music wants a body and that it reaches out to gymnastic, as did Greek music. In his work the visible becomes audible, and "all that is audible in the world likewise wants to emerge into the light and also become a phenomenon for the eye. . . . His art always conducts him along this twofold path, from a world as an audible spectacle [*Hörspiel*] into a world as visible spectacle [*Schauspiel*] enigmatically related to it, and the reverse." He further pronounces that "this constitutes the essence of the *dithyrambic dramatist*" and that it is "necessarily derived from the only perfect exemplar of the dithyrambic artist before Wagner, from Aeschylus and his fellow Greek artists" (*RW* 7; *KSA* 1.467).

Nietzsche seems to have come a long way from the thesis he argued in "On Music and Words," namely that the visible cannot produce the musical out of itself. What was once a one-way bridge has become a bustling intersection, with Wagner as flamboyant traffic cop. While Nietzsche might seem to be summarizing the thought of *The Birth of Tragedy*, he is both underlining the importance that the visual has there and according a generative power to the visual that he had explicitly denied it before. Although the *Birth* does not openly formulate Nietzsche's "one-way bridge" principle, it still abides by it. Nietzsche is drawn in this direction because he is writing of Wagner *in Bayreuth*, that is, in his own theater. The musician has established a site, he has produced an architecture, and now he has the apparatus to produce his own images as well as his own music.

Yet, at the time of writing *Wagner in Bayreuth*, Nietzsche had not yet beheld anything in this theater. On the basis of a few performances, especially one of *Tristan* in 1872, he is having a dreamy, phantasmatic experience. He projects his image of the successful theater. Perhaps he imagines himself as a *theoros*, the ambassador sent to observe the Greek games, since he emphasizes the kinship between what he hopes to see in Bayreuth and ancient gymnastics. If *The Birth of Tragedy* was the apologia for *Zukunftsmusik*, *Richard Wagner in Bayreuth* is the prolegomenon to a vision and an epiphany.

If we are to have such visions, it is only because the artist himself is a seer. It is in his light that we shall see the light of what will shine forth on the stage. Nietzsche describes the dithyrambic artist as a solar eye, a glance that illuminates and transforms: "His glance [*Blick*] falls *at once clear-sighted and lovingly selfless:* and everything he now illuminates with the twofold light of this glance is at once compelled by nature to discharge all its forces with fearful rapidity in a revelation of its most deeply hidden secrets: and it does so out of shame." We might be tempted to suppose that Nietzsche has merely adopted the familiar rhetoric of vision that typically accompanies any talk of revelation. That, together with his hyperbole, might lead us to ignore the possibility that he is making specific claims about the forms of dithyrambic visuality. But Nietzsche is concerned that we not read him this way, for he immediately continues: "It is more than a figure of speech [*Bild*] to say that with this glance he has surprised nature, that he has seen her naked: so that now she seeks to conceal her shame by fleeing into her antitheses. What has hitherto been invisible and inward escapes into the sphere of the visible and becomes appearance; what was hitherto only visible flees into the dark ocean of the audible: *thus, by seeking to hide herself, nature reveals the character of her antitheses.*" (*RW* 7; *KSA* 1.471). It is not just an image to say that the artist is responsible for extraordinary images. Wagner, or the dithyrambic artist, works at the point of exchange between the visible and the invisible, at what Merleau-Ponty would describe as their chiasm.

Artists of the highest kind, like Aeschylus and Wagner, are "sculptors [*Bildner*]," and the eyes of such plastic artists see the miracle of "a new visible world" (*RW* 9; *KSA* 1.490). Yet here Nietzsche seems to implicitly concede that there is something figurative about the title of sculptor, for he imagines that Wagner's work must inspire the jealousy of the plastic artist (one might find an affirmative instance of such agonistics in Kandinsky's relation to Wagner).[20] Nietzsche is reflective with regard to his terminology. He is speaking both from within and against a tradition in which arguments concerning the definition of the arts and their interrelations are prominent (as in Lessing, Hegel, and Schopenhauer). Yet Wagner must be thought of as an event, a disruption of geological proportion in relation to the conventional and philosophical distinction and system of the arts: "[H]is appearance in the history of the arts is like a volcanic eruption of the total undivided artistic capacity of nature itself after humanity had accustomed itself to seeing the arts isolated from one another as though this were an eternal rule. One can thus be undecided which name to accord him, whether he should be called a poet or a sculptor or a musician, each word taken in an extraordinarily wide sense, or whether a new word has to be created to describe him" (*RW* 9; *KSA* 1.485). As if to intensify the theme of the interconnection of the visual arts with others, Nietzsche invokes Raphael's *Saint Cecilia* once more. In a somewhat complicated figure, the image of the saint is to tell us something about how music enjoys itself when it has successfully surrounded itself with a magic circle. The happiest moments in music, found always in Wagner and occasionally in earlier works, are "rare moments of forget-fulness, when it speaks to itself alone and, like Raphael's Saint Cecilia, directs its glance away from its listeners, who demand of it only distrac-tion, merriment or scholarliness" (*RW* 9; *KSA* 1.490). Earlier the image was deployed in order to make vivid and visible the barrier between painting and music, and then between vocal and instrumental music. Now Cecilia is the musician who is transfixed by the music and oblivi-ous of her audience. Yet in Raphael's painting, Cecilia has no listeners to ignore, because her instruments lie broken and scattered at her feet. True, she is shown as raptly attentive to the music of this world, but it is the music of the angelic choir. The invocation of the painting pro-vides a visual equivalent of total absorption.

Yet it was not this absorption that Nietzsche experienced at Bay-reuth in July and August 1876. He was ill and his eyes troubled him terribly. What did he see and what did he fail to see? Nietzsche had been diffident about publishing *Richard Wagner in Bayreuth* and did so only after Heinrich Köselitz (Peter Gast) became involved in the project, taking dictation for parts of the manuscript. He completed the es-say in June 1876, and it was published in July, to coincide with the first opening of the Bayreuth festival. Already ill, Nietzsche seems to have been further unsettled by Bayreuth. The Wagners were consumed by their work on all aspects of the production, including replacing some of the performers and monitoring the income from ticket sales. Nietzsche was unable to stay for an entire rehearsal of *Götterdämmer-ung*. A few days later he attended the rehearsal of *Die Walküre* but left before the end. He explained in a letter to Elisabeth the next day: "Things are not right with me, I can see that! Continuous headache, though not of the worst kind, and lassitude. Yesterday I was able to listen to *Die Walküre*, but only in a dark room—to use my eyes is impossible [*alles Sehen unmöglich*]! I long to get away; it is too sense-less to stay. I dread every one of these long artistic evenings; yet I go to them" (*B* 5.181). Nietzsche escaped for a week to a boardinghouse in the small town of Klingenbrunn. He finally felt well enough to re-turn to Bayreuth, but all the signs are that he continued to be deeply unhappy with what he saw. Later in *Ecce Homo*, Nietzsche explains his response, dating the turn in his thought that led to *Human, All Too Human* to this time: "The beginnings of this book belong right in the midst of the first *Bayreuther Festspiele;* a profound alienation from everything that surrounded me there is one of its preconditions. Whoever has any notion of the visions [*Visionen*] I had encountered even before that, may guess how I felt when one day I woke up in Bayreuth. As if I were dreaming!" (*EH, HAH,* 2; *KSA* 6.323).

Nietzsche wrote *Wagner in Bayreuth* as a preparatory text for an initiatory vision set in a new sacred space. Like Aeschylus, Wagner was going to put on a display in which *Hörspiel* and *Schauspiel* were intricately interwoven; the spectacle was to serve as a model that might transform German reality. Perhaps this would begin with the way in which we present our images of ourselves in clothing and gesture, counteracting the deleterious effects of the opera and following the example of Aeschylus, who is credited with discovering the mobile architectural possibilities of the toga. Nietzsche had experienced such visions, as he says; but they were shown to have been nothing but dreams, private dreams or fantasies rather than the public dreams expected from a great artist.[21]

From the standpoint of *Ecce Homo,* all of those dreams and visions were projected onto Wagner. Nietzsche claims that he was really writing about himself, and proleptically of himself as the author of *Zarathustra.* "Instinctively," he says, "I had to transpose and transfigure [*transfiguriren*] everything into the new spirit I carried in me." Again it is a question of transfiguration, this time of what happens on the Wagnerian stage. Nietzsche could not put his reconstruction of the visual dynamics of ancient tragedy to the test by taking a seat in the Greek theater; his vision of its transfiguring power was safe. Yet what he saw as the fiasco of Bayreuth—the worst excesses of German philistinism—required an explanation, one that was only possible retrospectively, in line with his principle that in order to become what one is, one must not know what one is. For Nietzsche claims that he became the dithyrambic artist whom he had constructed out of the figures of Aeschylus and Wagner. Referring to *Wagner in Bayreuth,* he says: "[I]n all psychologically decisive places I alone am discussed—and one need not hesitate to put down my name or the word 'Zarathustra' where the text has the word 'Wagner.' The entire picture of the dithyrambic artist is a picture of the pre-existent poet of *Zarathustra,* sketched with abysmal profundity and without touching even for a moment the Wagnerian reality" (*EH, BT* 4; *KSA* 6.314). The "idea of Bayreuth," he continues, was a stand-in for the great noon, possibly "the vision of a festival that I shall yet live to see." And when Nietzsche rereads his earlier essay, what he finds as a proleptic analysis of *Zarathustra* is the account of his look, his glance. "The glance [*Blick*] spoken of in the seventh section is Zarathustra's distinctive glance. . . . At the beginning of section 9 the style of *Zarathustra* is described with incisive certainty and anticipated."[22] Here Nietzsche gives us some very specific directions to read certain passages of the Wagner essay as sketches of the poetics of *Zarathustra*, the book he regards as his greatest gift to humanity. These directions focus first on the glance, which he tells us is not just a figure of speech. Through his glance the artist sets up the exchange of the visible and the invisible, inaugurating a form of art that is not limited to conventionally distinct genres. The dithyrambic poet cannot be comprehended by divisions like those that Lessing makes between poetry and painting. Second, Nietzsche tells us that we should take the discussion of the difficulty of defining Wagner as poet, sculptor, or musician as a description of himself. And insofar as Wagner/Nietzsche is a poet, that passage declares, "he thinks in visible and palpable events, not in concepts." All of this suggests that the hopes, dreams, and fantasies having to do with an art that synthesized visionary images, music, and poetry is to be seen as realized in *Zarathustra*. Nietzsche is inviting us to read that book in a way that takes into account its visionary aspect. This is a challenge, for while *Zarathustra* has been read for what seemed to be abstractable theses, or appreciated (and condemned) for its hyperbolic style, and even compared to the libretto of an opera that would rival Wagner, it has not been seen as a work that explores and exploits the visual and visionary possibilities with which Nietzsche's dithyrambic artist works. Yet, as we shall see, the eye is not only active in *Zarathustra*; the glance of the eye, its many variations, and the very twinkling of the eye are among its chief themes.

five

In the Twinkling of an Eye: Zarathustra on the Gaze and the Glance

32 The Optics of Value

A classical strand in the philosophical tradition takes vision to be either a form of pure contemplation and unmediated spectatorial knowledge or at least the best analog that we have of these in our daily life. This is the tendency that finds expression in Plato's designating sight as "the noblest of the senses" or in Aristotle's constant appeal to the visual along the lines of the opening page of the *Metaphysics,* where he takes the delight we take in seeing to open up the path to speculation (contemplative mirroring) of being qua being: "All men by nature desire to know. An indication of this is the delight we take in our senses; for even apart from their usefulness they are loved for themselves; and above all others the sense of sight. For not only with a view to action, but even when we are not going to do anything, we prefer seeing (one might say) to everything else. The reason is that this, most of all the senses, makes us know and brings to light many differences between things."[1] Call this position ocularcentrism, as a number of critics have done. (Let us leave for another day the question whether Aristotle's "one might say" could mitigate the charge.) Other thinkers, especially in the twentieth century, have found that this model of vision is not only misleading but dangerous; one could mention Heidegger, Dewey, and Wittgenstein. Ocularcentrism presents vision as misleading in its assumption of a contemplative, unmediated, and decontextualized position; it would be dangerous insofar as it led us to imagine that the theoretical activity *(theoria)* was not imbued with desire and did not function as part of the gestures of power. The danger is that we take an interested, historically situated activity to be more or less than that and so preclude the possibility of a critical reflection on what our vision—meaning here either one of the senses or the theoretical venture itself—is doing. Since many of these criticisms claim a Nietzschean inspiration, it is not altogether surprising to find him advancing a similar critique. But if Nietzsche breaks with the ocularcentric tradition, he does so not in order to replace vision with the other senses, notably smell and hearing, as Eric Blondel comes close to suggesting, but in order to rethink what vision is.[2] In "On Immaculate Perception" (whose title parodies the Christian "immaculate conception"), Zarathustra denounces those who advocate a doctrine of pure sensory and theoretical vision as conscious or unconscious hypocrites. He constructs an astronomical parable or metaphor *(Gleichniss):* the moon has a bad conscience because he is not the pure reflection of the sun but is actually lecherous and jealous, wanting to share the nocturnal joys of lovers; similarly, the partisans of "immaculate perception" are full of the desire of the voyeur, a desire nonetheless, even if it refrains from immediate action:

> "This would be the highest to my mind"—thus says your lying
> spirit to itself—"to look at life without desire and not, like a dog,
> with my tongue hanging out. To be happy in looking, with a will
> that has died and without the grasping and greed of selfishness, the
> whole body cold and ashen, but with drunken moon eyes. This I
> should like best"—thus the seduced seduces himself—"to love the
> earth as the moon loves her, and to touch her beauty only with my
> eyes. And this is what the immaculate perception of all things shall
> mean to me: that I want nothing from them, except to be allowed
> to lie prostrate before them like a mirror with a hundred eyes."
> (Z II.15; *KSA* 4.157)

This alludes to Schopenhauer, who idealized the moon as symbolizing "a purely knowing consciousness."[3]

In the *Genealogy*, Nietzsche speaks of his project of a "physiology of aesthetics," a work that was never completed (*GM* III.8; *KSA* 5.356). But the idea surfaces in a number of the notes from the last two years of his writing. We could read *The Case of Wagner* as containing some hints toward a *Prolegomena to Any Future Aesthetics*, for Nietzsche will describe the basic concepts and questions of that pursuit in the epilogue as explicable in terms of ascending and descending life. Every age either embodies "the virtues of ascending life," or it "represents declining life." Each age seeks its own forms of life and expression, and each resists what characterizes the other. In summary fashion he says: "Aesthetics is tied indissolubly to these biological presuppositions: there is an aesthetics of *decadence* and there is a *classical* aesthetics— the 'beautiful in itself' [*Schönes an sich*] is a figment of the imagination, like all of idealism." So Nietzsche suggests that we require a fully embodied aesthetics, one that celebrates those forms of art that justify themselves solely "out of abundance, out of the overflowing richness of strength." What might this embodied, nonidealistic, anti-idealistic aesthetics look like? (Are there tastes of such a transvalued aesthetics in the post-Nietzschean twentieth-century aesthetics of an embodied subject—or experience—in John Dewey and Maurice Merleau-Ponty?) If we were to explore it further, we would surely want to understand its philosophical sensorium, what it has to say about the various senses and the way in which art cultivates, tranquilizes, intensifies, confuses, or challenges these. And then we would need to make sense of such remarks as these, also in the epilogue, just a paragraph past where we left Nietzsche denying the existence of a *Schönes an sich*. Having contrasted master morality with the morality of Christian value concepts, Nietzsche describes them as different forms of "optics" that must be understood as such. "These opposite forms in the optics of value are *both* necessary: they are ways of seeing, immune to reasons and refutations. One cannot refute Christianity; one cannot refute a disease of the eye" (*CW*, epilogue; *KSA* 6.51). As early as *The Birth of Tragedy*, Nietzsche had spoken of the "transfigured world of the eye." If Nietzsche did not develop the physiological aesthetics that he promised at the end of his career, he did write a narrative of the embodied eye and its glance in *Thus Spoke Zarathustra*. Kant and Hegel had made it clear within idealistic aesthetics that vision and hearing were the exclusively theoretical senses; in what follows I explore Nietzsche's alternative to this tradition, which he sees as another form of a disorder of the eye.

As we have seen, what recurs in recurrence is the *Augenblick,* the twinkling of the eye or moment of vision (sec. 10). English translations of
Nietzsche usually render this word simply as "moment," and so fail
to capture any of its visual associations. And while it is true that there
are many uses of the word in colloquial German in which those associations seem submerged or irrelevant, I suggest that they are not irrelevant in reading Nietzsche's highly poetic texts. Recall that in his early
writings he argued that poetry has an Apollonian tendency to evoke
visual images. So if he consistently employs a set of images, explicitly
concerned with variations on visual and optical themes, in a work whose
central teaching is sometimes said to be the eternal recurrence of the
Augenblick, we should attend to that imagery. Indeed, the passage in
"On the Vision and the Riddle" in which the thought of recurrence
first becomes explicit in *Zarathustra* involves a very definite visual scenario. On the way to reading that passage about what he elsewhere
calls the uncanny Medusa's head of eternal recurrence, we should see
how Nietzsche prepares the ground for this teaching about the meaning
of the twinkling of the eye—that which either can be dismissed without
a thought or can prove surprisingly momentous.

One noteworthy place in which Nietzsche's significant term enters
into German writing is in Luther's translation of the Bible. In Paul's
first letter to the Corinthians, we are told, as Luther renders it: "Siehe,
ich sage euch ein Geheimnis; Wir werden nicht alle entschlafen, wir
werden alle verwandelt werden; und das plötzlich, in einem Augenblick,
zur Zeit der letzten Posaune. Denn die Posaune wird erschallen, und die
Toten werden auferstehen unverweslich, und wir werden verwandelt
werden" (1 Cor. 15:51–52). The King James is similar: "Behold, I shew
you a mystery; We shall not all sleep, but we shall all be changed, In
a moment, in the twinkling of an eye [ῥιπῇ ὀφθαλμοῦ], at the last
trump: for the trumpet shall sound, and the dead shall be raised incorruptible, and we shall be changed" (the German *verwandelt* can be read
as "transformed," which has a stronger sense than "changed" and so
would be better suited to Nietzsche's appropriation of the term). Let
us consider the possibility that Paul's twinkling of the eye and Luther's
Augenblick continue to resonate in Nietzsche's use of the term. It has
frequently been observed that on one level all of *Thus Spoke Zarathustra* can be read as a parodic doubling of the Bible; and the Bible in
question is clearly the Lutheran one with which Nietzsche, son and
grandson of Lutheran pastors, had grown up. Parables about the eye
and metaphorical associations of bodily vision with spiritual vision are

constants throughout the Bible, and Jesus' healing of the blind can be taken as a way of making concrete the idea of a spiritual awakening. When the Jews dispute about whether Jesus is possessed, by a devil or demon, some ask rhetorically whether a demon can open the eyes of the blind (John 10:21). It is tempting to read the aphorism from *The Gay Science* that first announces the idea of eternal recurrence (*GS* 341; *KSA* 3.570) as a response to this talk about demons and blinding. Now it is a demon who whispers to us in our loneliest loneliness, insinuating that the glance of the eye recurs infinitely; that demon has the function of awakening us, of making the scales drop from our eyes. Many of the Bible's stories have to do with visions, dreams, and their interpretation and so lend themselves to representations like Raphael's *Transfiguration*. The title of *Thus Spoke Zarathustra* tells us that it contains and is about speeches; many of these speeches, too, are accounts of visions.

The moment of vision, this twinkling of the eye, is momentous for both Paul and Nietzsche. Paul is thinking of a unique and singular transformation, one that marks an absolute boundary between a "before" and an "after." Nietzsche thinks the *Augenblick* more generically; life or experience is a collection or assemblage of such moments, and the thought of recurrence does not encourage us to think of just one of these as a decisive hinge, unless it is that time when we are struck by the thought of recurrence itself or the "great noon," when it is suggested that the thought becomes decisive for humanity as a whole. Even these suggestions of a singular moment of vision must be qualified by the understanding of the thought of recurrence, which declares that *every Augenblick*, because it recurs eternally, is infinitely deep. In this sense Nietzsche's "most abysmal thought" would undermine any theory or approach that separates the parts of a life into a "before" and an "after." Yet because every moment is infinitely deep, we are invited to see it as such; in this sense every Nietzschean *Augenblick* can be as decisive, as momentous, as Paul's twinkling of the eye.[4] But granted this difference, what is it that leads Paul, Luther, and Nietzsche to employ a term with a specifically visual connotation? Perhaps nothing more is at stake than the designation of a brief period of time, something like the shortest perceivable duration, a phenomenological unit or slice of experience. In Paul's case (and a fortiori in that of his translator) we may assume that he is drawing on the long-standing association of vision with revelation, as in the saying that "now we see through a glass darkly, but then we shall see face to face." In the twinkling of an eye we will rise, in incorruptible bodies, which will be seen and recognized for what they are. On one reading, Nietzsche would be playing upon and extending this association of vision and revelation; now, with Emerson, he would be finding a way of pronouncing every moment holy or visionary.[5] Yet if this were all that was in question, why would Nietzsche have set the scene so carefully, embedding what is arguably his fullest account of the thought of recurrence in a chapter entitled "On the Vision and the Riddle [*Vom Gesicht und Räthsel*]," in a narrative that emphasizes its visual setting, includes a dispute over the meaning of a visual scene (the gateway inscribed *Augenblick*), and in which we are challenged by being asked "Is not seeing itself—seeing abysses?"

From the very beginning of *Zarathustra*, vision is in question. It is not just that there are the conventional associations between seeing and knowing that have been with us at least since Plato, but we hear of various types of the eye, notably the "evil eye" and its others, quiet or radiant eyes. Scenes like the one just described are set, and visual things or experiences—artifacts, dreams, visions—become subjects of close attention and interpretation.

Zarathustra's first speech, after ten years of silence, begins with an address to an eye, that is, to the sun. After comparing himself to this "overrich star" because he too has a need to "give away and distribute," he invokes a solar benediction: "So bless me then, you quiet eye that can look upon an all-too-great happiness without envy" (Z, prologue, 1; *KSA* 4.12).[6] The sun sees all; it is Apollo's star and it radiates without discrimination. It gives away its light and heat indifferently; at the end of the series of speeches that constitute part 1 of *Zarathustra*, there is a long discourse on "The Gift-Giving Virtue," in which Zarathustra offers an elaborate analysis of why gold is seen as the most valuable substance: "Because it is uncommon and useless and gleaming and gentle in its splendor; it always gives itself. Only as the image of the highest virtue did gold attain the highest value. Goldlike gleams the glance [*Blick*] of the giver" (Z I.22.1; *KSA* 4.97). Zarathustra is speaking about the golden handle of a staff given him as a farewell gift by his disciples; the handle represents a serpent coiled around the sun. So giving and solar radiance are connected at both the beginning and end of this series of speeches (like a cycle of the sun, perhaps) with the story of an eye. It is a quiet eye, one that gleams without envy. As the narrative of Zarathustra's adventures unfolds, the significance of such an eye becomes clearer, for it is contrasted with the eye of envy, or the "evil eye." In the world of *Thus Spoke Zarathustra*, we come to know someone by looking into their eyes and seeing whether they are radiant or envious. That a look can be full of meaning, that one can see depths in the eyes of the other, is a common conviction, but not one that is typically taken as thematic by philosophers. Here is Nietzsche describing the phenomenology of the glance or the look in his notebooks two years before the composition of *Zarathustra*: "'The soul is in the *eyes*': the accustomed form of movements and associated muscular contractions betrays what the eyes are usually used for. Thinkers have a full, clear, or piercing look [*Blick*]; the eye of the anxious person shies away *completely* from looking ahead straightforwardly; the envious one looks on sideways and wants to grab something. Even when we don't want to see in the service of these feelings, the position of the eyes still indicates the customary attitude" (*KSA* 9.24, 1[79]). Such recognitions are everywhere in *Zarathustra*. Just a few examples: the eyes of the lustful betray that they know nothing better than sex; "out of the eyes of your judges there always looks the executioner and his cold steel"; the "contorted eyes" of the priests reveal their shame and devotion; some lazily and self-righteously name their indolence as virtue and show this through their sleepy eyes, while others who cannot see anything high in man "call their evil eye virtue."[7] Many of the figures that Zarathustra encounters respond to something that they see in his eyes. The adder that bites him "recognized the eyes of Zarathustra, writhed awkwardly, and wanted to get away" (Z I.19; *KSA* 4.87); in the land of those who practice a virtue that makes small, Zarathustra's eyes give him away: "I walk among this people and I keep my eyes open: they do not forgive me that I do not envy their virtues. . . . And recently a woman tore back her child when it wanted to come to me. 'Take the children away,' she cried; 'such eyes scorch children's souls'" (Z III.5.2; *KSA* 4.212). In the merest exchange of glances, there can be a strong sense that this is someone for whom one has the deepest affinity or antipathy. After Zarathustra's address to the eye of the sun, there follows such a recognition scene with a religious hermit who saw him many years ago on his way up the mountain and whom he meets first on his descent. In his greeting the hermit declares, "Yes, I recognize Zarathustra. His eye is pure [*Rein ist seine Auge*], and around his mouth there hides no disgust" (Z, prologue, 2; *KSA* 4.12). Zarathustra is the man with a certain eye, an eye like the sun.

34 The Evil Eye and Its Radiant Other

Not every eye is pure, however. *Thus Spoke Zarathustra* is extraordinary among works of philosophy for the attention that it gives to the evil eye, or *böse Blick*. The good, pure, or quiet eye is explicitly contrasted with this envious one. The evil eye is part of an ancient and widespread set of folk beliefs. The general sense is that good fortune of any sort should be seen as something fragile and in need of protection, because there are envious agents who hate any obvious success or well-being. This envy is to be distinguished from jealousy or emulation; in jealousy we think that we deserve the honor or good that another has, while we emulate someone in order to achieve a similar good (as we might emulate an athlete). But in envy, properly speaking, we do not necessarily believe that we are equally deserving or that we are capable of attaining the goal that the other has; we simply resent the fact that the other has the good or has attained the goal. We cast an evil eye on the other's good fortune when we wish it destroyed or taken away, with no particular benefit to ourselves. In extreme cases we may even sacrifice ourselves to destroy the envied other or the good in question.[8] Nietzsche and Zarathustra recognize this as a folk belief, but that does not prevent them from endorsing it in a number of contexts. When Zarathustra condemns the "new idol" of the state, for example, he says, "Where there still is a people [*Volk*], it does not understand the state and hates it as the evil eye and the sin against customs and rights" (Z I.11; *KSA* 4.61). Speaking to the "brother" about "The Way of the Creator," Zarathustra warns him about the resentment he will attract from those whom he surpasses, which suggests the structure of the evil-eye syndrome in a nutshell: "You came close to them and yet passed by: that they will never forgive. You pass over and beyond them: but the higher you ascend, the smaller you appear to the eye of envy [*das Auge des Neids*]. But most of all they hate those who fly" (Z I.17; *KSA* 4.64). In the world of *Zarathustra*, the evil eye is regarded as a real threat, not merely as a folk superstition (Zarathustra is not above appealing to the wisdom of the people against special pleadings or superficial teachings; he does this forcefully in the pivotal chapter "On Redemption" when he replies to the hunchback who begs to be made whole. There, too, in a context having to do with natural gifts and resentment, he declares that the people are right in saying that if you take away the deformity of the cripple, you will also take away his spirit.) The meaning of vision is distorted by the envious who would like to think of themselves as the virtuous: "And some who cannot see what is high in humanity call it virtue that they see all-too-closely what is low in humanity: thus they call their evil eye virtue" (Z II.5; *KSA* 4.122). In the world of *Zarathustra*, the evil eye is always a possible threat; it may cast its gaze on anyone at any time, and it is prudent to be wary of it. There are biblical precedents; Jesus speaks several times of the evil eye, which the translators have frequently rendered simply as "envy."[9] In the parable of the laborers in the vineyard, those who were hired at the beginning of the day complain that they have received no more than those who arrived late; Jesus quotes the householder, who replies to this with "Is it not lawful for me to do what I will with mine own? Is thine eye evil because I am good?" (Matt. 20:15). The eye is also identified in the Gospels as the immediate source of sexual temptation, as in the famous passage that begins "And if thy right eye offend thee . . ." (Matt. 5:29). Zarathustra has no problem with sexual desire, and he uses the rhetoric of the eye to suggest that the true evil eye is the one that looks with hostility on the erotic. In the chapter "The Dancing Song," Zarathustra comes upon a number of girls dancing with one another, who become still and apprehensive when he appears. He reassures them that he is not the bearer of the evil eye: "Do not cease dancing, you lovely girls! No killjoy has come to you with evil eyes, no enemy of girls" (Z II.10; KSA 4.139).

To have an evil eye for something or somebody is to see that object or person in the worst possible light, to fix it with a gaze of disdain, contempt, and especially envy. It is to wish that the object of the gaze not shine forth, not be glorious, not be a center of radiance. Perhaps it is the eye that is singled out as the organ of envy because the envious are affronted by the very sight of that which arouses their hostility; they do not require an involvement by means of any of the senses that might be thought to be associated with more intimate contact. The evil eye neither sees disinterestedly nor looks on the world with joy. Beliefs and practices connected with the evil eye are pervasive in many cultures, especially those zero-sum societies in which one person's gain is necessarily another's loss. The worry that one's own luck or success will be the subject of a devouring and malicious envy is not unreasonable in those circumstances. The evil eye is reductionistic or nihilistic; it reduces whatever it sees to the lowest common denominator of sameness. If it cannot carry out its intended destruction in practice, it realizes it virtually in imagination, as Nietzsche points out in his frequent dissections of *ressentiment.* In such environments people go out of their way to conceal their good fortune from prying eyes; a beautiful, healthy child, for example, is potentially a prime target of the evil eye and can be protected by being hidden and by the use of charms or amulets, some of which are emblems of eyes. In *Mal Occhio,* Lawrence DiStasi, who grew up in a household that took for granted a belief in the evil eye, and in which an unmarried aunt practiced a cure for it, describes the attitudes that prevail in such a setting. He recounts an incident in which a beautiful baby who had been intensely admired by a stranger earlier in the day came down with a high, inexplicable fever, which then seemed to have been cured by his aunt's performing the prescribed ritual. His commentary on the episode emphasizes how normal it all seemed in the context and gives some clues as to why it is the eye that is thought of as the organ of envy (we might wonder: why should envy be localized in a particular sense?):

> [S]omeone could not help admiring the beauty of a child. That is really the idea that soaked through to the bone, that beauty and excellence attract the eye, and that the admiring eye thus attracted, no matter how benign it may appear, is *mal*, is evil, and capable of causing harm. Indeed, on the surface, or so it seemed to me at the time, beauty was as much the culprit as anything else, beauty stupidly prancing about naked, inciting all that praise. Whenever one was on display, therefore, either shining in one's best clothes, or prodded to sing or play piano or otherwise exhibit excellence, an uncomfortable feeling arose—the feeling that perhaps one would be better served by feigning a defect than yielding to perfection.[10]

At least since Plato, the eye has been thought of as the locus where beauty penetrates the soul or mind. While the Platonic tradition typically describes this entrance of beauty as the beginning of an ascent, folk wisdom is much more dubious, not because it disdains beauty but because it sees the world as pervaded by a conscious or unconscious envy of the beautiful that is centered in a monstrous eye. It is also possible to describe some rather complex religious and philosophical tendencies as forms of the evil eye. In *Twilight of the Idols*, Nietzsche says of Schopenhauer's doctrine of liberation from the will and tragic resignation that they constitute "the pessimist's perspective and 'evil eye'" (*T*, "Skirmishes," 24; *KSA* 6.127).

In "On the Tree on the Mountainside," Zarathustra offers a long discourse on envy and the evil eye. He notices—or, as the text has it, "his eye had noted"—that a youth was avoiding him. Finding him leaning against a tree, Zarathustra speaks to him in a parable:

> If I wanted to shake this tree with my hands I should not be able to do it.
> But the wind, which we do not see, tortures and bends it in whatever direction it pleases. It is by invisible hands that we are bent and tortured worst. (*Z* I.8; *KSA* 4.51)

The tree is moved by that which is not visible or tangible. Like natural motion, social and psychological motion (e-motion) need not be a response to grossly present pushes and pulls. Envy would be an exemplary case of such emotional action at a distance. Whereas love, hate, and friendship seem to presuppose some form of contact with their object, envy may thrive on absence. It is quite possible to envy those with whom I have little or no contact; their very celebration for their wealth, achievements, or power may distance them from me. The presence of the envied person may be disturbing, and so the envious one may seek to avoid this reminder of his unhappy condition. Nevertheless, the imagined superiority of the envied person will bend and torture us in the worst way; envy can become self-reinforcing, when reluctance to confront the actual figure leads the envier to further exaggeration and avoidance behavior. Elsewhere Nietzsche describes such silent envy: "Commonplace envy is accustomed to cackle as soon as the envied hen has laid an egg: it thereby relieves itself and grows gentler. But there exists a yet deeper envy: in such a case it becomes deathly silent and, wishing that every mouth would now become sealed, grows ever angrier that precisely this is what is not happening. Silent envy grows in silence" (*HAH, AOM*, 53; *KSA* 2.403). By speaking to the youth, Zarathustra aims at breaking this downward spiral of silent envy.

The young man confirms the analysis: "I hear Zarathustra, and just now I was thinking of him," he replies, standing up in confusion. That is, he confirms both Zarathustra's belief that his avoidance was due to obsession rather than indifference and the principle of emotional action at a distance, for it seems to him that his thoughts have led, as if magically, to Zarathustra's appearance. Zarathustra continues the parable of the tree, after he has attempted to calm the youth: "But it is with humanity as it is with the tree. The more strongly does it aspire to the height and light, the more strongly do its roots strive earthward, downward, into the dark, the deep—into evil." This is a dark saying, suggesting that the mutual dependence of aspiration and evil (in the form of envy) is a basic principle of human life. Some recent theories of justice, such as that of John Rawls, claim that envy can be eliminated or minimized by a system of social and economic arrangements that never rewards one group at the expense of another; but this claim, shaky enough on economic grounds, seems inadequate when we focus on such desires as those for athletic, romantic, or intellectual success.[11]

Stung by Zarathustra's saying, the young man confesses that he is disturbed and confused by the aspirations that he has stirred up in him. As he climbs higher, he finds himself alone and doubts his ambitions. He has experienced the envy of others who are suspicious of his climbing to the heights. He bursts out, "Behold, what am I, now that you have appeared among us? It is the *envy* of you that has destroyed me." Envy is socially pervasive. The youth is not only envious of the master but has experienced the envy of others. In the world of envy, the distinction between the envied and the enviers is functional and relative to specific contexts and situations. When we realize that there is no unique scale of attainment along which success or failure can be measured, we see that in many social situations, nearly everybody may be involved in envy. I may be envied for my good looks but envy others their wealth, health, social position, or any number of things. The anthropologist Oscar Lewis reports such a pervasive form of social envy, based on his observation of life in a Mexican village:

> The man who speaks little, keeps his affairs to himself, and maintains some distance between himself and others has less chance of creating enemies or of being criticized or envied. A man does not generally discuss his plans to buy or sell or take a trip. A woman does not customarily tell a neighbor or even a relative that she is going to have a baby or make a new dress or prepare something special for dinner. . . . There is greater readiness to commiserate in another's misfortune than to take joy in his success, resulting in a more widespread sharing of bad news than good. There is an almost secretive attitude toward good fortune and boasting is at a minimum. People . . . do not ordinarily advise each other where a good purchase or sale is to be made, how an animal can be cured, or in what ways a crop can be improved.[12]

Putting his arm around the youth and walking with him to comfort him, Zarathustra, as so often, offers an ocular diagnosis of his interlocutor's soul: "Better than your words tell it, your eyes tell me of all your dangers. You are not yet free, you still *search* for freedom. . . . And even the liberated spirit must still purify himself. Much prison and mustiness still remain in him: his eyes must still become pure" (Z I.8; KSA 4.53). The eyes must become pure or radiant, as Zarathustra describes the eye of the sun or as the hermit characterizes Zarathustra's eye. What began as a parable about invisibility and action at a distance has turned into a discussion of involuntary communication through the eyes. Perhaps the reason for the youth's evasion of Zarathustra is that he fears looking him in the eye. Zarathustra acknowledges that the evil eye is at work in all of this, disrupting the exchange of glances: "You still feel noble, and the others too feel your nobility, though they bear you a grudge and give you the evil eye" (Z I.8; KSA 4.53).[13] The episode ends with Zarathustra encouraging the young man to persevere in his ambitions. We, however, are left with the question why this lesson about envy has been couched in the language of the eye.

Jacques Lacan, with some debt to Maurice Merleau-Ponty, spoke of the gaze as a feature of the world, as having an existence that was not exclusively located in a human subject.[14] That perspective makes it possible to understand one aspect of the phenomenon of the evil eye that is sometimes thought of as a disembodied activity, that is, as a feature of a situation that is more inclusive than the human agents who inhabit it. It can seem as if the evil eye is hovering over us, waiting to blight any good fortune that it observes. Lacan, however, saw this relatively impersonal dimension of the gaze as tending toward the malevolent or at best the neutral, rather than the benevolent. He observes that "it is striking, when one thinks of the universality of the function of the evil eye, that there is no trace anywhere of the eye that blesses."[15] Perhaps Lacan is drawing upon Freud's suggestion that sight was the last of the human senses to be developed and that its present position of hegemony in human perception rests on a displacement of the others. In a long footnote to *Civilization and Its Discontents,* Freud speculates that human ancestors, finding their way about on all fours, tended to orient themselves by their tactile and olfactory sensibility. Consequently, it might be supposed that there is some lingering trauma connected with the shift from living on all fours and finding one's way about by smell and touch to the upright posture and the dominance of vision.[16] Yet Lacan would have been able to find such evidence of "the eye that blesses" in Nietzsche, who speaks frequently of the good, the purified, the clear, the quiet, and the radiant eye. Perhaps this does not have the status of a folk belief, with accompanying practices, but Nietzsche does seem to be drawing on a common vocabulary and store of images having to do with what happens in an exchange of looks or glances. In the *Phaedrus,* for example, Plato speaks of the communication of love through the eyes, in which one person's look is answered by another, and there is a reciprocal heightening of admiration and desire.[17] In addition to the "pure eye" recognized in Zarathustra by the hermit, Nietzsche writes in *Daybreak* of *"the purifying [reinmachende] eye."* There he contrasts two sorts of geniuses, those like Schopenhauer, whose penetrating thought is an extension of their nature or character, and those like Plato, who "possess the *pure, purifying eye* which seems not to have grown out of their temperament and character but free from these and usually in mild opposition to them, looks down on the world as a god and loves this god. But even they have not acquired this eye at a single stroke: seeing needs practice and preschooling, and he who is fortunate enough will also find at the proper time a teacher of pure seeing" (D 497; KSA 3.293). "Radiant eyes" have the capacity to bless and seduce: "*Applause itself as a continuation of the play*. Radiant eyes [*Strahlende Augen*] and a benevolent smile is the kind of applause rendered to the whole great universal comedy of existence—but at the same time a comedy within the comedy aimed at seducing the other spectators to a *'plaudite amici'*" (HAH, AOM, 24; KSA 2.288). The pure, radiant, clear eye is enthralled and entranced by the spectacle and has no need to dominate it. Eyes are not limited to the functions of objectifying and reducing but can also receive, honor, and bless. Yet Lacan may not have meant that there is no evidence of a radiant or blessing eye with regard to individuals; he could mean that when we speak of the eye in an impersonal way, as with the evil eye, there is no corresponding sense of an affirmative gaze or look. And while he may be right, insofar as there is no body of folk beliefs or practices connected with the good eye, Nietzsche at least can be seen as deploying the resources of language and philosophy in behalf of such a conception. *Zarathustra* is permeated with this theme, from the initial praise of the eye of the sun to the declaration in "Noontime" that one of the basic sources of happiness is the *"Augen-Blick."* The radiant eye is one that accepts and blesses its world; in contrast, the last men, of whom Zarathustra speaks in his address to the crowd gathered in the marketplace, *blink;* that is, they fail to look deeply, so they lack the intensity of either the evil or the radiant eye. The last men are the blinkers; their vision lacks all creativity. "The last men say 'We have invented happiness' and they blink"; Nietzsche repeats variants of this four times on one page, like a blinking that punctuates our encounter with a face. Blinking is an involuntary use of the eye; it is below the threshold of our attention span, so we are typically quite unaware that we are blinking, something that is quite clear when we see untrained talking heads on television.

We are constantly in danger of adopting the mode of the evil eye, as Nietzsche observes as late as *Twilight of the Idols*. There he suggests an analogy that we have already seen between the psychologist and the painter, both of whom run the risk of an excessive reflection and self-consciousness that could turn their vision against itself: "Experience as the *wish* to experience does not succeed. One *must* not eye oneself [*nach sich hinblicken*] while having an experience; else the eye becomes an 'evil eye.' A born psychologist guards instinctively against seeing in order to see; the same is true of the born painter. He never works 'from nature'; he leaves it to his instinct, to his *camera obscura*, to sift through and express the 'case,' 'nature,' that which is experienced. He is conscious only of what is general, of the conclusion, the result" (*T*, "Skirmishes," 7; *KSA* 6.115). One of the explicit themes of *Twilight* is the importance of the instincts, distinguished from the more primordial drives as the ways in which those drives have been shaped and given a relatively stable form by culture.[18] The painter's visual instincts, then, operate in a kind of camera obscura, behind his back. This suggests that Nietzsche would allow that there is a set of fundamental, biologically given limits to the sense of vision but that the sense is also shaped by history and culture. In a healthy person or a healthy culture, these givens will assume a certain form so that they generally operate without second-guessing and unnecessary reflection. To speak with Foucault, a genealogy and archaeology of vision are possible as the projects of clarifying the various *archai,* or principles of order and arrangement, that prevail in a given visual culture and exploring their transformations. Such genealogical or archaeological inquiry is to be contrasted with the sort of self-observation that Nietzsche is questioning. The latter attempts to catch an experience in the very process of its occurrence and so interferes with the experience itself. Genealogy is a much more distanced project of examining the grounds of a diverse range of practices; it is not immediately caught up in the impossible project of being simultaneously naive and reflective. The effort to observe one's own vision (literal or metaphorical) will lead to the construction of pictures (literal or metaphorical) that fail to hang together: "Then one lies in wait for reality, as it were, and every evening one brings home a handful of curiosities. But note what finally comes of all this: a heap of splotches, a mosaic at best, but in any case something added together, something restless, a mess of screaming colors. The worst in this respect is accomplished by the Goncourts; they do not put three sentences together without really hurting the eye, the psychologist's eye" (*T*, "Skirmishes," 7; *KSA* 6.115).

35 Zarathustra's Interpretation of Dreams

One place where Zarathustra shows himself susceptible to the threat of the evil eye is in the episode involving the soothsayer (*Z* II.19; *KSA* 4.172). Zarathustra hears the soothsayer speak of the great weariness that has descended upon mankind, a weariness "accompanied by a faith: 'All is empty, all is the same, all has been!'" The soothsayer might be thought to give voice to thoughts similar to those of the prominent pessimists of the nineteenth century, such as Schopenhauer and Eduard von Hartmann. He describes humanity's predicament in terms of the classical set of fears associated with the evil eye: "What fell down from the evil moon last night? In vain was all our work; our wine has turned to poison; an evil eye has seared our fields and hearts. We have all become dry." The narrative tells us that this prophecy touched Zarathustra's heart and made him weary, asking how he would be able to preserve his light through the depressing twilight that was descending. After grieving for three days, Zarathustra falls into a deep sleep, which we might think of as a way of conserving his light from the evil eye. When he awakes, he tells the disciples his dream and asks for their help in interpreting it. This is one of a number of prophetic visions or dreams related in the story of Zarathustra.

Before considering this dream as an apotropaic response to the threat of the evil eye, recall Nietzsche's characterization of the dream world, especially in *The Birth of Tragedy*, as an Apollonian realm of lucid images, with the suggestion that Apollo sometimes combines his role as healer with his oneiric gifts. Zarathustra relates these dreams and visions, they are visually well-defined, and they often hinge on specifically visual experiences. Part 2 of *Zarathustra* begins with such a dream, which is crucial in motivating the prophet to undertake a new series of teachings and a new phase of his self-overcoming ("The Child with the Mirror," Z II.1; *KSA* 4.105). In this case Zarathustra has no doubt about the meaning of the dream:

> Why was I so startled in my dream that I awoke? Did not a child step up to me carrying a mirror? "O Zarathustra," the child said to me, "look at yourself in the mirror." But when I looked into the mirror I cried out, and my heart was shaken: for it was not myself I saw, but a devil's grimace and scornful laughter. Verily, all-too-well do I understand the sign and admonition of the dream: my *teaching* is in danger; weeds pose as wheat. My enemies have grown powerful and have distorted my teaching till those dearest to me must be ashamed of the gifts I gave them. I have lost my friends; the hour has come to seek my lost ones.

Here too there is an evil-eye effect, and it is represented by the optical experience of seeing oneself hideously distorted in the mirror. Unlike Dorian Gray's portrait, which changes to reflect his invisible degeneration, the child's mirror reflects the distorted image of Zarathustra spread by his enemies. In the highly charged visual experience of the dream, Zarathustra is invited to look into a mirror where he appears as a devil. The child occupies an ambiguous position. As the child who emerges from "The Three Metamorphoses of the Spirit" that Zarathustra described in his initial speech, he is the figure of light, playfulness, and innocence; his acting as a messenger here could suggest both his help in offering a warning and his affiliation with the distortion of Zarathustra's visage. Despite this element of ambiguity, there is little question for Zarathustra about how to interpret the images of the dream; but this is not always the case.

The dream provoked by the encounter with the soothsayer, Zarathustra says when he awakes, "is still a riddle to me"; he is puzzled because "its meaning is concealed in it and imprisoned and does not yet soar above it with unfettered wings." Now the dream itself has to do with an experience of concealment, imprisonment, and locking away, which is followed by the liberation of a motley collection of flying things. Narrating his dream, Zarathustra explains that he was "a night watchman and a guardian of tombs upon the lonely mountain castle of death. . . . Life that had been overcome looked at me out of glass coffins." Although as a night watchman he has glass keys to open the great creaking gates of the castle, they fail to work for him; for when there are three great strokes like thunder at the door, he is impotent to move the gate even an inch. What the night watchman could not do is accomplished by a "roaring wind" that tears the gates apart and casts up a black coffin before him: "And amid the roaring and whistling and shrilling the coffin burst and spewed out a thousandfold laughter. And from a thousand grimaces of children, angels, owls, fools, and butterflies as big as children, it laughed and mocked and roared at me. Then I was terribly frightened; it threw me to the ground. And I cried in horror as I have never cried. And my own cry awakened me— and I came to my senses" (Z II.19; KSA 4.174).

What is the meaning of the dream? An eager disciple says that the master is both the wind and "the coffin full of colorful sarcasms and the angelic grimaces of life." Zarathustra seems uncomfortable with the interpretation, looking into the disciple's face for a long time and shaking his head. No further interpretation is offered, for at this point in the narrative, Zarathustra, as we soon learn from yet another dream in "The Stillest Hour," has not come to terms with his most difficult thought, the one that will receive its own phantasmatic presentation in "On the Vision and the Riddle." Perhaps the disciple's interpretation is correct but premature, for at this point in Zarathustra's career, he does not understand *how* he can be the liberating force that he dreams of. As in the earlier dream of the child with the mirror, this one involves an experience of being looked at, this time by the life overcome in glass coffins. There is something paralyzing about these looks or icy stares from behind the glass, and indeed they induce slumber in the night watchman, who both falls asleep (or into a sleeplike torpor) and is awakened, all still within his own dream. This is an Apollonian vision in which the dreamer says, in effect, "It is a dream. I will go on dreaming," even when the dream is dark and gloomy. Such dream-within-a-dream effects suggest the infinite depth, sometimes called an abyss, of the *Augenblick*. But recall that the dream is a response to Zarathustra's heart's being overcome by the teaching of the soothsayer. The evil eye has turned all life into corpses preserved under glass. Under glass the dead life is still visible, reminding the night watchman of what has been lost. These visions under glass are more frightening versions of the entombed divine glances and twinklings of the eye whose death was lamented in "The Tomb Song."

36 Vertigo

Life or what was once alive under glass: this recalls the still life, or *nature mort*. It is the object of what Foucault will call the clinical gaze, in which even the living is seen as if it were dead. Yet "only where there are tombs are there resurrections" (Z II.11; KSA 4.145); we get some sense of the resurrection of the *Augenblick* in the chapter "On the Vision and the Riddle," a chapter that interrogates the riddle of vision as well as some others. Zarathustra, sailing home, has had a vision, one that involved his being "cold and deaf from sadness." When he revives, he is impelled to relate this vision to the people on the ship, because he is a "friend" of those who travel far and take risks. Zarathustra salutes the bold "searchers and researchers [*Suchern, Versuchern*]": "You, drunk with riddles, glad of the twilight [*Zwielicht-Frohen*], whose soul flutes lure astray to every whirlpool, because you do not want to grope along a thread with cowardly hand; and where you can *guess*, you hate to *deduce*—to you alone I tell the riddle that I *saw*, the vision [*Gesicht*] of the loneliest" (Z III.2; KSA 4.197). So Zarathustra frames his account of the vision by seductively inviting an interpretation, an invitation that has been taken up by many of his readers. He reminds these nautical interpreters (or hermenauts) that he will be telling them of something that he *saw*. And the first thing he has to tell them, as he sets the scene, has to do with lighting and time of day: "Not long ago I walked gloomily through the deadly pallor of dusk [*leichenfarbne Dämmerung*]—gloomy and hard, with lips pressed together. Not only one sun had set for me" (Z III.2; KSA 4.198). A twilight the color of corpses: this recalls Zarathustra's dream of himself as a night watchman guarding the dead in their glass coffins. Death is made visible. In the *Dämmerung* light thickens and congeals. It is as if many suns had set; not only is the solar cycle turning into darkness, but all that the sun suggests of life, warmth, and illumination seems to be lost. There is no longer a sun overhead to whom Zarathustra can address the joyous words with which this book opened. It is indeed "the vision of the loneliest" that is staged here in these desolate surroundings. Zarathustra describes the painful and risky ascent of the treacherous mountain path, as he bears the burden of the spirit of gravity, the dwarf upon his back. In this account of a visionary or dreamlike experience, there is more visual detail, a more specific setting of the scene than in almost any of the wide-awake episodes of the book. It is still the case, even in a philosophical fiction that might be said to be visionary through and through, that the explicitly marked dream and the vision related as such have an Apollonian clarity and definition unobtainable elsewhere. The dwarf taunts him: "You threw yourself up high, but every stone that is thrown must fall, O Zarathustra, you philosopher's stone, you slingstone, you star-crusher!" Zarathustra explains to the sea voyagers that this intensified his sense of oppression and loneliness, and his narrative emphasizes that this phantasmatic experience is a veritable nested set of Chinese boxes of visions or dreams, one within the other: "I climbed, I climbed, I dreamed, I thought; but everything oppressed me. I was like one sick whom his wicked torture makes weary, and who as he falls asleep is awakened by a still more wicked dream."

In *The Birth of Tragedy* Nietzsche celebrated another type of dream within the dream, the sort in which the dreamer says triumphantly to himself, "It is a dream; I will dream on!" If what eternal recurrence teaches is that every *Augenblick* is infinitely deep, then these deeply embedded, abyssal visions, whether luminous and calm or oppressive and frightening, are symbols and suggestions of that depth, a depth that has no bottom. If Zarathustra is falling, as the dwarf threatened, from one wicked dream into another, he is also able, as a lucid dreamer, to take a position with regard to the complex dream itself. The position is to stop, to stand still, and to tell the dwarf, "It is you or I!" Zarathustra gives a speech in praise of courage, a virtue that he also exemplifies. Courage is defined as a slayer, and specifically as the slayer of dizziness or vertigo at abysses: "Courage also slays vertigo [*Schwindel*] at abysses: and where does the human being not stand at abysses? Is not seeing itself—seeing abyssses? [*Ist Sehen nicht selber—Abgründe sehen?*]" (Z III.2; KSA 4.199). There is no way of avoiding the abyss. Pity, Zarathustra says, is the deepest abyss, for once one looks into suffering, one sees that it is bottomless. This was the insight of Schopenhauer, in agreement with the religions of compassion and renunciation. Given that abyss, he thought that the only viable option was to remove oneself from the cycle of willing and suffering through art, saintliness, or philosophy. But Zarathustra sees another possibility that involves resolutely looking into the abysses that confront us willy-nilly; so he asks whether all seeing is not seeing abysses. The dwarf threatened Zarathustra with the abyss, with falling headlong into the depth from which he had climbed; and Zarathustra was simultaneously experiencing the abyss of the *Augenblick*, the sense of there being endless visions, terrifying in this case, nested within one another. Alfred Hitchcock's *Vertigo* raises similar questions. A man who lives in terror of heights "sees" his lover plunging to her death, only to discover that he has been the victim of an elaborate ruse in which one woman masqueraded as a man's wife so that the husband could murder her. But it takes time to work through the series of disguises, while the protagonist deals with the double (the phantasm or simulacrum), experiencing not only the dizziness caused by heights but also the vertigo produced by the doubling effect. Jimmy Stewart's character never musters the courage that Zarathustra summons against the dwarf.

My introduction of the film is meant to signal the way in which vertigo *(Schwindel)* is construed by both Nietzsche and Hitchcock as a visually mediated experience and one that can function metaphorically for all the challenges of life. Zarathustra's question "Is not seeing itself—seeing abysses?" can be read as a question about our ocular and perspectival experience. In one influential tradition, vision is what reveals things all at once; it is a mode of access to things in their sheer presence. The system of perspective elaborated by painters from Giotto through Raphael and the explicit and implicit appeal to metaphors such as the mind's eye or the dark cabinet (camera obscura) of the mind lend themselves to such a view. As we have seen, Nietzsche had already registered his criticism of "the one great Cyclops eye" of Socrates in *The Birth of Tragedy* and had suggested that the position of the spectator in the Greek theater, itself an emblem of an entire culture, involved at least two distinct perspectives. Now he has Zarathustra ask whether all vision does not involve a look into the abyss; I take this to mean, minimally, that all vision is indefinitely complex, that even in the twinkling of an eye there is layer after layer, perspective upon perspective. If vision never was what the great ordering systems of Renaissance painters or ocularcentric epistemologists took it to be, then it cannot serve as the ground or foundation that (cowardly) human beings are so prone to seek. For seeing is seeing *Abgründe*, that is, looking into areas where there is no ground, where the more intensely we look, the more the ground falls away.

The account of the vision continues with the introduction of a new scenario and a conflict of visual interpretations. Zarathustra challenges the dwarf again, declaring that he does not know his "abysmal thought." Although the spirit of gravity has threatened Zarathustra with falling into the abyss, he does not understand the nature of abysses; he cannot *think* the abyss, and he does not realize that we are always standing at the edge of abysses and always *seeing* abysses. When the dwarf jumps down from Zarathustra's shoulders, they become aware of a gateway *(Thorweg)* just where they have stopped. It is the meaning of this doorway that is at issue. The vision of the doorway needs to be interpreted. Now the doorway has a title or name, "Augenblick," which indicates that making sense of the doorway, a visual riddle, will contribute to understanding the moment of vision or twinkling of the eye. Knowing what is before them in *this* vision will have consequences for understanding what it can mean to be in the moment, to participate in a vision. The vision has to do, among other things, with the riddle of vision. Zarathustra presents part of the riddle to the one who has been weighing him down:

> "Behold [*Siehe*] this gateway! Dwarf!" I continued: "it has two aspects [*Gesichter*]. Two paths meet here; no one has yet followed either to its end.
>
> This long lane stretches back: it goes on for an eternity. And that long lane goes forward—that is another eternity.
>
> They contradict each other, these paths; they offend each other face to face:—and it is here at this gateway that they come together. The name of the gateway is inscribed above: "Augenblick."
>
> But whoever would follow one of them—on and on, farther and farther—do you believe, dwarf, that these paths contradict each other eternally?" (Z III.2; *KSA* 4.199–200)

The challenge is to *see* or behold the gateway, to see it intensely and perceptively, not to simply pigeonhole it within ready-made categories. Zarathustra's doubt that the dwarf can do this is signaled by his first commanding him to behold the sight and then addressing him contemptuously ("Dwarf!"). The gateway is said to have two aspects, faces, or *Gesichter*, the same term that appears in the title of the chapter and that Zarathustra uses to name what he will tell the sea voyagers. Those earlier uses of the word rely on its figurative sense of vision or apparition. More literally, a *Gesicht* is a face, a sight, or a look. To say that the gateway has two faces or two looks might mean at least two things. The most obvious one is what Zarathustra articulates in his very next sentence, "Two paths meet here." That is, the gateway has two sides or faces in that it can be seen as the terminus of two different paths. Even this observation requires an interpretation, because someone might think that there is only a single path that runs through the gateway. But perhaps it is misleading to speak of interpretation here, as if there were a meaning waiting to be discovered; Zarathustra is *defining* the moment of vision by explaining that it is to be seen as the confrontation of two ways or paths that run into one another. The *Augenblick* is a site of crisis or collision. And this is already to begin to introduce another way of understanding the claim that the gateway has a double aspect. The gateway is double in the first sense insofar as it can be seen as the terminus of either the path that leads backward or the one that leads forward (soon Zarathustra will identify these paths as leading into the past or the future, but he has not yet done so). A second sense in which the gateway is double is that, granted the first duplicity of aspect, there are two ways of seeing and understanding what is before them, that of Zarathustra and that of the dwarf. Every vision is multiple, which is simply to apply to *this* vision Zarathustra's principle that seeing itself is seeing abysses. (Let me suggest that frequently when Nietzsche or his characters say there are two of something—as in the distinction between the ethos of the masters and slave morality—what is meant is "at least two"; that is, the attribute of twoness is being cited in order to dispel the illusion that there is one and only one way of understanding or seeing the subject in question.) If Zarathustra's most abysmal thought includes the notion that every *Augenblick* is abyssal, then the multiplicity of *this* vision, the one that is marked or inscribed as *Augenblick,* makes it an exemplary instance of what it purports to illustrate.

In replying to Zarathustra, the dwarf seems oblivious to the hints that the former has provided concerning the doubleness (and the doubled doubleness) of the scene; but by offering his own reading or interpretation of the doorway, he confirms the point that it has (at least) two aspects: "'All that is straight lies,' the dwarf murmured contemptuously. 'All truth is crooked. Time itself is a circle.'" The dwarf again casts his evil eye. Earlier he evinced this envy in predicting, with malicious glee, that Zarathustra's ascent would necessarily lead to a precipitous fall. Now he turns his evil eye on a vision, one that has the potential to tell us about the depth of those twinklings of the eye that constitute our lives. Subjected to the *böse Blick* of dwarf vision, the infinite, abyssal depth of the *Augenblick* is reduced to the single, closed figure of the circle: a flat two-dimensional form, like the simplified diagram that an instructor might sketch on the blackboard to provide a first approximation of the thought of eternal recurrence. The evil eye seeks to reduce the object of its envy to the lowest common denominator; in philosophy it sometimes manifests itself in the claim that something is "nothing but" a devalued or neutral thing (as in the claims that mind is nothing but matter, universals are nothing but words, and so on).

Such reductionism is a facile evasion, Zarathustra admonishes the dwarf: "You spirit of gravity, do not make things too easy for yourself!" And again he insists that his adversary "behold this *Augenblick.*" As Wittgenstein said in a rather different context, "don't think but look!"[19] Don't settle for an easy generalization that conceals the problematic character of the subject. Zarathustra offers an alternative account of "this gateway *Augenblick,*" emphasizing again that this moment of vision is one that bears a name and an inscription. He is describing another face or aspect (*Gesicht*) that the dwarf ignored. On this interpretation, this twinkling of an eye is also a gateway, a place of transition, an opening to possibility, a clash of past and future; and as such, as a vision of what it is to be in the *Augenblick,* it offers an exemplary demonstration that we are always positioned at such critical junctures. Zarathustra's account of "this gateway *Augenblick*" falls into two sequential parts, one more general and one more specific. The general part seems to be a statement of what it is to be in any moment, although we may fail to realize it; the more specific aspect has to do with the particular setting of this experience: the scene in the gateway as he and the dwarf share a whispered colloquy, a spider crawling in the moonlight. Zarathustra's reply begins with the claim that whatever is possible must have already occurred; this is said not to suggest that there is no limit to the field of possibility (and occurrence) but to limit the field of possibility. So in thinking about time and what it means to always be standing in the moment, we should be struck by the radical finitude (as Heidegger might call it) of all that is, and especially of our actions, experiences, and choices:

> "Behold," I continued, "this *Augenblick!* From this gateway, *Augenblick,* a long eternal lane leads *backward:* behind us lies an eternity.
> Must not whatever *can* walk [*laufen*] have already walked by on this lane before? Must not whatever *can* happen have happened, have been done, have passed by before?"

To glibly assert that time is a circle is not yet to see that all possibilities have been realized, that there are no ghostly possibilities waiting to be actualized. And such an insight must apply to the very *Augenblick* that is the contested subject of the disputation with the dwarf. For the latter, with his contemptuous remark about the circle, imagines himself in a fantastic god's-eye position outside and above the circle of time and refuses to think what it means to be in the moment. But this is what Zarathustra insists he must do:

> And if everything has been there before—what do you maintain, dwarf, of this *Augenblick?* Must not this gateway too have been there before?
>
> And are not all things knotted together so firmly that this *Augenblick* draws after it *all* that is to come? *Therefore*—itself too? (Z III.2; *KSA* 4.200)

What the figure of the circle omits is the realization that we are, at any time, experiencing a twinkling of the eye that we have lived through before. The circle is perhaps the sort of theory inspired by the "one great Cyclops eye" of Socrates, an eye that cannot reflect on its own position or entertain alternative points of view. We cannot stand outside such a circle but must see that *this Augenblick* is one that has passed before. But it does not simply pass; Zarathustra earlier used the verb *laufen* to characterize whatever occurs, what passes on one of the long lanes. *Laufen* typically means to walk or to run and is used not only of humans and animals but of roads or paths. So the suggestion is that things are in motion, again contrary to the spatializing figure of the circle; the dwarf's diagrammatic reduction of eternal recurrence would be a fine example of what Bergson referred to as the spatialization of time.[20] *This* moment of vision is pulsing with the activity by which it runs and is drawn and by which it draws everything else, including itself.

Now Zarathustra points to the haecceity of the *Augenblick*, the thisness that seems to systematically escape the attention of the dwarf, who is repeatedly challenged to behold where he is:

> And this slow spider, which crawls in the moonlight, and this moonlight itself, and I and you in the gateway, whispering together, whispering of eternal things—must not all of us have been there before?
>
> —and return and walk in that other lane, out there, before us, in this long weird [*schaurigen*] lane—must we not return eternally?

What makes the lane weird, or uncanny, is the fact that we have been here before and will be here again. This means that all vision is of the infinitely deep, or the abyss. Typically, it is the visual scene that individualizes the *Augenblick:* the spider crawling in the moonlight and the moonlight itself. In the aphorism of *The Gay Science* that is frequently taken to be Nietzsche's first suggestion of eternal recurrence, the spider and the moonlight also appear (*GS* 341; *KSA* 3.570). There it is a demon who insinuates the idea; here it is Zarathustra rebuking the dwarf's simplistic evasions. In both cases the invitation is to single out a visionary moment, marked by an intensity of experience, the sort of moment that we encounter in our "loneliest loneliness." Yet in such moments we can still engage in a conversation of sorts; our internal demon or our spirit of gravity provokes or belittles us. In these conversations we try to make sense of those striking moments of vision.

37 The Nausea of Vision

So far Zarathustra has been recounting his talk with the dwarf. But now he tells the sea voyagers that he became silent, after speaking increasingly softly, "for I was afraid of my own thoughts and the thoughts behind my thoughts." At this point, he recounts, those thoughts were interrupted by hearing a dog howling. Perhaps this interruption is a diversion that intensifies his meditation. It recalls another experience, another *Augenblick,* one that returns as a forceful and poignant memory. This recollection comes from the most archaic strata of childhood memory, and it involves both a very specific scene and an emotional response, namely the feeling of pity, which Nietzsche and Zarathustra both denounce and struggle with interminably:

> Had I ever heard a dog howl like this? My thoughts raced back. Yes, when I was a child, in the most distant childhood:
> —then I heard a dog howl like this. And I saw him too, bristling, his head up, trembling in the stillest midnight when even dogs believe in ghosts:
> —and I took pity. For just then the full moon, silent as death, passed over the house, just then it stood still, a round glow—still on the flat roof, as if on another's property:—
> That was why the dog was terrified: for dogs believe in thieves and ghosts. And when I heard such howling again I took pity again. (Z III.2; *KSA* 4.201)

The howling of the dog summons up a distant childhood memory of another moonlit night. This is the only occasion in *Thus Spoke Zara-*

thustra when we hear about Zarathustra's childhood; the circumstances of his recall, in association with the vision of the gateway, should alert us to its significance. The dog of that memory was howling at the full moon, and the visual content of the remembered episode is very specific: the dog's posture and attitude, the full moon coming over the edge of the house. Again, one vision leads to another; earlier Zarathustra described his experience climbing up the mountain path as being like awakening from one dream into a more wicked one. Here the archaic remembered image is not more wicked, but it is uncanny as the still moon seems perched on the edge of the roof. And this vision, which recalls a strong feeling of pity, prepares the way for another that tests Zarathustra's struggle with pity. The mechanism of recall is explicitly laid out: wondering if he has ever heard such a canine howling, Zarathustra thinks back to an earlier, *uralt* memory, in a visual register. As in the art of memory recommended by ancient rhetoricians and refined by renaissance thinkers, the key to mnemonic mastery lies in visual images.[21]

In this final vision of the sequence, it is impossible to tell, after so many apparitions within apparitions, what the status of the new experience is: "Where was the dwarf gone now? And the gateway? And the spider? And all the whispering? Was I dreaming, then? Was I waking up? Among wild cliffs I stood suddenly alone, bleak in the bleakest moonlight." Now the same dog is howling. The dog, the moonlight, and possibly the natural surroundings establish some continuity in the scene despite the disappearance of the dwarf and the gateway. Again Zarathustra reminds his listeners of what he *saw*, and suggests that this part of his vision was the most uncanny:

> And verily, what I saw, I had never seen the like. A young shepherd I saw, writhing, gagging, in spasms, his face distorted, and a heavy black snake hung out of his mouth.
>
> Had I ever seen so much nausea and pale dread on one face? Had he fallen asleep? Then the snake crawled into his throat—and there bit itself fast. (Z III.2; *KSA* 4.201)

Nietzsche needs to emphasize that what Zarathustra sees is something remarkable, something perhaps scarcely ever seen, a unique vision. And in this chapter, "On the Vision and the Riddle," that is an invitation both to the sea voyagers and to Nietzsche's readers (who are being seduced into identifying themselves with those courageous guessers of riddles) to think about what it means to present such a tableau. If the first part of the vision was a meditation on the abyssal character of seeing, this second one emphasizes especially the struggle with pity, also described as an abyss, and it does so through the medium of a peculiar spectacle. In this evocation of the horrible, the disgusting, and the abject, we should recall Lessing's attempt to define the boundaries that would allow or disallow the incorporation of such scenes into the plastic or the literary arts. Although Nietzsche early signaled his project of overcoming Lessing's aesthetics, this vision, despite its nauseating character, does not violate the strictures laid down in *Laocoön*. What the writer has produced is, after all, verbal. While Lessing would presumably have found a visual depiction of this scene flagrantly disgusting and inappropriate, he acknowledges that poetry (or imaginative literature) has a much more extensive freedom in dealing with the painful and the ugly. Philoctetes may howl in pain (like a dog?) throughout most of a tragedy, but Laocoön may not emit a single shriek in a sculptural representation (or so Lessing supposed on the basis of somewhat inaccurate engravings). But this scarcely demonstrates that Nietzsche has accepted Lessing's principles. For as we have seen, the author of *Zarathustra* takes issue with the fundamental division of the arts that is inseparable from those principles. He understands the production of images as an essential aspect of the literary, and he rejects the modernist principle that calls for a strict division of verbal and visual arts.

Here, then, Nietzsche presents the offensive and ugly, a scene of nausea that itself provokes nausea. Zarathustra takes action:

> My hand tore at the snake and tore:—in vain! It did not tear the snake out of his throat. Then it cried out of me: "Bite it off! Bite it off!
>
> Bite the head off! Bite it off"—thus it cried out of me, my dread, my hatred, my nausea, all that is good and wicked in me cried out of me with a single cry.—

We and the sea voyagers are challenged to make sense of this, being reminded once more that the object of interpretation is above all a *visual* scene: "Guess me this riddle that I saw then, interpret me the vision [*Gesicht*] of the loneliest! For it was a vision and a foreseeing [*Vorhersehen*]." The series of questions that Zarathustra addresses to the "searchers and researchers"—Who is the shepherd? Into whose mouth will the snake crawl?—point first of all to himself, but also to anyone who will struggle seriously to digest or incorporate the thought of recurrence. (Nietzsche's notes, especially, frequently characterize the possible assimilation of the idea as a process of *Einverleibung* or incorporation.)[22]

The vision is one of abjection: grotesque, ugly, disgusting, and nauseating. In his notes Nietzsche calls the thought of recurrence a Medusa's head, which suggests that it is a terrible sight with the power to turn the viewer to stone: "In *Zarathustra* 4 the great thought as *Medusa's head:* all features of the world become rigid [*starr*], a frozen death's head" (*KSA* 11.360; 31[4]).[23] It is not immediately clear what this means. While the sketches for the fourth part of *Zarathustra* call for forty pages on the thought of recurrence as a Medusa's head, no such section was ever written. But a natural supposition is that the thought is horrifying and petrifying: as the demon says when he whispers this notion into the ear of the unsuspecting person who hears it for the first time, the thought could crush you. One way of responding to eternal recurrence is to be horrified that the moments of pain or nausea are fixed forever, frozen into stone. The challenge of the thought is to affirm recurrence despite the knowledge that all of these things have an infinite depth. This is the struggle that is foretold symbolically in the episode of the shepherd and realized more directly in "The Convalescent," when Zarathustra wrestles with his most abysmal thought. The terrible visage of Medusa was intensified by the snakes growing from her head. In the myth, all who beheld it were turned to stone. Vision becomes immobilized, held fast by something abhorrent. Certainly the scene with the shepherd, if it is a vision meant to be emblematic of recurrence, is already monstrous like the Medusa. If the many snakes growing from her head have been reduced to one, the nauseating idea of the snake planted in the throat makes up for this loss. However, this is not the last word about the "great thought" of recurrence; just as the threat of Medusa was mastered by a hero, so there is another way of taking this idea. As Perseus discovered, it was possible to avoid being turned to stone by a kind of visual trickery. Using his shield, he saw only the reflection of the head, which lacked the power of the original to petrify the viewer. So although the Medusa embodies the terror of the abyss, there are remedies. For Nietzsche in "The Dionysian Worldview," the Medusa story is an allegory of how the Greeks warded off the monstrosity that threatened to break into their lives: "To see its existence [*Dasein*] as it was in a transfiguring mirror [*in einem verklärenden Spiegel*] and with this mirror to protect itself against the Medusa—that was the inspired strategy of the Hellenic will just in order to be able to live" (*KSA* 1.560). The mirror is transfiguring, and transfiguration, as Nietzsche will confirm in his homage to Raphael, is the hallmark of Apollonian art. For the Greeks, Nietzsche says here,

Medusa is always a danger, but Apollo knows the trick of the mirror. Perseus's story continues: he not only evades transformation into stone, but by means of the ruse of the mirror and with the help of an eye stolen from two weird sisters, he succeeds in decapitating the monster. And now the head can be used to fend off attacks, especially attacks of the monstrous. Already in *The Birth of Tragedy* Nietzsche takes Perseus's heroism after the victory over the Gorgon to be symbolic of Hellenic culture's successful effort to ward off Asian excess: "For some time, however, the Greeks were apparently perfectly insulated and guarded against the feverish excitement of these festivals, though knowledge of them must have come to Greece on all the routes of land and sea; for the figure of Apollo, rising full of pride, held out the Medusa's head to this grotesquely uncouth Dionysian power—and really could not have countered any more dangerous force. It is in Doric art that this majestically rejecting attitude of Apollo is immortalized" (*BT* 2; *KSA* 1.32). If we think of the austere lines of Doric architecture and sculpture, we can recognize the gesture of rejection. But these works do not resemble the Medusa's head, except perhaps in being fearsome to their enemies. Some Doric temples do bear Gorgon figures or heads, although they tend to be somewhat austere in style.[24] Note that in the second, later passage from his first book, Nietzsche sees the head of the Gorgon as already severed and converted into a Greek weapon. In the earlier version, everything was more tentative; the Greeks were seen as existing in a perilous balance. They knew how to guard themselves against Medusa, by manipulating a mirror, but she was a real menace and there was no assurance that she could be eliminated. In both cases a war is being waged by means of fearsome images and optical tricks. When Nietzsche wants to think of the most extreme possibilities of the Greek world, he imagines the horror of an unseeable head or the monstrous Cyclops eye of Socrates.

To think of eternal recurrence, a thought presented in a vision with its own "grotesquely uncouth" dimension, as a Medusa's head might mean one of several things. The thought itself could be such as to turn those who looked at it or into it into stone, as suggested above. In that case we will need to approach it with mirrors; that is, we will need to produce surfaces through which we can see the contained and somewhat tamed image of its terrible face. Now in Nietzsche's account of the Greek mirror defense, he describes the mirror not as a sheer reflecting surface but as a transfigured representation of Greek life, as if Perseus had to hold his mirror-shield at just the right angle so that it would simultaneously reflect the Medusa's face to him and his own image back to himself. Or perhaps the suggestion here is that the

Greeks, by looking into the Apollonian mirror of their art, found themselves so transfigured that they could bear the terrors of life. The eternal recurrence would be an abyss that we are compelled to acknowledge but which we must warily avoid staring in the face. But if the recurrence is a decapitated Medusa's head, we get a different reading. The face still has its uncanny power, but it is now controlled by a hero (the *Übermensch?*) who knows how to direct it against others. In the sketch that calls the thought a Medusa's head, we are not told *for whom* the world is turned to stone. Perhaps not all who let this thought take possession of them will be frozen in terror or see the world as petrified; the demon in *The Gay Science* makes it clear that there are a number of possible responses. And in some of Nietzsche's earliest notes concerning the thought of recurrence in 1881, it is described as a selective, differentiating thought; the political consequence of the idea is to draw a sharp distinction between those who are invigorated by the thought and those who are utterly depressed by it (*KSA* 9.494; see sec. 70).

In an essay entitled "Nietzsche Medused," Bernard Pautrat elaborates the designation of Nietzsche's "great thought" as a Medusa's head.[25] Citing Freud, who said that the figure of Medusa was a symbol of castration, he claims that the thought has a double aspect for Nietzsche, comprising both the terror of death and absence and the fetish that the thinker desperately flourishes in order to deny the terror. Like the shoe glimpsed by the young boy in Freud's story, it is associated with the absence glimpsed under the woman's skirt—or by looking into the heart of being—and subsequently displayed or cherished to substitute for and deny the reality of the lack that was fleetingly perceived.[26] In this case the fetish is the thought itself, so frequently brandished, hinted at, cited, or expounded (but by figures other than Zarathustra—his animals, the Ugliest Man, or the dwarf) but never, on Pautrat's reading, presented, developed, and articulated in Nietzsche's voice. That Nietzsche would need to put the idea in the mouth of a spokesman and that even he would be egregiously reticent in explaining the thought itself would be a sign of the "logic of castration": the fetish is constantly in view in order to shield the writer (and us) from that which we refuse to think and see. So Pautrat does not find it surprising that while Nietzsche's notes indicate an awareness of the Medusa-like nature of the thought, the section on Medusa projected for *Zarathustra*, part 4, was never written. That absence is said to be simply the working out of the logic of castration, eliminating that level of analysis that might give away the game of fear, fetish, and denial. Similarly, Pautrat suggests that while Zarathustra (and Nietzsche in his notes) sometimes speaks of the great noon or midday, it never arrives. The fetish functions to assure deferral.

Freud's discussion of the fear of castration and the fetishism that responds to it depends upon a highly visual scenario of the young boy's startled discovery that women are not like him (or, alternatively, the young girl's discovery that the boy has something that she lacks). Like so many other scenarios of psychoanalysis (the primal scene, the mirror stage), it is described as an almost instantaneous moment of vision; *in the twinkling of the eye* the subject is changed forever, not as Paul has it, to rise with a visibly perfected body, but to grapple with the destiny of an inherently fragile and threatened corporeality. In this narrative, the subject concludes that the woman (or all women) has suffered a loss and that he is in danger of suffering the same, and then, denying all this as unthinkable, he finds a fetish that reinforces the denial. While Pautrat knows all this, he does not explicitly connect it with the visual dimension of recurrence as that thought is presented in Nietzsche's texts. The thought is a thought about the *Augenblick*, and it is debated with regard to the meaning of an image beheld in a vision, one designated by this term for a glance or a twinkling of the eye. It requires courage to look into the abyss, Zarathustra tells the seafarers, as he declares that vision itself involves such looking. If the abyss of vision is a Medusa's head, however, then we cannot look into it and survive. For Pautrat, eternal recurrence always involves thoughts of becoming and death, of that absolute absence that cannot be seen or imagined because we are no longer there as its subject. As a name for the unseeable, for that which offends vision, the Medusa's head warns us against looking into the abyss. Or we can employ a mirror as a shield (or a shield as a mirror) to protect ourselves against such a sight. Or (perhaps closer to what Pautrat understands as the function of the fetish) we can grasp the head ourselves in order to turn it against others.

39 High Noon: Hyphenating the *Augen-Blick*

Does the great noon never appear in Nietzsche's texts, as Pautrat claims? Certainly it never does as such, under that name. But in the fourth part of *Zarathustra*, the one that was to speak of the Medusa's head, there is a chapter called "Noontime [*Mittags*]" that articulates the theme of vision and the *Augenblick*. In the narrative that concludes the book, Zarathustra wanders through his mountain territory, assaulted by and responding to cries of distress uttered by the eight "higher men." If this part of *Zarathustra* is thought of as an anti-Wagnerian script or libretto, then all these cries constitute the wailing and lamenting that Plato would have banished from the theater and which Lessing noted in a tragedy like Sophocles' *Philoctetes*. This series of noisy, unsettling, and exhausting interruptions is brought to an end by the apparition of the figure known as Zarathustra's Shadow. The idea of running from one's own shadow is perhaps milked for more humor than it can yield. At first he only hears the Shadow's entreaties, but when he finally turns around to confront him, "laughing with his eyes and his entrails," he sees this spectral double in a way that alludes to the qualities of the phantasm: "when Zarathustra examined him with his eyes, he was startled as by a sudden ghost: so thin, swarthy, hollow, and outlived did this follower look" (Z IV.9; KSA 4.339). All of the higher men can be construed as parodies or isolated aspects of Zarathustra, so it is fitting that the last of them should be nothing but a shadow, a figure that evokes Jung's sense of this term, suggesting a dark, unacknowledged side of oneself, a sense that may indeed derive from this Nietzschean text.[27] In this episode the specter is given a voice with which to explain his phantasmatic existence: "I have already sat on every surface; like weary dust, I have gone to sleep on mirrors and windowpanes; everything takes away from me, nothing gives, I become thin—I am almost like a shadow." This darker side of Zarathustra confesses that he has been shadowing him in an endless quest for an authentic home or task, anticipating so many neo-Nietzschean spirits of the past century who were sensitive to the form of the master's aspiration but lacked any substance. It is the Shadow who articulates the thought "Nothing is true, all is permitted," which is frequently attributed to Nietzsche (who attributes it to the original band of Assassins [GM III.24; KSA 5.399]). But given over to the infinite possibilities of this "all is permitted," the Shadow has no idea what to pursue. Later, in the contest of songs at the festival staged by Zarathustra and the higher men, it is the Shadow who sings the song "Among Daughters of the Desert," which is notable for its confession of impotence by means of a parody of Luther's declaration "[H]ere I stand, I can do no other."

After sending this last partial self back to his cave (but how does a shadow separate itself from its substance?), Zarathustra encounters a new configuration of light and shade at "Noontime." Now he comes upon an old crooked and knotty tree, surrounded by a grapevine with attractive yellow fruit.[28] Since the narrative tells us that it is noontime and the sun stands straight over Zarathustra's head, we assume that the only shade available is under this large tree. He takes advantage of the opportunity to sleep, but the sleep described is rather peculiar, for it is one in which "only his eyes remained open" as they continue to enjoy and praise the sight of the tree. In this strange state of sighted sleep, Zarathustra has a conversation with his soul in which he describes himself as happy and quiet, peacefully experiencing the perfect world of noontime when everything comes to rest. So midday *has* arrived, at least in one sense, and it is a time of perfection. It also involves a vision, although in this case it is a pastoral vision beheld while asleep. This twinkling of the eye is not a Medusa's head but rather, like the landscapes of Claude Lorrain that Nietzsche invokes for similar reasons, an apparition of supreme calm. In this glance of the moment, whose punctuality will be marked in several ways, Zarathustra realizes what constitutes happiness: "Precisely the least, the softest, a lizard's rustling, a breath, a breeze, an *Augen-Blick*—it is *little* that makes the *best* happiness" (Z 277; *KSA* 4.344). Here, unusually and perhaps uniquely, Nietzsche hyphenates this word *Augen-Blick*.[29] Does this anomalous typography emphasize that one of the ingredients of happiness is a moment's glance of the eye, not just a brief interval of time? The play between two senses of *Augenblick* is at work here. The uncanny instantaneity of noon is also marked by the position of this chapter at the middle of the book's fourth part. At the end of this interlude, Zarathustra is awakened by a sunbeam falling on his face; that seems to imply that the sun, and so the location of the tree's shadow, has moved. He addresses the heaven, as he did once earlier in "Before Sunrise," apostrophizing it as the "cheerful, dreadful abyss of noon!" So the abyss enters into the noontime. When was this abyss? The text is enigmatic here, for when Zarathustra awakens and gets up, we hear that the sun is still standing straight over his head, and the narrative voice remarks that "from this one might justly conclude that Zarathustra had not slept long." The "abyss of noon" is an uncanny interruption of the day, a solar moment that opens up into a time that seems never to have been, an intercalary moment. This was not a dream or a visionary apparition, but a seeing while asleep or a dreaming while awake. In this strange *Augenblick*, Zarathustra remarks that happiness requires only the *Augen-Blick*. The passage is rich in the affirmative halcyon tone that Nietzsche attributes to the voice of *Thus Spoke Zarathustra* (*EH*, preface, 4; *KSA* 6.259).[30]

In the hyphenation of the *Augen-Blick* we can discern the distinction between the gaze and the glance. The gaze is imperial, lofty, fixes its subject, immobilizes it, and lays it open to a totalizing inspection. The glance is fleeting, perspectival, and partial. To gaze into the abyss is to discover the limits of the gaze itself, to find out that it cannot always (perhaps it never can) achieve a dominating vision. The abyss of the *Augen-Blick* is approached by a series of glances, none of which pretends to optical hegemony. The reappearance of the *Augen-Blick* in part 4, not guillotined (as in Bataille's drawing) but marked by an internal division recalling the confrontation of ways and the invocation of the abyss in the scenario of "On the Vision and the Riddle," gestures toward the deconstruction of presence, not just of what has been called a metaphysics of presence, but of an aesthetics of presence. A rather long notebook entry of August 1881 appears just a few pages after Nietzsche first writes of eternal recurrence. The passage speaks of the *Augenblick*, situating it in relation to the greater and smaller errors of mankind. After suggesting that science tells us about things in terms of the conditions necessary for the existence of beings like ourselves, but that such knowledge has nothing to do with truth, Nietzsche enters a long dash and says:

> The species is the cruder error, the individual the more refined error, it comes *later*. The individual struggles for its existence, for its new taste, for its relatively *unique* position among all things—it considers these as better than the universal taste and despises the latter. It wants to *rule*. But then it discovers that it itself is something changing and has a taste that changes, with its subtlety it sees into the secret that there is no individual, that in the smallest twinkling of the eye [*im kleinsten Augenblick*] it is something other than it is in the next and that its conditions of existence are those of no end of individuals: *der unendlich kleine Augenblick* is the higher reality and truth, a lightning image [*Blitzbild*] out of the eternal flow [*Fluss*]. So the individual learns: how all *satisfying* knowledge rests on the crude error of the species, the subtler error of the individual and the subtlest error of the creative *Augenblick*. (*KSA* 9.501–2; 11[156])[31]

Even the "creative *Augenblick*" is an error, albeit the very subtlest one. Its splitting or hyphenation is a sign of its opening onto an abyss.

In offering this vision, Zarathustra implies that it is exemplary; not only will it tell us something about eternal recurrence, but the vision itself, like any *Augenblick*, recurs eternally. So dwelling with and meditating on this vision will both help us to understand the thought of recurrence and provide a sense of the abyss involved in all seeing. When the shepherd bites off the head of the snake, spews it out, and jumps up transformed and radiant *(ein Verwandelter, ein Umleuchteter)* by an extraordinary laughter, we are invited to imagine a transfiguration. Later in the episode of "The Convalescent," Zarathustra will be the one who wrestles with nausea and emerges transformed and singing. These transformations are another aspect or face of vision; we learned in Zarathustra's confrontation with the dwarf that that vision had (at least) two aspects or faces (the *Gesicht* has at least two *Gesichter*). Now the contrast between two sorts of vision, each attuned to different aspects, has become clear. The divergence between the evil and the radiant eye is realized in articulating how each deals with the *Augenblick*. It is always possible to see "nothing but" the lowest common denominator, the most minimal outline to which something can be reduced; but it is also possible to look into the depths of the disgusting and be transformed. "In the twinkling of an eye," as Paul said, we will be transformed; what Nietzsche depicts in the thought of recurrence is a mode of transformation that changes the way in which we understand and experience those twinklings, *Augenblicke*, or subtle errors that constitute our lives.

six

Foucault's Story of the Eye: Madness, Dreams, Literature

40 Painting and Pleasure: What Do Philosophers Dream Of?

In 1975 Foucault gave a short interview to the journal *L'Imprévu*, published under the title "What Do Philosophers Dream Of?" (*DE* 2.704–7). As this title might suggest, the tone of the interview is somewhat playful. The interlocutor, E. Lossowsky, begins by asking Foucault about his habits in reading newspapers and watching television. He presses him to say what it is that occupies his fantasies or daydreams, but the philosopher replies (ironically?) that he does not waste time. But the interviewer is not discouraged, and he asks whether Foucault attends to his surroundings when he travels, adding, "Don't you look at painting, for example?" Here Foucault is trapped and admits to being quite taken by painting. He says: "What pleases me precisely in painting is that one is truly constrained to look at it. There it is, it is my rest. It is one of the rare things on which I write with pleasure and without fighting with what it is. I believe that I have no tactical or strategic relation with painting." Foucault then mentions the work of Manet, who, he says, made startling works by taking a destructive or indifferent approach to all the aesthetic canons. He also admits to an interest in contemporary American painters, including the photo-realists, and is proud of having used the royalties from the second edition of *The History of Madness* to buy a painting by Mark Tobey (remember that Foucault added a plate of a group portrait by Frans Hals at the beginning of this edition; see sec. 3). But let me quote the conclusion of the interview, which makes a strong and surprising statement about Foucault's relation to painting.

> And then there are the photorealists. I had not been able to give an account of what it was that pleased me in them. Doubtless it was tied to the fact that they revel in the restoration of the rights of the image. And this after a long disqualification. For example, when the canvases of some hack [*pompiers*] painters like Clovis Trouille had been brought together in Paris (which is always a bit behind the times), I was suddenly struck by my pleasure in looking and at the pleasure of the viewers. It was a joy! A current passed around bodily and sexually. All at once it became self-evident what an unbelievable Jansenism painting had imposed on us for decades.
>
> —*Are you more sensitive to the work of painting than to that of literature?*
>
> Yes, very clearly so. I should say that I have never loved literature [*l'écriture*] so much. There is a materiality that fascinates me in painting.

The interviewer has succeeded in getting Foucault to confess some of the things that give him pleasure, despite his claim that he wastes no time. And Foucault has acknowledged taking pleasure even in the work of hack artists, simply because they exult in the image.[1] He knows what he likes and enjoys sharing the collective excitement of the crowd, even at a show that is a bit out of date. Abstraction appears as an *askesis*, a self-denial in the world of the visible. None of the artists Foucault chose to write about could be described as nonfigurative, although, like Magritte, they may take great liberties with the image. Most striking is that Foucault, who has had such an enormous effect on literary studies but a rather negligible one with respect to the history of art, confesses that he finds painting so much more affecting than literature. For a practitioner of genealogy, he is here strangely devoid of all suspicion concerning painting's possible complicity in structures of power. In claiming that he has no tactical or strategic relation with painting, he

seems oblivious to the strong rhetorical uses to which he puts his meditations on that art. Here Foucault sounds surprisingly close to a traditional aesthetic point of view, a perspective from which art would be
the object of a disinterested pleasure, although this is belied somewhat
by his recalling the wave of collective desire that ran through the crowd
at the gallery. Indeed, as we shall see, he tends to respond to literature
as a *voyant*, a seer, to adopt the term that Gilles Deleuze used to describe his friend. Foucault tends either to contrast literature with painting, so as to suggest the greater strength of visual art, or to read literature as itself a radiant source of images. Here he follows in Nietzsche's
footsteps (perhaps unknowingly), when the young classicist took issue
with Lessing and described Homeric poetry as a great garland of images
rather than as a continuous narrative.

41 The Difficulty of Silence

In a late essay on the music of Pierre Boulez, published just two years
before his death in 1984, Michel Foucault looks back on the relation
between theoretical discourse and the arts thirty years earlier, and in
a seemingly casual remark he suggests something about the situation
of philosophy and painting at the beginning of his own career: "Painting in those days was something to be talked about; at any rate, aesthetics, philosophy, reflection, taste—and politics, as I recall—felt they had
a right to say something about the matter, and they applied themselves
to it as if it were a duty: Piero della Francesca, Venice, Cézanne, or
Braque. Silence protected music, however, preserving its insolence.
What was doubtless one of the great transformations of twentieth-
century art remained out of reach for those forms of reflection, which
had established their quarters all around us, places where we risked
picking up our habits" (F 2.241; DE 4.219). There was indeed a great
deal of talk about painting then. Sartre was writing about Tintoretto
(and Venice) and projected a comprehensive study of the artist that
he never completed. Merleau-Ponty had published "Cézanne's Doubt,"
which developed a parallel between phenomenology and painting and
was concerned with the issues that led to his major essay "Eye and
Mind." The very title of André Malraux's ambitious *Voices of Silence*
indicated that the question of how painting could speak or be spoken
for was on the agenda. Political questions also arose; the young Foucault seems to have been disturbed by the French Communist Party's
condemnation of Louis Aragon for publishing Picasso's portrait of Sta-
lin in violation of the canons of socialist realism; he apparently let his

party membership lapse shortly after this incident.[2] Here, as elsewhere, Foucault voices a certain suspicion about the value of all this talk; in the essay on Velazquez's *Las Meninas* that was to become his signature piece on painting, he speaks of "a language inevitably inadequate to the visible fact," of the "infinite relation of language to painting," and declares that "[n]either can be reduced to the other's terms: it is in vain that we say what we see" (*OT* 9; *MCh* 25). Foucault was unable to resist the temptation to speak of painting, even if he had his doubts about the value of the enterprise. The observation in the Boulez essay expresses a wish, tinged perhaps with irony, that the arts might maintain an insolent resistance to the threatened incursions of the word. Yet Foucault did contract the habit of discoursing on the visual, a habit that runs throughout his published work.

A brief dossier on the manifestations of this habit is in order. In the early pages of *The History of Madness,* Foucault writes of Bosch, Breughel, and others who treat the theme of the ship of fools; these passages are matched by those at the book's end where he comments on the more recent insights into madness offered by Goya and Van Gogh (as well as by the writings of Nietzsche and Sade). *The Birth of the Clinic* is concerned with the development of a certain kind of medical gaze, one that transforms the lived body into a virtual corpse; but Foucault passes from analysis of the dry language of the clinic to the display of death in the painting of the nineteenth century, in "the savage, castrated death of Goya, the visible, muscular, sculptural death offered by Géricault, the voluptuous death by fire in Delacroix" (*BC* 171). The celebrated essay on *Las Meninas* appeared first as a separate article before being incorporated into *Les mots et les choses;* and some readers have overlooked the fact that the problematic of the painting returns at a much later and crucial stage in the text, where Foucault describes the construction of the figure of man as "enslaved sovereign, observed spectator" (*OT* 312; *MCh* 323). If this figure haunts Velazquez's painting as implicitly but not actually there, and then looms large in the self-portraits of such nineteenth-century painters as Cézanne and Van Gogh, it is one whose disappearance is foreshadowed in a striking visual image from the end of the same book, when Foucault imagines how, given some unpredictable and disruptive event, "one can certainly wager that man would be erased, like a face drawn in sand at the edge of the sea" (*OT* 387; *MCh* 398). We know that he planned a book on Manet, and in an essay on Flaubert, he places the painter in the world of the museum; various reports and fragments of this abandoned Manet project have emerged, suggesting that, like Clement Greenberg, Foucault saw the painter as the hinge of the modernist movement. The essay on Magritte, *This Is Not a Pipe*, contains a capsule history of the relation between images and words; dating from the same time is a surprising review of Erwin Panofsky's *Studies in Iconology*. A long paragraph on Andy Warhol develops some remarks by Gilles Deleuze on the simulacrum, and related themes in more recent art are explored in two essays on artists who confound conventional distinctions between painting and photography, Gérard Fromanger and Duane Michals; the theme is also taken up in a study of Klossowski, which connects it with "the order of Noon and of eternal recurrence" (*F* 2.128; *DE* 1.330). Still other essays treat of contemporary artists best known in France, such as Paul Rebeyrolle and Maxim Defert.

This brief inventory of Foucault's writing on the visual arts would be incomplete if it omitted mention of a broader concern with the nature of visuality and visual culture. One of Foucault's earliest publications is his study of Ludwig Binswanger, "Dream, Imagination, and Existence," an essay that, like *The Birth of Tragedy* (and unlike Freud), develops a highly visual theory of the dream, engaging along the way with Sartre's theory of the image. A literary analysis, the reading of Bataille's *Story of the Eye*, takes the recurrent figure of the eye to be associated with philosophy's impossible desire to see everything without acknowledging its own roots in the body, its obsession with transforming the ophthalmic into the purely optical. The study of Raymond Roussel, which grew from an essay on "seeing and saying," becomes an exploration of the uncanny figure of the labyrinth that was so fascinating for Nietzsche. The books devoted to madness, the clinic, and to *Surveillance and Punishment* (as the title of the "prison book" should be translated) are marked by a concern with architecture and the spatial organization of experience; great set pieces like the vivid description of a grotesque execution in the latter study are paired with analyses of the Panopticon and its regime of the gaze. A notice of Boulez and Chereau's 1976 version of Wagner's *Ring* cycle emphasizes the visual dimension of the staging, renewing Nietzsche's analysis of a century earlier.

Was Foucault simply in the grip of certain habits of thought that he had absorbed from Malraux, Merleau-Ponty, Sartre, and others? Or does the concern with painting and the visual play a more constitutive role in his thought? Is it nothing more than a coincidence or a residue of early training that so many of the memorable "scenes" of his writing are commentaries on visual works or evocations of things to be seen? Given Foucault's intense concern with Nietzsche, it is striking that a number of his texts, notably those on Magritte and Klossowski, succeed in focusing attention on the specifically visual character of the theme of recurrence (chap. 11). One of the few writers to address these questions is Deleuze, whose own thematization of the theater of philosophy helped to provoke Foucault's exploration of the visual simulacrum. Deleuze claims that the relation between visual display and discursive articulation is a constant theme of Foucault's work. He suggests, in effect, that to understand the latter's philosophical project, we must understand that he is always working with various forms of parallelism, contrast, and intertwining of these two modes, acknowledging, of course, that Foucault's way of introducing the visual is by way of linguistic description (except for the occasional use of plates and illustrations). Deleuze sees the relation of the visible and the articulable as frequently antagonistic. As in the quotations above from the essay on Velazquez, Foucault can deny that the two are isomorphic, while also acknowledging that they can intersect in various ways, as in the study of Magritte, which treats the title painting as an "unraveled calligram." Deleuze suggests a rather Kantian reading of Foucault's procedure, in which statements play the role of concepts and the visible plays the role of intuition: "The statement has primacy by virtue of the spontaneity of its conditions (language) which give it a determining form, while the visible element, by virtue of the receptivity of its conditions (light), merely has the form of the determinable."[3] And he reads Foucault as acknowledging all of the following relations simultaneously between the visible and articulable: "the heterogeneity of the two forms, their difference in nature or anisomorphism; a mutual presupposition between the two, a mutual grappling and capture; the well-determined primacy of the one over the other."[4] One is tempted here to say that Deleuze is proposing a way of making sense of Foucault's fundamental mode of philosophical *Darstellung* or presentation, a way that could not be reduced to either the intuitive or the conceptual (to borrow Kantian terms once more). So we may venture the hypothesis that in examining what Foucault has to say about the visual, whether in the form of a meditation on the paradoxes of representation in *Las Meninas* or in an analysis of the architectonics of the Panopticon, more is at stake than his simply "applying" a certain critical or philosophical insight to a specific "field" or "region"; it is also a question of how thought proceeds. Foucault's juxtaposition of the visible and the linguistic may be as significant for his way of thinking as are Plato's use of the dialogue form, Descartes's sequence of meditations, or Hegel's dialectical structuring of a series of positions of thought in the *Phenomenology of Spirit*. However, I reserve judgment on whether Deleuze's contrast of spontaneous language and passive visuality is the most adequate way of characterizing the contrast between the two modes (sec. 63).

All of this suggests that Foucault's deep and continuing interest in Bataille may have had at least as much to do with his interrogation of the optical unconscious of Western thought as with the not unrelated themes of sexual, social, and literary transgression. These concerns emerge in "A Preface to Transgression," Foucault's 1963 homage to Bataille, but let us concentrate on how they are focused in terms of the eye. The eye is both passive and active, both radiant and receptive. This is what Nietzsche, a common source for both writers, dramatized in *Zarathustra*, and Foucault seems to speak for both himself and Bataille when he says: "The eye is mirror and lamp; it discharges its light into the world around it, while in a movement that is not necessarily contradictory, it precipitates this same light into the transparency of its well. . . . It is the figure of being in the act of transgressing its own limit." The eye, then, is a preeminently liminal organ, one addressed to both interior and exterior. Foucault shows how we can read Bataille's many stories of the eye—from his early novel to *The Tears of Eros*—as examinations of this doubled figure and of the role that it plays in philosophy. If Plato pronounced vision to be the "noblest of the senses," and if the tradition has continued to accord the eye at least a metaphorical hegemony, it is because the physical eye, the optical instrument, can always be seen as the external representative of a deeper vision, a more spiritual eye: "[B]ehind this particular eye, there exists another and, then, still others, each progressively more subtle until we arrive at an eye whose entire substance is nothing but the transparency of its vision. This interior movement is finally resolved in a nonmaterial center where the intangible forms of truth are created and combined, in this heart of things which is the sovereign subject" (*LCMP* 45; *DE* 1.244–45). All of idealism, what Foucault calls a "philosophy of reflection," then, is generated (or is at least granted a powerful rhetorical and persuasive force) by a certain metaphorical transformation of the organ of sight. We may be reminded of Nietzsche's question and answer: "What then is truth? A mobile army of metaphors, metonymies, and anthropomorphisms."[5] In this case the figure would not be merely one among others, however, but the very one that makes it possible to imagine truth as more than figurative, the one that allows us to say, for example, that it is not simply in the eye of the beholder. In examining this figurative idealization, which Foucault believes has been laid bare by Bataille, we might also think of Kant, who, in a memorable figure of his own, criticized the idealizing movement of those who believe in the possibility of human beings attaining a sheer intellectual intuition; it is as if, he says, a bird proud of its ability to fly in the atmosphere were to think that it could now take wing beyond the very medium that enables its flight.

Foucault schematizes the pattern of Bataille's narratives of the eye in order to show how these stories resist idealization: "Bataille reverses this entire direction: sight, crossing the globular limit of the eye, constitutes the eye in its instantaneous being; sight carries it away in this luminous stream (an outpouring fountain, streaming tears and, shortly, blood), hurls the eye outside of itself, conducts it to the limit where it bursts out in the immediately extinguished flash of its being. Only a small white ball, veined with blood, is left behind, only an exorbitated eye to which all sight is now denied" (*LCMP* 45; *DE* 1.245). Bataille thus reverses an idealizing figuration with a materializing one, one that risks a certain physiological reductionism. The series of degradations to which the eye is subjected in the stories is understood not only or even primarily as a sequence of sadistic torture but as a way of displaying the fleshly, ophthalmic resistance of the eye to philosophy's desire to superimpose a pure, disembodied vision on the actual organ of sight. To associate the eye with blood, tears, sex, and death is to show the impossibility of what Nietzsche called "immaculate perception." At the extreme the eye is blind, excavated from its socket, leaving behind a blank place in the skull; in this way "the philosophizing subject has been dispossessed and pursued to its limit" (*LCMP* 46; *DE* 1.245). Erotic ecstasy has a similar structure. When the eyes are upturned, showing only or mostly the whites, in "*la petite mort*" of sexual *jouissance*, there is also a dispossession and a blinding. Foucault reads Bataille in terms of his search for these limiting situations that disclose the impossibility of the hyperbolic hopes that philosophy builds upon this uncanny liminal organ; and this helps to explain the deep structure of Bataille's fictions: "The upturned eye discovers the bond that links language and death at the moment that it acts out this relationship of the limit and being; and it is perhaps from this that it derives its prestige, in permitting the possibility of a language for this play. Thus, the great scenes that interrupt Bataille's stories invariably concern the spectacle of erotic deaths, where upturned eyes display their white limits and rotate inwards in gigantic and empty orbits" (*LCMP* 47; *DE* 1.246).

Bataille, then, is a thinker of limits. His "Preface to Transgression," like Kant's *Critique of Pure Reason*, develops the dialectical contradictions that necessarily follow upon the attempt to jump outside of our own skin, to find an eye behind the eye. Here a pattern of idealization and resistance comes to the fore, a pattern repeated in all of Foucault's explorations of visual art and culture, or of what might be called visual regimes; a visual regime would simply be an arrangement under which there are privileged, hegemonic ways in which spectacles or displays are organized according to a set of typically implicit standards so as to privilege some sights and perspectives over others, and eyes are habituated to expect these visions and not others. In the case of Bataille, it is the eye of metaphysics or idealism that is undermined by its fleshy, sexual, and mortal other. In his reading of *Las Meninas*, Foucault will show that the apparently all-seeing eye of classical painting, the one that seems to look out on the world as through a window, is revealed as necessarily unable to reflect on itself. The regime of the medical clinic that would subject the body to the neutral and impersonal gaze of the accredited professional, the licensed and credentialed observer, is doubled by the grotesque scenes of death and madness (Goya, Delacroix, Van Gogh) that throw in our faces another side of the reduction of the body to its lifeless anatomy. In the disciplinary world of the Panopticon, a world under total surveillance, the art of Manet and of the modernist project suggests a different way of seeing, a flattening out of the painting that allows vision to become experimental and playful rather than tied to a need to catalog the behavior of a population. More recently, there has been a certain division or *partage* of the image, such that painting and photography have come to be seen as antitheses, with painting being a spontaneous art and photography the guarantor of veridical perception, a role that suits it to be the purveyor of news in the mass media and of the advertising that fuels them; but in the work of artists like Andy Warhol, Gérard Fromanger, and Duane Michals, Foucault sees that this dichotomy is challenged and the authority of photography (and its sales pitch) is undercut.

43 Return of the Phantasm: Dream Vision

Well before his essay on Bataille, Foucault gave a major place to the visual in one of his first published texts, "Dream, Imagination, and Existence," ostensibly a commentary on Ludwig Binswanger's "Dream and Existence," but more than that an essay in which he develops a theory of the oneiric image that emphasizes its visual character, offers an existential reading of the dream as a major mode in which we project the form of our destiny, and criticizes Freud for having an overly reductive account of the dream. The dream here becomes a preeminent form of human imagination. There is an intriguing parallel with Nietzsche, whose *Birth of Tragedy* begins with a consideration of the two states generative of art, dream and intoxication. The first philosopher invoked in that first book is Lucretius: "It was in dreams, says Lucretius, that the glorious divine figures first appeared to the souls of men: in dreams the great shaper beheld the splendid bodies of human beings; and the Hellenic poet, if questioned about the mysteries of poetic inspiration, would likewise have suggested dreams. . . . The beautiful *Schein* of the dream worlds, in which every man is truly an artist, is the prerequisite of all plastic art, and, as we shall see, of an important part of poetry also" (*BT* 1; *KSA* 1.26). So from the beginning, it appears, Nietzsche and Foucault are linked as theorists of the dream, of visual culture and visual art, of *Schein* and the simulacrum. The latter is Lucretius's term for the images that float through the ether, the objects of all perception, whether waking or sleeping. It is a term that Deleuze will adopt from Plato and the Epicureans and that Foucault will eventually adopt from Deleuze (see chap. 11). Foucault criticizes Freud for having an overly textual and linguistic approach to the dream; this parallels Nietzsche's implicit criticism of Aristotle and almost the entire post-Aristotelian tradition for reducing tragedy to plot, with an accompanying demotion of music and spectacle. This is the reduction that already begins, according to the *Birth*, with the "one great Cyclops eye of Socrates"; Aristotle simply disagrees as to the intelligibility and the ethical meaning of tragedy once it has been so reduced. To some extent Foucault anticipates the opposition between Jacques Lacan and Jean-François Lyotard about the role of image and language in Freud's dream theory. For Lacan, Freud has a linguistic account of the dream; the images of which the dream consists are essentially, as Freud declares, a rebus, or picture puzzle, which has a linguistic equivalent. According to Lyotard, it is the constant tension between language and image that characterizes the Freudian dream, and art generally.[6]

What we might call the Nietzschean or Lyotardian side of Foucault's dream book is its insistence on image and imagination; there is even a suggestion that the main literary genres can be understood in terms of typical forms of dream imagination. Against any linguistic reductionism, Foucault insists on the importance of dream space and dream landscape. Yet this most Heideggerian of Foucault's texts also deviates from Nietzsche in its account of the dreamer's position with regard to his or her own dream. For Nietzsche, in the *Birth of Tragedy*, there is something impersonal or naive about the dream and the art that both illuminates it and is derived from it. For Foucault, who is sympathetically developing a strain of Heideggerian existential phenomenology that underlies Binswanger's work, the dream is a form of *Existenz*; he writes: "In the dream, everything says 'I,' even the things and the animals, even the empty space, even objects distant and strange which populate the phantasmagoria. . . . To dream is not another way of experiencing another world, it is for the dreaming subject the radical way of experiencing its own world" (*DX* 59; *DE* 1.100). By the time he came to write *The Order of Things*, Foucault would doubtless have rejected the subjectivism of this formulation as part of the thought characteristic of the epoch of man, and he might have seen this kind of fascination with the dream as one manifestation of the return and retreat of the origin, which displays the instability of "man and his doubles."

What is notable about this early text is that, like *The Birth of Tragedy*, it situates its subject in an irreducibly visual perspective. If art is, as Socrates says in the *Sophist*, "a waking dream," then understanding the dream's visual dimension will yield a distinctive conception of art. This approach provides an important corrective to some attempts to categorize Foucault as a linguistic reductionist; the same applies to many others who are considered to be poststructuralists.[7] Such readings often proceed by citing the importance of Nietzsche for these thinkers; but I have suggested some reasons for thinking that we may be ready for a different approach to both thinkers, to their relationship, and to the way in which they theorize the relationship between the linguistic and the visual.

Perhaps this attention to the dream points to a concern with activities and practices that have been marginalized by normalizing disciplines and institutions but that persist in forms that can be unearthed and articulated for the possibilities of resistance that they present to those forces and their discourses. In *The Care of the Self*, Foucault mines ancient dream books, volumes that claimed to decode the meaning of dreams, in order to determine what some of the main ethical issues of the time were. This concern is perhaps not surprising, given that a French thinker, and a dreamer of powerful dreams, is usually taken to have inaugurated modern philosophy with the thought that he might always be dreaming. An important aspect of Foucault's exchange with Derrida over the opening of Descartes's *Meditations* is the claim that Descartes was able to accept the hypothesis that he was dreaming, but not that he was mad, the point being that dreaming is a doubt that can eventually be disposed of, while the supposition that one is mad is to disqualify oneself from rational discourse.[8]

Foucault's essay "Dream, Imagination, and Existence" has been described as his most Heideggerian text; this is not surprising, given Binswanger's debt to Heidegger. If so, it fills a significant gap in the Heideggerian world, for there appears to be no thematization of the dream in Heidegger. The essay is Heideggerian insofar as it suggests that the dream must be understood as a fundamental projection of the dreamer's ontological possibilities. Like Nietzsche, unmentioned in the dream essay, Foucault thinks of the dream as a very much like a work of art. Indeed, at the end of the essay he argues that a full phenomenological account of the dream must deal with its public expressions or analogs in works of art and the imagination, and he claims that "every act of imagination points implicitly to the dream" (DX 67). There are some reasons for wondering how seriously we should read this early essay on the dream. For example, Foucault claims that the result of his analysis will be to provide the outlines of "an anthropology of art," a project that he goes so far as to sketch by distinguishing the three modes of epic, lyric, and tragic. While this is a very traditional set of poetic genres, Foucault's understanding of them is not in terms of the dialectic of subject and object, which rules in such philosophical analyses as those of Hegel, Marx, and the young Lukacs. Instead, he sees them as developing three different axes or dimensions of the dream. In *The Order of Things*, as we know, Foucault questions such anthropological projects; there he argues that they are all variations on the problematic of "man and his doubles," in which modern thought is tied to the ambiguities implicit in the project, most familiar to philosophy in Kant, of trying to explain the nature and possibility of knowledge through an inquiry into man's finitude; limits paradoxically become enabling. From this perspective, Kant, Marx, the early Heidegger, and phenomenological projects of the sort undertaken in Foucault's dream essay would all be variations on one and the same enterprise, all suspect forms of an inquiry that must lead to the aporias of the transcendental and the empirical, the cogito and the unthought, and the return and retreat of the origin. One can imagine the Foucault of this archaeological standpoint observing his younger self's efforts rather skeptically, perhaps seeing the dream essay as one more valiant attempt to unearth and bring to light the obscure origins of human imagination, only to have them disappear into the darkness of the unconscious. What better example of the thematics of the return and retreat of the origin than the project of deriving the forms of art and imagination from the dream? Such an effort would appear to be a footnote to what Foucault calls that "experience of Hölderlin, Nietzsche, and Heidegger, in which the return is posited only in the extreme recession of the origin—in that region where the gods have turned away, where the desert is increasing, where the *techne* has established the dominion of the will" (OT 334; Mch 345). The heroic position that Foucault sometimes seems to accord to Novalis and some other German romantics could also be taken as signs that this is a juvenile piece. My own thought is that while he might have distanced himself from this early work, we can see some of its themes resonating in his later writings, as Nietzsche both criticized and loved his own firstborn *Birth of Tragedy* in the new preface he wrote for the 1886 edition (sec. 79).

There are, then, several themes worth attending to in the dream essay (as I will call it). First, Foucault argues strongly for the centrality and significance of the *image* in the dream. This has an immediate polemical relevance to what he sees as the limits of Freud's approach, which is said to pass all too quickly over the image in order to arrive at the more accessible field of the linguistic. The upshot is that "psychoanalysis has never succeeded in making images speak" (*DX* 38). On this view, Freud is an iconoclast, an enemy of images, perhaps following the ancient Mosaic prohibition in his own way. Later, Lyotard criticized Lacan for having elided the visual dimension of the dream; he suggested that Freud already was working with the confrontation and exchange between the visual and the verbal in a way that Lacan's linguistic structuralism could not accommodate. More generally, we can connect Foucault's attempt to give the image its due in the context of the dream analysis with his constant concern with the visual dimension, a concern that runs through his works and which has been noted by Deleuze.

A second emphasis in the dream essay is on the spatiality of existence. Apparently following Heidegger and extending his thought to the dream, Foucault understands the dream as a projection of meaning in which the human being encounters its freedom and its finitude and grapples with the question of authenticity. Yet Foucault apparently reverses the early Heidegger's emphasis on temporality as a more significant dimension of human existence than spatiality. Although Foucault has much to say about temporality, death, and destiny in the dream, he seems at least on the verge of subordinating time to space. This articulation of dream space is clearly indebted to Heidegger's account of being-in-the-world, *Umsicht*, and related notions. Dream space, despite its distensions and compressions, is an oriented space; it is (in Sartrean language) "hodological," marked by paths that can always be connected to a "homeward road" (*DX* 60; *DE* 1.102). While talk of the "homeward road" may recall some of the nostalgia one finds in such Heideggerian essays as "Building, Dwelling, Thinking," this emphasis on spatiality as such could be seen as anticipating Foucault's later concern with various forms of institutional space, architecture, and geography. The analysis of the asylum, the medical clinic, and the Panopticon all hinge on comprehending how forms of power and discourse are complicit with structures of space and visibility. The space of grotesque execution and the closed scenario of the Panopticon, both evoked in *Discipline and Punish,* can be read as frightening dreams of spatial possibilities. In this respect it would be fruitful to think of reading Foucault's discussion of urban and institutional spaces alongside the analyses of Walter Benjamin; in the *Arcades Project* the latter explicitly appeals to the logic and grammar of the dream in order to make sense of the spaces of the city. Benjamin's theme of the labyrinth draws on a traditional poetic dream or nightmare that Foucault was to find relevant in his book on Raymond Roussel.[9] The principle announced in the dream essay is that "the forms of spatiality disclose in the dream the very 'meaning and direction' of human existence" (*DX* 60; *DE* 1.101). A number of Foucault's accounts of paintings and other works of art read as essays in discovering the dream behind the image. Consider the oneiric ekphrasis of Magritte's *Ceci non pas une pipe,* in which Foucault imagines the painting as the dream set for all of us, in our roles as teachers and students, perplexed by reference. It is a long passage. I simply recall: "Everything is solidly anchored within a pedagogic space. . . . From painting to image, from image to text, from text to voice, a sort of imaginary pointer indicates, shows, fixes, locates, imposes a series of references, tries to stabilize a unique space" (*TNP* 29; *CP* 36).

In his dream essay, Foucault distinguishes three basic dimensions or forms of the dream that give rise to three types of art. These dimensions are variations on the possibilities of light and space. The epic type is based on modulations of the near and far and so includes departures, voyages, and circumnavigations; the lyric mode has to do with the opposition and alternation of solar and nocturnal themes; and the tragic form involves a structure of ascent and fall. If we were to compare this typology of genres with those prominent in the aesthetics of German idealism, we would be struck by the way in which Foucault's schema passes over both the dialectic of subject and object and the attempt to determine the artistic or poetic genres in terms of temporal modalities (past, present, future).

In the dream essay, Foucault claims that death is an essential theme of the dream, since the dream is a projection of the possibilities of existence and an encounter with destiny. He writes: "Death is experienced as the supreme moment of that contradiction, which death constitutes as destiny. Hence the meaningfulness of all those dreams of violent death, of savage death, of horrified death, in which one must indeed recognize, in the final analysis, a freedom up against a world" (*DX* 54; *DE* 1.94). While we might be tempted to dismiss Foucault's intense interest in death as a theme of the dream on the grounds that he himself had dismissed such concerns with *Existenz* by the time of "Man and

His Doubles," it is worth noting that death is again made thematic in his treatment of Andy Warhol and in the late essay on Duane Michals (secs. 77, 79).

44 Temptations: Bosch and Other Visionaries

Is Foucault a Platonist? He seems to agree with the thought of the *Sophist* that art is a waking dream, a visionary production that enters into the public space. In this respect Foucault would also be something of a Freudian, making allowances for his profound differences with these two thinkers of the metaphysics of vision. So the *Histoire de folie*, where he might be said to be engaging with both Platonic reason and the Freudian attempt to make sense of and contain madness, is framed, like so many of Foucault's texts, by the invocation of paintings or other visual images. It is a question at one end of depictions of madness, as in Renaissance versions of the ship of fools, and at the other of art in the wake of Goya, who (along with Sade) is said to mark the era in which "unreason has belonged to whatever is decisive, for the modern world, in any work of art: that is, whatever any work of art contains that is both murderous and constraining" (*MC* 228; *HF* 660). Prominent among Goya's heirs is Van Gogh, who knew that his madness was incompatible with his work and so confirmed that "madness is the absolute break with the work of art" (*MC* 230; *HF* 662).

At the beginning of *Histoire de folie*, Foucault offers an extended analysis of the "Ship of Fools" theme in a number of Renaissance texts and paintings. He emphasizes the distinction between the literary or philosophical, on the one hand, and the imagistic on the other. Here "painting engages in an experiment that will take it farther and farther from language," as the image allows itself to explore the cosmic dimensions of madness and the monstrous animality that reveals "the secret nature of man" (*MC* 26; *HF* 33–34). The literary representations of madness at this time, for example Erasmus's *Praise of Folly* or Brant's *Ship of Fools*, treat it as an occasion for moral satire and instruction, and "[n]othing suggests those great threats of invasion that haunted the imagination of the painters" (*MC* 33; *HF* 43). What are these threats of invasion? Foucault returns several times to Bosch's *Temptation of Saint Anthony* (the version in Lisbon), as well as to works by Brueghel, Dürer, and Bouts. Later he will write an afterword for a new edition of Flaubert's *Temptation*, in which he draws an analogy between the encyclopedic culture of the museum and the writer's use of the legends of Saint Anthony to summon up a vast array of heretical and threatening thoughts and images, that is, of invasive phantasms. The theme seems to be made for the painter, for it invites the visionary and oneiric art to engage in a doubling, to produce a vision of visions, a simulacrum of the simulacra haunting the saint. For Foucault this painting and others in its genre mark a break with earlier depictions of the grotesque and fantastic. During the preceding two centuries, he points out, a leading theme of Christian painting was mortality; the dance of death was a frequent subject. Now "[i]n the last years of the [fifteenth] century this enormous uneasiness turns upon itself; the mockery of madness replaces death and its solemnity. From the discovery of that necessity which inevitably reduces man to nothing, we have shifted to the scornful contemplation of that nothing which is existence itself" (MC 24; HF 31). It is only at a first glance that the literary and plastic expressions of this theme seem to echo one another. The iconography of the paintings follows that of texts like those of Brant and Erasmus. Yet there is something more vivid, more invasive, in the visual work. It is here, at the beginning of what was to become a vast narrative of the construction of the modern subject, a story that unfolds through the struggle of reason and madness, the formation of the clinical gaze, and the regimes of disciplinary surveillance whose sign is the Panopticon, that Foucault makes a point of noting the incommensurability of the word and the image. While it is true that he will later suggest that writers from Flaubert to Bataille and Artaud have incorporated some of the disturbing powers of the sixteenth-century painters in literary form, the decisive separation or *partage* of word and image in the art and writing of the time reveals a power in the visual to introduce humanity to the powers of madness:

> Between word and image, between what is depicted by language and what is uttered by plastic form, the unity begins to dissolve; a single and identical meaning is not immediately common to them. And if it is true that the image still has the function of *speaking*, of transmitting something consubstantial with language, we must recognize that it no longer says the *same thing;* and that by its own plastic values painting engages in an experiment that will take it farther and farther from language, whatever the superficial identity of the theme. Figure and speech still illustrate the same fable of folly in the same moral world, but already they take two different directions, indicating in a still barely perceptible scission, what will be the great line of cleavage [*partage*] in the Western experience of madness. (MC 26; HF 33–34)

It is not only a question of the *partage* of reason and madness, important as this certainly is; Foucault makes the point more generally a few years later in a review of two books by the art historian Erwin Panofsky (just then translated into French). To some readers Panofsky's studies of iconology might seem to be quite heavily textual, relying on his reconstruction of the painter's religious and philosophical learning. The art historian's magisterial erudition would seem to be in the service of a somewhat traditional *Geisteswissenschaft* of the sort that Foucault placed in archaeological brackets just the year before in *Les mots et les choses;* indeed, there he goes out of his way in his reading of Velazquez to avoid just the sort of historical contextualization that Panofsky conducts with great grace and aplomb. Foucault reads Panofsky rather differently, and his judgment is more interesting for what it tells us about his own sense of the relation between the visual and the discursive than as an explication of the art historian's theoretical orientation. "Panofsky eliminates the privilege of discourse. Not in order to assert the autonomy of the figurative universe, but to describe the complexity of their relations: chiasm, isomorphism, transformation, translation, in a word all of the festoon [*feston*] of the *visible* and the *sayable* that characterize a culture in a moment of its history. . . . Everything that men make is not, in sum, a decipherable murmur. Discourse and the figure each have their own mode of being; but they entertain complex and tangled relations. The task is to describe their reciprocal functioning" (*DE* 1.621).

If Foucault had indeed picked up the habit of speaking of painting, he also added another level to it rather quickly, that is, the ability to thematize that very speaking and to interrogate the relation between the figurative and the discursive. It is this project that Foucault begins to undertake in the *Histoire de la folie* and which continues through his writings on such recent figures as Warhol, Michals, and Fromanger. It is not as an art historian or a critic that he approaches the paintings and photographs, but as an archaeologist or a cartographer (Deleuze's expression), who would ascertain the specific topography of word and image. Specifically, in the paintings of Bosch and his contemporaries, Foucault finds a way in which visual art opens itself up to the dream. He agrees with Emile Mâle that during a certain period of the Middle Ages, and within definite limits, there was a strict parallelism of word and image; the figures of art could be read semiotically as transcriptions of texts (Bible, commentary, philosophy) (*MC* 26; *HF* 34). Yet a change occurs at that point (roughly around 1500) when the meaning of the image becomes too heavy and rich for such a reduction to be plausible.

The power of the image is "no longer to teach but to fascinate," so meaning appears in a new form: "Meaning is no longer read in an immediate perception, the figure no longer speaks for itself; between the knowledge which animates it and the form into which it is transposed, a gap widens. It is free for the dream" (MC 27; HF 34). The dream, we recall, is the site where the paths of our existence are mapped out. It is where man "has known since antiquity, that . . . he encounters what he is and what will be, what he has done and what he is going to do, discovering there the knot that ties his freedom to the necessity of the world" (DX 47; DE 1.85). Now Foucault is treating works like Bosch's *Temptation of Saint Anthony* as public or collective dreams, as Nietzsche took Raphael's *Transfiguration* to be an Apollonian vision that the great "naïve" artist had managed to project for the audience of his time. It is an index of what links and separates the two thinkers that they both accord a certain prominence to a Christian painting at relatively early points in their philosophical careers, that they manage to evade the most obvious Christian meanings of these works (Foucault says nothing about the virtuous resistance that the saint makes to the images), and that they choose such different paintings and painters as the subjects of ekphrasis. It is as if the implicit hallucinatory visions of Raphael's possessed boy had taken the most definite and multifarious shapes, or the strange carnivalesque beings that took flight in Zarathustra's dream of the night watchman had materialized in a series of unearthly landscapes.

In Foucault's reading of the Lisbon *Temptation*, he eventually focuses on one odd figure, a head without a body, that addresses the saint directly at the center of the triptych (fig. 9). Characteristically, Foucault prepares the ground for his encounter with this figure by examining its predecessors, stressing the diacritical differences between superficially similar images. Following the art historians to a certain point, he reminds us of the development of the gryllos, grotesque human faces set in the bellies of monsters, which were meant to show "how the soul of desiring man had become a prisoner of the beast." The shift occurs when it is no longer illicit desire that torments the human being (represented in the form of the ascetic hermit) but the terror of nonmeaning, the possibility of the impossibility of making sense. Consider, then, Foucault's extended ekphrasis of the exchange of looks between the saint and the uncanny head to his right:

> [W]hat assails the hermit's tranquility is not objects of desire, but these hermetic, demented forms which have risen from a dream, and remain silent and furtive on the surface of a world. In the Lisbon

Figure 9. Hieronymous Bosch (ca. 1450–1516), *Temptation of Saint Anthony* (central panel). Museu Nacional de Arte Antiga, Lisbon. Giraudon/Art Resource, New York

Temptation, facing Saint Anthony sits one of those figures born of madness, of its solitude, of its penitence, of its privations; a wan smile lights this bodiless face, the pure presence of anxiety in the form of an agile grimace. Now it is exactly this nightmare silhouette that is at once the subject and object of the temptation; it is this figure which fascinates the gaze of the ascetic—both are prisoners of a kind of mirror interrogation, which remains unanswered in a silence inhabited only by the monstrous swarm that surrounds them. The gryllos no longer recalls man, by its satiric form, to his spiritual vocation forgotten in the folly of desire. It is madness become Temptation; all it embodies of the impossible, the fantastic, the inhuman, all that suggests the unnatural, the writhing of an insane presence on the earth's surface—all this is precisely what gives the gryllos its strange power. The freedom, however frightening, of his dreams, the hallucinations of his madness, have more power of attraction for fifteenth-century man than the desirable reality of the flesh. (*MC* 28; *HF* 35–36)

For Foucault these figures are above all silent; the knowing look on their faces says that they understand more than could possibly be said, that whatever is said will vanish into an abyss of nonmeaning. In the *Transfiguration* madness can be dispelled by the magnificent appearance of the healing god of vision; in this world it asserts an ineluctable right because it is the very substance of vision. The looks exchanged between the saint and the gryllos displace any discursive interchange; in this "mirror interrogation," each sees his own madness in the face of the other. The strange figure instantiates "the pure presence of anxiety," an anxiety that, as Heidegger would remind us, cannot be reduced to any nameable fear. To be human is to be in question, but the question is one that is experienced not through a language that would be at least minimally reassuring in its conceptuality, but in the mad look of the other. An enormous amount of labor has gone into the attempt to decipher the haunting paintings of Bosch, as if their challenge could be analyzed in terms of the esoteric beliefs of a secret cult or an idiosyncratic transformation of an archive of more or less traditional symbols. Foucault is claiming, in effect, that however far our researches might take us into the history of art or religion, we will be left at bottom with that mad exchange of looks, where the saint and his dreamed or hallucinated other know that there is no truth beyond their mutual and necessarily silent interrogation. So far as we have a position in this picture, we identify with the saint. While we know that we should be looking into the interior, where the religious rite proceeds, with the established image of the crucifix, we are forever distracted by these haunting figures that cannot be exorcized in the space and time of the painting.

Foucault claims that the image, at least in this time and place, has the power of suspending our customary connection with the world. It may be with the example of surrealism in mind that he attempts to spell out the revelatory dimension of pictures like Bosch's *Temptation*, Brueghel's *Dulle Griet*, Thierry Bouts's *Hell*, and Dürer's *Four Horsemen of the Apocalypse*:

> It is in the space of pure vision that madness deploys its powers. Phantasms and dangers, pure appearances of the dream and the secret destiny of the world—there madness maintains a primitive force of revelation: the revelation that the oneiric is real, that the thin surface of illusion opens onto an unrecoverable depth, and that the scintillating instantaneity of the image leaves the world a prey to the disquieting figures that prolong its nights; and the inverse but equally lamentable revelation, that the entire reality of the world will be absorbed one day in the fantastic Image, in the moment midway between being and nothingness that is the delirium of pure destruction; the world is no more, but night and silence are still not entirely closed within it; it flickers in a final radiance, at the extreme of a disorder that immediately precedes the monotonous order of completion. It is in this immediately abolished image that the truth of the world is lost. All of this web of appearance and the secret, of the immediate image and the hidden enigma is deployed in fifteenth century painting as *the tragic madness of the world*. (HF 45–46)

For Foucault, as for Nietzsche, painting is a creature of dreams and night.[10] Yet while *The Birth of Tragedy* sees the plastic arts as shining visions of clarity, here painting hovers in a space of complete indeterminacy, a place that puts all discursive assumptions of order into doubt.

45 Fantasia of the Library: The Birth of Literature out of the Spirit of Painting

On Foucault's account, it will take almost four hundred years for something like this unconstrained life of the phantasm to enter into literature, with Flaubert's version of the *Temptation of Saint Anthony*. In this book, Foucault says that Flaubert may have been responding to a "new imaginative space," with its own "domain of phantasms" that spring not from the night but from "zealous erudition," that is from the realm of books and the library (*LCMP* 90; *DE* 1.297). Yet even here, he suggests in his essay "Fantasia of the Library," it is an inspiration from painting that leads to the bibliomanic explosion of the novel. In the text Saint Anthony lights a torch and opens a book as soon as his disturbing visions begin to appear. Foucault points out that the same action is to be found in "Breughel the Younger's" painting of the temptation topos "that so impressed Flaubert when he visited the Balbi collection in Genoa and that he felt had incited him to write *The Temptation*" (*LCMP* 94; *DE* 1.300).[11] He attributes an enormous importance to this fantastic text of Flaubert's, suggesting not only that it haunts all his other works but also that "it dreams other books, all other books that dream and that men dream of writing," and in so doing it makes modern literature possible, as in Mallarmé, Joyce, Roussel, Kafka, Pound, and Borges; now, he says, "the library is on fire" (*LCMP* 92; *DE* 1.298). In this extraordinary narrative, literature assumes its modern form through a painterly inspiration. And aside from Foucault's reference to Breughel the Younger, he constructs an analogy between Manet and Flaubert. The former is the first "museum" painter, the first whose works refer to the whole tradition of painting and to paintings as seen in the context of the museum; it is a position that André Malraux will describe as having displaced all earlier attitudes to art. Similarly, the writer works in relation to all earlier texts, to the vast archive of literature (itself a relatively recent invention), in order to evoke a "Fantasia of the Library." This is a theme that will deserve more attention when we consider Foucault's account of Manet and modernist painting as forms of visual resistance to the panoptical visual regime (sec. 65).

The essay on Flaubert offers a stunning scenic and theatrical analysis of the novel, an analysis that does indeed read it as the construction of a series of phantasms, the linguistic analog of a Bosch or Breughel *Temptation;* it is a reading that transforms what some commentators have seen as defects of the text into its distinctive strengths and that would position it as an exemplar of what the critic Joseph Frank has called "spatial form" in literature.[12] The novel is alleged by some to have a merely episodic structure, to heap one bizarre scene upon another, drawing indiscriminately from a miscellaneous reading in the history of religion and folklore. Foucault argues that once we understand the *Temptation*'s fundamental mode of presentation, we can also recognize its careful construction. The first thing to understand is that the text "challenges the priority of its printed signs and takes the form of a theatrical presentation." At one time, he adds, Flaubert had intended the book to be something like an epic drama, an analog of Goethe's *Faust*, a script to be recited and staged. On this interpretation, "[p]rint can only be an unobtrusive aid to the visual" (*LCMP* 93; *DE* 1.300). Within this context, which is also reminiscent of the puppet theater, we are presented with a complex series of visions within visions. The initial setting of the scene is in a "natural theater" at the top of a mountain, a half-moon space that functions as a stage on which further scenes will unfold. Without repeating here Foucault's detailed analysis of the series of visions within visions for which this setting serves as a *dispositif*—a series that he illustrates diagrammatically with numbered sections or events—note how he diagrams this structure as positioning the reader as a virtual spectator: "This arrangement allows the reader (1) to see Saint Anthony (3) over the shoulder of the implied spectator (2) who is an accomplice to the dramatic presentation: the effect is to identify the reader with the spectator. Consequently, the spectator sees Anthony on the stage, but he also sees over his shoulder the apparitions presented to the hermit, apparitions that are as substantial as that of the saint" (*LCMP* 97; *DE* 1.303). This analysis recalls the perspectivist account of the Greek theater in *The Birth of Tragedy*, which explains how the Athenian spectator sees from two places at once and manages to assume a virtual identity through a visual identification with the chorus. Flaubert then offers a modern, textual, and literary analog of Nietzsche's alternative to "the one great Cyclops eye" of Socrates, insofar as he constructs the novel as the site of "the simultaneous existence of multiple meanings" (*LCMP* 99; *DE* 1.304).

For Foucault the series of visions is a series of transformations. He remarks on the inversions of temporal order and the sudden shifts from the everyday scenes of Alexandria to the earliest beginnings of life. It is as if Flaubert were heading toward a Nietzschean revelation: "[B]eyond this primordial cell from which life evolved, Anthony desires an impossible return to the passive state prior to life: the whole of his existence is consequently laid to rest where it recovers its innocence and awakens once again to the sound of animals, the bubbling fountain, and the glittering stars. The highest temptation is the longing to be another, to be all others; it is to renew identifications and to achieve the principle of time in a return that completes the circle. The vision of Engadine approaches" (*LCMP* 101; *DE* 1.306). "The vision of Engadine" is Foucault's somewhat esoteric designation of Nietzsche's experience of eternal recurrence in the Swiss mountains, the one that he marks as "beginning of August 1881 in Sils-Maria, 6000 feet over sea level and much higher beyond all human things" (*KSA* 9.494; 11[141]). Flaubert's *Temptation* is the desire to be another. As Nietzsche says in *The Gay Science*, if this thought ever took hold of you, it would either crush you or turn you into another (*GS* 341; *KSA* 3.570), and in a letter to Jakob Burckhardt during his breakdown, he famously declares, "I am all the names of history" (*B* 8.578). The visions of Saint Anthony are all such possibilities of transformation, of becoming all those names. Foucault calls Nietzsche's "most abysmal thought" a *vision*, following the language of "On the Vision and the Riddle." Flaubert is said to stage a series of visions, visions of possible transformation, that anticipates the Nietzschean revelation.[13]

A pattern emerges in Foucault's early essays on literature. The earliest form of his study of Roussel is entitled "Seeing and Saying in Raymond Roussel." Now Foucault finds in Flaubert an approach to that visionary revelation. He writes on Bataille, exploring his figure of the eye, which turns out to be a figure for the philosophy of reflection. Bataille recognized the optical, ophthalmic, and visionary character of Nietzsche's thought of recurrence. The Flaubert essay was originally a postface to a German translation of the novel, so the introduction of Nietzsche may have had a specific resonance with his readers. When Foucault prepared a French edition of the essay in 1967, he added a series of twelve illustrations of a number of the fantastic apparitions, mostly of Hindu or Buddhist inspiration, that are summoned up in the novel. His own text aspires to the visual.

seven

Critique of Impure Phenomenology

46 Merleau-Ponty's Evasion of Nietzsche:
Misreading Malraux

What Foucault claims to have learned or to have understood more clearly from Panofsky was both the irreducibility of the visual in visual art and the necessity for a vigilant attention to the various ways in which the visual is articulated at different historical moments; he found there a confirmation of his own project of developing an archaeology of visual regimes. The first point sounds like a phenomenological principle. As Foucault came of philosophical age in the 1940s and 1950s, one of the "habits" that he might have picked up could very well have been that of speaking of painting with the voice of phenomenology, a voice that spoke most resonantly in the work of Merleau-Ponty. Yet the habit or tendency of Merleau-Ponty's thought about art is in some tension with the archaeological work that Foucault began to carry out in the 1960s.[1] In the essay on *Las Meninas*, Foucault is already engaged in providing a critique of phenomenology and articulating an archaeological alternative to it, a theme that will loom large in *Les mots et les choses*, where phenomenology is eventually seen as caught up in the aporias of "Man and His Doubles." To understand the polemical force of Foucault's writing on painting, it will be instructive to see how Merleau-Ponty addressed the question of art and history and to examine Foucault's response.

The conflict between phenomenology and a more radically historical approach to art is one that Merleau-Ponty had already begun to wrestle with, notably in the critical essay "Indirect Language and the Voices of Silence," which is an extended consideration of André Malraux's work. Put very schematically, Merleau-Ponty wants to interrogate what he sees as Malraux's capitulation to History (with a capital *H*) and to the introduction of what he calls the "Hegelian monstrosity" of the superartist who is at work through the succession of styles that is the history of art in the world of the museum, a monstrosity that is magnified in the imaginary museum with its proliferation of inescapable images in print and on screen. To this History Merleau-Ponty opposes what he repeatedly calls *presence*, although this is not a presence devoid of history, nor even of Hegel, when Hegel is properly understood in terms of a work that overcomes any simple binary distinction of internal and external perspectives and in terms of an advent of cultural meaning that is indefinitely fecund in events. Against what he takes to be Malraux's false Hegelianism of a succession of phases of the *Weltgeist*, Merleau-Ponty champions a true Hegel, who, in certain passages of the *Phenomenology of Spirit*, wrote insightfully of an embodied activity in which there is a constant reciprocity and interplay of inside and outside, intention and consequence, "so the Hegelian dialectic is what we call by another name the phenomenon of expression, which gathers itself up and launches itself again through the mystery of rationality" (*MPA* 110). I suggest that Malraux's work is best seen as not being Hegelian in the crude or false sense; and I also suggest that the "true" Hegelianism favored by Merleau-Ponty is the limited aesthetic of a specific era. Malraux's rethinking of the history of art ought rather to be seen as Nietzschean and proto-Foucauldian. It is not logic, not even the logic of the master-slave dialectic, that governs the history of art in *The Voices of Silence*, but a succession of unpredictable events, of more or less global shifts in visual regime, such as those associated with art's movement from churches and palaces to the museum and then the expansion of the imaginary museum through photographic means of reproduction.

There is an implicit politics in this critique: Merleau-Ponty is suggesting that Malraux, the Gaullist minister of culture, who proclaims the inevitability of an all-embracing global culture, a religion of art that exists simultaneously in cathedrals like the Louvre and the Metropolitan (its Catholic form) and in the sober (Protestant) home worship whose Bible is the book of color plates or the glossy magazines where even the advertisements quote Velazquez or Picasso, is subscribing to a philosophy of history hardly distinguishable from that of the Stalinists of the thirties who invoked an incontestable form of historical inevitability. Just as Malraux claims that the sense of a painting, the oeuvre of a painter, or the significance of a style is almost totally a function of the styles that have succeeded it, with each accession to the imaginary museum capable of transforming its past, so the Stalinists (whose arguments Merleau-Ponty had flirted with in *Humanism and Terror*) claimed that being on the wrong side, or being accused (as in the purge trials), showed that one was "objectively" a traitor or saboteur. To these "monstrosities" Merleau-Ponty opposes a phenomenology of expression, perception, and history (with a very small *h*). Painting can attain its apotheosis in the Museum only because "painting exists first of all in each painter who works, and it is there in a pure state, whereas the Museum compromises it with the somber pleasures of retrospection. . . . the Museum converts this secret, modest, non-deliberated, involuntary, and in short, living historicity into official and pompous history" (*MPA* 99). The alternative is to "put painting back into the present" (*MPA* 100).

In both this essay and "Eye and Mind," the valorization of presence in painting is carried further in the homage paid to the *hand* of the painter. Merleau-Ponty attempts to demonstrate the presence of the hand and its independence of the reproductive techniques of the imaginary museum, which is capable of finding the "same" style in a large sculpture or a tiny coin through the use of photography and change of scale. Since the hinge of "Indirect Language" is painting's relation to speech and literature, it is odd that the example of this inalienable presence of the hand is not the painter's brushstroke but handwriting, which is taken to be the exemplum of style (*MPA* 102–3). Later we will be told that despite this appeal to the signature, painting is *not* writing.

While we might sympathize with Merleau-Ponty's humanistic defense of the painter against an autonomous History, we should also note some of the extreme maneuvers and positions that this defense imposes on him; and we should ask whether and to what extent he is justified in his implicit dismissal of the Museum and its culture; is he able, for example, to provide an alternative way of comprehending the massive power of our era's artistic institutions, or must he treat them as mere parasitic excrescences on the "pure" body of art and painting, which could be diagnosed, if not removed, by a rigorous phenomenology? Such a phenomenology would understand its political and ethical obligation of recalling men to the sober reality of their work and their situation in the world. Because Merleau-Ponty attempts to distinguish the genuine contemporaneity of painting from the spurious, overheated quest for novelty that he finds as an ingredient in museum culture, he entitles himself to relegate the painting of his own day to a very minor and derivative position. In the following condemnation, he does not even dignify the painters dismissed by mentioning their names, although he is always specific in praising Cézanne, Klee, or Matisse.

> Today's painting denies the past too deliberately to be able to really free itself from it. It can only forget it while it profits from it. The ransom of its novelty is that in making what came before it seem to be an unsuccessful effort, it foreshadows a different painting tomorrow which will make it seem in turn to be another unsuccessful effort. Thus painting as a whole presents itself as an abortive effort to say something which still remains to be said. Although the man who writes is not content to simply extend existing language, he is no more anxious to replace it by an idiom which, like a painting, is sufficient unto itself and closed in upon its intimate signification. (MPA 116)

What is described here, first of all, is the dynamic of modernism, a dynamic obviously fueled by the Museum's thirst for ever-new styles. The same dynamic was being described simultaneously across the Atlantic, where New York had "stolen the idea of modern art," as a heroic conquest of the conditions of painting itself whereby the apparent limitations of the flat canvas were transformed into its resources and strengths (Merleau-Ponty's essay was published in *Les Temps Modernes* in 1952 at the height of the cold war and of the apotheosis of Jackson Pollock).[2] This is the position of Clement Greenberg, for example, whose thought bears some interesting aesthetic and political parallels to Malraux's and who may be said to have retained in his art criticism much of the philosophy of history that he had apparently abandoned in his political development.[3] There is something quixotic and cavalier in Merleau-Ponty's evaluation of modernism, since it very seldom engages with specific works or the discourses that surround them. Second, if we attend closely to the rhetoric of this passage and to the astounding final section of the essay in which it is embedded, we notice that what begins as a negative appraisal of contemporary painting expands into a criticism of painting in general when it is compared with literature or writing. Whereas the essay began by deploying Saussure's diacritical account of language to suggest that all meaning lies in the interstices, so that language in the narrow sense has no special claim to priority or explicitness in relation to painting, it concludes by setting out a series of distinctions between painting and writing that all hinge on the failure of presence. By speaking of its truth, speech gives us the past in its presence, while painting remains unreflective and is much more subject to the passage of time—its presence is obscured (*MPA* 117). To hold on to the presence of painting, then, Merleau-Ponty has had to first reject modernism and then admit that painting fails in presence after all; so its voices become voices of silence in quite another sense than the one he introduced earlier. They are now only mute gestures that lack the living presence of speech. While rejecting the supposed monstrous Hegelianism of the Museum's art-spirit, Merleau-Ponty has subscribed to the very traditional system of the arts that Hegel formulated more systematically than anyone else, according to which art becomes more truthful as it approaches the condition of spoken language. Finally, he seems to confess his inability to provide an institutional account of the power and scope of the culture of the imaginary museum, an analysis that could provide a significant alternative to those of Malraux, Benjamin, and Baudrillard (for example). At the end of "Eye and Mind," Merleau-Ponty states the position that is necessary if one wants to avoid such an analysis of the powers and institutions within which paintings circulate, their meanings are fixed or altered, and styles and painters are canonized or decanonized. Although he hedges this statement around with a number of qualifications, he does say that "the very first painting in some sense went to the farthest reach of the future" (*MPA* 149).

I suspect that Merleau-Ponty has incorporated more of the philosophy of the museum than he acknowledges, and perhaps this should not be surprising, for what is vehemently denied is often implicitly accepted. As Malraux points out, the rise of the relatively portable easel painting to its paradigmatic position in the world of the visual arts is a specific historical phenomenon whose genealogy can be traced. For centuries the most forceful forms of "painting" were stained glass windows and frescoes, works whose mobility has become imaginable only very recently. The Museum accepted what was portable (often what was carried off by military or economic conquest, as in the institutions over which Malraux presided). But then artists began to paint specifically for the museum, the gallery, or the private collector (which are affiliated institutions), so that the easel painting (or the portable sculpture) became the measure for all of the arts. In tracing this genealogy, let us not forget that Malraux too evades some difficulties. *The Voices of Silence* seems to speak a double language, one affirming that the history of art must be what the Museum has made of it, and another suggesting that we have access to other, alternative histories. When Malraux says, for example, speaking of stained-glass, polychrome wood-carving, and similar arts, that "during the Middle Ages there existed a sort of cinema in colors of which no trace has survived," we are reminded of Heidegger's reading of the sentence of Anaximander in which he uncannily announces that the very trace of the original ontological difference has fallen into oblivion.[4]

Merleau-Ponty was right in responding to the incoherence of such a position and in claiming that it referred in some way to the possibility of an ever-renewed perception of the past; however, his own writings about art and painting assume the primacy of the portable painting. This becomes clear in "Eye and Mind" when he offers a critique of Descartes's conception of vision. He carefully demonstrates the limitations of the theory of the *Dioptrics* with its emphasis on line drawings, its reduction of vision to physical contact, and its exclusion of the phenomena of hiddenness and obstruction that characterize perception in the world. Merleau-Ponty goes on, quite plausibly to suggest that Descartes is indebted to the monocular and immobile models of vision put forward by Renaissance painter-philosophers like Alberti. But he retains the most general frame of this model, that is, the framed portable picture, in his own thought on painting, as when he turns from his critique of Descartes to an impressive narrative of the "modern history of painting and its efforts to detach itself from illusionism and to acquire its own dimensions" (*MPA* 139); this narrative again construes painting as a highly autonomous art whose recent triumphs are marked by the work of Cézanne, Klee, and Matisse. Nothing in this account would help to explain the explosion of art forms since 1960 that have challenged and undercut first the traditional primacy of the portable painting and second the metaphysics and politics of the Museum itself; think of works that break or challenge the frame, for example minimalist art, conceptual art, various forms of ephemeral and performance art, earthworks like Robert Smithson's *Spiral Jetty*, and site-specific works of public art like Richard Serra's *Tilted Arc*.[5]

This difficulty in theorizing the contemporary, either in the sense of the art of today or in the more important one of contemporaneity as such, is signaled by another move that Merleau-Ponty makes in rewriting Malraux's metanarrative of art's history. He correctly recounts the three basic phases of that metanarrative:

At first, art and poetry are consecrated to the city, the gods, and the sacred, and it is only in the mirror of an external power that they can see the birth of their own miracle. Later both know a classic age which is the secularization of the sacred age; art is then the representation of a Nature that it can at best embellish—but according to formulas taught to it by Nature herself. . . . [He is then led to] define modern painting as a return to subjectivity—to the "incomparable monster"—and to bury it in a secret life outside the world. (*MPA* 84)

In rethinking this story, Merleau-Ponty offers a finely nuanced phenomenology to suggest that neither we nor the painter need choose between nature and the self, between representation and expression. But what has happened in this account to the city and the gods? Can we assume that painting is to be understood as an advent that moves chiasmically between the visible and the invisible without reference to these powers? Is this elision the price to be paid by a phenomenology that seeks to preserve the presence of painting against the demonic transformations threatened by History? Would recurring to the city and the gods compel Merleau-Ponty to ask in a more detailed way how the arts are shaped in both crude and subtle ways by the institutions, knowledges, and practices that surround them? Does the effort to articulate a fully embodied and contextualized view of the perceiving subject founder on an aestheticism that, in a fully traditional manner, takes art to rise above the conflicts and impositions of the political?

Merleau-Ponty reads Malraux somewhat eccentrically when he calls him a Hegelian. It would be more useful to think of the position of the *Voices* as a variant of Nietzschean thought, in several respects. Malraux, like Nietzsche in *The Birth of Tragedy* and in *Human, All Too Human,* rejects the idea that art has a continuous and logical development; the perspective of the museum and the later one afforded by the easy availability of photographic reproduction have clearly come about as the result of developments that are not strictly internal to the concept of art. Malraux is acutely aware of the enormous shifts that have occurred in our entire orientation to art because of these changes. The pages that Foucault devotes to the museum in "Fantasia of the Library" are easily compatible with Malraux's narrative and may very well owe something to it. In explaining his claim that "Flaubert is to the library what Manet is to the museum," he analyzes the rise of modernism in a passage that could be equally at home in a text by Malraux:

Déjeuner sur l'Herbe and Olympia were perhaps the first "museum" paintings, the first paintings in European art that were less a response to the achievement of Giorgione, Raphael, and Velazquez than an acknowledgment (supported by this singular and obvious connection, using this legible reference to cloak its operation) of the new and substantial relation of painting to itself, as a manifestation of the existence of museums and the particular reality and inter-dependence that paintings acquire in museums. . . . [The works of Flaubert and Manet] were not meant to foster the lamentations—the lost youth, the absence of vigor, and the decline of inventive-ness—through which we reproach our Alexandrian age, but to un-earth an essential aspect of our culture: every painting now belongs within the squared and massive surface of painting and all literary works are confined to the indefinite murmur of writing. (*LCMP* 92–93; *DE* 1.298–99)

Although Hegel does not precisely lament our living in an Alexandrian age and never uses the phrase "death of art," which is frequently attrib-uted to him, he does indeed declare that "art on its highest side is a thing of the past," a thesis to which neither Foucault nor Malraux would subscribe (sec. 75). Nietzsche, who later accused *The Birth of Tragedy* of being too Hegelian, was more anxious in that work about the possibility that Hegel may have been right, if the "death of art" is taken to be an empirical description, and *did* use the adjective "Alex-andrian" to describe his present; he desperately staked everything on the gamble of a Wagnerian rebirth, which would be a living perfor-mance that would escape from the confines of museum and archive. Only later did he suggest that an affirmative transvaluation of the Al-exandrian dimension of late Western culture was possible, as when he speaks in *Beyond Good and Evil* of how our encyclopedic study of the "costumes" of the past has "prepared [us] like no previous age for a carnival in the grand style, for the laughter and high spirits of the most spiritual revelry" (*BGE* 223; *KSA* 5.157).

The "truth" of Merleau-Ponty's charge of Hegelianism against Malraux (speaking of truth here in a vulgarized Hegelian sense) is that the latter does seem to opt for a somewhat uncritical concept of the *Zeitgeist*, a fundamental unity underlying all of the culture and thought of an era that would overwhelm the possibility of individual expression. Foucault has been accused of a similarly cavalier tendency to subsume all of the thought, writing, and art of a time under the sway of a specific epistemic regime. Yet Foucault distinguishes between appeals to such idealistic concepts as *Geist*, or spirit, and his own at-tempt to articulate the distinctions between various eras in terms of the prevalence of specific discursive forms or visual practices. It may finally be impossible to identify Malraux's perspective with either Hegel's or Nietzsche's; certainly *The Voices of Silence* comprehends a rich variety of outspoken voices that do not always sort well with one another. There is a strain of heroic humanism in this work that resembles some of the individualistic rhetoric to be found in Nietzsche, but which is not to be identified with the deepest tendencies of his thought; and Foucault, following a more subtle Nietzschean inspiration, would surely take issue with such passages. Yet there are also pronouncements like this, which verge on what I have been calling a visual archaeology and which would not be out of place in Nietzsche's meditation *On the Advantage and Disadvantage of History for Life:* "[M]ankind proceeds in terms of metamorphoses of a deep-seated order, it is not a matter of mere accretions or even of a continuous growth. . . . Thus our culture is not built up of earlier cultures reconciled with each other, but of irreconcilable fragments of the past. We know that it is not an inventory, but a heritage involving a metamorphosis; that the past is something to be conquered and annexed; also that it is within us and through us that the dialogue of Shades (that favorite art-form of the rhetorician) comes to life."[6] This deep-seated metamorphosis is something that Merleau-Ponty could not accept in Malraux's thought about art; Foucault offers his own version of it in framing his most celebrated discussion of painting, which implicitly takes issue with his phenomenological predecessor and his habits of thought.

47 Cézanne or Velazquez: What Is an Artist?

Michel Foucault's *Les mots et les choses* begins with a celebrated discussion of a very celebrated painting, Diego Velazquez's *Las Meninas* (fig. 10). It has been suggested that it is the only book of philosophy to begin with an ekphrasis, that is, a verbal description of a work of visual art.[7] Recently the painting has occupied a striking position in the Prado at the far end of a long room devoted to Velazquez; the actual depth of the exhibition space extends the interior depth of the painting so as to capture and fix the viewer's gaze. Even in reproductions it exercises a similar fascination on critics, art historians, and even the occasional philosopher. Foucault's essay itself has added to the vigorous discussion that circles around this compelling and enigmatic work, which the Italian painter Luca Giordano called the "theology of painting." It would be a theology insofar as it shows something about the ultimate structures and causes of painting by gathering together in a hierarchical order all of the elements of the art. Foucault's question to

Figure 10. Diego Velazquez, *Las Meninas*, 1656. Museo del Prado, Madrid. Alinari/Art Resource, New York

this work of what he calls the classical age, the age of representation, is whether the god of this theology is necessarily a *deus absconditus,* that is, the god of Pascal rather than Descartes; things get complicated when we realize that this "god" is that strange being, man, who, according to Foucault, appears only upon the ruins of the classical age.

Art historians have attempted to determine the precise meaning of *Las Meninas* within its seventeenth-century Spanish context, deploying the resources of historical learning, stylistics, and iconology; the identities of all the figures in the scene and even the subjects of the dim paintings on the walls (Rubens's versions of stories from Ovid) seem to have been ascertained. We have learned that this was a world in which Spanish painters were striving to have their vocation acknowledged as one of the liberal arts, as it already was in Italy; and it was one in which Velazquez aspired to the recognition marked in the painting by his wearing the cross of Saint James (or Santiago) (according to one tradition this mark of esteem was awarded by Philip IV, the sovereign whose shadowy image is apparently mirrored in the painting, who conferred it upon his court painter by taking up the brush himself in order to add it to the canvas).[8]

What Foucault's essay has provoked, at least in the Anglophone world, is mostly a series of critical responses that develop or take issue with his interpretation of the spatial structure of the painting, that is, its system of perspective. On his reading the place of the models (the king and queen presumably reflected in the mirror), that of the actual painter (not the image of Velazquez that looks out on us from the canvas), and that of the spectator all converge. Since these are all implicit functions that are not displayed in the painting, their oscillating coincidence would strengthen Foucault's idea that there is an essential gap or absence in this painting, one that can be read symptomatically or archaeologically as an indication that this work, which so carefully catalogs all of the aspects and dimensions of representation, must necessarily fail to represent the process of representation itself. If this is so, as Foucault claims, then the painting is perfectly suited to emblematize the "classical age" itself, the era of linear, graphic, Cartesian representation that came to an end when Kant and others called upon us to ask how the activity of representation itself was possible. (Readers of Foucault will recognize that I use Descartes and Kant as shorthand here; it is part of his purpose to show us that the great epochs of thought can be understood in ways that do not accord genius status to such familiar figures of philosophical history or an exclusive canonical status to their texts.)

Much discussion of Foucault's interpretation has focused on the question of whether he got the perspectival system of *Las Meninas* "right," that is, on questions such as whether the lines of sight that would locate the positions of model, spectator, and artist actually coincide, and it has been assumed that if they do not, his reading is insupportable.[9] Such criticism ignores the possibility that the painting might just have the visual and perceptual effect described by Foucault, even if a technical reconstruction yields a slightly different structure. There are clear cases in which Velazquez can easily be seen to have violated strict principles of perspective; in the *Rokeby Venus,* a cupid holds up a mirror in which we see the face of Venus but which, on a strict perspectival system, ought to reflect her hip. We will better see the point of Foucault's ekphrasis and of another later passage in *Les mots et les choses* on the same painting, by considering the way in which his descriptive analysis of this work of visual art constitutes a critique of Maurice Merleau-Ponty, who was intensively concerned with the art of Paul Cézanne, and whose essay "Cézanne's Doubt" stands as the introductory, signature piece of the book *Sense and Non-Sense.* Indeed, in the preface to that series of essays, Cézanne appears as the sign of the general possibility of expression and communication. After suggesting that the way in which meaning is created, expressed, and understood in art is a model for comprehending how any meaning is possible, Merleau-Ponty adds: "But the meaning of the work for the artist or for the public cannot be stated except by the work itself: neither the thought which created it nor the thought which receives it is completely its own master. Cézanne is an example of how precariously expression and communication are achieved. Expression is like a step taken in the fog—no one can say where, if anywhere, it will lead."[10] Cézanne stands as an example for all forms of expression and the creation of meaning, even with regard to the political, as Merleau-Ponty claims in the last sentences of the preface. He suggests that Cézanne's doubt whether his painting had any value and would be understood is closely analogous to a "man of good will [who] comes to doubt that lives are compatible with each other when he considers the conflicts in his own particular life" and to the generalized doubt "whether the human world is possible." And the hope that is the other side of Cézanne's doubt is formulated in this way: "But failure is not absolute. Cézanne won out against chance, and men, too, can win provided they will measure the dangers and the task."[11]

Two philosophers, then, each inaugurate a book by appealing to the work of a specific artist: in one case the point is that the struggle with visual meaning provides an example of the universal quest to establish meaning (artistic, philosophical, political) in a world where we will never be complete masters and will always be dealing with the chaotic, the ambiguous, and the unreasonable; in the other case, the painter exemplifies a well-structured, well-defined way of establishing meaning, which nevertheless, seen from a later vantage point, is disclosed as harboring a peculiar lack or absence at what might be its very center.

Although Foucault deliberately refrains from sketching any of the psychological and biographical information concerning Velazquez that

Merleau-Ponty provides about Cézanne, the contrast between the two artists is striking. Velazquez was the court painter of a monarch; in this position he claimed, at least implicitly, to be authorized by a long humanistic tradition, going back to Pliny's stories about the relation between Alexander the Great and his painter, Apelles. Cézanne had no official status; he rejected the artistic life of Paris and was lonely, tortured, suspicious, and verged on paranoia. He was unrecognized for the most part, and when his work attracted attention, it was scorned or ridiculed as an example of how not to paint. Merleau-Ponty uses Cézanne's life as a way of reflecting on the successes and limits of psychoanalysis, with reference to Freud's biography of Leonardo; he wants to demonstrate the way in which the painter exemplifies the ambiguity of a freedom that is situated. He suggests that the artist's anguish demonstrates "how each life muses over riddles whose final meaning is nowhere written down" (*MPA* 75). Foucault is not at all interested in Velazquez's life, nor does he deal with the lives of the artists that he discusses elsewhere, such as Bosch, Goya, René Magritte, Andy Warhol, and Duane Michals. Even if he were to agree with Merleau-Ponty on the exemplary value of Cézanne's life and work for the modern epoch, he would want to explain why this exemplarity is specifically modern. He would enclose both Cézanne and Merleau-Ponty within the same archaeological brackets, confirming the profound affinity sensed by the philosopher, while also demonstrating its limits.

Foucault's suspicions concerning the idea of the autonomous artist and the cult of genius are well known from his essay "What Is an Author?" which details some of the ways in which the "author-function" has changed over time and has varied when deployed with respect to various arts or in science or philosophy. So we would hardly expect him to take as a given Merleau-Ponty's concern with Cézanne's interior life. So far as psychoanalysis has something to tell us about any artist, it would, on this view, have a decentering tendency rather than confirming the tradition of the sovereign creator, a tradition whose traces can be seen even in Merleau-Ponty. Foucault considers one version of a psychoanalytic account of the literary artist in his essay on Laplanche's study *Hölderlin et le question du pére*. There he explains how the modern conception of the artist has developed in a series of stages that includes, very prominently, the schema of the career of the painter that assumed canonical form in Vasari's *Lives*. The painter comes to assume the characteristics of the epic hero: his genius makes itself known in infancy; he displaces his master; he hides his work until complete, then reveals it to great admiration (like the hero who enters masked into combat). This assumption of powers happens at a point when culture becomes attuned to what the artist offers: "The heroic dimension passed from the hero to the one whose task it had been to represent him at a time when Western culture itself became a world of representations" (*LCMP* 73; *DE* 1.193). In a world of representations, the one who succeeds at representing becomes a hero. In the *Iliad* Hector found some consolation for his fate by declaring that the gods bring sufferings on men in order to transform them into subjects of song; this implies an unbridgeable gap between hero and artist. But now the artist acquires the power both to act and to represent at once, through the possibility of self-portraiture: "The painter was the first subjective inflection of the hero. His self-portrait was no longer merely a marginal sign of the artist's furtive participation in the scene being represented, as a figure hidden at the corner of the canvas; it became, at the very center of the work, the totality of the painting where the beginning joins the ending in the absolute heroic transformation of the creator of heroes" (*LCMP* 74; *DE* 1.194). Self-portraiture, or at least our reading of it in these terms, reaches a zenith in the nineteenth century, in the work of such haunting faces as Cézanne's and Van Gogh's. It is this kind of reading that Foucault finds in Merleau-Ponty. We will return to the question of self-portraiture once we have seen why the latter takes Cézanne to be an exemplary painter and why the former begins his archaeology with Velazquez.

48 The Painter as Phenomenologist

What is it, then, that Merleau-Ponty finds in Cézanne's life and work? The very title of the essay, "Cézanne's Doubt," links the painter to the philosophical tradition and suggests the daemonic dimension of his enterprise. Here Cézanne is paired most obviously with Descartes; not with the Descartes who reduced vision to a form of blindness in the *Dioptrics*, but with the philosopher who contended with demons in undertaking a program of radical doubt and in interrogating inherited traditions of thought. As Merleau-Ponty explains in the *Phenomenology of Perception*, Descartes is to be admired for this reflexive movement of relentless inquiry, but not for its premature deviation into a dualistic system.[12] This is Descartes seen through the eyes of Husserl, whose *Cartesian Meditations* take root in and refuse to leave that level of vigilant questioning of the constitution of the subject and experience that is suppressed in Descartes's third meditation with the introduction of a metaphysical argument for the existence of God. This vigilance, which led Husserl repeatedly to rethink the question of the starting point and to call himself a "perpetual beginner" in philosophy, is evoked by the first sentences of Merleau-Ponty's essay, emphasizing the tentative characteristic of all *essais*, whether in philosophy or painting: "He needed one hundred working sessions for a still life, five hundred sittings for a portrait. What we call his work was, for him, only an essay, an approach to painting."[13] And he quotes these words of the artist's self-doubt, which are not only personal but have to do with the possibility of painting itself: "Will I ever arrive at the goal, so intensely sought and so long pursued? I am still learning from nature, and it seems to me I am making slow progress" (*MPA* 59). The portrait of Cézanne as phenomenologist, on the model of Husserl and Merleau-Ponty, is reinforced later on when we are told that "[e]xpressing what *exists* is an endless task," where the emphasis is not on the question of whether painting mirrors an external reality (terms that would be rejected here), but on the infinite levels of analysis that are possible in reconstituting the genesis of the visible (*MPA* 66). The same thought can be expressed differently by saying that "[h]e was, in any case, oriented toward the idea of an infinite Logos" (*MPA* 69).

Already in the *Phenomenology of Perception*, Merleau-Ponty had developed a comprehensive, if largely implicit, analogy between the work of Cézanne and the phenomenologist, that is, between Cézanne and himself. The force of the analogy in Merleau-Ponty's work is stronger than he explicitly acknowledges and is one that shapes and discloses his conception of philosophy as well as of painting. The identification is announced in the coda of the book's preface, where it is suggested that phenomenology is much more than a particular school of philosophy: "If phenomenology was a movement before becoming a doctrine or a philosophical system, this was attributable neither to accident, nor to fraudulent intent. It is as painstaking as the works of Balzac, Proust, Valery or Cézanne—by reason of the same kind of attentiveness and wonder, the same demand for awareness, the same will to seize the meaning of the world or of history as that meaning comes into being. In this way it merges into the general effort of modern thought."[14] In the *Phenomenology of Perception*, Cézanne is cited more frequently than any other figure except for a very few philosophers and psychologists. Typically, he appears either in order to clarify a major claim concerning the nature of perception or, more significantly, to provide a model for phenomenological inquiry itself. Cézanne speaks in Merleau-Ponty's text when it is a question of knowing what it is like to disclose an immanent meaning in things, to criticize the false separation of the senses, to show that there is a primordial expression independent of the human world, to perceive depth directly, or to overcome the misleading notion that we see meanings in things only through a process of association.[15]

Most of these themes return in a concentrated form in "Cézanne's Doubt." Phenomenological analysis, whether in Husserl or Cézanne, involves a rigorous suspension of our natural or commonplace beliefs and our commitments in the world, especially those that incline us to see it as an inhabitable place, instrumentally available to human beings: "We live in the midst of man-made objects, among tools, in houses, streets, cities, and most of the time we see them only through the human actions which put them to use. We become used to thinking that all of this exists necessarily, unshakeably. Cézanne's painting suspends these habits of thought and reveals the base of inhuman nature on which man has installed himself" (MPA 66). This, we might say, is the painterly *epoché* that is required to disclose the structure of visibility. If Cézanne seems like a strange, neurotic, anguished, and isolated figure, we ought not to reduce his work to pathological symptoms; rather we should see that a certain degree of solitude, self-questioning, and distance are the conditions of the painterly phenomenological project. These enable that sense of wonder which is the perpetual (and not merely historical) beginning of philosophy: "Only one emotion is possible for this painter—the feeling of strangeness—and only one lyricism—that of the continual rebirth of existence" (MPA 68).

Out of this infinite project, Merleau-Ponty highlights a number of Cézanne's phenomenological discoveries. In contrast to the impressionists, who wanted to reproduce an instantaneous vision and thus dissolved objects within a larger atmosphere, Cézanne insisted on the obstinacy of the object: "[I]t seems subtly illuminated from within, light emanates from it, and the result is an impression of solidity and material substance" (MPA 62). Implicit in this stylistic move is a refusal to divorce sight from touch or from the temporal experience in which vision is always more than a momentary impression; it is the latter that should be thought of as an abstraction, rather than considering the object as a construct. When Merleau-Ponty describes Cézanne as returning to the object, or when he approvingly cites those sayings in which he submits to the authority of "nature," we can hear an echo of Husserl's motto "[B]ack to the things themselves." Cézanne discovered, for example, that the photograph is not an unimpeachable authority concerning vision; nearby objects appear smaller and distant ones larger than they would in a photograph.[16] And "[t]o say that a circle seen obliquely is seen as an ellipse is to substitute for our actual perception what we would see if we were cameras; in reality we see a form which oscillates around the ellipse without being an ellipse" (MPA 64).

It is such effects as the oscillation around the ellipse that we find unsettling at first in Cézanne. But from Merleau-Ponty's point of view, what is happening is that Cézanne is suspending the natural standpoint, that which we think we know, based on "objective" evidence like the photograph (or on other pictorial conventions), and allowing things to "oscillate" or "vibrate"; he is expressing and communicating the ambiguity of experience. So, like the philosophical phenomenologist, the artist takes a step back from ordinary experience in order to disclose how meaning comes to be: "He did not want to separate the stable things which we see and the shifting way in which they appear; he wanted to depict matter as it takes on form, the birth of order through spontaneous organization" (MPA 63–64).

We find an account of one of these forms of meaning in Merleau-Ponty's discussion of the perception of depth. Some classical theorists of vision (Berkeley, for example) attempt to reinforce their claims by describing visual experience as being formally akin to pictures or paintings, which, it is said without further argument, are completely without depth.[17] Certainly this is true of paintings, if we take them simply as panels (disregarding the three-dimensionality of brush strokes on canvas), but the question is whether depth is perceived or inferred, and the answer is not to be found by appealing from vision in general to the seeing of paintings, when the same question can be raised about paintings themselves; Merleau-Ponty raises this question in the chapter "Space" in the *Phenomenology of Perception*, just after a discussion of Cézanne and the stereoscope: "The perspective drawing is not first of all perceived as a drawing on a plane surface, and then organized in depth. The lines which sweep towards the horizon are not first given as oblique, and then thought of as horizontal. The whole of the drawing strives toward its equilibrium by delving in depth. The poplar on the road which is drawn smaller than a man, succeeds in becoming really and truly a tree only by retreating towards the horizon. It is the drawing itself which tends toward depth as a stone falls downwards."[18]

On Merleau-Ponty's view, Cézanne's works are successful not only in disclosing the ambiguous riches of vision, but in thematizing some of the very questions that we might have thought could be raised only from outside the painting. He seems to suggest that what the philosopher does by shaping language into prose, Cézanne does wordlessly in his work. As with the practice of phenomenology, such a painting (on Merleau-Ponty's reading) does not merely present us with a result (an assertion or an image) but also shows us something of the process by which its discoveries are made, so that they can be reenacted (if not in the medium of print or paint) by the reader or the viewer.

It is essential for the role played by Cézanne in Merleau-Ponty's philosophy that his paintings and his general project of painting remain unfinished and open. The doubt that he exemplifies is a radical openness to the promptings of perception. Foucault chose rather to focus on a painting that strikes us as a polished and perfected masterpiece. We might also note that Merleau-Ponty, despite his emphasis on concrete experience, never discusses at length any specific painting by Cézanne (or any other artist); Foucault, who will be attempting to raise some questions about "the analytic of finitude" and "the analysis of actual experience," which Merleau-Ponty exemplifies, begins with a detailed account of *Las Meninas*. It is as if the later thinker is showing that he can outdo the phenomenologist by providing the concrete analysis of a visual experience that we might have expected from the earlier one.

While Merleau-Ponty attempted to work out a general approach to the chiasm of the visible and the invisible, Foucault finds the relation literalized in a specific work in a way that leads us to reflect on the archaeology of the visual. Merleau-Ponty concluded "Eye and Mind" by collapsing archaeology (in the ordinary, more limited sense) into history, suggesting that "the very first painting in some sense went to the farthest reach of the future"; there is a continuity, then, that overrides changes in style, meaning, convention, and historical context. This is also the point of Merleau-Ponty's critique of Malraux.

Yet there is a problem in taking Cézanne as a painter whose work can contribute to understanding this continuity. For many people Cézanne is an unsettling artist; those who appreciate the impressionists can still be disturbed by his attempts to go beyond classical perspective and to exhibit what Merleau-Ponty urges us to think of as a perception in constant process of formation, a process that refuses to settle down into a pattern that we have come to expect through the abstractions of rationalist or empiricist habits. Merleau-Ponty, then, attempts to normalize this painter whose work is so intensely defamiliarizing, taking him as the emblem of painting itself. In his ekphrasis of Velazquez, Foucault responds in effect by defamiliarizing a painting that we thought we knew; however puzzling we might have found its play of positions and looks, we did not previously see it as quite so uncanny.

One sense of archaeology, drawing on the practice that ordinarily goes by that name, is the articulation of diverse cultural levels *(archai)* that are typically separated by radical breaks. At an archaeological site, one identifies a number of artifacts at the same level that belong to a single social or cultural order: they manifest certain affinities of style and meaning that may be apparent only to an outside observer. As an archaeologist of the visual, Foucault aims at showing us what is distinctive about the way that a certain epoch structures the relation between the visible and the invisible, what is seen and what is said. This is why he explicitly refuses to name the figures in the painting (or defers such identification as long as he can); he does not want to be complicit with a historical approach that would insert the painting into a familiar narrative of life at court, of the contrast between the beautiful *infanta* and her grotesque attendants, or with anecdotes about the relation between a painter and his royal patron. All such readings, he implies, would have the effect of distracting us from seeing the painting in its archaeological specificity, as it displays the signature mode of its epoch; in this case that mode amounts to exhibiting every variation on representation except that gesture in which the question of the possibility of representation is asked and perhaps answered.

Foucault's initial description of *Las Meninas* encourages us to see the painting in terms of certain disconnections and oscillations that are difficult to make sense of in a phenomenology like Merleau-Ponty's. The painter, we are told, "is standing back from his canvas," disengaged for the moment from the process of expression. Expression itself, whose continuity is so important for Merleau-Ponty, is in a certain sense effaced from this picture. The eye and the hand are not, for the moment, part of a single activity: "The skilled hand is suspended in midair, arrested in rapt attention on the painter's gaze; and the gaze, in return, waits upon the arrested gesture" (OT 3; Mch 19). The suspension in the painting serves as an *epoché*, perhaps an *epoché* of phenomenology itself. The painter is not the origin of meaning, as Cézanne and all that he stands for are for Merleau-Ponty, but one element among others in a comprehensive tableau or diagram of the functions of representation.

Foucault deploys Merleau-Ponty's language of the visible and the invisible against its author's aims as he fills out his account of Velazquez's picture. He sees the relation of the visible and the invisible in the painting as a series of sharp oppositions, rather than as a chiasm in which there is a constant and fluid exchange. In this painting, we are told, the contents of the canvas whose back we see and the models and spectators who are the objects of the painter's gaze are always and necessarily invisible to us, although it is implied that they are visible to the painter as he is depicted in the painting. We might say that the painting can be seen as thematizing the resistance and ineluctability of the invisible: "The tall, monotonous rectangle occupying the whole left portion of the real picture, and representing the back of the canvas within the picture, reconstitutes in the form of a surface the invisibility in depth of what the artist is observing: that space in which we are, and which we are" (*OT* 4; *MCh* 20).

It is not that communication and expression are infinitely open projects, always on the way, as in the work of Cézanne, who struggled heroically with his doubts to the very end, but rather that the painting under analysis is a sort of machine or matrix guaranteeing that every perspective will be rigorously limited by its inverted form, that every form of visibility will be delimited by an invisibility; and it is not that these oppositions and interchanges will form a spiral of deepening meaning but that the viewer will necessarily be caught up in a structure allowing no escape and no progress: "[T]he observer and the observed take part in a ceaseless exchange. No gaze is stable, or rather, in the neutral furrow of the gaze piercing at a right angle through the canvas, subject and object, the spectator and the model, reverse their roles to infinity" (*OT* 4–5; *MCh* 20–21).

This reversal to infinity is a parodic or degraded version of the reciprocity of the visible and the invisible that Merleau-Ponty was exploring in his last, unfinished book; a typical passage from the crucial chapter of *The Visible and the Invisible*, "The Intertwining—The Chiasm," describes the way in which the world of visibility opens up beyond a solipsistic or narcissistic enclosure because of our being situated among a plurality of those who see: "As soon as we see other seers, we no longer have before us only the look without a pupil, the plate glass of the things with that feeble reflection, that phantom of ourselves they evoke by designating a place among themselves whence we see them: henceforth, through other eyes we are for ourselves fully visible."[19] If he had been able to respond to Foucault, he might have argued that such effects are a limiting case, which occurs only on the ground of a more primordial union of expression. Foucault anticipates such a reply in several ways. First, he attempts to show that the structure of *Las Meninas* is typical of the way in which the visual and the discursive are structured in the classical age of representation; as such, it cannot be dismissed as a curiosity (there was good reason for calling it the theology of painting). Second, Foucault will be arguing that the phenomenology of expression to which Merleau-Ponty appeals, and which he finds exemplified in Cézanne, is itself a historical artifact. Just as Cézanne is not a timeless painter but a creature of modernity, so Merleau-Ponty's phenomenology is just one more variation, even if the most recent one, on the philosophical schools that attempt to provide an analytic of finitude.

Here Foucault's analysis dovetails with some familiar tendencies in art theory: a critic like Clement Greenberg can suggest that we recognize Cézanne, Manet, and Picasso as alternative versions of the same artistic quest, centered on the question of how to accept the limitations of the flat canvas, rather than pretending, as in some earlier modes of art, that the pictorial rectangle is a window on the world. Greenberg explicitly compares this modernist move in painting with the modern turn in philosophy taken by Kant. On this account, the classical rationalist metaphysicians (Descartes, Spinoza, Leibniz) simply took for granted that thought could mirror reality. Kant began to ask what the conditions were under which human thought was possible; in each case what seemed to be a limit (at first unsuspected or ignored) is turned into a ground of knowledge.[20] Foucault wants to show that such apparently diverse thinkers as Kant, Marx, and the early Heidegger have a deep archaeological affinity, insofar as they are all concerned with the parallel question of how the limitations of a finite being can be the grounds of a profound knowledge of man and his possibilities. While the modern era may argue as to whether these limitations are best understood in terms of sensibility and the categories of the understanding, the necessity of labor and productivity, or death and anxiety, such disputes rest on a common set of unspoken assumptions about what questions are to be framed and what will count as an answer to them.

Part of Foucault's defamiliarization of Velazquez's painting is his demonstration that it does *not* belong to the modern era, the time of man. Just as pre-Kantian philosophers and scientists took the process of representation for granted, so did its painters. If Foucault had paused to examine the case of Cézanne, he might have agreed to a large extent with Merleau-Ponty that this was an artist who was always seeking the roots of visual experience and exploring his own involvement in the genesis of pictorial meaning. In other words, his paintings would be the visual equivalent of the philosophical quest shared by Kant, Marx, the early Heidegger, and Merleau-Ponty. A self-portrait by Cézanne or Van Gogh speaks to us of this attempt to catch in the act the way in which the subject is both origin and end, subject and object of meaning, revealing both a triumph of revelation and the necessary limitations that call for further exploration.

50 The Mirror of the Sovereign

Las Meninas makes its return later in *Les mots et les choses* in the section entitled "Man and His Doubles"; this is also the part of the text that contains a densely allusive critique of Merleau-Ponty. Just as Foucault's ekphrasis of Velazquez's painting refrains so far as possible from naming the characters it depicts, so his portrait of the philosophy of "actual experience" refuses to name the thinker who most obviously exemplifies it. When Foucault does return to the painting, it is to recon-figure or rewrite it. He speaks of the necessity of introducing a new figure into his analysis, "a character who has not yet appeared in the great classical interplay of representations." And he proposes to look "for the previously existing law of that interplay in the painting of *Las Meninas*, in which representation is represented at every point" (*OT* 307; *MCh* 318–19). The law of representation, it seems, is to point toward something or someone absent, and this personage is

> [a]t once object—since it is what the artist is copying onto his can-vas—and subject—since what the painter had in front of his eyes, as he represented himself in the course of the work, was himself, since the gazes portrayed in the picture are all directed toward the fictitious position occupied by the royal personage, which is also the painter's real place, since the occupier of that ambiguous place, in which the painter and the sovereign alternate, in a never-ending flicker, as it were, is the spectator, whose gaze transforms the paint-ing into an object, the pure representation of that essential absence. (*OT* 308; *MCh* 319)

In classical thought, Foucault adds, this personage who represents him-self and recognizes his reflection in the representation is never to be found. Classical painting can be characterized in the same way, and Velazquez's painting serves as a diagram of both. The name of the fig-ure, of course, is *man*, who came into existence only in the eighteenth century and is already disappearing. Man would be both subject and object, both the agent and the patient of the analytic of finitude by which he seeks to know himself.

If the underlying episteme of an entire era, such as the classical age, can be understood by analogy with a painting, then perhaps the modern epoch, the age of man, can also be comprehended by focusing on the self-portrait of the modern artist. Foucault attempts to suggest what such an epistemological-painterly portrait might be, in the wake of the collapse of classical discourse:

> [I]n the profound upheaval of such an archaeological mutation, man appears in his ambiguous position as an object of knowledge and as a subject that knows: enslaved sovereign, observed spectator, he ap-pears in the place belonging to the king, which was assigned to him in advance by *Las Meninas*, but from which his real presence has

for so long been excluded. As if, in that vacant space toward which Velazquez's whole painting was directed, but which it was, nevertheless, reflecting only in the chance presence of a mirror, and as though by stealth, all the figures whose alternation, reciprocal exclusion, interweaving, and fluttering one imagined (the model, the painter, the king, the spectator) suddenly stopped their imperceptible dance, immobilized into one substantial figure, and demanded that the entire space of the representation should at last be related to one corporeal gaze. (*OT* 312; *MCh* 323)

In the section devoted to "Man and His Doubles," Foucault is intent on exposing the ways in which the figure that emerges as "enslaved sovereign, observed spectator" is ceaselessly and necessarily tormented by the need to satisfy conflicting requirements; man is enmeshed in a series of doublets or double binds. To take only the first of these, "he is a strange empirico-transcendental doublet, since he is a being such that knowledge will be attained in him of what renders all knowledge possible" (*OT* 318; *MCh* 329). On the one hand, man is open to empirical investigation; he can be studied by psychology, sociology, and the other human sciences, which go hand in hand with his brief career on the world's stage. On the other hand, what is promised as the fruit of these inquiries is an understanding of the basic or transcendental conditions that allow him to know anything at all. An analytic of finitude must somehow reconcile these two emphases, but competing versions of that analytic tend either to deviate toward one pole or the other or to fluctuate between them. Foucault finds the cases of Comte and Marx instructive, because each is committed simultaneously to a discourse that is grounded in observation (of man as a social, historical, or laboring being) and yet which anticipates the results of that investigation to project an eschatological limit or culmination (the realization of the scientific age, the overcoming of alienated labor and of class society); it is this latter telos that provides the perspective from which the earlier observations make sense, yet it is the observations that were supposed to ground the projected end. These two thinkers, with their very different programs and politics, turn out to be "archaeologically indissociable" and to demonstrate how, within the analytic of finitude, "man appears within it as a truth both reduced and promised" (*OT* 320; *MCh* 331).

Foucault observes a kind of precritical naïveté in the fluctuations that such thought forces itself to undergo. It is understandable, then, that modern philosophy would look for some other way of pursuing an analytic of finitude, one that would not blindly or unconsciously suffer such fluctuations but would somehow make them into thematic material that it describes and comprehends. Even within the "Kantian" era of man, which is committed to investigating the conditions of knowledge, there is the possibility of reflecting on the dialectical contradictions generated by the first attempts of this sort.

It is at this point that Merleau-Ponty enters Foucault's archaeological analysis, although without being named. In searching for a philosophy that would somehow escape both "the order of reduction" and "the order of promise," thought is tempted by the possibility of "a discourse . . . which in relation to quasi-aesthetics and quasi-dialectics would play the role of an analytic which would at the same time give them a foundation in a theory of the subject and perhaps enable them to articulate themselves in that third and intermediary term in which both the experience of the body and that of culture would be rooted. Such a complex, over-determined, and necessary role has been performed in modern thought by the analysis of actual experience." We can see that Foucault's archaeology here touches on Merleau-Ponty and the kind of thinking that he represents as he designates other features of the philosophy of actual experience. These include the thematization of ambiguity itself; if the more naive versions of the analytic oscillated unreflectively between positivistic and eschatological alternatives, this more vigilant type of philosophy will take such movement as its focus. Since "actual experience is . . . both the space in which all empirical contents are given to experience and the original form that makes them possible in general and designates their primary roots," it is the locus of the body as irreducibly social and of culture as historically sedimented (*OT* 320–21; *MCh* 331–32). Foucault has performed something like a deduction of the central features of Merleau-Ponty's thought, showing that such a philosophy is an almost inevitable development, once one is committed to the project of an analytic of finitude.

It is appropriate, then, that Merleau-Ponty was fascinated by the work of Cézanne, although Foucault does not note this explicitly. Nevertheless, much of what Merleau-Ponty praises in Cézanne is what we would expect on the basis of Foucault's sketch of the philosophy of actual experience. Cézanne's work is said to be poised at the junction of nature and culture: "[O]nly a human being is capable of such a vision which penetrates right to the root of things beneath the imposed order of humanity" (*MPA* 67). A parallel ambiguity emerges in Merleau-Ponty's project of situating Cézanne's freedom; in doing so he attempts to stake out a position that strikes a subtle balance between a number of approaches to understanding how human beings give meaning to their situation. Whereas Cézanne was at first portrayed as the model of the phenomenological artist, here he becomes the illustration of what it means to be free in a world that is not of one's own making. The aim now is to show how there is an "emerging order" in a life, one that transcends the binaries of freedom and determinism or will and circumstances; in this respect Merleau-Ponty's essay parallels the *essai* he attributes to Cézanne of overcoming the duality of the impressionists and the old masters, that is, of sensation versus judgment, of nature versus composition, and of primitivism versus tradition (*MPA* 62–63). The reflective and discursive project of the philosophical phenomenologist doubles the work of the phenomenological painter. This is a motif that surfaces repeatedly in Merleau-Ponty, in which painting is a mute phenomenology and phenomenology is a discursive painting.

51 "Enslaved Sovereign, Observed Spectator"

The crucial painted analog of man as thematized by Foucault, that "enslaved sovereign, observed spectator" might well be Cézanne, staring out at us and himself from one of those self-portraits where he looks to his right, always somber, his pupils at the right edge of his eyes; even in the *Self-Portrait with Rose Background* (ca. 1875; fig. 11) the warmth of the setting fails to soften the seriousness of the gaze of this figure, who combines the many functions that were dispersed in earlier painting. Master or sovereign of the painted field, he is also enslaved by the limits of representation, beset by those very doubts that Merleau-Ponty saw as constitutive of his project. As a spectator he is simultaneously observed, constantly the object of his own obsessive gaze. We could see similar qualities in the self-portraits of Van Gogh, including his notorious depiction of himself with a bandaged ear, the sign of a self-wounding that can be read as part of his anguished commitment to explore his own finitude. If man is disappearing, it may be because his simultaneous assumption of all of those functions and roles was just too much for him; perhaps he is perishing of his own solemnity. It is as if the painter had been forced to assume the position of the mad genius, as Foucault observes in his articulation of the fate of the Vasarian model of the artist: "The space cleared in the decline of heroism, a space whose nature was suspected by the sixteenth century and one which our present culture cheerfully investigates in keeping with its basic forgetfulness, is ultimately occupied by the 'madness' of the artist; it is a madness which identifies the artist to his work and which makes him different—from all those who remain silent—and it also situates the artist outside his work when it blinds him to the

Figure 11. Paul Cézanne, *Self-Portrait with Pink Background*, ca. 1875. Private collection, France. Erich Lessing/Art Resource, New York

things he sees and makes him deaf even to his own words" (*LCMP* 75; *DE* 1.194). Is it not this strange oscillation between the inside and the outside that makes the self-portraitist along the lines of Cézanne or Van Gogh an enslaved sovereign and observed spectator?

Hugh Silverman has looked carefully at Cézanne's self-portraiture from the perspective of Merleau-Ponty, enriched by a consideration of Jacques Lacan's mirror stage, in which the infant is supposed to establish and confirm his or her sense of identity by realizing that the image in the mirror is indeed herself or himself.[21] As Silverman suggests, a self-portrait is always a portrait of oneself as both same and other. A mirror image will establish a left-right reversal; even if the artist employs a double mirror to correct for this, the element of depth is lacking in the flatness of the mirror. Yet the mirror(s) may help in the project of coming to terms with the appearance of that which we never really quite see, ourselves: "The mirror makes what is invisible visible. When painting himself from the image in the mirror, Cézanne takes what is typically invisible to him and brings another invisible—the one that accompanies all his seeing—and produces another visible which is the self-portrait."[22] The analysis helps to articulate the way in which Merleau-Ponty's thought about vision and painting is implicitly oriented to the question of self-portraiture, and it suggests that the genre as conceived by the philosopher will necessarily be an exploration of the exchange between the seer and the seen, even and especially when the two are aspects of the same. Foucault's question still arises: Should such self-portraiture and the philosophy of "actual experience" that both explores it and doubles it be understood as the universal fate of the visual and painting? Or should they be analyzed as what happens when art and thought set themselves the task of comprehending that figure who is "enslaved sovereign, observed spectator"?

In order to pose these questions with some intensity, Foucault has to establish some distance between himself and the epoch that he is analyzing. His account of *Las Meninas* sets up such a distance by implicitly suggesting at the verbal level that there is an identity of writer and reader; the text of his essay constantly insinuates a "we" to whom the paradoxes and absences of the painting become apparent. This is to perform and resolve on the discursive level the equivalent of what is said to be unresolvable within the visual world of the painting. In a certain sense, Foucault has assumed the position of man in his ekphrasis in order to demonstrate the absence of man in the painting. When the painting reappears in Foucault's text, the "we" disappears; now he will write simply that "man appears in his ambiguous position as an object of knowledge and as a subject that knows." A "we" is no longer needed to confirm our distance from this painting, because what we are now required to take our distance from is that very self-knowing subject that says "we." Man is the figure "towards which Velazquez's whole painting was directed, but which it was nevertheless reflecting only in the chance presence of a mirror" (*OT* 312; *MCh* 323). That somewhat ghostly mirror becomes an essential apparatus in the age of man and his doubles, both as a figure for the attempt to catch oneself in the very act of knowing oneself and in its literal role as a device in which the artist aims to see and show himself in the process of seeing.

If Foucault were to describe Cézanne's self-portraits as he has articulated the philosophy of Merleau-Ponty and the other analysts of finitude, he would need to establish a distance corresponding to the steps backward that he takes from *Las Meninas*. This is the project that he never explicitly carried out but whose outlines I am attempting to sketch. At the very end of *Les mots et les choses*, Foucault employs a visual trope to speak of the "wager that man would be erased, like a face drawn in sand at the edge of the sea" (*OT* 387; *MCh* 20). In that text it is language that is on the horizon, already overtaking and displacing man. In the visual register, such an alternative perspective is offered by the art of the simulacrum that Foucault celebrates in Warhol, Magritte, and Michals. Work of that sort allows him to exclaim, at the conclusion of *This Is Not a Pipe:* "A day will come when, by means of similitude relayed indefinitely along the length of a series, the image itself, along with the name it bears, will lose its identity. Campbell, Campbell, Campbell, Campbell" (*TNP* 54; *CP* 79). In contrast with the sort of self-portraiture that might epitomize the painting of the era of man, this would be an art that practices an *askesis* of identity, as a Warhol image of Elvis, Jackie, Mao—or, most strikingly, himself—is repeated to the point where it is emptied of meaning. Artists like Cézanne were attempting to establish and reveal their identities, even in struggling with all the elements of otherness in that process; the artist of the succeeding (postmodern?) age sacrifices not only his or her own identity but also the identity of the image itself, which, repeated indefinitely, is transformed like a mantra through that very repetition. It is this erasure by which we might finally free ourselves from the icons of self-portraiture that still haunt our visual horizons.

eight

Seeing and Saying: Foucault's Ekphrasis of *Las Meninas*

52 What's in a Name?

The title given to this celebrated painting is traditional, and indeed it is now unavoidable. The two simple words that designate what has been called "the theology of painting" are as arbitrary and as necessary as the names of God. Only very slowly did the picture acquire its title; and this suggests that its history may have something to tell us about the complex relation of words and images. The first written record of the work occurs in a 1666 inventory of the Alcazar, ten years after its composition and five years after the death of Velazquez; it is a description, not a title: "*La señora Emperatriz con sus damas y una enana,*" or "Her royal highness accompanied by her ladies and a dwarf." In 1734 a new inventory finally accords it a name: *The Family of King Philip IV.* This title, or a variant, seems to have endured for some time; in 1800 there is an allusion to "the famous picture called *The Family.*" The painting came into the Prado in 1819, at the founding of the museum; a catalog of 1843 lists it as "a painting called *Las*

Meninas." The changing descriptions and titles appear to have a genealogical significance, raising questions of legitimacy. At the date of the
painting in 1656, Philip IV and Mariana had failed to produce a surviv-
ing male heir. In the most absolute of European monarchies, with its
patriarchal expectations, there was a crisis of succession. The queen was
unsuccessful in her effort to obtain that right for her own daughter,
Maria Theresa, who is markedly absent from this "family" painting.
Over the next few years, Velazquez painted a series of portraits of the
Infanta Margarita, who occupies the center of this work. In 1661 the
royal couple managed to produce their ill-fated son, known as El Hechi-
zado, Carlos the Bewitched, who ruled incompetently for a few years
until his death in 1700.[1] There is a shift, then, from titles based around
the idea of the family to *"Las Meninas."* The earlier titles could be
serving as conscious or unconscious signs of the genealogical problem
of the royal family; by the nineteenth century it was possible to see
the painting as having apparently put the family into a secondary position while focusing on the ladies-in-waiting and other attendants.
Rather than pointing to the absence of an heir, the new title could be
read as indicating a leveling or democratic gesture in which the royal
child and even her attendants displace the sovereign. This painting, at
least, does not have an absolutely legitimate title, one whose authority
would stem unequivocally from the hand and words of the artist. Is
this the general condition of painting? How effective can any language
be in rendering the sense of a visual work of art? Is the relationship
between verbal discourse and pictorial presentation not timeless and
invariable but something that means quite different things when we
are speaking (as we do, interminably) of a Bosch, a Velazquez, a Manet,
or a Magritte? This is an issue of paramount importance for Foucault,
who says in his essay on the painting that "the relation between language
and painting is an infinite relation. . . . Neither can be reduced to the
other's terms: it is in vain that we say what we see" (*OT* 9; *Mch* 25). I
take this to be the central thought of the essay on *Las Meninas*, or, to
be faithful to Foucault's title, *"Les suivantes."* Commenting on his own
elision of the proper names of the figures in the painting, Foucault says:

> [T]he proper name, in this particular context, is merely an artifice:
> it gives us a finger to point with, in other words to pass surrepti-
> tiously from the space where one speaks to the space where one
> looks; in other words, to fold one over the other as though they
> were equivalents. But if one wishes to keep the relation of language
> to vision open, if one wishes to treat their incompatibility as a start-
> ing point for speech instead of an obstacle to be avoided, so as to

stay as close as possible to both, then one must erase those proper names and preserve the infinity of the task. (*OT* 9–10; *MCh* 25)

This is not an empty or merely ironic gesture, a traditional expression of wonder, and a confession of the impotence of one's own speech. It is rather an intervention in an all-too-easy commerce between words and images, the marking of a space for questioning. How odd, then, that the many responses to Foucault's essay have proceeded on the assumption that he intended to "get it right," to deliver the truth about the painting to us in words, and then have attempted to show us how he erred (for example, by misreading the system of perspective) and have offered what is presumably a fuller, more accurate account of the painting in their own language.

53 Ekphrasis

How far can the writer succeed in offering a verbal version—poetic, literary, critical, or philosophical—of a work of art? There must, we suspect, be some limit to this process, some point at which the sheerly visual, in its color, form, size, texture, and its very presence, resists translation into language. And yet the genre and tradition of ekphrasis persists and emerges in new and unexpected places (on Nietzsche and ekphrasis, see secs. 19, 26). Foucault's *Les mots et les choses* begins with a celebrated description of Velazquez's *Las Meninas*, which finally sees the painting as an emblem of the nature of representation in the Cartesian or "classical" era, as Foucault calls it in his Gallocentric fashion, that exposes the inability of representation to finally turn upon and represent itself. It is, as Claude Gandelmann remarks, perhaps the only book of philosophy to begin with an ekphrasis.[2]

I want to read this ekphrasis, which has still scarcely been read; the reading will explore the principles of Foucault's ekphrasis with an eye to exposing their philosophical roots and to raising some questions about the possibility and limits of the linguistic description that he provides and of the genre for which it serves as such a distinguished and unusual example. Like the painting that is its subject, this ekphrasis of *Las Meninas* can be understood on several different levels. As with the painting, some of these levels are not immediately apparent; in particular its readers have not seen that the essay thematizes and takes a position on the relation between its own linguistic form and the picture that it describes. But the writing is not without signposts to let us know what is at stake. As Foucault says, we ought to take the incompatibility of language and the visible as the "starting point for speech," so that the entire essay can be read as an articulate response to the gap between the seen and the said. In this respect Foucault's "*Las Meninas*" is analogous to *Las Meninas* itself, which can be read first, as by Carl Justi in the nineteenth century, for example, as a masterpiece of realism, anticipating impressionism, or, as is more common now, as a work that involves a complex reflection on the very conditions of pictorial presentation and representation.[3] So the essay can be read as a description of the painting or as an analysis of what is involved in giving such a description. Sympathetic philosophers have tended to see it as articulating the aporias of what Foucault calls classical representation, focusing on his claim that the three crucial poles of that process, the artist (the one who represents), the model (that which is represented), and the spectator (to whom the representation is communicated), are all themselves represented in dispersed form in the painting and yet fail to coincide. A number of critics, however, have challenged Foucault's reading of the painting on the grounds that he simply misunderstands its use of perspective: while he claims that the mirror at the back of the room and at the center of the canvas contains the reflection of the king and queen, who are presumed to be Velazquez's models for the canvas he is painting (but whose back is turned to us), these critics have argued that a strict orthogonal and perspectival look at the painting shows that the mirror must be reflecting what is on the canvas in front of the painter whom we see pausing in his work. Given this apparent error, it is sometimes implied, Foucault's use of the painting to exemplify the problematics of classical representation becomes questionable. Others have observed that the canvas on which the painter is working is rather too large for a double portrait, so that we might be less certain that the mirror reflects what Velazquez is painting.[4] Some art historians have also complained that Foucault's reading of the painting simply ignores the historical context, the purpose, and even the architectural setting of the picture, which have to do (although there is hardly any unanimity about this) with Velazquez's demonstration of the status he has achieved as painter and courtier, with the problematic elevation of painting to the rank of the liberal arts in Spain, or with the teachings of a humanism oriented to the court that sees painting, especially that of the state portrait, as tending to ennoble and idealize its models. Foucault is seen as having gotten the painting wrong, either by failing to do a careful internal inspection of the picture's systematic perspective or by neglecting its specific historical context in order to make it an emblem of knowledge and representation at the origin of the Cartesian, representational, or classical era. Most of these alternative responses to Velazquez's painting contain valuable suggestions for thinking about the work and the possibilities that it opens for reflecting on the resources of the pictorial and the relevance of historical contextualization.

And yet (here I echo Foucault, echoing Heidegger's "Und dennoch" in his evocation of a certain world and earth in a painting by Van Gogh), and yet I want to say that something of significance in and about Foucault's text has evaded the critics.[5] Just as almost every reading of the painting acknowledges that there is much more here than immediately meets the eye, that it is a work that brings us up short, subjecting us to breaks and reversals of understanding and vision, so there are strategies of transformation, identification, and reversal at work in the rhetoric of Foucault's ekphrasis of this painting that in part echo and in part contrast with what we see there under his guidance.

Perhaps we should not be asking the question whether Foucault got the painting "right" but should be looking more carefully at what he says and how he says it. And we ought not to forget the Nietzschean question "Now that God is dead, who is speaking?" that is never absent from his writings and that can never be answered with the assurance reserved for such questions in the theological era.[6] It is more than a question of the infinite or indefinite fecundity of works of art (or great works), of their lending themselves to apparently endless interpretations. In introducing his own graceful and illuminating reading of the painting in terms of the reciprocity of gazes that it provokes, Leo Steinberg says: "Writing about a work such as *Las Meninas* is not, after all, like queuing at the A&P. Rather, it is somewhat comparable to the performing of a great musical composition of which there are no definitive renderings. The guaranteed inadequacy of each successive performance challenges the interpreter next in line, helping thereby to keep the work in the repertoire."[7] Without engaging the aesthetics of infinity, going back at least to Kant's "aesthetic idea," that Steinberg appeals to here, there is a further difference between the painting and its verbal commentaries than that between the musical score and its performance. The score is the sort of thing that is or ought to be performed, while the painting is meant to be viewed. If there is an analogy, it should be between writing about musical works or performances and writing about paintings. The question posed by an ekphrasis is not whether it exhausts the sense of its subject but how language is related to the visible.

What sort of text is this essay on *Las Meninas*, how does it intersect with the painting that is its object, how does it address the question of its own discourse, what voice speaks here, and whom is it addressing? The practice of ekphrasis can be conducted with various degrees of sophistication. Naive description either does not confront the question of its own limits, assuming that there is nothing problematic in making paintings speak, or, at the other extreme, it retreats behind an expressive and impressionistic discourse that concedes its own impotence in rendering the visual, collapsing into a series of gestures toward the celebrated work. Foucault's writing is traversed by a sense of the relative independence of the verbal and the visual, of the way in which they can sometimes uncannily coalesce while at others they necessarily fail to coincide.

There are constant reminders of the discrepancy between these two modes. If there is no pristine vision, we need to be careful in accounting for the interplay of various modes of imaging and the discursive forms that reinforce, contradict, or fail to intersect with them. In his study of Foucault, Gilles Deleuze emphasizes the agonistic theme that sometimes describes the relation of the visible and the articulable. Foucault can deny that the two are isomorphic while also acknowledging that they can intersect in various ways. Deleuze suggests a rather Kantian reading of their relations, in which statements play the role of concepts and the visible plays the role of intuition: "The statement has primacy by virtue of the spontaneity of its conditions (language) which give it a determining form, while the visible element, by virtue of the receptivity of its conditions (light), merely has the form of the determinable."[8] And he reads Foucault as acknowledging all of the following relations simultaneously between the visible and articulable: "the heterogeneity of the two forms, their difference in nature or anisomorphism; a mutual presupposition between the two, a mutual grappling and capture; the well-determined primacy of the one over the other."[9]

How, then, should we read an essay that opens a book devoted to an archaeological investigation in which profoundly different uses of language are found to be crucial for understanding the various strata of knowledge that Foucault excavates, a book recording the complex dance of visual or tabular and linguistic modes as they advance toward one another or retreat? We might read not simply to open our eyes to a painting or even to its relations with the forms of discourse to which it may be analogous, but in order to comprehend the construction and movements of this writing, the way in which it makes its appeal to us and in which it alternately approaches and takes a step back from its subject, as the painter does in relation to his canvas.

54 Construction of the "We"

Certainly one of the major themes of Foucault's essay is that a certain sort of subject, one who later receives the name "man," is absent from the painting. But who, what subject, is marking that absence in the essay devoted to Velazquez's work? Toward the end there is a strong and clear statement detailing the way in which the various functions of representation are dispersed and fail to coincide in *Las Meninas*. Three functions or positions—painter (of *Las Meninas* itself), model, and spectator—are all, he says, to be found at the same point outside the painting; they are indicated and located by a series of reflections, looks, and converging lines. But of course they *cannot* coincide, because each is distinct; the distinction is emphasized, Foucault thinks, by their dispersion in various projected forms in the painting itself: the painted painter, the reflected sovereign models, and the man in the doorway, who embodies the spectatorial function within the painting. Everything conspires to produce gaps, absences, and dispersions of what might have been unified:

> It may be that, in this picture, as in all the representations of which it is, as it were, the manifest essence, the profound invisibility of what one sees is inseparable from the invisibility of the person seeing—despite all mirrors, reflections, imitations, and portraits.
>
> . . . it is not possible for the pure felicity of the image ever to present in a full light both the master who is representing and the sovereign who is being represented.
>
> . . . in the midst of this dispersion which it is simultaneously grouping together and spreading out before us, indicated compellingly from every side, is an essential void: the necessary disappearance of that which is its foundation—of the person it resembles and the person in whose eyes it is only a resemblance. (*OT* 16; *MCh* 31)

Yet the failure to coincide, the dispersion of the various components or poles of the picture, stands in contrast to what is accomplished linguistically in the text of the essay. For there we (readers and viewers) seem to glide effortlessly into identifying ourselves with that gaze and look, with that voice that guides us through the complexity of the painting. Eschewing any preliminary information about the date, the place, the circumstances of the painting or its painter, without locating it in the seventeenth-century Spanish court, this voice speaks to us of what we *see*, of the painter stepping back from his canvas, pausing in the midst of his work (or on the verge of undertaking it), giving in to that mingled fascination of vision and thought in which we too are soon caught up. Foucault quickly establishes a *collective subject* for the ekphrasis, one constructed almost imperceptibly and effortlessly by means of his opening description of the painter. The painter is first introduced without any reference to a viewer or writer: "The painter is standing a little back from his canvas." But in the next paragraph, he is positioned in relation to "the spectator at present observing him" (*OT* 3; *MCh* 19). So someone (Foucault, ourselves, a generalized spectator, like "the reader" so often invoked in the texts of literary criticism) is watching. And this spectator's presence is underlined further by the language of visibility and invisibility that follows his (or her, but Foucault uses the masculine form) introduction. By the third paragraph, however, the generalized spectator has been gathered up into a "we," a first person plural constituted by the ekphrasis itself, as it shows how that subject is implied by the painter's gaze: "The painter is looking, his face turned slightly and his head leaning toward one shoulder. He is staring at a point to which, even though it is invisible, we, the spectators, can easily assign an object, since it is we, ourselves, who are that point: our bodies, our faces, our eyes" (*OT* 4; *MCh* 20).

"We, the spectators": once this identification is made, it continues throughout the essay. (Just a few pages later we are again identified as "the spectators—ourselves" [*OT* 6; *MCh* 22].) This is a we that clearly includes the writer or the voice of the ekphrasis. We spectators have been evoked simultaneously, it seems, by the look of the painter and (much less obviously) by the text that puts that look into words. We spectators are also we readers. Once this collective subject has been established, it becomes easier to accept what that text says, because, after all, it speaks from our position and names our place. If within and without the painting, "no gaze is stable," if "subject and object, the spectator and the model, reverse their roles to infinity," no such oscillation disturbs what might be called the internal structure of the collective spectator, the "we," which now becomes complicit in the complex discussion of the painting's feints, dislocations, and reversals that occupies the rest of the essay. It may be the case that insofar as we are in the position of the spectator and cannot see the image (our image?) on the canvas within the painting, "we do not know who we are." But no such uncertainty infects the collective self that is observing and recording these ambiguities.

Notice that the identity insinuated between ourselves, "we" readers and viewers, and the writer or the voice of the ekphrasis is in an important respect the opposite of what the text tells us is happening in the painting. There, it turns out, everything is dispersions, gaps, and absences. Here, on the side of language, an identification is performed which the essay denies to the painting. We spectators, since we are merely spectators, are seized and commanded by "the painter's sovereign gaze": "As soon as they place the spectator in the field of their gaze, the painter's eyes seize hold of him, force him to enter the picture, assign him a place at once privileged and inescapable, levy their luminous and visible tribute from him, and project it upon the inaccessible surface of the canvas within the picture" (*OT* 5; *MCh* 21). There is room for some difference here in understanding our relation to the gaze of the painter and other figures. It might be described as involving a greater degree of reciprocity, as a Hegelian or Sartrean play of looks, as in Leo Steinberg's formulation: "If the picture were speaking instead of flashing, it would be saying: I see you seeing me—I in you see myself seen—see you seeing yourself being seen—and so on beyond the reaches of grammar."[10] Such articulations may not be beyond the reach of grammar; they simply involve an infinite series, a *mise-en-abîme* of grammatical operations. But the painting in fact does not speak but shows, and because of this silence it allows both for a trapped spectator and for one caught up in an endless exchange or reciprocity of looks (which may be another form of trap). What transpires in this painting occurs in the twinkling of an eye and is the reciprocity of looks that can be described as a twinkling of the eye. To speak with Nietzsche, the picture is both abyss and *Augenblick*.

Yet, since it is "we" who, in Foucault's essay, are writing and speaking with him, we enjoy a certain freedom in relation to these gazes, however they are described. As readers and speakers, we are not so riveted to our place; we are released from the tyranny of the painter's gaze and allowed to take our distance from the picture, with the freedom to step back from our position as its implied spectators in order to take account of the phenomenon of the painting as a whole.

John Searle seems to agree with Foucault, on the whole, that "we" spectators are seized and trapped by the painter's gaze, insofar as that look suggests that there is a unique place mapped out for us, an angle from which we must view the painting, and a single correct perspectival way of apprehending it.[11] The question, often, is not whether we are trapped but just where the trap is located. There are many questions to be raised about such readings of the painting, including these: Is there, for this painting or in general, a single determinate position that is required of the viewer? Does the picture have a single, fixed perspective? And even if it does, does this cancel out our impressions of the painting that may be at variance with it?[12]

What Foucault's text does is to offer us a way out of the traps of the visual (however they may be described and analyzed) by seducing us into an identity with the magisterial voice that leads us through the labyrinth of the painting. And although the painting itself appears to depict a moment frozen in time, a moment therefore susceptible to an analysis that parcels out the various functions of artist, model, and spectator, the "we" who are the subject of the ekphrasis are involved in a narrative, a process of discovery, that is emphasized by Foucault's rhetoric. For example, it is only after a number of experiences that we are said to perceive the mirror at the back of the room, an image that is at first not distinguishable from the painted images on the back wall. Foucault stages this as a triumphant episode in a story of desire finally satisfied: "It offers us at last that enchantment of the double that until now has been denied us" (OT 7; MCh 22–23). The distinction between the instantaneity of the painting and the linguistic narrative could be construed in terms of Lessing's familiar distinction between arts of space and arts of time. Following the instruction of the expert leading us through the Prado of the imagination necessarily takes time; but the epiphanies that we reach are in themselves timeless, like the suspended moment in which we see ourselves recognized by the figures in the painting. Foucault's intensification of temporality serves to convince us that we are involved in a common quest, even though what we are exploring is so static a thing as a painting.[13]

Las Meninas is a work of complex shifts and displacements. The attention of almost all the figures is focused on a point outside the painting, a point that Foucault suggests is occupied simultaneously and inconsistently by the model, ourselves ("we spectators"), and the painter of the actual canvas. In asking just what or who occupies this place for the personages within the painting, its internal spectators, it seems natural to look at the mirror (or what appears to be such), which seems to reflect the same figures that draw the attention of the Infanta, her attendants, and the painter behind his canvas. And indeed, this is what Foucault tells us about the mirror: "What it is reflecting is that which all the figures within the painting are looking at so fixedly" (OT 8; MCh 24). But the question has been raised whether the painting's perspective really allows such a reflection of the model or whatever occupies that position. A strict perspectival construction suggests that the mirror reflects what is on the canvas within the painting, rather than figures supposed to be outside it. Of course, if what is being painted on the canvas is indeed modeled on figures taken to be just beyond the space of the painting, then they would indeed be the "same" figures as are depicted on the canvas.[14] In that case Foucault would still be able to claim that the model, we spectators, and the painter of Las Meninas all seem to be in the same position, although he would not be able to base that claim on the laws of perspective. So far as it is in doubt whether the mirror at the back of the room reflects the models

Figure 12. Diego Velazquez, *Venus at Her Mirror (The Rokeby Venus)*, 1644–48. National Gallery, London. Foto Marburg/Art Resource, New York

who stand outside the painting or the figures depicted on the canvas itself, it is worth noting that in the *Rokeby Venus*, Velazquez employs a mirror within the painting that, by principles of strict perspective, could not reflect the woman's face but would have to contain the image of her left hip and torso (fig. 12).[15] Granted that the architectural setting of *Las Meninas* lends itself much more to a perspectival reading, it is still the case that Velazquez could tamper with perspective when it came to mirrors. It is even possible to read the mirror as not reflecting anything at all, either within or beyond the painting, but to see it as a painting of a mirror, as do Paul Claudel and George Kubler.[16] Socrates affected to look down on painting because it does no more than mirror the visible world. Here, if we accept the suggestions of Claudel and Kubler, the "mirror," which plays the role of a naturally produced image within the painting, would be seen as the product of complex artifice. This would contribute to the play of reversals that constitutes the painting and might, from Foucault's point of view, be one more indication of the absence of man from the picture.

55 The Vanishing Subject of Vision

Foucault does not stress the perspectival necessity of his reading but rather wants to articulate what it means for these three functions to be projected at the same place and yet fail to coincide. When he recalls the painting much later in the book, in order to explain the emergence of man, that construction of the analytic of finitude, it is in order to sketch a transformation of these three functions, a painting of an imaginary scene in which they would come to coincide. In reading this ekphrasis of a nonexistent painting that reverses the one that we have been examining, Foucault speaks again of the mirror as prefiguring what now emerges as the inevitable subject of knowledge. To see the force of this transposition, one does not have to decide whether the mirror in *Las Meninas* reflects the models directly, by the mediation of what is on the canvas whose back is turned to us, or whether in fact it is really a painting of a mirror:

> [I]n the profound upheaval of such an archaeological mutation, man appears in his ambiguous position as both an object of knowledge and as a subject that knows: enslaved sovereign, observed spectator, he appears in the place belonging to the king, which was assigned to him in advance by *Las Meninas*, but from which his real presence has for so long been excluded. As if, in that vacant space towards

which Velazquez's whole painting was directed, but which it was nevertheless reflecting only in the chance presence of a mirror, and as though by stealth, all the figures whose alternation, reciprocal exclusion, interweaving, and fluttering one imagined (the model, the painter, the king, the spectator) suddenly stopped their imperceptible dance, immobilized into one substantial figure, and demanded that the entire space of representation should at last be related to one corporeal gaze.

Several things stand out in this passage. Foucault passes from his description of an actual painting toward gesturing at a work that does not exist, yet which exemplifies the hegemonic view that holds sway from Kant through Marx, phenomenology and the human sciences. It is an image that would codify and reaffirm the basic assumptions of that era that, as Foucault sees it, have only recently begun to erode. Moreover, this ekphrasis refers to the earlier one, but in a curiously impersonal manner, when it recalls "the figures whose alternation, reciprocal exclusion, interweaving and fluttering *one imagined* [*soupçonait*]" (*OT* 312; *MCh* 323; my emphasis; the French has the suggestion of "surmised" or "suspected"). It is no longer acknowledged that this "one" was once a "we," a collective subject in which both the author and the reader were complicit. We readers, at this point, have come to a stage of distance and separation from our earlier versions, ourselves having changed places like the many roles and functions that our former selves discerned in the painting. Could it be that in order to detect the absences of *Las Meninas*, we had to assume something like the role of man, the subject whose exclusion we then discerned in terms of its effects but which has just now been named? Since this naming is tantamount to displaying its own limits, it is appropriate that we take our distance from that earlier subject and describe in impersonal terms that which was once our own project.

However, something like this *Entfremdungseffekt* already made itself felt in the earlier essay, which is divided into two numbered parts. The break between those two parts marks a specific change in voice and point of view; it is an alteration that catches its readers off guard and may produce a dislocation that is both like and unlike those evoked by the painting, some of which they have just been analyzing. In this shift, Foucault says that we have perhaps been too ascetic in our description, because we have refrained from naming the people in the painting and acknowledging that they are specific historical figures. Rather than pursue to infinity a language inadequate to the visible fact, why not name Velazquez, the Infanta Margarita, Philip IV, his wife Mariana, and the others whom we see? Yet that alternative is no sooner temptingly held out as a promise by which the painting could acquire a fuller and more specific meaning for us by establishing a rich context for it, than its possibility is rejected, in the passage already cited where we are told that "the relation of language to painting is an infinite relation."

While reading the first part of this essay, "we spectators" were indistinguishable from the speaking or writing voice that led us through the painting's complexities and announced the revelation of the mirror. The very construction of that "we" depended upon a certain implicit faith in the ability of language to describe what we were seeing and on our confidence that the voice we attended to both spoke for us and was a reliable guide to the painting. Now the proper name is denounced as a trap or artifice, one that would give us an illusion of security; it would encourage us "to pass surreptitiously from the space where one speaks to the space where one looks." What the proper name would lead us to believe is that we have closed the gap between speech and vision. We might think here of the way in which many art historians make the meaning of the painting hinge on the relation between Philip IV and Velazquez, or on the latter's aspiration to demonstrate that painting is truly a liberal art; in such readings, and *reading* is indeed the operative word, the figure named is endowed with a history and intentions that go far beyond the visible and may induce us to lose sight of it. (Foucault himself is not faithful to the protocol of erasure; just a few pages later he is speaking of the "princess," and "the attendants" [OT 12; MCh 27]).

These reflections, these inverted mirrorings of the confidence in language that we have enjoyed up until this point of the essay, lead to a resolution to be scrupulous in the assumptions we make about speech and painting; from now on ekphrasis will be conducted in full awareness of the difference between the two modes: "[O]ne must erase those proper names and preserve the infinity of the task. It is perhaps through the medium of this gray, anonymous language, always over-meticulous and repetitive because too broad, that the painting may, little by little, release its illuminations" (OT 9–10; MCh 25). Yet the discovery we have made concerning the gap between language and the visible is a discovery we have made together. The fundamental positions mapped out by the painting have failed to coincide, and language can no longer be assumed to be adequate to the visible, but "we" are still together to observe and comment on these discrepancies and to formulate protocols for our further work with the painting, such as this: "We must therefore pretend not to know who is to be reflected in the depths of that mirror, and interrogate that reflection in its own terms" (*OT* 10; *MCh* 25). We can be secure, it seems, in framing the painting by erasing the proper names and their many ramifications in history and rumor; we need not be concerned, as are the art historians, with the genre of the state portrait, the status of the painter at court, or the texts in Velazquez's library.

The reversal here parallels some of those that take place in viewing the painting and which we have just been recording. Whereas the painting might be taken superficially as simply a scene of court life, a shift occurs in which we realize that we ourselves are the object of gazes from within the painting; this is what Foucault designates as our sense of being trapped. The awareness that in using language we are necessarily at a certain distance from the visible may indeed free us from that trap, but it effects its own reversal of position. The break between the two parts of Foucault's "*Las Meninas*" is perhaps like the pause, the step back taken by the painter, with which the essay's account of the painting begins. If he has been painting, he now seems to be thinking, reflecting and considering his next move; we, having been engaged in describing the painting that we see, have taken our own step back to consider the rhetorical art presupposed by our own practice.

The role of the speaker and writer in which we become complicit is essential, yet we may fail to notice or thematize it, despite the various signs that there is something to be attended to. In this respect that role occupies a place in the essay paralleling that of the mirrored sovereigns in the painting. As Foucault describes the latter, it is a center to which no one within the painting attends: "Of all these figures represented before us, they are also the most ignored, since no one is paying the slightest attention to that reflection which has slipped into the room behind them all, silently occupying its unsuspected space; in so far as they are visible, they are the frailest and most distant form of all reality. Inversely, in so far as they stand outside the picture and are therefore withdrawn from it in an essential invisibility, they provide the center around which the entire representation is ordered" (*OT* 14; *MCh* 29). Our position, the fact that it is we, Foucault, or an "anonymous spectator" who strategically produces and constructs the ekphrasis, is a center that may easily escape the attention of readers in their haste to get at the truth of what they see.

Incidentally, what Foucault has to say about the mirror's angle of incidence is not exactly what it is usually represented to be. After encouraging us to interrogate its reflection in its own terms, he immediately says: "First, it is the reverse of the great canvas represented on the left." This is the *first* thing that we should note, and we are not told at this point whether the mirror image reflects the canvas directly or whether it happens to show us what is on the canvas because it is reflecting the models for the painting that we do not see. Later on, Foucault will indeed imply that the mirror reflects the models directly and that it could just as well have reflected the artist and the spectator: "[I]n the depths of the mirror there could also appear—there ought to appear—the anonymous face of the passer-by and that of Velazquez" (OT 15; MCh 30). And while this seems to mean that the mirror reflects the place where the actual model is standing, the remark is framed by a context in which the emphasis is not on the internal perspectival system of the painting but rather on the commerce between what is inside the painting and what is outside it. Foucault is saying that the meaning "we spectators" find in the mirror, so luminous and so close to the center of the composition as it is, is an apparent opening to what lies beyond the scene enclosed within Las Meninas. In general, this is what mirrors do: they open up another space, one that lies in front of them. In this case "the function of that reflection is to draw into the interior of the picture what is intimately foreign to it; the gaze which has organized it and the gaze for which it is displayed." Foucault is interested in how the painting constructs or implies a position for its spectator, its model, and its painter that are outside, beyond, and in front of its frame; this construction is not primarily an effect of the internal perspectival system of the picture but is rather established by an apparent convergence of looks and the mirror. There are lines that issue from the mirror, from the eyes of the princess and from the gaze of the painter. These lines "converge at a very sharp angle, and the point where they meet, springing out from the painted surface, occurs in front of the picture, more or less exactly at the spot from which we are observing it" (OT 13; MCh 28). Central to Foucault's ekphrasis is the definition of the spectator as having a place beyond and outside the painting, as standing in the position at which the most penetrating gazes from within the painting look out. Even if "we spectators" have become serially interchangeable with the "anonymous passer-by," our station has been defined; as viewers we are outside the painted surface, which nevertheless implicates or summons us, while as speakers or writers our language leaves us outside the visual in a quite different sense. These are two distinct forms of externality, one in the visible and one in the linguistic mode.

Foucault's essay is a sustained meditation on the relationship between the visible and the invisible. From its beginning he names, articulates, and orders the various ways in which these dimensions are implicated with one another: the canvas whose back is turned to us is invisible, yet its models (or itself) are reflected in the mirror; the presence of these models, of a spectator, and of the painter of the main painting itself are demanded by the picture yet are necessarily outside of the range of sight; the figures in the painting, who form a spectacle for us, cannot see the tableau that they form (except insofar as this scene is observed from the rear by the man in the doorway); the painter's figure itself is visible only because he has stepped back from the canvas, and when he moves back to work on it, rendering it visible to himself, he will become invisible to us. The play or chiasm of the visible and invisible was the subject of Merleau-Ponty's final meditations, his incomplete book and working notes, *Le visible et le invisible*, having been published just a few years before *Les mots et les choses*. While the essay on *Las Meninas* could be taken to be exploring the same theme as did Merleau-Ponty, here everything has been altered. It is no longer a question of a constant relation between the visible and the invisible, but of the way in which their movements are now understood within the context of specific visual and cognitive regimes or practices, as is suggested in Foucault's statement: "It may be that, in this picture, as in all the representations of which it is, as it were, the manifest essence, the profound invisibility of what one sees is inseparable from the invisibility of the person seeing—despite all mirrors, reflections, imitations, and portraits" (*OT* 16; *MCh* 31). As the rest of the book makes clear in its exploration of the classical episteme of representation, this principle is meant to hold (although in different ways) within both the visible and the discursive realms. Language that represents, whether it is a question of understanding speech and grammar, of the classifications of natural history, or of the exchanges by which wealth circulates, must remain unspeakable, unrepresentable, and—Foucault will frequently say—invisible to itself. The very gestures of a painting like *Las Meninas* must remain inaccessible to classical discourse. If that work is indeed the "theology of painting," as Luca Giordano said, it may be so insofar as, like classical theology, it works within a space of representation in which both the last word and the originating word are reserved for a speaker who is necessarily outside that space. Theology, in this sense, perhaps comes closer than any other classical discourse to acknowledging its own limits. The painting, too, in its own way, suggests the absence that is necessarily at its heart, as Foucault says in the last lines of the essay:

> [R]epresentation undertakes to represent itself here in all its elements, with its images, the eyes to which it is offered, the faces it makes visible, the gestures it calls into being. But there, in the midst of this dispersion which it is simultaneously grouping to-

gether and spreading out before us, indicated compellingly from every side, is an essential void: the necessary disappearance of that which is its foundation—of the person it resembles and the person in whose eyes it is only a resemblance. This very subject—which is the same—has been elided. And representation, freed finally from the relation that was impeding it, can offer itself as representation in its pure form. (*OT* 16; *MCh* 31)

These are judgments that cannot be expressed by or in the painting itself, for the "very subject . . . has been elided" who would be in a position to articulate them in the visible mode. The fullness of the play of the visible and the invisible is necessarily invisible within the realm of the painting. In this respect, Foucault has no quarrel in principle with those art historians who take a position like Jonathan Brown's, that "[t]he approach to the painting through application of post-structuralist and critical theory is intrinsically interesting, especially where it shows how contemporary ideas about art can be applied to works created in earlier periods. But its value for understanding the picture within an historical framework is intentionally limited."[17] Foucault is indeed concerned to make inescapable the gap between what we are able to say about the painting and what the painter, the king, or informed observers in the seventeenth century would have been able to say about it. An explication of the latter discourses, actual and possible, requires inquiries that involve biographical research, a knowledge of the Spanish court and the architecture of El Escorial, and an understanding of the ancient and humanist texts that Velazquez read. Every ekphrasis, we might say, is specific to one or another discursive regime, one or another episteme.

Yet this sense of the variability of regimes and epistemes seems to undercut the authority and identity of the writer of the ekphrasis. And in the case of the descriptions of the visual in Foucault's texts, the problem is compounded by the fact that it is not simply that we are in a position to perceive the instability of that writer or voice but that the "I" or "we" of the text must also be assumed to know it. In this sense, the instability of the spectator now begins, on reflection, to infect the position of the speaker or writer. If it is true that "we do not know who we are," that we oscillate between seeing and being seen, because we do not know what the painter is doing on his canvas, it is also the case that we do not know whether the position we speak from is that of an episteme that can be both depicted and erased by another hand or another era. We too stand at a peculiar juncture of the visible and the invisible, whence we encounter once more the celebrated difficulty of identifying the place from which Foucault speaks, and the continuing relevance of the Nietzschean question "Now that God is dead, who is speaking?" And how then do we read the absences of the "theology of painting" after the death of God? But we may still wonder whether some trace or shadow of the viewer remains here and, if so, what that observer looks like in turn. Notoriously, Foucault thematized his efforts to evade identification in the form of a brief dialogue at the close of the introduction to *The Archaeology of Knowledge*—and he does so in specifically visual and spatial terms. The dialogue itself has the effect of fragmenting and dispersing the writer's persona; we cannot say that it is Foucault who speaks here; it is a voice that has been conjured up by his text. Here that unnamed and disembodied voice speaks of preparing a labyrinth for himself, one "in which I can lose myself and appear at last to eyes that I will never have to meet again. I am no doubt not the only one who writes in order to have no face. Do not ask who I am and do not ask me to remain the same: leave it to our bureaucrats and our police to see that our papers are in order. At least spare us their morality when we write" (*AK* 17; *AS* 28). *And when we look,* as is implied by the visual figures here, which conjure up the image of the voyeur, who sees from the depths of his labyrinth, appears only fleetingly to eyes that will never reinspect him, and manages to shed his face. The masked, abyssal voice of the archaeologist is not so different from the oracular voice that speaks in Foucault's ekphrases. The precarious balancing act here is to speak of painting while systematically managing to avoid situating oneself as speaking as this or that person, from this or that position. But Nietzsche, who preceded Foucault with a rhetoric of the labyrinth and the mask, did not always imagine that the one who looks can also effect such an escape from the gaze, for he issued this cautionary note: "[W]hen you look long into an abyss, the abyss also looks into you" (*BGE* 146; *KSA* 5.98).

nine

Toward an Archaeology of Painting

Archaeology and Genealogy of the Visible

Given Foucault's general concern with power and his explicit research on the great medical and penal institutions of the nineteenth century, with their technologies of surveillance, systems of "isolating visibility," and the formalization of the clinical gaze, it may seem surprising that the essay on *Las Meninas* alludes to relations of power in only the most glancing way.[1] It is acknowledged, rather grudgingly, that this is a court painting, that the figures in the mirror are the sovereign and the queen, that the young girl in the center is the Infanta, and that it is at least possible to know the identity of the attendant figures. Yet Foucault, as we have seen, proposes a way of reading the painting that will minimize all these factors. He does this within a work that proposes to develop an archaeology of the human sciences; and, so far as it is archaeological, *Les mots et les choses* is concerned with explaining how certain discursive practices and forms of knowledge are constituted. In order to explore the way in which painting and other forms of making visible are implicated in structures of power and resistance, it will be useful to situate them with respect to what Foucault understands by archaeology and genealogy.

There is a distinction to be made between archaeology and genealogy, one not always explicitly or clearly made by Foucault, that may help to clarify matters. Archaeology is directed primarily toward describing how the disciplines that establish truth are constituted in a variety of contexts and cultures. Genealogy is concerned more with understanding how formations of power function; these formations involve various types of knowledge. Consider the following formulations of the task of archaeology:

> I have tried to disengage an autonomous domain which would be that of the unconscious of science, of the unconscious of knowledge [*savoir*], which would have its own rules, like the unconscious of the human individual similarly has its rules and determinations.[2]

> It is these rules of formation, which were never formulated in their own right, but are to be found only in widely differing theories, concepts, and objects of study, that I have tried to reveal, by isolating, as their specific locus, a level that I have called, somewhat arbitrarily perhaps, archaeological. Taking as an example the period covered in this book, I have tried to determine the basis or archaeological system common to a whole series of scientific "representations" or "products" dispersed throughout the natural history, economics, and philosophy of the Classical period. (*OT*, foreword, xi)

Foucault admits that he has perhaps "somewhat arbitrarily" adopted the term *archaeology* for his procedure. In a highly visible review of the English translation of *The Order of Things*, George Steiner seized on this admission and claimed that Foucault was indebted to Freud for this usage.[3] In a seigniorial reply to Steiner and to one of his French critics, in which he attempts to anatomize the basic forms of critical distortion, Foucault challenges this desire to locate his thought (and so minimize its originality) by countering with another genealogy for the term: "That word ought to locate itself somewhere, thinks Mr. Steiner. Let's give it to Freud. Mr. Steiner does not know that Kant used this word in order to designate the history of that which renders necessary a certain form of thought. I have pointed to this use, however, in another text. Certainly I would not presume that Mr. Steiner should read me. But he should leaf through Kant. I well know, however, that Kant is not as fashionable as Freud."[4] Foucault is having his fun with Steiner here (whom he refers to as a journalist), accusing him ultimately of purveying a critical fiction, founded on distortions and poor erudition, as if it were a responsible review. He responds to the assignment of archaeology to Freud with the more formidable invocation of Kant, as if to demonstrate that Steiner has hardly scratched the surface of the book and his thought. Foucault says that he has indicated the reference to Kant elsewhere, and this was no doubt in *The Archaeology of Knowledge,* where he invokes Kant, along with Husserl and Merleau-Ponty, as exemplars for his own project of freeing the history of thought from "transcendental narcissism" (*AK* 203; *AS* 265). Just as Kant showed that the validity of physics does not imply that the mind has a direct grasp of things in themselves, so Husserl is said to have shown that mathematics requires no such consciousness, and Merleau-Ponty is credited with demonstrating something similar of the perceptual world. Of course these demystifying projects are still, from Foucault's point of view, entangled with transcendental illusions of their own, as he argues in "Man and His Doubles."

The editors of Foucault's posthumous *Dits et écrits* claim that there is a more specific source for the reference to Kant in the response to Steiner. They cite Kant's incomplete essay "What Real Progress Has Metaphysics Made in Germany since the Time of Leibniz and Wolff?" (*DE* 2.221 n).[5] There Kant considers whether a "philosophical history of philosophy" is possible, and he contrasts a "philosophical archaeology" with a merely historical or empirical approach to such a history. For Kant, philosophical archaeology is deeper than an empirical history because it deals with necessities drawn from the nature of human reason. While Foucault would reject this, he would accept the contrast of a mere recounting or chronicle of the history of thought and systems with an approach like his own that traces the deeper and more implicit protocols of thought. Kant's rather neglected essay is the philosopher's most significant attempt to describe his own project in historical terms and to provide some indication of how to write the history of thought. In its drawing of a sharp line between critical and precritical metaphysics, it shows how major discontinuities between distinct epochs of thought can be discerned, even within national traditions that largely share a common terminology. If we decouple Kant's "archaeology" from a teleology that leads to his own critical philosophy and concentrate instead on the notion of crisis, we can see how Foucault would have found this an exemplary archaeological text.[6]

In his somewhat arbitrary rewriting of the Kantian archaeology, which he acknowledges as such, Foucault does not explicitly develop the analogy between his notion and the discipline of excavating and analyzing traces of the past which usually goes by that name. Yet that resonance is unavoidable (and clearly at the basis of Steiner's reference to Freud). So it will be useful to attempt to articulate their similarity. The archaeologist, who deals with (usually extinct) cultures, will typically be examining a set of remains and traces that she or he believes belong together, and on the basis of this evidence, he or she will formulate some ideas about how these different artifacts and marks, products both intentional and inadvertent, constitute parts of a meaningful arrangement of life. A particular style of pottery, a certain kind of burial mound, a way of laying out living spaces, the hunting or gathering of certain foods and their consumption, and a habitual way of disposing of the society's trash will make sense as components of a single way of life. This is, very generally speaking, the structuralist dimension of archaeology. The archaeologist will usually be curious whether the culture she has excavated and reconstructed is the only one to be found on its site, and so she will dig more deeply. Frequently, the result is to find another layer of artifacts, buildings, and traces beneath the one already studied. Here too the task will be to make sense of what has been unearthed, and the act of making sense will find different rules, styles, and arrangements obtaining among the various components of the culture. The process of discovery and excavation will be limited only by the resources of the archaeologist and the materials that lie beneath the surface; in principle the dig can go on as long as it yields results. The more cultures are discovered, the greater are the conceptual resources of the archaeologist for making sense of each one. For she begins to acquire a set of schemata or patterns that she can try out on the data presented by each level in the excavation; increasingly she makes sense of these cultures diacritically, comparing the ways in which one group arranges such things as eating, shelter, and defensive operations with the ways other groups manage their affairs. In most cases the members of the different groups would not be able to formulate their rules and procedures themselves; they see them not as one possible set of practices among others but simply as the way things are done, the way ordained by custom, the gods, or the nature of things. In contrast to the discipline of history, archaeology will not assume that there is a continuous path of development that links the cultures discovered. The archaeologist tends to focus rather on what renders these different cultures distinct, what, for example, separates early from late Minoan or Harappan from Indus. In looking at a succession of cultures that have successively occupied the same site, the archaeologist is sensitive to disruptive and catastrophic events that contribute to the sudden transformation of a culture or its displacement by another, such as natural disaster, climatic change, disappearance of a food supply, epidemic, war, or invasion. To adapt the procedures of the field archaeologist to the archives of Western culture and science, as Foucault does, is to engage in a parallel practice. The archaeologist of the human sciences will probably begin his inquiry where he is; if he is a student of psychology, like the young Foucault, he may begin with the institutions and uncertainties characterizing what is called "mental illness"; these are centered around asylums, licensed therapists, legitimation of treatment by the legal and medical professions, and the regular use of certain treatments. To see the deeper structure and tendencies of the disciplines associated with that concept, he will compare them with the practices of some previous eras. So he discovers, for example, not a constant "mental illness," which would be timelessly invariant, but, in the fifteenth and sixteenth centuries, a notion of madness as tragic knowledge that yields cosmic insights. Later this is displaced by another conceptualization and institutionalization of the mad in which their idleness is a reason for confinement and correction. "Mental illness" can now be described as the successor subject of hysteria, which is the successor subject of madness, and so on. Archaeology deals with the texts, practices, disciplines, and theories that contribute to constituting and dealing with these subjects.

Is there an archaeology of the visible? We have seen that in *Histoire de la folie*, Foucault appeals to the painting of Bosch, Brueghel, and others at the beginning of his study in order to contrast the tragic knowledge of the fifteenth- and sixteenth-century painters with what he sees as the attempt to domesticate madness in such literary works as Sebastian Brant's *Ship of Fools* and Erasmus's *Praise of Folly*. Here it would seem that the discursive and the visual operate along two parallel and contrasting tracks. Painting, or at least certain paintings, is associated with what seems to be a more authentic experience of madness than that seen in literary texts. This is accomplished through an openness to the dream and a confrontation with the inevitability of death. To pursue the valorization of Bosch and his contemporaries along these lines could suggest that they have some privileged access to "madness itself," a madness that simply is what it is, independently of specific traditions and cultural contexts. This is an unpromising direction of thought for two reasons. It is unhistorical and nonarchaeological to look at *these* paintings as if they stood outside such contexts. Art historians debate the specific iconological meaning of these fantastic visions and speculate concerning the particular position to be assigned to the painters on the spectrum of religious orthodoxy and heterodoxy. These inquiries are difficult and must, from a later Foucauldian perspec-

tive, reflect the discipline of art history. We suppose that similar principles will characterize the analysis of *any* visual work, including those
that are conventionally classified as innocent, naïve (Nietzsche's term
for Raphael), or the product of the folk.[7] This is the point that I take
Foucault to be making in the criticism of Merleau-Ponty embedded in
Les mots et les choses and anticipated by Malraux.

An archaeology of the visible, then, must attempt to understand
the changing practices, expectations, and disciplines that are concerned
with the production, display, and interpretation of visual artifacts. Foucault never explicitly attempts to develop such an archaeology, but he
provides several indications of how it might proceed. His analyses of
specific painters, works, and styles provide the outlines of such an archaeology of Western painting, and we have already begun to see the
emergence of this outline in Foucault's commentaries on Bosch and
his contemporaries and on Velazquez. We can highlight three avenues
toward an archaeology of the visible in Foucault's writing; these are
not the only such suggestions in his work, but they are indicative of
the most promising directions for this project. The first two are more
or less explicit in reflections on specific works of art in *The Order of
Things* and *This Is Not a Pipe;* the third is to be found in a general
reflection in *The Archaeology of Knowledge* on the possibility of developing archaeologies that are not tied directly to the episteme. The approaches to be explored are not completely consistent with one another.
While we will want to note the differences and possible conflicts among
them, it may be useful to see them not as baldly contradictory, but as
a series of attempts to sketch just what an archaeology of the visible
might look like.

57 From Renaissance Similitude to Postmodern Simulacrum

In *Les mots et les choses,* an avowedly archaeological work, Foucault
is concerned above all with the structure and function of discourses,
that is, of disciplines whose medium is language. Yet the signature piece
of this archaeology is the essay on *Las Meninas,* and the painting makes
an important second appearance later in the book when Foucault wants
to explain the rise of that uncanny doublet, man, who steps into the
empty place that has been reserved for him in the painting. So it is
appropriate to ask whether the archaeology of the epistemic regimes
mapped in this text can be extended to the visual. Are there parallels
between the four distinctive ways of knowing that Foucault considers
here and some forms of visual art? Consider first a brief sketch of the

epochs discussed in *Les mots et les choses* (we can think of an epoch, in accordance with its etymology, as a bounded delimitation).[8] In the Renaissance, Foucault says, the guiding principle or *episteme* of knowledge is resemblance, especially of part to whole or microcosm to macrocosm. Disciplines such as numerology and astrology, not to mention the philosophy of the day, delighted in finding resemblances and analogies between high and low, the plants and the stars, man and the cosmos. In what Foucault calls the classical age—roughly that ushered in by Cartesian philosophy and the new physics—the aim is complete representation, a total anatomy and system, an inventory by genus and species, as in taxonomic natural history or in the metaphysics of Leibniz and Wolff. In the succeeding era, marked philosophically by Kant's Copernican turn, questions are raised about the possibility of such unlimited representation. How, after all, is representation possible? If all representation occurs through the agency of finite subjects, limited by such things as the forms of intuition (space and time) and the categories (e.g., causality), then we require an analytic of finitude, that is, an account of how the very limitations of the finite beings that we are render possible what knowledge we may have. From this perspective Kant, Marx, and Heidegger are archaeological bedfellows, each attempting to show by emphasizing one aspect of our finite condition—phenomenal knowledge, the labor process, or mortality—how we can know what we do. In this epoch of "Man and His Doubles," we are dealing with the figure of man, "enslaved sovereign, observed spectator," a figure ambiguously positioned between the transcendental and the empirical, the cogito and the unthought, and the retreat and return of his own origin, an origin that, as soon as it seems to be recaptured, recedes again into obscurity. Finally, Foucault discerns on the horizon a successor epoch to this last one, when the figure of man will be washed away like a drawing in the sand, to be replaced by the return of language and the ascendancy of the simulacrum.

Consider now four epochs of painting that might be said to correspond to these discursive and epistemic regimes. In the Renaissance era of resemblance, analogy rules; there is an attempt to include as many dimensions of the cosmos as possible in the picture. In Brueghel's *Harvesters*, for example, the exhausted peasants sprawled in the fields resemble the very sheaves of wheat that they have just gathered and shaped or the roots of the trees against which they lie. Leonardo's famous figure of a man with outstretched limbs inscribed in a circle, emblem of the mutual reflection of microcosm and macrocosm, is paradigmatic of this age and its visuality. Erwin Panofsky's *Studies in Iconology* is typical of the kind of reading that these works appropriately receive. Such images draw on a wide spectrum of myth, philosophy, and curious erudition, their implicit principle being that all forms of knowledge can be mapped onto one another and reflect one another in mutually illuminating ways. In the classical age of painting (very roughly from 1600 to 1800), attention shifts from resemblance to representation, and the painter displays a mastery of visual effects of every sort, including the texture of a fur or a rug in Vermeer or the glint of a peeled lemon in a Dutch still life. It is in the context of this delineation of the epoch of representation and its contrast with the succeeding period that Foucault analyzes the puzzles and paradoxes of *Las Meninas*. This masterpiece seems to inventory all the possible objects, dimensions, and techniques of representation. It represents everything but the possibility of representation itself, a lacuna that is made evident to our later eyes by the wavering place of model, painter, and spectator in the virtual space in front of the painting. If what fills this space in the analytic of finitude is man knowing himself through his own limitations, as in Kant's Copernican revolution, what sort of painting might be appropriate to such a discursive regime? As I suggested earlier, we might think of such self-portraits as those of Cézanne and Van Gogh. Here the painters do not present themselves as serene masters, as Velazquez appears in *Las Meninas*, who preside over the totality of representation. They are engaged in anguished self-exploration; they know that representation depends on them and returns to them, rather than being supported in the nature of things. Even a still life by Van Gogh is still a form of self-portrait, or "personal object," as Meyer Schapiro argued in his response to Martin Heidegger.[9] From the perspective of "Man and His Doubles," even such styles as impressionism and expressionism, which are usually held to contrast sharply with each other, would be variant modes of exploring the artist's finitude. Is there a form of art that follows such visual exploration of the self in the way that the emergence of language follows the Kantian problematic? As should already be apparent, it would be an art of similitude, of the matrix, the grid, and the simulacrum. It is the art that Foucault analyzes in his discussions of Magritte, Warhol, Michals, and Fromanger. This is the kind of art that might be drawn in the sand after the figure of man had been washed away. This very figure of figuration, the sketch in the sand, is suggestive of the conception of the diagram, deployed in *Discipline and Punish* and further articulated by Deleuze (sec. 63). The archaeology of vision would be an inquiry into the structure and succession of various diagrams that are the nerve of visual regimes. What could be misleading about this figure of figuration would be the possible implication that a diagram is reducible to some specific, fixed, graphic pattern such as a blueprint.

This archaeological sketch builds on the general schema of *Les mots et les choses*, emphasizing the essay on *Las Meninas*. It would make sense of Foucault's various writings on the artists of similitude just cited. Yet Foucault himself has little to say about the visual art of the Renaissance, aside from his discussions of Bosch and Breughel in the context of the history of madness. However, some remarks toward the end of *Histoire de la folie* are suggestive and need to be read carefully in light of the question whether there is a timeless and ahistorical madness that stands in contrast with the archaeology of the discourses and practices that surround it. There Foucault says that

> the Goya who painted *The Madhouse* must have experienced before that grovel of flesh in the void, that nakedness among bare walls, something related to a contemporary pathos: the symbolic tinsel that crowned the insane kings left in full view suppliant bodies, bodies vulnerable to chains and whips, which contradicted the delirium of the faces, less by the poverty of these trappings than by the human truth that radiated from all that unprotected flesh. The man in the tricorne is not mad because he has stuck an old hat upon his nakedness; but within this madman in a hat rises—by the inarticulate power of his muscular body, of his savage and marvelously unconstricted youth—a human presence already liberated and somehow free since the beginning of time by his birthright. (MC 224; HF 654–55)

Here Foucault seems to be saying that Goya's painting discloses a "human truth" or "human presence" that he has experienced himself as a "contemporary pathos," or, in other words, an essential human reality that surfaced again in Goya's time after a period of submergence. Goya (along with Sade) is said to have given the Western world "the possibility of transcending its reason in violence, and of recovering tragic experience beyond the promises of dialectic" (*HF* 228). Like some of the remarks in "Stultifera Navis," the book's first chapter, these appear to appeal to painting, or at least to a painting with a certain connection to madness, as an avenue to an eternal tragic experience. Yet Foucault is not making such an appeal, for he goes on to contrast Goya's presentation of madness with that of Bosch and Breughel. After posing the question whether the monster whispering to *The Monk* is the same as the gnome or gryllo who catches the eye of Bosch's *Saint*

Anthony, he proceeds to insist on their difference in a way that begins to articulate an important distinction between a Renaissance art of cosmic analogies and a modern one of human self-interrogation. Speaking of the monstrous forms that loom up in these images, he says: "For Bosch or Brueghel, these forms are generated by the world itself; through the fissures of a strange poetry, they rise from stones and plants, they well out of an animal howl; the whole complicity of nature is not too much for their dance. Goya's forms are born out of nothing: they have no background, in the double sense that they are silhouetted against only the most monotonous darkness, and that nothing can assign them their limit, and their nature." Foucault goes on to detail the way in which the absence of a detailed background and the indeterminacy of features other than those of the figures contributes to this sense of forms being "born out of nothing." And yet, as we read on, we see that this dark night is not totally impersonal but a dark night of the soul: "[I]n that night man communicates with what is deepest in himself, and with what is most solitary. . . . Goya's *Idiot* who shrieks and twists his shoulder to escape from the nothingness that imprisons him—is this the birth of the first man and his first movement toward liberty, or the last convulsion of the last dying man?" (*MC* 225; *HF* 655). Something new arises in Goya's painting, Foucault is arguing. The night of his pictures may be the night of "classical unreason," in the sense of "classical" that characterizes the world from the time of the great confinement and Descartes through that of Kant and the early psychiatrists; but in that night, man is now the center, a center reflecting on itself. This man seeks his origin in an anguished solitude and finds that it constantly retreats from him. The madman could be the emblem of modern thought, which is condemned to "repeat repetition" and to "the experience of Hölderlin, Nietzsche, and Heidegger, in which the return is posited only in the extreme recession of the origin—in that region where the gods have turned away, where the desert is increasing, where the τέχνη [*technē*][10] has established the dominion of its will" (*OT* 334; *MCh* 345). So Foucault, more specifically the Foucault of *The Order of Things*, might begin to fill out the archaeology of painting derived from its articulation of four discursive regimes with his own earlier analyses of Bosch and Goya. And his subtle reading of the latter, which has a tighter line of thought than its lyrical language at first suggests, also serves to make possible a clearer view of the tragic experience of madness that he finds exemplified in the former. We can now understand his comments about the natural and cosmic dimensions of that experience in Bosch (and others) as pointing to the context of the world of analogy and resemblance, or microcosm and macrocosm, that is the fundamental Renaissance episteme.

58 Klee, Kandinsky, Magritte

The essay on Magritte is one of the few places where Foucault explicitly sketches a narrative sequence of a series of alterations in Western painting. It is the source of a second possible archaeology of painting. The account focuses on the relation between words and images; as such it leads quite smoothly into the discussion of Magritte's *This Is Not a Pipe* as an "unravelled calligram." In a section of the essay entitled "Klee, Kandinsky, Magritte," Foucault argues that the names of these three artists mark three successive departures from the two principles that, he believes, dominated Western painting for the previous five centuries. The first of these "asserts the separation between plastic representation (which implies resemblance) and linguistic reference (which excludes it)" (*TNP* 32; *CP* 39). What this means is that words and images are of two different orders, and this entails that one will always dominate the other. Words may be primary, as when pictures are used to illustrate a text, say of an encyclopedia or reference book. Language will be subordinate when it is one of several items depicted in an image, for example in a Vermeer painting of a woman reading a letter or in a Holbein portrait with a painted inscription of the subject's name. Even if actual paintings and texts complicate these relations, the two orders remain distinct. Paul Klee is credited with overcoming this principle "by showing the juxtaposition of shapes and the syntax of lines in an uncertain, reversible, floating space (simultaneously page and canvas, plane and volume, map and chronicle)" (*TNP* 33; *CP* 40–41). Foucault points to the importance of the arrows that appear so frequently in Klee, making explicit not only the movement to be attributed to an element in a painting, like a boat moving down the river, but displaying the way in which painting generally directs the viewer's attention, encouraging the reading of a painting in a certain way. What is relatively implicit in the left-to-right pattern of reading in Holbein's portrait *Thomas Godsalve and His Son John* becomes manifest in Klee's use of the arrow.[11] We should notice that the era in which words and images are of two separate orders does not coincide very neatly with the archaeological divisions that we have extrapolated from Foucault's analysis of the human sciences; the period of five hundred years that is said to be governed by the principle of separation would include the epochs of the Renaissance, the classical age, and the modern period. It would not be deeply anomalous to recognize a *langue durée* during which a principle such as this obtained and within which there were other marked differences. Yet if Foucault had addressed this question directly, we would be on firmer ground in attempting to make sense of his incipient archaeology of painting.

Klee plays an important role in this archaeology. In an interview given shortly after the publication of *The Order of Things*, Foucault was asked if there was a painting that had the same exemplary significance for contemporary times as *Las Meninas* had for the classical age. Without hesitation or qualification, he answered that Klee's painting played such a role; he did not single out a specific work but referred to the general style and approach of the artist. At least at that time, then, Foucault was ready to accept the notion that there could be an archaeology of forms of visual art that paralleled the one he had articulated for the discourses of the human sciences and their predecessor and successor subjects. This impression is strengthened by the emphasis in Foucault's response on the knowledge or know-how *(savoir)* that is key to Velazquez's and Klee's achievement.

> It seems to me that Klee's painting best represents, in terms of our century, what Velazquez was able to do in relation to his. To the extent that Klee made to appear in visible form all of the gestures, acts, graphisms, traces, lineaments, surfaces, which are able to constitute painting, he made the very act of painting the manifest and brilliant knowledge [*savoir*] of painting itself.
>
> His painting is not *art brut*, but a painting recaptured by the knowledge of its most fundamental elements. And these elements, apparently the most simple and spontaneous, the very ones that do not appear and that it seems never ought to appear, it is these that Klee distributes over the surface of the painting. *Las Meninas* represents all the elements of representation, the painter, the models, the brush, the canvas, the image in the mirror, they decompose painting itself into the elements that would make a representation.
>
> Klee's painting composes and decomposes painting into the elements which, on account of their being simple, are no less supported, haunted, and inhabited by the knowledge of painting.
> (*DE* 1.544)

Painting, then, is a discipline, or a disciplined practice, which can be articulated in terms of a variety of techniques, procedures, and forms of *savoir*. Foucault's remarks about Klee can be read as pointing to the way in which his works present an array of features that inventory aspects of painting that would earlier have been submerged in a "finished" canvas: drawing with all its hesitations and second thoughts, the application of paint, the spectrum of color, the varying textures of canvas and other surfaces (including collage), and the words that, in a title or a discourse supposedly external to the painting, would provide a linguistic supplement to a visual image. Velazquez seems to have understood the *savoir* of painting in a specifically classical way; everything has to do with the painter producing a representation of a particular subject. Klee, in contrast, is concerned with those dimensions and presuppositions of painting that are not themselves obviously visible, the elements that render visibility possible. His focus is neither on representation nor on self-exploration, but on those gestures, acts, graphisms, and manipulations of media that constitute the art of painting. Foucault says something similar in another interview from the same time; in the context of a discussion of Breton and surrealism, he compares Klee and Nietzsche: "I have the impression that there are two great families of founders. There are the builders who place the first stone, and there are the diggers and excavators. Perhaps in our uncertain space, we are closer to those who excavate: to Nietzsche (instead of Husserl), to Klee (instead of Picasso)" (*F* 2.171; *DE* 1.554). This suggests that Klee is not to be taken simply as an expression of an era—which would turn Foucault's archaeology into the Hegelianism that he contests—but as its patient explorer, one who succeeds at articulating the diverse elements of painting, laying them out for inspection and analysis. Nietzsche described his own inquiry in *The Birth of Tragedy* in similar terms: "It becomes necessary to level the artistic structure [*kunstvolle Gebäude*] of the *Apollonian culture*, as it were, stone by stone, till we catch sight of [*erblicken*] the foundations on which it rests" (*BT* 3; *KSA* 1.34). The suggestion that Klee, too, is an archaeologist may cast some light on Foucault's understanding of Velazquez and the role that the essay on *Las Meninas* plays in *The Order of Things*. For if Velazquez and Klee are engaged in analogous enterprises, then *Las Meninas* will also be seen not as an expression of the *Zeitgeist* but as an attempt at an inventory of the visual regime of the classical era, with its apparatus of painting and its assumptions concerning the sovereign gaze.

Foucault identifies a second principle as having ruled Western painting, one that "posits an equivalence between the fact of resemblance and the affirmation of a representative bond" (*TNP* 34; *CP* 42). By virtue of this principle, any form in a painting that resembles an object or another figure is taken to be a representation of that thing.

Kandinsky is the name that Foucault associates with the interrogation and abandonment of this principle:

> The rupture of this principle can be ascribed to Kandinsky: a double effacement simultaneously of resemblance and of the representative bond, by the increasingly insistent affirmation of the lines, the colors that Kandinsky called "things," neither more nor less objects than the church, the bridge, or the knight with his bow. . . . when asked "what it is" [this painting] can reply only by referring itself to the gesture that formed it: an "improvisation," a "composition"; or to what is found there: "a red shape," "triangles," "purple orange"; or to tensions or internal relations: "a determinant pink," "upwards," "a yellow milieu," "a rosy balance." (*TNP* 34–35; *CP* 43–44)

The shapes in these paintings, then, need not be taken as representing anything, even if they do happen to resemble certain objects. Resemblance is dismissed as irrelevant to the project of art. As with the first principle, Foucault's interest is focused on questions having to do with knowledge and meaning. It might be objected that this skews the understanding of painting in a rather intellectualist direction and tends to exclude what, at least since Kant, we have called the aesthetic. Yet it should be clear that Foucault is not attempting to provide an exhaustive account of the painters and styles that he discusses. Instead, he concentrates on those fundamental assumptions that render painting possible and which are subject to archaeological mutation. To foreground the "aesthetic" with its emphasis on feeling and on an experience independent of knowledge and will would be to homogenize strata of art that are quite diverse. As the eighteenth century discovered, the aesthetic attitude is remarkably adaptable; now one can assume it in the presence of a Byzantine icon or a Kandinsky composition. But this homogenization runs the danger of blinding us to significant differences, just as a phenomenology like Merleau-Ponty's limits our range of perception.

On the basis of his remark in the interview cited above, we might have expected that Foucault would give extended attention to Klee, as the painter whose art is emblematic of the twentieth century. Yet even in the casual context of an interview, Foucault does not suggest that Klee embodies the spirit of the age; it is rather that he exhibits the *savoir* of painting in exemplary fashion and perhaps that one of his pictures could be used to make a diagnosis of the episteme of his time as *Las Meninas* can be analyzed to show what was characteristic of the classical age. Such a treatment might deploy such an analysis to explain what is missing in Klee's work, the equivalent of the absence of man that we later viewers can discern as the implicit absence in Velazquez's picture. Yet precisely because Klee is an artist of our time, or more specifically of Foucault's time in 1966 when he answered the interviewer's question, there was no later position available from which he could have perceived the diacritical difference between the art of Klee and that of a successor period. As it turned out, Foucault turned his eye toward Magritte. We will follow his analysis later (chap. 11); now let us simply note his claim that, despite Magritte's apparent separation of text and image and his constant use of representational elements, he in fact combines both Klee's and Kandinsky's alternatives to the laws formerly governing painting, constituting "on the basis of a system common to them all, a figure at once opposed and complementary" (*TNP* 35; *CP* 45). This suggests that, from a considered archaeological view, Foucault finds Magritte to be the more typical artist of the twentieth century. For an art historian or a critic, this may seem to be a shocking judgment in the age that produced Picasso and cubism, Pollock and abstract expressionism, and a host of other figures and movements; but it is not the sort of judgment that comes as a total surprise from the archaeologist who confessed that he had altered "the calendar of saints and heroes" in his account of the epochs of the human sciences (*OT*, foreword, x).

59 Archaeology without the Episteme?

Toward the end of *The Archaeology of Knowledge,* as if in a postscript, Foucault raises the question of whether there might be archaeologies that were not oriented exclusively to the sciences, and he suggests that painting would be a good subject for such an alternative approach. Until this point he has been developing a set of categories for understanding the ways in which sciences constitute themselves and analytic strategies by means of which we can mark the *archai* of such sciences and the succession of quite different forms that they may take. If we have been following Foucault, we have been learning to free ourselves from the simplifications of traditional intellectual history, such as the assumption of the importance of the individual author or genius and the prevalence of continuous development. The question is this: "[B]y confining itself up to now to the region of scientific discourses, has archaeology been governed by some insuperable necessity—or has it provided an outline, on the basis of a particular example, of forms of analysis that may have a much wider application?" Foucault confesses, "I am not sufficiently advanced in my task to answer this question," yet he goes on to imagine several possibilities, notably having to do with sexuality, political knowledge, and painting. This is an intriguing list, given the later series on *The History of Sexuality* and works such as *Discipline and Punish,* which take up the political theme in a certain way. Although Foucault did not write an equivalent study of painting, his remarks provide a suggestive sketch of how it might proceed. Since these are the only remarks he explicitly addressed to the project of an archaeology of painting, I will reproduce and comment on them. Foucault begins by giving a brief account of some of the options available to an art history that would be oriented either to reconstructing the intentions of the artist or placing works of art within a broader cultural and intellectual context: "In analyzing a painting, one can reconstitute the latent discourse of the painter; one can try to recapture the murmur of his intentions, which are not transcribed into words, but into lines, surfaces, and colors; one can try to uncover the implicit philosophy that is supposed to form his view of the world. It is also possible to question science, or at least the opinions of the period, and to try to recognize to what extent they appear in the painter's work" (*AK* 192; *AS* 251). Foucault reminds us that a hermeneutical project directed to the painter's intention necessarily deals with an elusive subject; the artist's discourse is latent or implicit, since it is not put into language but is to be reconstructed from the visual evidence (remembering that "evidence" is what strikes the eyes, what is manifest to the *video*). That some painting, like Klee's and Magritte's, deploys language in complex ways does not alter the situation but simply makes it more complex because these are painted words. The painter's intentions are a "murmur," because she does not formulate them linguistically in the first instance but addresses herself to marking the canvas. And while one can insert a painting into a history of ideas, Foucault implies that he would be suspicious of this for the same reasons that he has been criticizing traditional intellectual history throughout the *Archaeology.* The typical assumptions of such history privilege continuity and homogeneity, failing to acknowledge the discursive formations that ground the ideas or sciences whose story they tell. This sort of approach reduces the painter to being the mouthpiece of the *Zeitgeist,* an expression fundamentally indistinguishable from others. Painting becomes the vehicle of philosophy or science, an illustration of the history of ideas. Yet for Foucault there is no "history of ideas," as if they generated and succeeded one another in some autonomous space. If philosophy and science must be understood as discursive practices, a history of ideas would be at best a shorthand for naming and classifying those practices, not an independent field of development. To make painting an epi-phenomenon of such an allegedly autonomous process would be to en-gage in a doubly idealistic reduction, excluding or minimizing much of what specifically pertains to the practice of painting, what Bourdieu terms the *habitus.*

There is an alternative: "Archaeological analysis would have an-other aim: it would try to discover whether space, distance, depth, color, light, proportions, volumes, and contours were not, at the period in question, considered, named, enunciated, and conceptualized in a dis-cursive practice; and whether the knowledge that this discursive prac-tice gives rise to was not embodied perhaps in theories and speculations, in forms of teaching and codes of practice, but also in processes, tech-niques, and even in the very gesture of the painter" (*AK* 192; *AS* 251). So archaeology would concentrate on neither the murmuring intention of the painter nor the general cultural history within which her work is embedded. We might note in passing that the provisional archaeol-ogy of painting that we speculatively derived from *The Order of Things* could be said to be concerned with the latter, although Foucault's ar-chaeology of knowledge is quite distinct from the history of ideas as usually practiced. An archaeology more specific to the practice of paint-ing would be concerned with discursive practices, both explicit and implicit. The "forms of teaching and codes of practice" that Foucault mentions are scarcely unknown to the history of art. The study of acad-emies, guilds, painters' workshops, and the documents and institutions of art education have become standard concerns among scholars. Yet there is perhaps a certain antiquarian flavor in the way such studies have been undertaken; Foucault encourages an exploration of the dis-courses associated with teaching and practice that would emphasize the way in which they function as a "positive unconscious," to borrow a term from his investigation of the sciences. Moreover, he envisions an approach that would see a continuity between the discursive formula-tions surrounding practice and the way in which the knowledge *(savoir)* embodied in these formulations is also incorporated into the entire atti-tude and position of the painter, her processes, techniques, and ges-tures. This talk of embodied knowledge begins to sound like Merleau-Ponty's description of the painter's situation, as when he says that "it is by lending his body to the world that the artist changes the world into paintings" or declares that "to understand these transubstantiations we must go back to the working actual body . . . that body which is an intertwining of vision and movement."[12] Yet Merleau-Ponty seems to divorce this working body with its implicit knowledge from the discur-sive practices within which the artist works. The model for the phenomenologist, again, is an idealization of a painter like Cézanne, conceived as working in splendid isolation and giving himself up to the landscape to let it become visible through him. "Cézanne's artist," Merleau-Ponty tells us, "speaks as the first man spoke and paints as if no one had ever painted before. . . . Before expression, there is nothing but a vague fever, and only the work itself, completed and understood, will prove that there was *something* rather than *nothing* to be found there. Because he has returned to the source of silent and solitary experience on which culture and the exchange of ideas have been built in order to take cognizance of it, the artist launches his work just as a man once launched the first word."[13] For Foucault, embodied practice, the *savoir* implicit in the artist's gesture, is not at "the source of silent and solitary experience" but is continuous with a language and a discursive community. That Merleau-Ponty reverts to figures connected with speech is symptomatic. He wants to think of the artist as being in the position of inventing a language for herself, rather than as always working within a context already discursively limited.

It could be that such a phenomenological tendency to minimize the linguistic is one of Foucault's targets as he continues to develop his sketch of what an archaeology of painting might do:

> It would not set out to show that painting is a certain way of "meaning" or "saying" that is peculiar in that it dispenses with words. It would try to show that, at least in one of its dimensions, it is discursive practice that is embodied in techniques and effects. In this sense, the painting is not a pure vision that must then be transcribed into the materiality of space; nor is it a naked gesture whose silent and eternally empty meanings must be freed from subsequent interpretations. It is shot through—and independently of scientific knowledge [*connaissance*] and philosophical themes—with the positivity of a knowledge [*savoir*]. (*AK* 194; *AS* 253)

Again Foucault insists that there is no "pure vision." Such a vision has been the object of an illusory philosophical desire from Plato through phenomenology. Critics have celebrated with awe the painters who they thought were gifted with such vision of the world and had successfully transcribed it; the reception of the impressionists provides a host of examples. In his essay on Bataille, Foucault argued that the figure or ideal of such a pure vision was essential to generating a philosophy of reflection, one that claimed a position of pure knowledge (sec. 42). Nietzsche made a parallel claim in his critique of "immaculate perception," which attempted to reveal the subtext of desire and envy underlying the praise of purity (sec. 32). Here Foucault mentions several ways in which painting might be thought to involve a pure vision. It could be imagined that such a vision is nondiscursive. While abstract expressionist painters rejected the idea of representing the visual field of everyday life, they and their advocates sometimes claimed that they were involved in embodying a purely expressive or constructive vision. They tended to speak ironically of any attempt to give a verbal account of their work either as process or product. Now such antilinguistic rhetoric appears as the code of an esoteric priesthood, striving to maintain a certain awe for their hierophantic mysteries among the adepts and adherents of their cult. Writing just a few years after the zenith of abstractionism, Foucault maintains that painting ought not to be thought of as a "naked gesture"; here one thinks of the claims that painting was sheer performance or action, necessarily falsified by all later interpretation, as if there could be human gestures that did not take place within a discursive space. Action and performance are embodiments, to be sure, but they are embodiments of techniques and discourses, among other things. The painters of the 1950s had not returned to a primal innocence but had formed a certain community with its own standards and vocabulary.

ten

Visual Regimes and Visual Resistance:
From the Panopticon to Manet's *Bar*

60 Nietzsche and the Theater of Cruelty

Foucault acknowledges Nietzsche's example and his priority in the genealogical investigation of institutions and practices. This priority extends to the rhetorical structure of some of their signature texts, and specifically to the way in which visual scenes are suggested or described. *Discipline and Punish* opens with a lurid account of the execution of the regicide Damiens, in which a series of tortures, some carried out in clumsy and incompetent fashion, are pictured in excruciating detail. Similar scenes are evoked in *On the Genealogy of Morality*, which precedes *Discipline and Punish* with its analysis of how torture and festive cruelty contributed to constituting that strange being, the autonomous subject, "an animal with the right to make promises" (*GM* II.1; *KSA* 5.291). Nietzsche wants to show us what strangely ambiguous ascetic, self-regulating creatures we have become, and he does so by tracing the peculiar history that leads from the public tortures and displays of cruelty among the Greeks, Romans, and earlier

Germans to the world in which human beings become their own judges, torturers, and hangmen, carrying out an internal, self-inflicted punishment whose affective intensity overshadows the merely physical pain of those antecedent practices. In the second essay of the *Genealogy*, "'Guilt,' 'Bad Conscience,' and the Like," he starts out to write a Foucauldian "history of the present," a history that would not take the present as normative and inevitable, but as the subject for an inquiry that would defamiliarize it by disentangling the varied strands of development and the histories that have constituted it. Beginning with "the end of this tremendous process, where the tree at last brings forth fruit . . . we discover that the ripest fruit is the *sovereign individual*" (*GM* II.2; *KSA* 5.293). Let us not assume that this autonomy is simply the essential condition of humanity. Rather, let us ask: Where does this sovereign individual come from? How is such a person constituted? In telling the story that will answer these questions, Nietzsche, like Foucault after him, is drawn repeatedly to certain spectacles, to scenarios of torture and cruelty. It is telling that, typically, after indulging in a detailed description of certain horrific practices, he will take a step back, declaring that the evocation of terrifying scenes has not yet directly located the institution of the bad conscience (see, for example, *GM* II.8, where Nietzsche says, after several pages of such descriptions, "To return to our investigations . . ."). We are reminded of the story that Socrates tells in the *Republic* of the man who, unable to resist the desire to look upon a ghastly scene of mutilated bodies, finally gives in and cries out to his eyes, "There, ye wretches, take your fill of the fine spectacle!"[1] Part of what Nietzsche sets out to explain is how the exaction of public pain could be the compensation for an unpaid debt, and the explanation lies in the fact that human beings enjoy spectacles of cruelty. Moreover, the principle receives a cosmic legitimation in the form of a theological theatrocracy:

> "Every evil the sight of which edifies a god is justified": thus spoke the primitive logic of feeling—and was it, indeed, only primitive? The gods conceived as the friends of *cruel* spectacles—oh how profoundly this ancient idea still permeates our European humanity! Merely consult Calvin and Luther. It is certain, at any rate, that the *Greeks* still knew of no tastier spice to offer their gods to season their happiness than the pleasure of cruelty. With what eyes do you think Homer made his gods look down upon the destinies of men? What was at bottom the meaning of the Trojan Wars and other such tragic terrors? There can be no doubt whatever: they were intended as *festival plays* for the gods. . . . The entire mankind of

antiquity is full of tender regard for "the spectator," as an essentially public, essentially visible world which cannot imagine happiness apart from spectacles and festivals. (*GM* II.7; *KSA* 5.305)

Nietzsche too assumes the position of an Olympian producer and spectator of such cruel scenes, as he makes his reader squirm, reminding her or him of the tortures in which the species has delighted since prehistory. Indeed, his own text mimes the trajectory of a certain Aristotelian dimension of tragedy, as it induces the movements of reversal and recognition *(anagnorisis* and *peripeteia)* in his reader or spectator. Nietzsche sprinkles his pages with a detailed catalog of cruel spectacles. Those of the ancient Germans—including tearing apart or trampling by horses, boiling in oil, flaying alive, and cutting flesh from the chest—turn out to be echoed in Foucault's ghastly account of the execution of the regicide Damiens, which opens *Discipline and Punish.* The scapegoating of Don Quixote at the court of the duchess, itself literary and imaginary, suggests that high culture, too, is full of vicarious enjoyments of this sort. But then we are brought up short by the declaration that "in the days when mankind was not ashamed of its cruelty, life on earth was more cheerful than it is now that pessimists exist" (*GM* II.7; *KSA* 5.302). We are tempted at first to regard those practices and pleasures as disgusting and reprehensible; then we are forced to admit that we too share in them more than we acknowledge, and finally we are presented with the claim that a life structured by an internal theater of cruelty is less vital, more melancholy than that of our "primitive" ancestors.

Nietzsche was responding to a nineteenth-century tendency to rewrite history, especially Christian history, in aesthetic terms. One of his bêtes noires, Ernest Renan, had produced a seven-volume *History of the Origins of Christianity* that revolved around a number of actual and imagined spectacles, including the vision of the risen Christ and the martyrdom of the Christians in the Roman gladiatorial games.[2] Renan saw Nero as the inventor of a new aesthetic, and although he explicitly regarded him with extreme abhorrence, his readers (including Nietzsche) could not help thinking that his narratives were written with a good bit of salacious interest. Consider this fragment of Renan's rather perverse account of the arena under Nero, which can be juxtaposed with those given by both Nietzsche and Foucault of the cruel spectacle:

> It was a day of note for heaven when Christian chastity, up till then carefully hidden, appeared in the full light of day, before fifty thou-

sand spectators, and posed as in a sculptor's studio in the attitude of a virgin awaiting death. Revelations of a secret unknown to antiquity, startling proclamation of the principle that modesty has a voluptuous charm and a beauty all its own! . . . In gaining the applause of a connoisseur so exquisite, of a friend of Petronius, who perhaps saluted the *moritura* with one of those quotations from the Greek poets which he loved, the timid nudity of the young martyr came to rival the self-assured nudity of a Greek Venus. When the brutal hand of that exhausted world, which sought its entertainment in the torments of a poor girl, had torn off the veils of Christian chastity, she might exclaim: "I also am beautiful." It was the principle of a new art. Blossoming forth under the eyes of a Nero, the aesthetics of the disciples of Jesus, up until then self-unconscious, owed the revelation of its magic to the crime which, tearing off its vesture, deflowered it of its virginity.[3]

Such passages render perspicuous Nietzsche's disgust with Renan, whom he was reading in the months just preceding the writing of the *Genealogy*, which is so concerned with the aesthetics of the cruel spectacle. Deleuze recalls these themes in Renan in attempting to clarify Foucault's aesthetics of existence. He also suggests that Renan can be seen as a predecessor of Heidegger, along with Nietzsche and Alfred Jarry, insofar as he conceives of the aesthetic taking priority over the cognitive and the moral.[4] Deleuze is not endorsing the tone or content of Renan's Christian aesthetic but rather pointing out that he was sensitive to the invention of new modes of subjectification. It is this similarity, presumably, that led an otherwise perceptive early reader of Nietzsche, Georg Brandes, to stress his affinities with Renan.[5] Yet it is also this common element that pushed Nietzsche to insist on their differences, as he does in remarking on the historian's voyeuristic aesthetics: "I know of nothing that excites such disgust as this kind of 'objective' arm-chair scholar, this kind of scented voluptuary of history, half parson, half satyr, perfume by Renan, who betrays immediately with the high falsetto of the applause what he lacks, *where* he lacks it, where in this case the Fates have applied their cruel shears with, alas, such surgical skill!" (*GM* III.26; *KSA* 5.406). Here, of course, Nietzsche forms part of the circuit, preferring to identify with the castrating Fates (or Nero) rather than with the new Christian aesthetic.

All these stories of the cruel spectacle have an oedipal resonance. Oedipus, the man of keen eye, begins by seeking the cause of Thebes's pollution. He discovers that he himself is to blame, and his self-punishment is to tear out his eyes, renouncing the outward-directed vision that has led him astray. Nietzsche, who boldly begins the *Genealogy* by taking on the role of the inquirer into the history of morality, a field that has hardly been surveyed, ends by discovering that we are, collectively, much more cruel to ourselves than we suspected, that we are our own worst enemies. What this realization may require is a sacrifice or at least a transformation of our own science, the very discipline that we imagined we were following when we joined Nietzsche in his inquiries into a tangled and complex history. For at the end of the *Genealogy*, he asks, "What Is the Meaning of Ascetic Ideals?": art, philosophy, the ascetic priesthood itself, science, history, and contemporary atheism are considered—in that sequence—in terms of their varying and increasing involvement with the deep motives of asceticism. We discover that the ethos of nineteenth-century science [*Wissenschaft*] is the pursuit of religious aims under another sign. The scientist mimes Christian morality by being willing to sacrifice himself for the truth. In offering up his own hypothesis to the falsification of others in the scientific community (which extends indefinitely into the future), he practices the Christian virtues of faith, hope, and charity, reserving final judgment and reward for an afterlife that has displaced heaven and installed it in a distant, shadowy, and ever-receding future. We learn that science "opposes and fights not the ascetic ideal itself, but only its exteriors, its guise and masquerade, its temporary and dogmatic hardening and stiffening" (*GM* III.25; *KSA* 5.402). Science discounts the visual, the scenic, in struggling against these surfaces. But science betrays its own quest for the invisible, or the inner law, insofar as it fails to see that its own deepest tendency as practice is indistinguishable from that of religion. The reconciliation of science and religion was a frequent theme for nineteenth-century thinkers; Nietzsche's position is formally similar to some of those who welcomed such a union (his contemporary Charles Peirce, for example) but he has transvalued the equation.[6]

We are forced to acknowledge that much deeper than the opposition between science and religion is the one between science and poetry, the one that is marked by "Plato versus Homer" (*GM* III.25; *KSA* 5.402). It was tragedy that was depicted in the *Republic* as the greatest enemy of philosophy and science, tragedy that had the most dangerous appeal to those "lovers of sights and sounds" who were so easily seduced by its spectacle and watering of the dangerous emotions. The *Genealogy* has been reviewing and analyzing forms of the cruel spectacle, beginning with two quotations from Tertullian and Thomas Aquinas, which demonstrate that Christianity does not abandon the structure of the spectacle but simply reverses the positions of spectator and victim. The lengthy passage from Tertullian is drawn from his screed against the theater, *De Spectaculis,* and indulges in imagining a series of scenes in which philosophers, actors, and statesmen become the objects of a Christian audience gleefully rejoicing in their tortures. Nietzsche, in his management of these many scenarios, orchestrates a tragic rather than a scientific text, one that proposes a self-sacrifice of the oedipal scientist. *Discipline and Punish* limits its scope to the last two hundred years but follows a strikingly similar pattern. The spectacle of Damiens's execution is played off against the new theater of the Panopticon. It is a contrast between the public display of cruelty through an assault on the body and the insidious imposition of forms of surveillance insinuating themselves into the very interior of the prisoner, indeed constituting that interior, so that he becomes at once observer and observed, an abject version of the "enslaved sovereign, observed spectator" to which *Las Meninas* had pointed.

Like Nietzsche, Foucault seems to invite us to think that the world was much more cheerful then, when executions were still festive occasions, and he notes with pleasure that one reason for the suppression of this mode was its tendency to encourage acts of resistance among the crowd. And the consequence of the contrast is a deep suspicion directed toward modern science, at least to the "human sciences," which are now seen to be part and parcel of those mechanisms for generalized surveillance of self and others. In "Nietzsche, Genealogy, History," Foucault argues that genealogy involves "the sacrifice of the subject of knowledge" (*LCMP* 162; *DE* 2.154–55); here he echoes the ironic moment of recognition prepared for the historian of morals in the *Genealogy.* We will never again be able to assume that naive attitude toward the human sciences, resembling the naïveté that Nietzsche adduces in the first words of the preface to his own *Genealogy,* when he declares that "we people of knowledge" or "we who recognize everything" *(Wir Erkennende)* fail to recognize ourselves. If we do not literally give up the sciences as the result of either genealogy, we can never view them as we once did. Perhaps, like Thomas Kuhn, we will see them as structured by periodic revolutions akin to the stylistic inventions of art. Foucault's version of this is to suggest that the human sciences form an intimate dimension of carceral society: "If after the age of 'inquisitorial' justice, we have entered the age of 'examinatory' justice, if, in an even more general way, the method of examination has been able to spread so widely throughout society, and to give rise in part to the sciences of man, one of the great instruments for this has been the multiplicity and close overlapping of the various mechanisms of incarceration" (*DP* 305; *SP* 311–12).

The scene of the execution of the regicide Damiens in 1757 occupies a position in *Discipline and Punish* that is structurally analogous to the Boschian images of *The Ship of Fools* and *The Temptation of Saint Anthony* that were summoned up at the beginning of the *Histoire de la folie* or to that of the ekphrasis of *Las Meninas* in *Les mots et les choses*. Both the first chapter of *Discipline*, "The Body of the Condemned," and "Stultiferia navis" exploit the possibility of visualizing a world that has vanished but still hovers over us as a specter or haunts our dreams. Discourses that are all too human, all too comfortable— of "humane" punishment of criminals or treatment of the mad, or a "humanism" that takes us to be the very source that renders representation possible—are called into question by images, images that vividly present other forms of life. There is a madness of excess in the evocation of Damiens's execution, as if all concerned were acting out the terrible possibilities that Bosch or Grünewald saw in a dream vision. Like Nietzsche, who quotes a text of Tertullian to evoke a scene of cruelty, Foucault quotes from a contemporary report (in the *Gazette d'Amsterdam*) in presenting us with the spectacle of punishment. *Discipline and Punish* is concerned in part with how the modalities of vision were transformed from the time of such "gloomy festivals" to the universal inspection and self-inspection of panoptical institutions. The public execution of Damiens was a sovereign display of power; monarchy insists on showing the populace what it can do and that it is the agent that orchestrates such visibilities. In this respect, executions and other public punishments are not dissimilar to royal celebrations and other festivities. The royal portrait, too, is a virtual presentation of the sovereign's power. Velazquez, let us recall, was a court painter, and his work was expected to disseminate the virtual body of the king and, if circumstances allowed, to show that the dynasty was productive of legitimate heirs. If, in *Las Meninas*, Velazquez concentrated on the Infanta (before the birth of Philip's son) and consigned the sovereign couple to a dim reflection in a mirror, he may have been testing the limit of such expectations, but he was not transgressing them. There, after all, was the possible heiress to the throne, with parents looking on. And the sovereign gaze, so closely associated with the systematic deployment of perspective in the era of absolute monarchy, is the fundamental presupposition of the painting. In the great public executions, the sovereign acts through his agents and the people look on; it is also a part of the process that the criminal is expected to *observe* the torture of his own body, so long as he is conscious. Damiens looks down on himself as his flesh is being torn away. Foucault articulates the analogy by invoking Ernst Kantorowicz's brilliant study *The King's Two Bodies*, which distinguishes the fragile and mortal body from the incorruptible one with its own iconography and system of public ritual. The condemned man, Foucault suggests, is the opposite and plays this role in his own theater: "In the darkest region of the political field the condemned man represents the symmetrical, inverted figure of the king" (*DP* 29; *SP* 37).

All of this changes in the next century. Foucault describes a series of steps leading to a radical shift in the ordering of the visible and the invisible. The result is that "punishment will tend to become the most hidden part of the penal process. . . . its effectiveness is seen as resulting from its inevitability, not its visible intensity" (*DP* 9; *SP* 16). In becoming more "humane," punishment also becomes more devious, for "justice no longer takes responsibility for the violence that is bound up with its practice." The change is described as a shift in modes of vision, a narrative technique that Foucault also employed in his account of the medical gaze: "Now the scandal and the light are to be distributed differently; it is the conviction itself that marks the offender with the unequivocally negative sign: the publicity has shifted to the trial, and to the sentence" (*DP* 9 ; *SP* 16). Before the construction of panoptical architecture, with its new distribution of the seen and the unseen, there is the introduction of the guillotine. It was an egalitarian method of execution and was novel in this respect; decapitation had been the least shaming of judicial forms of meting out death; now it was available to all, not just the nobility. At first used in public, it retains something of the spectacle: "Death was reduced to a visible, but instantaneous event" (*DP* 13; *SP* 20). Foucault is at pains to trace the gradual disappearance of such display, as the heads of the convicted were shrouded before execution and the guillotine finally hidden away within the prison, with provision made for the prosecution of unauthorized witnesses to the operation of the guillotine. In this narrative it is as if a malign force were gradually veiling all traces of the administration of capital punishment. Discourse follows suit, beginning to speak now of the soul, rather than the body, as the real object of the punitive apparatus.

Yet, despite all this talk of the soul and the proliferation of discourses and disciplines purporting to address the soul of the criminal (or the institutionalized), there is nevertheless a production of an architecture of seeing and being seen, a new distribution of the visible and the invisible. While we come to focus on seeing certain things, that is, when we direct our gaze at the prisoners in their cells, at the students in their schools, or at ourselves, suitably framed, we do not see the apparatus of sight, of our visual regime. It is this historical unconscious of the optical that Foucault's reading of Bentham and of the nineteenth century's structures of surveillance attempts to uncover.

62 Bentham and Plato as Philosopher-Architects

Martin Heidegger was also an archaeologist of visibility, although his most trenchant observations on this subject did not concern the old shoes of van Gogh or the temple at Paestum. He understood the Western philosophical project as the pursuit of presence, a pursuit that typically clothed itself in the language of vision, supposing that vision makes things present to us in a way that no other sense does. In "Plato's Doctrine of Truth," he squarely assigns the responsibility for philosophy's obsession with the visible on the thinker of the *eidos* (εἶδος: originally a visible form or shape). Plato was a geometer who had found in the visual the alternative to the fusion and immersion of the oral culture. Throughout his grand narrative of philosophy's pursuit of presence, Heidegger tells us how *eidos* is replaced by a series of fundamental concepts that appeal to sight and the eye: *evidentia* (as in *video*), the *lumen naturale*, and finally the *Augenblick* of Nietzsche.[7]

Does Foucault fail to take Bentham seriously as a philosopher? His utilitarianism is scarcely mentioned, let alone thematized and criticized. We can guess what Foucault thought about utilitarianism most directly through his apparent acceptance of Nietzsche's judgments on it, most notably in his reading of the *Genealogy* (*LCMP* 139; *DE* 136).[8] Or does Foucault take Bentham to be a philosopher in a very serious way, when he sees his project as emblematic of a new architecture of power and a new regime of the eye? Perhaps Bentham is one of those Nietzschean (or Platonic) philosopher-legislators, "master builders" who seem to build for the ages (*GS* 356; *KSA* 3.595). In any case, Foucault's studied indifference to the career of the author here is consistent with his archaeological approach; he engages in a similar avoidance of the careers of Velazquez and Magritte and refuses to attempt to reconstruct their intentions. For Foucault the *Panopticon* is a text that offers a diagram for a social arrangement; its place within Bentham's oeuvre is at most a secondary consideration.[9] If the carceral society has faded into the shadows much faster than the Rome whose builders were so admired by Nietzsche (and by some of his most perverse disciples), it may have less to do with the comparative "vision" of its philosopher-architects than with the rapidly accelerating rate of technological change; Nietzsche, no less than his contemporaries, but also certainly no more, failed to see what lay ahead in the transformation of space.

Next to Bentham's *Panopticon* we should read Plato's myth of the cave. Both figure a relation of truth and vision. Plato's tale is a myth or a story; it is a narrative that explains the way in which vision, although subject to constraints and illusions, can realize its potential to see the very source of light and so of its own activity. The gradual liberation of the cave's prisoners marks the stages in a ladder of vision that moves from the flimsiest of simulacra to human artifacts, to natural things, and to the sun itself. It is also a story of how embodied human beings assume power over themselves, learning to move at will, to direct the eyes, and to develop a coordination of eye, hand, and limb. It is, then, above all a story of education, of being led out of a certain darkness into the light.[10] Teachers are a necessary part of education, and in Plato's story the educators are known to those whom they liberate from their bonds. In Foucault's reconstruction of Bentham, there is no narrative, no myth, because the emphasis is on a given structure, a structure that is simply taken for granted in the carceral world. It is a structure that renders sight possible, and so it is unlikely to be seen for itself unless we engage in archaeological and genealogical researches predicated on the suspicion that things could be otherwise.

63 Panopticon

Martin Jay claims that for Foucault the Panopticon is the emblem not only of the carceral society but also of the malignity of vision (sec. 2). He sums up the position that he takes Foucault to be articulating, with reference especially to *Discipline and Punish* and its account of Bentham's architecture of surveillance: "Vision was still the privileged sense, but what that privilege produced in the modern world was damned as almost entirely pernicious."[11] I have argued that this is a misunderstanding of Foucault, who has no arguments that vision is generally dangerous; he is an archaeologist of the visual, alert to the differential character of various visual regimes. And within the space of a certain epoch or culture, he is alert to disparate and possibly conflicting visual practices.

This said, Foucault's reading of Bentham's apparatus is indeed the analysis of an "evil eye," transformed into architecture. As he says in an interview, "the perfected form of surveillance consists in a summation of *malveillance*" (PK 158; DE 3.201). Foucault prepares the way for this reading by reviewing the procedures of individualization, surveillance, and normalization that were employed with regard to lepers and the plague. The core of these procedures consists in segmenting and individualizing the population to be observed and controlled, on the one hand, and, on the other, in rigidly applying a binary system of classification: "mad/sane; dangerous/harmless; normal abnormal" (*DP* 199; *SP* 232). What Bentham did was to combine in one efficient figure and structure what had required a number of dispersed efforts in a situation like the policing of a plague-ridden town. The prison is like Plato's cave, a total, closed optical system completely sequestered from the outside world; the cave is a prison, because its residents are confined by force. In the *Republic* Socrates asks his interlocutors to imagine a place where men have been shackled since birth, their eyes directed unavoidably to a screen of images, a series of shadows projected from behind the cave dwellers. He explains the apparatus for the production of images and the restraint of prisoners in some detail. Foucault indicates that the Panopticon ranks with this greatest set scene in philosophy when he says that "the tendency of Bentham's thought is archaic in the importance it gives to the gaze; but it is very modern in the general importance it assigns to techniques of power" (*PK* 160; *DE* 3.202). Bentham indeed is quite explicit in his ocularcentrism: "Preach to the eye, if you would preach with efficacy. By that organ, through the medium of the imagination, the judgment of the bulk of mankind may be led and moulded almost at pleasure. As puppets in the hands of the showman, so would men be in the hands of the legislator, who, to the science proper to his function, should add a well-informed attention to stage-effect."[12] This was the man who refused to take a final bow from the world's stage, ensuring that his body would be permanently on view at University College London. As Jacques-Alain Miller comments, "every utilitarian system is of necessity theatrical—in that not only does everything in it serve some end, but that everything in it has meaning."[13]

Foucault follows the Platonic pattern. After describing the architecture of the place—a ringed structure with a center tower, segmented cells with two windows allowing for inspection—he populates the Panopticon, although now he is describing a site that is not simply of the imagination, but a type that flourished for a century (figs. 13, 14):

> All that is needed, then, is to place a supervisor [*surveillant*] in a
> central tower and to shut up in each cell a madman, a patient, a condemned man, a worker or a schoolboy. By the effect of backlighting,
> one can observe from the tower, standing out precisely against the
> light, the small captive shadows [*silhouettes*] in the cells of the pe-

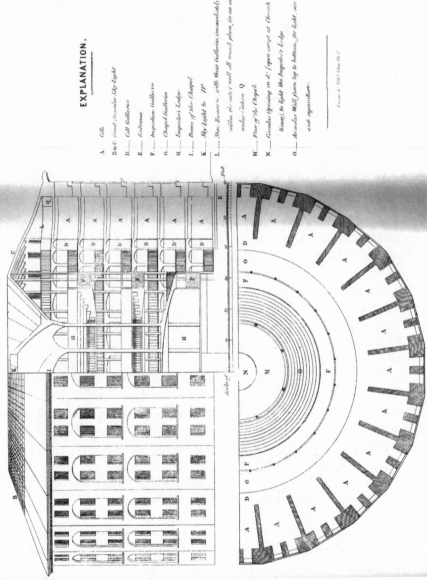

A General Idea of a PENTENTIARY PANOPTICON in an Improved, but as yet (Jan.y 23.d 1791). Unfinished State.

See Postscript References to Plan, Elevation, & Section (being Plate referred to as N.º 3).

EXPLANATION.

A. _____ Cells.

B & C. Great circular Sky-Light.

D. _____ Cell Galleries.

E. _____ Entrances.

F. _____ Inspection Galleries.

G. _____ Chapel Galleries.

H. _____ Inspector's Lodge.

I. _____ Dome of the Chapel.

K. _____ Sky-Light to D.º

L. _____ Store Rooms &c. with their Galleries; immediately within the outer wall all round, place for an annular Cistern Q.

M. _____ Floor of the Chapel.

N. _____ Circular Opening in d.º (open except at Church times), to light the Inspector's Lodge.

O. _____ Annular Well, from top to bottom, for light, air, and separation.

Figure 14. Stateville Prison, nineteenth century

riphery. They are like so many cages, so many small theatres, in which each actor is alone, perfectly individualized and constantly visible. The Panoptic mechanism [*dispositif*] arranges spatial unities that make it possible to see constantly and to recognize immediately. (*DP* 200; *SP* 233)

While Plato's prisoners took shadows for reality, Bentham's are themselves transformed into silhouettes, objects of observation. Those trapped in the cave are part of an audience; the inhabitants of the Panopticon are, each one of them, the solitary actors of their own theaters. The *dispositif* of the structure is in many ways the inverse of Nietzsche's conception of the Greek theater. There the audience is aware of itself as a collective; it focuses on the action that occurs in the center, where actors ritually make themselves into objects of display; and the audience has a double perspective, looking down on the actors on the *skene* while looking up at them as they identify with the chorus

Figure 13. Jeremy Bentham, *Plan of the Panopticon. The Works of Jeremy Bentham*, ed. John Bowring (New York: Russell and Russell, 1962), 4:172–73.

in the *orchestra*. This last feature involves the tragic perspectivism that Nietzsche saw as having been overwhelmed by the "one great Cyclops eye" of Socrates. As the organizers of the shadow plays in Plato's cave were invisible to the spectators, the overseers in the Panopticon are hidden from the inmates. While the naive cave prisoners never suspected the presence of these puppet masters, it is essential to the Panopticon that those confined there understand that they may be under surveillance at any time. The consequence of deviance is punishment, so these subjects of the institution must assume that they are actually under constant surveillance, since the latter is always possible. The effect, then, is to depersonalize the surveillance function and to generalize it so far that the inmates necessarily become observers of themselves. All of this is tied up with the arrangement of visibility:

> Hence the major effect of the Panopticon: to induce in the inmate a state of conscious and permanent visibility that assures the automatic functioning of power. So to arrange things that the surveillance is permanent in its effects, even if it is discontinuous in its action; that the perfection of power should tend to render its actual exercise unnecessary; that this architectural apparatus should be a machine for creating and sustaining a power relation independent of the person who exercises it; in short, that the inmates should be caught up in a power situation of which they are themselves the bearers. (*DP* 201; *SP* 234)

As with the construction of Plato's cave, the result is a system that comes to seem natural and inevitable. The genius of Bentham's design, of his "simple idea in architecture," is that it transforms the inmates from passive subjects to active workers at their own surveillance and normalization.[14] The "simple idea" involves constructing the entire system around a fiction, using the "utterly dark spot" of the central observation tower to promote the idea that surveillance is total and unremitting. As Miran Božovič points out, Bentham was also a theorist of fictions; the idea of the Panopticon hinges upon a fictional gaze, a simple architectural equivalent of the traditional eye of God (like conscience, whose construction is traced by Nietzsche). Like God, the inspector cannot actually appear to the eyes of the inmates, for then he will be seen as limited in vision, perspective, and location; rather, in Božovič's formulation, "the inspector is *apparently omnipresent precisely insofar as he is not really present.*"[15] However frightening and ghoulish the regentesses that Hals had depicted might be, as well as all those guards and officials that they represent, they were still visible to the inhabitants of the institution. Terror is increased exponentially with Bentham's invention of a depersonalized gaze.

What Nietzsche did not seem to suspect, or at least what he did not speak of, was that the internal theater of conscience could be given an architectural foundation in the organization of space and visibility. Foucault has produced a demonstration of the *dispositif* that enables what Nietzsche called the ascetic ideal, that ideal that is able "to *exploit* the bad instincts of all sufferers for the purpose of self-discipline, self-surveillance [*Selbstüberwachung*], and self-overcoming" (GM III.16; KSA 5.375). If Nietzsche thought that such practices and attitudes required a religious or ideological source of support, Bentham and Foucault know that there is a simpler route to self-surveillance. Nietzsche calls on us to have "fresh air! and keep clear of the madhouses and hospitals of culture!" (GM III.14; KSA 5.371). Part of what these institutional and hypertrophied versions of Socratic Cyclopism lack is multiplicity of perspective. If Nietzsche speaks of madhouses and hospitals somewhat metaphorically, Foucault fills out these suggestions with an analysis of Bentham's plans as realized in iron and stone, plans that lead to a machine of visibility that functions almost automatically:

> The Panopticon is a machine for dissociating the see/being seen dyad: in the peripheric ring, one is totally seen, without ever seeing; in the central tower, one sees everything without being seen.
>
> It is an important mechanism, for it automatizes and disindividualizes power. Power has its principle not so much in a person as in a certain concerted distribution of bodies, surfaces, lights, gazes; in an arrangement whose internal mechanisms produce the relation in which individuals are caught up. (DP 201–2; SP 235)

Bentham imagined devices for going very far in the dissociation of the "see/being seen" dyad. Realizing that prisoners must be brought together for religious services, he needs to minimize their ability to look at one another and to exchange looks with any inspectors or visitors at the services. So the technician of vision hit upon the expedient of masking the prisoners, with masks corresponding to their offenses. In this inversion of the Greek theater, the congregation is masked rather than the actors. Bentham himself notes that in designing a "masquerade," he is moving into the space of theater, and he acknowledges that the Starchamber and the Inquisition, whatever their evils, "must at least be allowed to have had some knowledge of *stage effect.* Unjust as was their penal system in its application, and barbarous in its degree, the skill they displayed in making the most of it in point of impression, their solemn processions, their emblematic dresses, their terrific scenery, deserve rather to be admired and imitated than condemned."[16] In *Zarathustra* Nietzsche tells a story that relies on the reciprocity of the relation of seeing and being seen; individuals look into each other's eyes and faces, reading meaning and response. Merleau-Ponty makes the relation ontological; for him it is a defining property of being human that the one who sees can also be seen. Bentham shows that such reciprocity is not inevitable. Whether it obtains or not will be a function of the frame of viewing, of the distribution of visibility and its activities.

Foucault reinforces his treatment of the Panopticon as a work of visual art (as well as a mechanism) by contrasting Bentham's creation with pictorial representations and fantasies of its predecessor institutions. So in commenting on the principle of the building that "visibility is a trap," he explains the distinction between such a structure and the more overtly frightening visions of Goya: "[T]his made it possible—as a negative effect—to avoid those compact, swarming, howling masses that were to be found in places of confinement, those painted by Goya or described by Howard" (*DP* 200; *SP* 234). And a few pages later: "As opposed to the ruined prisons, littered with mechanisms of torture, to be seen in Piranesi's engravings, the Panopticon presents a cruel, ingenious cage" (*DP* 205; *SP* 239). The visions of Goya and Piranesi are dominated by death, secrecy, madness, and the labyrinth. As nightmares of confinement, they are alive with something of the force of the madness in the revelatory paintings of Bosch and his contemporaries. Yet the Panopticon has the banality and the power of the actual: "But the Panopticon must not be understood as a dream building: it is the diagram of a mechanism of power reduced to its ideal form; its functioning, abstracted from any obstacle, resistance or friction, must be represented as a pure architectural and optical system: it is in fact a figure of political technology that may and must be detached from any specific use" (*DP* 205; *SP* 239).

Gilles Deleuze makes much of Foucault's idea of the diagram, a term that in fact appears fairly rarely in his writing.[17] He understands the diagram as "a map, a cartography that is coextensive with the whole social field," and sees it as historical and changeable, making history "by unmaking preceding realities and significations, constituting hundreds of points of emergence or creativity."[18] Deleuze is one of the few commentators on Foucault to have focused on his concerns with the visual; he argues that the visible and the articulable form a duality in Foucault comparable to Kant's binary of a passive sensibility and a spontaneous conceptuality, allowing for the fact that Foucault's categories, unlike Kant's, are radically historical. But, contra Deleuze, Foucauldian visibility ought not to be considered a passivity. The most coherent view of the matter, I propose, is that the boundary between the two, as well as the particular form that each one takes, is historically or archaeologically variable; the point is made fairly clearly, in a context specific to painting, in *This Is Not a Pipe* (*TNP* 32–35; *CP* 39–45). In any case, Deleuze sees the diagram, as understood in *Discipline and Punish*, as the one place in which Foucault "expressly overcomes the dualism of his earlier books," for he now understands the diagram and the mechanism as "a mushy mixture of the visible and the articulable."[19] The elucidation highlights Foucault's conception of visibility as historical spatiality and distinguishes the mobile, flexible aspect of the diagram from the very specific forms it receives in Bentham's blueprints (his diagrams in a narrow sense) or in specific realizations of panoptic architecture.

64 The Visual State

Nietzsche, writing in the later nineteenth century, as the state was consolidating itself and casting off its older associations with the person of the sovereign, has Zarathustra denounce the state as "the new idol" (in a chapter by that name). While we may have some misgivings about the contrast that he draws between the *Volk* and the *Staat*, we can hear an anticipation of Foucault in Zarathustra's jeremiad: "Where there is still a people, it does not understand the state and hates it as the evil eye and the sin against custom and rights" (Z I.11; *KSA* 4.61). For Foucault the Panopticon is the diagram of a truly impersonal evil eye, giving an oddly literal turn to Nietzsche's figure. He offers an archaeological account of social forms of visibility that, like Nietzsche's histories, contrasts the ancient form of the theater with recent techniques of observation and with the emergence of the modern state. Foucault does not cite Nietzsche here but (in one of his excursions of esoteric erudition) paraphrases the historian N. H. Julius, who "gave this society its birth certificate" just a few years after Bentham published his proposals. Julius developed a contrast between ancient and modern regimes of visibility. The principle of the *polis*, he suggested, was the spectacle: "'To render accessible to a multitude of men a small number of objects': this was the problem to which the architecture of temples, theaters and circuses responded." In these spectacles blood flowed, so that society was reinvigorated with a sense of collective strength. This is the diagram of ancient philosophy as well as of the theater in the narrow sense. The captives of the *Republic* are liberated from a theater of error in order to participate in a theater of truth. Bound in their seats at first, they are analogous to the citizens who are in thrall to the spectacles and teachings of the poets. The process of *paideia* leads them out of the cave to a new collective experience of the truth. Socrates' critique of tragedy is in fact an *agon* in which dialectics takes the place of drama. Modernity poses itself a different problem, again quoting Julius: "To procure for a small number, or even for a single individual, the instantaneous view of a great multitude . . . by using and directing towards that great aim the building and distribution of buildings intended to observe a great multitude of men at the same time" (*DP* 216–17; *SP* 252). Julius was able to see the conditions of our seeing: he saw that we are a society of surveillance, not of the spectacle. The state assumes the form of a giant unblinking eye, a realization Foucault finds acknowledged in the transitional figure of Napoleon, who marks the threshold between ritual sovereignty and modern surveillance. His comment on this "individual who looms over everything with a single gaze, which no detail, however minute, can escape" recalls the grandiose portraits of the Emperor by David and Ingres: "As a monarch who is at one and the same time a usurper of the ancient throne and the organizer of the new state, he combined into a single symbolic, ultimate figure the whole of the long process by which the pomp of sovereignty, the necessarily spectacular manifestations of power, were extinguished one by one in the daily exercise of surveillance, in a panopticism in which the vigilance of intersecting gazes was soon to render useless both the eagle and the sun" (*DP* 217; *SP* 253). This helps to explain how Hölderlin (in *Friedensfeier*) managed to fuse Napoleon with Christ, how Hegel reported seeing him ride through the streets of Jena as "the world-spirit on horseback," and how Nietzsche idealized him as the last great man of Europe. It may also have some bearing on Nietzsche's own poetics of eagle and sun, in *Zarathustra*, as the nostalgia for a more personal eye preceding the evil eye of the modern state.

65 Shutters and Mirrors: Manet Closes the Panopticon Window

Foucault lectured on Manet when he taught in Tunisia in 1968. He planned a book on the artist and signed a contract to write and publish it with the provisional title *Le noir et la surface*.[20] Foucault abandoned the idea, although there are student notes of his lectures; while we might speculate that this had something to do with the political upheaval of that year and the turn that his thought took with *Discipline and Punish*, we note that he continued to write on painting and the visual arts, publishing the much expanded version of the essay on Magritte in 1973 and an essay on the artist Fromanger in 1975, as well as other short pieces on artists such as Paul Rebeyrolle. Foucault's concern with the visual did not come to an end. It has been suggested that some of Foucault's apparently rather diverse books can be read as complementary pairs, for example the study of Roussel and *The Birth of the Clinic*, both of which deal with variations on the relationship between seeing and saying; one concentrating on the way in which the relation is articulated in a public, institutional, and disciplinary space, and the other examining an artist's exploration of some rather esoteric alternatives to prevailing discursive regimes. Similarly, I propose that the aborted work on Manet could form a pair with *Discipline and Punish*.[21] The project apparently survives only in traces, through the unauthorized student transcription of some of the lectures.[22] These traces can be supplemented by the discussion of Manet in "Fantasia of the Library," where he appears as the painter of the museum era, in parallel with Flaubert as the writer of the age of the library. Since the Manet project was not realized, this pairing is my own reconstruction. Both the book and the lectures treat highly powerful and influential diagrams of the visible, one directed at positioning individuals as objects of surveillance and self-surveillance, the other at transforming painting from an art of the illusory viewing of an imaginative space into an organon for the contemplation of surfaces without depth, opening onto nothing but themselves. In this respect the art that follows Manet's innovations can be construed as a form of resistance to the society of surveillance. This would help to confirm and explain the general conviction that the avant-garde had tendencies toward social deviation and rebellion that were not reducible to the obvious political commitments or bohemian life styles of its members.[23]

Foucault might argue that within the realm of visibility that emerged in nineteenth-century Europe, there are both regimes of surveillance and forms of resistance. Some of these forms of resistance inhabit the panoptical institutions themselves, such as the individual or collective strategies and tactics by which prisoners sought to escape or at least hide from the watchful eyes of their jailers. Foucault himself was quite seriously involved with groups working for prisoners' rights and prison reform, and he argued that forms of power are necessarily intertwined with forms of resistance. In his essay "Lives of Infamous Men," he traces the paradoxical route by which the monarchy and police machinery of a century or two earlier helped to generate unanticipated forms of action and expression among the very people it was intended to control. As police power expanded, there was a rationalization of administration through the keeping of detailed and individualized records of offenders and deviants, from accusation to incarceration. An entire apparatus of *lettres de cachet* or king's orders, along with police reports, came into being. As Foucault notes, these practices "usually evoke only the despotism of an absolute monarchy." Yet typically the *lettre de cachet* was requested by a family member or a neighbor. Punishment or internment would then become a matter for the authorities charged with investigating and verifying accusations. This practice empowered the accusers, people who would otherwise have had little influence with regard to such matters: "[P]olitical sovereignty penetrated into the most elementary dimension of the social body. . . . providing one knew how to play the game, every individual could become for the other a terrible and lawless monarch" (F 3.167–68; DE 3.247). This pattern is meant to suggest that the exercise of power always involves unintended consequences and invites strategic responses by those who are its objects. So far the discussion of the reciprocal involvement of regime and resistance has been confined within certain institutions, such as the prison and the policing of accusations. Could a form of power holding sway within a certain institution or sector of society be answered by a movement of resistance in another? Could the museum or the salon foster alternatives to a society of surveillance? Foucault seems to suggest something of this sort, and with reference to the visual, in *The Birth of the Clinic*. There the anatomical gaze, which objectifies the human being through the virtual reduction of living to dead bodies is paralleled by a new sensibility with respect to death in nineteenth-century painting. In clinical medicine, "death brings to truth the luminous presence of the visible" (BC 165; NC 169). Yet contemporary art also becomes concerned with death in "the savage, castrated death of Goya, the visible, muscular, sculptural death offered by Géricault, the voluptuous death by fire in Delacroix." It is as if painting were responding to the protopositivism of medicine by insisting on the utter individuality of death, which has now "left its old tragic heaven and become the lyrical core of man: his invisible truth, his visible secret" (BC 171–72; NC 175–76). Analogously, I suggest, we can think of the art of modernity as a response to the society of surveillance; this response does not consist so much in altering the character of the object seen as in reconfiguring the entire dynamics and the diagram of vision and its objects. What might appear to be a move in the direction of formalism within the practices of art can suggest a way of seeing that offers an alternative to panoptical inspection.

What remains of Foucault's lectures on Manet does not, at first, seem very novel to art-historical ears. He begins by stressing the remarkable reversal that the painter effected in the way that painting presents itself to its audience. At least since the quattrocento, Foucault tells us, painting attempted to obscure and veil everything connected with the materiality of its medium. The spectator was invited to see a rectangular, two-dimensional canvas (or some analogous flat surface) as a window on the world. Painters strove to intensify this effect by employing perspective, emphasizing oblique or spiral lines that distracted one from the rectilinear frame of the canvas, deploying a finely modulated palette of colors, suggesting sources of illumination internal to the "world" of the painting, and, in general, doing everything possible to make the canvas function as an illusionistic or theatrical space. Manet's disruption of this tradition consisted in such gestures as allowing the flat, rectilinear surface of the painting to become an ineluctable dimension of its presence, eliminating the appearance of internal illumination, and making use of forceful colors, including black, in a nonillusionistic manner.

So far Foucault's understanding of Manet seems to dovetail with that of critics like Clement Greenberg. Greenberg saw Manet's work as a decisive step in the development of modernism, and he understood modernism as that reflective movement in which a discipline or practice explicitly reflects upon its own conditions of possibility. If this has a Kantian ring, it is because Greenberg does take Kant's critical turn to be an exemplary modernist moment that has been followed by parallel developments in the arts (sec. 15). On this understanding, classical metaphysics (as in Descartes, Spinoza, and Leibniz) assumed that it was possible to describe the structure of the world by the use of reason and that the purified grammar and syntax of human language were adequate to the task. They were like painters who thought that the tools of their art were sufficient for creating windows on the world. Kant asked about the status of such assumptions, pointing to the fact that we always bring with us the forms of intuition (space and time) and the categories (such as causality) that allow us to construct a coherent world of experience. He wanted to direct attention to these as conditions or limits of our knowledge; in realizing these limits, we would lose our naive confidence that we had access to things in themselves, but we would gain the assurance that in analyzing such conditions, we were on much firmer ground, a ground that could in fact be mapped prior to any specific experience. Painting would make an analogous transcendental movement in exchanging a model of universal representation or picturing for one in which it acknowledged its own dependence on conventions of flatness, rectilinearity, and the like. Michael Fried has claimed that Manet is the "first post-Kantian painter" who made self-consciousness into "the great subject of his art."[24] It is this kind of reflective step that Foucault understands as essential to the construction of the figure of man, conceived as the "enslaved sovereign, observed spectator" who finds resources in his own limitations. However, Foucault differs with Greenberg on a crucial point. For Greenberg, as for Kant, the transcendental movement described, whether for knowledge or for painting, is one in which the discipline discovers its own intrinsic nature: on this view knowledge simply is, always was, and always will be the application of the forms of intuition and the categories to the raw material of experience, and painting is similarly just the application of paint to a two-dimensional material surface. Foucault makes no such claims, and it is part of his archaeological project to suggest that the Kantian project and all of its relatives that circle around the figure of man are forms of thought with a sway that is limited to a specific epoch. These variations on the analytic of finitude fail to discern their own archaeological limitations. We can recognize the fecundity of Kant's or Manet's work without assuming that they have once and for all set philosophy on the sure (and only) path of a science or given to painting the universal principle that it must follow henceforth.

Foucault organizes his discussion of Manet's style around three topics: the painter's articulation of space and the flatness of the image; the treatment of lighting, involving the elimination of any represented illumination in the painting; and the positioning of the viewer, a theme whose importance he also stressed in his reading of *Las Meninas*. While these are relatively standard art-historical themes, and the scholarly Foucault could be assumed to have been reading widely and promiscuously as usual in preparing his lectures, a few points stand out, even in this pedagogical context, that resonate in intriguing ways with some of his other concerns. Like a number of other critics, he observes that Manet frequently structures his paintings, such as *Music in the Tuileries* or *Masked Ball at the Opera* (fig. 15), in terms of rather strongly defined vertical and horizontal axes that emphasize the flat and rectilinear canvas by creating only a very shallow space with constant reminders of the structure of the medium. His comments on the *Masked Ball* emphasize a further aspect of the painting that this shallow space renders possible. Above the men and women depicted at ground level, we see the lower edge of a balcony, which offers a rather truncated view of more figures: "Here the opening ironically displays only feet, stockings, and so on, so everything begins anew, as if it were the same scene in infinite repetition: it works like a carpet, a wall or a

tapestry, with the ironic addition of two little feet that indicate the phantasmatic character of this space, which is not the real space of perception but one that gives once more the mutual play of the surface and the colors that are distributed from top to bottom of the painting and are infinitely repeated."[25] It is not only that Manet leaves us in no doubt about the flatness of his surfaces; he makes these surfaces a field for an endless repetition of colors and forms. This is a theme that Foucault also develops in his essay on Magritte (sec. 72). He elaborates it further in his analysis of Manet, for example in his description of the wall in *The Execution of the Emperor Maximilian* as a redoubling of the canvas itself in its flat featurelessness, recalling the blank support that we know to be the ground of the painting. It brings to mind his concern with Nietzsche's thought of eternal recurrence, a concern that also surfaces in "Fantasia of the Library," where Flaubert is said to launch a literary development that helps to prepare the way for "the vision of Engadine." Once again the absence of depth is associated with the recurrence of the phantasm. Figures are not individualized in depth, as they are in the Panopticon, but become subjects for repetition.

In the diagram that runs through the painting of Manet, Foucault finds a renunciation of the traditional means of illumination and the conventions of making people and things visible. *The Fifer* was ridiculed by the critics at first for its flatness. Foucault explains this effect in terms of the artist's use of light. The boy stands on no discernible surface other than the small shadows cast by his feet, shadows that suggest the figure is illuminated simply by the same light in the actual space of display that makes visible the painting itself. Standing in no real space, the boy hangs "in the void," Foucault says, or as Nietzsche might put it, "in the abyss."[26] If painting no longer evokes a theater of light, neither does it reveal a coherent relation between the looks that are internal to it and their objects. Persons in Manet's works look out beyond the canvas, or to the side, but in any case we typically know nothing about the target of their gaze. *Gare St.-Lazare* (fig. 16) achieves its flatness with a network of horizontal and vertical lines. The two figures face in opposite directions, and we see nothing of what they are looking at. The woman looks attentively forward, apparently having raised her head from her book; the young girl looks back toward the railway yard, but the steam from a passing train has thrown up a cloud obscuring whatever she might be observing. Foucault suggests that Manet tempts us to go around the canvas, to change our position, in order to see what the observer in the painting sees. The work forces a sense of invisibility upon us: "It is this play with invisibility, enabled by the

flatness of the canvas, that Manet carries out within the painting itself. It is the first time that painting gives us something that shows us an invisible: the looks are there in order to indicate to us that there is something to see, something that on account of the nature of the canvas itself is necessarily invisible."[27] In writing of *Las Meninas*, Foucault spoke of the position in front of the canvas that was successively occupied by observer, artist, and model. If there was an undecidability in the oscillation among the three kinds of occupants of that place, we still knew something about what, outside the painting, was attracting the attention of the figures within the depicted scene. We understood that what had been captured was a passing moment, an almost instantaneous glance of the eye, in which the painter, the Infanta, and the courtiers suddenly found their attention drawn by one or more people arriving in a space directly in front of them. In the Panopticon the gaze is mobilized and fixed on each individual; it is a floating or functional gaze that need not appear as the look of anyone in particular. In Manet looks meet no object, no person, even though we see their source. What we see, then, is an eye disconnected from a content of vision.

A similar effect is achieved in paintings that show figures who are looking with some degree of concentration but in different directions; the object of their vision is unknown, and they share no glances among themselves. *The Balcony* is such a painting, one that combines Manet's characteristic modes of constituting space and light (fig. 17). The painting is rigorously framed by green shutters and railing. Whereas the conventional painting before Manet might pose as a window looking out on the world, or represent a window as the source of illumination, in *The Balcony* we look into a window that repeats the shape of the canvas. Or, rather, we are invited to look into it, but in fact we cannot make out very much: the dim figure of a young man, some very obscure pictures on a wall.[28] The window is an obstacle to sight rather than its enabler. It becomes a flat surface like the canvas. Three figures stand on the balcony, in front of the window that does nothing to make them visible. They look out in three different directions, none of them looking at either of the others. Foucault reads these figures as occupying a strangely liminal space:

> On the border of light and shadow there are three figures who hover in the air in a certain way and have almost no surface on which to stand, so that the little foot of Berthe Morisot's sister [the young woman on our right] hangs down, as if there were nothing there on which she could place it (as in Giotto's *Il dono del mantello*). The figures are suspended between darkness and light, be-

Figure 17. Édouard Manet, *The Balcony*, 1868–69. Musée d'Orsay, Paris. Réunion des Musées Nationaux/Art Resource, New York

tween the inside and the outside, between the room and the open space. They are simply there: two white ones, one dark, like three musical notes; they leave the shadows in order to reach the light; the whole has something of the raising of Lazarus about it, on the border of life and death. Magritte, the surrealist, has painted a variation on this picture in which he has presented the same elements, but has replaced the three figures with three coffins. It is precisely this border of life and death which becomes manifest through the three figures. All of them look attentively at something that we do not see.[29]

Manet, then, has brought the frame into the work; the *parergon* has become the *ergon*. And the frame's function is not to make an interior visible, as in the Panopticon, but to produce an uncanny space in which figures hover between life and death. It is as if we were being told: "Do not imagine that you can look into the interior; all that you will be able to see is the surface and the phantasmatic figures who appear there." The proper place for viewing such a picture is the museum, where we can understand it as a commentary on other strategies of viewing. The museum as transformed by Manet's paintings becomes a space for seeing flat images; the images no longer function as virtual windows on the world. In a society that has instituted so many windows and guard towers of surveillance, the closed structure of the museum turns our eyes toward another kind of activity.

According to the transcripts, Foucault's lectures end with a consideration of *A Bar at the Folies-Bergère* (fig. 18); this is appropriate, for it is probably Manet's most challenging painting and has been the subject of many interpretations since the essays of T. J. Clark from the 1970s. It serves Foucault as a site for examining the role of the viewer in Manet's work. As he notes at the beginning, since almost all of the picture is occupied by the large mirror behind the bar, the painting constitutes a "double negation of depth," both because it is a painting and because its representation is almost entirely devoted to the mirror, itself a flattening out of the scene it reflects. His analysis proceeds by demonstrating a number of ways in which the *Bar* must appear incoherent from the standpoint of traditional conceptions of perspective. These constitute what Foucault calls "three systems of disunity," as exemplified by the following incoherences: the painter must be assumed both to be directly in front of the woman at the bar and also to our left, in order to both see her frontally and see her reflection; the man who appears speaking to the barmaid in the mirror ought also to be visible in front of the bar, but he is absent; the barmaid is looking

Figure 18. Édouard Manet, *A Bar at the Folies-Bergère*, 1882. Courtauld Institute Galleries, London. Foto Marburg/Art Resource, New York

outward and slightly upward in the frontal image but looks somewhat downward in the mirror.[30] These discrepancies are well known; others noted by critics include such inconsistencies as the position of the mirrored bottles on our left, which are at the rear of the bar but reflected as if they were at its front, the incongruous location of the label in the reflection of the leftmost bottle, and the situation of the reflected bar, appearing to float without support, suggesting that the bar that it mirrors may also be a floating phantasm. The inventory of these asymmetries could be expanded, but enough has been said to see how Foucault arrives at the conclusion that it is impossible to know where we should be positioned to see what we see and that Manet has broken with "the entire tradition of classical painting" in not determining, by means of perspective, where the painter must be located in order to paint the picture as he does. "Classical painting," it seems, is the painting especially of the "classical age," which offers a systematic apparatus of "lines and perspectives" to establish the painter's ideal location, as Foucault described it in the case of *Las Meninas*. The lecture breaks off with the following observation, worth quoting at length because the text is not easily accessible:

> With this technique Manet has deployed the property of painting
> according to which it is not a normative space whose presentation
> fixes the viewer at a single point, but is, rather, a space in relation
> to which one can assume varied positions: the viewer moves in
> front of the painting which the light hits directly from the front.
> The verticals and horizontals are constantly doubled, and the dimen-
> sion of depth is excluded; in this way the canvas begins to come into
> view in its *physis* and to incorporate all its properties in one mode
> of presentation. Manet did not discover non-representational paint-
> ing, since everything with him is representational. But he incorpo-
> rated the basic material elements of the canvas in the presentation.
> He was on the verge of discovering the image as object and the
> painting as object. That was the fundamental condition required to
> free them from representation altogether one day and to deploy the
> surfaces solely in terms of their own properties, their material prop-
> erties.[31]

Foucault's last comments characterize Manet in a way that parallels his account of Marx, Nietzsche, and Freud as founders of certain forms of discourse (*DE* 2.564–79). These three initiate modes of discourse that require a continuous and open-ended body of commentary, criticism, and elaboration of their texts and theories; they open up discursive worlds in which, for example, Freudian categories are invoked in order to criticize some of Freud's own claims, as in many discussions of the feminine. Similarly, Manet makes possible a variety of styles of painting, including all the forms of nonrepresentational painting, that flourished in the twentieth century. If Marx, Nietzsche, and Freud are founders of discursivities, Manet is the founder of a mode of visibility; in that mode artists like Kandinsky, Klee, Pollock, and Rothko play roles analogous to those that Rank, Jung, Lacan, and Laplanche play in exfoliating, reinterpreting, and deforming the work of Freud. Moreover, although Foucault does not say this, the effects of the many forms of visibility that can trace their genealogy to Manet are arguably more pervasive in everyday life than the discursivities associated with Marx, Nietzsche, and Freud, having insinuated themselves into the practices of art, advertising, architecture, and all the visual media. In this respect "Manet" stands for the transformation, deployment, and development of a form of visibility that can be compared with the discipline and surveillance whose names are "Bentham" and "Panopticon."

The painting, then, is no longer a window through which we look from a given position. The illusion is peeled away, revealing a flat canvas, structured by lines that parallel its edges and encrusted with paint. Or if we want to call the painting a window, it is a closed one; we end up looking at the surface of the window itself, rather than through it. Merleau-Ponty was fascinated by the dimension of depth and attempted to explain painting's mysterious ability to evoke it; this picture refuses that dimension. Nor is the painting a mirror. Plato long ago suggested an analogy between visual art and the mirror; he has Socrates say that the painter is like an artist or craftsman *(technites)* who "takes a mirror and carries it about everywhere," producing the appearance of all things in heaven and earth.[32] If the mirror in the painting is a stand-in for the canvas, then the breakdown of the mirroring relation leads to the discovery that the painting does not reflect the world. In *Las Meninas* the mirror was the device by means of which the positions of painter, spectator, and model were established, even if their identities oscillated through their assignment to a common location.

Now the painting becomes the inverse of the Panopticon. The "central lodge" of the latter is the undisputed point of view for the inspector, a position from which every prisoner appears in the window of his or her cell. Bentham tells us that the activity of the inspectors is like the common occupation of looking out the window; for the inspectors "[i]t will supply in their instance the place of that great and constant fund of entertainment to the sedentary and vacant in towns— the looking out of the window. The scene, though confined, would be a very various, and therefore, perhaps, not altogether an unamusing one."[33] The entire *dispositif* is based on the fiction that each window is constantly under observation. All becomes completely transparent. For Manet, and the painting he initiates, the position of the viewer is systematically indeterminate. For both the viewer and the man in the top hat, we can say, with Carol Armstrong, that "spectatorship is defined by dislocation."[34] Far from being a window or a mirror, the canvas reveals itself as an opaque surface, whose materiality is undeniable. At the same time, the painting reminds us in manifold ways of the play of phantasms, through its reflections that are not (true) reflections and its images whose status is put into question by those problematic reflections. The look itself becomes thematic in the gaze of the barmaid, the exchange of glances with the customer in the mirror, and the looks of the men and women in the balcony, especially the woman with opera glasses and the man in the top hat who could be a double of the customer (as such he could be the displaced substitute for the figure who is absent from the space in front of the bar). We can connect this deployment of the look and the phantasm with the painting's explicit subject matter, having to do with the world of commodities and advertising. Much critical energy has been occupied in discussing whether the barmaid offers herself for sale; this possibility cannot be excluded, nor can it be definitely confirmed. One reading that floats through the literature like an errant phantasm suggests that we think of the entire scenario as the customer's dream; this take on the painting would allow us to see it as a play of indeterminate desire.[35] In any case, the bottles of beer, wine, and champagne, the availability of the spectacle (marked by the strange, dangling legs of the trapeze artist), and the attractive surfaces and textures all combine in a phantasmagoria that is the painterly equivalent of the world of glittering commodities of which Walter Benjamin wrote in the *Arcades Project*. The Folies-Bergère itself is a site of illusion, the illusion of a community of classes and social groups that otherwise observed fairly sharp distinctions. The repeated doubling of objects and figures in the mirror suggests a logic of the simulacrum, as we see that what the reflections copy are not originals. We remember Nietzsche's question, "[I]s not seeing itself seeing abysses?" The question arises in the context of a narrative that broaches the thought of eternal recurrence, a thought that Nietzsche was developing in the same years, 1881–82, that Manet was painting the *Bar*. In detecting resonances of recurrence in Manet's painting, Foucault is alert to the prevalence of this figure in post-1870 Europe, as was Benjamin, who saw the thought as especially strong in the Paris of this time.[36]

It is remarkable that Foucault never broaches the question of gender in his lectures on Manet, the painter of *Olympia* and *Luncheon on the Grass* as well as the *Bar*. This might be chalked up to the unfinished and occasional status of these talks, but it is also the case that there is hardly a whisper of such issues in the discussion of *Las Meninas* or in that of Magritte, who certainly offers a full supply of nude female bodies and their parts that both invite and offer a critique of the "male gaze." In his narrative about the sexual excitement that swept through the gallery where "realistic" hack images were being displayed, Foucault seems to credit this to an enthusiasm for the image as image (as opposed to abstraction), rather than to any specific interest in the content (yet some of the pictures of Clovis Trouille, whom he mentions, verge on soft-core pornography). Critics of the *Bar* are fascinated with the figure(s) of the woman, who seems to oscillate between Madonna and whore; such indeterminacy and doubling reinforce Foucault's reading of the painting on a level of social and sexual content that he notes mostly in the case of panoptical institutions. Bataille certainly did not ignore these themes in his study of Manet. Directed toward a broad audience, his book for the Skira series emphasizes, among other things, that Manet's paintings frequently involve the "sacrifice of the subject"; this could certainly be said of the present case, where only the reflection of the gentleman at the bar remains.[37]

Foucault abandoned the book on Manet in 1968, reportedly destroying whatever drafts and notes he had accumulated.[38] He did not explicitly articulate the relation I have suggested between the visual regime of the Panopticon and the visual resistance embodied in the work of the painter and the artistic movement that he initiated. However, the surrender of this project did not entail a sacrifice of his continuing concern with modes of visibility, including those of painting, and other arts of vision and space; that concern is evident in the post-1968 essays on Magritte, Fromanger, Rebeyrolle, and Michals and in a variety of briefer allusions to other artists.

66 Wanderers and Shadows

If Manet has rendered the place of the viewer and the artist indeterminate, Foucault has done something analogous in his relationship to his writing. The philosopher's critics have been acutely attentive to what appear to be changes of position in regard to major themes and methods from one text to the next. To these Foucault replied, even anticipating further critiques of this sort, in the introduction to *The Archaeology of Knowledge*. There he conducts a dialogue with an imaginary interlocutor, one who asks: "Aren't you sure of what you're saying? Are you going to change yet again, shift your position according to the questions that are put to you, and say that the objections are not really directed at the place from which you are speaking?" (*AK* 17; *AS* 28).

This internal and imagined dialogue bears comparison with those that Nietzsche constructs, especially in *The Wanderer and His Shadow*. That text, the concluding section of *Human, All Too Human*, is framed by two such dialogues, which suggests that the 350 intervening aphorisms are to be considered as aspects of an internal conversation of a polytropic self. Surprised in the opening dialogue by his speaking Shadow, the Wanderer is forced to thematize the play of light and shadow, so acknowledging a certain distance from the optics and metaphysics of presence. He confesses: "You will know that I love shadow as much as I love light. For there to be beauty of face, clarity of speech, benevolence and firmness of character, shadow is as needful as light. They are not opponents: they stand, rather, lovingly, hand in hand, and when light disappears, shadow slips away after it." We suppose that the two now settle down to a conversation echoed in some way by the text that bears their names (or descriptions). But the communication of this colloquy is hedged about with restrictions. In keeping with his retiring nature, the Shadow begs the Wanderer to "promise that you will tell no one how we talked together!" The Wanderer knows well that a flat transcription would lack the appropriate shadings: "*How* we talked together? Heaven defend me from long-spun-out literary conversations. . . . A conversation that gives delight in reality is, if transformed into writing and read, a painting with nothing but false perspectives; everything is too long or too short. But shall I perhaps be permitted to tell *what* it was we were in accord over?" (*HAH, WS*, prefatory dialogue; *KSA* 2.537–39). This is the visual protocol for reading the aphorisms that follow (including two that we have interrogated at some length dealing with Raphael and with the landscapes of Claude and Poussin: secs. 11, 21). Each aphorism has to be read as if it were a form of dialogical chiaroscuro. The dialogue is explicitly taken up by the two designated speakers again at the conclusion of the text. As daylight disappears, the Shadow must reckon with his own imminent disappearance. All that the Wanderer can do now for his own Shadow is to move in such a way as to prevent his being swallowed up in the encroaching *Dämmerung*. Begging for a small favor, the Shadow recalls a philosophical anecdote. All the Wanderer can do is this: "Nothing, except that which the philosophical 'dog' [Diogenes the Cynic] desired of the great Alexander: that you should move a little out of the sunlight, I am feeling too cold" (*HAH, WS*, concluding dialogue; *KSA*

2.703–4). Of course once the Wanderer steps out of the light, the Shadow disappears, and the conversation (and the book) come to an end. This is Nietzsche's way of suggesting that thought occurs neither in the glaring Platonic sunlight nor in its all-too-facile negation, but in the flickering, twilight play of light and shadow. The authorial voice becomes a function of this play, embodying the wandering or nomadic life of the mind and of writing.

It is as if Foucault had also generated a shadow self that followed him about, always just a step or so behind in his attempt to recreate and chart his itinerary. Readers find this strange, a response that is not unlike the puzzled reactions of the first set of viewers of Manet's *Bar*, who could not make sense of the position virtually attributed to them by the painting or the implied location of the painter. Their impatience found expression not only verbally but in visible forms, in satirical cartoons that either "corrected" or questioned the perspective of the painting and the oddness of the mirror. Manet was not able to reply in kind to those critics of this, his last major painting, completed while he was dying of the illness that would finish him off in a year. In the essay "Different Spaces," Foucault suggests that mirrors are precisely intermediate spaces between the utopia and the heterotopia. The mirror is a "placeless place," and so a utopia, so that "I am over there where I am not, a kind of shadow that gives me my own visibility." But the mirror really exists and its reflection displaces me: "Due to the mirror I discover myself absent at the place where I am, since I see myself over there" (*F* 2.179; *DE* 4.756). The mirror is a way of having and losing oneself; it is perhaps more ambiguous than the Lacanian mirror, which stabilizes an otherwise volatile identity in a specular image.

In the spirit of the hide-and-seek of Manet's mirror, Foucault, like one of the momentary and partial selves mobilized in Nietzsche's dialogues, responds defiantly and famously to the rather plodding critic, asking whether the latter really imagines that he has not all the time been preparing a labyrinth for himself, one "in which I can lose myself and appear at last to eyes that I will never have to meet again. I am no doubt not the only one who writes in order to have no face. Do not ask who I am and do not ask me to remain the same: leave it to our bureaucrats and our police to see that our papers are in order. At least spare us their morality when we write" (*AK* 17; *AS* 28). The faceless writer is the counterpart of Nietzsche's wandering aphorist or of Manet's elusive painter, the one who presents his work in terms of a triple system of disunity. The visual and spatial language of this exchange— the labyrinth, the unique and momentary appearance to the eyes of the other, the absence of the face—all of this reinforces the mobile quality of Foucault's thought, one of the characteristics that Deleuze found so appealing. In the virtual visit to the gallery that defamiliarized our viewing of *Las Meninas*, we at least thought that we could trust our guide, the expert who spoke with great authority on the structure of the painting; but much later, in the unfolding of *Les mots et les choses*, that guide disappeared, and we were even told at the book's conclusion that the very figure of "man," which we thought we had discovered as the unthought foundation of the painting, would quite possibly vanish altogether, and soon, "like a face drawn in sand at the edge of the sea." In his reply to his own shadow, Foucault tells us that we have failed to understand his compositional principles. It is the bureaucrats and the police who are charged with surveillance (the librarians will have no trouble in cataloging a series of books under the name "Foucault"). Their methods, derivative from Benthamite practices and disciplines, will unfailingly yield results in their own terms, through systems of inspection and classification. Yet Manet, in a Paris whose Hausmannisation had rendered everything visible while enabling various forms of surveillance, managed to devise a mode of painting that offered an alternative, the sketch of an activity of visual resistance. Foucault invites us to *see* his own writing as the equivalent of that practice, one that liberates surfaces as such, rather than imposing classical, Cyclopean grids that promise depth but provide only the meager satisfaction of filling in the contents of a monotonous matrix.

67 The Prison of the Gallery and the Force of Flight

A brief essay by Foucault extends his treatment of visual confinement and strategies of resistance and rebellion. In 1973 Paul Rebeyrolle, a French painter who has attracted the interest of Sartre and Foucault, but who is not so well known outside of France, exhibited a series of ten paintings, simply entitled *Dogs*.[39] Each one shows a dog in captivity, in various stages of struggle, suffering, or defeat. The same basic vocabulary is employed in each image: a single dog, the indication of a cage constructed with a wire lattice and a wooden frame, sometimes a glimpse of the sky. Each cage has a window, offering a minimal view of what lies outside. All is done in a thick impasto, whose rough texture emphasizes the physicality of imprisonment and its sufferings; coarse strips of wood are glued to the canvas. The series was reproduced in the art periodical *Derrière le Miroir*, which is published in a large folio edition, with an essay by Foucault, "La force de fuir" (*DE* 2.401–5). From the images in the folio, it appears that the paintings were hung without frames against a wall of dark, unpainted brick, a setting that would have intensified the claustrophobic atmosphere of the ten pictures. Foucault, involved then with the politics of the prison as well as with the articulation of its panoptical diagram (*Surveillance and Punishment* was published two years later, in 1975), found this series emblematic of the condition of confinement and the dream of escape. In his published and unpublished remarks on Manet, he had sketched the idea of the museum as an enclosed and totalizing space, parallel to but contesting the optical machinery of the Panopticon. In the 1967 essay "Different Spaces," he suggested that both the prison and the museum were "heterotopias," spaces existing outside the norms of the culture.[40] Now he addresses paintings that not only depict captivity but are situated in a gallery space that evokes the form of the prison. In this ekphrasis, as in that of *Las Meninas*, he insists on giving voice to the position that is forced upon the viewer, who is caught or trapped not by the gaze of the figures in a painting, but by images of imprisonment arrayed in a space of confinement. The first lines of the essay spell out the conditions of this constriction of vision as well as the visions of constriction it displays:

> You have entered. Here you are held fast by ten pictures, that circle a room in which all the windows have been carefully closed.
>
> In prison, in your turn, like the dogs that you see standing on their hind legs and butting up against the grillwork?

These are dogs, not human beings, and there is nothing here to suggest a particular location. But this very abstraction from human ethnicity and geography brings to mind the many actual prisons of the time that lie beyond the virtual prison of the gallery with its shuttered windows: "It is not about the prisons of Spain, Greece, the USSR, of Brazil or Saigon; it is about *the* prison. But the prison—as Jackson has attested—is today a political place, that is, a place where forces arise and show themselves, a place where history takes shape, and whence time arises" (*DE* 2.401). In 1973 Foucault's readers would have needed no explanation that it was George Jackson's *Prison Letters* to which he referred, and the atrocities at Attica in New York state were fresh enough that there was no need to mention them. Jackson was a young black militant, whose letters, published as a book, outlined a revolutionary and internationalist Marxist critique of capitalism and racism; the book was published in 1970 with an introduction by Jean Genet, famous for his own prison writings.[41]

Earlier Rebeyrolle had painted other series of animals, *Birds* and

Frogs, which involved variations on form, color, and movement. But this group of pictures is different; it "forms an irreversible series, an eruption that cannot be mastered." Yet Foucault does not mean that they constitute a continuous narrative. What emerges in the series, he says, is a movement of escape. The series "rather than narrating what has occurred, transmits *(fait passer)* a force whose history can be narrated as the wake of its flight and its liberty. Painting has at least this in common with discourse: when it transmits a force that creates history, it is political." Rebeyrolle's paintings of the *Dogs* accomplish this political movement by their construction of the motif of windows and the use of wooden sticks and bars, and through the direction they give to the movement of flight. Here the windows are completely blank and neutral. Unlike the windows of classical painting that project an interior into the external world, they reveal only "a pure outside, neutral, inaccessible, without any figure." The wooden strips impose the dimension of verticality on the paintings; here, Foucault argues, verticality is not simply a spatial dimension; it is the dimension of power. "The window and the stick are both opposed to one another and constitute a couple, like power and impotence." Flight and escape are not oriented toward the window, which is an illusory exit. We are reminded of Magritte's windows, which turn out to be false exits, blending with pictures or mirrors. The window is a means of inspection; it is part of the apparatus of power and the diagram of surveillance. To leave through the window is to leave that apparatus intact. Like Manet, but in a very different key, Rebeyrolle drains the window of its phantasmatic power, and he teaches this ancient lesson: "In human struggles, nothing great ever passes by way of the windows, but everything, always, by the triumphant crumbling [*l'effondrement*] of the walls." Gérard Fromanger, who will be the subject of another Foucault essay, transforms well-known photographs of the Toul prison rebellion, in which the exultant convicts occupy the roof (sec. 78; fig. 23). In his essay on the dream, Foucault identifies the vertical dimension of ascent and fall with the tragic (secs. 43, 78). There is a Nietzschean resonance here also, as in Zarathustra's delirious encomia on flight as the achievement of freedom.

Unlike his *Birds*, Rebeyrolle's *Dogs*, as Foucault points out, are animals of the ground, not the air. In a complex philosophical conceit, he recalls Spinoza's saying that language can be confusing when it applies the same name to the animal that barks and to a celestial constellation. But Rebeyrolle's dog, he says, is both a barking animal and a "terrestrial constellation." Painting, at least here, becomes a meditation on the process of human liberation in a society where there is all too much in the way of surveillance. It does this not through the creation of imaginary windows, like the classical images presupposed by the mirror play of a Velazquez, but by challenging the *dispositif* of painting as window; enclosing the viewer in the simulacrum of a prison, it demonstrates that the way out, the "thought of the outside," is to vault over the walls of the structure itself.[42]

Summing up the effect of the series that culminates in a leap, Foucault shows how it has transformed the relative position of subject and viewer:

> Rebeyrolle has found the means of making the force of painting [*peindre*] pass in a single gesture into the vibration of the painting itself [*la peinture*]. The form is no longer charged with representing force by means of its distortions; force no longer has to jostle with form to come to light. The same force passes directly from the painter to the canvas, and from one canvas to the following one; from a trembling prostration, then from pain borne all the way to a quiver of hope, to the leap, to a flight without end, from this dog, who, circling around you, has left you alone in the prison where you find yourself enclosed, dizzied by the passage of this force, now already distant from you and of which you see only traces—the traces of what has "flown the coop" [*se sauve*]. (*DE* 2.404–5)

As in the account of *Las Meninas*, we discover that the drama really revolves about ourselves. And if that painting left us in the most ambiguous of positions, confused by our shifting identity with painter and model, this series has shaken us by reinforcing the sense of enclosure that was enforced by the constriction of the forbidding gallery space and the dogs struggling against their cages of wire and wood. This pictorial space is political, and we are left to reflect on a world of prisons, literal and virtual.

eleven

Pipe Dreams: Recurrence of the Simulacrum in Klossowski, Deleuze, and Magritte

68 Simulacra, or Floating Images

Michel Foucault invokes Andy Warhol at the very end of *This Is Not a Pipe,* at the end of a chapter entitled "Seven Seals of Affirmation," so that the words must be read with a Nietzschean resonance, echoing Zarathustra's "Seven Seals," which itself parodically recalls John's Apocalypse.[1] To the Johannine end of time, Nietzsche and Foucault oppose both a radical novelty and a reorientation of the sense of temporality and historicity: "A day will come when, by means of similitude relayed indefinitely along the length of a series, the image itself, along with the name it bears, will lose its identity. Campbell, Campbell, Campbell, Campbell" (*TNP* 54; *CP* 79). If John's Apocalypse offers a revelation through a complex series of images, Foucault proposes that the image will lose its identity and its name in the Warholian revelation. A flat, immobilized image will usher in a new form of temporality. In Flaubert's phantasms Foucault saw the approach of the "vision of Engadine," Nietzsche's *Augenblick* of eternal recurrence, as eternal recurrence of the *Augenblick,* and that vision has a further manifestation in Pop Art and its affines. Andy (so familiar has he become, like "Claude" in the English eighteenth century) has become a flash point for posing questions on the one hand about the very definition of art, as in the theory of Arthur Danto, and, on the other, about the commodified world of late capitalism and its spectacles. An artist who arouses the intellectual passions of Anglo-American philosophical aesthetics and those of that culture's own cultural theorists must be an emblematic figure indeed. In cases of such overdetermined interest within a certain critical community, it should be worthwhile to step outside its bounds just a bit, by seeing how such work manifested itself to a French thinker who had been rethinking a German philosopher's thoughts about images, time, and history. But we are getting a bit ahead of the story.

Magritte is known as a surrealist, a painter who transforms reality, one who brings forth fantasies, dreams, and impossible combinations (the face as sexual torso in *The Rape,* the bizarrely gigantic flower of *The Tomb of the Wrestlers*); Warhol's art borrows the unmistakable images of the everyday: celebrities, front-page newspaper photos, or commercial products (Marilyn who needs no last name, a generic car crash, the Campbell's Soup that was Warhol's regular lunch). Yet Magritte achieves his effects by alienating the everyday from its customary context, and Warhol's products render the banal perspicuous in its banality. Foucault sees both bodies of work in terms of a cluster of notions—similitude, simulacrum, eternal recurrence, and affirmation—that are variations on and extensions of Nietzsche's thoughts in the daring articulations of Pierre Klossowski and Gilles Deleuze.

The images of Magritte, the once esoteric surrealist, have become standard quotations on book covers and in advertising; similarly, and for the same reasons, Foucault might say, Magritte's deformations and inventions have analogs and descendants in the realm of a photographically based art that addresses questions of commodification and repetition (chap. 12). Before confronting these developments in greater depth, that is, with proper respect to their shimmering play of surfaces, I read Foucault's essay on Magritte as an instance of ekphrasis. This ekphrasis grows out of a circulation of texts among Klossowski, Deleuze, and Foucault, a dizzying interchange of positions on the phantasm, the simulacrum, and the interpretation of eternal recurrence that exhibits some of the same qualities as its subject matter. What is unusual about this variation on an ancient genre is Foucault's claim that Magritte's painting *already* speaks. The consequence is a significant complication in the task of the writer on art; as Foucault said in *Les mots et les choses*, "the relation between painting and language is an infinite relation." If this holds even of a classical painting like *Las Meninas*, there is an additional fold introduced when painting foregrounds the question of the relationship between word and image, as it does in the work of Magritte. Klossowski's writing also plays upon that relationship; he theorizes the question of the image and the phantasm (as in his texts on Nietzsche), fictionalizes it (as in *Diana at Her Bath* and *The Baphomet*), and produces drawings, paintings, and films, including one of the latter, *Hypothesis of the Lost Painting*, that renders problematic the connection between the temporality of narrative and the timelessness of painting. It is, in effect, one more challenge to Lessing's bifurcation of the literary and the visual.

Before entering into the labyrinthine and simulacral play among Deleuze, Klossowski, and Foucault, note that Foucault's reading of Magritte is by no means the importation of philosophy into an alien context. From the start the painter's art is a form of seduction and provocation directed toward philosophy. The inscription and the paintings it identifies that find their way into Foucault's title put into question the very possibility of reference and the relationship between language and the world. (It will be useful to recall that the title Magritte gave to the painting Foucault examines most intensely is *Les deux mystères*). Another painting, *Hegel's Holiday*, depicting an open umbrella supporting a glass of water, suggests perhaps that the philosopher is above all interested in producing a shelter against alterity and accident; even when on vacation he does not forget his *Regenschirm* ("rain-shield," more expressive here than "umbrella").[2] *La philosophie dans le boudoir* echoes Sade's title; its nightgown with breasts of flesh and its high-heeled shoes with real toes also, like so much of Magritte's work, pose an undecidable oscillation between the inside and the outside, appearance and reality, the drapery or covering and the naked truth presumed to underlie it. If there are temptations to philosophy here, they no longer include some of the familiar gestures toward a philosophy of the visual found in earlier painting. The issue of a reciprocity of gazes that arises in *Las Meninas*, where we are uncertain whether and how the positions of model, painter, and spectator intersect, is not present. Nor does Magritte play with any of the conventions of self-portraiture that explore the possibility of man's attaining self-knowledge. The image now is left on its own.

This tendency of the image to float free is implicit throughout Foucault's essay and explicitly there in its rhetoric. In discussing the 1966 painting *Les deux mystères* (fig. 19), in which a pipe drawn on a blackboard with the inscription "*Ceci n'est pas une pipe*" is echoed, supple-

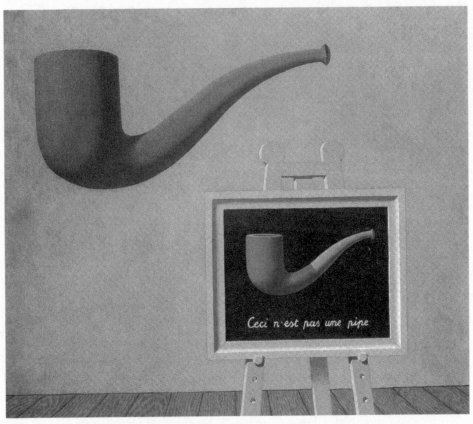

Figure 19. René Magritte, *Les deux mystères*, 1966. Private collection. Photothèque R. Magritte–ADAGP/Art Resource. © 2003 C. Herscovici, Brussels/Artists Rights Society (ARS), New York

mented, and contradicted by the image of a larger pipe that seems suspended above it in the air, he speaks of the latter as "floating," as a "simple notion or fantasy of a pipe," and asks whether it is an "emanation, a mist just detaching itself from the painting" (*TNP* 16–17; *CP* 12–13). This language might appear metaphorical or even whimsical, which it is, but it also stands in a rather rigorous relation to the conception of the simulacrum developed by Deleuze, and through that intermediary Foucault is putting Magritte into dialogue with a certain "anti-Platonic" aspect of Plato and with Lucretius's theory of perception.[3] Deleuze had written of *Alice's Adventures in Wonderland*, proposing to explain its paradoxical logic and texture by introducing certain Stoic concepts of the event and the surface, speaking of "the faint incorporeal mist that escapes from bodies, a film without volume that envelops them."[4] In general, there is a strong parallel between Deleuze's reading of Lewis Carroll and Foucault's of Magritte: both writer and painter emerge as artists of the surface and the simulacrum. This dialogue continues when Foucault goes on to speak of a form that "reascends to the ethereal realm," of similitudes being "born of their own vapor and . . . ris[ing] endlessly into an ether where they refer to nothing more than to themselves" (*TNP* 22, 54; *CP* 24, 79). Recall that Nietzsche incorporated Burckhardt's judgment on Raphael's *Transfiguration,* namely, that it contained the first truly successful floating figure in Italian art; yet Nietzsche, in naming that figure as Apollo, rather than Christ, made him the very generator of images.

An appendix to Deleuze's *Logic of Sense,* "The Simulacrum and Ancient Philosophy," asks what it might mean to follow Nietzsche's injunction to reverse Platonism. In going back to a neglected theme in Plato himself and to Lucretius, something of an outsider in relation to the philosophical canon, Deleuze proposes to excavate neglected possibilities from within the tradition for valuing a certain multiplicity. This repeats Nietzsche's gesture at the beginning of *The Birth of Tragedy,* where he recalls Lucretius's theory of the dream (and so of the phantasm and the simulacrum) in order to make sense of Apollonian art. Deleuze focuses his efforts at first on a reading of Plato's *Sophist.* In this dialogue an important distinction between the legitimate icon or copy, on the one hand, and the wayward phantasm or simulacrum, on the other, is illustrated by an analogy drawn from the visual arts. As Deleuze observes, "the Platonic dialectic is neither a dialectic of contradiction nor of contrariety, but a dialectic of rivalry [*amphisbetesis*], a dialectic of rivals and suitors."[5] The rivalry when vision is in question is not only between philosophy and its competitors but also among various forms of the visual. There is a hierarchy of visual powers, productions, and forms of knowledge, including dreams, reflections, illusions, objects perceived in a variety of contexts and perspectives, healthy and diseased eyes, and the eye of the soul. In the *Sophist* the Stranger asks: "And what shall we say of human art? Do we not make one house by the art of building, and another by the art of drawing, which is a sort of dream created by man for those who are awake?"[6]

In what might be called a strong and even violent reading of the dialogue, Deleuze sees the *Sophist* as releasing these dreams, as Plato's thought is shaken by the possibility that there may be no absolute model to which various images must be referred: "[I]t may be that the end of the *Sophist* contains the most extraordinary adventure of Platonism: as a consequence of searching in the direction of the simulacrum and of leaning over its abyss, Plato discovers, in the flash of an instant, that the simulacrum is not simply a false copy, but that it places in question the very notions of copy and model."[7] This disturbance creates an opening for the Nietzschean project, for "'to reverse Platonism' means to make the simulacra rise and to affirm their rights among icons and copies."[8] Deleuze then explicitly associates Nietzsche's reversal of Platonism with a certain understanding of the image, an understanding that restores the image not in a kind of atomic identity (as in the thought of the British empiricists), but in its indefinite multiplicity. And in a move that will echo (or be simulated) in Foucault's essays on Deleuze and Magritte and in his remarks on Warhol, Deleuze associates this rise of the simulacrum with the eternal recurrence and exemplifies it by the phenomenon of Pop Art. Here the recurrence is understood not as a way of organizing chaos but as the circulation of simulacra; in the eternal recurrence, there is no genuine or authentic model of which the infinitely many recurrences or simulacra are copies. The recurrence might be rethought as the reign of the simulacrum itself and the expulsion of the Platonic model: "[I]t does not make *everything* come back. It is still selective, it 'makes a difference,' but not at all in the manner of Plato. What is selected are all the procedures opposed to selection; what is excluded, what is *made not* to return, is that which presupposes the Same and the Similar, that which pretends to correct divergence, to recenter the circles or order the chaos, and to provide a model or make a copy." Modernity is said to be "defined by the power of the simulacrum" (in 1969, the date of Deleuze's work, there was virtually no talk of the postmodern). In this connection a distinction is made between the artificial, which is in good Platonic terms simply "a copy of a copy," and the simulacrum, for which that hierarchy no longer obtains. That which might appear at first as artificial can be transformed or transvalued: "The artificial is always a copy of a copy, which should be pushed *to the point where it changes its nature and is reversed into the simulacrum* (the moment of Pop Art)."[9] If Warhol's images at first appear to be merely copies, reproductions of well-known images of Coca-Cola bottles or of photographers' shots of Marilyn or Elvis, this marks their status as artifice; but what appears as artificial from a Platonic perspective can be "reversed" by a mode of presentation that makes it multiply and proliferate indefinitely so as to erase what would have been its source and center.

Foucault develops Deleuze's suggestions about the role of the simulacrum in Pop Art in his essay "Theatrum Philosophicum," which is devoted to a review of Deleuze's *Difference and Repetition* and *The Logic of Sense*. Foucault sees Andy Warhol's art as genuinely revelatory in a way that complements his analysis of Magritte:

This is the greatness of Warhol with his canned foods, senseless acci-
dents, and his series of advertising smiles: the oral and nutritional
equivalence of those half-open lips, teeth, tomato sauce, that hy-
giene based on detergents; the equivalence of death in the cavity of
an eviscerated car, at the top of a telephone pole and at the end of
a wire, and between the glistening, steel blue arms of the electric
chair. "It's the same either way," stupidity [*bêtise*] says, while sink-
ing into itself and infinitely extending its nature with the things it
says of itself; "Here or there, it's always the same thing; what difference if the colors vary, if they're darker or lighter. It's all so sense-
less—life, women, death! How ridiculous this stupidity! [*Comme
est bête la bêtise!*]." But in concentrating on this boundless monot-
ony, we find the sudden illumination of multiplicity itself—with
nothing at its center, at its highest point, or beyond it—a flickering
of light that travels even faster than the eyes and successively lights
up the moving labels and the captive snapshots that refer to each
other to eternity, without ever saying anything: suddenly, arising
from the background of the old inertia of equivalences, the striped
form of the event tears through the darkness, and the eternal
phantasm informs that soup can, that singular and depthless face.
(*LCMP* 189; *DE* 2.293–94)

69 *Diana at Her Bath:* Theophany as Vision and Text

What is "the eternal phantasm?" Foucault's most significant early engagement with such issues appears in his essay of 1964, "The Prose of
Actaeon," devoted to the work of Klossowski. The essay's title refers
to the writer's subtle and phantasmagoric retelling of the myth of Diana and Actaeon in *Le bain de Diane,* which Foucault pronounces to be
"doubtless of all the texts of Klossowski, the one closest to that brilliant
light—but very dim for us—from whence the simulacrum comes to
us" (*F* 2.132; *DE* 1.335). He had met Klossowski a year or so earlier,
and his praise for the thinker of the simulacrum was matched by the
latter's dedication of his last novel, *The Baphomet,* to Foucault in 1965.
The Baphomet is an allegorical and gnostic transformation of the doctrine of eternal recurrence into the process of metempsychosis in the
context of a fantastic story of the medieval and heretical Knights Templar.[10] *Diana at Her Bath* is the attempt to reconstruct, to imagine once
more, an archaic experience of an image, a vision, and a story that, the
author says, "comes down to us like the light of constellations which

for us are now extinct."[11] The story of Diana and Actaeon, as we know it, centers around a vision, the vision that Actaeon has of the nude Diana at her bath. But things are not as simple as this version implies; with impressive erudition, Klossowski argues that the form of the story we know (notably from Ovid's *Metamorphoses*) is rather late (no earlier than Callimachus in the fourth century B.C.E.) and that we must attempt to see what it might have meant to an earlier humanity "that has vanished to the point that the term 'vanished' no longer has any meaning—despite our ethnologies, all our museums and everything else."[12] Like Heidegger reading the saying of Anaximander, Klossowski undertakes to recreate a lost possibility of thought, one that has been buried over and disguised by millennia of readings and interpretations. In this case what is to be approached is not just a text whose thought is virtually unthinkable for us, but a story whose understanding involves possibilities of vision and imagination that are for us invisible. In other words, *Diana at Her Bath* undertakes an archaeology of vision.

Perhaps the most difficult notion of the archaic visual regime is that of theophany, the self-manifestation of divinity, which Klossowski strives to explicate by means of the concepts of phantasm and simulacrum. How mad to think of the gods appearing in visible guise! The ancients cannot make use of the concept of incarnation as deployed by Christianity—and evaded in Nietzsche's substitution of Apollo for Christ—for gods do not literally become men. In a long explanatory note to *Diana*, Klossowski (an ex-seminarian) comments on Augustine's attempt to construe the pagan gods as demons. The argument in *The City of God* goes like this: the Roman gods commanded that they be represented, with all their conflicts and amours, in the first stage shows. The gods thus reveal themselves as debased in their adulteries, incests, thefts, and lies; such beings can only be demonic.[13] Klossowski transvalues this position, drawing on the traditions of gnosticism, in which appearances float freely, independent of any higher world. Yet while gnosticism sees these appearances as the sign of this world's irremediable corruption, Klossowski valorizes the phantasms and simulacra as glittering, shimmering, and dazzling; if they can be seductively misleading, they also give *jouissance*. In *Diana at Her Bath*, Klossowski simply deploys these notions, but in his writings on Nietzsche, he offers a definition of the phantasm and the simulacrum. In *Nietzsche and the Vicious Circle*, he explains that the phantasm is the involuntary product of impulses (what Nietzsche speaks of as *Triebe*, *Instinkte*, and so on). Simulacra are skillful reproductions of a phantasm "by which humanity can *produce* itself, through forces that are thereby exorcized and dominated by the impulse."[14]

In *Diana* the gods also produce simulacra. Actaeon is haunted by the idea of beholding Diana nude, but the goddess's nude body is a form or simulacrum she assumes, having made a pact with a demon (not an evil being but an intermediary between men and gods). Knowing Actaeon's passion, Diana is seduced by the thought of her own image, so that she too is caught up in the play of images. Nude at the bath, reflected in the pool, there is from the beginning a redoubling of simulacra, anticipating a reciprocity of glances, and an intertwining of fantasies: "All the while, invisible Diana contemplates Actaeon imagining the goddess naked. The deeper he sinks into his reverie, the more Diana assumes bodily shape. . . . the wish to see her own body involves the risk of being defiled by a mortal's gaze, and with this risk the representation of, and then the desire for, defilement enters the goddess's nature. . . . this body, in which she will manifest herself to herself, she actually borrows from Actaeon's imagination."[15]

"The Prose of Actaeon" is a meditation on Klossowski's thought of the simulacrum, one that explores the sensibility of modernity in the light of the barely recoverable world of demonic simulacra. Foucault asks us to consider the possibility that the demon is not the evil other but "the Same, the exact Likeness." Christianity saw its Temptations (and we can certainly think of its *Saint Anthonys* here) in terms of the appearance of strange animals and nameless monsters. But "what if the contest unfolded in a mirror space?" Christianity also knew this experience, insofar as it elaborated a demonology, a skeptical epistemology that would leave us in uncertainty about the source of images. Even the appearances of witches and the devil might be God's simulations, meant to test our faith. Descartes, pushing the hypothesis of the evil demon to its extremity, is said to have put an end to this crisis of thought, even inaugurating an oblivion that there was ever a generalized anxiety about simulacra. Later, in *The Order of Things*, Foucault will elaborate this archaeological insight in providing an overview of the Renaissance world of analogy and similitude, a world of indefinitely many corresponding and overlapping images.

Foucault sees Klossowski and Nietzsche as providing analogous responses to the oblivion that has overtaken that world: "*Incipit* Klossowski, like Zarathustra. And in this somewhat obscure and secret face of Christian experience he suddenly discovers (as if it were its double, perhaps its simulacrum), the resplendent theophany of the Greek gods" (F 2.125; DE 1.327). The reference is to *Twilight of the Idols*, a book whose title refers to the last flickerings of light from the images that hold modernity captive. More specifically, it is to the last lines of the famous section "How the True World Finally Became a Fable," a passage that can be read as a story of the image. It suggests that the binary opposition between the real and the apparent worlds, which was given its first canonical philosophical form by Plato and then underwent a series of transformations through Christian, Kantian, and positivistic versions, can finally be overcome. While it might seem that abandoning the concept of the true world would lead to the conclusion that "only the apparent world is left," Nietzsche points out that the concept of a sphere of appearance is strictly correlative with that of the true world; if appearance is the other of that world, then the downfall of the senior partner must entail the disappearance of the junior: *"with the real world we have also abolished the apparent world!"* (T, "True World"; KSA 6.81). Foucault and Klossowski read Nietzsche as teaching that we are left not with appearances as full and present counterparts of a world behind the scenes but that we must rethink experience in terms of categories that acknowledge the constant play of presence and absence. The mythological version of this is theophany as the manifestation of simulacra, mediated by the demonic. Is it any surprise, then, that, as Foucault points out, Nietzsche also invokes a demon when he first broaches the thought of eternal recurrence, a thought of the recurrence of the *Augenblick?* This is precisely what he does in *Gay Science* (GS 341; KSA 3.570) where the demon calls on us "in our loneliest loneliness" to imagine recurrence. Is this not to think the twinkling of the eye as simulacrum, and might we not, liberated from the binary opposition of appearance and reality, hail the demon as a god?

70 Vicious Circles

In *Nietzsche and the Vicious Circle* (1969) Klossowski develops and extends the reading of eternal recurrence whose hints Foucault detected in his earlier writings. For Klossowski, Nietzsche is a thinker who wrestles with his own tendencies to delirium and dissolution by seeking a doctrine, a teaching that allows him to interpret his struggles as strength. *Amor fati* entails an affirmation of the cycles of highs and lows of mood, health, and fortune that constituted the life of the shy, isolated, and modestly pensioned professor, who was, in fits and starts, producing that extraordinary written corpus that he imagined would split the history of humanity in two. In Klossowski's analysis it is precisely the play between Nietzsche's lived body and the body of his writings that offers a purchase from which to understand his philosophical project. It is not a question of reducing the thinker to his psychic and corporeal frailties and eccentricities, as so many psychologists have undertaken to do. Rather, Klossowski sees Nietzsche as having understood that all thought is necessarily caught up in the tension between the involuntary phantasms that are products of our impulses and the just-as-inevitable desire for lucidity and communication. Nietzsche is the thinker who comes to see all of our thinking as a fallacious commentary on an unknown play of forces, so that "the only conceivable lucidity would be to admit our state of servitude."[16] His experience of eternal recurrence, marked in his notebooks of August 1881 as occurring "six thousand feet beyond man and time," was a vision of dissolution and transformation, a revelation of how all things, caught up in the cycle of becoming, must sacrifice any claim on a substantial identity. This is the experience in which Nietzsche speaks of the discovery that "there is no individual," that the species, the individual, and even the *Augen-blick* are progressively more subtle errors (*KSA* 9.500–502; see secs. 33, 36, 39). Klossowski demonstrates acutely that the thought of recur-rence tends to weaken any sense the individual might have of his or her identity. In thinking the thought through, I know that I have for-gotten and remembered it an infinite number of times. I cannot by means of the thought establish any priority for one or another of the moments of my existence; each unfolds into its infinite repetitions, its simulacra. Unlike such great teleological and organizing thoughts as Christianity and Marxism, the thought does not offer a way of dividing my life into a before and an after, and I think this also about that mo-ment, when in August 1881, or Paris 1935, or St. Paul, Minnesota, in 1957, I first experienced the thought. Of course, I might be born into a society that takes this thought for granted, as Indians are born into one that takes reincarnation for granted; this would make the idea even more difficult for me to privilege any specific *Augenblick*. What the thought can do for me *now* is to make me more lucid about the servi-tude of all thought, by reminding me of my insubstantiality, my tran-sience, my metamorphosis.[17] Klossowski said this allegorically in one way in *Diana* and in another in *The Baphomet*. Both books constitute daring philosophical readings of ancient stories; like some of the great neo-Platonic and kabbalistic commentators on Homer or the Bible, Klossowski offers a philosophical reading of a legend, whether of an-cient metamorphosis or of an esoteric cult among the Knights Templar. His unclassifiable texts are in one dimension exegeses or retellings of myth, history, and legend from the standpoint of eternal recurrence. In the case of *Diana*, the emphasis is on what we might call the Apol-lonian aspect of the eternal recurrence, the multiplication, exfoliation, and folding over of shining simulacra. *The Baphomet* shows the meta-morphosis and dissolution of the soul into a series of "breaths," a term that evokes the earliest words for soul in Indo-European languages (like *psuche*), so undercutting the apparent dualism of a world in which disembodied bits of consciousness float and wander, by suggesting that there is something corporeal about these "souls," even if most subtly attenuated.

In *Nietzsche and the Vicious Circle*, Klossowski explores Nietzsche's oscillation between his singular and idiosyncratic experience of the return in Sils-Maria and his experimentation with making the teaching public, both in his notes, sketches, and plans and in the published works, notably *Zarathustra*. Struggling with the possibility that the "thought of thoughts" might be nothing more than an expression of his delirium, the philosopher sought ways of confirming the doctrine and making it publicly acceptable. According to Lou Salomé, he even considered scientific arguments drawn from physics, and in an anticipation of the career of his "son" Zarathustra, he proposed at one point to study the natural sciences for ten years, during which he would maintain a public silence, and then come forth as the teacher of recurrence.[18] Although this plan was soon abandoned, others came to fruition. Klossowski offers a nuanced account of Nietzsche's rhetorical strategies for announcing and teaching the doctrine. He assembles a number of notes that speak of the philosopher, described variously as experimenter or imposter, as being in command of the "beautiful simulacra [*Trugbilder*]"; in possession of these, they suggest, to an as yet unidentified constituency, "*Let us be the deceivers and the embellishers of humanity!*—In fact, this is precisely what a philosopher is" (*KSA* 11.699–700).[19] For Klossowski, Nietzsche's *teaching* of recurrence, as opposed to his *experience* of it, consists of deploying images, that is, simulacra, which will have a persuasive power and serve as a great organizing principle, if not for Western society at large, then for a "conspiratorial" group of thinkers who will use the thought to conduct great cultural experiments as they confront the question "who will be the lords of the earth?" He praises Nietzsche's great insight into the progressive industrialization of the world, the accompanying hypertrophy of gregarious tendencies, and the rise of scientism and technocracy. In the hands of the conspirators, the idea of recurrence would be a way of countering or co-opting these trends. Ultimately Nietzsche's enlightened philosophers are caught in a contradiction between their seeking an aim and a meaning for existence by means of the thought of recurrence and the way in which the content of the thought, pursued to its depth, denies the possibility of such an aim and meaning.

The ideas that Foucault and Deleuze seem to have carried away from Klossowski's analysis are these: a radically anti-individualist reading of the thought of recurrence, according to which it is my self-dissolution and metamorphosis that are brought about by the return, rather than any eternalizing of myself as a self-identical, substantial "I"; the notion of the thought as a phantasm that could be propagated by simulacra; and the conception of a practice or strategy in which images and simulacra could be mobilized as a form of resistance directed against the homogenizing forces of industrialization, commodification, and rampant gregariousness. Given the example of Klossowski's own experimentation with the visual, Foucault was ready to find signs of a similar practice in an artist like Magritte.

71 Déjà Vu: Recurrence of the Image, Once More

Klossowski, then, comes very close to suggesting that there is or could be a Nietzschean practice of the visual arts or visual culture that would deploy simulacra in the interest of experimentation with a decentered conception of the human and a corresponding resistance to prevailing disciplines. Echoes of Klossowski's views, and a more explicit development of this possibility in visual culture, are to be found in Deleuze's comments on Pop Art and in Foucault's readings of Magritte, Warhol, Fromanger, and Michals. What none of the three thinkers note explicitly in their juxtaposition of Nietzsche's thought of recurrence with a certain transformation of the *visual* image, is that this association is already present in Zarathustra's most extended speech on the recurrence, whose title already indicates an optical theme: "Vom Gesicht und Räthsel." What recurs in the recurrence is the *Augenblick*, the twinkling of the eye (sec. 32). Nietzsche sets a specifically visual scene for Zarathustra's confrontation with the dwarf who embodies the spirit of gravity here, describing a walk through "the deadly pallor of twilight" leading to a gate bearing the inscription *Augenblick* and at which two paths confront or abut one another. At this gateway Zarathustra challenges the dwarf to say what he *sees*, and he replies dismissively (as "stupidity" responds to Warhol's multiples in Foucault's scenario): "'All that is straight lies,' the dwarf murmured contemptuously. 'All truth is crooked; time itself is a circle.'" "So what?" or "What's the difference?" is the response of the dwarf and of stupidity to the actuality or possibility of a certain repetition.

This is the background of Foucault's ekphrasis of Warhol, when he speaks of the "eternal phantasm" or "the striped form of the event." Mark Taylor has said that art like Warhol's exhibits a style of thought that he calls "logo centrism," that is a stress on the recognizable logo or label of the celebrity, commodity, instantly recognizable symbol, or scene that constitutes the occasion for a multiplication of the image.[20] What Foucault says about these images, apparently produced to infinity, is that it is precisely the form of their presentation, multiplication, and indefinite proliferation that releases them from the circle of the logo and precipitates an abyssal vision that calls for a focus on the moment of vision, just as the thought of eternal recurrence is meant to provoke an attention to experiences that goes beyond fitting them into one or another conventional narratives that we might tell about our lives. This is what Foucault says about that thought, just a few pages after the passage on Warhol:

> As for the Return, must it be the perfect circle, the well-oiled millstone, which turns on its axis and reintroduces things, forms, and men at their appointed time? Must there be a center and must events occur on its periphery? . . . perhaps like the young shepherd we must break this circular ruse—like Zarathustra himself who bit off the head of the serpent and immediately spat it away. . . . Aeon [the Stoic contrast to Chronos, of which Deleuze writes] is *recurrence* itself, the straight line of time, a splitting quicker than thought and narrower than any instant. It causes the same present to arise—on both sides of this indefinitely splitting arrow—as always existing, as indefinitely present, and as indefinite future. (*LCMP* 192–93; *DE* 2.96)

This conception of the recurrence contributes to Foucault's analysis of the circulation of similitudes in Magritte and to his announcement: "A day will come when, by means of similitude relayed indefinitely along the length of a series, the image itself, along with the name it bears, will lose its identity." Foucault's last book before the Magritte essay, *Les mots et les choses*, also concluded with the apocalyptic pronouncement, described again as an effacement or erasure, "that one can certainly wager that man would be erased, like a face drawn in sand at the edge of the sea." These two vanishing acts are intimately connected insofar as it is the same factors that will destabilize the reign of man and that of the representational image.

Let us look more carefully now at the argument of *This Is Not a Pipe* with these erasures in mind. At the beginning of Foucault's bravura ekphrases of the two versions of the painting that include those words, he wants to insist that the genre presupposed by what we are beholding is not the painting or picture in general but the calligram. Especially the second painting, the one with two pipes (or their images, their simulacra) must be understood as based on a fusion of the visual and the linguistic, the imaged and the written: "The operation is a calligram that Magritte has secretly constructed, then carefully unravelled" (*TNP* 20; *CP* 19). From the outset, then, Foucault's essay will have complicated the traditions and conventions of the ekphrasis, just as Magritte's painting will have deformed some of the conventions and traditions of the Western pictorial mode since the Renaissance. For the ekphrasis ordinarily supposes that the writer (possibly a poet, critic, or philosopher) makes a painting speak; the account that she provides gives a voice to that which is silent (as André Malraux, for example, becomes a ventriloquist of *The Voices of Silence*). But if what is to be described *already* speaks, indeed if it seems to speak of itself, then the writer is not bringing a voice to the voiceless but entering into a conversation already begun. In the calligram, words and letters are arranged so as to suggest forms that evoke objects or themes that are themselves topics of or commentaries on their text. Eventually Foucault suggests that Magritte's pipe paintings are responses to one of Apollinaire's calligrams, "*Fumées*," that itself shapes its words into the image of a pipe. The calligram then challenges the very conditions that make the ekphrasis possible: "The calligram uses that capacity of letters to signify both as linear elements that can be arranged in space and as signs that must unroll according to a unique chain of sound. As a sign, the letter permits us to fix words; as line, it lets us give shape to things. Thus the calligram aspires playfully to efface the oldest oppositions of our alphabetical civilization: to show and to name; to shape and to say; to reproduce and to articulate; to imitate and to signify; to look and to read" (*TNP* 21; *CP* 21–22).

Zarathustra's discourse on the abyss involved in "seeing itself" is also based on a vision that, if not precisely a calligram, also mixes inscription and image. The problem of naming or inscribing the moment, graphically presented by the word *Augenblick* that marks the gateway, is a disruption of the *topoi* of reference, indexicality, and temporality in Western thought. Already ingredient in the sayings of Heraclitus is the impossibility of holding fast the passing moment, a theme that received a magisterial treatment from Augustine, who insisted on the impossibility of naming the present, which must immediately escape before its name is pronounced. Hegel, at the beginning of the *Phenomenology of Spirit*, proposes that one who believes in the fullness and cognitive certainty of the moment ought to try the experiment of writing down or describing that realization; experience will teach that "now it is night" or "now it is day" will be quickly falsified by the passage of time.[21] The inscription on Zarathustra's gateway offers an affront to these philosophies, by writing the name of the moment, *Augenblick*, in stone. The dwarf produces a variant of the standard philosophical response to the problematic by insisting on the movement or flow of time and neglecting the inscription of the moment, its intensity or *haecceitas*.

The paradox of Magritte's inscription, like Zarathustra's, is that it subverts the function of the "legend," that which is to be read, and so undermines the distinction erected by Lessing between the plastic and the verbal:

> Magritte seemingly returns to the simple correspondence of the image with its legend. Without saying anything, a mute and adequately recognizable figure displays the object in its essence; from the image, a name written below receives its "meaning" or rule for usage. Now, compared to the traditional function of the legend, Magritte's text is doubly paradoxical. It sets out to name something that evidently does not need to be named (the form is too well known, the label too familiar). And at the moment when he should reveal the name, Magritte does so by denying that the object is what it is. (*TNP* 23–24; *CP* 25–26)

7̄2̄ Epistemology at the Blackboard

In Foucault's ekphrasis of *Les deux mystères*, a complicated story is told that involves a variety of actions, voices, and events. The "pipe on the blackboard," accompanied by the words *"Ceci n'est pas une pipe,"* written in an all-too-schoolmasterly hand, is taken to be part of a classroom demonstration. In this case the lesson is an essential step in philosophy: do not confuse images and things. The picture of a pipe, for all its resemblance to the real thing, is certainly not smokable or even tangible. Foucault's *prosopopeia* puts this lesson into the mouth of a pedagogue, so that the whole scene of instruction becomes animated by his interchange with his students. As soon as the teacher speaks, he is compelled by the lesson that he would teach to criticize what he has just said: "But why have we introduced the teacher's voice? Because scarcely has he stated, 'This is a pipe,' before he must correct himself and stutter, 'This is not a pipe, but a drawing of a pipe,' 'This is not a pipe but a sentence saying that this is not a pipe,' 'The sentence "this is not a pipe" is not a pipe,' 'In the sentence "this is not a pipe" *this* is not a pipe: the painting, written sentence, drawing of a pipe—all this is not a pipe'" (*TNP* 30; *CP* 37–38). At least since Plato's *Cratylus*, philosophy has been trying to teach the lesson that one ought not to assimilate words and things, that the order of language must not be confounded with that of the world. And yet as soon as the philosopher speaks, even if the lesson is well taken, questions can arise about that speech itself: the problems that were expelled from the object language may surface in the metalanguage. Of course the regress can be brought to a halt by invoking something like Russell's theory of types, so that rigorous distinctions can be enforced between the various levels of language. But this break may seem abrupt and artificial; if the status of the metalanguage is left open, the conscientious philosopher may have worries like those of the teacher in Foucault's scenario.

In all of this concern for precision in speech and the avoidance of error, there is a certain obsession with that which is excluded. We might say that the progressive attempts to evade the false identification of words, images, paintings, indexical signs, and inscriptions with their objects or referents is haunted by the specter that it seeks to exorcize. And this is the very scene that Foucault sees Magritte as enacting for us:

> Negations multiply themselves, the voice is confused and choked. The baffled master lowers his extended pointer, turns his back to the board, regards the uproarious students, and does not realize that they laugh so loudly because above the blackboard and his stammered denials, a vapor has just risen, little by little taking shape and now creating, precisely and without a doubt, a pipe. "A pipe, a pipe," cry the students, stamping away while the teacher, his voice sinking ever lower, murmurs always with the same obstinacy though no one is listening, "And yet it is not a pipe." He is not mistaken. (*TNP* 30; *CP* 37–38)

And yet he is not completely right either, for what he fails to acknowledge is the "vapor," the floating image or simulacrum that complicates his negations and distinctions. The pedagogical scene constructed here (is it Magritte's or Foucault's?) pertains not only to philosophy's concern with language and reference, but also to the way in which painting has been constituted. The anecdote told of Zeuxis and Parrhasius is paradigmatic: the first painted grapes so realistic that birds tried to eat them; the latter presented him with a draped painting that was to be the rival of that one, but the drapery in fact *was* the painting, and when Zeuxis asked for it to be unveiled, he had to confess that Parrhasius was the superior painter. Painting has had to flirt with the possibility of producing an illusion of the real or a substitute for it, while at the same time preserving a distance from it (as in the ironic distance of the master of the *trompe-l'oeil*). It is this entire history that is condensed, dramatized, and transformed in Foucault's *mise-en-scène*.

73 Resemblance and Similitude

In Magritte, says Foucault, we have "An art of the 'Same,' liberated from the 'as if.' We are farthest from *trompe-l'oeil*" (*TNP* 43; *CP* 60). In the longest chapter of his essay "Seven Seals of Affirmation," he brings together a Nietzschean conception of recurrence and affirmation with Deleuze's notion of the simulacrum. Everything hinges on the distinction between resemblance and similitude: "Resemblance has a 'model,' an original element that orders and hierarchizes the increasingly less faithful copies that can be struck from it. Resemblance presupposes a primary reference that prescribes and classifies. The similar develops in series that have neither beginning nor end, that can be followed in one direction as easily as in another, that obey no hierarchy, but propagate themselves from small differences, among small differences" (*TNP* 44; *CP* 61).

Note that Foucault no longer uses the term *resemblance* in the same sense that he did in *Les mots et les choses*. There resemblance and similitude are both modes of the analogical thinking of the Renaissance, in which the world is seen as a great web of corresponding parts and aspects, linking texts and things and microcosm and macrocosm. Magritte wrote to Foucault after the publication of the earlier book, urging a distinction between resemblance and similitude, according to which things may or may not have relations of similitude with one another (green peas being his example of such things) but "[o]nly thought resembles. It resembles by being what it sees, hears, or knows; it becomes what the world offers it" (*TNP* 57; *CP* 86). Magritte is concerned to formulate a general distinction between two relations here and does not attend to the archaeologically specific context of Foucault's discussion of the way in which premodern knowledge was organized. In *This Is Not a Pipe*, the philosopher uses "resemblance" to designate a relationship of copying, in which a picture, for example, resembles its original by both referring to it and looking like it. Similitude, on the other hand, has become strictly a relation among images without any reference to an external model or a primary instance.[22]

The difference between resemblance and similitude can be described in economic terms as a distinction between appropriation and circulation. Resemblance refers back to an original, to which it belongs and to which it remains subordinate. Similitude is a continuous movement that "circulates the simulacrum as an indefinite and reversible relation of the similar to the similar." What has been erased in similitude is any trace of monarchy or sovereignty; when Foucault says that the latter notions have no place in Magritte, there is surely an echo of the essay on *Las Meninas*, in which the position of the sovereign and the claims of representation are intimately bound together. In discussing the ironically titled *Representation*, Foucault notes how a smaller part of the painting, framed by a balustrade, repeats precisely the scene of the larger picture. The title and the suggestion of a *mise-en-abîme* structure make this work into a tableau of representation or visual presentation itself (representation here is reduced to the presentation of similitude), analogous to the function that Velazquez's painting has with respect to the classical episteme.[23] Foucault remarks that the two images in their similitude are sufficient to generate an infinite series and consequently to abolish any sovereign or monarchical principle: "Even as the exactness of the image functioned as a finger pointing to a model, to a sovereign, unique and exterior 'pattern,' the series of similitudes (and two are enough to establish a series) abolishes this simultaneously real and ideal monarchy" (*TNP* 44–45; *CP* 62). And he asks, "Is it not the role of resemblance to be the sovereign that makes things appear?" (*TNP* 46; *CP* 66).

So there is an analogy between more overtly political regimes of vision and the forms taken by visual art. In the age of sovereignty, as Foucault emphasizes in *Discipline and Punish*, it is the sovereign, his proxy, or the effects of his power that are put on display; this is also the grand age of the portrait, first of royal or aristocratic personages, second, by approximation, of the successful bourgeoisie. The world of political sovereignty requires that originals take precedence over their representations, as the sovereign must be the authentic source of all political acts. In the world of similitude, power circulates from image to image or site to site. In *Las Meninas*, as described by most commentators (and Foucault does not exclude this interpretation), the painter and some of the other figures depicted seem to have paused in their activities to give their attention to the king and queen who have just entered the room. They, or their images on the canvas (and we need not decide between these two possibilities) are reflected in the mirror at the back of the room (and that framed image may even be the painting of a mirror); the painting as a whole embodies the aesthetics of sovereignty both in its commitment to resemblance and in its presentation of the panorama of royal power—king and queen, princess, attendants, and Velazquez himself, who is both an artist of resemblance and an ambitious courtier whose painting has plausibly been read as an attempt to provide a royal legitimation for the art of painting as well as to certify his own position at court.[24]

According to Foucault, the carceral society replaces sovereignty with a structure of power in which no central figure is on display. Uniformity is enforced by the architectures, regulations, and protocols of power, which circulate without end; the gaze is mobilized and no longer exclusively exercised by or directed at any one person. The art of similitude proceeds by means of an analogous circulation of images cut loose from any original. Power, as Foucault insists, is productive and not merely repressive (as the theories based on sovereignty declare); this principle has consequences at several levels. If panoptic machinery produces delinquencies, docile bodies, and perversions, the art of circulating similitudes has the power to eviscerate the supposed original meaning of the image and to force upon us the sense of an indefinite repetition. In this mode of repetition and the simulacrum, "[s]imilitude multiplies different affirmations, which dance together, tilting and tumbling over one another" (*TNP* 46; *CP* 65–66). The echo of the rhetoric of dancing and affirmation from the descriptions of the eternal recurrence in *Zarathustra* seems more than accidental (see the chapters "The Convalescent," "The Other Dancing Song," and "The Seven Seals (or The Yes and Amen Song)." It is in this spirit that Foucault explains how the drawing that resembles a pipe and the text that resembles a text subvert their own resemblance in order to generate "an open network of similitudes" in which explicit negations are transvalued into affirmations: "Each element of 'this is not a pipe' could hold an apparently negative discourse—because it denies, along with resemblance, the assertion of reality resemblance conveys—but one that is basically affirmative: the affirmation of the simulacrum, affirmation of the element within the network of the similar" (*TNP* 47; *CP* 67).

Foucault then proposes to "establish the series of these affirmations," by exploring the different voices that speak in "this is not a pipe." Affirmation is always multiple because it is beyond limit and restriction. Nietzsche asked, "Now that God is dead, who is speaking?"; the question asks whether with the disappearance of the sovereign center there is no longer an authoritative subject to ground texts or utterances (as in the higher criticisms of the Bible and the Homeric question that are paradigmatic for his own work as a philologist). In the wake of the decline of resemblance, linked as it is to the fate of sovereignty, Foucault asks of Magritte's painting, "Who speaks in the statement?" and proceeds to detail seven speakers: the lower pipe, the higher pipe, the inscription, the text and the lower pipe in unison, the two pipes speaking together, the text and the higher pipe, and a "dislocated voice" that speaks of all the painting's elements. (Foucault's principle, as adapted from Deleuze: two are enough to generate a series. Here the series stops with seven, which chimes with the title of the section. Titles, in this book so concerned with titles, must be read as an aspect of Foucault's affirmation of the multiple.) If the lower pipe insists that it is only a drawing, this insistence is echoed and amplified by the higher one, which acknowledges itself to be a "cloudy similitude, referring to nothing," and the other voices add their own variations, "tilting and tumbling over one another." In "The Seven Seals" of Nietzsche's *Zarathustra*, the speaker disperses himself into various voices and functions (e.g., "If I am fond of the sea . . . ," "If my virtue is a dancer's virtue . . . ," "If ever I spread tranquil skies over myself . . ."). What all the voices affirm, in chorus, is the eternal recurrence, the infinite depth of the moment that is experienced as repeated without limit. The moment-of-vision or twinkling of the eye *(Augenblick)* is no longer a mere appearance to be grounded upon or to refer to a more substantial reality; it has acquired its own depth (Z 3.16; *KSA* 4.287–91).

This is analogous to what happens to similitude among the seven affirmations—"seven discourses in a single statement"—that issue from Magritte's painting: "Henceforth similitude is restored to itself—unfolding from itself and folding back upon itself. It is no longer the finger pointing out from the canvas in order to refer to something else. It inaugurates a play of transferences that run, proliferate, propagate, and correspond within the layout of the painting, affirming and representing nothing" (*TNP* 49; *CP* 71). Let us be careful about this "affirming and representing nothing." It is not that there is no affirmation, Foucault seems to be saying here, but that nothing *is* affirmed. It is the affirmation of similitude as sheer image, emptied of meaning and reference. In "Theatrum Philosophicum" Foucault speaks of "the sudden illumination of multiplicity itself—with nothing at its center, at its highest point, or beyond it." Foucault might seem to teeter here on the brink of nihilism, recalling Nietzsche's principle that "humans would rather will nothingness than *not* will" (*GM* III.28; *KSA* 5.412). The disappearance of the center could be taken as a cause for lamentation or as the impetus for a series of desperate efforts to substitute another version of the center for the one that has been lost. Or it might be celebrated as it is here in the form of a dance of similitude.

Characteristically, Foucault speaks in the passage quoted above of the fold *(pli)* of similitude, "unfolding from itself and folding back upon itself." This somewhat elusive notion seems to designate what happens when resistance becomes itself a structure of power; it is not interiority in the classical sense of subjectivity but the inside of the outside, a doubling. For example, as Deleuze suggests, Foucault's late analysis of the Greeks outlines a form of doubling in which one gains mastery over oneself; the *use* of pleasure is not to be driven by it but to take it as an occasion for self-regulation.[25] So here folding and unfolding are to be understood as the diagram created by similitude in which seriality, difference, and repetition efface sovereignty, representation, and originality. What is put into play is neither the regime of the sovereign gaze nor the panoptical apparatus but a visual practice that confutes both through the mobilization and multiplication of the phantasm.

twelve

The Phantasm in the Age of
Mechanical Reproduction

74 Warhol and His Doubles: One Brillo Box or Many?

"Campbell, Campbell, Campbell, Campbell." The logo, label, or title is repeated four times at the end of the brief book on Magritte. Four is the number of multiplicity, the minimum necessary to generate a matrix. It is something other than monism, dualism, or the trinity, which figures so prominently in Christianity and in Hegelian philosophy, which claimed to provide a logical version of that religion. Magritte opens up a world of multiplicity or sheer difference. Foucault's understanding of "the sudden illumination of multiplicity itself" can be thrown into relief by considering another philosophical reading of Warhol, one quite influential in the Anglophone world. Arthur Danto's interpretation of Andy Warhol has been central to his philosophy of art since his first essay in this field, "The Artworld" (1964). The comparison is rendered more intriguing by the fact that at around the same time, Danto helped to inaugurate a tendency among Anglo-American philosophers to take Nietzsche more seriously; his book *Nietzsche as Philosopher* signaled by its title that its subject was no longer to be considered merely as a literary figure or a strange psychological case. Two figures who might have been dismissed as peripheral or even rather silly were thus elevated to positions of philosophical legitimacy. Although Foucault gave less extensive attention to Warhol, his comments (developing those of Deleuze) reveal a markedly different way of understanding his accomplishment. In some respects this difference is parallel to one in the American and European receptions of Warhol's work: while his compatriots still tend to see him as a publicist for the consumer culture, artists like Sigmar Polke and Gerhard Richter have articulated a deeply ambivalent strain in his innovative images. Finally, the distinction involves two quite different responses to Hegel and his thesis concerning the dissolution *(Auflösung)* of art (sometimes referred to misleadingly as its death). Danto can be credited with introducing a strongly historical perspective into aesthetics; but we can use his reading of Warhol to contrast a self-confessed, if reformed, Hegelian sense of history with a Foucauldian archaeology.

Danto has sometimes expressed his own sense of the apparent incongruity involved in the fact that he takes seriously Warhol's *Brillo Boxes* and images of Campbell Soup cans, an art that not only appears superficial but seems to glory in its superficiality. Danto regards Warhol (with a good bit of irony) as a genuinely philosophical artist, one who in his view is "the nearest thing to a philosophical genius the history of art has produced."[1] Warhol's genius, as Danto explains it, was to have realized that the nature or content of a visual surface alone could never be a necessary or sufficient condition for something being a work of art. Danto has frequently recalled his revelatory experience in 1964 when, seeing Warhol's *Brillo Boxes* at a gallery, he realized that it had posed the question "What is the difference between a work of art and a mere thing?" The answer that Danto gave in his seminal essay "The Artworld," and that he later elaborated in *The Transfiguration of the Commonplace* and many other writings, is that something becomes a work of art, or enters the art world, insofar as it is enabled or enfranchised by a certain theoretical context. Theory is not external to the production and understanding of art but constitutes things as art and constitutes the art world itself. For Danto this realization was sparked by his experience of Warhol in the way that Aristotle's conception of tragedy, the West's first major theory of art, was provoked by his meditating on Homer and Sophocles, an analogy playfully suggested by Danto himself: "Aristotle is shown contemplating the bust of Homer, but Danto . . ."[2]

Foucault, as we have seen, also views Warhol as a revolutionary artist whose work is emblematic of a major shift in our relationship to images. Yet what Foucault emphasizes about Warhol's work is quite distinct from what Danto stresses. Foucault sees the point of Warhol's productions in their repetitions, multiplicities, and proliferations of what we call "the same" image (although what is meant by the same is precisely an issue for Foucault and Deleuze): Campbell Soup cans, Brillo boxes, faces of Marilyn Monroe or Jackie Kennedy arrayed in series, grids, or matrices that could go on to infinity. Danto, in contrast, is struck by the fact that a *single* Warhol Brillo box is indistinguishable from a Brillo box on a supermarket shelf. This is enough, for him, to suggest the philosophical question "Why were *these* boxes art when their originals were just boxes?"[3] The force of Danto's question is heightened when we learn that the Brillo box was designed by James Harvey, whose day job as a commercial artist supported his work as an abstract expressionist painter (Harvey at one time threatened to sue Warhol for plagiarism).[4] As we will see, it is significant that Danto speaks here of "boxes" or the equivalent in the plural; however, he thematizes the issue of indiscernibility rather than plurality. The same emphasis is apparent at the beginning of *The Transfiguration of the Commonplace*, where Danto asks us to imagine a set of six square red canvases, each with a different title and a different meaning, ranging from "The Red Sea" to a Communist "Red Square" to an abstract "Red Square" after the manner of Malevich.[5] The point in producing this *Gedankenexperiment* is that each one of these painting is distinct in meaning from the others. What might appear to be a series is, in fact, an assemblage of unique works, each one enfranchised in the art world by a different convention (representationalism for "The Red Sea," ideological symbolism for the Communist "Red Square," and abstraction for "The Red Square" à la Malevich.

Let us join Danto as he stands at the Castelli Gallery, asking himself why Warhol's *Brillo Boxes*, unlike its apparent double in the supermarket, is a work of art. In "The Artworld" he writes:

> Mr. Andy Warhol, the pop artist, displays facsimiles of Brillo cartons, piled high, in neat stacks, as in the stockroom of the supermarket. . . . [W]e may forget questions of intrinsic value and ask why the Brillo people cannot manufacture art and why Warhol cannot *but* make artworks. . . .
>
> What in the end makes a difference between a Brillo box and a work of art consisting of a Brillo box is a certain theory of art. It is the theory that takes it up into the world of art, and keeps it from collapsing into the real object it is. Of course, without the theory,

one is unlikely to see it as art, and in order to see it as part of the
artworld, one must have mastered a good deal of artistic theory as
well as a considerable amount of the history of recent New York
painting.[6]

At this point in the argument, Danto introduces the conception of
an artistic matrix, generated by the availability of artistic predicates,
such as "is representational" or "is expressionist," and he demonstrates
that at any time such a matrix will allow 2^n possible "styles" or forms
of art, (where n equals the number of artistically relevant predicates).
Several consequences of the matrix are then derived: every addition of
a new artistic predicate will double the number of possible art forms,
the addition of new predicates will retroactively affect the ways in
which it is possible to think of past works, created before that predicate
was available, and any insistence that all art (or art selected for a specific
purpose, such as an exhibition) be characterized by one predicate (and
not its negation) such as "is representational" will reduce the number
of possible styles to $2^n/2$. Presumably the artistic predicate introduced
by Warhol was something like "is indistinguishable from a real thing,"
where "real" has the sense, at least, of "nonartistic."
    What is especially interesting for understanding the later narrative
of art after modernism, as fashioned by Danto, is the contrast he draws
between a "purist" approach to art, based on an implied appeal to the
style matrix, and Warhol's innovation. The purists here are artists like
Ad Reinhardt, who reduced his paintings to black canvasses—that is,
the purists of recent times (and a fortiori the last purists, if art has in
some sense come to an end). They have worked their way through
modernism, successively giving up pretensions to optical realism, all
reference to the visual world, and finally any claim to individual expression. It is an important part of Danto's argument to show that purism
is mistaken in thinking that it has identified the essence of art: "[N]otice
that, if there are m artistically relevant predicates, there is always a
bottom row with m minuses. This row is apt to be occupied by purists.
Having scoured their canvasses clear of what they regard as inessential,
they credit themselves with having distilled out the essence of art. But
this is just their fallacy: exactly as many artistically relevant predicates
stand true of their square monochromes as stand true of any member
of the Artworld, and they can *exist* as artworks only insofar as 'impure'
paintings exist."
    After explaining that an "artistic breakthrough" consists in intro-
ducing a new artistic predicate that adds a row to the matrix, Danto
goes on to speak of Warhol's art so as to suggest that that is precisely

what it did, thus shattering the illusions of the purists: "Brillo boxes enter the artworld with that same ironic incongruity the *commedia dell'arte* characters bring into *Ariadne auf Naxos*. Whatever is the artistically relevant predicate in virtue of which they gain their entry, the rest of the Artworld becomes that much the richer in having the opposite predicate available and applicable to its members. And to return to the views of Hamlet . . . Brillo boxes may reveal us to ourselves as well as anything might: as a mirror held up to nature, they might serve to catch the conscience of our kings."[7]

Now I have rehearsed these important passages from "The Artworld" both in order to highlight Danto's explicit claim about Warhol and the art world and also to emphasize some assumptions he makes and consequences he draws that are not so explicit and have not been much noticed. First, the explicit claim is that Warhol shows us that artworks may be visually indiscernible from real things and so adds a whole new row to the matrix. He bursts the bubble of abstract expressionist or hard-edge purism in the way that the heavy and all-too-serious tone of tragic opera is transformed when Richard Strauss introduces a troupe of comic singers onto the same stage. ("Pop" could be the sound of the bubble bursting.) The criticism of the dogmatic purism of the American artists of the 1950s is a recurring theme in Danto's writing: "Artmaking in New York in the 1950's transpired in a mist of romantic theorizing and an almost religious celebration of what one might call the blood and flesh of painting, namely the material stuff of art. . . . It was a dour, puritanical period when artists walked Tenth Street in their paint-streaked garments to demonstrate their oneness with their art, and gathered at The Club to shout themselves out over minute questions of orthodoxy."[8] Implicit in Danto's argument is a far-reaching metanarrative concerning the meaning of the history of art that could, without too much of a stretch, be called Hegelian.

75 Hegelian Themes: On the Comedy of Art and Its Death

Danto's celebration of the comic has two Hegelian aspects: it marks the supremacy of thought or theory over the material, and it suggests the Hegelian view of history (or at least the history of art) as tending toward an ever-greater self-consciousness in which the art spirit *recognizes* what it has been doing in all of its earlier incarnations. Comedy, Danto would seem to argue along with Hegel, is more profound than tragedy. While Danto will later develop and articulate this comic Hegelian theme, a theme, by the way, that greatly qualifies what might otherwise be a gloomy meditation on the end of art, there are two aspects of the concluding paragraph of "The Artworld" quoted above ("Brillo boxes enter the artworld . . .") to which I wish to call attention. Both help to mark some differences with Foucault and to confirm the essentially Hegelian tendencies of Danto's own thought. These are the mention of "Brillo boxes" (plural) and the notion that Warhol's art can serve its contemporaries as a significant means of self-knowledge. Although Danto occasionally speaks of the Brillo boxes in the plural, he has little to say, here or elsewhere, about the effect or significance of the fact that these boxes are indeed many. Perhaps the closest he comes to emphasizing this point is in his observation that by using mechanical means of reproduction, Warhol demonstrates that the touch of the artist's hand is not necessarily required for the making of art. While Walter Benjamin developed such observations in his essay "The Work of Art in the Age of Mechanical Reproduction," in order to suggest that it is just such changes that rob the work of its traditional aura, Danto could be seen as insisting that, regardless of the use of such techniques and the production of multiples, a certain theoretical matrix gives even the *Brillo Box*, which is indistinguishable from a Brillo box, the special status or aura that makes it continuous with other works in the art world. Moreover, Danto points out that the choice of images (whether commercial products like Brillo or Campbell's Soup or instantly recognized figures like Jackie, Mao, or Elvis) confirms and reinforces the artist's physical independence of his work as well as the project of turning the mirror on consumer society. Yet even in recognizing this, Danto speaks of the production of identical objects in such a way as to elide the fact that what is most characteristic of Warhol's work (after 1962 anyway) is the presentation of these repeated objects in a grid or series—a roomful of Brillo boxes, a rectangle of thirty Mona Lisas, a room plastered with wallpaper repeating the blank gaze of a cow—in which repetition is not just implicit in the artist's practice but is intrinsic to the work's reception by the viewer. So Danto in 1987, just after Warhol's death: "Once the mechanical, and hence the precisely repetitious, had become the form and substance of the new art, the barriers were removed against its mass production, so that the artwork could be a kind of industrial product and the studio itself a kind of factory [Recall that Warhol's studio was called The Factory]."[9] It is not just that indefinitely many of these images can be and are produced, but that many are simultaneously presented so as to suggest the effect of infinite replication.

Finally there is Danto's humanistic reading of Warhol's work as serving "to catch the conscience of our kings." Danto, engaged as he is in "deep interpretation" of Warhol's art, is not necessarily claiming that the artist aimed consciously at provoking such self-knowledge (although Warhol wrote and said a number of things that would support such a view—but then, he said many other things that would not). Rather Danto is making the (traditional) Hegelian point that art at its highest is a reading, articulation, and presentation of the collective soul (spirit or *Geist*) to itself:

> The images he singled out and displayed—of Marilyn, Jackie, Liz, Elvis, Mickey, Campbell's soup—define our common consciousness, for we are bonded through the fact that we recognize, instantly and without having to be told, who or what these are. This is so even if, or especially because, we have never seen the originals. . . . The collective work of Warhol is less a portrait of contemporary consciousness than it is contemporary consciousness itself, objectified in the images that express our fantasies and feelings. . . . In this sense *we are one with this artist*, whose own image is almost unique among artists; it has a reality on a par with his subjects, with which it is one.[10]

There is a deep affinity that links these three positions: the supremacy of theory, the idea of art as self-knowledge in which artist, audience, and work are ultimately identical, and the conception of art as achieving a comic end or resolution in which it comes to know the meaning of its own past. The confluence of these positions leads to the claim, cited above, that "with the philosophical coming of age of art, visuality drops away." Putting it very briefly, Danto's philosophy of art eliminates or drastically reduces the role of ekphrasis, the verbal account of visual works, which has played such a large role in visual aesthetics. If a *Brillo Box* is indiscernible from a Brillo box, there is little point in describing its visual appearance or effect; it raises philosophical questions not through its appearance but through its status as a work of art. Yet there are philosophically oriented descriptions or ekphrases of Warhol's work, notably the ones offered by Deleuze and Foucault, that challenge Danto's interpretation of that art and are embedded in an approach that perhaps bears a relationship, however revisionary, to the tradition of ekphrasis analogous to the relation that Danto's theory sustains with Hegel's.

I call the principle of Danto's philosophy of art Hegelian because for Hegel the history of art consists in a march to comic self-consciousness. Indeed, Danto's comments on Warhol's achieving an identity as both subject and object of art that puts him at one with its audience can be read as a slightly modified version of Hegel's account of Greek comedy, which is for him the "death" or end of Greek art (and because of the special role of Greek art, it is a paradigm for art's *telos* generally). In tragedy, let us recall, the actor wears a mask, perhaps analogous to the purist pose of 1950s painters. In comedy, Hegel says, the self "plays with the mask": "The religion of art is consummated and has completely returned into itself. . . . it is the individual consciousness in the certainty of itself that exhibits itself as this absolute power. . . . This unity, too, is not unconscious. . . . on the contrary, the actual self of the actor coincides with what he impersonates, just as the spectator is completely at home in the drama performed before him and sees himself playing in it."[11]

For Hegel this comic resolution is the fulfillment of art's destiny, a resolution of its aims, which is sometimes described as its death. Danto sometimes seems to share in this philosophical narrative of the death of art. Could it be that this story depends upon a certain reading of an exemplary artist or style, a reading that might have at least one plausible alternative? Danto has been taken to task by Rosalind Krauss for identifying the death of art with an art that, as it happens, seems to exemplify his own philosophical principles. The claims of this death, she says in effect, are greatly exaggerated.[12] We can imagine Krauss, as a theorist of the grid and the multiple, sympathizing with Foucault's account as opening up a way of understanding recent art in its novelty and productivity. As David Carrier has suggested in *Artwriting*, a book that owes much to Danto, claims about the death of art tend to enable certain kinds of narratives, which are then deployed precisely to validate this conclusion. Yet it is somewhat odd that Carrier cites Krauss and not Danto as such a death-of-art theorist.[13] His reason for doing so seems to be that he sees Krauss as claiming that the advent of photography has brought the traditional history of painting to an end, since exact replication of visual appearances or the mechanical production of a work of art is now possible. But from a Foucauldian perspective, it could be said that Krauss's emphasis on the photograph is a way of pointing out the new resources open to an art through use of the reproductions, grids, and series that photography makes possible. She would not be announcing the death of art but the death of a certain humanistic mode of art, as Foucault proclaimed the death of man. Surely if one were looking for an account of art's history (or archaeology) that would enable a conception of living art, one could do worse than look to Foucault, who sees exact resemblance as establishing a mode of repetition or the era of the simlulacrum rather than as foreclosing the possibilities of art. Could it be that the question of whether the history of art will have an advantage or disadvantage for life (as Nietzsche says) now depends on how we interpret a Brillo box or a soup can?

⁷⁶ Stupidity and the "Eternal Phantasm"

When Foucault comes to discuss Warhol, he implicitly rejects the three linked Hegelian positions shared by Danto. His remarks on this artist appear in the context of a reading of two books by Gilles Deleuze, during which he recalls how Flaubert's novel *Bouvard and Pécuchet* achieves an inspired presentation of the superficial and the entropic when it depicts its eponymous characters as abandoning their ambitions to return to their roles as mere copyists, turning out endless repetitions of the same thing. (Foucault is especially sensitive here, as he was in his essay *The Temptation of Saint Anthony*, to the way in which Flaubert's writing can be a prelude or a provocation to a certain kind of visual experience, to an explosion of images.) The suggestion that Foucault is pursuing a deep meaning here would be an oxymoron, but he clearly takes Flaubert's and Warhol's ways of presenting the identical and the repetitive to be distinctive operations, which, if they do not confirm or advance our quest for meaning, or for identifying with the artist or our own times, certainly do succeed in a kind of ascetic emptying out of meaning. But let us read Foucault's long paragraph on Warhol once more, repeating this meditation on repetition:

> This is the greatness of Warhol with his canned foods, senseless accidents, and his series of advertising smiles: the oral and nutritional equivalence of those half-open lips, teeth, tomato sauce, that hygiene based on detergents; the equivalence of death in the cavity of an eviscerated car, at the top of a telephone pole and at the end of a wire, and between the glistening, steel blue arms of the electric chair. "It's the same either way," stupidity says, while sinking into itself and infinitely extending its nature with the things it says of itself; "Here or there, it's always the same thing; what difference if the colors vary, if they're darker or lighter. It's all so senseless—life, women, death! How ridiculous this stupidity!" But in concentrating on this boundless monotony, we find the sudden illumination of multiplicity itself—with nothing at its center, at its highest point, or beyond it—a flickering of light that travels even faster than the eyes and successively lights up the moving labels and the captive snapshots that refer to each other to eternity, without ever saying anything: suddenly, arising from the background of the old

Figure 20. Andy Warhol, *Marilyn Monroe's Lips*, 1962. © 2003 Andy Warhol Foundation for the Visual Arts/ARS, New York. Photo copyright The Andy Warhol Foundation, Inc./Art Resource, New York

inertia of equivalences, the striped form of the event tears through the darkness, and the eternal phantasm informs that soup can, that singular and depthless face. (*LCMP* 189; *DE* 2.93–94)

For Foucault the serial, multiple, and repeated images of Warhol's art come into play precisely to destroy the relation of resemblance so crucial to Danto. According to Danto, when we look at a (single) Warhol Brillo box, we are forced to reflect on the fact that it is identical, so far as the eye can see, with an actual Brillo box. It is a theory that distinguishes Warhol's creation from its exact model in the supermarket. Danto would reject the "stupidity" that sees no point in this exact replication of the mundane. But in rejecting that response, Danto thinks like a Platonist, who sees the form or idea, not itself visible, that differentiates the artwork from a mere thing.

But was Warhol thinking like a Platonist? His work took a turn toward multiplicity and repetition in 1962. Before that year he produced a number of objects that take their themes and format from commercial products or popular images (comic strips, soup cans and the like), but in 1962 he begins to make multiples, such as paintings or silk screens of Campbell's Soup cans, Marilyn, Elvis, Coke bottles, Cadillacs, and dollar bills (fig. 20). In 1964 he begins to make three-dimensional replicas of soup cans and Brillo boxes, including the exhibition of Brillo boxes that caught Danto's attention. Warhol continued to make multiples of various sorts, sometimes with variations in the coloring of the repeated image, sometimes without variation (these include car crashes, race riots, electric chairs, atomic bombs, "Last Suppers," and images of Mao and of Joseph Beuys). Warhol's flip comments about his work often highlight this penchant for repetition and may take on a new resonance after considering Foucault's observations on "the sudden illumination of multiplicity itself." Consider, for example:

> I've been quoted a lot as saying "I like boring things." Well, I said it and I meant it. But that doesn't mean I'm not bored by them. Of course, what I think is boring must not be the same as what other people think it is, since I could never stand to watch all the most popular action shows on TV, because they're essentially the same plots and the same shots and the same cuts over and over again. Apparently, most people love watching the same basic thing, as long as the details are different. But I'm just the opposite: if I'm going to sit and watch the same thing I saw the night before, I don't want it to be essentially the same—I want it to be *exactly* the same. Because the more you look at the same exact thing, the more the meaning goes away, and the better and emptier you feel.[14]

This "better and emptier" can be heard as Warhol's way of marking something very much like Foucault's notion of the illumination of a multiplicity with "nothing at its center." Even Warhol's self-indulgently trivial book *The Philosophy of Andy Warhol (From A to B and Back Again)* makes the same point, at least by its subtitle. Historians of art and critics have tended to be sensitive to Warhol's multiples. Robert Rosenblum writes of the artist's tendency to create "a world of multiple replication, where even the artist's self-portrait is doubled as a means of diffusing any one-to-one focus on what might once have been a singular revelation of face and feeling at a particular time and place."[15] Foucault looks not at a single Brillo box, Campbell Soup can, or picture of Liz, Elvis, or Marilyn, but at the matrix, grid, or series in which these are repeated—if not to infinity, at least with the suggestion that the repetition could go on indefinitely. He would endorse the title of Warhol's multiples of the *Mona Lisa: Thirty Are Better Than One*. Of what does the "sudden illumination of multiplicity itself" consist? The images are freed of the bond of resemblance to their "original" and "refer to each other to eternity"; they do not ever *say* anything, because there is no longer a subject to which they refer and about which they would speak. Through repetition Warhol effects an emptying out of meaning, what the Greeks called a *kenosis,* that overcomes "the old inertia of equivalences." In claiming that "the eternal phantasm informs that soup can, that singular and depthless face," Foucault draws not on Platonic or Hegelian philosophy but on the ancient conception of the phantasm, especially as elaborated by Klossowski and Deleuze.

77 Pop without a Patriarch: Deleuze, Difference, and Warhol

The observations on Warhol that I have quoted appear toward the end of Foucault's essay "Theatrum Philosophicum"; it is devoted to Deleuze's books *Difference and Repetition* and *Logic of Sense,* which celebrate the effort to articulate a philosophy of the phantasm or the simulacrum. *Phantasm* is found in Plato's *Sophist,* which distinguishes between the levels of original, copy, and phantasm.[16] The Epicureans held that objects throw off or radiate infinitely many phantasms or simulacra, and so they are taken by Deleuze and Foucault as providing a model of thinking that avoids the closures and unities of Platonic or Hegelian dialectics.[17] Deleuze sees the Platonic project as a war with the phantasm, a war that forces Plato to acknowledge the name of his enemy. Deleuze's attempt to reverse Platonism (an effort at transvaluation in which he acknowledges Nietzsche as a precursor) consists, to put it very schematically, in replacing a representationalist image of thought with a form of thinking that understands difference and repetition as primary features of being that need not be traced back to concepts of identity and resemblance. Deleuze likens this revolution in thought to one that has occurred in the history of art: "[T]he theory of thought is like painting: it needs that revolution which took art from representation to abstraction. This is the aim of a theory of thought without image."[18] Painting abandons the image, but not visuality, through abstraction; Deleuze, who praises Foucault's diagrammatic thought, seems to allow a space for a thought that still works with the visual, even if it is not tied to a specific image. For such a thought, "there is no center, but always decenterings, series that register the halting passage from presence to absence, from excess to deficiency" (*LCMP* 165; *DE* 2.76). Even the nature of repetition is transformed in this perspective; it will no longer be a "dreary succession of the identical" but will manifest a "displaced difference" (*LCMP* 182; *DE* 2.88). That is, it is possible to emphasize the multiplicity in repetition, the fact that each repetition, as a repetition, is at least numerically different from other repetitions, rather than focusing on the object or original of that which is repeated.

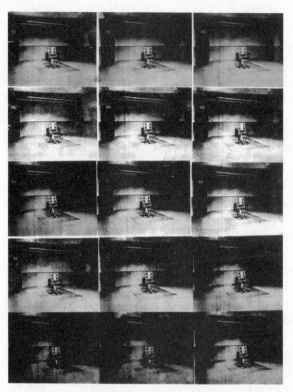

Let us now read Foucault's passage on Warhol more slowly (quoted in sec. 68). In this ekphrasis Foucault attempts to describe the visual impression or effect of seeing multiple images of Marilyn's lips, Campbell Soup cans, or electric chairs (fig. 21). Danto, by contrast, simply notes that these are all recognizable forms; they are all so well known, presumably, that there is no need to articulate what we see or might see when we look at them. The element of surprise or novelty in this art would come not from anything specific to our experience of seeing it, but from the question "Why is this art?" that it is said to raise. It is not that Danto has any incapacity for discussing visual art in a concrete way; quite on the contrary, he is an accomplished art critic, and it would be superfluous here to quote samples of his illuminating accounts of other artworks.[19] But it is precisely with regard to Warhol, whom he considers the closest thing to a philosophical genius in the history of art, that Danto becomes mute with respect to anything like a traditional, critical account of the work's look. At the point where art turns into philosophy, there is no need to see it simply as art. The tone of the canonical ekphrases in Western criticism, a tone that can be heard in Foucault's text, is quite different. Philostratus and Diderot, for example, writing in the third and the eighteenth centuries, are typically describing works that depict well-known events of myth or history or (in the case of some of the salon paintings that are Diderot's subject) domestic scenes whose iconological meaning is not obscure. But the ekphrases in their writings move beyond this recognition to a sense of wonder or astonishment at the way that the artist has handled these themes. The movement from recognition to wonder is often marked by a dialogical style. Philostratus's guide speaks to a boy, leading him through a complex gallery of paintings; the boy, it is said or implied, understands what is represented, but the docent goes beyond this recognition in encouraging him to see what is distinctive or unusual in the artistry that is displayed. Diderot frequently produces fictional dialogues about the works of the salon, creating literary and philosophical effects analogous to those in *Rameau's Nephew* or *D'Alembert's Dream;* as in a Platonic dialogue, it is what happens between the speakers, when one's observation builds upon or contradicts another, that helps to evoke the best conversations (actual or virtual) that we have about art.[20]

In Foucault's ekphrasis he imagines two voices or positions, one of which he calls "stupidity"; the other is unnamed, but the context, as we shall see, allows us to identify it with thought. Yet "stupidity" is not merely a way of designating a lack of intelligence or sensitivity, although it is not uncommon in this genre to contrast the perspective of those who just don't get it with that of those who do. Danto, for example, frequently has recourse to such a device, as in "The Artworld," where he invents a Mr. Testadura, who cannot see (or, specifically, cannot *tell*) the difference between the artwork that is a bed painted by Robert Rauschenberg and a bed (not an artwork) that just happens to be smeared with paint. As he does elsewhere, Danto introduces this fictional persona in order to demonstrate that the question "what is art?" arises in an interesting form only when we have two items, one being an artwork and one not, that are indiscernible in appearance. But this is not the purpose of Foucault's multiplication of voices in the text we are considering. What he understands by stupidity emerges in his discussion of *Bouvard and Pécuchet* and of Deleuze, who also uses the term in a technical sense. Foucault emphasizes the way in which Deleuze's two books bring together two markers of or ways of perceiving difference: through the event and the phantasm. The event is singular and, as event, escapes categories. The world, the self, and God are the traditional totalities by means of which the sheer difference of the event and the phantasm is obscured. Categorical thought, that is, thought in the service of categories, relentlessly carries out this process of unification and homogenization, and it leads ultimately to dialectical thought. "Difference can only be liberated through the invention of an acategorical thought," writes Foucault (*LCMP* 186; *DE* 2.91). Following Deleuze, he discerns two modes of breaking with categorical thought, stupidity and thinking. Stupidity is the first stage of a process that moves toward an illumination of difference; it is not to be despised altogether, but there is a danger of getting stuck in it, like Bouvard and Pécuchet, who disdain the mistakes of others but fail to think difference as such: "Thus, we court danger in wanting to be free from categories; no sooner do we abandon their organizing principle than we face the magma of stupidity. At a stroke we risk being surrounded not by a marvelous multiplicity of differences, but by equivalences, ambiguities, the 'it all comes down to the same thing,' a levelling uniformity, and the thermodynamism of every miscarried effort" (*LCMP* 188–89; *DE* 2.93).[21] *Thinking* acategorically means not simply accepting or embracing this stupidity but confronting it. And here, on the verge of his ekphrasis of Warhol, it may be more than an unreflective habit that leads Foucault to adopt philosophy's classical language of vision: "Stupidity is contemplated: sight penetrates its domain and becomes fascinated; it carries one gently along and its action is mimed in the abandonment of oneself; we support ourselves upon its amorphous fluidity; we await the first leap of an imperceptible difference, and blankly, without fever, we watch to see the glimmer of light return" (*LCMP* 189; *DE* 2.93). This helps us to read the passage that begins with "This is the greatness of Warhol." Stupidity not only says "It's the same either way," when confronted by these repetitious images; it also sinks into itself and extends itself by saying more. It displaces itself onto the objects seen when it says: "Here or there, it's always the same thing; what difference if the colors vary, if they're darker or lighter. It's all so senseless—life, women, death! How ridiculous this stupidity!" Foucault asks us to pay attention to what stupidity says, to see how it reveals itself when it speaks of what it sees. It notes differences, those of coloring, for example, in order to deny their relevance. And when it expands on what it sees, its choice of words is significant: "life, women, death!" It has already been suggested that it is the life of commodities that is at stake, and the fetishized images of sexual desire (as in the Marilyns) that are offered to us, along with the death that haunts the automobile crashes and the electric chairs. But are these not the themes or *topoi* of difference and repetition themselves?

Certainly this is what Deleuze suggested in *Difference and Repetition* when he came to speak of Warhol, whom he sees as (deliberately or not) doing much more than disclosing the common content of our culture to us. Here again it is Deleuze who finds the ethical and political meaning of art in its ability to thematize the repetition that is all around us:

> The more our daily life appears standardized, stereotyped and sub-ject to an accelerated reproduction of objects of consumption, the more art must be injected into it in order to extract from it that lit-tle difference which plays simultaneously between other levels of repetition, and even in order to make the two extremes resonate—namely, the habitual series of consumption and the instinctual series of destruction and death. Art thereby connects the tableau of cruelty with that of stupidity, and discovers underneath the consumption a schizophrenic clattering of the jaws, and underneath the most igno-ble destructions of war, still more processes of destruction.[22]

The truth of art is not in imitation, but in repetition. This "critical and revolutionary power" can "lead us from the sad repetitions of habit to the profound repetitions of memory and then to the ultimate repeti-tions of death in which our freedom is played out." Deleuze cites three examples of such art: the repetitive structure of modern music (e.g., Berg), the new novel or cinema (e.g., Butor, Resnais), and Pop Art, which he describes as having "pushed the copy, copy of the copy, etc., to that extreme point at which it reverses and becomes a simulacrum (such as Warhol's remarkable 'serial' series, in which all the repetitions of habit, memory and death are conjugated)."[23] Habit, memory, and death—these are echoed (repeated) in Foucault's evocation of advertis-ing images that call to mind the most banal routines of life and of the pictures of automobile crashes and the electric chair.

Together, Deleuze and Foucault suggest a strongly ethical reading of Warhol and Pop Art, one that becomes perspicuous in the light of Deleuze's essay "Lucretius and the Simulacrum." There Lucretius is portrayed as a great pioneer of philosophical naturalism, leading hu-mans away from the theological conceptions of the eternal and the tran-scendent. By producing a naturalistic account of the images that spur our fears and fantasies, he becomes a hero of philosophical liberation. Along with Spinoza and Nietzsche, he is both a great demystifier and an affirmative thinker who undermines the sources of anxiety. Lucre-tius did this by a now-implausible account of the dynamics of per-ception, in which he claimed that objects are constantly emitting the thinnest of films, which by accidental combination and variation can constitute the objects of baseless hopes and fears.[24] Warhol comes upon the scene in a world where the media of photography, television, and film are in fact constantly producing such simulacra, in a mechanical and electronic variation of Lucretius's theory that could not have been foreseen. The Foucauldian-Deleuzian reading of Warhol is that he shows us the very repetitive filminess of these fantasies, demonstrating their phantasmatic quality and so emptying them of the obsessive link with hope and fear that formerly held us captive.

Even more explicitly and repeatedly than Foucault, Deleuze associates the repetitions of the image with Nietzsche's thought of eternal recurrence, so that Warhol becomes, in effect, the illustrator of that thought within the world of commerce and mass art. It is a remarkable suggestion that the most deliberately "stupid" of twentieth-century painters should become the voice of the nineteenth-century's most abysmal, most difficult thought. Throughout *Difference and Repetition*, Deleuze plays a series of variations on Nietzsche's thought. Very early on he suggests that Nietzsche (along with Kierkegaard) must be thought of as having introduced a theatrical dimension into philosophy, as having found a way to embody or perform thought, not merely representing it. So he sees, as few other readers have done, that *Thus Spoke Zarathustra*, Nietzsche's self-styled "greatest gift" to mankind, needs to be staged, so far as possible: "*Zarathustra* is conceived entirely within philosophy, but also entirely for the stage. Everything in it is scored and visualized, put in motion and made to walk or dance. How can it be read without searching for the exact sound of the cries of the higher man, how can the prologue be read without staging the episode of the tightrope walker which opens the whole story?"[25] Deleuze opposes the theater of repetition to the theater of representation. The latter operates with words, faces, and characters in order to create the image of a stable world; the former deploys language, gestures, masks, phantoms, and specters, so as to act more directly on its audience, to force it into motion rather than producing only the image of motion. In coming to read (repeatedly) Nietzsche's narration of eternal recurrence, Deleuze insists that we miss the point of this thought if we imagine that it has to do with the reappearance of the same or the similar. It is just such identities that Nietzsche is challenging. Only differences return. The force of the "same" in the formula "eternal recurrence of the same" is simply that the different recurs in all its multiplicity; that is the "same" and nothing else. At the conclusion of *Difference and Repetition*, after having spoken of that repetition of simulacra in modern art which can counter the illusions of consumption, we learn that the content of the eternal return is "simulacra, and simulacra alone."[26] Nietzsche, Deleuze suggests allusively, explained this in that famous one-page history of philosophy, "How the 'True World' Finally Became a Fable: History of an Error," in *Twilight of the Idols*. That passage ought to be read, he claims, as "the history of representation, the history of the icons." Recall that the six "stages" of the history that Nietzsche relates are eminently theatrical and visual. Expanding on Deleuze's suggestion, let me sketch a way of reading this controversial little story as the outline of a theater of philosophy. Beginning with Plato, Nietzsche constructs a series of ways in which philosophy has represented the "true world" or has begun to dispense with it. Each stage is accompanied by a stage direction or setting, so that we might imagine the narrative as a sequence of tableaus. Consider, for example, the third or Kantian stage of the representational error:

> 3. The true world, unattainable, undemonstrable, cannot be promised, but even when merely thought of a consolation, a duty, an imperative.

> (Fundamentally the same old sun, but shining through mist and scepticism; the idea grown sublime, pale, northerly, Königsbergian.)

At first the true world was said to be accessible to the wise man; Plato claims to live in the truth, to have a vision of the Good, or, speaking analogically, of the sun. Then it is thought that such visions must be postponed, reserved for the pious or the virtuous after death (as Paul says, "now we see through a glass darkly, but then we shall see face to face"). Kant makes the true world into a world in itself, one that can at best be postulated rather than promised. He would like to see the sun, but his weather forecast is such that no true sighting is possible; only the aesthetic traces, such as those he analyzes in his theory of the sublime, give us a hint of what such a presentation would be. In this "history of the icons," each image, each stage setting supposes some modality of full presence. The metaphysics of presence not only requires an aesthetics of presence but is now seen to depend upon it. Nietzsche, who had developed a theater of philosophy, turned the table on his predecessors by reading them all, including the staid and apparently antitheatrical Kant, as actors and directors *manqué*. Following Kant, the positivists think that the true world must be intrinsically invisible, and the free spirits, following them, imagine that it can be abolished and so consider themselves set free to frolic in a world of appearances cut loose from their imaginary foundation. At this point, the stage directions become even more explicit:

> 6. We have abolished the true world: what world is left? The apparent world perhaps? . . . But no! With the real world we have also abolished the apparent world!

> (Mid-day; moment of the shortest shadow; end of the longest error; zenith of mankind; INCIPIT ZARATHUSTRA.)

"INCIPIT ZARATHUSTRA": in other words, the theater of Zarathustra begins here. The free spirits were still in thrall to the imagery of representational metaphysics, insofar as they supposed that what would survive the disappearance of the true world would be the appearances to which it was sometimes opposed and which were sometimes thought of as representing it. Such an "apparent world" would be a world of stable phenomena, appearances with a certain identity conceived after the manner of the abandoned true world. It would be still something of a shadow of the dead God (GS 108; KSA 3.467). To stage thought in the manner of Zarathustra, Deleuze and Foucault imply, would be to let the simulacra play, to let them float free of the illusory foundation. It is this angle of vision that is suggested by Nietzsche's talk of the abyss and of perspectivism; and it is the point of view for discerning the filmy simulacra in Magritte's paintings or the repetitive images of Warhol with "nothing at their center." To stage Zarathustra is to see things not with the hard stare of representational theater, but with a playful glance, in the twinkling of an eye.

78 Photogenic Painting: The Frenzy of the Circulating Image

Gérard Fromanger is a contemporary French artist not much known in the Anglophone world, where his work has seldom been exhibited. For a booklet accompanying a 1975 exhibition of Fromanger's work, "Le désir est partout," Foucault contributed an essay, "La peinture photogénique," situating the images in the context of a history of the complex relations between photography, painting, and related arts and techniques since the mid-nineteenth century. The essay positions Fromanger's paintings with respect to the culture of the mass image that they both reflect and resist. The exhibition and the booklet coincided with the publication of Discipline and Punish. "Photogenic Painting" is a statement of Foucault's view of the role of images in a hyper-commodified society. It may have been the political events of 1968 that led to the abandonment of the Manet project and a concentration on disciplinary institutions; here, in any case, is an analysis of how art might interrupt a world of manipulated advertising, publicity, and mass media. Contrary to some of his earliest comments on the Panopticon and to the views of a number of his critics, Foucault did not believe that the late twentieth century was a panoptical society; it is better described by Deleuze as a "society of control," in which power operates not by confining and conducting visual surveillance over individuals in prisons, hospitals, schools, and factories but by processes of encoding access, for example, by allowing some offenders limited freedom to leave their homes while their location is monitored by a transmitter that they wear, or by requiring a coded card for admission to various places, an admission that can be recorded and selectively allowed depending on status, time of day, or other variables. Video cameras and monitors in public and private places are typical devices of this arrangement or *dispositif*. The diagram that is the nerve of such apparatuses does not lend itself to the sort of architectural blueprint that Bentham supplied for the Panopticon, but it does involve a way of making things visible. Deleuze suggests that one day, if the society of control extends itself sufficiently, we may look back with nostalgia on the privacy of the dungeon.[27]

Foucault was interested in Fromanger's technique, his engagement with the *dispositif* of his art. He produces his images by projecting black and white photographs onto a canvas. The photographs often appear to be random shots of French street scenes, but they include prison revolts and pictures from China. Fromanger then paints over these images, with a palette of fairly bright and unmodulated colors. The resulting paintings often have a single dominant color, a hot red or a cool green, which transforms the black and white image. In some the artist's silhouette appears in black, superimposed on the image. After the trajectory defined by Velazquez and Cézanne, this is one place where "the figure of man is being erased," as signaled by this marking of the absence of the artist, who now becomes an enigmatic shade in the circulation of images. The use of photography as the ground of the image shows affinities with Warhol and some other Pop artists, but Fromanger does not usually engage in the production of multiples, like Warhol's many Maos or *Mona Lisas* (with at least one exception, noted below).

"Photogenic Painting" begins by challenging any simple and assured division between photography and painting; it attempts to undermine the bifurcated assignment of reality and fantasy that accords an epistemic authority to one and a claim to the aesthetic to the other. Foucault begins by quoting Ingres, the painter mischievously said by the Goncourts to be Raphael in the form of color photography (*KSA* 11.51).[28] Ingres reveals a tension in the earliest wave of established artistic response to photography. He says both that it is nothing more than "a series of manual operations" and that "it is very beautiful, but one cannot admit it." Foucault had rejoiced in the materiality of painting in the interview cited earlier, which appeared almost simultaneously with the essay on Fromanger (*DE* 2.704–7). So it is not surprising to find him celebrating a painting like this that embodies and responds to the undeniable corporeity of photography. Foucault replies to Ingres with a series of challenges: "And what if one were indeed to consider the series, and with it the series of manual operations to which painting too can be reduced? What if one were to follow the one with the other? And what if one were to combine them, alternate them, superimpose them, intertwine them, if one effaced or exalted the one by the other?" This statement of Fromanger's procedure, drawing on notions of parody, parasitism, and performativity, shows how a practice can insinuate itself deeply into another and so transform it. Foucault was exploring the possibility of developing such practices in relation to prisons and the administration of sexuality and with respect to the disciplines of the human sciences and philosophy. This is to defamiliarize the oppressive presence of the manufactured image while also suggesting the problematic position of the *aesthetic*, as represented by painting, so often taken to be a refuge from the regrettable banality of the mass image and thought, as in Kandinsky and Klee, to retain something of spirit. To Ingres's coy admission about the beauty of photography, Foucault replies that painting can produce its own form of uncanny and disturbing beauty by parasiting photography: "When painting re-covers the photograph, occupying it insidiously or triumphantly, it does not admit that the photograph is beautiful. It does better: it produces the beautiful hermaphrodite of instantaneous photograph and painted canvas, the androgyne image." Nietzsche, too, had spoken of the birth of tragedy as a sexual genesis, although he is far from explicit in welcoming the hermaphrodite and the androgyne. For Foucault this is not simply a novel possibility invented by the contemporary avant-garde or a gesture toward the pan-eroticism suggested by the exhibition's title, "Desire Is Everywhere." He explains the emergence of this new figure of visual desire by providing a genealogy of the relations between photography and other techniques of the image (painting, drawing, collage, and so on) that reminds us of that time of ferment and experimentation when photography was young, when "the years 1860 to 1880 witnessed a new frenzy for images" (*GF* 83; *DE* 2.707). That was also the time of Flaubert, Manet, and Nietzsche, those Foucauldian figures of resistance; we might wonder especially whether Nietzsche, whose archive of photographic portraits certainly exceeds in both quantity and notoriety that of any earlier thinker, could be considered a thinker of the photographic age. Things were different before the two arts arrived at their current arrangement, which has led to the sequestration of painting, to a hyperbolic puritanism and Jansenism of abstraction, and to the ceding of the public visual space to the rhetoric of commodity, entertainment, and political image.

In the hope of recovering the "madness" and "insolent freedom" that accompanied the birth of photography, Foucault offers a conspectus of some of the ways in which photographic images were transformed. The list is provided with materialistic glee as an extensive catalog, with reference to specific photographers, including for example, enhancing through touches of paint; painting a backdrop of scenery against which subjects could be photographed; reconstructing a tableau vivant of a painting in the studio and then photographing it; constructing a similar tableau vivant on the basis of a literary text, printing different negatives together; making a photographic collage and then rephotographing it; and working directly on the negative, for example to produce "Impressionist photo-paintings" (*DE* 2.708–9; *GF* 84–87). This echoes the passionate attachment to images that characterizes the opening of the *History of Madness*, which celebrated Bosch and other artists who allowed the astonishing phantasm to come forth: "Love of the image was ubiquitous, and pleasure was taken in it by every means" (*GF* 88; *DE* 2.710). Yet this great explosion of images has been suppressed by the professionalization of photography, the marginalization of the ingenious amateur, and the division of labor between those who take and deliver photographs. The ensuing diagnosis of the current state of the image is formulated as a political analysis in which the prevailing modes of visibility take on a sinister aspect:

> Painting, for its part, has committed itself to the destruction of the image, while claiming to have freed itself from it. Gloomy discourses have taught us that one must prefer the slash of the sign to the round-dance of resemblance, the order of the syntagm to the race of simulacra, the grey regime of the symbolic to the wild flight of the imaginary. They have tried to convince us that the image, the spectacle, resemblance, and dissimulation, are all bad, both theoretically and aesthetically, and that it would be beneath us not to despise all such folderols.

Foucault is not explicit in naming the authors of these "gloomy discourses," but he is writing not long after the high tide of structuralist analysis and of positions such as those of Guy Debord, who attempted to induce a general suspicion of the spectacle (but, as argued in sec. 2, these strictures do not apply to such thinkers as Derrida, Kristeva, and Lyotard).[29] What was liberating in the art instituted by Manet has become a straitjacket. Abstraction becomes a puritanical religion, and one cannot help thinking here of the story told by Serge Guibault, in which freedom from the representational image becomes an ideological fetish in the cold war, by which the United States congratulates itself on its artistic liberties and sets up an unanswerable contrast between Jackson Pollock and socialist realism.[30] Foucault's iconophilia is part of a general project of finding ways for the enjoyment of "bodies and pleasures," despite the disciplinary regimes to which they have been subjected, even the disciplinary regimes of socially established taste and criticism. The exuberance about the image recalls Nietzsche's fascination with the Apollonian phantasm; but it also dovetails with the work of Pierre Bourdieu, who argues that highbrow taste, with its preference for abstraction, is a dimension of social and intellectual capital at work, rather than a timeless "Kantian" apprehension of the aesthetic.[31] Foucault, we recall, could rejoice even in the unabashed kitsch of a Clovis Trouille, whose images would probably not fare very well with the upper strata in Bourdieu's study.

Foucault had earlier shared (an unacknowledged) common ground with a critic like Clement Greenberg in explaining Manet's work as the watershed allowing painting to focus on the specific characteristics of the canvas. Greenberg was suspicious of movements such as surrealism, which obviously delighted in the image. He took avant-garde and kitsch to be mutually exclusive opposites, but, as Foucault points out in the following observation, such oppositions mask a certain complicity that may deliver us to the actual power of the apparently despised and offensive other by their ascetic and puritanical commitment to an ideal claiming a transcendental legitimation. So kitsch returns with a vengeance, once art has surrendered the territory of everyday life to it, and it is now kitsch in the service of uncongenial forces. The argument above continues: "As a result of which, deprived of the technical ability to produce images, subordinated to the aesthetics of an art without images, subjected to the theoretical obligation to disqualify them, forced to read them only like a language, we could be handed over, bound hand and foot, to the power of other images, political and commercial, over which we had no power" (GF 88–89; DE 2.710). Fromanger's project, as Foucault understands it, is in part to awaken us to the power of those "political and commercial" images that fill the vacuum created by the asceticism of modern art and in part to produce images that open up new paths of circulation by parasiting on those. Wanting to make a space for a truly free art, modernist theory and practice turns into a self-denying asceticism, which fails to understand what it is doing within a larger economy. This is precisely what Nietzsche says in an analogous context, in *Toward a Genealogy of Morals*, about the modern conception of science as the pursuit of absolutely disinterested knowledge; so critics have sometimes been struck by the priestly aspect of the abstract expressionist painters with their horror of representation, their wearing paint-stained clothes as a badge of their labors, their insistence on the inadequacy of words to disclose the sense of their painting, amounting to a claim for the mystical incommunicability of its meaning other than through its sheer presence.[32]

This analysis sets the stage for Foucault's analysis of Pop Art and hyperrealism. They do more than simply rediscover the object; they "plug us into the endless circulation of images." That is, they provide a relay or a vantage point in that circulation which constitutes the prevalent form of visibility in our society. Rather than holding themselves aloof, these styles get down and dirty. Foucault remarks that these artistic modes are superior to "the games of the old days," when photography was in its infancy; they no longer have that trace of the hypocrisy or fraud that marked those experiments. And he adds, "but Fromanger in his turn goes further and faster" (*GF* 90–91; *DE* 2.711).

What impresses Foucault about Fromanger is the way he volatilizes the image. The paintings are based first on press photographs and later on random photos in the street. The more random the photo, the less likely it is to have a center or a privileged object, and so the more it will disclose an event; Fromanger uses this "to create a painting-event on the photo-event." Part of this is accomplished through his application of colors, which "establish distances, tensions, centers of attraction and repulsion, regions of high and low, differences of potential." Dispensing with the stage of drawing and outlining, he makes the painting into a kind of image-machine, the source of "an infinite series of new passages" for each viewer (*GF* 93; *DE* 2.712).

This general observation takes on a more determinate sense when we look at some of Fromanger's specific pictures. The first to which Foucault refers to are a series of a rebellion at Toul prison (fig. 22). He had just published *Discipline and Punish* and was involved in the work of the G.I.P., an organization that was working for prison reform and attempting especially to give prisoners a more public voice. Although stories of the rebellion were widespread and the news photo of prison-

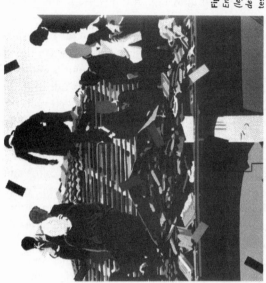

Figure 22. Gérard Fromanger, *En révolte à la prison de Toul I* (*left*) and *En révolte à la prison de Toul II* (*right*), 1974. Courtesy Gérard Fromanger

ers on the roof employed by Fromanger was well known, Foucault raised the question whether anyone had ever asked just what was happening in the photo. "What commentary has ever articulated the unique and multiple event which circulates in it? In scattering a handful of multicolored marks whose position and color are not calculated in relation to the canvas, Fromanger draws countless celebrations from the photograph" (*GF* 94: *DE* 2.712). Might Foucault be suggesting something like the following? In the world of instant news, these are simply dangerous men, enraged and destructive criminals rebelling against their condition. Their appearance on the roof is an act of desperation, an indication of the senselessness of their enterprise. If Fromanger leads us to think a bit more seriously about this event, we might see their emergence on the roof as a call to make their voices heard, to enter a more public space. The background of the image retains the grainy black and white texture of the newspaper photo in modulated form. The prisoners' faces had apparently already been masked; now the faces are invisible, by virtue of a mask, a monochromatic coloring, or simply their position. These colors and those of the rectangles scattered across the image give rise to "countless celebrations." Perhaps one must already be sympathetic to the plight of the prisoners to read the image in this way. Yet a viewer might begin to see the festive aspect of the rebellion, a festivity typical of rebellions, by asking why the painter has strewn *this* image with *these* colors.

Foucault sees these paintings not as "capturing" images but as "passing them on." Fromanger's technique, the "series of manual operations," becomes an outline of what his images do when sent forth into the public space. The painter follows a sequence from photo to slide to projection to painting; the process "ensures the transit of an image." The society of control also passes on and circulates images, but it does so in order to regularize and normalize activity. If Fromanger follows a counterdiagram of mobilizing the image, he suggests that the avenues of its passage are not only those of the governmental or corporate apparatus. Foucault notes that the street is not only the explicit subject of many of the paintings; it is also a figure for the movement they evoke:

> Each painting is a thoroughfare; a "snap" which rather than fixing the movement of things in a photograph, animates, concentrates and magnifies the movement of the image through its successive supporting media. . . . In [several] series he painted streets—the birthplace of images, images themselves. In *Desire is Everywhere* the images may well have been taken for the most part from the street, and named sometimes after a street, but the street is no longer given in

the image. Not that it is absent, but it is incorporated in some way in his technique. The painter, his gaze, the photographer who accompanies him, his camera, the photo he has taken, the canvas—all these form a long, speedy and crowded street, in which images advance and race towards us. The paintings need no longer represent the street; they are streets, roads, paths across the continents, to the very heart of China or Africa. (*GF* 95, 98; *DE* 2.713)

These are not Heidegger's irregular *Holzwege*, which are narrow, winding paths in the woods. The figure of the street suggests Derrida's urbanization of that metaphor as whatever renders possible iteration, that is, repetition and circulation.[33] As Foucault says, "multiple streets burst out from the same photograph." His first example is a series of at least sixteen paintings generated by a single photo of a black street cleaner (fig. 23). It is a simple picture, cropped from a much larger photo. The street cleaner stands at the door of his truck, holding a broom and wearing a large glove on the hand that we see. The many variations on this theme highlight or obscure the subject's face, the truck, or his activity. They vary from hot red to a black surface with a few circular cutouts, to carnivalesque plays of color. The titles suggest a variety of moods, situations, events. If Warhol's repetitions had the function of evacuating the meaning of the image, Fromanger's variations "liberate a whole series of events."

Foucault calls this iteration and circulation the "autonomous transhumance" of the image. Transhumance is the transference of grazing animals from one field to another, a zigzagging change of territory, akin to what Deleuze and Guattari call deterritorialization.[34] So an "autonomous transhumance" of the image is a nomadic wandering. By joining in this wandering, painters will "rediscover the crowd of amateurs, artificers, manipulators, smugglers, robbers, looters of images," says Foucault. The artist becomes a deviant rather than the high priest of a new form of purity. Her activity, like that of the smuggler or looter, is parasitic upon the standard forms in which the image circulates. She sends the equivalent of a computer virus into the image-machines of advertising, media, and state. The best video art has this character of deforming the most omnipresent "channel" of the image, performing it otherwise, liberating and multiplying the contents of the screen.[35]

Fromanger may not be a "great" painter like Bosch, Velazquez, Manet, and Magritte; but this is not Foucault's claim. He is interested in the possibility of an art that responds to the twentieth century's bifurcation of the image into a supposedly pure art and the public icons of consumption and power. Foucault's final comments on Fromanger

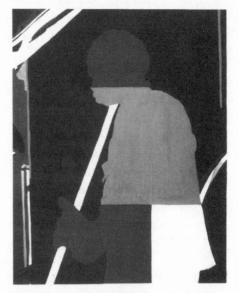

Rue de la mer, 1974

Rue de la saison des pluies, 1974

Wild Animal Street, 1974

Dance Street, 1974

Rue des animaux sauvages, 1974

Rue de la danse, 1974

Figure 23. Gérard Fromanger, *Sea Street, Rainy Season Street, Wild Animal Street, Dance Street,* 1974. Courtesy Gérard Fromanger

tell us that the exhibition closes on "two foci of desire," one of the rock singer Michel Bulteau at the Versailles Opera, the other of an amateur peasant painter in Hu-Xian. Two artists, two producers of images. In the first case, "everything is decomposed in the glitter of the pomp and the image discharges a volley of colors." Fromanger's title calls Bulteau "the greatest poet in the world," reflecting both the dazzling setting and an alternative to "great art." This artist appears in the image in drag, and as Foucault comments, "the mirror at Manet's *Bar* shatters into fragments." The painting does not stand still like a fetishized old master or the work of a revered abstract expressionist. It bursts in a celebration of color that contrasts strikingly with the blue face of Bulteau. The companion piece of the Chinese painter suggests a patient, obscure work in very simple surroundings. We are reminded that paintings are not windows by the four bands of color that occupy the window space on the left. The image, in its autonomous transhumance, shows that it can move into and through the same streets marked and traversed by the signs of convention.

79 What Do Photographers Dream Of? Duane Michals and the Uses of Pleasure

Foucault's last essay dealing with the visual arts is a contribution to a short publication on the North American photographer Duane Michals, titled simply "Thought and Emotion." The essay is concerned with phantasms and dream visions, so reading it in terms of Foucault's early *Dream and Existence*, which sketches a theory of the dream and of its role in art, may clarify some of the continuities and changes in his thought about the visual and the phantasmatic, as well as the conjunction of dream and art that also fascinated Nietzsche. At the same time, this text is contemporary with Foucault's concern with the process of subjectification and the aesthetics of existence, as in the later volumes of *The History of Sexuality* (*The Care of the Self* brings these themes together in its extended reading of the ancient dream book of Artemidorus).

Foucault acknowledges his affinity with Michals's working method; he describes it as expansive rather than developmental, referring to "methods like this which do not move forward like a developing oeuvre but rather spread out and open because they are themselves experiments: Magritte, Bob Wilson, *Under the Volcano*, *The Death of Maria Malibran*, and of course H.G." This little list, produced in a seemingly offhand way, is consistent with the theme of repetition and the simulacrum that pervades the discussion of Magritte, Warhol, Deleuze, and Klossowski. But it also suggests that we see Foucault's own writing as a ramifying experiment, a structure branching out simultaneously in a number of different directions (this may be the place to note that one of the pitfalls of reading Foucault in English translation is that the French *expérience* frequently has the sense of "experiment").[36] H.G. is Hervé Guibert, a friend, novelist, and photographic critic for *Le Monde*. Wilson's theater minimizes dramatic development and teleology for the sake of movement, gesture, and expression. Malcolm Lowry, the author of *Under the Volcano*, is mentioned one other time in an early interview, along with Robbe-Grillet, Borges, and Blanchot, as a writer who bears witness to the disappearance of man in the resurgence of language (*DE* 1.544). *The Death of Maria Malibran* is a film by Werner Schroeter; Foucault was quite taken by this director's work and conducted a long interview with him (*DE* 4.251–60).[37] Most of all, Foucault is saying something about his own working method; he would like to be seen as an experimenter, moving on from one problematic to another, rather than as developing a grand system. In a 1978 interview, he says, "I am an experimenter and not a theorist. . . . I'm an experimenter in the sense that I write in order to change myself and in order not to think the same thing as before" (*F* 3.240; *DE* 4.42). In this spirit Deleuze suggests that we read all of Foucault's writing, including interviews and occasional pieces, rather than privileging just his published books. More specifically, Deleuze claims that Foucault's "historical" works, such as *Discipline and Punish*, are always paralleled by interviews or shorter pieces that articulate the fundamental concerns of the analysis in terms of the contemporary situation, or (I add) in another register, say, in terms of the visual.[38] So the Manet book would have explored the development of visual practices, offering alternatives to the main directions of panopticism, while the Magritte essay and the remarks on Warhol situate eternal recurrence at the intersection of the visible and the discursive in twentieth-century imagery. From this perspective, the essay on Michals, like some of the other writings of Foucault's last five years or so, can be read in conjunction with *The Uses of Pleasure* and *The Care of the Self*. That reading would not be limited to seeing these "minor" works as applications of the books; it would also employ the essays and interviews to see what is involved in the self-fashioning that Foucault calls "an aesthetics of existence." In *The Care of the Self*, Foucault notes that the physicians and the writers on love (Ovid and Propertius, for example) testify to the power of visual images *(phantasiai)*, whether remembered, dreamed, or seen.[39] Since Michals is a gay man, much of whose work focuses on desire and gender, and a photographer who deforms the conventions of his art, his deployment of images as a means of self-fashioning, to create himself as a gift for the viewer, is amenable to Foucault's analysis.

The reflections on Michals begin rather disarmingly with a confession of impotence and a plea for indulgence. Foucault says, "I know a photograph is not something you talk about" ("TE" ix; *DE* 4.244). This calls attention to that gap between words and images marked in the essay on *Las Meninas* when he says that "the relation between painting and language is an infinite relation." It names the whole question of ekphrasis, raising the possibility that there can never be a smooth match or a substitution between words and images. Yet it also says something more specific about photography, which is taken to be an art of reality in which what you see is what you get. In 1980, two years before this essay, Roland Barthes had published his *Camera Lucida*, where similar questions are raised and in which the author asks us finally to understand photography by meditating on a photo that he does not show us, the one of his mother as a young girl in the winter garden (and by using a colored frontispiece photograph of a bedroom that is never discussed, thus constructing a chiasmus with the treatment of the winter garden picture). For Barthes, the point of this absence is the eventual discovery that his quest to find the meaning of photography was not a project of elaborating universal and impersonal truths about the art, as it had originally seemed, but a circuitous way of encountering his own passion and mortality.[40] What defines photography is the existential or indexical connection between the picture and an occasion of the past, the actual exposure of the film. Barthes thus proposes a deeply materialistic conception of the photographic medium, seemingly in agreement with a position like the one Foucault took in responding to Ingres. And ultimately, what photography meant was a specific connection with his past, or, more precisely, a past of his past, the image of his mother long before he was born. Foucault writes of his own pleasure in Michals's photos, but there is nothing absolutely personal or idiosyncratic about this pleasure. Like Barthes, he confesses that he is driven to speak about photography by a certain obscure necessity; he overcame his reluctance to speak of the photographs simply because they "move" him to an "indiscretion" and make him "want to talk about them, like trying to give a clumsy account of something which cannot be communicated" ("TE" ix; *DE* 4.244).

Foucault warns us that he is incapable of discussing the technical aspects of Michals's photos or their form *(plastique)*, but he says: "They attract me as experiments. Experiments that only he made, but which, in a way I don't completely understand, glide toward me—and,

I think, to whoever looks at them—evoking pleasures, anxieties, ways of seeing things, feelings I have already known or anticipate having to encounter one day; so that I must always ask myself whether these feelings are his or mine, even though I know well that I owe them to Duane Michals. "I am the gift I offer you," he says" ("TE" ix; *DE* 4.244). Michals's photographs are not records of individual experiences; in other words, they are not indexical, as in one of Barthes's definitions of the photograph (his Peircean definition). They are not the visual diary of a certain subjectivity. They are rather a set of experiments, conducted indeed by a specific individual, but available to others of an experimental spirit. Nietzsche frequently expresses a similar thought, as in *The Gay Science:* "[T]he great liberator came to me: the idea that life could be an experiment of the seeker after knowledge—and not a duty, not a calamity, not trickery" (*GS* 324; *KSA* 3.552). More specifically, Nietzsche defended Raphael against Michelangelo's charge that he had simply learned from tradition while Michelangelo had a natural talent. Instead, Raphael should be seen as a *"great learner"* (like Goethe), whose last series of works, which is epitomized by the *Transfiguration,* is the *"beginning* of a new plan of study" (*D* 540; *KSA* 3.309; see sec. 22). It is only retrospectively that Raphael becomes the paradigm of the classical as the fixed and stable. In pursuing an aesthetics of existence, fashioning one's life as a work of art, it is necessary to experiment with oneself and to learn from the experiments of others. It is in this sense that Michals offers himself as a gift. We learn something of his appearance and even his history from his photographs, as in the picture that comments on the letter he never received from his father.[41] Yet what he gives us most of all is not that biographical record but the example of his experimentation.

Michals experiments with photography, asking what will happen if the conventional dichotomy between an aesthetic, dreamlike painting and a documentary, factual photography is put into question. Again Foucault is concerned with the epistemic politics of the photographic medium. He highlights a quotation from Michals: "People believe in the reality of photographs, but not the reality of paintings. This gives photographs an advantage. The disadvantage is that photographers themselves believe in the reality of photographs." Foucault describes several of Michals's photographs that play with the line between painting and photography. They make their visual point by conjuring up evanescent, almost invisible objects, as if the camera had captured a spirit, an aura, or ectoplasm. We cannot tell, in one case of a young man with eyes closed, resting on a table, whether the painted forms of biscuits on the table are to be seen as "the dreamer's phantasm [*mes-*

sage de rêveur] or the actual, concrete object of our perception" ("TE" ix; *DE* 4.243–44). The dream image, that errant form of the visible, is conjured up again. Now the suggestion is not only that art derives from the phantasm but also that it can play with the line between phantasm and perception. It is akin to the thought of classical antiquity that visions and dreams are not simply located in our individual minds or brains but are sent by the gods or (in the version of Epicurus) spun off by objects and so have a certain substantiality.

Photography has been assigned the job of displaying reality, while the older art has the task of "painting an edge or brilliance, the dream element hidden within that reality" ("TE" ix; *DE* 4.245). It is the same division of labor, with its consequences for the distribution of the epistemic and the aesthetic, that Foucault discussed in the essay on Fromanger. Insofar as a photographer like Michals plays off his work against the expectation of reality, he sets up a situation in which the viewer must be simultaneously aware of the convention and its violation, the incursion of the dream or the phantasm. "To the photo itself, the act of taking photographs, the carefully composed scene he is photographing, and the complicated rite enabling him to photograph such a scene, he renders the power of the dream world and the invention of thought" ("TE" ix–x; *DE* 4.244). Such seeing requires a kind of double vision, something akin to the double point of view that Nietzsche discerned in the Greek theater and in the viewing of the *Sistine Madonna*. And just as Nietzsche reminds us of the *agon* of tragic and Socratic vision, so Foucault shows the *resistance* to prevailing visual regimes in the work of painters and photographers. Warhol, Michals, and Fromanger, the three visual artists after Magritte of whom Foucault takes notice, all question the mundane truthfulness of the photograph. Foucault sees in Michals's photos "a laugh in the face of hyperrealism" ("TE" x; *DE* 4.245). Similar observations could be and have been made about contemporary video artists like Gary Hill and Nam June Paik. For that matter, film played with the exchange of reality and phantasm for decades, although we are still recovering from the Hollywood realism of the 1940s and 1950s.

In addition to perspectivism, Foucault finds an anti-ocularism in Michals's work, directed against the "tyrannical, infallible eye" assumed to preside over photography. In attempting to "cancel out the ocular function of photography," Michals deploys a number of strategies. One of these is to "photograph evanescence itself": this is to allow the visible to escape. In doing this he refuses the role of the photographer who, like a big game hunter, captures or shoots his prey. If some of Michals's photographic series show a vanishing, others reverse this by depicting the invisible, or what is ordinarily taken to be so. So Foucault's list of figures that "haunt" the photographs of Duane Michals: "ectoplasms, seductive silhouettes from beyond, angels who through carnal knowledge of women lose their wings, souls like transparent bodies rising up, tearing themselves gradually from the naked sleepers of death" ("TE" 10; *DE* 4.246). If Heidegger elaborated a thought of art based on the idea of dwelling or inhabiting, Foucault suggests that art can also manifest a "haunting." Reading Foucault's early essay on the dream along with this analysis of Michals, we can imagine how he could make the claim that the dream is the source of that imagination that can issue in what Derrida has called a "hauntology."[42] The photograph becomes a fully materialized dream.

In the series *Alice's Mirror* (fig. 24) Foucault invites us to see some of Magritte's techniques at work as they are translated into photography: perfecting a form, draining it of reality, taking things outside their ordinary context. Michals often makes series of photographs with a common title that seem to tell a story. Ordinarily photographers, as Foucault observes, produce such series for one of three reasons: to construct a narrative, to show the passage of time (as in Muybridge's famous studies), or to "exhaust all the many contours of an object" (like Husserlian *Abschattungen*). Michals's series allow things to escape, rather than capturing them. *Alice's Mirror* begins with a Magritte-like scene in which the glasses, the instrument of vision, have been enormously magnified; this could be the Alice who went through the looking glass (perhaps in her dream). As the series progresses—or should we say regresses?—we find that objects are further diminished, turned into reflections, reflections within reflections, finally to be crushed and eliminated. It is a dream of loss, in which we find ourselves in a world that constantly withdraws from our efforts to seize it. It is also a self-referential work of art, one that demonstrates the iconoclasm of the imagination by deconstructing and then destroying (these are not identical steps) the image that it has established. Foucault sees such uses of the series as running against the grain of the photographic convention that uses snapshots to produce an image of temporal continuity. What Michals shows us is this: "[A]lthough time and experience/expériment [*expérience*] ceaselessly interact and play off one another, they are not part of the same world. Time may bring changes, ageing, death, but thought-emotion is the stronger; it, and only it, can see and show others its invisible wrinkles" ("TE" xii; *DE* 4.250). Foucault seems to have coined the term "thought-emotion" for this essay. It is roughly equivalent to what he called the movement of existence in the dream essay about thirty years earlier. In both contexts the work of the dream, imagination, or art is to explore a certain space, which, although it may be presented in a temporal sequence, is overshadowed by the dimensions of destiny and death that characterize existence. If man is in the process of vanishing, like an inscription on the shores of the sea, language and dreams remain.

Many of Michals's photographs carry his own inscriptions in a distinctive handwriting. Like Magritte's work, then, they complicate the relation of language and image. As Foucault notes, the usual function of labels, titles, and the like in photography is to fix the meaning of the photo by providing contextual information. But Michals's texts "are not there to fix the image, hold it fast, but rather expose it to invisible breezes" ("TE" xi; *DE* 4.247). The effect is to make the pictures circulate, both in the mind of the viewer and from one viewer to another. As with Fromanger, Foucault shows himself sensitive to any way of presenting the image that renders it less of a unique fetish and that lets it wander along unpredictable paths. In exploring the dream logic of Michals's photographs, Foucault goes beyond the themes of space and movement that characterize his discussions of the dream in his Binswanger essay. He also attends to the presence of language and to Michals's reference to narrative in the series of photos that he produces. Michals gives titles to his pictures and often, as Foucault notes, presents them "enveloped in rich tresses of words," typically written by hand on the paper of the print ("TE" xi; *DE* 4.247). Yet while titles and information usually function to affirm and expand the indexical function of photography, to elucidate and confirm its tie with reality, this is not the case with Michals. In "This Photograph Is My Proof" (fig. 25), the hand-written inscription reads: "This photograph is my proof. There was that afternoon, when things were still good between us, and she embraced me, and we were so happy. It did happen, she did love me. Look, see for yourself!" This protests too much on the fact of love; one could read this as a denial and describe it in Freudian terms as a secondary revision. Now, in retrospect, we see that expression on the woman's face somewhat differently than we would if there were no words. Is there something just a bit quizzical, a bit detached there? Is that a rather knowing hint of a Mona Lisa effect that the words help to suggest?

The painters of the late nineteenth century were postphotographic; they could use photography while distinguishing their art from that process. Michals has absorbed this history. He asks in effect why photography might not twist free of representation, developing its own way of dealing with light and its shadings. Michals realizes that because of the habitual documentary and representational expectations connected with photography, the artist can vividly materialize the ghostly;

Figure 24. Duane Michals, *Alice's Mirror*, 1974. Series of seven photographs. © Duane Michals. courtesy Pace/ MacGill Gallery, New York

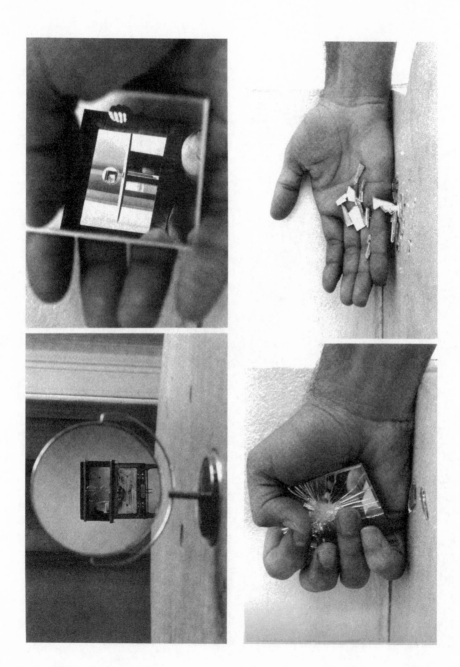

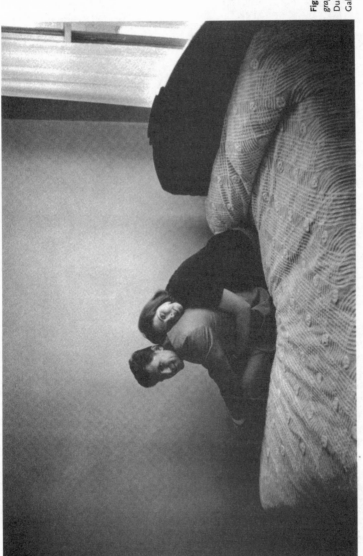

THIS PHOTOGRAPH IS MY PROOF

This photograph is my proof. There was that afternoon, when things were still good between us, and she embraced me, and we were so happy. It did happen. She did love me. Look see for yourself!

Figure 25. Duane Michals, *This Photo-graph Is My Proof*, 1974 photograph. © Duane Michals; courtesy Pace/MacGill Gallery, New York

yet the effect of his art will be to solicit or shake those expectations, rendering the medium more ghostly or *geistlich*. He says, "The things that interested me were all invisible, metaphysical questions: life after death, the aura of sex—its atmosphere rather than the mechanics—these are things you never see on the street. So I had to invent and make these situations to express and explore these things."[43]

Michals literalizes the idea of the otherworldly or oneiric shade. In a sequence like *The Spirit Leaves the Body*, the images and the title are quite directive, asking us to imagine a shade as it departs. We do not know whether the prone man is sleeping, perhaps dreaming, unconscious, or dead, although the starkness of the bed or platform on which he lies, his posture, and the fact that it does not change during the series, all suggest death. As the shadowy self rises from the pallet, it becomes both larger and more indistinct. While the last image of the sequence is almost indistinguishable from the first, we may have the sense that the spirit has filled the entire space rather than disappeared, while the body is left behind as starkly and bleakly as in Hans Holbein's *Dead Christ*, about which Julia Kristeva has written so perceptively.[44]

Consider now a few photographs, unmentioned by Foucault, that body forth the dream and the invisible. In a photograph of a male and female nude, two figures oscillate between the solid or fleshly and the ghostly; here the superimposition of negatives is made quite explicit (fig. 26). One might say that the use of black and white turns us all into shades, but here the effect is intensified. This couple are neither conventionally beautiful or handsome, nor are they ill-favored. Facing one another (a facing that we can see is an artifice of the camera), they could be everyman and everywoman. Either face can be seen as superimposed on or as overshadowed by part of the other's face. The man's head is turned at just enough of an angle to avoid a simple face-off in which there would be an excessive symmetry, for after all, there is difference here. The undulating line that goes down the middle of the picture creates or opens up a space of meeting, a meeting that does and does not take place. Notice that the only really dark or empty space is at the level of the genitals, where there is a natural recession of both bodies. The place where contact might be closest, amounting to possession or penetration, is left as a void, yet a void enclosed within the space of the bodies' intersections. If anything like penetration occurs here, it is in the two faces that face into one another and, more markedly, in the tip of the woman's breast, which seems to enter into the man's flesh. Bodies, fated to be apart or briefly together in ordinary circumstances, are liberated as shades to pass into one another. Or do they simply pass each other by? Are they "headed" through one an-

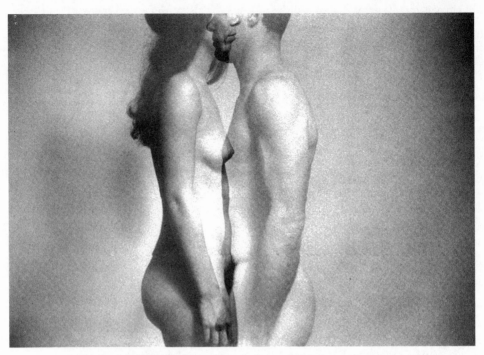

Figure 26. Duane Michals, *Male and Female*, 1963 photograph. © Duane Michals; courtesy Pace/ MacGill Gallery, New York

other? Notice that we see only a trace, a shade of the eyes, a little patch that could be the man's or the woman's eye or perhaps the intersection of the two. Do they see each other, or are they blind to one another? Does their vision merge? Or do they share a closed, blind eye? Are their "eyes wide shut," as one of our late animators of shades would have it? This could be Michals's *Traumnovelle*, a dream made visible.

Michals says, "Everything can be photographed, most of all the difficult things in life: anxiety, the afflictions of childhood, desires, nightmares. The things we can't see are the most meaningful."[45] Many of his photographs and sequences deal with gay affection and sexuality, matters that have for many years been closeted or forced into invisibility. Michals brings these things into the light, whether as fantasies or realities, including two homages to gay poets, Cavafy and Whitman. Yet the project of bringing the invisible to light is hardly limited to homoerotic themes, even when it is a question of sexual desire, although Michals's experiments in this direction are informed by a sensibility formed in terms of an acute awareness of the line between what can be generally shown and what must be hidden. Commenting on Michals's series *Things Are Queer*, which has no explicit reference to

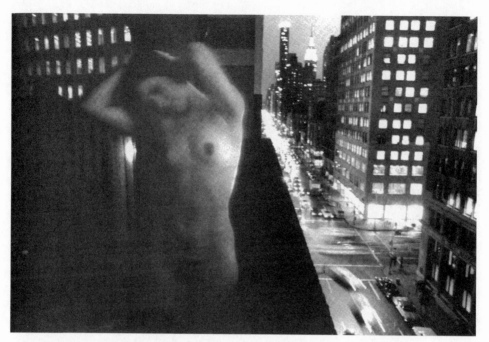

Figure 27. Duane Michals, *A Woman Dreaming in the City*, 1969 photograph. © Duane Michals; courtesy Pace/MacGill Gallery, New York

gay life or to sexuality, but which involves a number of shifts in framing and context, Jonathan Weinberg writes: "What is queer is the certainty by which we label things as normal or abnormal, decent and obscene, gay and straight."[46]

A pair of photographs highlights the theme of the dream: *A Woman Dreaming in the City* and *A Man Dreaming in the City* (figs. 27, 28). The woman might be on a balcony; there could be a window behind her reflecting the lights across the street, lights that have themselves become ghostly. She dreams in the city, a nocturnal metropolis where anonymity and solitude carry a strong erotic charge; the phantasmatic city of desire is suggested by soft focus, lights, and blurred traffic. Her body is centered, and the pose could almost be classical except for the exaggerated tilt of the head, indicating that she is asleep, yet standing. The differentiation of spaces is also dreamlike: the black diagonal that separates the woman's space from the outside of the street encloses her within a much more muted area, whose large dark swatches approach and give their own enigmatic quality to the pubic triangle. This is not a Nietzschean dream; Nietzsche, oddly enough, thought that dreams were well defined pictorially, with outlines as

Figure 28. Duane Michals, *A Man Dreaming in the City*, 1969 photograph. © Duane Michals; courtesy Pace/MacGill Gallery, New York

definite as Renaissance paintings. But this photograph evokes that sense of the archaic and the underworld emerging into and transforming the banality of the everyday that is the crown of our nocturnal experience.

In his dream essay, Foucault distinguishes three basic dimensions of the dream that give rise to three types of art. These are variations on the possibilities of light and space; think of them as the basic diagrams of the dream. The epic type is based on variations of the near and far, so it includes departures, voyages, and circumnavigations; the lyric mode has to do with the opposition and alternation of solar and nocturnal themes; and the tragic form involves a structure of ascent and fall. If we compare this typology of literary genres with those prominent in the aesthetics of German idealism, we are struck by the way in which Foucault's schema passes over both the dialectic of subject and object and the attempt to determine the artistic or poetic genres in terms of temporal modalities (past, present, future); the genres are all understood as forms of spatiality.[47] *A Woman Dreaming in the City* is a dream raised to the second power, since all art, on Foucault's early analysis, anyway, is generated by the dream. In the dream essay, Foucault says that to imagine is to dream oneself dreaming. Nietzsche makes a similar point in his analysis of Raphael's *Transfiguration*, in which the transfigured Christ is Apollo, the giver of dreams. The *Transfiguration* involves elements of both Foucault's lyrical and tragic modes. The light that transforms "Apollo" contrasts with the darkness of the area in which the disciples struggle to heal the possessed boy. In *A Woman Dreaming in the City*, reality has become blurry, dreamlike. Foucault writes in his dream essay that the imagination is iconoclastic: as an active power it refuses to fetishize the image, to give it a solidity and fixity that would detract from movements in and through imaginative space (*DX* 72; *DE* 1.116). The bright but indistinct lights of the street, the buildings across the street from the dreamer, and the towers in the distance offer a promise—hope, fulfillment, *jouissance*—envisioned by a woman whose blurred eyes suggest a sleepy oblivion to the ordinary world of well-defined, outlined structures. This woman could ascend to the height of those luminous towers; she could fall or throw herself over the ledge into the darker part of the street. In the dream essay, Foucault claims that death is an essential theme of the dream, since the dream is a projection of the possibilities of existence and an encounter with destiny. He writes: "Death is experienced as the supreme moment of that contradiction, which death constitutes as destiny. Hence the meaningfulness of all those dreams of violent death, of savage death, of horrified death, in which one must indeed recognize, in the final analysis, a freedom up against a world" (*DX* 54; *DE* 1.94). The tragic theme is also visible in *A Man Dreaming in the City*. Two vertical forms, marked as light and dark, offer possibilities of ascent and descent. The towering building in the distance is an attractive center of light, although the illuminated clock can also be read as a cancellation sign, suggesting that there is some barrier or prohibition blocking the ascent. The dreamer is fallen: stretched out horizontally, sleeping on what seems to be a very shallow ledge that may be just barely off the ground, only partially clothed, he lies as an object beneath the gaze of the hulking figure whom we read as a policeman because of the shape of his cap. He may also be an object of desire or of violence, what the dreamer hopes or fears. If the cancellation sign is the cancellation of time, of the passage that the clock would have told, then this dream is also an approach to death.

Foucault's archaeology is also the sketch of a series of forms of visual resistance. The spectacles by which sovereigns like Louis XIV and Philip IV advertised their power can be questioned by Velazquez's painting, which obscures the image of the king in a shadowy reflection in the depth of the picture, while the artwork ostensibly both obeys and models all the canons of proper representation. It is a dream in which the supreme figure of power is blurred in a mirror, invisible on the canvas whose back is turned toward us, and positioned in a perpetually oscillating space outside the picture. The emerging practices of surveillance typified by the Panopticon and the clinic are countered by those ways of seeing, like Manet's, which are commentaries on the art world of the museum. We are offered dreams rather than windows for the inspection of individuals. The museum embodies a practice of mastering the art of the past and the present in a space threatening to sap the vitality of images; that was part of what Hegel noted when he declared, at that time shared by the museum and the Panopticon, that art was a thing of the past and had now become a subject of science, a subject for disciplinary surveillance by art history, say, a *Fach* that his *Aesthetics* helped to invent. In a time with so much energy devoted to photographic and video documentation, to mechanized and routinized surveillance, an art like Michals's reminds us of the necessarily constructive dimension of those media and their tendency to generate ghosts and shades.

80 Retrospective

I introduced this series of essays by suggesting that we consider both Nietzsche and Foucault as experimental philosophers whose thought is open to a variety of currents, and I proposed to read them in terms of their engagement with visual art and visual culture. This might be seen as an eccentric approach with regard to both. Nietzsche's own eyesight was notoriously poor, and very few have previously supposed that he had much to say about these subjects. Foucault's best-known essay on art, "*Las Meninas*," is thought by many intelligent observers to rest on a misreading of the painting, and this philosopher is reputed in some circles to have regarded the entire visual world with acute suspicion, perhaps assimilating it all to the evil eye of the Panopticon. I hope to have shown that such views are partial, exaggerated, or irrelevant. We can go further and identify in Nietzsche the outlines of an archaeology of the visual that is articulated and amplified in Foucault. We can read Nietzsche's most abysmal thought, his thought of thoughts, that of the eternal recurrence of the *Augenblick*, not only as a thought presented in images but as one that has to do with the phantasm. In Foucault's adaptation of Deleuze's and Klossowski's reading of Nietzsche in terms of the phantasm and the simulacrum, and in his suggestion of how the theme of recurrence surfaces in Manet, Magritte, and Warhol, we see Nietzsche's uncanny thought assuming other visible shapes.

It takes some time to see the currents with which a philosopher is grappling and coming to terms; thinkers are frequently only partially aware of the context of their thought. Nietzsche and Foucault offer acute visions of past thinkers, frequently in terms that those thinkers themselves would certainly find puzzling. For example, in *The Uses of Pleasure*, Foucault attempted to situate a major aspect of Plato's thought in terms of a contemporary Greek problematic having to do with the question of how one should manage one's erotic life; and, with respect to the modern world, he argues that the growth of the human sciences is bound up with the establishment of a disciplinary society. In reading these two thinkers by mapping their encounters with the visual, I am of course influenced by the "visual turn" in what we still quaintly call humanistic studies, which now might concern themselves with everything from the Taliban's iconoclasm to the insidious suggestion of the Teletubbies program that the normal human condition is that of the cyborg, constantly wired into an apparently infinite network of visual images. Nietzsche and Foucault have contributed to the possibility of reading them, like other philosophers, in terms of cultural contexts that they did not fully thematize and articulate.

Foucault was a theorist of both power and resistance, and as such it should now be clear that he has much to offer to visual studies. His understanding of artists as diverse as Bosch, Velazquez, Manet, Magritte, and Warhol are exemplary experiments in understanding the very different forces and associations connected with the production and circulation of images in a variety of regimes of power and knowledge. Nietzsche was not indifferent to such concerns. He was a theorist of the power of the dream image, including that waking dream that we call art. He analyzed the structure of seeing in the Greek theater as an alternative to the Cyclopean eye of Socratic science that displaced the perspectivism of the tragic age. Nietzsche abandoned his early enthusiasm for Wagner, when he realized that his spectacles did not involve the renewal of that theater, a renewal that was in any case impossible. In *Thus Spoke Zarathustra*, he devised a story of the eye as part of a philosophical theater, with its evil and radiant eyes, its exchanges of looks, its gazes and glances, and its revelatory twinklings of the eye that he desperately hoped might displace the blinking of the last men, which he feared would become the hegemonic mode of vision. When Nietzsche speaks of the "great noon," he might seem to be repeating the heliocentrism and ocularcentrism of the tradition, according to which there will be a final disclosure, an ultimate vision; but we have seen that noon is no more and no less than a moment in the diurnal or the eternal cycles, and that it is always surrounded by shadows. The writer who had devised the couple of the wanderer and his shadow did not conceive of the possibility of an ultimate revelation based on the classical model of vision. Both thinkers were often highly suspicious of the traditional "God's eye" conception of vision that finds frequent expression in philosophy. But rather than rejecting this "noblest of the senses," they found ways of thinking of the visual differentially, in ways that exhibited its many historical forms. Nietzsche can speak for both when he expresses his perspectivism in a note entitled "Der Versucher." *Versucher* might be translated as seducer or tempter, but Nietzsche frequently plays upon the suggestion of the experimental spirit in this word and its cognates, as Foucault does with that of *expérience*.

The Experimenter

There are many sorts of eyes. The sphinx too has eyes: consequently, there are many sorts of "truths," and consequently there is no truth. (*KSA* 11.498)

This is only one of a rather surprising number of passages in which Nietzsche formulates a pluralistic attitude toward truth in visual terms. He is seen too frequently as simply dismissing the notion of truth altogether, but this is a hasty reading. Consider the celebrated line from "On Truth and Lie in an Extra-Moral Sense," "[W]hat then is truth? A mobile army of metaphors and metonymies, and anthropomorphisms"; truths are like coins that have lost their image *(Bild)* (*KSA* 1.880). Earlier in that essay, Nietzsche claimed that these metaphors and other tropes were complications and transformations of images, which suggests that while truth may not be one single, stable thing, it is not nothing. It is, indeed, a mobile deployment of images or their counters. I read Foucault as having elaborated this thought in the registers of both the discursive and the visible. In "The Experimenter" Nietzsche first puts truth in quotation marks, marking in this way the oddity of speaking of *plural* truths. By the time he gets to the conclusion of the aphorism, then, we should read "consequently there is no truth" as saying that there is no single, fixed truth. There is no monological, monocular truth, as might appear to an obsessive Cyclops eye. The sphinx poses riddles, not least to Oedipus, the man who thinks that all can be revealed, once and for all, to a hero of resolute vision. Oedipus fails to see that the sphinx also sees, and so he fails to see that he too is observed. If he managed to solve one riddle of the sphinx, thinking it the only one, he paid for his presumption with the sacrifice of his eyes. Nietzsche, who in many ways lived a gradual sacrifice of vision, saw at least that there was an alternative to both blindness and the one great staring eye. Directly after the aphorism of *Human, All Too Human*, in which he sketches what I have ventured to call an archaeology of vision by commenting on archaic cult images (sec. 6), Nietzsche asks, *Where must we travel* (HAH, AOM, 223; KSA 2.477–78). The topics might seem wildly unrelated, for the second aphorism has to do with contemporary people with access to the railroads; but just as he has suggested a differential conception of vision in the first of these sections, so he now explains that experienced travelers will become like the "hundred-eyed Argos," thinking themselves into and out of a dazzling variety of times and places. Argos does not have all possible eyes; but both Nietzsche and Foucault can help us to open or create some "windows of the soul" whose possibility we would otherwise scarcely have suspected.

Notes

Introduction

1. *KSA* 10.166; 4[194].

2. *BT* 3; *KSA* 1.34.

3. *F* 2.171; *DE* 1.554.

4. *DE* 2.401.

5. W. J. T. Mitchell speaks of a "pictorial turn" in *Picture Theory* (Chicago: University of Chicago Press, 1994), 11–34.

6. *November 2001:* I leave the text as originally written. Since September 11, 2001, the Taliban, or at least the Al Qaeda network that they harbored, have effectively dominated the imagery on American television screens; there is some irony here, given the Taliban's prohibition of television in Afghanistan. We have also learned that the director of the destruction of the Baniyam Buddha, Taliban leader Mullah Omar (who is not really a mullah), has a complex relation to the visual: he has only one eye (one was lost in fighting the Soviets), and he refuses to be photographed, since he believes that the traditional Islamic exclusion of images extends to photography and video; in this respect his position is more radically iconoclastic than that of his associate Osama bin Laden, who allows himself to be photographed and videoed and who apparently does not discourage the wide distribution of his image.

7. Hans Belting, *Likeness and Presence: A History of the Image before the Age of Art* (Chicago: University of Chicago Press, 1994); the German title is *Bild und Kult—Eine Geschichte des Bildes vor dem Zeitalter der Kunst.*

8. This is not the place to discuss in any detail how well founded this use of the Jewish *Bilderverbot* by various forms of iconoclastic theory and practice may be; for a comprehensive collection of sources and commentary on the subject, which suggests that the Jewish tradition is not as intolerant of all images as has sometimes been thought, see Vivian Mann, ed. *Jewish Texts on the Visual Arts* (New York: Cambridge University Press, 2000). For a commentary on the issues, see Kalman P. Bland, *The Artless Jew: Medieval and Modern Affirmations of the Visual* (Princeton, NJ: Princeton University Press, 2000).

9. Guy Debord's 1967 essay *Society of the Spectacle* (Detroit: Black and Red, 1983) introduced that term into the discussion of contemporary society and remains an important theoretical statement, as is recognized by Michael Hardt and Antonio Negri in *Empire* (Cambridge, MA: Harvard University Press); see esp. 188–89, 280–304, 321–23.

10. The literature on the philosophical appeal to vision is vast and growing. For a set of significant critical essays on this theme, see David Michael Levin, ed. *Modernity and the Hegemony of Vision* (Berkeley: University of California Press, 1993); cf. also Hans Jonas's essay "The Nobility of Sight: A Study in the Phenomenology of the Senses," in his *Phenomenon of Life: Toward a Philosophical Biology* (New York: Harper and Row, 1966), 135–56. In addition to and as a corrective to Martin Jay's *Downcast Eyes: The Denigration of Vision in Twentieth-Century French Thought* (Berkeley: University of California Press, 1993), David Michael Levin's *Philosopher's Gaze* (Berkeley: University of California Press, 1999) explores the meaning of vision as concept and metaphor in philosophers from Descartes to the late twentieth century.

11. For a helpful account of Heidegger's complex stance toward vision, see David Michael Levin, "Decline and Fall: Ocularcentrism in Heidegger's Reading of the History of Metaphysics," in *Modernity and the Hegemony of Vision*, ed. Levin (Berkeley: University of California Press, 1993), 186–217.

12. For Rorty and references to the pragmatic tradition, see Richard Rorty, *Philosophy and the Mirror of Nature* (Princeton, NJ: Princeton University Press, 1979), esp. 38–9, 143–44, 157–59, 162–63, 375–76.

13. Sigmund Freud, *Civilization and Its Discontents*, trans. James Strachey (New York: Norton, 1989), 54–55 n.

14. Erwin Straus, "The Upright Posture," in *Phenomenological Psychology*, by Erwin Straus, trans. Erling Eng (New York: Basic Books, 1966).

15. Jay, *Downcast Eyes*, 383–84. Cf. Jacques-Alain Miller, "Jeremy Bentham's Panoptic Device," *October* 41 (summer 1987): 3–29.

16. Celia Lury writes, citing Martin Jay, "Foucault remained unremittingly hostile to the power of vision," in *Prosthetic Culture: Photography, Memory, and Identity* (London: Routledge, 1998), 10.

17. I give a further account of Nietzsche's project of "overcoming Lessing's aesthetics" in sec. 14.

18. Jacques Derrida, *The Truth in Painting*, trans. Geoff Bennington and Ian McLeod (Chicago: University of Chicago Press, 1987), 23.

19. For a fuller account and further references, see my article "French Aesthetics: Contemporary Painting Theory," in *Encyclopedia of Aesthetics*, ed. Michael Kelly (New York: Oxford University Press, 1998), 2:235–40.

20. A sample of some studies of philosophers in the light of their relation to visual culture would include Pierre Maxime Schuhl, *Platon et l'art de son temps* (Paris: Presses Universitaires de France, 1952); Eva C. Keuls, *Plato and Greek Painting* (Leiden: Brill, 1978); Gilles Deleuze, *The Fold: Leibniz and the Baroque*, trans. Tom Conley (London: Athlone, 1993); Beat Wyss, *Hegel's Art History and the Critique of Modernity*, trans. Caroline Saltzwedel (New York: Cambridge University Press, 1999).

21. Nietzsche's references to the labyrinth and to the myth of Theseus, Ariadne, and Dionysus are frequent. For a provocative psychological reading in terms of homoeroticism and power, see Joachim Köhler, *Nietzsche and Wagner: A Lesson in Subjugation*, trans. Ronald Taylor (New Haven, CT: Yale Univer-

sity Press, 1998). Foucault's book on Raymond Roussel, *Death and the Labyrinth*, does not develop the theme as explicitly as the title might promise; but Foucault sometimes invokes the labyrinthine topos elsewhere, as in the introduction to *The Archaeology of Knowledge*, where he talks about preparing a labyrinth for himself "opening up underground passages, forcing [the discourse] to go far from itself, finding overhangs that reduce and deform its itinerary" (*AK* 17; *AS* 28); see sec. 66. The appeal to the figure of the labyrinth suggests that the "unthought" of this book, in the Heideggerian sense, is spatiality; it is addressed somewhat obliquely in chapter 4, where I explore Nietzsche on the *dispositif* of the Greek theater, and in chapter 10, which deals with the Panopticon. I hope to devote another study to some of the questions raised by the way in which space has to some extent "displaced" time in post-Kantian transcendental aesthetics.

22. Originally published under the title *Folie et déraison*, new ed. (Paris: Gallimard, 1972). This edition also includes Foucault's response to Derrida's reading of his account of Descartes on dreams and madness, "Mon corps, ce papier, ce feu." None of this material appears in the English edition, and none of it was reprinted in later French editions.

23. For a brief conspectus of some of this history and context, see Seymour Slive, ed., *Frans Hals* (London: Royal Academy of Arts, 1989), 362–69.

24. Gerald S. Davies, *Frans Hals* (London: G. Bell and Sons, 1902), 80.

25. P. J. Vinken and E. de Jongh, "De boosaardigheid van Hals' regenten en regentessen," *Oud Holland* 78 (1963): 1–26.

26. Seymour Slive, *Frans Hals* (New York: Phaidon Press, 1970), 1:210–15.

27. John Berger, *Ways of Seeing* (New York: Viking Press, 1973), 11–16. See also Peter Fuller, *Seeing Berger: A Revaluation of Ways of Seeing* (London: Writers and Readers Publishing Cooperative, 1980), 5–10. While in general agreement with Berger's Marxist reading of the painting, Fuller argues that he should give more attention to the human constants that allow us to make sense of the subjects' expressions.

28. Paul Claudel, *The Eye Listens*, trans. Elsie Pell (Port Washington, NY: Kennikat Press, 1969), 28–29.

29. Georges Bataille, *Story of the Eye*, trans. Joachim Neugroschel (San Francisco: City Lights Books, 1987), 98. The first edition of the novel appeared in 1928; *W.C.* was published in 1943 in *Le Petit*.

30. Lionel Gosman, *Basel in the Age of Burckhardt* (Chicago: University of Chicago Press, 2000), 350.

31. We can plausibly suppose that Nietzsche saw this famous painting in Basel, where he lived and taught for almost ten years. We could even imagine him thinking of it in connection with the dictum "God is dead." Dostoyevsky, who traveled to Basel to see the painting, has Prince Myshkin declare in *The Idiot*, "Why, some people may lose their faith by looking at that picture!" *The Idiot*, trans. David Magarshack (New York: Penguin, 1955), 236. See Julia Kristeva, "Holbein's Dead Christ," in *Black Sun: Depression and Melancholia*, by Julia Kristeva, trans. Leon S. Roudiez (New York: Columbia University Press, 1989).

32. See Oskar Bätschmann and Pascal Grenier, *Hans Holbein*, trans. Cecilia Hurley and Pascal Grenier (Princeton, NJ: Princeton University Press, 1997), esp. chap. 6, "The Portrait, Time, and Death," 149–93. Bätschmann and

Grenier do not comment on the left-to-right structure of the painting, although they do have useful observations concerning Holbein's use of script within his pictures.

33. Maurice Merleau-Ponty, "Eye and Mind," in *The Merleau-Ponty Aesthetics Reader,* ed. Galen Johnson (Evanston, IL: Northwestern University Press, 1993), 130.

34. R. J. Hollingdale, whose translation (London: Cambridge University Press, 1986) I am mostly following here, renders Nietzsche's *innere Phantasie* by "the imagination." While contemporary English spelling may be "fantasy," "phantasy" is a good enough transliteration of the Greek. I preserve the reference to the tradition connected with the Greek term, which Nietzsche, Foucault, Klossowski, and Deleuze typically presuppose. There is a suggestion of the *merely* and perhaps personally imaginary in "fantasy," but Nietzsche and Foucault both employ variants of the Greek, which can speak of the phantasm as a relatively free-floating thing. See secs. 19, 20, 43, 77, 78.

35. Paul Kristeller, "The Modern System of the Arts," in his *Renaissance Thought II: Humanism and the Arts* (New York: Harper & Row, 1965).

36. Belting, *Likeness and Presence.*

37. Ibid., 9.

38. André Malraux, *The Voices of Silence,* trans. Stuart Gilbert (Princeton, NJ: Princeton University Press, 1978), esp. pt. 1, "Museum without Walls."

39. Martin Heidegger, "Plato's Doctrine of Truth," trans. John Barlow, in *Philosophy in the Twentieth Century,* ed. Henry Aiken and William Barrett (New York: Random House, 1962), 3:261.

40. Ibid., 265.

41. Ibid., 267.

42. I have explored some of the limits of Heidegger's reading of Nietzsche in *Nietzschean Narratives* (Bloomington: Indiana University Press, 1989), where I questioned Heidegger's account of Nietzsche as the destined completion of Western metaphysics; in *Alcyone: Nietzsche on Gifts, Noise, and Women* (Albany: State University of New York Press, 1991), I argued that the three themes in the book's subtitle ought to be understood as counterconcepts to those of property, meaning, and man as understood in the metaphysical tradition.

Chapter One

1. Nietzsche to his mother, May 1885, *Selected Letters of Friedrich Nietzsche,* ed. and trans. Christopher Middleton (Chicago: University of Chicago Press, 1969), 242–43. For a critical review of the medical information concerning Nietzsche's eye troubles, see Pia Volz, *Nietzsche im Labyrinth seiner Krankheit: Eine medizinisch-biographische Untersuchung* (Würzburg: Königshausen und Neumann: 1990), 90–118.

2. For the halcyon, see Shapiro, *Alcyone.* For a scholarly overview of Claude's meaning for Nietzsche and some of the resonances of the encounter with the painter for other aspects of Nietzsche's thought about the arts, see Ingrid Schulze, *"Nietzsche und Claude Lorrain," Nietzscheforschung* 4 (1998): 217–25.

3. Fyodor Dostoyevsky, *The Possessed,* trans. Constance Garnett (New

York: Modern Library, 1936), 695. Julia Kristeva comments on Dostoyevsky's use of the painting in *Black Sun*, 201–3.

4. See Theocritus, *Cyclops (Idyll 11)*, and the account by William Berg in *Early Virgil* (London: Athlone Press, 1974), 8–12; in Ovid's *Metamorphoses*, trans. Frank Justus Miller (New York: G. P. Putnam's Sons, 1926), the story of Acis and Galatea is in bk. 13, lines 738–897.

5. Ovid, *Metamorphoses*, bk. 13, lines 851–53.

6. Martin Heidegger, "The Age of the World Picture," in *The Question concerning Technology*, trans. William Lovitt (New York: Harper and Row, 1977).

7. For a brief review of this thesis and of Claude's significance in the landscape tradition, see Gina Crandell, *Nature Pictorialized* (Baltimore: Johns Hopkins University Press, 1993), 59–82.

8. See Hubert Damisch, "Claude: A Problem in Perspective," in *Claude Lorrain, 1600–1682*, ed. Pamela Askew (Washington, DC: National Gallery of Art, 1984), 29–44.

9. See Crandell, *Nature Pictorialized*, 1–14 and passim.

10. This is the original version of parts of the passage from *Human, All Too Human, Assorted Opinions and Maxims*. Nietzsche's later citation in *Nietzsche contra Wagner* is somewhat abbreviated.

11. Jacques Derrida, *Speech and Phenomena, and Other Essays on Husserl's Theory of Signs*, trans. David Allison (Evanston, IL: Northwestern University Press, 1973), 95.

12. Cf. Gary Shapiro, *Earthwards: Robert Smithson and Art after Babel* (Berkeley: University of California Press, 1995), 65–69, which discusses the deconstruction of the *video* and the questioning of Cyclopean vision with reference to Smithson, Heidegger, and Derrida.

13. In March 1888, Nietzsche writes to Georg Brandes, the first scholar to lecture on his thought, offering an account of the ups and downs of his eyesight: "In my eyes, by the way, I have a dynamometer of my total condition: they are more durable than I had ever believed, as the main thing goes onward and upward—they have made a disgrace of the prophecies of the very best German ophthalmologists" (*B* 8.278). Nietzsche recognized that the many perspectives offered by his eyes corresponded to the many forms of his general way of life.

14. Ernst Bertram offers a reading of this and other passages on Claude in his *Nietzsche: Versuch einer Mythologie* (Berlin: Georg Bondi, 1922), 249–60; Bertram wants to demonstrate what is specifically German in the mythology that he takes Nietzsche to be constructing about the south. Insofar as a certain tradition would identify southern Europe as relatively timeless in comparison to the supposed historical dynamism of the north, this interpretation coincides with the one I am suggesting to a limited extent. The differences are perhaps more significant. Bertram, writing in the wake of the German defeat, was attempting to use Nietzsche in the cause of German nationalism; I am trying to show that Nietzsche was thinking of the case of vision, and the vision of beauty, with respect to some of what are generally taken to be the major themes of his philosophy, such as perspectivism, tragedy, and eternal recurrence. Bertram is one of the few writers on Nietzsche who has made the question of the philosopher's concern with the visual an explicit theme, and he argues that Nietzsche was scarcely interested in visual art or in his surroundings.

He claims that "Nietzsche was completely the grandson of the Protestant Reformation" in this respect (54). But he does this in the context of his essay "Ritter, Tod und Teufel" (in the book cited) in order to claim that Nietzsche had a singular interest in Dürer's image because of its implications for the German fate. Similarly, he claims that Nietzsche's references to Claude are symptomatic of his rethinking of the German longing for the south, rather than to be understood in the terms of a visual thematics having to do with the fragility of vision or the meaning of landscape. One notable exception to the general neglect of Nietzsche's concern with the visual is Vivetta Vivarelli, "'Vorschule des Sehens' und 'stilisierte Natur' in der *Morgenröthe* und der *Fröhlichen Wissenschaft,*" *Nietzsche-Studien* 20 (1991): 134–51. Vivarelli argues that in 1880–82 Nietzsche drew a "series of images" from the writings of Burckhardt, Stendhal, and Goethe on Italian art in order to "outline an anti-Schopenhauerian and anti-Wagnerian ethical model" (134). Vivarelli does not note that Nietzsche was concerned with Burckhardt's art writing at least as early as 1870.

15. For an excellent survey and contextualization of the pastoral and utopian dimensions of Claude's painting and of some of his contemporaries, see Margaretha Rossholm Lagerlöf, *Ideal Landscape: Annibale Caracci, Nicolas Poussin, and Claude Lorrain,* trans. Nancy Adler (New Haven, CT: Yale University Press, 1990), esp. 161–84.

16. Sir Joshua Reynolds, *Discourses on Art,* ed. R. B. Wark (San Marino, CA: Huntington Library, 1959), 255 (Discourse 14, Dec. 10, 1788).

17. John Ruskin, *Modern Painters* (London: George Allen, 1906), 1:xl–xliii. At the conclusion of an inventory of Claude's alleged inconsistencies, Ruskin writes: "This is, I believe, a fair example of what is commonly called an 'ideal' landscape; i.e. a group of the artist's studies from nature, individually spoiled, selected with such opposition of character as may insure their neutralizing each other's effect, and united with sufficient unnaturalness and violence of association to insure their producing a general sensation of the impossible" (xl).

18. *Conversations of Goethe with Eckermann,* trans. John Oxenford (New York: E. P. Dutton, 1935), 321. Nietzsche's verdict is recorded in *HAH, WS,* 109; *KSA* 2.599).

19. Jakob Burckhardt, *Der Cicerone* (Stuttgart: Alfred Kröner Verlag, 1964), 998–99.

20. There is a rich literature on Poussin's paintings of the Arcadian shepherds. Erwin Panofsky's classic essay *"Et in Arcadia Ego:* Poussin and the Elegiac Tradition," in his *Meaning in the Visual Arts* (New York: Doubleday, 1955), argues for a distinction between Poussin's two versions of the theme, in the first of which the subject of the inscription is "I, death," while in the other it is "I, the person interred in the tomb." Some critics, in keeping with a style of reading that allows for a greater multiplicity of meaning, have suggested more complex readings; see Louis Marin, "Towards a Theory of Reading in the Visual Arts: Poussin's *The Arcadian Shepherds,*" in *Calligram: Essays in New Art History from France,* ed. Norman Bryson (New York: Cambridge University Press, 1988), 63–90, and my discussion in *Earthwards,* 214–21.

21. The first inventory of the collection, dating from 1587, lists globes and maps, measuring devices, clocks and automata, a library of books oriented to Augustus's interests in geography and surveying, and, especially notable, the unicorn's horn that hung from the ceiling by a golden chain. By Nietzsche's time the old master paintings had a building of their own in the Zwinger complex; it had been designed originally by Gottfried Semper, but the architect's participa-

tion in the uprising of 1849 forced him to flee Dresden, and his plans were modified somewhat, over his protests lodged from Paris. Semper had the main responsibility not only for framing the old master paintings in Dresden but also for most of the theatrical, musical, and operatic performances that took place there, for he was also the architect of the *Hoftheater* and the *Opernhaus*. Nietzsche saw paintings, plays, and operas, especially Wagner's, through the frames that Semper fashioned. Wagner and Semper were close collaborators for a time, and during the height of his friendship with Wagner, Nietzsche read and annotated Semper's book on style, a reading that seems to have contributed to his reconstruction of the architectonics or framing of ancient tragedy and which shows an early interest in contemporary theories of the visual arts. After the bombing of Dresden in 1945, the hiding of most of the paintings, their removal to the Soviet Union, and the reconstruction of the Gallery, which reopened in 1956 (and was again closed for restoration after the reunification of Germany), the museum continues to exhibit Raphael's painting in a privileged position and to reproduce the "holy of holies" style of presentation for the entire collection that was confirmed in Semper's design.

22. Henner Menz, *The Dresden Gallery*, trans. Daphne Woodward (New York: Harry N. Abrams, 1962), 62. This book and the more recent *Gemäldegalerie Dresden—Alte Meister: Führer*, by Harald Marx (Leipzig: E. A. Seemann, 1994) are useful guides to the collection and its history.

23. See Belting, *Likeness and Presence*, chap. 20, "Religion and Art: The Crisis of the Image at the Beginning of the Modern Age," 458–90; the discussion of Calvinist history is on 460–61.

24. In a brilliant concluding section (ibid., 478–84), Belting explores the significance of the *Sistine Madonna* within this context, both in its original terms and in those of the romantics who came close to worshiping it in its Dresden setting. The painting was originally painted for the high altar of the church at the monastery of San Sisto, Piacenza; the two figures at the sides are the monastery's patron saints, Pope Sixtus and Saint Barbara. Before it was purchased for the Dresden royal collection by Augustus III (for a price that set a record for the nascent art market), there seems to have been little interest in the painting. Augustus was Catholic, so presumably more receptive to such pictures than some of his Protestant predecessors.

25. It is not surprising to learn that his earliest philosophical hero, Schopenhauer, had chosen to live in Dresden while writing *The World as Will and Representation* in 1814–18, a decision made largely on account of the city's artistic and cultural resources. On the verge of his move to the Saxon capital, he wrote to Karl August Böttiger, who was chief inspector of the Royal Museum of Antiquities in Dresden: "My better and real life are my philosophical studies, everything else is well subordinated to them, and is indeed no more than peripheral. However, being in the position to choose, I desire a place of residence which would offer me the beauties of nature, the pleasures of art, and the appurtenances of scholarship, and which would allow me to find the necessary repose. All of these, far though I have travelled, I have never found so happily combined as in Dresden, and it has therefore long been my wish to settle down there permanently. I am therefore very keen on going to Dresden." Schopenhauer to Böttiger, Apr. 24, 1814, quoted in Rüdiger Safranski, *Schopenhauer and the Wild Years of Philosophy*, Ewald Osers, trans. (Cambridge, MA: Harvard University Press, 1989), 191. Schopenhauer moved to Dresden the next month. The statement is full of Schopenhauer's characteristic arrogance, but it

exemplifies the taste of the century, in which Dresden was high on the list of cultural centers for the educated European. While working on his manuscript, Schopenhauer was a frequent visitor to the Dresden Gallery, and the pages of his major work devoted to art and religion contain a good number of references to the paintings of Raphael, Coreggio, and other artists whose works he saw there. His rival Hegel was not so well endowed with money and leisure, but he managed to make a two-week visit to the city, and the results of his survey of the Gallery are to be found in his *Lectures on Aesthetics*.

26. Edward Snow, *A Study of Vermeer* (Berkeley: University of California Press, 1994), 54.

27. Zeuxis was famous for having painted grapes so lifelike that the birds came down to peck at them; not to be outdone, in this art that may always be shadowed by the agon, Parrhasius invites his rival to his own studio to behold his response. Zeuxis arrives, sees a draped canvas, and asks the other painter to remove the drapery so he can view the painting. But the drapes were painted, showing that Parrhasius was able to confuse a skilled student of appearances, not only the birds, with the suggestion here being that they are painted by light, not merely by the hand of the artist. See Pliny, *Natural History*, trans. H. Rackham (Cambridge, MA: Harvard University Press, 1968), bk. 35.36.65–66.

28. In writing of Monet, John Sallis says, "What is painted is . . . the spread of light over all things, that is, the shining itself, that which ordinarily lets things be visible while itself remaining largely unseen." *Shades—of Painting at the Limit* (Bloomington: Indiana University Press, 1998), 48.

29. Arthur Schopenhauer, *The World as Will and Representation*, trans. E. F. Payne (New York: Dover Books, 1969), 1:221 (this work is cited hereinafter as WWR).

30. Caroline Schlegel's remark, in the *Athenaeum*, the house organ of early German romanticism, is quoted in Harald Marx, *Gemäldegalerie Dresden*, 184.

31. I assume that the landscapes are the three paintings in the Palazzo Doria that are mentioned in Burckhardt's *Cicerone* (1964), 998.

32. See Bernard Frischer, *The Sculpted Word* (Berkeley: University of California Press, 1982).

Chapter Two

1. Eric Blondel, *Nietzsche, the Body, and Culture*, trans. Seán Hand (Stanford, CA: Stanford University Press, 1991); see my review in *Man and World* (now *Continental Philosophy Review*) 26 (1993): 228–31.

2. Plato, *Republic*, 395e–396b; I've attempted to show the way in which Nietzsche responds to this proscription of the female voice in *Alcyone*, especially in the "Prelude" and in "Alcyone's Song: The Halcyon Tone." Perhaps the current study can be thought of as supplementing or paralleling that exploration of voice with an inquiry into vision, and so proceeding to adumbrate a study of Nietzsche's attempt to develop the equivalent of a transcendental aesthetic or a philosophy of embodiment and an embodiment of philosophy.

3. For a concise statement, see Gotthold Ephraim Lessing, *Laocoön: An Essay on the Limits of Painting and Poetry*, trans. Edward Allen McCormick (Baltimore: Johns Hopkins, 1984), 78–79.

4. Irving Babbitt, *The New Laokoon* (Boston: Houghton Mifflin, 1934);

Clement Greenberg, "Towards a Newer Laocoon," in *Clement Greenberg: The Collected Essays and Criticism*, ed. John O'Brian, vol. 1, *Perceptions and Judgments, 1939–1944* (Chicago: University of Chicago Press, 1986). Michael Fried, "Art and Objecthood," in his *Art and Objecthood: Essays and Reviews* (Chicago: University of Chicago Press, 1998).

5. Greenberg's classic and most influential statement of his position is found in "Modernist Painting," in *The New Art*, ed. Gregory Battcock (New York: Dutton, 1973). The indispensable commentary on Greenberg's statements on modernism is Thierry de Duve, *Kant after Duchamp* (Cambridge, MA: MIT Press, 1996), esp. 201–29; de Duve describes the project of this book as an archaeology of modernism, inspired by Michel Foucault. However, he does not develop the meaning of archaeology, other than to say it should be taken in Foucault's sense (73 n). On Greenberg and modernism, see also Shapiro, *Earthwards*, esp. 33–35; Mark Cheetham explores Greenberg's appeal to Kant's critical philosophy in *Kant, Art, and Art History* (Cambridge: Cambridge University Press, 2001), 87–100.

6. For a recent exploration of the parallels between Aeschylus and Wagner, see Michael Evans, *Wagner and Aeschylus* (New York: Cambridge University Press, 1982).

7. Many more recent readers would disagree with Nietzsche, who here seems to be following the general outlines of German philology, which since Friedrich Wolf tended to see the Homeric poems as stitched together from a number of diverse songs. In *Homer and the Heroic Tradition* (Cambridge: Harvard University Press, 1958), Cedric Whitman develops a powerful argument that the *Iliad* has a complex order akin to Greek geometrical art, in which incidents in two great leaves of the poem mirror each other; on this view the two leaves frame a central, more chaotic series of episodes, thus providing, in Nietzsche's terms, an Apollonian structure for a Dionysian wisdom.

8. In his *Aesthetics*, Hegel saw the epic as objective, the lyric as subjective, and the dramatic as the combination of the two; see Gary Shapiro, "Hegel on the Meanings of Poetry," *Journal of Aesthetics and Art Criticism* 1976 (fall 1976): 23–35.

9. The text is at *KSA* 7.359–69; a translation by Walter Kaufmann is reprinted as an appendix to Carl Dahlhaus, *Between Romanticism and Modernism: Four Studies in the Music of the Later Nineteenth Century* (Berkeley: University of California Press, 1980), 106–19; I have generally followed this translation.

10. I borrow the term *iconophobic* from W. J. T. Mitchell, *Iconology: Image, Text, Ideology* (Chicago: University of Chicago Press, 1986).

11. Merleau-Ponty, "Eye and Mind," 127.

12. Especially Nietzsche's early writing may be thought of as belonging to the tradition that E. M. Butler called *The Tyranny of Greece over Germany*. The German writers of the nineteenth century also tended to be in awe of the painters of the Renaissance, notably Raphael, Leonardo, and Michelangelo. Jakob Burckhardt, Nietzsche's colleague at Basel, can be considered as the inventor of this era in his *Civilization of the Renaissance in Italy*. Burckhardt's conception of Raphael as the exemplary Renaissance painter, which emerges in his writings on art, is discussed later (secs. 19, 20).

13. For a comprehensive discussion of Raphael's *Saint Cecilia* and its iconographic context, see Thomas Connolly, *Mourning into Joy* (New Haven, CT: Yale University Press, 1994).

14. Schopenhauer, *WWR*, 1:267.

15. Ibid., 1:25.

16. Jacob Burckhardt, *Cicerone*, trans. Mrs. A. H. Clough (London: John Murray, 1879), 144–45.

17. Lessing, *Laocoön*, 14–15.

18. Mitchell, *Iconology*, 110.

19. See *KSA* 14.52, where a discarded passage on a fresco by Bernardo Luini is recorded.

Chapter Three

1. For a classical account of ekphrasis, see Paul Friedländer, *Johannes von Gaza, Paulus Silentiarus und Prokopios von Gaza: Kunstbeschreibungen justinianischer Zeit* (Hildesheim, Germany: Georg Olms Verlag, 1969), 1–103; more recent studies, with ample references to ancient and modern literature, are James A. W. Heffernan, *Museum of Words* (Chicago: University of Chicago Press, 1993); and W. J. T. Mitchell, "Ekphrasis and the Other," in Mitchell, *Picture Theory*. In addition to Homer's account of the shield of Achilles, and Virgil's of Aeneas's, one should consult Philostratus the Elder, *Imagines*, trans. Arthur Fairbanks (New York: G. P. Putnam's Sons, 1931); see, for example, *Imagines* 1.9 (pp. 35–41) for the theme of the play between the seen and the unseen; a very suggestive recent study is Norman Bryson's essay "Philostratus and the Imaginary Museum," in *Art and Text in Ancient Greek Culture*, ed. Simon Goldhill and Robin Osborne (Cambridge: Cambridge University Press, 1994), 255–83. For descriptions of paintings that their authors could not have seen, see Pliny, *Natural History*, trans. H. Rackham (Cambridge, MA: Harvard University Press, 1968), bk. 35; and Franciscus Junius, *The Painting of the Ancients*, ed. Keith Aldrich, Philipp Fehl, and Raina Fehl (Berkeley: University of California Press, 1991).

2. Giorgio Vasari, *The Lives of the Artists*, trans. George Bull (New York: Penguin, 1965), 284.

3. Ibid., 320–21.

4. Burckhardt, *Cicerone* (1964), 812. See Hayden White, *Metahistory: The Historical Imagination in Nineteenth-Century Europe* (Baltimore: Johns Hopkins University Press, 1973), 251–62.

5. Burckhardt, *Cicerone* (1879), 139.

6. White, *Metahistory*, 252.

7. Ibid.

8. Raphael died on his thirty-seventh birthday (April 6, 1520). Nietzsche gives him only thirty-six years, perhaps thinking of his own father's death at that age.

9. Burckhardt said, for example in his *Reflections on History (Weltgeschichtliche Betrachtungen)*: "All high art arises when the soul is set mysteriously vibrating. What is released as a result of these vibrations no longer belongs to a particular individual or a particular time but functions as a symbol and acquires everlastingness." Quoted in Gosman, *Basel in the Age of Burckhardt*, 365.

10. Schopenhauer, *WWR*, 1:411. In addition to the *Sistine Madonna*, the Dresden Gallery, in the city where Schopenhauer composed his major work, is rich in Correggios that could sustain his remark.

11. S. J. Freedberg says that the two scenes are "irremediably disconnected" and "peculiar" in *Painting of the High Renaissance in Rome and Flor-
ence* (Cambridge, MA: Harvard University Press, 1961), 337. He qualifies this
judgment somewhat ten years later: "What Raphael has conceived in the *Transfiguration* no longer works as a genuinely synthetic image but as one in which
disparates have been forced to coexist; this forced unity has been made by an
overriding power of dramatic idea, supported by brilliantly contrived devices of
form. No work could demonstrate more clearly Raphael's continuing assertion
of basic classical principles and, at the same time, the strain and alteration of
such principles by new intentions. The *Transfiguration* shows, with almost schematic explicitness, the fault that has opened in the structure of classical style."
Painting in Italy: 1500–1600 (New Haven, CT: Yale University Press, 1971), 83.
And in the next decade, Freedberg speaks perhaps even more highly of the painting, describing its combination of the two scenes as taking place by a *"force
majeure,"* which produces the following effect: "This brilliant, daring and profoundly intelligent manipulation is the mainspring of the grand machinery of
form in the *Transfiguration*, and it is, as well, the source of its utterly commanding content, a content which, quite aside from any precise fact of narrative, exalts meaning to its highest pitch of climax and with no possibility of re-
mission holds it there." *Raphael, Michelangelo, and Others* (Poughkeepsie, NY:
Vassar College, 1983), 16. John Pope-Hennessy refers to the "two unrelated
scenes" in *Raphael* (New York: New York University Press, 1970), 73. E. H.
Gombrich speaks of the combination of the scenes as puzzling and "untenable,"
in *New Light on Old Masters* (Chicago: University of Chicago Press, 1986), 143.

12. The most frequent identification of the two figures on the left has been
that they are the patron saints of Narbonne Cathedral, Justus and Pastor; Giulio
de' Medici had commissioned the painting for Narbonne. The quotations are
from Matt. 17:2, 5. All quotations from the Bible are from the King James Version.

13. Johann Wolfgang von Goethe, *Italian Journey*, trans. Robert R. Heit-
ner (New York: Suhrkamp, 1989), 364.

14. Hegel, *Aesthetics*, trans. T. M. Knox (New York: Oxford University
Press, 1975), 2:860.

15. Von Löhneysen describes and richly documents the process by which
critics have ingeniously attributed various aspects of the painting to different
hands, especially to those of Giulio Romano. Wolfgang Freiherr von Löhneysen,
*Raffael unter den Philosophen, Philosophen über Raffael: Denkbild und Sprache
der Interpretation* (Berlin: Duncker und Humblot, 1992), 251.

16. Gordon Bendersky, M.D., argues for the postseizure character of the
boy and the scene in "Remarks on Raphael's Transfiguration," *Notes in the History of Art* (summer 1995): 18–25.

17. Nietzsche praises Burckhardt's *Cicerone* to his friend Carl von Gersdorff in 1872, when he learns that the latter is planning a journey to Italy: "[I]t
seems to me that one should wake up and fall asleep with the reading of Burckhardt's Cicerone: there are few books that can so stimulate *Phantasie* and prepare one for the impression of the artistic." Nietzsche to von Gersdorff, Oct. 18,
1872 (*B* 4.68). Similar enthusiasm is expressed in a card to Mathilde Maier of
Aug. 6, 1878 (*B* 5.345), and in a letter to his sister Elisabeth, to whom he had
just given a new edition of the book as a birthday gift (*B* 6.391).

18. *Schein* is conventionally translated (by Walter Kaufmann, for example)
as "appearance," but that term can be fraught with unnecessary metaphysical

and epistemological baggage, since it suggests the importance of a distinction between appearance and reality, or between that which gives rise to appearance and the appearance itself. Translating *Schein* simply as "illusion" or "mere appearance" (Kaufmann often chooses the latter) enforces the impression that Nietzsche is just following Schopenhauer here; but we can read the *Birth* more productively as adopting Schopenhauer in a much more tentative and provisional fashion. As John Sallis suggests, in *The Birth of Tragedy* "the word *Schein* will have to be read in its full range of senses: shine, look, appearance, semblance, illusion." John Sallis, *Crossings: Nietzsche and the Space of Tragedy* (Chicago: University of Chicago Press, 1991), 25. Sallis's chapter "Apollo—Shining Phantasy" (9–41) is illuminating on Apollonian vision.

19. See Emil Staiger, *"Ein Briefwechsel mit Martin Heidegger,"* in his *Die Kunst der Interpretation* (Zürich: Atlantis, 1955); and the discussion in Albert Hofstadter, *Truth and Art* (New York: Columbia University Press, 1965), 196–98.

20. Martin Heidegger, *Being and Time,* trans. Joan Stambaugh (Albany: State University of New York Press, 1996), 25.

21. Schopenhauer, *WWR,* 1:232.

22. Ibid., 1:209–10.

23. For an account of the *paragone* of the two painters, see Rudolf Preimesberger, "Tragische Motive in Raffaels 'Transfiguration,'" *Zeitschrift für Kunstgeschichte* 50 (1987): 89–115. Preimesberger's rich essay also argues for seeing the painting as alluding to the struggle between Christendom and Islam, suggesting that the "moonstruck" boy—the moon is reflected in water at the lower left of the painting—is to be seen as a symbol of the madness of the Turks (Islam being represented by the crescent moon). In addition, he sees Raphael as having adopted the pattern of reversal and recognition from Aristotle's *Poetics,* which was being discussed intensively at the time of the painting; on this reading Christ would be simultaneously revealed as God's son and in his miracle-working capacity. Such an Aristotelian interpretation, of course, runs counter to Nietzsche's nonnarrative way of construing the picture; the analysis given in *The Birth of Tragedy* does indeed explore the tragic motifs of Raphael's work, but on the basis of an understanding of tragedy that sets out to be quite different from Aristotle's.

24. Nietzsche may have been stimulated by Hölderlin's tendency to link Apollo and Christ, but here he would be substituting one for the other.

25. Louis Marin makes this point in his sensitive and complex essay "Transfiguration in Raphael, Stendhal, and Nietzsche," in *Nietzsche in Italy,* ed. Thomas Harrison (Saratoga, CA.: Anima Libri, 1988), 67–76. On his reading it is the collapse or syncopation of the earlier picture that allows the introduction of the lower scene (in the final version), and the inconsistency of the two parts of the painting helps to make it clear that what is seen now is *our* vision (73). Marin suggests that the painting prefigures the opposition announced in Nietzsche's final text, *Ecce Homo,* of Dionysus and the Crucified; yet in *The Birth of Tragedy* the floating figure is named as Apollo, rather than as Jesus or Christ. He also articulates an analogy between Nietzsche's reading of the painting and the passage of *Ecce Homo* in which Nietzsche declares that the riddle of his existence is that he is dead as his father but alive as his mother, and that he has a "dual descent, as it were, both from the highest and the lowest rung on the ladder of life"; it is as if Nietzsche is here describing himself in terms of "the composition and distribution of Raphael's *Transfiguration*" (76). Marin

points out that Nietzsche could not have known Stendhal's discussion of the *Transfiguration*, although he notes that Stendhal was among those who saw as problematic the apparent disjunction of the upper and lower scenes.

26. Bendersky, "Raphael's Transfiguration," 20.

27. Kaufmann translates "Und so möchte von Apollo in einem excentrischen Sinne das gelten . . ." as "And so, in one sense, we might apply to Apollo the words of Schopenhauer . . ."; this, like some other aspects of this translation, fails to convey some of the ways in which Nietzsche distances himself from Schopenhauer.

28. Burckhardt, *Cicerone* (1879), 145.

29. Burckhardt, *Cicerone* (1964), 857; I have generally followed the partial translation by Clough (1879), 145.

30. Ibid.

31. Belting, *Likeness and Presence*.

32. The question of how much Freud knew of Nietzsche's philosophy is a complex one. Freud said that he had never read more than a page of Nietzsche; he also declared that he had a greater self-knowledge than any man who had ever lived. See Ernest Jones's report of the Oct. 28, 1908, meeting of the Vienna Psychoanalytic Society in *Sigmund Freud: Life and Work* (New York: Basic Books, 1955), 2:385. Recent research makes a plausible case that Freud knew much more of Nietzsche's work than he ever acknowledged; see, for example, Ronald Lehrer, *Nietzsche's Presence in Freud's Life and Thought: On the Origins of a Psychology of Dynamic Unconscious Mental Functioning* (Albany: State University of New York Press, 1995).

33. See Friedrich Schiller, *Naive and Sentimental Poetry*, trans. Julius A. Elias (New York: Frederick Ungar, 1966).

34. As Vasari informs us, Raphael's painting was created in direct competition with Sebastiano's *Raising of Lazarus* (now in the National Gallery in London); both had originally been commissioned by Cardinal Giulio de' Medici for his church in Narbonne, France. One can imagine Nietzsche noting with interest the beauty brought about by such agonistic relations among painters. A. P. Oppé suggests, in effect, that Raphael's strength in this competition was his Apollonian spirit: "Raphael desired to give an exhibition not only of grouping, movement, and wide space, but also of the solid and brilliant delineation of form which was the truest characteristic of Florentine tradition, and the sharpest contrast to the sketchy and structureless creations of Sebastiano's superficial skill." *Raphael*, ed. Charles Mitchell (New York: Praeger, 1970), 120. For the apocalyptic reading of Raphael's painting, see Josephine Jungić, "Joachimist Prophecies in Sebastiano del Piombo's Borgherini Chapel and Raphael's *Transfiguration*," *Journal of the Warburg and Courtauld Institutes* (1988): 66–83.

35. Preimesberger, "Tragische Motive," 107.

36. August Wilhelm Schlegel, *Die Gemählde*, ed. Lothar Müller (Dresden: Verlag der Kunst, 1996), 104. Hegel takes the *Sistine Madonna* as an occasion for discussing the significance of prayer: "[P]rayer is itself satisfaction, enjoyment, the express feeling and consciousness of eternal love which is not only a ray of transfiguration shining through the worshipper's figure and situation, but is in itself the situation and what exists and is to be portrayed. This is the prayerful situation of e.g. Pope Sixtus in the Raphael picture that is called after him, and of St. Barbara in the same picture." Hegel, *Aesthetics*, 2:827.

37. Von Löhneysen, *Raffael*, 217; von Löhneysen reviews and documents the response to the painting, almost exclusively German (198–226).

38. Hegel sees the visual representation of the Christ child in Christian art as a manifestation of the truth of the incarnation, understood in terms of his philosophy of spirit. God becomes man, develops, and goes through the stages of human life as he completes and unfolds himself. In the *Aesthetics* he says, "So Raphael's pictures of the Christ-child, especially the one in the *Sistine Madonna* in Dresden, have the most beautiful expression of childhood, and yet we can see in them something beyond purely childlike innocence, something which makes visible the divine behind the veil of youth and gives us an inkling of the expansion of this divinity into an infinite revelation; and at the same time the picture of a *child* has justification in the fact that in him the revelation is not yet perfect." Hegel, *Aesthetics*, 2:823.

39. Schlegel, *Die Gemählde*, 129; cited in von Löhneysen, *Raffael*, 210.

40. Schopenhauer, *WWR*, 2:395.

41. Schopenhauer, *Parerga and Paralipomena*, trans. E. F. J. Payne (Oxford: Clarendon Press, 1974), 1:478.

42. Belting, *Likeness and Presence*, 483–84.

43. Nietzsche continues to praise Raphael in the wake of finishing the *Birth*. For Christmas 1871 his mother and sister sent him a print of the *Madonna della Sedia*, and he responds by reporting that his small room has become quite magnificent and takes the presence of the painting to be consonant with the imminent publication of his first book: "It also seems to me as if such a picture [*Bild*] is drawing me involuntarily toward Italy—and I almost think you have sent it to me as a temptation. I can't respond to this Apollonian effect in any other way than through my own Dionysian, that is Christmas Eve, and so through the Apollonian-Dionysian double effect of my book, that appears at New Year's" (*B* 265–66).

44. Schopenhauer, *WWR*, 1:411.

45. Hegel, *Aesthetics*, 1:9–11.

46. Burckhardt concludes his account of Raphael's *Transfiguration* with a similar remark, which clearly sums up his judgment on the artist's career: "Raphael was constantly endeavoring to master new methods of representation. As a conscientious artist he could do no less. Those who reproach him for it, and speak of decline, do not understand his inner nature. The ever-noble spectacle of Raphael's self-development as an artist is in itself worth more than any adherence to a particular stage of the ideal, for example, such as the *Disputà*, could be." *Cicerone* (1964), 858; Clough trans. (1879), 146. Cf. Nietzsche's note of 1880 in which he suggests that even the great "naïve style," which is "the highest in art," must be learned, but that this is not appreciated by the connoisseurs (*KSA* 9.352).

47. This emphasis on learning anticipates Nietzsche's remarks on the importance of learning to see (in *Twilight of the Idols*) and may reflect the intensive commitment in Basel to education in drawing, which was regarded, as Lionel Gosman says, as much more than an "idle supplement to education"; see Gosman, *Basel in the Age of Burckhardt*, 350.

48. See Jungić, "Joachimist Prophecies," 66–83.

49. In a note of 1885, Nietzsche implicitly classifies Raphael as being a dogmatic type, like Plato and Dante, and compares the three most famous artists of the Renaissance: "It requires a completely different kind of strength and flexi-

bility to remain within an incomplete system, with views that are free and unobstructed, than in a dogmatic world. Leonardo da Vinci stands higher than Michelangelo, Michelangelo higher than Raphael" (*KSA* 11.429; 34[25]).

50. In writing of Raphael's sensuality, Nietzsche may have been thinking of Vasari's report that his final illness was brought about by sexual dissipation; the artist had supposedly failed to tell his physicians of this, which led to their bleeding him, precisely the wrong procedure in the circumstances. Vasari, *Lives*, 320.

51. There is a parallel passage concerning the engraving in one of Nietzsche's notebooks of 1871: "We *do our duty and curse the monstrous burden of the present—we need* a special form of art. It offers us both duty and existence. Dürer's picture of knight, death, and devil as a symbol of our existence" (*KSA* 7.305; 9[85]). Around the same time there are two outlines, apparently of projected books, with chapter or section headings reading "Dürer, Ritter Tod."

52. The admirer was Adolf Vischer; see *B* 5.32, 36, 38.

53. See Erwin Panofsky, *The Life and Art of Albrecht Dürer* (Princeton, NJ: Princeton University Press, 1955), 152. Panofsky notes Dürer's familiarity with Erasmus's *Enchiridion*, in which he speaks of the "spooks and phantoms" that beset the way of the Christian but which can be ignored by the truly resolute.

54. Søren Kierkegaard, *The Concept of Anxiety*, trans. Reidar Thomte (Princeton, NJ: Princeton University Press, 1980), 130–32. For example, "[t]he most terrible words that sound from the abyss of evil would not be able to produce an effect like that of the suddenness of the leap that lies within the confines of the mimical" (131).

55. Burckhardt told his students of art history that "[t]he essential condition . . . for viewing works of art is that the eye must still be capable of seeing and must not yet have been dulled in relation to the visible world by overexertion or have become incapable of reacting to anything but the world of writing and prose." Quoted in Gosman, *Basel in the Age of Burckhardt*, 351.

56. There is perhaps some ambiguity in whether Nietzsche means to be speaking of Dürer's own clothing or that with which he dresses his figures; since he clothes the latter in contemporary fashions, the difference may be negligible.

Chapter Four

1. See Jacques Derrida, *The Politics of Friendship*, trans. George Collins (New York: Verso, 1997), 26–74.

2. See, e.g., Jürgen Habermas, "Knowledge and Human Interests: A General Perspective," in *Knowledge and Human Interests*, by Jürgen Habermas, trans. Jeremy J. Shapiro (Boston: Beacon Press, 1971), 301–2.

3. In translating *Bildnergott* as "sculptor god," we should be aware that *Bildner* is a rather rare term, which can be equivalent to *Bildhauer* (sculptor) or to the more general *Former* (former or molder); it is also an old synonym for *Erzieher* (educator) which seems especially appropriate since it would suggest, for Nietzsche, a teaching through images.

4. P. Christopher Smith, "From Acoustics to Optics: The Rise of the Metaphysical and Demise of the Melodic in Aristotle's *Poetics*," in *Sites of Vision: The Discursive Construction of Sight in the History of Philosophy*, ed. David M. Levin (Cambridge, MA: MIT Press, 1997), 69. Smith's essay provides a very

acute discussion of what he takes to be Aristotle's inconsistencies, stemming from his attempt to combine a recognition of tragedy's origins in ritual *mimesis* with an intellectualist focus on the intelligibility of the plot.

5. For a thorough and controversial account of Aristotle on the "parts" of tragedy, see Gerald F. Else, *Aristotle's Poetics: The Argument* (Cambridge, MA: Harvard University Press, 1967); Else suggests a number of complexities in the meaning of *opsis* (233–34) and *melos* (62–66). See 274–79 on the question whether Aristotle called *opsis* a "sweetening."

6. In a recent handbook, *The Ancient Theatre*, by Erika Simon, trans. C. E. Vafopoulou-Richardson (New York: Methuen, 1982), the author writes about this aspect of Greek theater: "The modern Greek performances have revived this oldest element of ancient drama in a remarkable way. The reason is that modern Greek choruses understand how to pray, dance, entreat and, above all, lament in the ancient manner, as hardly any other modern dramatic chorus can" (8).

7. For scholarly accounts of Greek tragic performance and theater, see Simon, *The Ancient Theatre*; A. W. Pickard-Cambridge, *The Theatre of Dionysus in Athens* (London: Oxford University Press, 1946); T. B. L. Webster, *Greek Theatre Production* (London: Methuen, 1956); and "The Origins of Tragedy" and "Tragedy in Performance," both in *The Cambridge History of Classical Literature*, vol. 1, *Greek Literature*, ed. P. E. Easterling and B. M. W. Knox (Cambridge: Cambridge University Press, 1985), 258–81.

8. Nietzsche did not make this point explicitly until *Twilight of the Idols*, sixteen years later. There he suggests that architecture is fundamentally different from the other arts in having broader scope and ambitions:

> The actor, the mime, the dancer, the musician, the lyric poet are fundamentally related in their instincts and essentially one, only gradually specialized and separated from one another—even to the point of opposition. The lyric poet stayed united longest with the musician, the actor with the dancer.—The *architect* represents neither a Dionysian nor an Apollonian condition; here it is the mighty act of will, the will which moves mountains, the intoxication of the strong will, which demands artistic expression. The most powerful men have always inspired the architects; the architect has always been influenced by power. Pride, victory over weight and gravity, the will to power, seek to render themselves visible in a building; architecture is a kind of rhetoric of power, now persuasive, even cajoling in form, now bluntly imperious. The highest feeling of power and security finds expression in that which possesses *grand style*. Power which no longer requires proving; which disdains to please; which is slow to answer; which is conscious of no witnesses around it; which lives oblivious of the existence of any opposition; which reposes in *itself*; fatalistic, a law among laws; *that* is what speaks of itself in the form of grand style. (*T* 10.11; *KSA* 6.118)

In some other late passages dealing with architecture, Nietzsche makes it clear that he is concerned with monumental building and city planning. In this vein he praises the layout of Turin and the aristocratic multiplicity of Genoa, where each palace institutes a unique perspective. The general feature of architecture in all of these accounts is that it establishes meaning, whether in the form of a "single commanding taste" as in Turin, or in the baroque churches that provide a space for transfiguration. For Turin see Nietzsche to Köselitz, Apr. 7, 1988 (*B* 8.284–86); on the baroque church, see *HAH, AOM,* 144; *KSA* 2.437–38. In *Daybreak* Nietzsche distinguishes Greek architecture from some of these more massive manifestations, noting that "at Paestum, Pompeii, and Athens, and with all Greek architecture, one is astonished at the smallness of the masses with which the Greeks contrive and love to express the sublime." The analysis of the Greek theater in *The Birth of Tragedy* is perhaps Nietzsche's most rigorous account of how a specific architectural structure works to make possible certain forms of meaning. For a series of essays exploring Nietzsche's thoughts concerning architecture, see Alexandre Kostka and Irving Wohlfarth, eds. *Nietzsche and "An Architecture of Our Minds"* (Los Angeles: Getty Research Institute, 1999), hereafter *"Architecture."* Surprisingly, none of the contributors discuss Nietzsche's analysis of the Greek theater. After commenting on the astonishing economy of Greek building, the passage in *Daybreak* concludes with a challenge to modernity to have the courage for its appropriate form of architecture: "Had we but will and daring enough for an architecture to match our own souls (we are too cowardly for that!)—then our prototype should be the labyrinth" (*D* 169; *KSA* 3.151). Although we do not dare to create such an architecture, he observes, we betray our labyrinthine proclivities in our music, where we mistakenly think that they are hidden. The Greek theater, where everything is on display and the center is manifestly visible and luminous, can be thought of as the antithesis of the labyrinth, where the center is hidden and the haptic dominates the optical.

9. Immanuel Kant, *Critique of Judgment,* trans. Werner S. Pluhar (Indianapolis: Hackett, 1987), sec. 14, p. 72 (Akademie edition, 226).

10. See Claudia Brodsky Lacour, "Architecture in the Discourse of Modern Philosophy: Descartes to Nietzsche," in *"Architecture,"* 19–34.

11. See Derrida, *Truth in Painting,* "Parergon." Derrida's claim is that despite the attempt of philosophical aesthetics to draw a sharp distinction between the allegedly extraneous frame and the intrinsic substance of the work, the frame is at least implicitly acknowledged as complicit with the work: "Philosophical discourse will always have been *against* the *parergon.* But what about this *against.* A *parergon* comes against, beside, and in addition to the *ergon,* the work done, the fact, the work, but it does not fall to one side, it touches and cooperates within the operation, from a certain outside. Neither simply outside nor simply inside" (54).

12. Jean-François Lyotard, *Les dispositifs pulsionnels* (Paris: Union Générale d'Editions, 1974), 268–69; I have used the translation in Geoffrey Bennington, *Lyotard: Writing the Event* (New York: Columbia University Press, 1988), 12–13.

13. With respect to the role of the mask and transformation, Nietzsche takes a position sharply opposed to Hegel's. In the chapter "Art-religion [*Kunstreligion*]" in *The Phenomenology of Spirit,* Hegel regards the separation between the actor and the character he plays, and between the audience and both, as carrying with it a dimension of the unintelligible, of a failure of reciprocity. Comedy, on the contrary, becomes for him a model of his own philosophical comedy of ultimate recognition and self-knowledge, insofar as the actor literally or metaphorically drops the mask and reveals that he, the audience, and the character portrayed are all on the same level, all intelligible to one another. See

G. W. F. Hegel, *The Phenomenology of Spirit,* trans. A. V. Miller (New York: Oxford University Press, 1977), 450; and Gary Shapiro, "Hegel's Dialectic of Artistic Meaning," *Journal of Aesthetics and Art Criticism* (fall 1976): 23–35.

14. Nietzsche, *Philosophy and Truth,* ed. and trans. Daniel Breazeale (Atlantic Highlands, NJ: Humanities Press, 1979), 85.

15. Burckhardt praises this fresco as one of the greatest works in northern Italy in *Cicerone* (1964), 821.

16. Luce Irigaray, *Speculum of the Other Woman,* trans. Gillian C. Gill (Ithaca, NY: Cornell University Press, 1985), 328–29.

17. Luce Irigaray, *Marine Lover of Friedrich Nietzsche,* trans. Gillian C. Gill (New York: Columbia University Press, 1991), 47.

18. Schopenhauer *WWR,* 2:22.

19. See, for example, *GS* 368; *KSA* 3.617: "I am essentially anti-theatrical" and "in the theater one is honest only in the mass; as an individual one lies, one lies to oneself." But this should be read in its context, in which Wagner is identified as "essentially a man of the theater." For a reading of *Zarathustra,* especially part 4, as an anti-Wagnerian libretto, see "Parasites and their Noise," in my book *Alcyone,* 53–107.

20. See Wassily Kandinsky, *Complete Writings on Art,* ed. Kenneth C. Lindsay and Peter Vergo (New York: Da Capo Press, 1994), e.g., 155, 260, 364, 889.

21. Foucault visited Bayreuth more than one hundred years later. His praise of the centennial production, conducted by Pierre Boulez and directed by Patrice Chereau, with scenic designs by Peduzzi, emphasizes the play between the musical and the visual; he claims that the production resurrects "The Imagination of the Nineteenth Century" (the title of his brief essay), citing especially its visual images. Foucault concludes that the production has rediscovered the contemporaneity of Wagner's music and has made Wagner himself into "one of our contemporary myths." There is no direct reference to Nietzsche's multiple and changing evaluations of Wagner, although Foucault's analysis could be compatible with several of them. More generally, we might say that it illustrates an archaeology of artistic reception, in sketching the way in which Wagner can become more contemporary through a version that intensifies a dated imagery; this could be seen as a suggestion about how the postmodern operates by means of a juxtaposition of the traditional and the contemporary (*F* 2.235–39; *DE* 4.111–15).

22. I have amended Nietzsche's text, which refers to "the seventh page." I am supposing that he or whoever transcribed his manuscript slipped; the extended passage on the glance of the dithyrambic artist is in the seventh *section* of the essay, not on its seventh page.

Chapter Five

1. Aristotle, *Metaphysics,* trans. W. D. Ross, 980a22–27.

2. See Blondel, *Nietzsche, the Body, and Culture,* 201–38.

3. Schopenhauer, *WWR,* 2:375 (chap. 30, "On the Pure Subject of Knowing").

4. The literature on Nietzsche's thought of eternal recurrence is extensive and continues to proliferate; see Gary Shapiro, *Nietzschean Narratives,* 78–96, and the works cited there, as well as chap. 11 of this book.

5. Cited in German on title page of the first edition of *The Gay Science* (1882); originally, Emerson wrote, "To the poet, the philosopher, to the saint, all things are friendly and sacred, all events profitable, all days holy, all men divine." "History," in Ralph Waldo Emerson, *Essays* (New York: Vintage Books, 1990), 12.

6. I discuss Nietzsche's play with an implicit seasonal solar mythology, by exploring his thought of the "halcyon" and the story of Alcyone, in *Alcyone,* 109–54. Derrida's essay "White Mythology: Metaphor in the Text of Philosophy" aims at uncovering a structure of solar protometaphors or philosophemes that underlie Western philosophical attempts to theorize metaphor. See "White Mythology," in *Margins of Philosophy,* by Derrida, trans. Alan Bass (Chicago: University of Chicago Press, 1982), 207–71.

7. For these "eye examinations," see (among others) Z I.13, *KSA* 4.69; Z I.19, *KSA* 4.88; Z II.4, *KSA* 4.118–19; Z II.5, *KSA* 4.121–22.Y

8. See Helmut Schoeck, *Envy: A Theory of Social Behavior,* trans. Michael Glenny and Betty Ross (New York: Harcourt, Brace, and World, 1970); George M. Foster, "The Anatomy of Envy: A Study in Symbolic Behavior," *Current Anthropology* 13 (1972): 165–202.

9. See esp. Matt. 20:15, Mark 7:22; and cf. Matt. 6:22–23, Luke 11:34.

10. Lawrence DiStasi, *Mal Occhio: The Underside of Vision* (San Francisco: North Point Press, 1981), 23–24.

11. Cf. John Rawls, *A Theory of Justice* (Cambridge, MA: Harvard University Press, 1971), 530–41.

12. Oscar Lewis, cited by Schoeck, *Envy,* 50–51.

13. Here both Hollingdale and Kaufmann translate *böse Blicke* as "evil glances," missing the systematic context of the phrase; elsewhere, however, both do usually translate *böse Blick* as "evil eye."

14. Cf. Jacques Lacan, *The Four Fundamental Concepts of Psychoanalysis,* trans. Alan Sheridan (New York: W. W. Norton, 1978), 67–78.

15. Ibid., 115.

16. Cf. Freud, *Civilization and Its Discontents,* trans. Joan Riviere (London: Hogarth Press, 1955), 77–78.

17. Plato, *Phaedrus,* 501c–d.

18. Cf. Daniel Conway, *Nietzsche's Dangerous Game: Philosophy in the Twilight of the Idols* (New York: Cambridge University Press, 1997), 30–34.

19. Ludwig Wittgenstein, *Philosophical Investigations,* trans. G. E. M. Anscombe (Oxford: Blackwell, 1997), par. 66.

20. See, e.g., Henri Bergson, *Creative Evolution,* trans. Arthur Mitchell (New York: Modern Library, 1944), chap. 1.

21. Cf. Frances Yates, *The Art of Memory* (Chicago: University of Chicago Press, 1974).

22. See, e.g., *KSA* 11.494, Nietzsche's first note on eternal recurrence, which speaks repeatedly of the process of *Einverleibung* involved in thinking and living the thought.

23. See also *KSA* 11.362, 11.363.

24. See, e.g., the west pediment of the temple of Artemis in Corfu (Korkyra), an Archaic structure dating from the early sixth century B.C.E.; Reinhard Lullies, *Greek Sculpture* (New York: Harry N. Abrams, 1960), pl. 18 and pp. 56–58.

25. Bernard Pautrat, "Nietzsche Medused," in *Looking after Nietzsche*, ed. Lawrence Rickels (Albany: State University of New York Press, 1990), 159–75 (the essay appeared first in French in 1972); in his book *Versions du soleil: Figures et système de Nietzsche* (Paris: Editions du Seuil, 1971), Pautrat provides an extensive discussion of Nietzsche's conception and use of figurative language, with some attention to solar metaphors.

26. Freud, "Fetishism" and "Medusa's Head," in *Sexuality and the Psychology of Love*, ed. Philip Rieff (New York: CollierMacmillan, 1963).

27. Jung, of course, is indebted to Nietzsche for his concept of the shadow; see Carl Jung, *Nietzsche's Zarathustra: Notes of the Seminar Given in 1934–39*, ed. James L. Jarrett (Princeton, NJ: Princeton University Press, 1988), 125–30, 1320–25, and other passages as cited in the editor's index.

28. The description of the tree echoes an earlier passage in which Zarathustra anticipates encountering his "children" as such trees. In "On Involuntary Bliss," he speaks of the "one single thing" for which he has sacrificed so much, "this living plantation [*Pflanzung*] of my thoughts and this morning light of my highest hope!" It is a garden on which he places these hopes, and he develops the figure at length: "My children are still verdant in their first spring, standing close together and shaken by the same winds—the trees of my garden and my best soil [*Erdreich*]. And verily, where such trees stand together there are blessed isles. But one day I want to dig them up and place each by itself, so it may learn solitude and defiance and caution. Gnarled and bent [*knorrig und gekrümmt*] and with supple hardness it shall then stand by the sea, a living lighthouse of invincible light" (Z III.3; *KSA* 4.204). The tree in "Noontime" is described as "bent and gnarled [*krummen und knorrichten*]" (Z IV.10; *KSA* 4.342).

29. It may be impossible to determine with certainty whether this hyphenation is Nietzsche's or that of a copyist or typesetter; but in the absence of such evidence, it can be assumed to be his own mark. In any case, as I believe the context makes clear, the notion of the *Augen-Blick* as internally split and abyssal does not depend solely on the vagaries of typography. One should compare the suggestiveness of this deformation of the word with Derrida's *différance*, in which the substitution of *a* for *e* marks the complex play of writing and speech; see Derrida, "Différance," in *Margins of Philosophy*, 1–27.

30. On the halcyon tone, see Shapiro, *Alcyone*, 109–48.

31. For a fine discussion of this passage, see Gerard Visser "Der unendlich kleine Augenblick," *Nietzsche-Studien* 27 (1998): 82–106.

Chapter Six

1. Clovis Trouille (1889–1975), whom Foucault mentions in the interview, was a popular painter whose rather kitsch oeuvre includes soft-core pornography. See Clovis Prévost, *Parcours à travers l'oeuvre de Clovis Trouille* (Paris: Edition Melie-s, n.d.); or www.trouille.com.

2. David Macey, *The Lives of Michel Foucault* (New York: Pantheon Books, 1993), 41.

3. Deleuze, *Foucault*, trans. Seán Hand (Minneapolis: University of Minnesota Press, 1988), 67. John Rajchman's very insightful essay "Foucault's Art of Seeing," *October* 44 (spring 1988): 88–117, begins by citing Deleuze on Foucault as a *voyant* or seer.

4. Deleuze, *Foucault*, 67–68.

5. Nietzsche, "On Truth and Lie in an Extra-Moral Sense" (*KSA* 1.880), English version in Nietzsche, *Philosophy and Truth*, 84 (translation modified).

6. See Jean-François Lyotard, "The Dream-Work Does Not Think," trans. Mary Lydon in *The Lyotard Reader*, ed. Andrew Benjamin (Cambridge, MA.: Blackwell, 1989), 19–55.

7. See Gary Shapiro, "Contemporary French Painting Theory," in *Encyclopedia of Aesthetics*, 2:235–40.

8. There is an important exchange between Foucault and Derrida on the relation between the *cogito* and madness in Descartes. Foucault claimed that there was an analogy as well as a near simultaneity between Descartes's supposed exclusion of the possibility that he might be mad, as he develops his thought in *Meditation I*, and the confinement of the mad in Paris and elsewhere in the mid-seventeenth century (*HF* 67–70). Derrida replied that Descartes did not exclude this possibility but in fact exacerbated it by considering the even more devastating hypothesis that the meditator might be dreaming. Derrida, "Cogito and the History of Madness," in his *Writing and Difference*, trans. Alan Bass (Chicago: University of Chicago Press, 1978), 31–63. Foucault responded in an essay appended to the 1972 edition of *HF* entitled "Mon corps, ce papier, ce feu" (*F* 2.393–418; *DE* 2.245–68). Although there is much discussion of dreams and hallucinations in this exchange, it is fundamentally limited to an epistemological context and does not contribute to the articulation of the phenomenology or historicity of dreams and related experiences.

9. See Gary Shapiro, "Ariadne's Thread: Walter Benjamin's Hashish Passages," in *High Culture: Reflections on Addiction and Modernity*, ed. Anna Alexander and Mark Roberts, 59–74 (Albany: State University of New York Press, 2003).

10. Foucault's emphasis on inner vision is significant. Painted depictions of the fantastic and demonic in the early modern period are almost exclusively limited to works of a "Northern" orientation that do not employ a system of strict quattrocento perspective, as if the latter style was concerned with opening the equivalent of a realistic window on the world and the former was directed to the evocation of internal visions. Claudia Swan has suggested that this distinction can be worked out rigorously, to the extent that there are no representations of the utterly fantastic, or of images sent by demonic forces, in paintings of the period that follow a method of strict linear perspective (personal communication, April 2001).

11. For Flaubert's first comments on the painting, see his *Correspondence*, ed. and trans. Francis Steegmuller (Cambridge, MA: Harvard University Press, 1980), 1:31. Although Flaubert attributes the painting to Breughel the Younger, this attribution is now in doubt; some art historians think the painter is Jan Mandijn (ca. 1500–1559). For a reproduction of the painting and some further discussion, see Adrianne J. Tooke, *Flaubert and the Pictorial Arts: From Image to Text* (New York: Oxford University Press, 2000).

12. Joseph Frank, *The Idea of Spatial Form* (New Brunswick, NJ: Rutgers University Press, 1991).

13. Did Nietzsche know Flaubert's *Temptation of Saint Anthony*? He certainly had read a number of the novels. There are two references to "Saint Anthony" (but not explicitly to the novel) in passages in the notebooks where Nietzsche is discussing Flaubert or other contemporary French writers (*KSA* 11.268, 428; 26[441], 34[23]).

Chapter Seven

1. Terminology can be problematic here, for Merleau-Ponty also speaks of the thought he is developing as an "archaeology," especially in the last few years of his life (which overlap with Foucault's early career); see, for example, *In Praise of Philosophy and Other Essays,* trans. John Wild and James Edie (Evanston, IL: Northwestern University Press, 1988), 72. Len Lawlor (to whom I owe the previous reference) argues in an unpublished paper that for the two thinkers, "archaeology" has common sources in Kant, Freud, and Husserl. Of these the Freudian usage (as in his extended comparison of the unconscious to Rome, where all its history occupies the same place) seems closest to the mundane sense of archaeology, concerned as it is with evaluating meanings and practices in terms of distinct stages and practices and relatively independent of the practitioners' self-descriptions. This mundane sense, I think, is at work in Foucault. Foucault at one point expresses a debt to Kant with regard to archaeology, perhaps thinking of the latter's contrast of natural history with an "archaeology of nature" that would investigate "the traces of nature's most ancient revolutions"; see *Critique of Judgment,* sec. 80, 82 n, where Kant mentions an archaeology of art (see sec. 56).

2. Cf. Serge Guilbault, *How New York Stole the Idea of Modern Art,* trans. Arthur Goldhammer (Chicago: University of Chicago Press, 1983). Around this time Harold Rosenberg's essays on the New York art scene appeared frequently in *Les Temps Moderne.* Merleau-Ponty was involved in editing the journal until he broke with Sartre (the chief editor) in 1952 over the latter's support of the French Communist Party. "Indirect Language" was his farewell essay, published in June and July of that year.

3. Cf. Clement Greenberg, "Modernist Painting" in *The New Art,* ed. Gregory Battcock (New York: Dutton, 1973).

4. Malraux, *Voices of Silence,* 50.

5. I have discussed some of the complexities of providing narrative accounts of the modern and the postmodern in *Earthwards;* see esp. chap. 1, "Postperiodization: Time and Its Surfaces." There are some resources for the discussion of art and the earth in Merleau-Ponty; see, for example, his remarks on Husserl, "The Earth Does Not Move," in "The Philosopher and His Shadow," *Signs,* trans. Richard C. McCleary (Evanston, IL: Northwestern University Press, 1964), 180–81.

6. Malraux, *Voices of Silence,* 633.

7. See Claude Gandelmann, "Foucault as Art Historian," *Hebrew University Studies in Literature and the Arts* 13, no. 2 (autumn 1985): 266–80; if there are other philosophical books that begin in this way, Foucault's is certainly the best-known among them. Merleau-Ponty begins *Sense and Non-Sense* with his essay on Cézanne; but the latter is not an ekphrasis of a single picture (indeed, there is little detailed comment on any specific painting), and the book itself, a set of essays on various topics, does not purport to have the unified structure of some of Merleau-Ponty's other books, even if it does claim to offer a number of related phenomenological explorations.

8. For some of the most comprehensive art-historical discussions of Velazquez and of *Las Meninas* in particular, see Jonathan Brown, *Images and Ideas in Seventeenth Century Spanish Painting* (Princeton, NJ: Princeton University Press, 1978); and Jonathan Brown, *Velazquez: Painter and Courtier* (New Haven, CT: Yale University Press, 1986).

9. A number of recent essays on *Las Meninas* refer critically to Foucault's essay and take it as a relatively immediate account of the painting, rather than emphasizing its own discursive form; these include John R. Searle, "*Las Meninas* and the Paradoxes of Pictorial Representation," *Critical Inquiry* 6 (1980): 177–88; Svetlana Alpers, "Interpretation without Representation, or The Viewing of *Las Meninas*," *Representations* 1 (Feb. 1983): 31–42; Leo Steinberg, "Velazquez's *Las Meninas*," *October* 19 (1981): 45–54; Joel Snyder and Ted Cohen, "Critical Response: Reflexions on *Las Meninas: Paradox Lost*," *Critical Inquiry* 7 (1980): 129–47; Joel Snyder, "*Las Meninas* and the Mirror of the Prince," *Critical Inquiry* 11 (June 1985): 539–72.

10. Maurice Merleau-Ponty, *Sense and Non-Sense*, trans. Hubert Dreyfus and Patricia Dreyfus (Evanston, IL: Northwestern University Press, 1964), 3.

11. Ibid., 5.

12. Maurice Merleau-Ponty, *Phenomenology of Perception*, trans. Colin Smith (New York: Humanities Press, 1962) (hereafter *PP*), pt. 3, chap. 1, "The Cogito," 369–409.

13. For Merleau-Ponty's emphasis on Husserl's project as a perpetual starting over, see "The Philosopher and His Shadow": "To say that he never succeeded in ensuring the bases of phenomenology would be to be mistaken about what he was looking for. The problems of reduction are not for him a prior step or preface to phenomenology; they are the beginning of inquiry. In a sense, they are inquiry, since inquiry is, as he said, a continuous beginning" (161). Forrest Williams traces the analogy between Cézanne's painting and phenomenology, culminating in the relations stressed by Merleau-Ponty, in "Cézanne and French Phenomenology," *Journal of Aesthetics and Art Criticism* 12 (1954): 481–92, reprinted in *MPA* 165–73.

14. Merleau-Ponty, *PP*, xxi.

15. See ibid., passim, but esp. 132 n, 197, 198, 260, 262, 318, 322, 323, 330.

16. Merleau-Ponty questions the authority of the photograph in a number of contexts. Acknowledging that the photograph of a horse in motion shows a position of the legs quite different from that found in a "lifelike" painting of a running horse, he argues that the truth is with the painting and not the photograph, citing Rodin's comment that "time never stops cold." "Eye and Mind," *MPA* 145.

17. Cf. George Berkeley, *A New Theory of Vision*, in *Works on Vision*, by Colin M. Turbayne, ed. George Berkeley (New York: Library of Liberal Arts, 1957); Edward Casey, "'The Element of Voluminousness': Depth and Place Reexamined," in *Merleau-Ponty Vivant*, ed. Martin C. Dillon (Albany: State University of New York Press, 1991), 1–29.

18. Merleau-Ponty, *PP*, 262.

19. Maurice Merleau-Ponty, *The Visible and the Invisible*, ed. Claude Lefort, trans. Alphonso Lingis (Evanston, IL: Northwestern University Press, 1968), 143. For some helpful discussions of Merleau-Ponty's difficult and provocative late thought, with some reference to this work, see Levin, *Philosopher's Gaze*, 195–233; Martin C. Dillon, *Merleau-Ponty's Ontology* (Evanston, IL: Northwestern University Press, 1997); and Gary Madison, *The Phenomenology of Merleau-Ponty* (Athens: Ohio University Press, 1981).

20. Clement Greenberg, "Modernist Painting," in *Modern Art and Modernism*, ed. Francis Frascina and Charles Harrison (New York: Harper and Row, 1982), 5–10.

21. Hugh Silverman, "Cézanne's Mirror Stage, *MPA* 262–77.

22. Ibid., 273.

Chapter Eight

1. For a useful summary of the genealogical facts and for an illuminating materialist reading of the painting, see Geoffrey Waite, "Lenin in *Las Meninas*: An Essay in Historical-Materialist Vision," *History and Theory* 25, no. 3 (1986): see 270–74 for a discussion of the problem of succession.

2. Gandelmann, "Foucault as Art Historian," 266–80.

3. Cf. note 9, chap. 7. A number of recent essays on *Las Meninas* refer critically to Foucault's essay and take it as a relatively immediate account of the painting, rather than emphasizing its own discursive form; these include Searle, "*Las Meninas* and the Paradoxes of Pictorial Representation," 177–88; Alpers, "Interpretation without Representation," 31–42; Steinberg, "Velazquez's *Las Meninas*," 45–54; Snyder and Cohen, "Critical Response," 129–47; Snyder, "*Las Meninas* and the Mirror of the Prince," 539–72. For an exception to this tendency, see Gandelmann, "Foucault as Art Historian," which places Foucault's essay within the philosophical project of *Les mots et les choses* and notes its affinities with the ancient tradition of ekphrasis.

4. See José López-Rey, *Velazquez: Painter of Painters* (Cologne: Taschen, 1996), 1:216; López-Rey is among those who, after considering the view that perspective requires the mirror to reflect what is on the canvas, continues to read *Las Meninas* as not allowing us to make any determination of the subject of the painter's work.

5. For Foucault's "And yet [*Et pourtant*]," see *The Order of Things*, 4. For Heidegger, see "The Origin of the Work of Art," in *Poetry, Language, Thought,* trans. Albert Hofstadter (New York: Harper and Row, 1971), 33.

6. Nietzsche poses the question in his notebooks. Previously the highest authority for a speech or discourse was God, but "now suppose that belief in God has vanished: the question presents itself anew: "who speaks?" (*WP* 275). Foucault recalls the question and notes Mallarmé's reply that what speaks is the word itself (*OT* 305–6; *Mch* 316–17).

7. Steinberg, "Velazquez's *Las Meninas*," 48.

8. Deleuze, *Foucault,* 67.

9. Ibid., 67–68.

10. Steinberg, "Velazquez's *Las Meninas*," 54.

11. Searle, "*Las Meninas* and the Paradoxes of Pictorial Representation," esp. 481–83.

12. Joel Snyder argues: "As viewers we need not occupy any particular place in order to take in everything most paintings have to offer. There is something confused and confusing about saying that because a picture is projected from a certain point we must place ourselves at that point to make sense of the picture," "*Las Meninas* and the Mirror of the Prince," 550. But what is true of "most paintings" may not be true here, and our position may be defined not so much by geometrical perspective, but by the gazes of the figures in the painting. Both Svetlana Alpers and Jonathan Brown have claimed that there is no exclusively correct perspectival reading of the painting, and Brown has drawn the corollary that we can therefore, for example, see the mirror as reflecting either the canvas or the model; as he puts it, "Velazquez's instinctive use of perspective de-

liberately accommodates both possibilities" (yet how does one do something of this nature both instinctively and deliberately?). Cf. Alpers, "Interpretation without Representation," 39; Brown, *Velazquez*, 260.

13. There are many antecedents of this narrative style of ekphrasis, going back at least to the *Imagines* of Philostratus (ca. 230 C.E.), in which a boy is led through a gallery by a connoisseur.

14. Joel Snyder, in "*Las Meninas* and the Mirror of the Prince," has argued that the mirror, in reflecting what is on the canvas that stands before Velazquez in the painting, is an image not of the optical image of the sovereigns, but of their ennobled appearance on the canvas; this, he maintains, is in accordance with the humanistic theory of painting that requires a state portrait to present an idealized version of its subject.

15. See Brown, *Velazquez*, 182.

16. See Paul Claudel, *L'oeil écoute* (Paris: Gallimard, 1946), 63; and George Kubler, "The Mirror in *Las Meninas*," *Art Bulletin* 67 (1985): 316. Kubler argues that if the image were in an actual mirror, reflecting either the canvas or the models, the figures of the king and queen would be much smaller than they appear in what he takes to be a painting of a mirror. And he points out that if the "mirror," which reverses images, is taken to be actual, that requires the king (whether in the painting whose back we see or standing before the scene of the whole painting) to be placed on the queen's left, which would be contrary to protocol. Following these suggestions, one might read the illusion of the mirror as itself alluding to the story, well known in the humanist literature of art, that Pliny reports about Zeuxis and Parrhasius. After Zeuxis made a painting of grapes that fooled birds into pecking at it, Parrhasius promised to do him one better. When Zeuxis arrived at the latter's studio and asked him to unveil the canvas, which was covered by drapery, Parrhasius revealed that the drapery itself was painted. The red drapery that is opened over the heads of the royal couple may allude to just this story. Art historians have emphasized a political reading of Pliny's stories about painters as relevant to Velazquez's ambition to achieve a higher rank and, simultaneously, to show that painting is one of the liberal arts, worthy of full royal patronage. In this case, the example from Pliny is that of Alexander the Great and Apelles, the painter with whom he is said to have been on intimate terms. But it may be that by relegating the royal pair to an illusory mirror, Velazquez is downplaying the political dimension with regard to the achievement of painterly immortality and choosing instead to succeed as a master of illusion. Political ambition would be superseded by the agonistics of the painter's art.

17. Brown, *Velazquez*, 303 n. 43.

Chapter Nine

1. For "isolating visibility," see "The Eye of Power" (*PK*, 146–65).

2. Foucault, "*Foucault répond à Sartre*," in *La Quinzaine Littéraire* 46 (Mar. 1–15, 1968): 21, cited and translated by Michael Mahon, *Foucault's Nietzschean Genealogy: Truth, Power, and the Subject* (Albany: State University of New York Press, 1992), 61.

3. George Steiner, "The Mandarin of the Hour—Michel Foucault" (review of *The Order of Things*), *New York Times Book Review*, Feb. 28, 1971, 8.

4. Foucault, "Monstrosities in Criticism," *diacritics* 1, no. 1 (fall 1971): 60; *DE* 2.221.

5. The editors simply say that this is the text that Foucault had in mind, although he never refers to it directly. Nevertheless, the suggestion is very plausible.

6. The reference to "philosophical archaeology" is in Kant, *Gesammelte Schriften* (Berlin: Walter de Gruyter, 1942), 20:341. See also Kant, *What Real Progress Has Metaphysics Made in Germany since the Time of Leibniz and Wolff?* trans. Ted Humphrey (New York: Abaris Books, 1983), which unfortunately does not contain the passage on "philosophical archaeology." The Royal Academy of Sciences in Berlin had announced a prize essay competition on the topic; Kant never submitted his essay, but he gave his various drafts on the subject to his friend Frederich Theodor Rink, who published them shortly after Kant's death in 1804.

7. See Gary Shapiro, "High Art, Folk Art, and Other Social Distinctions," in *The Folk: Identity, Landscapes, and Lores,* ed. Robert Smith and Jerry Stannard, University of Kansas Publications in Anthropology, no. 17 (Lawrence: Dept. of Anthropology, University of Kansas, 1989), 73–90.

8. Edmund Husserl's conception of the *epoché* or phenomenological bracketing also derives from this sense.

9. See Meyer Schapiro, "The Still Life as a Personal Object," in *The Reach of Mind: Essays in Honor of Kurt Goldstein* (New York: Springer, 1968), 203–9. Derrida's response to both Heidegger and Schapiro demonstrates that both art historian and philosopher are committed to an ontology of ownership, appropriation, and restitution. Derrida, "Restitutions," in *Truth in Painting,* by Derrida. Foucault could claim that such an ontology is precisely one that is to be expected in the era of "man and his doubles."

10. This is an allusion to Heidegger's conception of *technē* and technology, as in "The Question concerning Technology"; see *The Question concerning Technology,* 3–35. Heidegger's argument is that the modern world is subject to a massive discipline of enframing or *Gestell.* Heidegger leaves open the possibility that the "saving power" of art offers an alternative to the total domination of *Gestell,* thus suggesting a position that bears some resemblance to what I suggest below (chap. 10) is the Foucauldian position (never quite explicitly articulated by Foucault), that visual regimes, like others, generate characteristic forms of visual resistance. What Heidegger means by art, at least in the first instance, is poetry, as in the work of Hölderlin, whose lines "where danger is / there grows the saving power" he quotes here. Heidegger is committed to the priority of linguistic art over other forms, as noted by Derrida (sec. 2).

11. Late in his life, Martin Heidegger became an admirer of Klee; see Heinrich Petzet, *Encounters and Dialogues with Martin Heidegger,* trans. Parvis Emad and Kenneth Maly (Chicago: University of Chicago Press, 1993), 146–51.

12. Merleau-Ponty, "Eye and Mind," *MPA* 123–24.

13. Merleau-Ponty, "Cézanne's Doubt," *MPA* 69.

Chapter Ten

1. Plato, *Republic,* 440a.

2. See Gary Shapiro, "Nietzsche contra Renan," *History and Theory,* no. 2 (1982): 193–222; and Shapiro, *Nietzschean Narratives,* chap. 5, "The Text as Graffito: Historical Semiotics," where I suggest that *The Antichrist(ian)* should also be read, in part, as a response to Renan's history.

3. Ernest Renan, *Antichrist* (London: Mathieson, 1889), 90.

4. Gilles Deleuze, *Negotiations, 1972–1990,* trans. Martin Joughin (New York: Columbia University Press, 1995), 114; Deleuze, *Essays Critical and Clinical,* trans. Daniel Smith (Minneapolis: University of Minnesota Press, 1997), 54.

5. See Shapiro, "Nietzsche contra Renan," 221–22, where I suggest that Brandes's assimilation of Nietzsche to Renan, who was the much better known and more widely read author at the time, contributed to a misreading of the *Übermensch* and related ideas.

6. Peirce specifically argues that scientific method requires the Christian virtues of faith, hope, and charity; see "The Doctrine of Chances," in Charles Sanders Peirce, *Collected Papers,* ed. Charles Hartshorne and Paul Weiss (Cambridge, MA: Harvard University Press, 1965), vol. 2, par. 655 (pp. 399–400).

7. For Heidegger on the "unthought" visuality of philosophy's traditional conceptions, see "The End of Philosophy and the Task of Thinking," in *Basic Writings,* ed. David Farrell Krell (New York: Harper and Row, 1993), esp. 441–44; and Heidegger, "The Age of the World Picture," 115–54.

8. What is perhaps Nietzsche's most pointed critique of English philosophy is in *Beyond Good and Evil,* where he calls the utilitarians "ponderous herd animals" devoid of imagination (*BGE* 228; *KSA* 5.164) and describes the English as an "unphilosophical race" (*BGE* 252; *KSA* 5.195) and their thinkers generally (including Darwin, Mill, and Spencer) as "mediocre minds" (*BGE* 253; *KSA* 5.196). If Nietzsche had known Bentham's Panopticon writings, he might have shared some of Foucault's admiration for his architectonic genius.

9. In *Bentham's Prison: A Study of the Panopticon Penitentiary* (Oxford: Oxford University Press, 1993), Janet Semple presents a detailed history of Bentham's efforts to promote the Panopticon and his struggles with patrons and politicians. She defends the humanitarian and Enlightenment motivations of the project against Foucault's criticisms. However, in rebuking Foucault and others for their failure to place the Panopticon in a certain context, she assumes the priority of an intentionalistic and biographically oriented history that Foucault contests.

10. The literature on Plato's story of the cave and his analogy of the sun in the *Republic* is vast. In addition to Heidegger's essay, cited in the introduction, note 39, see Luce Irigaray, "Plato's Hystera," in *Speculum of the Other Woman,* trans. Gillian C. Gill (Ithaca, NY: Cornell University Press, 1985), 243–64.

11. Jay, *Downcast Eyes,* 383–84. Cf. Miller, "Jeremy Bentham's Panoptic Device," 3–29.

12. Jeremy Bentham, *Works,* ed. John Bowring (New York: Russell and Russell, 1962); Jeremy Bentham, *Rationale of Judicial Evidence,* in Benthan, *Works,* 6:321, quoted by Miller, "Jeremy Bentham's Panoptic Device," 15. Foucault himself does not quote this text.

13. Miller, "Jeremy Bentham's Panoptic Device," 15.

14. For the "simple idea in architecture," see Bentham, *The Panopticon Writings,* ed. Miran Božovič' (New York: Verso, 1995), 95.

15. See Božovič's very acute introductory essay "'An utterly dark spot,' " in Bentham's *Panopticon Writings,* which develops the interrelation of gaze and fiction, and the theological parallels, from a Lacanian point of view. The quotation is on 9.

16. Bentham, *Panopticon Writings,* 100–101.

17. In fact it is the preceding passage that Deleuze quotes in his analysis of the diagram. Deleuze, *Foucault*, 34.

18. Ibid., 34–35. Other discussions of the diagram and of the *dispositif* in Foucault can be found in these essays by Deleuze: "What Is a *dispositif?*" in *Michel Foucault: Philosopher*, trans. Timothy J. Armstrong (New York: Routledge, 1992), 159–68; and several essays in Deleuze, *Negotiations*, 92–96, 107, 117–18.

19. Deleuze, *Foucault*, 38–39.

20. Macey, *The Lives of Michel Foucault*, 189.

21. Denis Hollier, after noting the correspondence of *The Birth of the Clinic* and the book on Roussel, says that there is no book corresponding to *Discipline and Punish*. Denis Hollier, "The Word of God: 'I am Dead,' " in *Michel Foucault: Philosopher*, 138. My suggestion is that the Manet book could have been part of such a pair, given its exploration of a form of visibility that contrasts point by point with that of the Panopticon.

22. The transcript of the lectures was published, without authorization from Foucault's literary estate, as "La peinture de Manet," in *Les cahiers de la Tunisie: Numéro spécial: Foucault en Tunisie* (Tunis, 1989). I have had access to a copy of the handwritten transcript and to a German translation of the text: *Die Malerei von Manet*, trans. Peter Geble (Berlin: Merve Verlag, 1999), cited hereafter as *Manet*.

23. However, in the case of Manet, the relation between personal and artistic resistance may be overdetermined. Manet's father, Auguste, was a rigorous judge who served under Louis Napoleon, despite his own republican sentiments; he encouraged Édouard to follow a legal career and apparently accepted the young man's disinclination for the law only after he had twice failed his examinations. Nancy Locke has argued that Suzanne Leenhoof (Manet's frequent model), who entered the household as a music teacher for Édouard and his brother, conceived her child, Léon (born in 1852), with Auguste. As a married man and a senior judge, it would have been a great disgrace for Auguste to acknowledge the boy. Édouard married Suzanne in 1863 when Léon was eleven; Manet scholars have tended to suppose that he was the father, but he never acknowledged the boy as his, although his eventual marriage to Suzanne and the fact that neither was married at the time of conception would have made it possible for him to do so without scandal. Locke offers a subtle reading of a number of Manet's paintings in terms of the "family romance" constituted by this situation. For example, Léon appears in a number of paintings, and Locke makes a strong case for reading his figure, as in *Le déjeuener sur l'atelier*, as one that is ambivalently inside and outside a family circle. She adopts a Foucauldian perspective, based especially on the *History of Sexuality*, to investigate the complexities of the familial situation as it is worked out in the paintings; but she does not make any explicit use of Foucault's writing on Manet, on visual art, or on the legal and penal system in which his father worked and from which Édouard turned away. See Nancy Locke, *Manet and the Family Romance* (Princeton, NJ: Princeton University Press, 2001); I regret that this book came to my attention too late to make full use of it.

24. Michael Fried, *Three American Painters* (Cambridge, MA: Fogg Art Museum, 1965), 4–10, cited in Locke, *Manet and the Family Romance*, 180, n. 6.

25. *Manet*, 15–16.

26. Ibid., 30.

27. Ibid., 29.

28. Locke identifies the figure within as Léon (*Manet and the Family Romance*, 126); if so, then Manet might be indicating some resistance to looking at the family situation with a keen Panoptic surveillance.

29. *Manet*, 40–41. Foucault also discussed *The Balcony* in the interview "What Do Philosophers Dream Of?" (see sec. 40). There he speaks of the aggressive ugliness *(laideur)* of the painting, and he explains this ugliness as a deliberate flouting of or indifference to all aesthetic canons. Manet has done a number of things, he says, in comparison with which the work of the impressionists was "absolutely regressive" (*DE* 2.706).

30. *Manet*, 45.

31. Ibid., 46–47.

32. Plato, *Republic*, 596d–e.

33. Bentham, *Panopticon Writings*, 45.

34. Carol Armstrong, "Counter, Mirror, Maid: Some Infra-Thin Notes on *A Bar at the Folies-Bergère*," in *Twelve Views of Manet's Bar*, ed. Bradford R. Collins (Princeton, NJ: Princeton University Press, 1996), 37.

35. See Jack Flam, "Looking into the Abyss: The Poetics of Manet's *A Bar at the Folies-Bergère*," in Collins, *Twelve Views of Manet's Bar*, 173.

36. Walter Benjamin, *The Arcades Project*, trans. Howard Eiland and Kevin McLaughlin (Cambridge, MA: Harvard University Press, 1999), 101–19. Benjamin cites some of Auguste Blanqui's formulations of the thought of recurrence (112–15) as well as Nietzsche's (in his notes of 1883, Nietzsche himself refers to Blanqui's book, which argued for recurrence; *KSA* 10.560).

37. See Georges Bataille, *Manet*, trans. Austryn W. Wainhouse and James Emmons (New York: Skira, 1955), 52–53, 103.

38. See Macey, *The Lives of Michel Foucault*, 189.

39. For Sartre's essay on Rebeyrolle, *"Coexistences,"* see *Rebeyrolle: Peintures, 1963–1980* (Paris: Maeght Editeur, 1991).

40. The lecture "Different Spaces" was presented to the Architectural Studies Circle in 1967 but not published until 1984. There Foucault argues that while the nineteenth century may have been obsessed with the question of time, "the present age may be the age of space instead" (*F* 2.175; *DE* 4.752) and proceeds to offer a brief account of the modern desacralization of space, with the suggestion that this may be an incomplete project. Foucault describes several "heterotopias," places that are "outside" the normative locations of the culture, including hospitals, prisons, gardens, museums, and libraries. The museum is a heterotopia of "a time that accumulates indefinitely" (*F* 2.182; *DE* 4.759). Foucault's paragraph on gardens is intriguing, for it sketches the outlines of a possible archaeology of the arts of the environment and of the history of the aestheticization and construction of the natural. I have discussed Robert Smithson's historical and archaeological perspective on the aesthetics of the garden in *Earthwards*, 113–20.

41. George Jackson, *Soledad Brother: Prison Letters of George Jackson*, with an introduction by Jean Genet (New York: Coward-McCann, 1970). The rebellion at Attica Prison (September 1971) is surely part of the context of Foucault's references to prisons in the essay on Rebeyrolle, which appeared in 1973.

42. "The Thought of the Outside" is the title of Foucault's essay on Maurice Blanchot (*F* 2.147–69; *DE* 1.518–39).

Chapter Eleven

1. The Apocalypse or Revelation is a disclosure or a denuding; just as the Apocalypse is the last book of the Christian Bible, so Nietzsche's "Seven Seals" is the last chapter of *Zarathustra*'s third part, which was intended for some time to be the conclusion of the entire book (for a discussion of Nietzsche's ambivalence with regard to the privately and very sparsely distributed fourth part of the book, see *Alcyone*, "Parasites and their Noise," 53–105, esp. 54–59). See Jacques Derrida, "Of an Apocalyptic Tone Newly Adopted in Philosophy," trans. John P. Leavey Jr., in *Derrida and Negative Theology*, ed. Harold Coward and Toby Foshay (Albany: State University of New York Press, 1992), 25–71.

2. Cf. Jacques Derrida, *Spurs*, trans. Barbara Harlow (Chicago: University of Chicago Press, 1979). Magritte is unlikely to have known the now notorious sentence from Nietzsche's *Nachlass* on which Derrida plays variations.

3. A word about the relationship between Foucault and Deleuze is in order. The two philosophers began a friendship in 1962 when they first met. Although they ceased to see each other in 1977, after a political dispute, Deleuze, at least, had a continuing interest in Foucault's work. Deleuze published his important book *Nietzsche and Philosophy* in 1962, and some of the articles that were incorporated in *The Logic of Sense* (1969) were published from 1961 to 1967, including the studies of Plato and Lucretius that, I suggest, are significant for *This Is Not a Pipe*. In any case, the two were in regular contact during these years. The first version of Foucault's essay on Magritte appeared in 1968 and in expanded form (the basis for the English translation by James Harkness) in 1973; the latter includes a great deal more of the "Deleuzian" language of vapor, similitude, and simulacrum. During 1968 and 1969, the two published largely celebratory essays about one another's work. Deleuze's "New Cartographer" appeared in response to Foucault's *Archaeology of Knowledge*; Foucault published a brief review of *Difference and Repetition* (1968) in 1969 and a longer celebration of that book and of *The Logic of Sense* in "Theatrum Philosophicum" in 1970. Deleuze's book *Foucault* appeared in 1986, two years after the death of its subject, and included both previously published and new essays. For an insightful treatment of the dynamics of philosophical friendship, interchange, and gratitude between (and beyond) the two, see Eleanor Kaufman, "Madness and Repetition: The Absence of Work in Deleuze, Foucault, and Jacques Martin," in *Deleuze and Guattari: New Mappings in Politics, Philosophy, and Culture*, ed. Eleanor Kaufman and Kevin John Heller (Minneapolis: University of Minnesota Press, 1998), 230–50.

4. Gilles Deleuze, *The Logic of Sense*, trans. Mark Lester (New York: Columbia University Press, 1990), 10.

5. Ibid., 254. See Paul Patton, "Anti-Platonism and Art," in *Gilles Deleuze and the Theater of Philosophy*, ed. Constantin V. Boundas and Dorothea Olkowski (New York: Routledge, 1994), 141–56.

6. Plato, *Sophist*, 266.

7. Deleuze, *Logic of Sense*, 256.

8. Ibid., 262.

9. Ibid., 265.

10. For a brief account of some of the personal and philosophical relations between Foucault and Klossowski, see Macey, *The Lives of Michel Foucault*, 154–58. It should be noted that Klossowski is the brother of the painter Balthus.

11. Pierre Klossowski, *Diana at Her Bath*, trans. Stephen Sarterelli (New York: Marsilio Publishers, 1998), 3–4. The figure of light from a dead star that has not yet reached us is also used by Nietzsche; see *The Gay Science* 125 (*KSA* 3.480–82), where the madman says that this is our situation with respect to receiving the news of the death of God. For a reading of *Diana* in terms of the logic of the simulacrum (but without reference to Nietzsche), see Scott Durham, "From Magritte to Klossowski: The Simulacrum, between Painting and Narrative," *October* 64 (spring 1993): 17–33.

12. Klossowski, *Diana*, 3; for the claim about the relatively recent date of the familiar version of the story, see Klossowski's notes in *Diana* (78). For Foucault's reflections on the modern problematic of attempting to recover lost origins, see the section titled "The Retreat and Return of the Origin" (*OT* 328–35; *Mch* 339–46).

13. Klossowski, *Diana*, 82–84.

14. Klossowski, *Nietzsche and the Vicious Circle*, trans. Daniel Smith (Chicago: University of Chicago Press, 1997), 133.

15. Klossowski, *Diana*, 31–33.

16. Klossowski, *Nietzsche and the Vicious Circle*, 122–23.

17. For a fuller statement of the way in which thinking the thought of eternal recurrence weakens the identity of the thinker and puts the notion of personal identity into question, see my *Nietzschean Narratives*, 84–93. I take issue with Alexander Nehamas's reconstruction of the thought of recurrence (in his *Nietzsche: Life as Literature* [Cambridge, MA: Harvard University Press], 170–200), in which he argues that the thought is meant to reinforce the individual's sense of integrity and artistic unity.

18. Sketches of a physical "demonstration" of eternal recurrence are to be found in Nietzsche's notebooks, as in *WP* 1062–66.

19. Cited by Klossowski, *Nietzsche and the Vicious Circle*, 129–31. Some might see Klossowski's translation of *Trugbilder* as "simulacra" as somewhat forced; however, I am primarily interested here in his construction of Nietzsche as thinker of the phantasm and the simulacrum, so I simply note the question.

20. Mark Taylor, *Disfiguring: Art, Architecture, Religion* (Chicago: University of Chicago Press, 1992), 178–84; and my review "Go Figure! Refiguring *Disfiguring*," *Philosophy Today*, fall 1994, 326–33.

21. For Augustine's classical meditation on the elusiveness of the "now," see his *Confessions*, bk. 11, xiv–xxx; Hegel's discussion is in *Phenomenology of Spirit*, in the section of "Consciousness" entitled "Sense-Certainty: Or the 'This' and 'Meaning.'"

22. See Guido Almansi, "Foucault and Magritte," in *History of European Ideas* 3 (1982): 303–9; and Silvano Levy, "Foucault and Magritte on Resemblance," *Modern Language Review*, Jan. 1990, 50–56.

23. There is no *mise-en-abîme*, strictly speaking, here; the smaller scene repeats the larger one (a country house, a lawn with soccer players) but does not

include itself; that is, it does not encompass the part of the balcony and its odd architectural flourish that frames the scene for us.

24. Cf. Brown, *Images and Ideas in Seventeenth Century Spanish Painting;* and Brown, *Velazquez.*

25. See Deleuze, *Foucault,* 94–100.

Chapter Twelve

1. Arthur Danto, *Encounters and Reflections: Art in the Historical Present* (Berkeley: University of California Press, 1997), 287.

2. Ibid., 290.

3. Ibid., 288.

4. Benjamin Buchloh recalls the Warhol-Harvey relation in "Andy Warhol's One-Dimensional Art," in *Andy Warhol, a Retrospective,* ed. Kynaston McShine (New York: Museum of Modern Art, 1989).

5. Arthur Danto, *The Transfiguration of the Commonplace* (Cambridge, MA: Harvard University Press, 1981), 1–3.

6. Danto, "The Artworld," *Journal of Philosophy* 61 (1964): 581.

7. Ibid., 584.

8. Arthur Danto, "Who Was Andy Warhol," *Art News,* May 1987, 129.

9. Ibid., 131.

10. Ibid., 131–32, my emphasis.

11. Hegel, *Phenomenology of Spirit,* 452. Cf. my article "Hegel's Dialectic of Artistic Meaning," 23–35.

12. Rosalind Krauss, "Post-History on Parade," *New Republic,* May 25, 1987.

13. David Carrier, *Artwriting* (Amherst: University of Massachusetts Press, 1988), 87–91. In "Deaths of Art: David Carrier's Metahistory of Artwriting," *Leonardo* (1992), I have attempted to untangle some of the claims and counterclaims about which of these writers has announced the death of art.

14. Quoted in McShine, *Andy Warhol, a Retrospective,* 457.

15. Robert Rosenblum, in McShine, *Andy Warhol, a Retrospective,* 29.

16. See the *Sophist,* where the Stranger contrasts "two forms of the image-making art, the likeness making and the phantastic" (236); later he speaks of the phantasms of dreams and of waking life (266).

17. See especially the two essays included as an appendix to Deleuze's *Logic of Sense,* "Plato and the Simulacrum" and "Lucretius and the Simulacrum," 253–279.

18. Gilles Deleuze, *Difference and Repetition,* trans. Paul Patton (New York: Columbia University Press, 1994), 276.

19. Danto has been art critic for *Nation* since 1984; it is a position once held by Clement Greenberg, and the watershed involved in Greenberg's rejection and Danto's welcome of Pop Art says much about the importance of this strategic position. Among the collections of Danto's critical writings that contain brilliant descriptive analyses of visual art are Arthur Danto, *The State of the Art* (New York: Prentice Hall Press, 1987), *Encounters and Reflections,* and *Beyond the Brillo Box: The Visual Arts in Post-Historical Perspective* (New York: Farrar Straus Giroux, 1992).

20. For Philostratus, see chap. 8, note 13; the most accessible source of Did-

erot's descriptive work is Denis Diderot, *Diderot on Art*, trans. John Goodman, 2 vols. (New Haven, CT: Yale University Press, 1995).

21. See Deleuze, *Difference and Repetition:*

> This indeterminate or groundlessness is also the animality peculiar to thought: not this or that animal form, but stupidity. For if thought thinks only when constrained or forced to do so, if it remains stupid so long as nothing forces it to think, is it not also stupidity which forces it to think, precisely the fact that it does not think so long as nothing forces it to do so? Recall Heidegger's statement: "What gives us most cause for thought is the fact that we do not yet think." Thought is the highest determination, confronting stupidity as though face to face with the indeterminate which is adequate to it. Stupidity (not error) constitutes the greatest weakness of thought, but also the source of its highest power in that which forces it to think. Such is the prodigious adventure of Bouvard and Pécuchet or the play of sense and non-sense. (275)

22. Ibid., 293.

23. Ibid., 293–94.

24. In "Lucretius and the Simulacrum," Deleuze gives a detailed analysis of the Epicurean theory of knowledge and perception in its relation to the ethical; he explains Lucretius's goal of revealing the illusory quality of many of the images that disturb the soul. Like Lucretius, Deleuze is a philosophical naturalist, but not an atomistic materialist like Democritus. He amplifies the expressivism of Spinoza (and what could be called the "non-theological Leibniz") with three sources of more recent naturalism: a non-Hegelian Marx, a pluralistic Nietzsche, and an anti-oedipal Freud. Deleuze articulates a number of distinctions in Lucretius's *De Rerum Natura* with respect to perceptual elements: these can be divided into emanations from the depths of bodies (especially sounds, smells, tastes, and temperatures) and those "skins, tunics, or wrappings, envelopes or barks—what Lucretius calls simulacra and Epicurus calls idols," which are mainly visual, *Logic of Sense*, 273. In this typology, phantasms constitute a third species, compounded of simulacra but relatively independent of the objects that produce them and also more subject to change than simple simulacra. Phantasms in turn can be distinguished as theological, oneiric, and erotic. In addition to Nietzsche's interest in Lucretius and his theory of perception, we should note his early concern with Democritus, whose physics and psychology form the basis for those of Epicurus and Lucretius; see James I. Porter, *Nietzsche and the Philology of the Future* (Stanford, CA: Stanford University Press, 2000). Nietzsche's understanding of naturalism and materialism was formed in part through his study of Friedrich A. Lange's *History of Materialism* (first edition, 1866).

25. Deleuze, *Difference and Repetition*, 9. Elsewhere, and without reference to Deleuze, I have attempted to show the theatrical and operatic character of *Zarathustra*, especially of part 4; see *Alcyone*.

26. Deleuze, *Difference and Repetition*, 299.

27. Deleuze, "Postscript on Control Societies," in *Negotiations*, 177–82.

28. Nietzsche took extensive notes on the Goncourts' writing on painting; see the entries in the index of *KSA*.

29. See Debord, *Society of the Spectacle*. Debord is a much more totalizing and "Hegelian" thinker than Foucault, insofar as he claims that in advanced industrial societies, the social has condensed completely into the form of the spectacle. Foucault would respond to Debord (and to Jean Baudrillard) that any visual regime generates distinctive forms of resistance, so that its reign is necessarily partial.

30. Cf. Guilbault, *How New York Stole the Idea of Modern Art*.

31. Bourdieu writes, for example, that "acquisition of legitimate culture by insensible familiarization within the family circle tends to favour an enchanted experience of culture which implies forgetting the acquisition. The 'eye' is a product of history reproduced by education." *Distinction: The Judgment of Taste*, trans. Richard Nice (Cambridge, MA: Harvard University Press, 1984), 3. Compare Bourdieu's discussion of the social basis of "Kantian" formalism (41–50).

32. Arthur Danto writes, "It was a dour, puritanical period when artists walked Tenth Street in their paint-streaked garments to demonstrate their oneness with their art, and gathered at The Club to shout themselves out over minute questions of orthodoxy." "Who Was Andy Warhol," 129.

33. Derrida argues that the roads in even the remote Amazon jungle, which is one of the sites of Lévi-Strauss's *Tristes Tropiques*, are forms of writing and invitations to iteration; cf. Derrida, *Of Grammatology*, trans. Gayatri Spivak (Baltimore: Johns Hopkins University Press, 1976), 107–8.

34. As in *Anti-Oedipus*, published in 1972 with a foreword by Foucault; see Gilles Deleuze, *Anti-Oedipus: Capitalism and Schizophrenia*, trans. Robert Hurley, Mark Seem, and Helen R. Lane (Minneapolis: University of Minnesota Press, 1983).

35. I am thinking of video artists such as Nam June Paik, Bruce Naumann, and Gary Hill.

36. The unnamed translator of "Thought and Emotion" ignores this sense of *expérience*.

37. I have not been able to locate a copy of this film; Maria Malibran was a celebrated diva of the nineteenth century.

38. Deleuze, *Negotiations*, 106.

39. Foucault, *The Care of the Self*, trans. Robert Hurley (New York: Random House, 1986), 136–39.

40. See Gary Shapiro, "To Philosophize Is to Learn to Die," in *Signs in Culture: Roland Barthes Today*, ed. Steven Ungar and Betty McGraw (Iowa City: University of Iowa Press, 1989), 3–31.

41. Marco Livingstone, *The Essential Duane Michals* (New York: Little, Brown, 1997), 17.

42. See Jacques Derrida, *Specters of Marx*, trans. Peggy Kamuf (New York: Routledge, 1994), 10.

43. Quoted in Livingstone, *The Essential Duane Michals*, 8.

44. Cf. the introduction to this volume, sec. 5 and note 31.

45. Quoted in "TE" ix.

46. Jonathan Weinberg, "Things Are Queer," *Art Journal* 55, no. 4 (winter 1996): 11.

47. Compare, for example, Hegel's account of the epic, lyric, and dramatic forms as expressive of the temporal modalities, respectively, of past, present, and future. Hegel, *Aesthetics*, 2:1035–39.

Index

Aeschylus, 73, 151, 153–54
"age of art," 3–4
Alberti, L. B., 62
Alexandrian age, 224
Ambros, A. W., 75
Anschauung, 25, 73, 81, 131
anxiety, 211–12
Apollo, 97–100, 104, 106, 116,
   118, 133. *See also* Christ
Apollonian and Dionysian, 26,
   128–30, 136–38, 408n.43
   distinguished from Lessing's art
   categories, 70–71, 73–74
   in Raphael's *Transfiguration*,
   96–97, 101
   relation to music and image, 76,
   81–85, 133–34, 148–49
Aragon, Louis, 195
archaeology, 234–35, 268–69, 416n.1
   and genealogy, 266
   in Kant, 266–67
   of vision, 30–38, 49, 332 (*and
   see* chap. 9 passim)
archaeology of painting, 270–75;
   in contrast to science, 279–83
architecture
   Bentham and Plato and, 293–98
   of Greek theater, 137–44
   Wagner and, 152
   See also gallery; museum; Panopticon
Argos, 393
Aristophanes, 145
Aristotle, 55, 70, 287
   importance of tragic plot exaggerated by, 135–36, 202

and ocularcentrism, 157–58
on organic unity in art, 95–96
Armstrong, Carol, 316
artist, as hero, 229–30
Augenblick, 5, 53, 253
   and fragility of *video*, 53
   and Heidegger's metahistory of
   philosophy, 293
   as smallest error, 335
   in Nietzsche: splitting or hyphenation, 187–91, 414n.29;
   and visual dimension of eternal recurrence, 21, 37, 174, 337
   precedents in Paul and in Luther's Bible, 160–62
   translation as "moment" or
   "twinkling of the eye," 20,
   160–62
   See also eternal recurrence;
   phantasm; simulacrum
Augustine, 53, 149, 332, 339

Barthes, Roland, 377
Basel, 26
Bataille, Georges, 19–20, 190, 317
   on physical and philosophical
   eye, 199–201
   Story of the Eye, 19–20
Beethoven, Ludwig van, 81; *Ninth
   Symphony*, 81, 85, 87
Belting, Hans, 123
   on ages of art and image, 3, 33–
   34, 60–61, 103, 112
   on *Sistine Madonna*, 111–12,
   401n.24
Bendersky, Gordon, 100

429

Dresden Gallery, 26, 42, 58–67, 85, 401n.25
Dürer, Albrecht, *Knight, Death, and the Devil*, 118–26, 399n.14

ekphrasis, 206, 377
  as literary and rhetorical genre, 87–89
  and *"Las Meninas"*: as beginning of philosophical book, 225; as analysis of genre, 247–48 (*and see* chap. 8 passim)
  and *Les deux mystères (This is not a Pipe)*, 337–45; complicated by language in the painting, 326–27
  in Nietzsche, 133
  of Warhol's works, 359–63
El Greco, *Christ Healing the Blind Man*, 66
Emerson, Ralph Waldo, 162
Enlightenment, 21
envy, 164–70
Epicurus, bust of, 67–68
Erasmus, 123
eternal recurrence
  in Deleuze, 330
  in Foucault, 215–16, 316, 325–26, 338, 344–45
  in Klossowski, 331, 334–37
  in Nietzsche, 160–62, 174–91, 184–87, 325–26; as Medusa's head, 184–87
Euripides, 138, 143–45, 149
evidence, 1
evil eye
  Foucault and, 8, 18, 294, 301
  Nietzsche and, 22, 25, 163–72, 175, 301
exemplarity, 92
experiment, 375–78, 380, 392–93
eye, pure or radiant, 169–70. See also *Augenblick*; evil eye; gaze; glance; Nietzsche, eyesight

fashion (in clothing), 124–26
Feuerbach, Ludwig, 110
Flaubert, Gustave
  Bouvard and Pécuchet, 355, 360–61
  and Manet, 223–24
  Temptation of St. Anthony, 207–8
floating forms
  in Lucretius, 202

in Magritte's *Les deux mystères*, 102–3, 327–30, 341–42
in Raphael's *Transfiguration*, 101–3
Foucault, Michel, 61, 203
  as alleged critic of the visual, 8–10, 12
  on archaeology of vision, 171, 234–35
  as elusive author, 263, 317–19
  on Flaubert's *Temptation of St. Anthony*, 15, 207–8
  as illustrator, 12–14, 216
  not a linguistic reductionist, 203
  offers more specific analysis of painting than Merleau-Ponty, 234
  on painting and power, 193–94
  on pleasures of painting, 193–95
  relation to Nietzsche, 205, 263, 390–93 (*see also* dreams and dreaming, parallels of Nietzsche and Foucault on; eternal recurrence; language and writing; Panopticon, Foucault's views on related to Nietzsche's; visual art, in Foucault and Nietzsche)
  on specific artists and their works: Bosch's *Temptation of St. Anthony*, 210–13; Gérard Fromanger, 365–75; Frans Hals's *Regentesses*, 13–18; Magritte's *Les deux mystères*, 206, 325–29, 340–42; Manet, 302–17, 320; Velazquez's *Las Meninas*, 12, 47, 62, 95, 108, 201, 234–239, 243–44, 291, 310, 343–44 (and see chap. 8 passim); Andy Warhol, 325, 347–49, 355–63
  survey of writings on visual art, 196–97
  on twentieth-century French philosophy and painting, 195
  writings: *Archaeology of Knowledge*, 267, 279–83, 317–20; *Birth of the Clinic*, 304; *History of Madness*, 12–18, 207–13, 269, 273–74; *Order of Things*, 203–4, 225–27, 235–41, 243–244, chap. 8 passim, 266–75, 320, 342–43; *Care of the Self*, 203, 375; *Discipline and Punish*, 206, 285, 287, 290–302, 343–44; *This is not a Pipe*, 275–79, 301, 325–29, 338–45; *Uses of Pleasure*, 391

Schopenhauer (*continued*)
  as symbol of Dürer knight, 121, 124–25
  on theater as epistemological model, 149
science and art, 289–90
Searle, John, 253
self-portrait, 230, 237–38, 242–43
Semper, Gottfried, 59–60, 151
Semple, Janet, 421n.9
shadow, 105–6, 188, 318–19
shining. See *Schein*
Silverman, Hugh, 242–43
simulacrum, 102–3, 106, 202, 208, 358, 427n.24 (*and see* chap. 11 passim); distinguished from phantasm by Klossowski, 332. *See also* phantasm
Slive, Seymour, 17
Smith, P. Christopher, 135
Snow, Edgar, 62
Socrates, 144. *See also* Cyclops
Sophocles, 71, 130, 183, 188
spatiality, in Foucault's theory of dream and art, 205–6
Stateville Prison, 297
Steinberg, Leo, 249, 253
Steiner, George, 267
Straus, Erwin, 7
stupidity, 355, 360–63
suspicion, 21
Swan, Claudia, 415n.10

Taliban, 2–5, 395n.2
Taylor, Mark, 337–38
Teletubbies, 4–5
Tertullian, 289–90
theater
  of cruelty, in Nietzsche, 285–90
  Flaubert's *Temptation of St. Anthony* as, 214–16
  Wagner's, 127–29, 150–56
theater, Greek
  optics of, chap. 4 passim
  Panopticon and, 297–99
Theocritus, 56
Tobey, Mark, 194
tragedy
  ancient (*see* theater, Greek)
  as concerned with suffering, not action, 136

tragic hero, as optical illusion, 129–30
transcendental aesthetic, 9, 138
transfiguration, 113–15, 128–29, 139, 159, 184–85. *See also* Raphael, *Transfiguration*
Trouille, Clovis, 194

Van Dyck, Anthony, 85
Vasari, Giorgio, 31, 89, 91, 229, 241
Velazquez, Diego
  Las Meninas, 225–29, 234–44 (*and see* chap. 8 passim); perspective in, 227–28; as theology of painting, 225–26; title and historical context, 245–46
  Venus at her Mirror (Rokeby Venus), 229, 255
Vermeer, Jan, *Girl Reading a Letter*, 62–64
vertigo, 174–77
Vertigo (Hitchcock), 176
video, 1, 50–51
Virgil, 56
vision. *See* archaeology, of vision; *Augenblick*; ekphrasis; eye; ocularcentrism; phantasm; simulacrum; words and images
Visser, Gerard, 414n.31
visual art, in Foucault and Nietzsche: abyssal and perspectival effects in painting, 108; elision of Christian aspects of paintings, 210; parallel discussions of Raphael and Magritte, 102–3, 329
visual regime, 2–6, 200–201; and visual resistance, 379 (*and see* chap. 10 passim)
visual turn, 1, 10, 12, 391

Wagner, Cosima, 122
Wagner, Richard, 69–70, 72, 84–85, 120–21, 127–28, 150–56
Warhol, Andy, 114, 325–26, 330–31, 347–62, 366, 373
  Lavender Disaster, 359
  Marilyn Monroe's Lips, 356
White, Hayden, 90
Wilamowitz-Moellendorff, Ulrich von, 150
Winckelmann, Johann Joachim, 35, 71–72, 109, 120, 150–51